# T H E
# H I V
# D R U G
# B O O K

# THE
# HIV
# DRUG
# BOOK

PROJECT INFORM'S COMPREHENSIVE, ILLUSTRATED GUIDE TO
THE MOST-USED HIV/AIDS TREATMENTS. THE ONLY REFERENCE
THAT LISTS AND DESCRIBES ALL THE DRUGS USED BY PEOPLE
WITH HIV, THEIR EFFECTS AND INTERACTIONS.

INTRODUCTION
BY MARTIN DELANEY
PROJECT INFORM FOUNDING DIRECTOR

EDITOR
STEVEN PETROW (FIRST EDITION)
PROJECT INFORM STAFF (SECOND EDITION)

PRINCIPAL AUTHOR
BRIAN KEARNEY, PHD (FIRST EDITION)
PROJECT INFORM STAFF (SECOND EDITION)

DESIGNER
TOM MORGAN & PROJECT INFORM STAFF (SECOND EDITION)

COVER DESIGN
TAI LAM WONG

POCKET BOOKS
New York   London   Toronto   Sydney   Tokyo   Singapore

## DISCLAIMER

*The HIV Drug Book* is intended to help people become better informed medical consumers and to familiarize them with the most recent information about drugs that are presently used to treat HIV/AIDS. The information in this book is intended to supplement, not replace, the medical advice of a trained health care professional. No description of off-label uses of drugs or experimental drugs listed herein should be construed as an endorsement of those uses or drugs. Only a physician can prescribe drugs and their precise dosages. All matters regarding your health require medical supervision. The authors, medical advisers, and publisher disclaim any liability arising directly or indirectly from use of this book.

Efforts have been made to photograph and reproduce accurately the drugs contained in the color inset; variations of size or color can be expected as a result of the printing and production. Readers are cautioned not to confuse brand name drugs with their generic counterparts, and vice versa. Readers should not rely solely on the photographs contained herein to identify specific pills, but should rely on their physician's or other health care provider's prescription as dispensed by the pharmacist. All interior photographs have been provided by Medical Economics.

An *Original* Publication of POCKET BOOKS

POCKET BOOKS, a division of Simon & Schuster Inc.
1230 Avenue of the Americas, New York, NY 10020

Library of Congress Catalog Card Number 95-23034

ISBN: 0-671-01490-0

First Pocket Books revised trade paperback printing February 1998

10 9 8 7 6 5 4 3 2 1

POCKET and colophon are registered trademarks of
Simon & Schuster Inc.

Printed in the U.S.A.

# CONTENTS

## DRUG PROFILES

# ADVISERS AND CONTRIBUTORS

## MEDICAL ADVISORY BOARD

THE FOLLOWING PEOPLE SERVED ON OUR MEDICAL ADVISORY BOARD AND GAVE GENEROUSLY OF THEIR TIME AND EXPERTISE TO REVIEW THE CONTENTS OF THIS BOOK:

| | |
|---|---|
| DONALD I. ABRAMS, MD | SAN FRANCISCO GENERAL HOSPITAL |
| ROBERT BOLAN, MD | PACIFIC FAMILY PRACTICE, SAN FRANCISCO |
| MARCUS A. CONANT, MD | SAN FRANCISCO |
| JUDITH FEINBERG, MD | UNIVERSITY OF CINCINNATI |
| JUSTIN MCARTHUR | JOHNS HOPKINS UNIVERSITY, BALTIMORE |
| ANNE PETRU, MD | CHILDREN'S HOSPITAL, OAKLAND |
| PHILIP PIZZO, MD | NATIONAL CANCER INSTITUTE, BETHESDA |
| MICHAEL SAAG, MD | UNIVERSITY OF ALABAMA, BIRMINGHAM |
| ROBERT SCHOOLEY, MD | UNIVERSITY OF COLORADO, DENVER |
| SAMUEL B. TUCKER, MD, MPH | UNIVERSITY OF CALIFORNIA, SAN FRANCISCO |
| DIANE WARA, MD | UNIVERSITY OF CALIFORNIA, SAN FRANCISCO |
| CATHERINE WILFERT, MD | DUKE UNIVERSITY MEDICAL CENTER, DURHAM |

# ADVISERS AND CONTRIBUTORS

**CONTRIBUTORS:**

THE FOLLOWING PEOPLE CONTRIB-
UTED MATERIAL TO THIS BOOK:

Donald I. Abrams, MD
Ben Cheng
Steven G. Deeks, MD
Martin Delaney
John Gilmore, MD
Reena Lawande
Sharon Lee, MD
Brenda Lein
Marcia McLain
Charles Steinberg, MD
Joel Thomas
Paul A. Volberding, MD

**EDITORIAL ADVISORY BOARD**

THE FOLLOWING PEOPLE SERVED ON THE
EDITORIAL ADVISORY BOARD:

Ben Cheng
Martin Delaney
Reena Lawande
Brenda Lein

**BOOK PROJECT DIRECTOR**

Ben Cheng

# INTRODUCTION

## BY MARTIN DELANEY

The HIV/AIDS epidemic that began in the early 1980s and continues unabated to this day has forever changed the face of modern medicine. On the most obvious level, the epidemic has led to a more realistic appraisal of the limitations of medicine in society. We now understand that disease can't always quickly be conquered by a single pill and HIV and AIDS may represent a life-long battle for those infected. More importantly, the epidemic has led to a necessary new paradigm in the doctor-patient relationship, one in which HIV-related information and knowledge have become recognized as critically important tools of healing.

The need for this new paradigm is nowhere more evident than in the seemingly endless and growing list of medications, experimental drugs, and supplements routinely used in the treatment of HIV/AIDS. The nature of this disease–and the fact that no single treatment provides a cure outright–brings doctor, patient, and loved ones into near constant discussion of a bewildering array of therapies and how to use them. The wave of advances in therapy that began in late 1995 have further heightened the demand for well-informed doctors working with well-informed patients.

Basic knowledge of the drugs prescribed, including their possible side effects and other drug interactions, is only a starting point to empowerment. Today, the HIV-infected person must also become a strategist, concerned at every step with the long-term consequences of each decision about therapy. Moreover, the complexity of using the new treatments has made patient adherence as important as any of the drugs themselves. Hundreds of thousands of HIV-infected people face the daily challenge of incorporating complex and rapidly changing therapy regimens into their lifestyles.

These changes have led to a complete overhaul of *The HIV Drug Book* in its second full edition. Dozens of new therapies have been added along with a much wider presentation of the practical guidelines and suggestions Project Inform has always been known for.

Since its inception, Project Inform has sought to give people the tools they need to make sense of the myriad treatment decisions facing them. *The HIV Drug Book* is designed to provide a single, authoritative reference and medical strategy guide for using the treatments most commonly used by people with HIV and AIDS. The book goes far beyond the normal list of HIV-specific

---

*MARTIN DELANEY IS THE FOUNDING DIRECTOR OF PROJECT INFORM.*

medications, incorporating all of the common antibiotics, painkillers, anti-depressants, and experimental drugs that many people with this disease take.

Written in the language of the lay reader–with patients, caregivers, friends, and family members in mind–this book should be equally useful to physicians, who themselves must struggle daily to keep up with the information in this rapidly changing field. People living with HIV disease, we hope, will find personal empowerment in this book by understanding–independently of their physician–the medications they are using. For the physician, this book offers simplicity and clarity in the form of a readily accessible reference to the medications and strategies routinely used across the spectrum of HIV infection. For the caregiver, the most obvious benefit should be an increased level of comfort in taking care of someone with HIV disease. Far too often, caregivers are left with the thankless task of sorting, counting, and arranging the daily intake of medication. Those tasks become far less daunting when the caregiver has a complete reference guide, replete with names, dosages, warnings, interactions, and illustrations.

When Project Inform first sprang to life as a small service agency in 1985, we naively expected that our work would be completed within six months. Then, we assumed, the "standard" systems for educating patients and physicians about a new disease would be taking over. Little did we know that there was no "standard" educational system for HIV or any other disease. Over the next ten years, Project Inform became a primary source of treatment information for hundreds of thousands of HIV-affected people and their physicians worldwide. In its wake were created the treatment-information departments and newsletters of dozens of other AIDS service organizations that eventually came to see medical education as a key aspect of their work.

One of the great lessons in AIDS recounted by both physicians and people with HIV has been the realization that well-informed people simply make far better partners in health care. And, when knowledge is shared, everyone benefits and the risk of error on any individual's part is diminished. We hope that this new and extensively updated edition of *The HIV Drug Book* will improve patient care for all people living with HIV disease.

# PREFACE

## BY DONALD I. ABRAMS, MD

"Knowledge equals power." I learned that lesson at the beginning of the AIDS epidemic, even before the slogan became a popular call to arms of the HIV activist community. In the early 1980s, as I was finishing my long years of medical training and starting my career as a physician and academic, I quite naively felt that I knew it all. With five years of medical school, followed by two residencies (three years of internal medicine and three years of oncology training), not many people knew more about cancer, infectious diseases, or clinical trials–or so I thought.

I was wrong. Who could have imagined that solutions to the mysteries and complexities presented by what became known as AIDS wouldn't come as quickly or easily as they had for Legionnaires' disease or toxic shock syndrome? It took years before we had a name for AIDS, and even more years before we could identify the virus and begin to test for the infection. Aggressive chemotherapy did not work. Reference books were useless. In this day of the magic bullet, our gun–our entire arsenal–proved empty. As a profession, we physicians suddenly began to realize the limits of our power and knowledge.

At the same time HIV-infected people and their advocates began to speak up demanding treatment advances, faster drug approvals, and greater access to clinical trials *and* began giving us advice about what drugs we should be testing, how the trials should be designed, and who should be included. Because the medical establishment was too slow in testing new treatments, individuals and groups began importing drugs that they thought might work. The community created networks to inform itself and others about possible treatment options and strategies. Then, our patients began coming to us–their healthcare providers–with questions about therapies we'd never even heard about. "Wait a minute!" I said to myself. "This is not how I thought my 'noble' profession would be." Not coincidentally, AIDS threatened medicine and physicians' egos at the same time it threatened the public health.

Time passed, people died, and we still had few answers and fewer intelligent options to offer. Activists and advocates continued to press for more research dollars, community-based research, and speedier results. The physician community began to realize that its patients and advocates were making a lot of good points. In the second decade of this devastating epidemic, the us-versus-

*DONALD I. ABRAMS, MD, IS ASSISTANT DIRECTOR OF AIDS ACTIVITIES AT SAN FRANCISCO GENERAL HOSPITAL.*

them mentality is being replaced by a unified attack against a common enemy: HIV. The doctor-patient relationship has been redefined in a positive and invigorating way for all of us. A new, urgent model of community and patient activism has emerged. I, and many of my colleagues, encourage and expect patients to keep abreast of research and treatment options, to keep their ears to the underground, and to share with us everything they learn about possible HIV treatments.

With all the medications people with HIV disease are taking and all the potential new therapies they hear about, it's a challenge to keep the information straight and to learn about possible drug interactions and side effects. *The HIV Drug Book* is unique because it provides the consumer and the physician an invaluable resource that is user-friendly, accurate, and entirely up-to-date. With general information about the drugs, their use in special populations, and important entries on drug and food interactions, Project Inform's comprehensive and illustrated handbook will arm us all with one of the most valuable weapons we have in fighting HIV infection: knowledge.

KNOWLEDGE = POWER!

# FOREWORD

**BY JOEL THOMAS**

As a person with HIV disease, I have received treatment information from Project Inform that has saved my life, or at the very least, extended it for many healthy, active years. I have learned how to educate myself about HIV and AIDS, how to select and form a partnership with a doctor, how to analyze the various therapies I might choose to take, and most importantly, I have learned how to become a fighter in the battle against HIV. This learning did not occur overnight: in fact, it began twelve years ago when I learned I was infected. People often ask me what's the most important thing I've learned. I tell them, "If I can do it, anybody can do it."

In September 1985, I received a positive antibody test for HIV and began following the progress of my infection with blood tests, first every six months, and then every month as my CD4+ cells began to drop. In late 1988, at a routine monthly checkup, my doctor informed me that my CD4+ cells had dropped another 50 points (to 300) and my p24 antigen level (an indication of viral activity) was rising at an alarming rate. Coupled with the previous months of declines, this was very bad news.

At the time I had been on AZT–then the only licensed drug for HIV infection–for nearly a year. Even with AZT, I was clearly losing the battle with HIV. I turned to my doctor, scared to death, and asked, "What am I going to do?" He patted my hand as if I were a little old lady and told me that "we" would just have to wait. As I left his office, it was only too clear what "we" were waiting for: "we" were waiting for me to die. Frankly, that plan of nonaction was completely unacceptable to me. I knew then that as long as there were any rational therapies I could try, approved by the FDA or not, I would not sit by and slip gently into that good night. I became angry at my doctor's passivity, so angry that I proceeded to do what seemed at the time to be one of the riskiest things I have ever done: I fired my doctor. Ironically, firing my doctor signaled the beginning of my fight and my quest to stay alive in the face of this horrible disease.

The fight for my life was on. Not being a fool, I quickly realized that firing my doctor would not in itself prevent my disease from progressing. I began asking anyone and everyone I knew for names of other physicians. I knew what I wanted. I wanted a doctor with whom I could form a working partnership. I'd had enough of one-sided affairs. Until this time I had chosen doctors

---

*JOEL THOMAS IS A FORMER MEMBER OF PROJECT INFORM'S BOARD OF DIRECTORS AND A LONGTIME AIDS ACTIVIST.*

at random. Now I wanted another person on my side. I wanted someone to suggest new ideas. I wanted a doctor who agreed with the idea that I had the right to try any treatment I felt would benefit me. I called and visited several docs. A month later, I found the first of two doctors with whom I formed a health partnership.

With the input of my new doctor, I began taking compound Q, a nonapproved experimental drug that was showing some promise in community trials. Almost simultaneously, my doctor enrolled me in the ddI expanded access program, in effect making me one of the first to rely on "combination therapy" to fight HIV. I quickly saw the benefits of having a physician who is a full partner and not an adversary, and who is aggressive in fighting for my life.

At the same time I was searching for my doctor, I was also gathering information. In 1985, when I first tested positive for HIV, there were few, if any, reputable organizations gathering and disseminating AIDS information. Initially, I attempted to do my own research, spending long hours at the University of California, San Francisco, Medical Library. A lot of my time was wasted because I simply didn't know how to search for the type of medical and technical data I wanted. But, the folks at UCSF were helpful, and within days I was able to do on-line searches for information about HIV disease (including that found in periodicals, journals, and various medical newspapers). Slowly, but surely, I began to understand the language and vocabulary in which the articles were written. In a few short weeks, I had learned a lot about HIV/AIDS and more about medicine in general. Most importantly, I came to understand that if *I* could find the information, anyone could. Curiously, as my knowledge expanded, so did my involvement with the HIV/AIDS community. In 1988 I found Project Inform, then a three-year-old organization.

Over the years, my involvement with Project Inform has become the mainstay of my treatment program. Initially, I attended monthly town meetings to keep up-to-date on new information. As my involvement with Project Inform increased, I began volunteering for shifts on the hotline. Incoming calls are fielded by volunteers who have had extensive training. The information I got from the training—listening to my fellow Hotline operators and from the callers—has been invaluable to me. Project Inform also publishes fact sheets on the various HIV-related diseases, including the latest medications both approved and experimental. I relied on the *PI Perspective,* the journal that covers the latest happenings in the world of HIV and AIDS, including both medicine and politics. My first love, however, was Project Inform's town meetings. The town meetings became a vital link for me to the most current medical news and helped me to become involved with the advocate/activist community. Eventually I became a part of the information-gathering and disseminating process at Project In-

form. My involvement with PI was and has always been about self-empowerment and taking control of my disease.

No one at Project Inform has ever suggested that I take a particular drug. PI helped me to understand that I had choices and that some of those choices were better proven than others. Information about my disease gave me a solid foundation, but the real battle began when I needed to think about various HIV therapies.

In 1987, when I swallowed my first AZT capsule, I knew little about HIV infection. I relied solely on my physician's directives, but quickly became increasingly familiar with the various drugs, particularly the antiviral compounds known as nucleoside analogs. Since those early days, I have moved on to other antivirals and combinations of antivirals, and I continue to be extremely aggressive in the treatment of my disease. I never stop learning about the newest therapies available, antiviral therapies as well as therapies to prevent opportunistic infections. I know if I am going to stay alive, I must keep current with all the advances.

Recently I began receiving bad laboratory test results again. I saw that my CD4+ count drifted lower with every test, but most importantly, I was feeling tired much too often. I took more tests, and I didn't like what I found: the virus was active and I knew what was down the road if I didn't stop this viral onslaught. I had heard of an approved drug–hydroxyurea–that was being used experimentally to treat HIV. I learned more about this compound and it seemed like the most rational choice that I could make. At the very least, this drug offered me a chance to fight. I had made another aggressive choice and this new treatment seems to be helping.

Now I think back to my first doctor who recommended that "we" wait. Had I taken his advice, there is little doubt in my mind that I would be dead now. When I think back to 1985 and my total lack of knowledge and compare it to what I have now, I feel powerful. The self-empowerment and self-determination that I have achieved as a result has sustained me through these often difficult and painful years. Information about the disease and treatments are important, but more helpful is being in this fight together with your friends, family, and colleagues. I cherish the friends I've made in this battle. Much of my fighting spirit came from being involved and doing battle with the political and medical establishments. Although I chose to become a political fighter, you don't have to become a member of a political group to fight for your life. Not everyone needs to be or wants to be an activist, but everyone can do many of the things that have kept me alive in the face of incredible odds. As I've said so many times before, "If I can do it, anyone can do it."

# HOW TO USE THIS BOOK

*The HIV Drug Book* is designed to be reader-friendly for easy access to crucial information about the most commonly used HIV medications. The book is formatted for quick reference and written in non-technical language for people living with HIV disease, their caregivers, loved ones, and for health care providers. The text reflects the most current medical knowledge and standard medical practices. *The HIV Drug Book,* like medications, should be used in consultation with your health care provider. The core of the book consists of profiles of the medications most commonly used by people with HIV disease. The decision as to which drugs were to be included was based on an exhaustive survey of HIV primary-care physicians and clinicians nationwide.

## HOW TO FIND YOUR PRESCRIPTION

The easiest way to find a specific medication is in the master drug index located at the end of the book. The index contains all the names by which a drug may be known (brand or trade name, generic, popular, scientific, and experimental code name). As long as you know one name for a particular drug, the index will direct you to the specific entry. A separate index of drug classes lists all the medications covered in the book for each specific class (e.g., antiviral, antibiotic, antifungal).

## HOW THE DRUG PROFILES ARE STRUCTURED

The book is structured by drug classes. Seventeen classes are contained in *The HIV Drug Book*: antibiotics, anticancer, antidiarrheal, antifungal, antihistamines, antinausea/antivomiting, antiprotozoal, antiseizure, antiulcer, antiviral, antiwasting, corticosteroids, immune-based therapy, neuropathy drugs, pain relievers, psychoactive drugs, and vaccines. Within each class, FDA-approved drugs are listed alphabetically and each is fully profiled. Some experimental treatments that are either widely available or expected to be approved are treated the same way. Other experimental drugs are discussed at the end of this section. The introduction to each drug class contains a list of all medications discussed in that section for easy reference and provides an overview of how that class of drug is used by people living with HIV disease.

## THE PROFILES

Each drug is listed by its most commonly known name. The profiles contain the following information:

**BRAND NAME-S (MANUFACTURER-S)**

**TYPE OF DRUG:** This entry describes the general drug class of each medication.

**USED FOR:** Conditions for which the drug is usually prescribed are highlighted. This includes FDA-approved uses as well as off-label uses commonly prescribed by doctors. (Once a drug is approved by the FDA, physicians may prescribe it for other conditions and diseases. This is called off-label use of a drug. If a drug is not approved by the FDA for HIV, it doesn't mean you shouldn't use it if your doctor prescribes it. Become fully aware of its indications and discuss them with a physician.

**GENERAL INFORMATION:** This entry provides basic information on how a drug works and how it is similar to or different from other drugs in its class. This section also discusses how the drug is administered (most medications are taken orally, however some are administered via inhalants or by injection, requiring special instructions before use) and discusses how the drug is generally used by people with HIV.

**TREATMENT:** This entry describes currently recommended treatment regimens and doses for adults and children. The dosage prescribed by a doctor may or may not be the same as listed here; dosages vary based on an individual's body weight and overall health, other medications, and symptoms. Ask your health care provider about any discrepancies.

**PREVENTION:** Drugs used to prevent initial infections will include this entry. It describes how the drug is used for this purpose.

**MAINTENANCE:** Drugs used to prevent recurrent infections will include this entry. It describes how the drug is used for this purpose.

**CAUTIONS AND WARNINGS:** This section tells readers about possible allergic reactions, known toxicities, and other conditions that should be discussed with a doctor before a drug is prescribed. It also lists the precautions necessary for safe use.

**SIDE EFFECTS:** Common, less common, and rare side effects are outlined in detail to help readers better understand what to expect from medications. This information is especially important to people with HIV/AIDS and provides a "reality check" to help determine if a new or unusual symptom is related to the disease or is a drug side effect. Side effects can be psychological as well as physical. **PREGNANCY/BREAST-FEEDING:** Pregnant women or those nursing

newborns need up-to-date information on how specific drugs can harm or help their fetus or baby. Although few drugs have been specifically tested in pregnant women because of the potential harm to the fetus, this entry reports all known cautions and relevant information. If pregnant or anticipating pregnancy, talk to a doctor in detail about specific medications.

**USE IN CHILDREN:** Children's bodies are different from adults' and HIV affects children differently from adults. For this reason, drugs may work differently in a child. Relevant information is included here.

**USE IN THE ELDERLY:** Seniors often have different responses to medications because our bodies change as we age. This entry describes how older people's reactions and symptoms may be different, and how drug dosages should be adjusted. Special attention is paid to drug interactions common to seniors.

**DRUG INTERACTIONS:** This entry describes how the medication reacts with other drugs and what medications should not be taken at the same time. As more and more drugs have become available for the treatment and prevention of specific diseases and conditions, the possibility of problematic drug interactions has increased and is a far more common problem than drug overdoses. Drug interactions with other medications, alcohol, and other substances can be harmful and may, in some cases, be fatal. Project Inform's Drug Interaction Chart (pages 622 - 654) describes many of the major interactions for the most commonly used anti-HIV medications. Because of the risk of drug interactions, it is important that you consult your doctor before adding any medication to your treatment regime.

**FOOD INTERACTIONS:** In general, food affects absorption of medication, and this section tells readers whether or not to take a particular drug with or without food.

**OTHER DRUGS USED FOR SIMILAR CONDITIONS:** This entry gives a listing of other commonly prescribed medications used for similar symptoms or illnesses. This information may be helpful in discussing treatment options with a doctor.

**COMMENTS:** This entry provides Project Inform's most up-to-date information, assessment, or evaluation of the medication.

## EXPERIMENTAL DRUGS

Experimental drugs are also listed by class depending on how they are currently being tested for treatment of HIV and other related diseases. The availability of medications referenced in this section may be limited. A few are approved for specific HIV use; most are available through clinical trials, expanded-access, or compassionate-use programs. Inclusion here does not constitute endorsement of use.

## OTHER FEATURES OF THE BOOK

- How to choose an HIV-knowledgeable doctor
- How to manage medications
- Guidelines for healthful eating and nutrient supplementation
- Alternative and holistic medicine
- How to avoid fraudulent AIDS therapies
- Information on clinical trials and experimental treatments

Full-size color reproductions of many of the drugs profiled are included in a sixteen-page section.

The chapters at the end of the book include Project Inform's Guide to the Management of Opportunistic Infections, information on how to use Project Inform and its treatment information hotline, Project Inform's Drug Interaction Chart, a comprehensive and up-to-date resource guide (with listings of national, state, and local AIDS organizations, buyers' clubs, mail-order pharmacies, treatment-information publications, and more), as well as a glossary of important terms used in the book.

The master index at the very end of the book is designed to help readers find drug entries easily. Drugs are listed by their most common name as well as other known names.

# DRUG PROFILES

# ANTIBIOTICS

Antibiotics are some of the most commonly used drugs in the United States today. In people with HIV, they are prescribed to treat or prevent a wide variety of bacterial infections. Since penicillin was first introduced in the early 1940s, many different classes of antibiotics have been developed. They have different chemical structures and are effective against different bacteria. Some have a broad spectrum of activity, meaning that they are effective against a wide range of bacteria. Some are effective against only a few specific organisms.

Depending on the drug and the concentration used, antibiotics either kill bacteria (are bactericidal) or slow bacterial multiplication (are bacteriostatic) so that the body's immune system can eliminate it. Antibiotics that belong to the penicillin or cephalosporin classes are bactericidal; they prevent bacteria from building strong cell walls. As susceptible bacteria take up liquid and swell, they burst and die. Antibiotics of other classes generally work inside bacteria, preventing the production of key proteins or RNA. This may be lethal in itself or it may stop the bacteria from multiplying.

Because of the danger of drug interactions and producing antibiotic-resistant organisms through the inappropriate use of antibiotics, these drugs should only be used under the guidance of a physician who is knowledgeable about the entire range of medications being taken by the individual.

In some cases, antibiotics increase the risk of fungal disease by altering the natural "flora" of "friendly" bacteria that keep fungi in check in the body. For this reason, some people use acidophilus supplements when taking antibiotics in order to restore the natural balance and reduce the risk of fungal infections.

The antibiotics covered in this section are listed below by class.

## PENICILLINS

The penicillins were one of the first classes of antibiotics developed. Because they have been so widely used, resistance to them has developed and they are ineffective against many strains of bacteria. Penicillins also often cause allergic reactions. The penicillins profiled are:

- amoxicillin
- ampicillin
- dicloxacillin
- penicillin

## CEPHALOSPORINS

Cephalosporins are broad-spectrum antibiotics similar in chemical composition to the penicillins. They are often used when penicillin treatment is inef-

fective. People who are allergic to the penicillins may also be allergic to the cephalosporins. The following cephalosporins are profiled:
- cefaclor
- cefepime
- cefixime
- ceftriaxone
- cefuroxime

## AMINOGLYCOSIDES

The aminoglycosides are broad-spectrum antibiotics that are usually reserved for when other antibiotics are not effective. They are given by injection and have potentially serious side effects. The aminoglycosides profiled are:
- amikacin
- gentamicin
- streptomycin

## MACROLIDES

The macrolides are broad-spectrum antibiotics similar in structure to erythromycin. Because they have potentially serious side effects, they are usually reserved for cases where penicillins or cephalosporins are not appropriate. The macrolides profiled are:
- azithromycin
- clarithromycin
- erythromycin

## TETRACYCLINES

The tetracyclines have a broader range of activity than any other class of antibiotics. However, their widespread use has led to bacterial resistance to them, and they are ineffective against many previously susceptible bacterial strains. A major drawback to their use is that they can permanently discolor developing teeth. The tetracyclines profiled are:
- doxycycline
- tetracycline

## ANTIMYCOBACTERIALS

This class contains a group of chemically diverse antibiotics that are effective against certain strains of *Mycobacterium,* the microorganisms responsible for *Mycobacterium avium* complex (MAC), tuberculosis, and leprosy. Because *Mycobacterium* are so resistant to drug treatment, combinations of these drugs are generally used over long periods of time to eradicate these infections. The two most widely used drugs for the treatment of MAC are the

macrolides azithromycin and clarithromycin (listed on page 23). Other antimycobacterials profiled include:

- ciprofloxacin
- clofazimine
- ethambutol
- isoniazid
- ofloxacin
- pyrazinamide
- rifabutin
- rifampin

Amikacin is an aminoglycoside antibiotic (listed on page 23) also used in combination therapy to treat mycobacterial infections.

## OTHER ANTIBIOTICS

Antibiotics that are profiled in this section but are not included in any of the classes above are:

- chloramphenicol
- ciprofloxacin
- clindamycin
- furazolidone
- meropenem
- vancomycin

In addition, brief descriptions of experimental therapies for bacterial infection are included at the end of this section. They include:

- sparfloxacin

# AMIKACIN

## BRAND NAME (MANUFACTURER)
Amikin (Apothecon)

## TYPE OF DRUG
Antibiotic

## USED FOR
Amikacin is used to treat serious bacterial infections, specifically infections of the respiratory tract, blood, bones, joints, central nervous system, skin, soft tissue, abdomen, and urinary tract. It is also used to treat infections that occur after severe burns and surgery. For most bacterial infections, amikacin is not the physician's first choice. It is used primarily when the bacteria causing the infection cannot be controlled by less toxic alternatives.

In people living with HIV, amikacin is sometimes used as part of combination therapy to treat *Mycobacterium avium* complex (MAC) when other treatments have failed. It is also occasionally used as part of combination therapy for tuberculosis in HIV-positive people when other drugs are not appropriate.

## GENERAL INFORMATION

Amikacin belongs to a class of antibiotics called aminoglycosides, which include kanamycin, gentamicin, and streptomycin. Aminoglycosides prevent susceptible bacteria from making proteins, stopping their growth and preventing them from multiplying.

Amikacin is available as a solution for injection into a vein or a large muscle.

## TREATMENT

A 1997 U.S. Public Health Service Task Force recommends treating MAC with either azithromycin or clarithromycin plus at least one other drug such as ethambutol or rifabutin. Ciprofloxacin and amikacin are also used as part of the combination regimen. In combination therapy for MAC, azithromycin is generally taken at a dose of 500-600 mg per day. It should be noted that the Division of AIDS of the National Institute of Allergy and Infectious Diseases recently recommended that clofazimine not be used since the addition of the drug did not result in any added benefit and may result in increased risk of death.

Amikacin is commonly prescribed for people who do not respond after two to six weeks of treatment with the oral drugs. As part of combination therapy to treat MAC, amikacin is injected at 10 mg per kg of body weight per day. The dose should not exceed 1.5 g per day. The usual duration of treatment for MAC is one month, but maintenance therapy is usually lifelong. Treatment may be repeated, but the risk of hearing loss on retreatment is significant, especially in people infected with HIV.

The dosage of amikacin is often decreased for people with poor kidney function to reduce the risk of side effects.

## CAUTIONS AND WARNINGS

Amikacin should not be used by people with known allergies to it or other aminoglycoside antibiotics.

Because of the drug's potential toxicity to the kidneys, people who use amikacin should take extra fluids during treatment. The drug may cause irreversible hearing loss before it is readily noticeable. Deafness in the higher frequencies usually occurs first and can be detected only by special testing. The risk of hearing loss is greater for those with reduced kidney function.

Because amikacin may partially treat and mask the symptoms of tuberculosis, it is important to be tested for tuberculosis before starting amikacin

therapy for MAC. Amikacin should be used with caution in people with myasthenia gravis or Parkinson's disease because aminoglycoside antibiotics may aggravate muscle weakness.

Strict adherence to the anti-MAC regimen prescribed by a physician decreases the likelihood of developing resistant organisms.

The amikacin injection solution contains sulfite, which can cause allergic reactions in people with sulfite sensitivity.

### SIDE EFFECTS

Sustained use of amikacin can result in hearing loss, loss of balance, or both. Rarely, its use may result in acute muscle paralysis or the inability to breathe. It can be toxic to the kidneys and, less frequently, causes vertigo (dizziness), numbness or tingling in the skin, twitching, and convulsions.

### PREGNANCY/BREAST-FEEDING

Amikacin has not been formally studied in pregnant women. Aminoglycoside antibiotics can cross the placenta and cause fetal harm. Several women who have taken streptomycin, a related aminoglycoside antibiotic, have had children with total, irreversible hearing loss. While this side effect has not been observed in the children born to women taking amikacin during pregnancy, the potential for harm exists. Pregnant women should discuss the benefits and potential risks with their physician before taking this drug.

HIV can be passed from a woman to her child through breast milk. In areas where nutritionally sound alternatives are readily available, breast-feeding is discouraged for HIV-positive women. While it is not known if amikacin passes through breast milk, women should consider alternatives to breast-feeding while taking it because of the potential toxicity of the drug.

### USE IN CHILDREN

Amikacin can be used in children, although gentamicin is generally used first. Very young or premature children do not have fully developed kidneys and may be more susceptible to side effects of amikacin. Dose reductions in these cases may be necessary.

### USE IN THE ELDERLY

Older adults may be more susceptible to the side effects of the drug and may require reduced doses.

### DRUG INTERACTIONS

Beta-lactam-type antibiotics (penicillins or cephalosporins) may enhance amikacin activity.

Inability to breathe because of muscle paralysis has been reported following the use of aminoglycoside antibiotics. This is more likely when these antibiotics are used together with anesthetics, tubocurarine, succinylcholine, decame-

thonium, or in people receiving massive transfusions of blood treated with citrate to prevent clotting.

Concurrent and/or sequential use of bacitracin, cisplatin, amphotericin B, cephaloridine, paromomycin, viomycin, polymyxin B, colistin, vancomycin, or other aminoglycosides should be avoided. The concurrent use of amikacin with potent diuretics should be avoided since some diuretics by themselves may cause hearing loss.

### FOOD INTERACTIONS
None reported.

### OTHER DRUGS USED FOR SIMILAR CONDITIONS
For the treatment of MAC. Clarithromycin or azithromycin are the preferred drugs. Either one is usually used in combination with ethambutol, rifabutin, rifampin or ciprofloxacin. Amikacin is usually reserved for disease that doesn't respond to the initial combination.

### COMMENTS
In the early stages of the AIDS epidemic, many physicians thought treating MAC was futile. Mycobacteria are notorious for becoming drug resistant and effective treatment requires several different drugs (some with severe side effects). A combination regimen of clarithromycin, rifabutin and ethambutol was significantly superior to ethambutol, rifampin, clofazimine, and ciprofloxacin for treating MAC and prolonging survival.

With the development of new drugs and combinations that have fewer side effects, however, the attitude of many physicians has changed. Treating MAC is likely to prolong survival, reduce symptoms, and improve quality of life.

# A M O X I C I L L I N

### BRAND NAME (MANUFACTURER)
Amoxil (SmithKline Beecham); Moxilin (International Ethical); Wymox (Wyeth-Ayerst)
Amoxicillin + Clavulanate: Augmentin (SmithKline Beecham)

### TYPE OF DRUG
Antibiotic

### USED FOR
Amoxicillin is used to treat a wide variety of bacterial infections, including those of the ear, digestive tract, respiratory tract, skin, and urinary tract.

In people with HIV, amoxicillin is used specifically to treat bacterial inflammation of the sinuses (sinusitis), diarrhea caused by *Salmonella*, and vaginal ulcers (chancroid) caused by *Haemophilus ducreyi*. In clinical trials, it has

also been used in combination with clavulanate for the treatment of bacterial pneumonia.

## GENERAL INFORMATION

Amoxicillin belongs to the penicillin class of antibiotics, which work by interfering with a susceptible bacteria's ability to build cell walls. Amoxicillin is converted by the body into the antibiotic ampicillin. The primary difference between the two is that amoxicillin is resistant to acid in the stomach, which means that more of the active drug gets into the intestines where it is absorbed.

In the last few years, bacteria have increasingly become resistant to penicillin-type antibiotics. This resistance may occur more frequently in the HIV-positive population because of the widespread use of antibiotics. In cases of resistance, additional antibiotics that kill bacteria by a different mechanism are often needed. For example, amoxicillin is commonly used in combination with clavulanate. The amoxicillin kills a broad range of bacteria, and the clavulanate kills bacteria that are resistant to amoxicillin. Together they are effective in controlling infection. The disadvantage of this combination is an increased risk of side effects.

## TREATMENT

For most infections, the adult dose of amoxicillin is 250 mg, taken every eight hours. Children weighing under 20 kg (44 lb.) usually receive 20 mg per kg of body weight per day, divided into equal doses given every eight hours. For more severe infections or those caused by less susceptible bacteria, the dosages may be increased.

## CAUTIONS AND WARNINGS

People who know they are allergic to any penicillin-type antibiotic should not take amoxicillin, as there is a chance they will be allergic to it as well.

As with any antibiotic, it is important to take amoxicillin for the entire length of time indicated by the physician. Even after symptoms disappear, the bacteria may continue to multiply in the body. The infection may quickly recur if the drug is stopped prematurely.

## SIDE EFFECTS

Amoxicillin is generally well tolerated. The most common side effects of amoxicillin are minor and include rashes, heartburn, nausea, vomiting, or diarrhea. These side effects are more likely to occur in people who are allergic to penicillin or have a history of allergy, asthma, or hay fever. Rarely, some people taking amoxicillin experience agitation, anxiety, insomnia, dizziness, confusion, or behavioral changes.

**PREGNANCY/BREAST-FEEDING**

Amoxicillin has not been formally tested in pregnant women. In animal studies, the drug did not impair fertility or cause fetal harm, but it is not known whether the same would be true for humans. Pregnant women are encouraged to discuss the benefits and potential risks of amoxicillin with their physician before deciding to use it.

HIV can be passed from a woman to her child through breast milk. In areas where nutritionally sound alternatives are readily available, breast-feeding is discouraged for HIV-positive women. Amoxicillin is excreted in human milk, and use by nursing women may cause their infants to become allergic to the drug.

**USE IN CHILDREN**

Amoxicillin is routinely used for children at the doses described on page 28. Newborns have immature kidneys and clear ampicillin more slowly from their bodies. These children may need lower doses.

**USE IN THE ELDERLY**

No dose adjustments are necessary for older adults with normal kidney and liver function. Dose reductions may be necessary for older adults with reduced kidney or liver function.

**DRUG INTERACTIONS**

Some antibiotics, including chloramphenicol, erythromycin, sulfonamides, or tetracyclines, may reduce the effectiveness of amoxicillin. Oral contraceptives may be less effective when taking amoxicillin and increased breakthrough bleeding may occur.

Using amoxicillin and allopurinol together may result in a higher risk of skin rashes. Probenecid may increase blood levels of amoxicillin and increase the risk of amoxicillin-related side effects.

**FOOD INTERACTIONS**

Amoxicillin may be taken with or without food.

**OTHER DRUGS USED FOR SIMILAR CONDITIONS**

Other penicillin-type antibiotics, including penicillin or ampicillin, are sometimes used in place of amoxicillin. For *Salmonella* infections, trimethoprim/sulfamethoxazole, ciprofloxacin, or chloramphenicol may be used. For the treatment of vaginal infections, azithromycin, ceftriaxone, doxycycline, ofloxacin, erythromycin, or ciprofloxacin may be used.

# AMPICILLIN

**BRAND NAMES (MANUFACTURERS)**
Omnipen (Wyeth-Ayerst); Unasyn (Roerig/Pfizer)

**TYPE OF DRUG**
Antibiotic

**USED FOR**
Ampicillin is used to treat a wide variety of bacterial infections, including those of the ear, digestive tract, respiratory tract, skin, and urinary tract.

In people with HIV, ampicillin is frequently used for the treatment of diarrhea caused by *Salmonella,* and it is used less frequently for intestinal pain and diarrhea caused by the bacterial pathogen *Shigella.*

**GENERAL INFORMATION**
Ampicillin belongs to the penicillin class of antibiotics, which work by interfering with a susceptible bacteria's ability to build cell walls. Ampicillin is similar in structure to the antibiotic amoxicillin. In fact, amoxicillin is converted to ampicillin by the body. The primary difference between the two is that amoxicillin is resistant to acid in the stomach, which means that more of the active drug gets into the intestines where it is absorbed. The other major difference is that amoxicillin is less effective than ampicillin against diarrhea caused by *Shigella,* because it stays in the cells lining the gut (where *Shigella* multiplies) for a shorter period of time.

Ampicillin is available in capsules, powder for oral suspension, and as a solution for injection. It is most commonly taken orally.

**TREATMENT**
For most infections, the usual adult dose of ampicillin is 250 mg taken every eight hours. Children weighing under 20 kg (44 lb.) usually receive 20 mg per kg of body weight per day, divided into equal doses given every eight hours. For more severe infections or those caused by less susceptible bacteria, the dosages may be increased.

**CAUTIONS AND WARNINGS**
Ampicillin should not be used by people who know they are allergic to it or to any of the other penicillins.

As with any antibiotic, it is important to take ampicillin for the entire length of time indicated by the physician. Even after symptoms disappear, the bacteria may continue to multiply in the body. The infection may quickly recur if the drug is stopped prematurely.

**SIDE EFFECTS**
Ampicillin is generally well tolerated. The most common side effects of ampicillin are minor and include rashes, heartburn, nausea, vomiting, or diar-

rhea. These side effects are more likely to occur in people who are allergic to penicillin or have a history of allergy, asthma, or hay fever. Rarely, some people taking ampicillin experience agitation, anxiety, insomnia, dizziness, confusion, or behavioral changes.

**PREGNANCY/BREAST-FEEDING**

Ampicillin has not been formally tested in pregnant women. In animal studies, the drug did not impair fertility or cause fetal harm, but it is not known whether the same would be true for humans. Pregnant women are encouraged to discuss the benefits and potential risks of ampicillin with their physician before deciding to use it.

HIV can be passed from a woman to her child through breast milk. In areas where nutritionally sound alternatives are readily available, breast-feeding is discouraged for HIV-positive women. Ampicillin is excreted in human milk, and use by nursing women may cause their infants to become allergic to the drug.

**USE IN CHILDREN**

Ampicillin is routinely used for children at the dosages described above. Newborns have immature kidneys and clear ampicillin more slowly from their bodies. These children may receive lower doses.

**USE IN THE ELDERLY**

No changes in dosage are required for elderly adults with normal kidney function. Reduced doses may be required for older adults with impaired kidney function.

**DRUG INTERACTIONS**

Some antibiotics, including chloramphenicol, erythromycin, sulfonamides, or tetracyclines, may reduce the effectiveness of ampicillin. Oral contraceptives may be less effective when taking ampicillin.

Using ampicillin and allopurinol together may result in a higher risk of skin rashes. Probenecid may increase blood levels of ampicillin and increase the risk of ampicillin-related side effects.

**FOOD INTERACTIONS**

Ampicillin should be taken at least one-half hour before or two hours after meals to ensure maximum absorption of the drug.

**OTHER DRUGS USED FOR SIMILAR CONDITIONS**

For the treatment of *Salmonella* infections, amoxicillin, trimethoprim/sulfamethoxazole, and ciprofloxacin are alternatives to ampicillin. For *Shigella,* trimethoprim/sulfamethoxazole is usually the treatment of choice.

# AZITHROMYCIN

**BRAND NAME (MANUFACTURER)**
Zithromax (Pfizer)

**TYPE OF DRUG**
Antibiotic/antiprotozoal

**USED FOR**
Azithromycin is used to treat mild-to-moderate bacterial infections, specifically infections of the respiratory tract and skin caused by *Haemophilus* or *Streptococcus*. For these infections, azithromycin is used primarily when other less toxic antibiotics like penicillin cannot be used. Azithromycin is also used to treat pneumonia and pelvic inflammatory disease. Azithromycin is also commonly used to treat sexually transmitted infections caused by *Haemophilus* or *Chlamydia*. It is not effective when used alone to treat gonorrhea or syphilis.

In people infected with HIV, azithromycin is often used as part of combination therapy to treat or prevent *Mycobacterium avium* complex (MAC). Azithromycin is also sometimes used to treat the HIV-related protozoal infections cryptosporidiosis and toxoplasmosis. The FDA has approved azithromycin for the prevention of MAC disease.

**GENERAL INFORMATION**
Azithromycin is a derivative of erythromycin and belongs to a class of antibiotics called macrolides. Macrolides stop bacteria from making proteins, which prevents them from multiplying. Although used primarily to treat bacterial or protozoal infections, azithromycin is sometimes used to prevent infection.

Azithromycin is available as capsules, tablets, and as a solution for oral administration or intravenous injection.

**TREATMENT**
For most respiratory or skin infections, azithromycin is taken in a dose of 500 mg on the first day followed by 250 mg once daily on days two through five. For treatment of chancroid or chlamydia in people with healthy immune systems, the recommended dose is 1,000 mg taken only once. In people with HIV, a follow-up dose after three to seven days may be necessary. A 1997 U.S. Public Health Service Task Force recommends treating MAC with either azithromycin or clarithromycin plus at least one other drug such as ethambutol or rifabutin. Ciprofloxacin and amikacin are also commonly used as part of the combination regimen. In combination therapy for MAC, azithromycin is generally taken at a dose of 500–600 mg per day. It should be noted that the Division of AIDS of the National Institute of Allergy and Infectious Diseases recently recommended that clofazimine not be used since

the addition of the drug did not result in any added benefit and may result in increased risk of death.

If effective in treating acute episodes of MAC in people with HIV, azithromycin therapy should be continued for life.

For toxoplasmosis, azithromycin has been studied alone and in combination with pyrimethamine, but given the small amount of information available, no firm recommendations can be made regarding the use of azithromycin for toxoplasmosis.

There is little consensus on appropriate treatment for cryptosporidiosis. Intravenous azithromycin is one treatment being tested in clinical trials. The doses used vary from 500 to 1,800 mg daily, and the early results of the trials suggest the drug may have some effect.

### PREVENTION

A 1997 U.S. Public Health Service Task Force recommends that people with less than 50 CD4+ cells receive either clarithromycin or azithromycin to prevent MAC. If clarithromycin or azithromycin cannot be tolerated, rifabutin is recommended as an alternative. Use of these antibiotics must be weighed against the potential side effects and the possibility that the MAC bacteria may develop resistance over time.

In one study, incidence of MAC in people using azithromycin was 65% less than those taking only a placebo. Another study compared azithromycin alone to rifabutin alone to the combination of the two. The study found that azithromycin was as effective as rifabutin in preventing MAC disease. The combination of the two was even more potent, but was associated with much higher side effects than either monotherapy treatment.

### CAUTIONS AND WARNINGS

Azithromycin should not be used by people who know they are allergic to it or any of the derivatives of erythromycin.

Azithromycin should be used with caution in people with impaired liver function, since the drug is eliminated from the body by the liver.

The bacteria that cause MAC and tuberculosis are similar. Treating MAC can mask the symptoms of tuberculosis; consequently, people considering preventive therapy for MAC should first be tested for tuberculosis.

### SIDE EFFECTS

Most side effects related to azithromycin occur in the digestive tract, including nausea, vomiting, loose stools, diarrhea, and abdominal pain. Rare, but potentially serious, side effects include swelling of blood vessels and damage to the liver. There have been some reports that azithromycin may cause hearing loss.

Rare but serious allergic reactions have also been reported in people taking azithromycin. Because the drug stays in the body long after people stop taking it, allergic reactions can occur even after therapy is stopped.

**PREGNANCY/BREAST-FEEDING**

Azithromycin has not been formally studied in pregnant women. In animal studies, it did not cause fetal harm, but whether this is true in humans is not known. It is also not known whether azithromycin crosses the placenta, but the chemically related antibiotic erythromycin does. Pregnant women are encouraged to discuss the benefits and potential risks of using azithromycin with their physician before making a decision whether or not to use the drug.

The 1997 U.S. Public Health Service Task Force recommends that pregnant women be offered preventative therapy against MAC. Azithromycin should be considered the drug of choice and clarithromycin should only be used if no alternative therapy is appropriate.

HIV can be passed from a woman to her child through breast milk. In areas where nutritionally sound alternatives are readily available, breast-feeding is discouraged for HIV-positive women. It is not known whether azithromycin is excreted into breast milk. Because of the potential toxicity of the drug, women should consider alternatives to breast-feeding while taking it.

**USE IN CHILDREN**

Azithromycin has been approved by the FDA for the treatment of otitis media (ear infection), and pharyngitis/tonsillitis (inflammation of the pharynx resulting in a severe sore throat).

The 1997 U.S. Public Health Service Task Force recommends that children under 13 years of age with advanced HIV disease receive either clarithromycin or azithromycin to prevent MAC. The following guidelines have been established: children over six years of age and less than 50 CD4+ cells; children aged 2-6 years and less than 75 CD4+ cells; children 1-2 years and less than 500 CD4+ cells; and children under 12 months of age and less than 750 CD4+ cells should all be offered preventative therapy.

**USE IN THE ELDERLY**

A dosage adjustment does not appear necessary for healthy elderly people with normal kidney and liver function. Reduced doses may be required for older adults with impaired liver or kidney function.

**DRUG INTERACTIONS**

Antacids that contain aluminum or magnesium decrease blood levels of azithromycin. Azithromycin may increase the blood thinning effect of warfarin. Azithromycin may increase levels of theophylline, phenytoin, and rifabutin in the body, potentially increasing the risk of side effects from these drugs.

**FOOD INTERACTIONS**

Azithromycin should be taken at least one hour before or two hours after meals, because food in the stomach reduces absorption of the drug by 50%. Azithromycin tablets and oral solution can be taken with or without food.

**OTHER DRUGS USED FOR SIMILAR CONDITIONS**

Clarithromycin is the primary alternative to azithromycin in combination with other drugs for the treatment of MAC. For prevention of MAC in people with CD4+ counts less than 50, the Public Health Service Task Force recommends using clarithromycin or azithromycin. Rifabutin should only be used if clarithromycin or azithromycin cannot be tolerated.

For the treatment of cryptosporidiosis, alternatives to azithromycin being tested include paromomycin, octreotide, atovaquone, Immuno-C, NTZ, and bovine colostrum, although the effectiveness of each of these agents against cryptosporidiosis has not been fully determined.

Sulfadiazine combined with pyrimethamine is standard therapy for treatment of toxoplasmosis. When sulfa drugs cannot be tolerated, pyrimethamine can be combined with clindamycin or azithromycin. Atovaquone, a drug with activity against toxoplasmosis, is being tested alone and in combination.

The emphasis in managing toxoplasmosis is shifting from treatment to prevention. People who have antibodies to the protozoa and CD4+ counts less than 100 are at risk for the disease. Prophylactic drug combinations including trimethoprim/sulfamethoxazole (Bactrim or Septra) or dapsone plus pyrimethamine have been effective in preventing initial infection.

For treatment of chlamydial infections, azithromycin is often the drug of choice because it can be taken in a single dose while other therapies may require up to four doses a day for seven to ten days. Doxycycline, ofloxacin, and erythromycin are alternatives.

**COMMENTS**

In the early stages of the AIDS epidemic, many physicians thought treating MAC was futile. Mycobacteria are notorious for becoming drug resistant, and effective treatment requires several different drugs (some with severe side effects). However, a combination regimen of clarithromycin, rifabutin, and ethambutol was shown to be effective and significantly superior to ethambutol, rifampin, clofazimine, and ciprofloxacin for treating MAC and prolonging survival.

With the development of new drugs and new combinations that have fewer side effects, however, the attitude of many physicians has changed. Treating MAC is likely to prolong survival, reduce symptoms, and improve quality of life.

Prevention and early detection of cryptosporidiosis are high priorities because treatment of the full-blown disease in people with advanced stages of AIDS is only moderately successful. Because the value of antibiotics and antiparasitic drugs in preventing the spread of the disease has yet to be determined, the focus must remain on preventing the spread of the microorganism through contaminated water or feces. Thorough hand washing and sterilization of surfaces with full-strength bleach for fifteen minutes, 5% ammonia (a capful of ammonia in a quart of water) for more than fifteen minutes, or heat to greater than 113°F for thirty minutes have proven effective at killing cryptosporidia. Water filters with a one-micron or smaller pore size have also been effective at screening out the microorganism.

# CEFACLOR

**BRAND NAME (MANUFACTURER)**
Ceclor (Lilly)

**TYPE OF DRUG**
Antibiotic

**USED FOR**
Cefaclor is used to treat infections of the ears, respiratory tract, urinary tract, and skin. In people infected with HIV, it is occasionally used in combination with antihistamines to treat inflammation of the sinuses.

**GENERAL INFORMATION**
Cefaclor is an orally administered, broad-spectrum antibiotic that belongs to a class called cephalosporins. These antibiotics are structurally similar to the penicillin-type antibiotics, and some people who are allergic to penicillin may also be allergic to cefaclor.

**TREATMENT**
The usual adult dose of cefaclor is 250 mg taken every eight hours. For more severe infections, higher doses may be needed.

**CAUTIONS AND WARNINGS**
Cefaclor should not be used by people who know they are allergic to it or any of the other cephalosporin antibiotics.

It is important to take cefaclor for the entire time indicated by the physician, usually seven to fourteen days. If the drug is stopped too soon, resistant bacteria may grow, and the infection could recur.

### SIDE EFFECTS

About 2.5% of people taking the drug experience digestive tract side effects including diarrhea. Few people taking the drug experience allergic reactions, nausea, or vomiting.

### PREGNANCY/BREAST-FEEDING

Cefaclor has not been formally studied in pregnant women. In animal studies, it did not cause fetal harm, but it is not known whether this is true for humans. Pregnant women are encouraged to discuss the benefits and potential risks of cefaclor with their physician before deciding to use the drug.

HIV can be passed from a woman to her child through breast milk. In areas where nutritionally sound alternatives are readily available, breast-feeding is discouraged for HIV-positive women. Cefaclor is excreted in human milk. Because the effect of the drug on nursing infants is unknown, women are encouraged to consider alternatives to breast-feeding while using it.

### USE IN CHILDREN

Cefaclor is routinely used in children at a dose of 20 mg per kg of body weight per day, divided into three equal doses taken eight hours apart. Higher doses may be required for more serious infections, up to a maximum dose of 1 g per day. The drug is not recommended for children under one month of age, because their kidneys are not fully developed.

### USE IN THE ELDERLY

In general, the dose does not need to be adjusted in elderly people who have normal kidney and liver function. Reduced doses may be required for older adults with impaired liver or kidney function.

### DRUG INTERACTIONS

Probenecid may increase the concentrations of cefaclor in the blood and increase the risk of side effects. The side effects of furosemide, bumetanide, ethacrynic acid, colistin, vancomycin, polymyxin B, and aminoglycoside antibiotics may be increased by cefaclor.

### FOOD INTERACTIONS

Food may interfere with the speed at which cefaclor is taken up into the body, although it doesn't affect the total amount absorbed.

### OTHER DRUGS USED FOR SIMILAR CONDITIONS

Ampicillin, chloramphenicol, trimethoprim/sulfamethoxazole, amoxicillin, ceftriaxone, or cefotaxime are antibiotics that can be used in place of cefaclor for many different types of infection. The choice usually depends on side effects and the drug resistance of the particular pathogen causing the infection.

# CEFEPIME

**BRAND NAME (MANUFACTURER)**
Maxipime (Bristol-Myers Squibb)

**TYPE OF DRUG**
Antibiotic

**USED FOR**
Cefepime is used for bacterial infections of the skin and urinary tract and for pneumonia.

**GENERAL INFORMATION**
Cefepime is a broad-spectrum antibiotic of the cephalosporin class. It is generally not the first-choice therapy for most bacterial infections because it cannot be taken orally. It is particularly useful when the infection is in the brain or another part of the central nervous system, and when the bacteria is resistant to penicillin or the oral cephalosporins. Cefepime weakens cell walls of newly formed bacteria.

As with most antibiotics, resistance to cefepime will almost inevitably develop, and inappropriate use of the drug (not taking the amount prescribed) may hasten the appearance of resistant strains.

Cefepime is available for intravenous injection.

**TREATMENT**
For most infections, the adult dose of cefepime is 0.5 to 2 g given twice a day. Cefepime should be given by intravenous injection over a 30-minute period. People with kidney impairment should use a lower dose. A further dose reduction is necessary for women with kidney impairment.

**CAUTIONS AND WARNINGS**
Cefepime should not be taken by people who know they are allergic to it or other cephalosporin, penicillin, or beta-lactam classes of antibiotics.

Cefepime, like all other cephalosporins, can cause kidney damage. Since the drug is primarily excreted by the kidney, dose reduction will be necessary for people with impaired kidney function.

People taking cefepime may need supplements of vitamin K if they have low vitamin K synthesis or low vitamin K reserves. Cefepime may interfere with blood clotting, and vitamin K is essential to the clotting process. Consequently, people living with hemophilia should use cefepime with caution.

Cefepime should be used with caution in people with a history of digestive tract disease, especially inflammation of the colon, because these people are at higher risk of digestive tract side effects, including diarrhea, nausea, vomiting, or fungal infection of the colon.

**SIDE EFFECTS**

Common side effects include pain, tenderness, or hardness at the injection site. Rash, diarrhea, nausea, vomiting, fever or chills, and deficiencies in red or white blood cells occur less frequently.

**PREGNANCY/BREAST-FEEDING**

Cefepime has not been formally studied in pregnant women. Although cephalosporin antibiotics are considered relatively safe for use during pregnancy, cefepime should be used only if clearly needed.

HIV can be passed from a woman to her child through breast milk. In areas where nutritionally sound alternatives are readily available, breast-feeding is discouraged for HIV-positive women. Small concentrations of cefepime pass through human milk, but the drug is considered safe for newborns.

**USE IN CHILDREN**

Cefepime is not recommended for children under 12 years of age because its safety and effectiveness have not been formally studied or established for them.

**USE IN THE ELDERLY**

Elderly people with normal kidney and liver function should be able to take cefepime without dosage modification. Older adults with impaired kidney function may require reduced doses.

**DRUG INTERACTIONS**

Probenecid may increase blood levels of cephalosporins, potentially increasing the risk of side effects. High doses of the aminoglycoside class of drug and potent diuretics (such as furosemide) may increase the risk of kidney toxicities when used with cefepime.

**FOOD INTERACTIONS**

Cefepime is not an oral medication; consequently, food does not affect its absorption into the body, and the drug may be taken with or without food.

**OTHER DRUGS USED FOR SIMILAR CONDITIONS**

Ampicillin, chloramphenicol, trimethoprim/sulfamethoxazole, amoxicillin, ceftriaxone, or cefotaxime are antibiotics that can be used in place of cefepime for many different types of infection. The choice usually depends on side effects and the drug resistance of the particular pathogen causing the infection.

# CEFIXIME

**BRAND NAME (MANUFACTURER)**
Suprax (Lederle)

**TYPE OF DRUG**
Antibiotic

**USED FOR**

Cefixime is used for bacterial infections of the urinary tract, throat, and ear. It is also used to treat bronchitis and gonorrhea.

**GENERAL INFORMATION**

Cefixime is a broad-spectrum antibiotic of the cephalosporin class. Cefixime weakens cell walls of newly formed bacteria.

As with most antibiotics, resistance to cefixime will almost inevitably develop, and inappropriate use of the drug (not taking the amount prescribed) may hasten the appearance of resistant strains.

Cefixime is available in tablets and suspension for oral administration.

**TREATMENT**

The usual dose of cefixime is 400 mg once daily or 200 mg twice daily. People with kidney impairment should use a lower dose.

**CAUTIONS AND WARNINGS**

Cefixime should not be taken by people who know they are allergic to it or other drugs in the cephalosporin class of antibiotics.

Cefixime, like all other cephalosporins, can cause kidney damage. Since the drug is primarily excreted by the kidney, dose reduction will be necessary for people with impaired kidney function.People with kidney dysfunction are also at increased risk for developing seizures if the dosage is not reduced.

Cefixime should be used with caution in people with a history of digestive tract disease, especially inflammation of the colon, because these people are at higher risk of digestive tract side effects, including diarrhea, nausea, vomiting, or fungal infection of the colon.

**SIDE EFFECTS**

Common side effects include diarrhea, abdominal pain, and nausea.

**PREGNANCY/BREAST-FEEDING**

Cefixime has not been formally studied in pregnant women. Although cephalosporin antibiotics are considered relatively safe for use during pregnancy, cefixime should be used only if clearly needed.

HIV can be passed from a woman to her child through breast milk. In areas where nutritionally sound alternatives are readily available, breast-feeding is discouraged for HIV-positive women. It is not known whether cefixime passes through human milk, but the drug is considered safe for newborns.

**USE IN CHILDREN**

Cefixime is not recommended for children under 6 months of age because its safety and effectiveness in this age group have not been formally studied or established. For children over 6 months of age, cefixime is usually given as an oral suspension at a dose of 8 mg/kg once a day or as two divided doses

at 4 mg/kg every 12 hours. Children over 12 months of age should be given the adult dose.

**USE IN THE ELDERLY**
Elderly people with normal kidney and liver function should be able to take cefixime without dosage modification. Older adults with impaired kidney function may require reduced doses.

**DRUG INTERACTIONS**
None reported.

**FOOD INTERACTIONS**
Cefixime may be taken with or without food.

**OTHER DRUGS USED FOR SIMILAR CONDITIONS**
Ampicillin, chloramphenicol, trimethoprim/sulfamethoxazole, amoxicillin, ceftriaxone, or cefotaxime are antibiotics that can be used in place of cefixime for many different types of infection. The choice usually depends on side effects and the drug resistance of the particular pathogen causing the infection.

# CEFTRIAXONE

**BRAND NAME (MANUFACTURER)**
Rocephin (Roche)

**TYPE OF DRUG**
Antibiotic

**USED FOR**
Ceftriaxone is used for bacterial infections of the lower respiratory tract, skin, urinary tract, bones and joints, abdomen, and blood. It is also used for pelvic inflammatory disease and meningitis.

Ceftriaxone is often used by women with HIV for gynecological infections, including vaginal ulcers (chancroid), chlamydia, syphilis, and gonorrhea.

**GENERAL INFORMATION**
Ceftriaxone is a broad-spectrum antibiotic of the cephalosporin class. It is generally not the first-choice therapy for most bacterial infections because it cannot be taken orally. It is particularly useful when the infection is in the brain or another part of the central nervous system, and when the bacteria is resistant to penicillin or the oral cephalosporins. Ceftriaxone weakens cell walls of newly formed bacteria.

**TREATMENT**
For most infections the adult dose of ceftriaxone is 1 to 2 g given once a day or divided into two equal doses. The total daily dose should not exceed 4 g.

For treatment of gonorrhea or chancroid, a single 250 mg dose injected into a muscle is usually sufficient.

For most infections, the dosage for children is 50 to 75 mg per kg of body weight per day. The total daily dose should not exceed 2 g. For treatment of meningitis, children generally receive 100 mg per kg of body weight per day, not to exceed 4 g per day. The usual duration of therapy for meningitis is seven to fourteen days.

### CAUTIONS AND WARNINGS

Ceftriaxone should not be taken by people who know they are allergic to it or other drugs in the cephalosporin class of antibiotics. Drugs related to penicillin (ampicillin, amoxicillin, etc.) are similar in structure to cephalosporins. It is possible that someone allergic to penicillin will also be allergic to ceftriaxone, although the risk is small.

Ceftriaxone, like all other cephalosporins, can cause kidney damage. Since the drug is metabolized by both the kidney and the liver, impaired function in either should not require dose reductions. If both the liver and the kidneys are not working properly, a dose reduction may be required.

People taking ceftriaxone may need to take supplements of vitamin K if they have low vitamin K synthesis or low vitamin K reserves. Ceftriaxone may interfere with blood clotting, and vitamin K is essential to the clotting process. Consequently, people living with hemophilia should use ceftriaxone with caution.

Ceftriaxone should be used with caution in people with a history of digestive tract disease, especially inflammation of the colon, because these people are at higher risk of digestive tract side effects, including diarrhea, nausea, vomiting, or fungal infection of the colon.

### SIDE EFFECTS

Common side effects include pain, tenderness, or hardness at the injection site. Rash, itching, fever or chills, blood-clotting disorders, and deficiencies in red or white blood cells occur less frequently. Diarrhea is common among people taking ceftriaxone, but nausea and vomiting occur less often.

### PREGNANCY/BREAST-FEEDING

Ceftriaxone has not been formally studied in pregnant women. Although cephalosporin antibiotics are considered relatively safe for use during pregnancy, ceftriaxone should be used only if clearly needed.

HIV can be passed from a woman to her child through breast milk. In areas where nutritionally sound alternatives are readily available, breast-feeding is discouraged for HIV-positive women. Small concentrations of ceftriaxone pass through human milk, but the drug is considered safe for newborns.

**USE IN CHILDREN**

Ceftriaxone has been used extensively in children at the dosages described on page 41 (see Treatment). It should not, however, be given to children with symptoms of liver problems because of the risk of serious side effects.

**USE IN THE ELDERLY**

Elderly people with normal kidney and liver function should be able to take ceftriaxone without dosage modification. Older adults with impaired liver or kidney function may require reduced doses.

**DRUG INTERACTIONS**

Probenecid may increase blood levels of cephalosporins, potentially increasing the risk of side effects.

**FOOD INTERACTIONS**

Ceftriaxone is not an oral medication; consequently, food does not affect its absorption into the body, and the drug may be taken with or without food.

**OTHER DRUGS USED FOR SIMILAR CONDITIONS**

For treatment of chancroid (vaginal ulcers), azithromycin, amoxicillin/clavulanate (Augmentin), erythromycin, and ciprofloxacin are alternatives to ceftriaxone. Azithromycin or ceftriaxone are often used first, because they require only a single treatment. Erythromycin, amoxicillin/clavulanate, and ciprofloxacin require treatment over a number of days and may be prescribed if azithromycin or ceftriaxone are ineffective or not tolerated.

For treatment of gonorrhea, many antibiotics are safe and effective. Alternative treatments to ceftriaxone include cefixime, ciprofloxacin, azithromycin, erythromycin, and ofloxacin. During pregnancy, the drug of choice is cefuroxime because of its safety profile.

For treatment of chlamydial infections, azithromycin is often the drug of choice because it can be taken in a single dose while other therapies may require up to four doses a day for seven to ten days. Doxycycline, ofloxacin, and erythromycin are alternatives.

# CEFUROXIME

**BRAND NAME (MANUFACTURER)**

Ceftin (Glaxo Wellcome); Kefurox (Lilly); Zinacef (Glaxo Wellcome)

**TYPE OF DRUG**

Antibiotic

**USED FOR**

Cefuroxime is used to treat bacterial infections of the ear, respiratory tract, skin, sinuses, bones and joints, and urinary tract.

**GENERAL INFORMATION**

Cefuroxime is a broad-spectrum antibiotic belonging to the cephalosporin class. It works by preventing susceptible bacteria from building strong cell walls. The drug is available as tablets, an oral suspension, and a solution for injection. The different forms are taken up differently by the body and require different doses. The oral suspension is intended primarily for children. The tablets are used for mild-to-moderate infections, and the solution for injection is used for more serious infections.

**TREATMENT**

Commonly used adult doses of the tablets range from 250 to 500 mg taken twice a day for ten days. Uncomplicated urinary tract infections are treated with 125 to 250 mg taken twice daily for seven to ten days.

The dose of the oral suspension varies between 20 and 30 mg per kg of body weight per day for ten days, depending on the infection.

The solution for injection is administered at 750 mg to 1.5 g every eight hours depending on the condition. For severe or complicated infections, 1.5 g every eight hours is recommended. Life-threatening infections or infections due to less susceptible organisms may require 1.5 g every six hours. These dosages may need to be reduced for people with severely impaired kidney function.

**CAUTIONS AND WARNINGS**

Cefuroxime should not be used by people who know they are allergic to it or any other cephalosporin antibiotic. It is possible that someone allergic to penicillin will also be allergic to cefuroxime, although the risk is small.

**SIDE EFFECTS**

The most common side effects include diarrhea, nausea, vomiting, and abdominal pain. These side effects occur more frequently at higher doses of the drug.

**PREGNANCY/BREAST-FEEDING**

Cefuroxime has not been formally studied in pregnant women. In animal studies, the drug did not cause fetal harm, but it is not known whether the same would be true for humans. Although cephalosporin antibiotics are considered relatively safe for use during pregnancy, cefuroxime should be used only if clearly needed. Pregnant women are encouraged to discuss the benefits and potential risks of cefuroxime with their physician before deciding to use the drug.

HIV can be passed from a woman to her child through breast milk. In areas where nutritionally sound alternatives are readily available, breast-feeding is discouraged for HIV-positive women. Cefuroxime is excreted in human milk. Because of the potential toxicity of the drug, women are encouraged to consider alternatives to breast-feeding while using it.

### USE IN CHILDREN

Cefuroxime has been extensively studied in children between the ages of three months and twelve years. The oral suspension is the usual form children take, but they can also take the tablet if they can swallow it whole. Five percent of children studied didn't like the taste of the oral suspension.

### USE IN THE ELDERLY

No dosage adjustments are necessary in older people with normal kidney function. No differences were seen in clinical trials comparing the drug's effectiveness and safety in people above or below the age of sixty-five. Reduced doses may be required for older adults with impaired kidney function.

### DRUG INTERACTIONS

Probenecid may increase the concentrations of cefuroxime in the blood and increase the risk of side effects. The side effects of furosemide, bumetanide, ethacrynic acid, colistin, vancomycin, polymyxin B, and aminoglycoside antibiotics may be increased by cefuroxime.

### FOOD INTERACTIONS

Cefuroxime may be taken with or without food.

### OTHER DRUGS USED FOR SIMILAR CONDITIONS

Cefaclor, cefixime, and cephalexin are equivalent alternatives. Penicillin-type antibiotics (penicillin, ampicillin, amoxicillin, etc.) can also be used for similar conditions. The drug of choice usually depends on side effects and the drug-resistance profile of the particular pathogen causing the infection.

# CHLORAMPHENICOL

### BRAND NAME (MANUFACTURER)

Chloromycetin (Parke-Davis); Elase-Chloromycetin (Fujisawa)

### TYPE OF DRUG

Antibiotic

### USED FOR

Chloramphenicol is a broad-spectrum antibiotic used to treat a number of bacterial infections, including *Salmonella* infections, meningitis caused by *Haemophilus influenzae*, rickets, and cholera.

In HIV-infected people, chloramphenicol is most frequently used to treat *Salmonella* infections that cause severe diarrhea.

### GENERAL INFORMATION

Chloramphenicol is used for serious infections caused by organisms that are resistant to other antibiotics or when other antibiotics are not tolerated. There are significant side effects with chloramphenicol, so it should only be used

when necessary. Chloramphenicol prevents multiplication of susceptible bacteria by preventing them from making strong cell walls and essential proteins.

*Salmonella* infection is twenty times more common in people with AIDS than in the general population. In people with healthy immune systems, the infection is rarely treated, but symptoms tend to be much more severe in immuno-compromised people and require intervention.

Chloramphenicol comes in tablets, ointment, and solution for injection.

## TREATMENT

The typical dosage of chloramphenicol for adults is 50 mg per kg of body weight per day divided into equal doses at six-hour intervals. In exceptional cases, 100 mg per kg per day may be required, but this dose is usually lowered as soon as possible. Impairment of kidney or liver function may require dose reduction. Children are given the same dosage, based on weight, as adults.

## CAUTIONS AND WARNINGS

Chloramphenicol should not be taken by anyone with a known allergy to it. During extended therapy, physicians often monitor the levels of chloramphenicol in the blood. If the drug causes significant decreases in red or white blood cells, it should be discontinued.

Repeated treatment with the drug should be avoided if at all possible to reduce the risk of serious side effects.

## SIDE EFFECTS

Although rare, the most serious side effect of chloramphenicol is bone marrow suppression. The bone marrow is the site where white blood cells, red blood cells, and platelets (particles involved in blood clotting) are produced. Chloramphenicol can cause serious and sometimes fatal bone marrow suppression even weeks or months after therapy is stopped. For this reason, most physicians recommend its use only when other drugs are ineffective or not tolerated.

Minor side effects include nausea, vomiting, diarrhea, and other digestive tract disturbances. Headache, mild depression, mental confusion, short attention span, and impaired thinking have also been noted. Inflammation of nerves in the eyes has been reported, especially after long-term use. Rarely, fever, rashes, swelling, itching, and other allergic reactions may occur.

## PREGNANCY/BREAST-FEEDING

Chloramphenicol readily passes through the placenta. Although it appears safe during early pregnancy, it can cause severe side effects in newborns whose mothers take the drug in late pregnancy or during labor. Given the potential toxicity to newborns, chloramphenicol should be used in pregnant women only when there is no alternative.

HIV can be passed from a woman to her child through breast milk. In areas where nutritionally sound alternatives are readily available, breast-feeding is discouraged for HIV-positive women. Small amounts of chloramphenicol can pass through breast milk and cause side effects in infants. Because of the potential toxicity of the drug, women should consider alternatives to breast-feeding while taking it.

**USE IN CHILDREN**
High levels of chloramphenicol have been detected in newborn infants given the drug. Because newborns have immature liver and kidney function, these high drug levels puts them at risk for gray baby syndrome. For this reason, infants require close monitoring of their drug levels by their physician.

**DRUG INTERACTIONS**
Chloramphenicol can increase the blood levels of dicumarol, phenytoin, phenobarbital, tolbutamide, and chloropropamide, increasing the risk of side effects. Acetaminophen and penicillin may increase the levels of chloramphenicol in the blood, potentially increasing the risk of side effects.

Chloramphenicol can reduce the effectiveness of iron, vitamin B, and cyclophosphamide.

Chloramphenicol should not be used with other drugs that suppress bone marrow function (AZT, ganciclovir, or cancer treatments, for example), because their side effects may be additive.

**FOOD INTERACTIONS**
Chloramphenicol is absorbed most effectively when taken on an empty stomach. It should be taken one hour before or two hours after a meal.

**OTHER DRUGS USED FOR SIMILAR CONDITIONS**
Ampicillin is the most frequently used treatment for *Salmonella* infection. If the bacteria is resistant to ampicillin or if there is a penicillin allergy, chloramphenicol, trimethoprim/sulfamethoxazole, or cephalosporin are alternatives. For chronic infection, ciprofloxacin may be useful.

# CIPROFLOXACIN

**BRAND NAME (MANUFACTURER)**
Cipro (Bayer); Ciloxan (Alcon)

**TYPE OF DRUG**
Antibiotic

**USED FOR**
Ciprofloxacin is a broad-spectrum antibiotic of the quinolone class. It is used for infections of the lower respiratory tract, skin, bones and joints, digestive

tract, and urinary tract and for sinusitis. Quinolone antibiotics are effective against many bacteria resistant to other antibiotics, including the penicillins and cephalosporins.

In people with HIV, ciprofloxacin is often used as part of combination therapy to treat *Mycobacterium avium* complex (MAC) and used alone to treat diarrhea caused by *Salmonella* or *Shigella* infection. It is also used in travelers with HIV to prevent bacterial infection.

## GENERAL INFORMATION

Ciprofloxacin was the first antibiotic in the quinolone class to be approved by the FDA. It works against susceptible bacteria by attaching to their cell walls and preventing multiplication. It is available as tablets, solution for intravenous injection, and eye drops.

## TREATMENT

For most uses, the oral formulation of the drug is preferred because it is easier to take. Two hundred milligrams of the injectable drug is equivalent to 250 mg of the oral drug.

For urinary tract infections, the usual dose of the drug is 250 to 500 mg taken twice daily. For lower respiratory tract infections, the recommended dose is 500 to 750 mg taken twice daily.

A 1997 U.S. Public Health Service Task Force recommends treating MAC with either azithromycin or clarithromycin **plus** at least one other drug such as ethambutol or rifabutin. Ciprofloxacin and amikacin are also commonly used as part of the combination regimen. In combination therapy for MAC, azithromycin is generally taken at a dose of 500-600 mg per day. It should be noted that the Division of AIDS of the National Institute of Allergy and Infectious Diseases recently recommended that clofazimine not be used since the addition of the drug did not result in any added benefit and may result in increased risk of death. For combination therapy of MAC, ciprofloxacin is generally used at a dose of 500 to 750 mg taken twice daily.

Diarrhea caused by *Salmonella* or *Shigella* infection often responds to ciprofloxacin. The standard dose for infections caused by *Salmonella* is 500 mg taken twice daily for seven days. For *Shigella,* 500 mg taken four times a day for seven days is used.

In general, ciprofloxacin treatment is continued for two days after symptoms of infection disappear, and the usual duration is somewhere between seven and fourteen days. However, prolonged therapy may be required for certain conditions. Bone and joint infections may require treatment for four to six weeks or longer. If recurrences of diarrhea are frequent, long-term suppression therapy with ciprofloxacin may be appropriate.

The dose of ciprofloxacin may need to be reduced in people with impaired kidney function.

**CAUTIONS AND WARNINGS**

Ciprofloxacin should not be used in people allergic to it or to any antibiotics in the quinolone class. When taking the drug, it is a good idea to drink extra fluids to reduce the risk of kidney-related side effects.

Quinolones make some people sensitive to sunlight. Excessive sunlight should be avoided while taking the drug.

As with all quinolones, caution is recommended when the drug is used by people with a history of central nervous system disorders, since neurological side effects may be more common in these people.

**SIDE EFFECTS**

The most frequently reported side effects of ciprofloxacin include nausea, diarrhea, vomiting, abdominal pain/discomfort, headache, restlessness, and rash.

Convulsions, pressure on the brain, and psychotic episodes have been reported by some people taking quinolones. These drugs may also cause tremors, light-headedness, confusion, and hallucinations in rare cases.

Serious and potentially fatal allergic reactions have occurred after initial use of ciprofloxacin. The drug should be discontinued at the first sign of rash or other allergic symptom, and a physician should be contacted immediately.

**PREGNANCY/BREAST-FEEDING**

In animal studies ciprofloxacin increased the risk of spontaneous abortions, but it did not appear to cause birth defects. In formal studies of pregnant women, ciprofloxacin did not cause birth defects. Pregnant women are encouraged to discuss the benefits and potential risks of ciprofloxacin with their physician before making a decision about taking the drug.

HIV can be passed from a woman to her child through breast milk. In areas where nutritionally sound alternatives are readily available, breast-feeding is discouraged for HIV-positive women. Ciprofloxacin is also excreted in human milk. Because of the potential toxicity of the drug, women should consider alternatives to breast-feeding while taking it.

**USE IN CHILDREN**

In studies of juvenile animals, ciprofloxacin has been shown to cause permanent damage to cartilage. For this reason, the drug was not routinely used in children when it was first approved by the FDA. Since then, more than fifteen hundred children (most with cystic fibrosis) have been given ciprofloxacin in clinical studies. The drug was effective for nearly 100% of bacterial infections treated in children, and side effects occurred in 5% to 15% of children who received the drug. No cases of cartilage damage were observed.

**USE IN THE ELDERLY**

Older adults may be more susceptible to the side effects of the drug and may require reduced doses.

**DRUG INTERACTIONS**

Antacids containing magnesium hydroxide or aluminum hydroxide (e.g., Maalox, Mylanta, Gaviscon, etc.) may reduce the absorption of ciprofloxacin into the body by as much as 90%. For people taking ddI, ciprofloxacin should be taken two hours before or after taking ddI because ddI tablets and powder contain an antacid.

Ciprofloxacin causes increased theophylline levels and an increased risk of developing central nervous system side effects. If ciprofloxacin and theophylline must be used together, theophylline levels must be carefully monitored. This combination has been fatal in some cases.

Ciprofloxacin increases caffeine concentrations. Probenecid increases serum levels of ciprofloxacin. Ciprofloxacin enhances the blood-thinning effect of warfarin. Combined use of ciprofloxacin and cyclosporine may cause impairment of kidney function.

**FOOD INTERACTIONS**

Food slows the absorption of ciprofloxacin but does not affect the total amount absorbed. The drug may be taken with or without food.

**OTHER DRUGS USED FOR SIMILAR CONDITIONS**

For MAC treatment, ethambutol or rifabutin may be substituted for ciprofloxacin when used in combination with azithromycin or clarithromycin.

For treatment of bacterial infections causing diarrhea, amoxicillin, ampicillin, or trimethoprim/sulfamethoxazole may be used instead of ciprofloxacin.

For most bacterial infections, there is no single "definitive" treatment. The choice of drug will depend primarily on which drugs can be tolerated, which side effects a person is at risk for, and which drugs are effective for the particular organism.

# CLARITHROMYCIN

**BRAND NAME (MANUFACTURER)**

Biaxin (Abbott)

**TYPE OF DRUG**

Antibiotic

**USED FOR**

Clarithromycin is used to treat mild-to-moderate bacterial infections, specifically infections of the respiratory tract, skin, and soft tissue caused by *Streptococcus, Haemophilus, Moraxella, Staphylococcus, and Mycobacterium.* Addi-

tionally, clarithromycin is approved for the treatment of duodenal ulcers associated with *helicobacter pylori* when used in combination with omeprazole or ranitidine (see section on antiulcer drugs).

In people infected with HIV, clarithromycin is most often used as part of combination therapy to treat or prevent *Mycobacterium avium* complex (MAC).

**GENERAL INFORMATION**

Clarithromycin is a derivative of erythromycin and belongs to the macrolide class of antibiotics. All the macrolides work by stopping susceptible bacteria from making proteins, thus preventing them from multiplying. The different antibiotics in this class are effective against similar types of bacteria, but there are slight differences among these antibiotics. Clarithromycin is available as tablets and powder for oral suspension.

**TREATMENT**

A 1997 U.S. Public Health Service Task Force recommends treating MAC with either azithromycin or clarithromycin **plus** at least one other drug such as ethambutol or rifabutin. Ciprofloxacin and amikacin are also commonly used as part of the combination regimen.

In combination therapy for MAC, clarithromycin is generally taken at a dose of 500 mg twice a day. Uncomplicated respiratory infections (caused by a single type of bacteria) in people with healthy immune systems usually require lower dosages (250 to 500 mg, twice daily) for up to fourteen days.

If effective in treating acute episodes of MAC in people with HIV, clarithromycin therapy should continue for life to prevent recurrent MAC infection.

**PREVENTION**

A 1997 U.S. Public Health Service Task Force recommends that people with less than 50 CD4+ cells receive either clarithromycin or azithromycin to prevent MAC. If clarithromycin or azithromycin cannot be tolerated, rifabutin is recommended as an alternative. Use of these antibiotics must be weighed against the potential side effects and the possibility that the MAC bacteria may become resistant to a drug when used as a single agent for prevention of the disease. If resistance to a drug should develop during preventive therapy and the drug cannot be given at higher doses, the drug will probably have lost its effectiveness in that person for treatment of active infection.

Results from one study of seven hundred volunteers with CD4+ counts less than 100 that compared clarithromycin (500 mg twice daily) to a placebo for the prevention of MAC found that there was a 68% reduction in risk of developing MAC while on clarithromycin compared to a placebo. However, of fifteen people in the study who were treated with clarithromycin and de-

veloped MAC, nine also developed resistance to the drug, which limited their future treatment options.

### CAUTIONS AND WARNINGS

Clarithromycin should not be used by people who know they are allergic to it or to any other macrolide antibiotics.

Clarithromycin is eliminated from the body by the kidneys. People with reduced kidney function should use the drug with caution, and dose reductions may be required.

MAC and tuberculosis are caused by closely related bacteria. Treatment of MAC with clarithromycin may partially treat tuberculosis and mask its symptoms, so it is important to be tested for tuberculosis before starting any drug for the prevention or treatment of MAC.

In three different studies for the treatment of MAC, higher doses of clarithromycin (1,000 mg twice a day) was associated with increased risk of death.

### SIDE EFFECTS

The most frequent side effects of clarithromycin observed in clinical trials of people with AIDS include nausea and vomiting, which were reported by more than 7% of people taking the drug. Abdominal pain, rash, and abnormal taste were reported by more than 3% of volunteers in clinical trials. Diarrhea, gas, and headache were reported by 1% to 3%.

Clarithromycin may also cause reversible hearing loss, but this side effect is rare.

### PREGNANCY/BREAST-FEEDING

Clarithromycin has not been formally tested in pregnant women. The drug caused birth defects in all laboratory animals tested, and although this does not necessarily mean that the same would be true in humans, it is wise to use the drug during pregnancy only when there is no alternative.

The 1997 U.S. Public Health Service Task Force recommends that pregnant women be offered preventative therapy against MAC. Azithromycin should be considered the drug of choice and clarithromycin should only be used if no alternative therapy is appropriate.

HIV can be passed from a woman to her child through breast milk. In areas where nutritionally sound alternatives are readily available, breast-feeding is discouraged in HIV-positive women. It is not known if clarithromycin passes into breast milk, but similar drugs do. Because of the potential toxicity to the newborn child, women should consider alternatives to breast-feeding while taking it.

**USE IN CHILDREN**

Clarithromycin has been approved by the FDA for the treatment of otitis media (ear infection), MAC, sinusitis, uncomplicated skin infections and pharyngitis/tonsillitis (inflammation of the pharynx resulting in a severe sore throat).

In children, the recommended dosage as part of combination therapy for MAC is 7.5 mg per kg of body weight twice daily with a maximum daily dose of 1,000 mg.

In one clinical study of clarithromycin for the treatment of MAC, twenty-four children (1.7 to 20.6 years of age) were given clarithromycin up to a dosage of 15 mg per kg of body weight twice a day. The children were taking AZT, ddI, or ddC and had CD4+ counts less than 27. Clarithromycin was well tolerated at all dose levels tested. Only one child developed a serious side effect (high-frequency hearing loss). Clinical improvement occurred at all dose levels, but symptoms generally returned within six to twelve weeks. The researchers concluded that clarithromycin had some transient clinical benefit when used alone, but the recurrence of the disease underscored the need for combination therapy.

**USE IN THE ELDERLY**

In clinical trials, the frequency of side effects in younger and older adults was the same, but older adults may be more susceptible to the side effects of the drug and may require reduced doses.

**DRUG INTERACTIONS**

Clarithromycin levels are increased by both indinavir and ritonavir. Clarithromycin may increase the blood levels of theophylline, carbamazepine, cyclosporine, digoxin, triazolam, and phenytoin. Use of clarithromycin with astemizole or terfenadine may increase the risk of heart problems. Clarithromycin may reduce AZT levels in the blood.

Clarithromycin can double rifabutin levels, and rifabutin may decrease clarithromycin levels by 50%. This combination may increase the risk of painful eye inflammation (uveitis), arthritis, joint pain, and tenderness or pain in muscles.

**FOOD INTERACTIONS**

Clarithromycin may be taken with or without food.

**OTHER DRUGS USED FOR SIMILAR CONDITIONS**

Azithromycin is the primary alternative to clarithromycin in combination therapy for MAC. However, if someone is unable to tolerate clarithromycin because of gastrointestinal side effects, it is unlikely he or she will be able to tolerate azithromycin either.

For prevention of MAC in people with CD4+ counts less than 50, the Public Health Service Task Force recommends using clarithromycin or azithromycin.

Rifabutin should only be used if clarithromycin or azithromycin cannot be tolerated.

## COMMENTS

In the early stages of the AIDS epidemic, many physicians thought treating MAC was futile. Mycobacteria are notorious for becoming drug resistant, and effective treatment requires several different drugs (some with severe side effects). However, a combination regimen of clarithromycin, rifabutin, and ethambutol was shown to be effective and significantly superior to ethambutol, rifampin, clofazimine, and ciprofloxacin for treating MAC and prolonging survival.

With the development of new drugs and new drug combinations that have fewer side effects, however, the attitude of many physicians has changed. Treating MAC is likely to prolong survival, reduce symptoms, and improve quality of life.

# CLINDAMYCIN

## BRAND NAME (MANUFACTURER)

Cleocin (Pharmacia & Upjohn)

## TYPE OF DRUG

Antibiotic/antiprotozoal

## USED FOR

Clindamycin is used to treat bacterial infections of the respiratory tract, skin, abdomen, pelvis, and female genital tract.

In HIV-positive people, clindamycin is often used to treat *Pneumocystis carinii* pneumonia (PCP), toxoplasmosis encephalitis, and pelvic inflammatory disease.

## GENERAL INFORMATION

Clindamycin is one of relatively few oral antibiotics effective against anaerobic pathogens, microbes that can grow without the presence of free oxygen. The drug is available as capsules, flavored granules, a solution for intravenous injection, a topical gel, a lotion, a topical solution, and as a vaginal cream.

For people infected with HIV, clindamycin is used primarily in combination with the antimalarial drug primaquine to treat mild-to-moderate PCP in people who have failed or cannot tolerate trimethoprim/sulfamethoxazole (Bactrim/Septra). People with mild cases of PCP often take the oral form of clindamycin immediately. People with moderate cases of the disease sometimes initially receive clindamycin intravenously and then switch to the oral drug.

A few small studies have confirmed the effectiveness of clindamycin/primaquine for mild-to-moderate PCP. In one small study comparing the combination to Bactrim/Septra, both treatments were equally effective in suppressing the infection. Another study determined that the combination of clindamycin/primaquine was as effective as trimethoprim plus dapsone for the treatment of PCP.

Clindamycin has also proven effective in treating encephalitis (inflammation of the brain) caused by the protozoal pathogen *Toxoplasma gondii*. In one small study, clindamycin used in combination with the antimalarial drug pyrimethamine quickly suppressed the disease in most people treated. The majority of responders improved after a single week, and only a few quit taking the drug because of side effects. Clindamycin has also been used effectively in combination with sulfadiazine and pyrimethamine to treat toxoplasmosis.

For pelvic inflammatory disease, intravenous clindamycin can be combined with intravenous or intramuscular injections of gentamicin to treat acute infection, followed by gentamicin as maintenance therapy to prevent recurrence of the disease.

## TREATMENT

The dosage and administration of clindamycin varies depending on the disease and which formulation of the drug is used. For most bacterial infections, the adult oral dose is 150 to 300 mg taken every six hours. Higher doses are used for more severe infections.

In clinical studies for PCP, intravenous clindamycin was used at a dose of 600 mg every six hours for ten days followed by oral clindamycin at a dose of 450 mg every six hours for eleven days. Lower doses were used for volunteers who weighed less than 132 pounds. Corticosteroids or antihistamines were used at the same time to reduce the severity of side effects.

For treatment of toxoplasmosis, clindamycin is usually given orally at a dose of 600 mg every six hours for three to six weeks, in combination with pyrimethamine and sulfadiazine. Because these drugs interfere with vitamin B uptake, folinic acid or leucovorin calcium is usually added.

Clindamycin at 300 mg every six hours in combination with pyrimethamine and sulfadiazine is sometimes used to prevent recurrent toxoplasmosis infection in people who have already been previously treated.

## CAUTIONS AND WARNINGS

People who know they are allergic to clindamycin or lincomycin should not take either drug. Because clindamycin may stimulate the growth of a bacterium called *Clostridia* in the colon and cause a potentially fatal condition

called colitis, clindamycin is usually used only when other less toxic drugs have failed.

Mild cases of colitis caused by the drug generally improve when the drug is stopped. Moderate to severe cases may require treatment, usually with the antibiotic vancomycin. If significant diarrhea develops while taking clindamycin, a physician should be contacted and the therapy stopped.

### SIDE EFFECTS

The most significant side effect associated with the use of clindamycin is severe colitis, which is a potentially fatal superinfection caused by *Clostridia,* as described above. Severe and persistent diarrhea (occasionally bloody) and severe abdominal cramps are the first signs of colitis. People who experience these side effects should contact their physicians immediately.

Allergic reactions, including rashes, are the most common side effects. Nausea, vomiting, diarrhea, jaundice, and abnormal liver function have also been reported.

### PREGNANCY/BREAST-FEEDING

Clindamycin has not been formally studied in pregnant women. When taken during pregnancy, clindamycin can be found in high concentrations in fetal blood and tissues. It is not known whether the drug poses a significant risk to fetal development. Pregnant women are encouraged to discuss the benefits and potential risks of clindamycin with their physician before deciding to take the drug.

HIV can be passed from a woman to her child through breast milk. In areas where nutritionally sound alternatives are readily available, breast-feeding is discouraged for HIV-positive women. Clindamycin is excreted in human milk. Generally, with medical supervision, clindamycin is considered safe for use by nursing women.

### USE IN CHILDREN

There is an oral formulation of clindamycin specifically designed for children. It is used primarily when other less toxic alternatives are not effective or tolerated. Clindamycin is most often used in children at a dose of 8 to 16 mg per kg of body weight per day, but doses up to 25 mg per kg of body weight per day may be used for severe infections. In general, children who take the drug experience side effects at similar rates as adults.

### USE IN THE ELDERLY

Older people may be less able to tolerate the diarrhea that sometimes occurs with clindamycin. These people should report any change in bowel frequency to their physicians.

**DRUG INTERACTIONS**

Erythromycin may reduce the effectiveness of clindamycin. Codeine, hydrocodone, oxycodone, diphenoxylate (Lomotil), or atropine may prolong or worsen the diarrhea associated with the use of clindamycin. The absorption of clindamycin into the body may be slowed down by kaolin-pectin (Kaopectate).

**FOOD INTERACTIONS**

Clindamycin should be taken with a full glass of water or with food to minimize stomach upset.

**OTHER DRUGS USED FOR SIMILAR CONDITIONS**

For many of the bacterial infections treated with clindamycin, erythromycin is an effective alternative. However, erythromycin does not have as wide an antibacterial range as clindamycin. While clindamycin is effective against staphylococcus infections, erythromycin is not.

For treatment of PCP, TMP/SMX (Bactrim/Septra) is the drug of choice because it has been extensively studied and used in clinical practice. Pentamidine, dapsone with or without trimethoprim, and atovaquone are also treatments for PCP.

For treatment of toxoplasmosis, the standard therapy is pyrimethamine in combination with sulfadiazine. Azithromycin and atovaquone in combination with sulfadiazine or pyrimethamine may also be useful.

For treatment of pelvic inflammatory disease, clindamycin in combination with gentamicin or doxycycline plus a cephalosporin antibiotic (generally cefoxitin or cefotetan) are the most commonly used alternatives.

# DICLOXACILLIN

**BRAND NAME (MANUFACTURER)**
Pathocil (Wyeth-Ayerst)

**TYPE OF DRUG**
Antibiotic

**USED FOR**

Dicloxacillin is used primarily to treat infections caused by staphylococcal bacteria that are resistant to penicillin. In people infected with HIV, dicloxacillin is routinely used to treat staphylococcal infections of the skin and hair follicles. It is also used occasionally as maintenance therapy to suppress recurrent staphylococcal infections.

## GENERAL INFORMATION

Dicloxacillin is a penicillin-type antibiotic with a narrower spectrum of use than penicillin, but it is effective against bacteria that produce beta-lactamase, a protein that makes bacteria resistant to penicillin. Dicloxacillin is the drug of choice for staphylococcal infections in hospitals, because penicillin-resistant staphylococcal bacteria are most frequently found there. As more penicillin-resistant bacteria are found outside hospitals, especially in people with impaired immune systems, dicloxacillin is being used more frequently.

As with most antibiotics, resistance to dicloxacillin will almost inevitably develop, and inappropriate use of the drug (not taking the amount prescribed) may hasten the appearance of resistant strains.

Dicloxacillin is available as capsules and solution for oral administration.

## TREATMENT

The usual dose to treat mild to moderate infections in adults and children weighing 88 pounds or more is 125 mg taken every six hours. For children who weigh less, the recommended dose is 12.5 mg per kg of body weight per day, divided in four equal doses. Higher doses may be required for more severe infections.

For mild to moderate staphylococcal infections of hair follicles in HIV-positive people, the recommended dose is 500 mg taken four times a day for seven to fourteen days. For more severe infections, 600 mg of rifampin a day may be used in combination with the dicloxacillin. Rifampin is normally continued for five days.

## CAUTIONS AND WARNINGS

Dicloxacillin should not be used by people who know they are allergic to it or to any other penicillin-type antibiotics.

For serious or life-threatening infections, oral penicillins like dicloxacillin should not be used first, because they generally take longer to work than intravenously administered penicillins.

## SIDE EFFECTS

Dicloxacillin often causes digestive tract side effects that include nausea, vomiting, stomach upset, gas, or loose stools. As with other penicillins, allergic reactions such as skin rashes, redness, and itching may occur when taking dicloxacillin.

## PREGNANCY/BREAST-FEEDING

Dicloxacillin has not been formally studied in pregnant women or animals. Pregnant women are encouraged to discuss the benefits and potential risks of dicloxacillin with their physician before deciding to use the drug.

HIV can be passed from a woman to her child through breast milk. In areas where nutritionally sound alternatives are readily available, breast-feed-

ing is discouraged for HIV-positive women. Dicloxacillin may be excreted in human milk. Because there is little information about the effect of the drug on newborns, women are encouraged to consider alternatives to breast-feeding while using it.

### USE IN CHILDREN
Children routinely use dicloxacillin at the doses described above without unexpected side effects.

### USE IN THE ELDERLY
No alterations in dose are recommended for older adults with normal liver and kidney function. Dose reductions may be necessary for older adults with impaired liver and kidney function.

### DRUG INTERACTIONS
Probenecid may increase the blood concentrations of dicloxacillin, potentially increasing its side effects. Dicloxacillin may reduce the effectiveness of oral contraceptives.

### FOOD INTERACTIONS
Dicloxacillin is absorbed best when taken on an empty stomach, preferably one to two hours before meals.

### OTHER DRUGS USED FOR SIMILAR CONDITIONS
Oral erythromycin and topical mupirocin are alternative treatments for staphylococcus infections of the skin or hair follicles.

Oxacillin and nafcillin are commonly used to treat staph infections.

# DOXYCYCLINE

### BRAND NAME (MANUFACTURER)
Bio-Tab (International Ethical); Doryx (Parke-Davis); Monodox (Oclassen); Vibramycin (Pfizer)

### TYPE OF DRUG
Antibiotic

### USED FOR
Doxycycline is used to treat a wide variety of bacterial infections, including Lyme disease, Rocky Mountain spotted fever, mycoplasma infections, typhus fever, respiratory tract infections, bacillary angiomatosis, and traveler's diarrhea, among others.

In women infected with HIV, doxycycline is used to treat chlamydial infections and is used in combination with cefoxitin or cefotetan for the treatment of pelvic inflammatory disease. For people who are allergic to penicil-

lin or who have infections resistant to penicillin, doxycycline is an effective alternate for the treatment of syphilis.

### GENERAL INFORMATION

Doxycycline is a broad-spectrum antibiotic derived from tetracycline. The drug works by interfering with the production of proteins in susceptible bacteria, which prevents them from multiplying. Because doxycycline is chemically similar to tetracycline, bacteria that are resistant to one of the antibiotics may also be resistant to the other.

Doxycycline is available in tablets, capsules, oral suspension, oral syrup, and solution for injection.

### TREATMENT

The adult dose of doxycycline is usually 100 mg taken twice a day on the first day, followed by 100 mg taken daily thereafter. The duration of treatment varies by infection, but routinely lasts seven to fourteen days, longer for syphilis or bacillary angiomatosis.

Children above the age of eight weighing 100 pounds or less generally receive 2 mg of doxycycline per pound of body weight the first day, followed by 1 mg per pound of body weight daily thereafter.

People taking doxycycline are encouraged to drink plenty of fluids to reduce the potential for irritation of the esophagus. If irritation occurs, taking the drug with food or milk may help.

The metabolism of doxycycline does not appear to be altered in people with reduced kidney or liver function, and people with these conditions require no modifications in use.

### CAUTIONS AND WARNINGS

Doxycycline should not be used by anyone with a known allergy to it or any other derivatives of tetracycline. Some formulations of doxycycline contain sulfite preservatives and should be used with caution in people with known allergies to sulfites.

Doxycycline may cause sensitivity to sunlight, which may result in severe sunburns. People taking the drug should avoid bright sunlight or ultraviolet light, and the drug should be stopped at the first sign of skin redness.

### SIDE EFFECTS

Side effects of doxycycline use include nausea, vomiting, changes in appetite, and inflammation around the anus or genitals. The drug may also cause allergic reactions. Tetracyline drugs can also cause discoloration of developing teeth.

Rarely, anemia, increased susceptibility to infections, bleeding, and increased pressure within the brain (reversible) have also been reported.

**PREGNANCY/BREAST-FEEDING**

Doxycycline is not recommended for pregnant women. In animals, tetracyclines cross the placenta, often causing death to embryos and retardation of skeletal development in fetuses. The drug has not been formally studied in pregnant women, but the children of some women who have taken the drug during the last half of pregnancy developed permanent discoloration of teeth.

HIV can be passed from a woman to her child through breast milk. In areas where nutritionally sound alternatives are readily available, breast-feeding is discouraged for HIV-positive women. Doxycycline is excreted in human milk. Because of the potential toxicity of the drug, women are encouraged to consider alternatives to breast-feeding while using it.

**USE IN CHILDREN**

Doxycycline is not recommended for children under the age of eight. When used for premature children, it has caused decreases in bone growth rates. When used in children when their teeth enamel is being formed, it can cause permanent discoloration of teeth. The risk of these side effects is related to the dose used. Children over six years of age are not usually depositing enamel on their front teeth and are unlikely to experience teeth discoloration after using doxycycline.

**USE IN THE ELDERLY**

No changes in dose are recommended for elderly adults.

**DRUG INTERACTIONS**

Doxycycline decreases blood-clotting times and may require dosage adjustment for people taking warfarin. The uptake of tetracyclines, including doxycycline, is reduced when taking bismuth subsalicylate (Pepto-Bismol) or antacids.

Doxycycline may reduce the effectiveness of oral contraceptives and may interfere with the activity of penicillin. Barbiturates, carbamazepine, and phenytoin decrease the half-life of doxycycline, potentially reducing its effectiveness.

The concurrent use of tetracycline and methoxyflurane has been reported to result in fatal kidney damage.

**FOOD INTERACTIONS**

The uptake of doxycycline is not markedly affected by food, but food may be taken if the drug causes stomach upset.

**OTHER DRUGS USED FOR SIMILAR CONDITIONS**

Penicillin G is the recommended treatment for syphilis. Doxycycline or tetracycline may be used when penicillin is not tolerated or effective, but neither drug is as effective as penicillin.

For the treatment of pelvic inflammatory disease, a combination of clindamycin and gentamicin can be substituted for the combination of doxycycline plus a cephalosporin antibiotic (usually cefoxitin or cefotetan).

For treatment of chlamydial infections, azithromycin is often the drug of choice because it can be taken in a single daily dose while other therapies may require up to four doses a day for seven to ten days. Doxycycline, ofloxacin, and erythromycin are alternatives.

Erythromycin is an effective alternative to doxycycline for the treatment of bacillary angiomatosis.

# ERYTHROMYCIN

**BRAND NAME (MANUFACTURER)**
Akne-mycin (Hermal); Benamycin (Dermik); E-Mycin (Knoll); ERYC (Parke-Davis); Erycette (Ortho); EryPed (Abbott); Eryzole (Alra); Ilotycin (Dista); Theramycin Z (Medicis)

**TYPE OF DRUG**
Antibiotic

**USED FOR**
Erythromycin is a broad-spectrum antibiotic used for a wide variety of bacterial infections, including those of the upper and lower respiratory tract, middle ear, skin, eyes, digestive tract, and urinary and genital tracts.

In people infected with HIV, erythromycin is often used to treat chancroid (vaginal ulcers), *Chlamydia,* bacterial pneumonia, diarrhea caused by *Campylobacter,* and bacillary angiomatosis.

**GENERAL INFORMATION**
Erythromycin is a naturally occurring product derived from a strain of *Streptomyces.* The drug belongs to the macrolide group of antibiotics, which includes azithromycin and clarithromycin, among others. Erythromycin inhibits production of protein in susceptible bacteria, preventing them from multiplying.

Erythromycin is available in a wide variety of forms, including tablets, capsules, solution for intravenous injection, eye ointment, oral drops, and oral suspension.

**TREATMENT**
The adult dosage of erythromycin varies from 250 to 500 mg taken four times a day. The duration of treatment varies from seven days to three weeks or more, depending on the type of infection.

**CAUTIONS AND WARNINGS**

Erythromycin should not be used by anyone with a known allergy to it or the other macrolide antibiotics, such as clarithromycin, azithromycin, or clindamycin.

Because erythromycin may be toxic to the liver, it should be used with caution by people with impaired liver or kidney function.

**SIDE EFFECTS**

The most common side effects of erythromycin are dose-related reactions in the digestive tract, including vomiting, abdominal pain, diarrhea, and changes in appetite. Abnormal liver function may occur in some people; inflammation of the colon has been rarely reported.

Isolated reports of central nervous system side effects have occurred after the use of erythromycin. These have included confusion, hallucination, seizures, and vertigo (dizziness).

Allergic reactions, abnormal heart rhythms, and reversible hearing loss have also been reported. Hearing loss occurred primarily in people with poor kidney function using high doses of the drug.

**PREGNANCY/BREAST-FEEDING**

Erythromycin has not been formally studied in pregnant women. In animal studies, it did cross the placenta in small amounts, but there was no evidence that the drug caused fetal harm. It is not known whether the same would be true in humans. Pregnant women are encouraged to discuss the benefits and risks of erythromycin with their physician before deciding to use the drug.

HIV can be passed from a woman to her child through breast milk. In areas where nutritionally sound alternatives are readily available, breast-feeding is discouraged for HIV-positive women. Erythromycin is excreted in human milk. Because newborns have immature kidneys, which makes them more susceptible to the drug's side effects, women are encouraged to consider alternatives to breast-feeding while using it.

**USE IN CHILDREN**

Erythromycin is used for a number of bacterial infections in children. The recommended dose is determined by age, weight, and severity of infection. Normal doses range from 30 to 50 mg per kg of body weight per day. More severe infections may require higher doses.

**USE IN THE ELDERLY**

Older adults may be more susceptible to the side effects of the drug and may require reduced doses.

**DRUG INTERACTIONS**

Erythromycin may increase levels of theophylline, digitoxin, aminophylline, oxtriphylline, warfarin, carbamazepine, cyclosporine, hexobarbital, and phenytoin, which may increase the risk of side effects from these drugs.

The use of lovastatin in combination with erythromycin has caused muscle degeneration in seriously ill people.

**FOOD INTERACTIONS**

Coated erythromycin tablets, erythromycin estolate and erythromycin ethylsuccinate can be taken with food or milk to reduce stomach upset. Other erythromycin products should be taken on an empty stomach, preferably one hour before or two hours after meals.

**OTHER DRUGS USED FOR SIMILAR CONDITIONS**

For most infections treatable with erythromycin, penicillin is often the alternative of choice. For treatment of active chancroid infection, azithromycin, ceftriaxone, amoxicillin, or ciprofloxacin may be used.

For treatment of chlamydial infections, azithromycin is often the drug of choice because it can be taken in a single daily dose while other therapies may require up to four doses a day for seven to ten days. Doxycycline, ofloxacin, and erythromycin are alternatives.

# ETHAMBUTOL

**BRAND NAME (MANUFACTURER)**
Myambutol (Lederle)

**TYPE OF DRUG**
Antibiotic

**USED FOR**
Ethambutol is used as part of combination therapy for the treatment of mycobacterial infections, specifically tuberculosis and *Mycobacterium avium* complex (MAC).

**GENERAL INFORMATION**
Ethambutol is a narrow-spectrum antibiotic. It is effective against microorganisms belonging to the genus *Mycobacterium,* but it is not active against other bacteria. For treatment of MAC, ethambutol is most often combined with clarithromycin or azithromycin.

Tuberculosis is usually treated with a drug regimen that includes isoniazid, pyrazinamide, and rifampin. Ethambutol is added to the combination when the pathogen becomes resistant to isoniazid, if isoniazid or rifampin cannot be tolerated, or if the tuberculosis has spread from the lungs to the central

nervous system or other places in the body. Tuberculosis is an airborne disease; therefore, everyone in the household of someone who has the disease should be tested and treated as appropriate.

Ethambutol is available as tablets for oral administration.

### TREATMENT

A 1997 U.S. Public Health Service Task Force recommends treating MAC with either azithromycin or clarithromycin plus at least one other drug such as ethambutol or rifabutin. The following drugs are also commonly used as part of the combination regimen: ciprofloxacin and amikacin. In combination therapy for MAC, azithromycin is generally taken at a dose of 500-600 mg per day, and clarithromycin is taken at 500 mg twice a day. It should be noted that the Division of AIDS of the National Institute of Allergy and Infectious Diseases recently recommended that clofazimine not be used since the addition of the drug did not result in any added benefit and may result in increased risk of death.

Fifteen milligrams per kg of body weight in a single daily dose is the most commonly used dose of ethambutol when used in combination therapy for MAC or tuberculosis. The manufacturer recommends increasing the dose to 25 mg per kg of body weight per day for people who have received previous drug therapy for their mycobacterial infections. After sixty days, the lower dose should be resumed.

A reduced dose may be required for people with impaired kidney function.

It is extremely important to complete the full course of treatment for tuberculosis. Because it takes so long to eradicate the microorganism, people are often tempted to stop taking the drugs after symptoms disappear. However, stopping therapy early increases the chance the disease will recur and contributes to the development of strains of the mycobacteria that are resistant to multiple drugs. Multiple-drug-resistant tuberculosis is extremely difficult to treat and is often fatal (even in people with healthy immune systems).

### CAUTIONS AND WARNINGS

Ethambutol should not be used by anyone with a known allergy to it.

People with inflammation of the optic nerve should not use the drug because of the increased risk that the drug may impair vision. Because ethambutol may impair vision, eye examinations should be done routinely in people taking the drug. If vision is affected, it is wise to assume that the drug is causing the side effect. Therapy should be stopped and a physician should be contacted.

As with any drug, blood counts, kidney function, and liver function should be monitored in people using the drug for long periods of time.

## SIDE EFFECTS

A serious side effect of ethambutol is a decrease in visual acuity. This side effect is more likely to occur when the drug is taken for extended periods of time or at high doses. It is usually reversible if the drug is stopped, but it may take weeks or months for vision to return to normal.

Other side effects include rashes, joint pain, changes in appetite, nausea, vomiting, stomach upset, abdominal pain, fever, malaise, headache, dizziness, mental confusion, disorientation, and hallucinations. Peripheral neuropathy (numbness, tingling, or pain in the legs, hands, or feet) has been reported infrequently.

## PREGNANCY/BREAST-FEEDING

Ethambutol has not been formally studied in pregnant women. In animal studies, the drug caused fetal abnormalities, but it is not known whether the same would be true for humans. There have been no reports of fetal harm in the small number of pregnant women who have used the drug, but the available information is too limited to conclude that the drug is safe for all women during pregnancy. Pregnant women are encouraged to discuss the benefits and potential risks of the drug with their physician before deciding to use it.

HIV can be passed from a woman to her child through breast milk. In areas where nutritionally sound alternatives are readily available, breast-feeding is discouraged for HIV-positive women. It is not known whether ethambutol is excreted in human milk. Because of the potential toxicity of the drug to newborns, women are encouraged to consider alternatives to breast-feeding while using it.

## USE IN CHILDREN

Ethambutol is used in combination drug therapy for children with MAC or tuberculosis with the same cautions and warnings as for adults, at dosages appropriately adjusted for body weight. The drug may not be appropriate for children who are too young to be tested and monitored for drug-induced loss of vision. For these children, streptomycin is often substituted.

## USE IN THE ELDERLY

Older adults may be more susceptible to the side effects of the drug and may require reduced doses.

## DRUG INTERACTIONS

Aluminum-containing antacids may decrease uptake of ethambutol.

## FOOD INTERACTIONS

Ethambutol may be taken with or without food.

## OTHER DRUGS USED FOR SIMILAR CONDITIONS

The combination of isoniazid, pyrazinamide, rifampin, and either ethambutol or streptomycin is the therapy of choice for tuberculosis in people with

HIV. For tuberculosis that is resistant to two or more drugs in the standard therapy, a combination of at least three other antibiotics should be used. Some of these drugs include amikacin, kanamycin, capreomycin, ciprofloxacin, ofloxacin, sparfloxacin, ethionamide, cycloserine, streptomycin, and para-aminosalicylic acid. Treatment should continue for at least eighteen months.

**COMMENTS**

In the early stages of the AIDS epidemic, many physicians thought treating MAC was futile. Mycobacteria are notorious for becoming drug resistant, and effective treatment requires several different drugs (some with severe side effects). However, a combination regimen of clarithromycin, rifabutin, and ethambutol was shown to be effective and significantly superior to ethambutol, rifampin, clofazimine, and ciprofloxacin for treating MAC and prolonging survival.

With the development of new drugs and new combinations that have fewer side effects, however, the attitude of many physicians has changed. Treating MAC is likely to prolong survival and reduce symptoms and improve quality of life.

# FURAZOLIDONE

**BRAND NAME (MANUFACTURER)**
Furoxone (Roberts)

**TYPE OF DRUG**
Antibiotic

**USED FOR**
Furazolidone is used for the treatment of bacterial or protozoal diarrhea.

**GENERAL INFORMATION**
Furazolidone is a broad-spectrum antibiotic available as tablets and liquid for oral ingestion. The drug attacks a number of different metabolic activities within bacteria and protozoa, which minimizes the risk of resistance.

Diarrhea should normally respond to therapy within two to five days. If a satisfactory response is not obtained within seven days, it indicates that the pathogen is not susceptible to the drug, and different therapy should be started.

**TREATMENT**
The average adult dose of furazolidone is 100 mg, taken four times a day. Children five years of age and older usually receive between 25 and 50 mg four times a day.

The average adult dose of the liquid is two tablespoons, taken four times daily. For children five and older, one-half to one tablespoon is often used. Lower doses are used for children between one month and four years of age.

**CAUTIONS AND WARNINGS**

Furazolidone should not be used by anyone with a known allergy to it. Even small amounts of alcohol should be avoided when taking the drug and for four days afterward, because the combination can cause flushing, pain in the neck and head, difficulty breathing, and elevated temperature.

Furazolidone is a weak monoamine oxidase (MAO) inhibitor, which means that it inhibits the destruction of certain neurotransmitters, resulting in increased levels of them in the central nervous system. Furazolidone has the potential to cause low blood pressure and low blood sugar when used with other known MAO inhibitors, tyramine-containing foods (beans, yeast extracts, unpasteurized cheeses, beer, wine, pickled herring, chicken livers, and fermented products), nasal decongestants containing phenylephrine or ephedrine, amphetamines, certain sedatives, tranquilizers, or narcotics. The risk of this side effect is low in adults who take the drug at the recommended dose for five days. The risk increases with the dose and duration of therapy.

**SIDE EFFECTS**

Furazolidone is generally well tolerated with few side effects. It may cause a brown coloration of the urine. Allergic reactions, including a fall in blood pressure, fever, joint pain, and rash have been reported in a few people taking the drug. Nausea, vomiting, headache, or malaise occur occasionally and may be minimized or eliminated by dose reduction or withdrawal of the drug.

Furazolidone may cause increased destruction of red blood cells, possibly leading to anemia, in certain ethnic groups of Mediterranean and Near East origin and in African-Americans.

**PREGNANCY/BREAST-FEEDING**

Furazolidone has not been formally studied in pregnant women. In animal studies, it did not cause fetal harm, but it is not known whether this would be true for humans. Pregnant women are encouraged to discuss the benefits and potential risks of furazolidone with their physician before deciding to use the drug.

HIV can be passed from a woman to her child through breast milk. In areas where nutritionally sound alternatives are readily available, breast-feeding is discouraged for HIV-positive women. It is not known whether furazolidone is excreted in human milk. In infants under one month of age, the drug may cause severe anemia. Because of this potential toxicity, women should consider alternatives to breast-feeding while taking furazolidone.

**USE IN CHILDREN**

Furazolidone has been used effectively in children older than one month. Infants under one month should not receive the drug because of the possibility of severe anemia.

**USE IN THE ELDERLY**

No dosage modifications are necessary for older adults with normal liver and kidney function.

**DRUG INTERACTIONS**

Alcohol, MAO inhibitors, nasal decongestants, sedatives, antihistamines, tranquilizers, and narcotics may increase the risk of serious side effects caused by furazolidone. See "Cautions and Warnings" section for more information.

**FOOD INTERACTIONS**

Tyramine-containing foods may increase the risk of side effects caused by furazolidone.

**OTHER DRUGS USED FOR SIMILAR CONDITIONS**

Because of its potential food and drug interactions, furazolidone is not the treatment of choice for any bacterial or protozoal diarrheal infection. The preferred drug depends on the particular microbe causing the symptoms. Furazolidone is used primarily for infections caused by the protozoa *Isospora belli* in cases where trimethoprim/sulfamethoxazole (TMP/SMX) is not effective or cannot be tolerated.

# GENTAMICIN

**BRAND NAME (MANUFACTURER)**

Garamycin (Schering); G-myticin (Pedinol)

**TYPE OF DRUG**

Antibiotic

**USED FOR**

Gentamicin is used to treat bacterial infections of the blood, central nervous system (meningitis), urinary tract, respiratory tract, digestive system, skin, bone, and soft tissue. In women living with HIV, gentamicin is used to treat pelvic inflammatory disease, a condition that develops when sexually transmitted infections such as chlamydia or gonorrhea are left untreated.

**GENERAL INFORMATION**

Gentamicin is a broad-spectrum antibiotic of the aminoglycoside class, available in a variety of forms including topical cream, eye drops, ointment, and a solution for injection. It works by interfering with production of proteins in bacteria, which ultimately kills them.

Gentamicin is relatively toxic when compared to other antibiotics used for similar conditions. It is used primarily when less toxic antibiotics are not effective or cannot be tolerated. Gentamicin works best when combined with drugs from other antibiotic classes.

To treat acute pelvic inflammatory disease, caused by an untreated sexually transmitted disease that may result in tubal scarring and infertility, gentamicin is combined with intravenous injection of clindamycin.

**TREATMENT**

Standard gentamicin may be injected intravenously or into a large muscle. The intravenous injection is used for severe infections of the blood or when the individual is in shock.

For most infections, standard gentamicin is used at a dose of 3 mg per kg of body weight per day, split into three equal doses. Higher doses are used for more severe infection. Lower doses may be required for people with reduced kidney function.

The recommended dose for children is higher: 5 to 7.5 mg per kg of body weight per day. Newborns receive lower doses.

The usual duration of treatment is seven to ten days. Difficult or complicated infections may take longer and thus require monitoring of blood, kidney, and nerve function.

**CAUTIONS AND WARNINGS**

Gentamicin should not be used by anyone with a known allergy to it or to other aminoglycoside antibiotics, including streptomycin, erythromycin, azithromycin, clarithromycin, etc.

Kidney function and hearing should be closely monitored in people taking gentamicin because of its potential side effects. Taking plenty of fluids while using gentamicin may reduce the risk of kidney damage.

Gentamicin injectable solution contains sodium bisulfite and should not be used by people with sulfite allergies.

**SIDE EFFECTS**

The most serious potential side effects of gentamicin are kidney toxicity and damage to the eighth cranial nerve, which controls hearing. Symptoms of the nerve damage may be hearing loss, dizziness, roaring in the ears, or tingling or acute pain in the extremities. The risk of these side effects is low in people with normal kidney function using recommended doses, but they occur more frequently in people who take high doses for extended periods of time and those who have a preexisting kidney impairment.

Other side effects reported for gentamicin include difficulty breathing, confusion, depression, decreased appetite, weight loss, changes in blood pressure, rash, itching, swelling in the throat, fever, headache, nausea, vomiting, in-

creased salivation, stomach upset, lung damage, hair loss, joint pain, inflamed liver, and enlarged spleen.

### PREGNANCY/BREAST-FEEDING

Gentamicin has not been formally studied in pregnant women. Streptomycin, which is another antibiotic of the aminoglycoside class, can cause irreversible birth defects when given to pregnant women, but serious side effects to the mother or fetus have not been reported in pregnant women using gentamicin. Women are encouraged to discuss the benefits and potential risks of the drug with their physician before deciding to use it during pregnancy.

HIV can be passed from a woman to her child through breast milk. In areas where nutritionally sound alternatives are readily available, breast-feeding is discouraged for HIV-positive women. It is not known whether gentamicin is excreted in human milk. Because of the potential toxicity of the drug in newborns, women are encouraged to consider alternatives to breast-feeding while using it.

### USE IN CHILDREN

Gentamicin has been used effectively in children for serious bacterial infections.

### USE IN THE ELDERLY

Older adults may be more susceptible to the side effects of the drug and may require reduced doses.

### DRUG INTERACTIONS

The antibacterial effect of gentamicin may be increased by penicillin, ampicillin, carbenicillin, nafcillin, or oxacillin.

Concurrent and/or sequential use of cisplatin, kanamycin, amikacin, neomycin, polymyxin B, colistin, paromomycin, streptomycin, tobramycin, vancomycin, and viomycin increases the risk of gentamicin-related kidney and nerve damage.

Concurrent use with diuretics, such as ethacrynic acid or furosemide, should be avoided, since the diuretics by themselves may cause hearing loss and may increase the blood levels of gentamicin, increasing the risk of side effects.

### FOOD INTERACTIONS

None reported.

### OTHER DRUGS USED FOR SIMILAR CONDITIONS

For pelvic inflammatory disease, a combination of cefoxitin or cefotetan and doxycycline may be used instead of a combination of clindamycin and gentamicin. The choice often depends on which combination is better tolerated.

For treatment of chlamydial infections, azithromycin is often the drug of choice because it can be taken in a single daily dose while other therapies

may require up to four doses a day for seven to ten days. Doxycycline, ofloxacin, and erythromycin are alternatives.

# ISONIAZID

**BRAND NAME (MANUFACTURER)**
Nydrazid (Apothecon)
Rifampin + Isoniazid: Rifamate (Hoechst Marion Roussel)
Rifampin + Isoniazid + Pyrazinamide: Rifater (Hoechst Marion Roussel)

**OTHER NAME**
INH

**TYPE OF DRUG**
Antibiotic

**USED FOR**
Isoniazid is used for the treatment of pulmonary tuberculosis in combination with other agents such as rifampin, pyrazinamide, and ethambutol.

**GENERAL INFORMATION**
Isoniazid is a narrow-spectrum antibiotic that works against the bacteria that cause tuberculosis. It is available as a solution for injection, tablets, or capsules. Because isoniazid is normally used with other drugs when treating tuberculosis, a number of combination products have been developed. Rifamate is the brand name of capsules containing 300 mg rifampin and 150 mg isoniazid. Rifater is the brand name of tablets containing 120 mg rifampin, 50 mg isoniazid, and 300 mg pyrazinamide. The injectable form of isoniazid is used when digestive tract conditions (diarrhea, vomiting, etc.) prevent the person from taking the oral drug.

**TREATMENT**
Tuberculosis may progress more rapidly in people infected with HIV, but it is almost always curable if treated. Tuberculosis is an airborne disease; therefore, everyone in the household of someone who has the disease should be tested and treated as appropriate.

The disease is usually treated with a combination of several antibiotics. The U.S. Centers for Disease Control recommends that isoniazid (300 mg per day) be combined with at least two other antibiotics, generally rifampin (450 to 600 mg per day) and pyrazinamide (20 to 30 mg per day). Ethambutol (15 to 25 mg per kg of body weight per day) or streptomycin (15 mg per kg of body weight per day) are added to the regimen if the disease is resistant to isoniazid, if the individual cannot tolerate full doses of isoniazid or rifampin,

or if the disease has spread from the lungs to the central nervous system or other organs.

Pyrazinamide is normally taken for the first two months. The duration of treatment with the other drugs is debatable. Recommendations range from six months to indefinitely. The consensus is that isoniazid and rifampin should be continued for at least seven months after the mycobacteria that causes tuberculosis is not detectable in the blood. Ethambutol or streptomycin should be taken for at least six months after the mycobacteria disappear.

It is extremely important to complete the full course of treatment for tuberculosis. Because it takes so long to eradicate the microorganism, people are often tempted to stop taking the drugs after symptoms disappear. However, stopping therapy early increases the chance that the disease will recur and contributes to the development of strains of the mycobacteria that are resistant to multiple drugs. Multiple-drug-resistant tuberculosis is extremely difficult to treat and is often fatal (even in people with healthy immune systems).

### MAINTENANCE/PREVENTION

It is not clear whether lifelong maintenance therapy is required to prevent recurrence of tuberculosis in people infected with HIV. However, since the drug is relatively well tolerated, many physicians recommend that their patients take isoniazid (300 mg per day) indefinitely.

People who have tested positive for tuberculosis but don't have signs of active disease may benefit from preventive drug therapy. Standard preventive therapy includes isoniazid (300 mg per day) for twelve months along with pyridoxine (vitamin $B_6$). The vitamin is added to reduce the chance of isoniazid-associated peripheral neuropathy, nerve damage characterized by numbness, tingling, or pain in the extremities.

### CAUTIONS AND WARNINGS

Isoniazid should not be used by anyone with a known allergy to it, or by anyone who experiences severe side effects while taking the drug. People with a history of liver disease should take the drug with caution, and their liver function should be routinely monitored. If severe hepatitis occurs after treatment with isoniazid, the drug should be stopped until the hepatitis resolves.

### SIDE EFFECTS

Severe and sometimes fatal noninfectious hepatitis (inflammation of the liver) may occur in people who have taken isoniazid. This side effect may develop months after initiating therapy with the drug. The risk is age related, from zero for people under the age of twenty up to 2.3% for people between fifty and sixty-four years of age. People sixty-five years of age and older have a

small risk of contracting hepatitis. Daily alcohol consumption significantly increases the risk of hepatitis in all these age groups.

Vitamin $B_6$ deficiency is sometimes observed in adults taking high doses of isoniazid. It can be reversed by taking vitamin $B_6$ supplements.

Peripheral neuropathy is the most common toxic effect of the drug. It occurs more often in those taking higher doses and those who are malnourished. Other side effects include fever and rashes.

### PREGNANCY/BREAST-FEEDING
Isoniazid has not been formally studied in pregnant women. In animal studies, the drug caused an increased rate of spontaneous abortions, but did not cause birth defects. It is not known whether this would be true in humans. Pregnant women are encouraged to discuss the benefits and potential risks of isoniazid with their physician before deciding to use the drug.

HIV can be passed from a woman to her child through breast milk. In areas where nutritionally sound alternatives are readily available, breast-feeding is discouraged for HIV-positive women. Isoniazid is excreted in human milk. Because of the potential toxicity of the drug to newborns, women are encouraged to consider alternatives to breast-feeding while using it.

### USE IN CHILDREN
Tuberculosis in children is treated essentially the same way as in adults, using doses of isoniazid and the other drugs appropriately adjusted for weight or body surface area.

### USE IN THE ELDERLY
Older adults may be more susceptible to the side effects of the drug and may require reduced doses.

### DRUG INTERACTIONS
Isoniazid may increase blood levels of acetaminophen, carbamazepine, and phenytoin, potentially increasing the risk of their side effects. Daily alcohol consumption combined with isoniazid use may increase the risk of liver damage. Similarly, rifampin may increase the risk of liver damage caused by isoniazid.

Corticosteroids reduce isoniazid levels, potentially reducing the antibacterial effectiveness of the drug. Isoniazid may decrease fluconazole, itraconazole, and ketoconazole levels, potentially reducing their effectiveness.

Sulfonylureas taken with isoniazid may increase the risk of high blood sugar levels.

Antacids can reduce the uptake of isoniazid and should be used either two hours before or after taking the drug. However, one study found that the specific antacids in two ddI tablets had no significant effect on the uptake of isoniazid, suggesting that ddI and isoniazid may be taken simultaneously.

**FOOD INTERACTIONS**

Isoniazid should be taken on an empty stomach, at least one hour before or two hours after eating, because food may reduce the drug's uptake.

**OTHER DRUGS USED FOR SIMILAR CONDITIONS**

Combinations containing isoniazid are the therapy of choice for tuberculosis. When isoniazid is ineffective or not tolerated, other drugs can be substituted. For tuberculosis that is resistant to two or more drugs in the standard therapy, a combination of at least three other antibiotics should be used. Some of these drugs include amikacin, kanamycin, streptomycin, levofloxacin, capreomycin, ciprofloxacin, ofloxacin, sparfloxacin, ethionamide, cycloserine, and para-aminosalicylic acid. Treatment should continue for at least eighteen months.

# MEROPENEM

**BRAND NAME (MANUFACTURER)**

Merrem (Zeneca)

**TYPE OF DRUG**

Antibiotic

**USED FOR**

Meropenem is used for meningitis and bacterial infections in the abdomen.

**GENERAL INFORMATION**

Meropenem is a broad-spectrum antibiotic of the carbapenem (beta-lactam) class. It is generally not the first-choice therapy for most bacterial infections because it cannot be taken orally. Meropenem weakens cell walls of newly formed bacteria.

As with most antibiotics, resistance to meropenem will almost inevitably develop, and inappropriate use of the drug (not taking the amount prescribed) may hasten the appearance of resistant strains.

Meropenem is available for intravenous injection.

**TREATMENT**

The usual dose of meropenem is 1 gram every 8 hours by intravenous injection. The drug is usually given over a 15- to 30-minute period. People with kidney impairment should use a lower dose. A further dose reduction is necessary for women with kidney impairment.

**CAUTIONS AND WARNINGS**

Meropenem should not be used by people who know they are allergic to it or to any of the other carbapenem-type antibiotics.

People with neurological disorders (seizures, etc.) or kidney dysfunction are at increased risk for neurological side effects.

### SIDE EFFECTS
Most commonly reported side effects of meropenem include nausea, vomiting, diarrhea, headache, inflammation at the injection site, and rash.

### PREGNANCY/BREAST-FEEDING
Meropenem has not been formally studied in pregnant women. In animal studies meropenem did not cause harm to the fetus. However, pregnant women are encouraged to discuss the benefits and potential risks of meropenem with their physician before deciding to use the drug.

HIV can be passed from a woman to her child through breast milk. In areas where nutritionally sound alternatives are readily available, breast-feeding is discouraged for HIV-positive women. It is not known whether meropenem is excreted in human milk. Because there is little information about the effect of the drug on newborns, women are encouraged to consider alternatives to breast-feeding while using it.

### USE IN CHILDREN
The safety and effectiveness of meropenem has been established in children over the age of 3 months. The dose of meropenem is usually 20–40 mg/kg every 8 hours. The drug is given by intravenous injection over a 15–30-minute period.

### USE IN THE ELDERLY
No alterations in dose are recommended for older adults with normal kidney function. Dose reductions may be necessary for older adults with impaired kidney function.

### DRUG INTERACTIONS
Probenecid increases the blood concentrations of meropenem, potentially increasing its side effects. Use of the two drugs together is not recommended.

### FOOD INTERACTIONS
Meropenem is not an oral medication; consequently, food does not affect its absorption into the body, and the drug may be taken with or without food.

### OTHER DRUGS USED FOR SIMILAR CONDITIONS
The choice of drug usually depends on side effects and the drug resistance of the particular pathogen causing the infection.

# OFLOXACIN

### BRAND NAME (MANUFACTURER)
Floxin (McNeil)

**TYPE OF DRUG**
Antibiotic

**USED FOR**
Ofloxacin is a broad-spectrum antibiotic of the quinolone class. It is used for infections of the lower respiratory tract, skin, prostate and urinary tract, as well as for gonorrhea and chlamydia. Quinolone antibiotics are effective against many bacteria that are resistant to other antibiotics, including the penicillins and cephalosporins.

In people with HIV, ofloxacin is sometimes used as part of combination therapy to treat *Mycobacterium avium* complex (MAC) and to prevent and treat tuberculosis.

**GENERAL INFORMATION**
Ofloxacin works against susceptible bacteria by attaching to their cell walls and preventing multiplication. It is available as tablets and solution for intravenous injection.

**TREATMENT**
The dose of ofloxacin tablets is usually 200 to 400 mg twice daily. The same dose is used when ofloxacin is given by intravenous injection and must be administered over 60 minutes. The length of time on ofloxacin depends on the particular bacterial infection.

The dose of ofloxacin may need to be reduced in people with impaired kidney function; further reduction may be necessary if the patient is female.

**CAUTIONS AND WARNINGS**
Ofloxacin should not be used in people allergic to it or to any antibiotics in the quinolone class. When taking the drug, it is a good idea to drink extra fluids to reduce the risk of kidney-related side effects.

Quinolones make some people sensitive to sunlight. Excessive sunlight should be avoided while taking the drug.

People taking antidiabetic medications should have their blood glucose levels carefully monitored while taking ofloxacin.

As with all quinolones, caution is recommended when the drug is used by people with a history of central nervous system disorders, since neurological side effects are more common in them.

**SIDE EFFECTS**
The most frequently reported side effects of ofloxacin include nausea, diarrhea, vomiting, insomnia, dizziness, headache, restlessness, and rash.

Convulsions, pressure on the brain, and psychotic episodes have been reported by some people taking quinolones. These drugs may also cause tremors, light-headedness, confusion, and hallucinations in rare cases.

**PREGNANCY/BREAST-FEEDING**

Ofloxacin has not been formally studied in pregnant women. In animal studies with 10-50 times the equivalent human dose, ofloxacin did cause harm to the fetus, but it is not known whether the same would be true in humans. Pregnant women are encouraged to discuss the benefits and risks of ofloxacin with their physician before making a decision about taking the drug.

HIV can be passed from a woman to her child through breast milk. In areas where nutritionally sound alternatives are readily available, breast-feeding is discouraged for HIV-positive women. Ofloxacin is also excreted in human milk. Because of the potential toxicity of the drug, women should consider alternatives to breast-feeding while taking it.

**USE IN CHILDREN**

Ofloxacin is not recommended for children under 18 years of age because its safety and effectiveness have not been formally studied or established for them.

**USE IN THE ELDERLY**

Older adults may be more susceptible to the side effects of the drug and may require reduced doses.

**DRUG INTERACTIONS**

For people taking ddI or antacids containing magnesium hydroxide or aluminum hydroxide, ofloxacin should be taken two hours before or after taking those other medications.

Ofloxacin may cause increased theophylline levels and an increased risk of developing central nervous system side effects. If ofloxacin and theophylline must be used together, theophylline levels must be carefully monitored.

Probenecid and cimetidine are likely to increase blood levels of ofloxacin. Ofloxacin may enhance the blood-thinning effect of warfarin. Combined use of ofloxacin and cyclosporine may cause impairment of kidney function.

**FOOD INTERACTIONS**

Ofloxacin tablets should not be taken with food.

**OTHER DRUGS USED FOR SIMILAR CONDITIONS**

For treatment of bacterial infections causing diarrhea, amoxicillin, ampicillin, or trimethoprim/sulfamethoxazole may be used instead of ofloxacin.

For most bacterial infections, there is no single "definitive" treatment. The choice of drug will depend primarily on which drugs can be tolerated, which side effects a person is at risk for, and which drugs are effective for the particular organism causing the infection.

# PENICILLIN

**BRAND NAME (MANUFACTURER)**
Bicillin (Wyeth-Ayerst); Wycillin (Wyeth-Ayerst); Ledercillin (Lederle); Pen-Vee (Wyeth-Ayerst); Veetids (Apothecon)

**TYPE OF DRUG**
Antibiotic

**USED FOR**
Penicillin is used to treat a wide variety of bacterial infections of the respiratory tract, digestive tract, urinary tract, skin, mouth, and ears. Penicillin is also prescribed for less common conditions such as scarlet fever and infections of the heart.

Penicillin is also used to treat syphilis.

**GENERAL INFORMATION**
Penicillin was one of the first antibiotics to be discovered, purified, and used to treat bacterial infections. Penicillin interferes with a bacterium's ability to build cell walls, which prevents it from multiplying. Penicillin G, also known as benzylpenicillin, is normally used by injection to treat serious bacterial infections that don't respond to other treatments. Because penicillin G is not very effective when taken orally, a modified form of penicillin, called penicillin V, was developed. It is readily absorbed when taken with food, and its effects are more reliable than those of other oral penicillins. However, it is not recommended for acute stages of serious infections or in people with nausea, vomiting, or other conditions that may interfere with oral absorption of the drug.

Penicillin is available as tablets, solution for oral administration, and solution for intravenous administration.

**TREATMENT**
The recommended dosage and administration of the drug varies depending on the condition and the form of penicillin used. For adults, the dosages generally range from 125 to 500 mg, taken three to four times a day.

For treatment of syphilis in women with HIV, penicillin G administered as a single intramuscular injection is often used. Some physicians recommend additional treatment, such as one dose a week for three weeks or other antibiotics in addition to penicillin.

**CAUTIONS AND WARNINGS**
Serious and potentially fatal allergic reactions have occurred when using penicillin. Although these reactions are more common with the injectable form of the drug, they also occur when taking penicillin by mouth. Penicillin should

not be used by anyone with a known allergy to it or any of the other penicillin-type antibiotics, including ampicillin, amoxicillin, and cloxacillin.

People who have multiple allergies or asthma are more likely to be allergic to penicillin. About 5% of people who are allergic to penicillin will also be allergic to cephalosporin antibiotics, such as cefaclor, cefoxitin, etc.

Prolonged use of penicillin may result in superinfection by other bacteria. Should superinfection occur, appropriate antibiotic therapy should be taken. Acidophilus supplements are used by some people to restore the natural balance between bacteria and fungi in the body.

Chronic use of penicillin may lead to the development of bacterial strains resistant to it.

### SIDE EFFECTS

The most common reactions to penicillin include nausea, vomiting, stomach upset, diarrhea, and black, hairy tongue. Allergic skin reactions and anaphylactic shock occur less frequently. Rarely, bone marrow toxicity, nerve damage, or kidney damage may occur, but usually only after high-dose administration of injectable penicillin.

### PREGNANCY/BREAST-FEEDING

Penicillin has not been formally studied in pregnant women, although it is commonly prescribed for them. Penicillins do cross the placenta and should be used only if absolutely necessary. Pregnant women are encouraged to discuss the benefits and potential risks of penicillin with their physician before deciding to use it.

HIV can be passed from a woman to her child through breast milk. In areas where nutritionally sound alternatives are readily available, breast-feeding is discouraged for HIV-positive women. Small amounts of penicillin pass into breast milk. It is generally considered safe to use while breast-feeding, but in some cases, it may sensitize the infant to penicillin, possibly causing a lifelong allergy. In addition, it may cause stomach upset, diarrhea, or other side effects in newborns. Women are encouraged to consider alternatives to breast-feeding while using penicillin.

### USE IN CHILDREN

Children can use penicillin at dosages adjusted for weight and age.

### USE IN THE ELDERLY

Older adults may be more susceptible to the side effects of the drug and may require reduced doses.

### DRUG INTERACTIONS

Bacteriostatic antibiotics such as chloramphenicol, erythromycin, tetracycline, or neomycin may reduce the effectiveness of penicillin. Probenecid may increase

blood levels of penicillin, potentially increasing the risk of drug-related side effects.

Penicillin may interfere with the effectiveness of oral contraceptives and increase the blood-thinning effects of anticoagulants such as warfarin.

### FOOD INTERACTIONS
Penicillin should not be taken with fruit juice or carbonated beverages because the acid in them can destroy the drug. For most-consistent blood levels of oral penicillin, it may be taken with food.

### OTHER DRUGS USED FOR SIMILAR CONDITIONS
A wide variety of oral and injectable antibiotics may be used in place of penicillin, depending on the condition. In general, the choice of antibiotic depends on the particular organism causing the infection. For treatment of syphilis in women with HIV, penicillin G is usually the drug of choice. When it is ineffective or not tolerated, doxycycline or tetracycline may be substituted, but they are generally not as effective.

### COMMENTS
Because penicillin was one of the first antibiotics developed and because it has been so widely used, resistant strains of bacteria have developed and spread throughout the years, and now are fairly common. Because the different penicillins are similar in chemical structure, organisms that are resistant to one are likely to be resistant to many. For these strains, other types of antibiotics or combinations of penicillins with other types of antibiotics (such as clavulanate) may be needed to control the infection.

# PYRAZINAMIDE

### BRAND NAME (MANUFACTURER)
Pyrazinamide USP (Lederle)
Rifampin + Isoniazid + Pyrazinamide: Rifater (Hoechst Marion Roussel)

### OTHER NAME
PZA

### TYPE OF DRUG
Antibiotic

### USED FOR
Pyrazinamide is used in combination with other antibiotics for the treatment or prevention of active tuberculosis.

### GENERAL INFORMATION
Pyrazinamide is a narrow-spectrum antibiotic that works against the bacteria that cause tuberculosis. It is available in tablet form and in a combina-

tion product called Rifater that contains 300 mg pyrazinamide, 120 mg rifampin, and 50 mg isoniazid.

## TREATMENT

Tuberculosis may progress more rapidly in people infected with HIV, but if treated, it is almost always curable. Tuberculosis is an airborne disease; therefore, everyone in the household of someone who has the disease should be tested and treated as appropriate.

The disease is usually treated with a combination of several antibiotics. The U.S. Centers for Disease Control recommends that isoniazid (300 mg per day) be combined with at least two other antibiotics, generally rifampin (450 to 600 mg per day) and pyrazinamide (20 to 30 mg per day).

Pyrazinamide is normally taken for the first two months of treatment. Isoniazid and rifampin are continued for nine to twelve months, at least seven months after the mycobacteria are not detectable in the blood. Ethambutol or streptomycin should be taken for at least six months after the mycobacteria disappear.

It is extremely important to complete the full course of treatment for tuberculosis. Because it takes so long to eradicate the microorganism, people are often tempted to stop taking the drugs after symptoms disappear. However, stopping therapy early increases the chance the disease will recur and contributes to the development of strains of the mycobacteria that are resistant to multiple drugs. Multiple-drug-resistant tuberculosis is extremely difficult to treat and is often fatal (even in people with healthy immune systems).

## MAINTENANCE/PREVENTION

People who have tested positive for tuberculosis but don't have signs of active disease may benefit from preventive drug therapy. Standard preventive therapy includes isoniazid (300 mg per day) and pyridoxine (vitamin B6), taken daily for twelve months. Because this course of treatment takes so long, many people don't complete it.

## CAUTIONS AND WARNINGS

Pyrazinamide should not be used by anyone with a known allergy to it. The drug can cause serious liver toxicity and should be used with caution by people with liver conditions. Pyrazinamide may cause elevated levels of urea in the blood, which may result in symptoms of gout (painful arthritis caused by accumulation of uric acid in the joints). If symptoms of gout or liver damage appear while taking pyrazinamide, the drug should be discontinued.

## SIDE EFFECTS

The most common side effects of pyrazinamide are nausea, vomiting, joint pain, and muscle pain. The most serious side effect is liver damage, which occurs rarely. Other side effects include loss of appetite, fever, acne, sensitiv-

ity to light, difficulty urinating, kidney damage, rashes, itching, and reduced blood cell and platelet counts.

### PREGNANCY/BREAST-FEEDING

Pyrazinamide has not been formally studied in pregnant women or animals. Pregnant women are encouraged to discuss the benefits and potential risks of pyrazinamide with their physician before deciding to use the drug.

HIV can be passed from a woman to her child through breast milk. In areas where nutritionally sound alternatives are readily available, breast-feeding is discouraged for HIV-positive women. It is not known whether pyrazinamide is excreted in human milk. Because of the potential toxicity of the drug to newborns, women are encouraged to consider alternatives to breast-feeding while using it.

### USE IN CHILDREN

Tuberculosis in children is treated essentially the same manner as in adults, using doses of pyrazinamide and the other drugs appropriately adjusted for weight or body surface area.

### USE IN THE ELDERLY

Older adults may be more susceptible to the side effects of the drug and may require reduced doses.

### DRUG INTERACTIONS

None reported.

### FOOD INTERACTIONS

Pyrazinamide may be taken with or without food. Rifater tablets should be taken one hour before or two hours after eating, because the absorption of isoniazid is greatest on an empty stomach.

### OTHER DRUGS USED FOR SIMILAR CONDITIONS

A combination of isoniazid, rifampin, and pyrazinamide is the treatment of choice for non-drug-resistant tuberculosis. Ethambutol (15 to 25 mg per kg of body weight per day) or streptomycin (15 mg per kg of body weight per day) is added to the regimen if the disease is resistant to isoniazid, if the individual cannot tolerate full doses of isoniazid or rifampin, or if the disease has spread from the lungs to the central nervous system or other organs.

For tuberculosis resistant to two or more drugs in the standard therapy, a combination of at least three other antibiotics should be used. Some of these drugs include amikacin, kanamycin, capreomycin, ciprofloxacin, ofloxacin, sparfloxacin, ethionamide, cycloserine, and para-aminosalicylic acid. Treatment should continue for at least eighteen months.

# RIFABUTIN

**BRAND NAME (MANUFACTURER)**
Mycobutin (Pharmacia & Upjohn)

**TYPE OF DRUG**
Antibiotic

**USED FOR**
Rifabutin is used for the prevention of *Mycobacterium avium* complex (MAC) disease in people with advanced HIV infection. It is also used in combination with other drugs for the treatment of active MAC disease.

**GENERAL INFORMATION**
Rifabutin is a narrow-spectrum antibiotic effective against *Mycobacterium*. It is a synthetic chemical derived from the antibiotic rifamycin and is closely related to the tuberculosis drug rifampin. Rifabutin works by interfering with synthesis of RNA in susceptible bacteria, which prevents them from multiplying.

In two clinical studies where rifabutin was compared to a placebo for prevention of MAC disease in people with HIV and CD4+ counts less than 200, those receiving rifabutin were 30% to 50% less likely to develop MAC infections detectable in the blood than those on placebo. In addition, the people using rifabutin had fewer symptoms of MAC disease, including fever, night sweats, weight loss, fatigue, abdominal pain, anemia, and liver impairment.

Rifabutin is available as tablets for oral administration.

**TREATMENT**
A 1997 U.S. Public Health Service Task Force recommends treating MAC with either azithromycin or clarithromycin **plus** at least one other drug such as ethambutol or rifabutin. Ciprofloxacin and amikacin are also commonly used as part of the combination regimen. In combination therapy for MAC, azithromycin is generally taken at a dose of 500-600 mg per day, and clarithromycin is taken at 500 mg twice daily. It should be noted that the Division of AIDS of the National Institute of Allergy and Infectious Diseases recently recommended that clofazimine not be used since the addition of the drug did not result in any added benefit and may result in increased risk of death.

**PREVENTION**
A 1997 U.S. Public Health Service Task Force recommends that people with less than 50 CD4+ cells receive either clarithromycin or azithromycin to prevent MAC. If clarithromycin or azithromycin cannot be tolerated, rifabutin is recommended as an alternative. Use of these antibiotics must be weighed against the potential side effects and the possibility that the MAC bacteria

may become resistant to a drug when used as a single agent for prevention of the disease, making the drugs less effective in treatment of active MAC disease.

## CAUTIONS AND WARNINGS

Rifabutin should not be used by anyone with a known allergy to it or any other rifamycin derivatives (including rifampin).

The bacteria that cause MAC and tuberculosis are similar. Treating MAC can mask the symptoms of tuberculosis; consequently, people considering preventive therapy for MAC should first be tested for tuberculosis.

Rifabutin prophylaxis should not be used by people with tuberculosis, because mycobacteria often become resistant to rifampin after extended use of rifabutin. When this happens, rifampin loses its effectiveness as a treatment for tuberculosis.

Urine, feces, saliva, perspiration, tears, and skin may be colored brown-orange in people taking rifabutin. Soft contact lenses may be permanently stained.

## SIDE EFFECTS

Rifabutin is generally well tolerated. In clinical trials, about 16% of people taking the drug stopped therapy because of side effects. The most common side effects were discolored urine, stomach upset, and rashes. Reduced counts of certain white blood cells also occurred. Painful inflammation of the eye (called uveitis) has been reported in some people receiving rifabutin, particularly in people taking high doses (greater than 300 mg/day) and those receiving fluconazole or clarithromycin, drugs that increase blood levels of rifabutin. If inflammation of the eye occurs while taking rifabutin, the drug should be stopped and a physician should be contacted.

## PREGNANCY/BREAST-FEEDING

Rifabutin has not been formally studied in pregnant women. In animal studies, the drug caused spontaneous abortions and other fetal harm, but it is not known whether the same would be true in humans. Pregnant women are encouraged to discuss the benefits and potential risks of rifabutin with their physician before deciding to use the drug.

The 1997 U.S. Public Health Service Task Force recommends that pregnant women be offered preventative therapy against MAC. Azithromycin should be considered the drug of choice and clarithromycin should only be used if no alternative therapy is appropriate.

HIV may be passed from a woman to her child through breast milk. In areas where nutritionally sound alternatives are readily available, breast-feeding is discouraged for HIV-positive women. It is not known whether rifabutin

is excreted in human milk. Because of the potential toxicity of the drug, women are encouraged to consider alternatives to breast-feeding while using it.

## USE IN CHILDREN

The safety and effectiveness of rifabutin have not yet been established by formal studies. In limited clinical experience, children have used the drug in combination with other antibiotics with side effects similar to those observed in adults. Although a wide range of doses have been used for children, there is no evidence that a dosage greater than 5 mg per kg of body weight per day is useful.

The 1997 U.S. Public Health Service Task Force recommends that children under 13 years of age with advanced HIV disease receive either clarithromycin or azithromycin to prevent MAC. The following guidelines have been established: children over six years of age and less than 50 CD4+ cells; children aged 2-6 years and less than 75 CD4+ cells; children 1-2 years and less than 500 CD4+ cells; and children under 12 months of age and less than 750 CD4+ cells should all be offered preventative therapy.

## USE IN THE ELDERLY

The metabolism of rifabutin is only slightly affected by age. No alterations in dosage or administration are necessary for most elderly people.

## DRUG INTERACTIONS

Rifabutin should not be used in combination with ritonavir as this may increase the risk of side effects. Rifabutin will decrease blood levels of nelfinavir, indinavir and saquinavir while indinavir and nelfinavir will significantly increase the blood levels of rifabutin. Rifabutin may decrease the effectiveness of analgesics, anticoagulants (like warfarin), barbiturates, diazepam, disopyramide, estrogen, mexiletine, oral contraceptives, progesterone, and verapamil. In addition, rifabutin may decrease the blood levels of clarithromycin, corticosteroids, cyclosporine, dapsone, delavirdine, itraconazole, ketoconazole, quinidine, sulfonylurea drugs, and theophylline.

Fluconazole or clarithromycin may double rifabutin blood levels, increasing the risk of rifabutin-related side effects, including painful inflammation of the eye (uveitis).

## FOOD INTERACTIONS

High-fat meals may slow the absorption of rifabutin without affecting the total amount of drug absorbed. If rifabutin upsets the stomach, it may be taken with food.

## OTHER DRUGS USED FOR SIMILAR CONDITIONS

Clarithromycin and azithromycin are the primary alternatives to rifabutin for the prevention of MAC. For prevention of MAC in people with CD4+ counts less than 50, the U.S. Public Health Service Task Force recommends using

clarithromycin or azithromycin. Rifabutin should only be used if clarithromycin or azithromycin cannot be tolerated.

**COMMENTS**
In the early stages of the AIDS epidemic, many physicians thought treating MAC was futile. Mycobacteria are notorious for becoming drug resistant and effective treatment requires several different drugs (some with severe side effects). However, a combination regimen of clarithromycin, rifabutin and ethambutol was shown to be effective and significantly superior to ethambutol, rifampin, clofazimine, and ciprofloxacin for treating MAC and prolonging survival.

With the development of new drugs and new drug combinations that have fewer side effects, however, the attitude of many physicians has changed. Treating MAC is likely to prolong survival and reduce symptoms and improve quality of life.

# RIFAMPIN

**BRAND NAME (MANUFACTURER)**
Rifadin (Hoechst Marion Roussel); Rimactane (Novartis)
Rifampin + Isoniazid: Rifamate (Hoechst Marion Roussel)
Rifampin + Isoniazid + Pyrazinamide: Rifater (Hoechst Marion Roussel)

**TYPE OF DRUG**
Antibiotic

**USED FOR**
Rifampin in combination with other antibiotics is used primarily for the treatment of pulmonary tuberculosis.

**GENERAL INFORMATION**
Rifampin is a narrow-spectrum antibiotic that works against *Mycobacterium*, the bacteria that cause tuberculosis and MAC. It is available as a solution for injection and capsules for oral administration. Because rifampin is normally used with other drugs when treating tuberculosis, a number of combination products have been developed. Rifamate is the brand name of capsules containing 300 mg rifampin and 150 mg isoniazid. Rifater is the brand name of tablets containing 120 mg rifampin, 50 mg isoniazid, and 300 mg pyrazinamide. The injectable form of rifampin is used when digestive tract conditions (diarrhea, vomiting, etc.) prevent a person from taking the oral drug.

**TREATMENT**
Tuberculosis may progress more rapidly in people infected with HIV, but if treated, it is almost always curable. The disease is usually treated with a

combination of several antibiotics. The U.S. Centers for Disease Control recommends that isoniazid (300 mg per day) be combined with at least two other antibiotics, generally rifampin (450 to 600 mg per day) and pyrazinamide (20 to 30 mg per day). Ethambutol (15 to 25 mg per kg of body weight per day) or streptomycin (15 mg per kg of body weight per day) are added to the regimen if the disease is resistant to isoniazid, if the individual cannot tolerate full doses of isoniazid or rifampin, or if the disease has spread out of the lungs to the central nervous system or other organs.

Pyrazinamide is normally taken for the first two months. The duration of treatment with the other drugs is a matter of some controversy. Recommendations range from six months to indefinitely. The consensus is that isoniazid and rifampin should be continued for at least seven months after the mycobacteria are not detectable. Ethambutol or streptomycin should be taken for at least six months after the mycobacteria disappear.

It is extremely important to complete the full course of treatment for tuberculosis. Because it takes so long to eradicate the microorganism, people are often tempted to stop taking the drugs after symptoms disappear. However, stopping therapy early increases the chance the disease will recur and contributes to the development of strains of *Mycobacterium* that are resistant to multiple drugs. Multiple-drug-resistant tuberculosis is extremely difficult to treat and is often fatal (even in people with healthy immune systems).

**MAINTENANCE/PREVENTION**

People who have tested positive for tuberculosis but do not have signs of active disease may benefit from preventive drug therapy. Rifampin plus pyrazinamide is one of the combinations being tested in clinical trials.

**CAUTIONS AND WARNINGS**

Rifampin should not be used by anyone with a known allergy to it or any other drug derived from rifamycin (including rifabutin).

Because rifampin can cause severe liver toxicity, it should be used with caution in people with preexisting liver damage. Physicians will generally periodically monitor the liver function of people on rifampin.

**SIDE EFFECTS**

The most common side effects of rifampin are flu symptoms, heartburn, upset stomach, loss of appetite, nausea, vomiting, gas, cramps, diarrhea, drowsiness, headache, menstrual irregularities, dizziness, fever, pain in the extremities, confusion, blurred vision, numbness, and allergic reactions.

Rarely, reduced number of platelets (particles involved in blood clotting), swelling of the face and extremities, kidney toxicity, and liver toxicity have occurred in people taking the drug.

Rifampin may cause a red-orange color in the urine, feces, saliva, sweat, and tears of the people who take it. It may cause permanent discoloration of soft contact lenses.

### PREGNANCY/BREAST-FEEDING
Rifampin has not been formally studied in pregnant women. In animal studies, the drug caused spontaneous abortions and birth defects, but it is not known whether the same would be true in humans. In limited clinical experience, rifampin caused postnatal bleeding in the mother and infant when taken during the last few weeks of pregnancy. Pregnant women are encouraged to discuss the benefits and potential risks of rifampin with their physician before deciding to use the drug.

HIV may be passed from a woman to her child through breast milk. In areas where nutritionally sound alternatives are readily available, breast-feeding is discouraged for HIV-positive women. Rifampin may be excreted in human milk. Because of the potential toxicity of the drug to newborns, women are encouraged to consider alternatives to breast-feeding while taking it.

### USE IN CHILDREN
For treatment of tuberculosis, the recommended drug combinations for children are the same as for adults, with doses adjusted for weight. The recommended dose of rifampin for children is 10 to 20 mg per kg of body weight, not to exceed 600 mg per day.

### USE IN THE ELDERLY
Older adults may be more susceptible to the side effects of the drug and may require reduced doses.

### DRUG INTERACTIONS
Rifampin may decrease the effectiveness of analgesics, anticoagulants (like warfarin), barbiturates, diazepam, digitalis, disopyramide, estrogen, methadone, mexiletine, oral contraceptives, progesterone, and verapamil. In addition, rifampin may decrease the blood levels of corticosteroids, cyclosporine, dapsone, delavirdine, itraconazole, ketoconazole, quinidine, sulfonylurea drugs, and theophylline. Probenecid may increase rifampin levels in the blood, potentially increasing the risk of side effects. Halothane may increase the risk of rifampin-related liver toxicity.

### FOOD INTERACTIONS
Because food reduces the absorption of rifampin, the drug should be taken one hour before or two hours after meals. It is best to take the drug at the same time every day, because taking the drug irregularly increases the chance of experiencing "flu-like" side effects.

**OTHER DRUGS USED FOR SIMILAR CONDITIONS**
Combinations including isoniazid, rifampin, and pyrazinamide are standard therapy for tuberculosis. When these drugs are ineffective or not tolerated, at least three other antibiotics can be used, based on the drug sensitivity of the organism causing the disease. Some of these drugs include amikacin, kanamycin, streptomycin, ciprofloxacin, capreomycin, ethionamide, cycloserine, and para-aminosalicylic acid. Experimental drugs being tested in clinical trials include levofloxacin and sparfloxacin. Treatment should continue for at least eighteen months.

# S T R E P T O M Y C I N

**BRAND NAME (MANUFACTURER)**
Streptomycin USP (Roerig/Pfizer)

**TYPE OF DRUG**
Antibiotic

**USED FOR**
Streptomycin is used to treat a number of moderate to severe bacterial infections, including tuberculosis, plague, and chancroid (vaginal ulcers). In people with HIV it is used rarely to treat *Mycobacterium avium* complex (MAC) when less toxic alternatives are not effective or appropriate.

**GENERAL INFORMATION**
Streptomycin was one of the first antibiotics of the aminoglycoside class, which includes kanamycin, gentamicin, and amikacin. Aminoglycosides prevent susceptible bacteria from making proteins, which stops their growth and prevents them from multiplying.

Streptomycin was the first drug with proven effectiveness against the mycobacteria that cause tuberculosis, but because of its toxicity and the development of alternatives, streptomycin is no longer first-line therapy for tuberculosis or other bacterial infections.

Streptomycin is available as a solution for intramuscular injection.

**TREATMENT**
Tuberculosis may progress more rapidly in people infected with HIV, but it is almost always curable if treated. The disease is usually treated with a combination of several antibiotics. The U.S. Centers for Disease Control recommend that combinations of isoniazid, rifampin, and pyrazinamide be used as first-line therapy against tuberculosis. Streptomycin or ethambutol are added to the regimen if the disease is resistant to isoniazid, if the individual cannot

tolerate full doses of isoniazid or rifampin, or if the disease has spread out of the lungs to the central nervous system to other organs.

It is extremely important to complete the full course of treatment for tuberculosis. Because it takes so long to eradicate the microorganism, people are often tempted to stop taking the drugs after symptoms disappear. However, stopping therapy early increases the chance the disease will recur and contributes to the development of strains of *Mycobacterium* that are resistant to multiple drugs. Multiple-drug-resistant tuberculosis is extremely difficult to treat and is often fatal (even in people with healthy immune systems).

Streptomycin must be administered intramuscularly, usually into the large muscles of the buttock or mid-thigh. Injection sites should be alternated. The dosage schedule varies, depending on the infection, the age and weight of the individual, and the concurrent use of other drugs. Streptomycin is usually administered as a single daily injection.

**CAUTIONS AND WARNINGS**

Streptomycin should not be used by anyone with a known allergy to it or the other aminoglycosides. People with reduced kidney function may be at increased risk of side effects, especially hearing impairment. Early signs of damage to the nerves involved in hearing include headache, nausea, vomiting, or loss of balance. Streptomycin should be used only when facilities are available to test for the nerve damage that results in hearing loss.

The streptomycin injection solution contains sulfites and should not be used by anyone with a sulfite allergy.

**SIDE EFFECTS**

Nausea, vomiting, vertigo, flushing, skin rashes, and swelling are common side effects of streptomycin. Less frequently, deafness, severe peeling of the skin, anaphylactic shock, muscle weakness, vision impairment, and bone marrow toxicity occur. Rarely, kidney toxicity may occur.

**PREGNANCY/BREAST-FEEDING**

Streptomycin is not recommended for use during pregnancy. The drug crosses the placenta and can cause irreversible hearing loss or other side effects in children born to mothers who took the drug during pregnancy. Women are encouraged to use effective contraception while using the drug.

HIV may be passed from a woman to her child through breast milk. In areas where nutritionally sound alternatives are readily available, breast-feeding is discouraged for HIV-positive women. Streptomycin may pass into human milk. It is poorly absorbed from the gut and breast-feeding is not recommended.

### USE IN CHILDREN

Children are given streptomycin at dosages adjusted for weight, without unexpected side effects. The drug should be given with caution in very young children for whom hearing loss may be difficult to detect. In addition, a syndrome of apparent central nervous system depression, characterized by stupor, coma, and suppression of breathing, has occurred in very young infants using the drug at high doses. It is important that children not receive doses higher than those recommended by their physicians.

### USE IN THE ELDERLY

Older adults may be more susceptible to the side effects of the drug and may require reduced doses.

### DRUG INTERACTIONS

Use of streptomycin together with ethacrynic acid, mannitol, furosemide, and other diuretics may increase the risk of hearing loss.

Other drugs that can cause nerve or kidney damage (e.g., neomycin, kanamycin, gentamicin, cephaloridine, paromomycin, viomycin, polymyxin B, colistin, tobramycin, cyclosporine, foscarnet, and certain chemotherapy agents) may increase the risk of these side effects from streptomycin and should be avoided when possible.

The nerve damage caused by streptomycin can result in respiratory paralysis, especially when the drug is given soon after the use of anesthesia or muscle relaxants.

### FOOD INTERACTIONS

Streptomycin is administered by injection, so food does not affect the drug's absorption into the body.

### OTHER DRUGS USED FOR SIMILAR CONDITIONS

For treatment of tuberculosis, the recommended drugs are listed above. For other infections, a wide variety of other aminoglycosides and other types of antibiotics may be substituted for streptomycin. The choice generally depends on which antibiotics the organism is susceptible to and which can be tolerated by the individual. In virtually all cases, use of streptomycin is reserved for when less toxic alternatives are not effective or tolerated.

# TETRACYCLINE

### BRAND NAME (MANUFACTURER)

Achromycin (Lederle); Topicycline (Roberts); Panmycin (Pharmacia & Upjohn); Sumycin (Squibb); Tetracyn (Pfizer)

**TYPE OF DRUG**

Antibiotic

**USED FOR**

Tetracycline is used for the treatment of a wide variety of bacterial infections, including diarrhea and dysentery caused by *Shigella,* chronic infections of the prostate gland, pelvic inflammatory disease, urinary-tract infections, acne, atrophic ulcers (sores in the mouth), and acute bronchitis, among others. For people with HIV, it is used to treat bacterial infections of the gut when other standard treatments are not effective or tolerated.

**GENERAL INFORMATION**

Tetracycline is a relatively old, broad-spectrum antibiotic used to treat a wide variety of bacterial infections. At commonly used dosages, the drug does not kill bacteria; rather it prevents them from growing or multiplying, providing the immune system the ability to destroy the infection.

Tetracycline is available in a wide variety of forms, including tablets, capsules, oral suspension, topical solution, and eye drops.

**TREATMENT**

For most systemic bacterial infections, the adult dose ranges from 250 to 500 mg, taken four times a day. Children aged nine and older generally receive a dosage of 10 to 20 mg per pound of body weight per day, divided in four equal doses. The topical solutions and eye drops should be used as directed by a physician.

**CAUTIONS AND WARNINGS**

Tetracycline should not be used by anyone with a known allergy to it or any similar drug, including doxycycline, demeclocycline, meclocycline, oxytetracycline, or minocycline. The drug should not be used by anyone with impaired liver or kidney function or anyone with difficulty urinating, because of the potential for serious side effects.

People taking high doses of tetracycline should avoid bright light or sunlight, because the drug reduces the body's natural protection against ultraviolet radiation.

Some formulations of tetracycline (e.g., the topical solution) contain sulfites and should not be used by people with sulfite allergies.

**SIDE EFFECTS**

The most common side effects of tetracycline are stomach upset, nausea, vomiting, diarrhea, and rash. Less common side effects include hairy tongue and itching. Rare side effects include loss of appetite, skin reactions, fever, chills, anemia, discoloration of the skin, kidney toxicity, and liver toxicity.

**PREGNANCY/BREAST-FEEDING**

Tetracycline taken during pregnancy, especially the third trimester, can cause severe birth defects. It should not be used by pregnant women.

HIV may be passed from a woman to her child through breast milk. In areas where nutritionally sound alternatives are readily available, breast-feeding is discouraged for HIV-positive women. Tetracycline can pass through breast milk and severely retard growth of the infant's skull, bones, and teeth. It should not be used by breast-feeding women.

**USE IN CHILDREN**

The drug is generally not recommended for younger children because it may cause permanent discoloration of teeth or abnormal or retarded development of the skull, bones, and teeth. There are exceptions, however. For example, tetracycline is used for young children to treat Rocky Mountain spotted fever because the illness justifies the risk. Tetracycline is routinely used in children over the age of six because the enamel on the front teeth has been deposited by then.

**USE IN THE ELDERLY**

Older adults may be more susceptible to the side effects of the drug and may require reduced doses.

**DRUG INTERACTIONS**

Tetracycline may interfere with the activity of penicillin-type antibiotics. The two types of antibiotics should be used together with caution.

Antacids (like those in ddI preparations), mineral supplements, and multi-vitamins containing bismuth, calcium, zinc, magnesium, and iron may reduce the absorption of tetracycline into the body. Tetracycline should be taken two hours before or after taking these other compounds.

Cimetidine may reduce the amount of tetracycline absorbed. Tetracycline may increase the blood levels of digoxin. Tetracycline may also reduce the amount of insulin necessary in diabetics.

Tetracycline may reduce the effectiveness of oral contraceptives.

**FOOD INTERACTIONS**

The antibacterial activity of tetracycline may be neutralized when taken with food or milk. The drug should be taken one hour before or two hours after meals.

**OTHER DRUGS USED FOR SIMILAR CONDITIONS**

For most bacterial infections, the penicillins are preferred to tetracycline, because they have fewer serious side effects. For treatment of chlamydia (which may lead to pelvic inflammatory disease), azithromycin is often the drug of choice because it can be taken in a single daily dose while other therapies may re-

quire up to four doses a day for seven to ten days. Doxycycline, ofloxacin, and erythromycin are alternatives.

For treatment of pelvic inflammatory disease, either cefotetan or cefoxitin with doxycycline or clindamycin with gentamicin are recommended. Tetracycline may be used when these other combinations are ineffective or not tolerated.

# VANCOMYCIN

**BRAND NAME (MANUFACTURER)**
Vancocin HCl (Lilly)

**TYPE OF DRUG**
Antibiotic

**USED FOR**
Vancomycin is a final stage drug used to treat serious infections caused by strains of staphylococcal bacteria that are resistant to methicillin or other penicillins or cephalosporins. Intravenous (IV) vancomycin is used for staphylococcal endocarditis, systemic bacterial infection in the blood (septicemia) and infections of the bone, lower respiratory tract and skin. The oral form of vancomycin is used to treat enterocolitis, an infection of the gastrointestinal tract, and colitis caused by C. *difficile* after antibiotic use.

**GENERAL INFORMATION**
Vancomycin is a type of antibiotic that works by inhibiting the cell walls of bacteria and thereby preventing bacteria from multiplying. Vancomycin is effective for bacteria that may already be resistant to penicillins or cephalosporins or various antimicrobial drugs.

As with most antibiotics, resistance to vancomycin will almost inevitably develop, and inappropriate use of the drug (not taking the amount prescribed) may hasten the appearance of resistant strains.

Vancomycin is available as tablets or as a solution for intravenous injection.

**TREATMENT**
For intravenous vancomycin in adults, the recommended daily dose is 2 g administered either as 500 mg every 6 hours or 1,000 mg every 12 hours. The IV doses should be given at no more than 10mg/min or over a period of at least 60 minutes, whichever is longer. In children, the IV dose should be 10 mg/kg per dose given every 6 hours. For infants and newborns, the dose should begin at 15 mg/kg and reduce to 10mg/kg every 12 hours during the first

week of life and then every 8 hours thereafter. Again, the doses should be administered over 60 minutes.

The recommended dose for oral vancomycin is a total daily dose of 500 mg to 2 grams divided into 3–4 doses each day for 7–10 days. In children, the usual daily dosage is 40 mg/kg in 3–4 divided doses for 7–10 days. Total daily dosage should not exceed 2 grams in children.

**CAUTIONS AND WARNINGS**

Vancomycin should not be used in people allergic to it.

IV vancomycin should only be administered over a period of at least 60 minutes because rapid administration may be associated with hypotension or cardiac arrest (although rare).

Some people taking vancomycin experience hearing loss that may be transient or permanent, although this occurs most in people given an overdose or who have underlying hearing loss already.

People with previous kidney problems should be aware that high prolonged blood levels of vancomycin can cause kidney toxicity.

**SIDE EFFECTS**

After a rapid IV administration, people may experience an allergic reaction to the drug, including side effects such as hypotension, wheezing, shortness of breath, hives, or itching.

Rare cases of kidney failure, hearing loss, reversible neutropenia, and reversible agranulocytosis have been noted. Other infrequent side effects may include fever, nausea, chills, or rashes.

**PREGNANCY/BREAST-FEEDING**

In one controlled study of vancomycin in pregnant women, there was no hearing loss or kidney toxicity in the newborn children. However, because the study was small and mothers were only given vancomycin during the second and third trimesters, it is not known whether vancomycin can cause fetal harm. It is also not know if vancomycin can affect fertility as no reproduction studies have been performed. Pregnant women are encouraged to discuss the benefits and potential risks of vancomycin with their physician before making a decision about taking the drug.

HIV can be passed from a woman to her child through breast milk. In areas where nutritionally sound alternatives are readily available, breast-feeding is discouraged for HIV-positive women. Vancomycin is also excreted in human milk. Because of the potential toxicity of the drug, women should consider alternatives to breast-feeding while taking it.

**USE IN CHILDREN**

Vancomycin can be given to children but blood levels should be monitored carefully. Use of the drug along with anesthetic agents in newborns and infants has resulted in some cases of skin redness (erythema) and flushing.

**USE IN THE ELDERLY**

Older adults may be more susceptible to the side effects of the drug and may require reduced doses.

**DRUG INTERACTIONS**

Administration of vancomycin with anesthetic drugs has been associated with erythema (skin redness) and flushing, as well as potentially life-threatening allergic reactions. These may be minimized by administering vancomycin as a 60-minute infusion prior to giving the anesthetic drug.

**FOOD INTERACTIONS**

No information available.

**OTHER DRUGS USED FOR SIMILAR CONDITIONS**

Nonresistant staphylococcus infections can be treated using various penicillins or cephalosporins, but IV vancomycin is the only drug that can treat resistant strains of staphylococcal bacteria.

To treat *C. difficile* infections in the gut, first-line therapy generally includes oral metronidazole (Flagyl).

For most bacterial infections, there is no single "definitive" treatment. The choice of drug will depend primarily on which drugs can be tolerated, which side effects a person is at risk for, and which drugs are effective for the particular organism.

# ANTIBIOTICS

## EXPERIMENTAL DRUGS

The following drug is being tested for the treatment of bacterial infections in people with HIV.

**SPARFLOXACIN (ZAGAM)**

Sparfloxacin is also a member of the quinolone family of antibiotics and is approved for the treatment of several types of bacterial infections. In laboratory studies it has activity against tuberculosis and *Mycobacterium avium* complex (MAC). It is available in a compassionate use program for individuals with multiple-drug-resistant tuberculosis who are resistant to conventional therapy.

# ANTICANCER DRUGS

Normally, the body's cells grow, divide, develop, and die according to a specific, highly regulated plan laid out in its DNA. Soon after an egg is fertilized, some cells are committed to become the nervous system; others become the skin; and still others become the skeleton, internal organs, blood, or other components of the body. Not only do the cells "know" when to divide and what function they will perform, they also know when to stop dividing. If something interferes with the DNA instructions that tell cells when to stop dividing, uncontrolled cell growth and division may occur. This condition is known as a cancer or malignancy, and the growth is called a tumor. The type of cancer is determined by the location and the kind of cells that are multiplying. For example, lymphoma is uncontrolled multiplication of lymph cells; cervical cancer is uncontrolled multiplication of the cells of the cervix.

People living with HIV are at higher risk for certain types of cancers than the general population. Because the immune system attacks malignant cells as well as microorganisms that cause infection, severe immunosuppression leaves the body increasingly susceptible to cancer. And as people with HIV live longer with lower CD4+ counts because of the successful prevention and treatment of opportunistic infections, cancers may become even more common in people with AIDS.

Kaposi's sarcoma (KS) and non-Hodgkin's lymphoma (NHL) are the two most common malignancies found in people with AIDS. KS generally starts as a skin malignancy that can spread internally throughout the body if left unchecked. It is found primarily in gay men and is now believed to occur only when a person is infected with human herpes virus-8 (HHV-8). NHL, in people with AIDS, is a rapidly progressing cancer of the lymph nodes. It occurs approximately sixty times more frequently in people living with HIV than the general population, and it is common in both men and women with HIV.

Because KS and NHL also occur in HIV-negative people, treatments for the cancers were developed before the AIDS epidemic began. However, these treatments are generally less effective for people with HIV than the general population, at least in part because people with suppressed immune systems often cannot tolerate full doses of chemotherapy drugs because of bone marrow toxicity or an increased risk of opportunistic infections. Drugs that stimulate the bone marrow (colony-stimulating factors like G-CSF or GM-CSF) can counteract the bone marrow toxicity of chemotherapy. They are being tested in clinical trials to determine whether they will permit higher (potentially more effective) doses or provide longer benefit when standard doses of chemotherapy are used by people with AIDS-related cancers.

Nausea and vomiting are common side effects of drugs used to treat cancer. They may be managed by diet (eating mild or bland foods such as white rice), eating small and frequent meals, or by taking antiemetic drugs such as granisetron or ondansetron. See the chapter on nutritional therapies and the antinausea/antivomiting drug section for more details on treating these side effects of chemotherapy.

Treatment of KS on the skin may include surgical excision, radiation, cryotherapy (freezing the lesions), or drugs injected directly into lesions. Advanced-stage KS that has spread throughout the body is usually treated with systemic drugs. In people with KS who have not previously received antiretroviral therapy (AZT, etc.), the cancer often regresses when antiretroviral therapy is started. For people who have already started antiretroviral therapy before KS develops, individual drugs such as vinblastine, vincristine, etoposide, bleomycin, doxorubicin, or alpha interferon have been used, but more commonly, combinations of drugs (such as BV, ABV, or VV; see below) are used for advanced stages of the disease. In general, the individual's condition, including CD4+ count, extent of disease, and history of prior opportunistic infections, is more important than the drugs used in predicting whether a person will respond to treatment.

Similarly, treatment of AIDS-related NHL usually consists of combination chemotherapy (some commonly used regimens are described below). Again, a person's condition is a better predictor of response to treatment than the combination of drugs used. Overall, about half of the people who receive drug treatment for AIDS-related lymphoma have a complete response, but the disease usually returns rapidly. Higher success rates are achieved with people with higher CD4+ counts (greater than 200).

The dosing schedules for AIDS-related malignancies vary widely, depending on the condition of the person being treated and the physician's experience with the protocol. The following combination protocols are used to treat KS or NHL in people with HIV.

## KS COMBINATION CHEMOTHERAPY

**V V COMBINATION**

| | |
|---|---|
| **DRUGS** | vincristine and vinblastine |
| **ADMINISTRATION** | Vincristine and vinblastine are administered intravenously one day a week on alternate weeks. The vinblastine is reduced when leukocyte or platelet counts drop severely. The vincristine is stopped when neurological side effects occur. |

**SIDE EFFECTS** The side effects of this combination are mainly neurological, including muscle weakness. Severe bone marrow suppression occurs less frequently.

## BV COMBINATION

**DRUGS** bleomycin and either vincristine or vinblastine

**ADMINISTRATION** When bleomycin and vincristine are used together, the drugs are often administered every two weeks intravenously. When bleomycin and vinblastine are used together, the drugs may be administered on alternate weeks.

**SIDE EFFECTS** Peripheral neuropathy caused by vincristine is the primary side effect of the combination. Bone marrow toxicity is also seen in people with low bone marrow reserve. In one study where bleomycin was used with vinblastine, more than half of the responders experienced an opportunistic infection, perhaps because of vinblastine suppression of bone marrow.

## ABV COMBINATION

**DRUGS** doxorubicin (**Adriamycin**)
bleomycin
vincristine or vinblastine

**ADMINISTRATION** Similar to BV combination with doxorubicin added to the protocol.

**SIDE EFFECTS** Bone marrow suppression and neurological damage (including peripheral neuropathy) are the most serious side effects of ABV.

# NHL COMBINATION CHEMOTHERAPY

## CHOP COMBINATION

**DRUGS** cyclophosphamide
doxorubicin (hydroxydaunomycin)
vincristine (Oncovin)
prednisone

**ADMINISTRATION** Cyclophosphamide, doxorubicin, and vincristine are administered on day 1. Prednisone is administered on days 1 through 5. The cycle is repeated every 21 to 28 days.

**SIDE EFFECTS** Bone marrow toxicity is the major side effect of CHOP.

## M-BACOD COMBINATION

**DRUGS**
methotrexate
bleomycin
doxorubicin (Adriamycin)
cyclophosphamide
vincristine (Oncovin)
dexamethasone
leucovorin

**ADMINISTRATION** Bleomycin, doxorubicin, cyclophosphamide, and vincristine are administered intravenously on day 1. Dexamethasone is taken orally on days 1 to 5. Methotrexate is administered intravenously on day 15, followed by leucovorin to counteract the vitamin B deficiency caused by methotrexate. In one clinical trial, cytosine arabinoside was administered directly into the spinal column on days 1, 8, 21, and 28 in an attempt to prevent central nervous system (CNS) relapse. Radiation may be used when CNS or bone marrow involvement is known. Cycles are repeated every 28 days.

**SIDE EFFECTS** Bone marrow toxicity was the most common side effect of therapy. Even when half-dose therapy was used in clinical trials, approximately 60% of participants developed a deficiency of white blood cells called neutrophils.

**COMMENTS** Because full-dose m-BACOD cannot be tolerated by many people with HIV, a low-dose combination of the drugs has been tested in clinical trials. About half the people participating achieved a complete response, but opportunistic infections occurred in 20% of them, despite prophylaxis for *Pneumocystis carinii* pneumonia.

Other, more toxic NHL therapy is also used, but there is no good evidence at this time that it works any better than CHOP or m-BACOD.

Human chorionic gonadotropin (HCG) is an approved therapy, used primarily to treat hormone deficiencies. It is also being tested as a possible treatment for KS, and as such, it is described in this section.

A number of experimental KS and NHL therapies are discussed briefly at the end of this section. They include:

- rPF4
- SP-PG
- TNP-470
- OPC-8212

- tretinoin
- cidofovir
- foscarnet
- mitoguazone

# BLEOMYCIN

**BRAND NAME (MANUFACTURER)**
Blenoxane (Bristol-Myers Squibb Oncology)

**TYPE OF DRUG**
Anticancer agent

**USED FOR**
Bleomycin has been used in the treatment of head and neck cancers, Hodgkin's disease, lymphomas, and testicular cancer. In people living with HIV, bleomycin is most often used alone or in combination with other chemotherapy drugs for the treatment of AIDS-related lymphoma (primarily non-Hodgkin's lymphoma, NHL) and advanced Kaposi's sarcoma (KS).

**GENERAL INFORMATION**
Bleomycin is a mixture of naturally occurring proteins purified from a species of *Streptomyces*. It is available only as a solution for injection. The drug works by interfering with the production of DNA, which prevents tumor cells from multiplying.

Although bleomycin can be used by itself to treat cancers, it is used more frequently in combination with other chemotherapy drugs. The rationale is that different drugs have different ways of working and different side effects. By combining drugs, it is often possible to come up with a more effective treatment with reduced side effects and less risk of developing drug-resistant tumors.

For the treatment of KS in people infected with HIV, bleomycin is often used with vincristine or vinblastine in a combination called BV. It is also used with doxorubicin (Adriamycin) plus vinblastine or vincristine in a combination called ABV. The number of people whose KS is successfully treated varies from study to study. Factors likely to affect response include stage of disease, other opportunistic infections, prior treatment with chemotherapy, or lower CD4+ counts. A recent study showed that a liposomal formulation of doxorubicin (Doxil) when used alone is more effective in treating KS and less toxic than the BV combination. Doxil alone was also significantly less toxic than a combination of Doxil, bleomycin, and vincristine.

For the treatment of AIDS-related lymphoma, bleomycin is used in a combination of drugs called m-BACOD, which consists of methotrexate, bleomycin, doxorubicin, cyclophosphamide, vincristine, dexamethasone, and leucovorin. Clinical studies show that complete remission of disease is possible after treatment, but the cancer commonly recurs after a short period of time. Full-dose m-BACOD is toxic to bone marrow, and many HIV-positive individuals cannot tolerate it. To overcome this limitation, some people also use

drugs known as colony-stimulating factors (e.g., G-CSF, commonly known as Neupogen), which stimulate bone marrow production of blood cells. Another option has been to use a low-dose version of the combination. In clinical trials of this low-dose regimen, about 50% of volunteers experienced a complete remission of their lymphoma, but the effect was usually short-lived. These results are similar to those achieved with the full-dose version of the combination, but with fewer dose-related side effects. People with less invasive disease, no prior AIDS-defining illness, and no bone marrow or central nervous system involvement are more likely to respond to treatment for AIDS-related lymphoma. The most important predictor of success is not the drugs used, but the CD4+ count of the individual at the time the cancer is diagnosed.

**TREATMENT**
The dose and schedule of administration of bleomycin varies depending on the type of disease and the other drugs being administered at the same time.

Granisetron or ondansetron are often used concomitantly to reduce or prevent the nausea caused by the bleomycin-containing combinations.

**CAUTIONS AND WARNINGS**
Bleomycin is highly toxic. It should not be used by people who know they are allergic to it, and it should be used only in a setting where careful observation by health care professionals experienced in its use is possible. Because the drug can cause serious lung or kidney damage, it should be used with extreme caution in people with reduced kidney or lung function. When used in combination with other chemotherapy drugs, bleomycin may cause lung damage at lower doses.

Because bleomycin makes lung tissue more sensitive than normal, people who have received it are at greater risk of developing breathing complications when oxygen is administered during surgery.

Because of the risk of serious, drug-related birth defects, women are encouraged to use effective birth control while using bleomycin.

**SIDE EFFECTS**
The most serious side effect of bleomycin is toxicity to the lungs, which occurs in approximately 10% of those treated. About 1% of people treated with the drug have died from pulmonary fibrosis, a condition in which the lung tissue becomes fibrous and unable to perform properly. This side effect occurs more frequently in people over the age of seventy and in those who receive a cumulative dose of more than 400 units of the drug, but it is not possible to predict whether an individual will experience this side effect. The earliest symptom is difficulty in breathing, which should be reported immediately to the physician.

Severe allergic reactions have been reported by 1% of people with lymphoma receiving the drug. These reactions usually occur after the first or second dose of the drug. The most frequent side effects are allergic skin reactions, which occur in about 50% of people who take the drug.

Fever, chills, and vomiting are also frequently reported side effects. Changes in appetite and weight loss are common and may persist long after the drug is stopped.

### PREGNANCY/BREAST-FEEDING

Bleomycin has not been formally studied in pregnant women, but it is highly toxic to rapidly dividing cells, such as those in a malignant tumor or in a fetus. Consequently, it has significant potential for causing fetal harm. Pregnant women are encouraged to discuss the benefits and potential risks of bleomycin with their physician before deciding whether or not to use the drug.

HIV can be passed from a woman to her child through breast milk. In areas where nutritionally sound alternatives are readily available, breast-feeding is discouraged for HIV-positive women. Bleomycin may be excreted in human milk, and given the drug's potential toxicity, women should consider alternatives to breast-feeding while using it.

### USE IN CHILDREN

Physicians generally treat KS and AIDS-related lymphoma in children with the same drugs used in adults, at doses adjusted for weight or body surface area. In general, the drugs have similar response rates and side effects in children as in adults.

### USE IN THE ELDERLY

In people over seventy years of age, there is a higher risk of toxicity to the lungs. For these people, the value of treatment must be weighed against the increased risk of potentially fatal side effects.

### DRUG INTERACTIONS

When used with foscarnet, amphotericin B, ganciclovir, AZT or other anti-cancer agents, bleomycin side effects may occur at lower dosages. Serious side effects have been reported in people using bleomycin together with vinblastine or cisplatin.

### FOOD INTERACTIONS

None reported.

### OTHER DRUGS USED FOR SIMILAR CONDITIONS

For lymphoma, a commonly used treatment is a chemotherapy combination called CHOP, which consists of cyclophosphamide, doxorubicin, vincristine, and prednisone. There are no clinical studies directly comparing CHOP and m-BACOD for the treatment of AIDS-related lymphoma, so it is not possible to say one is more effective than another. The choice of treatment often comes

down to which combination is best tolerated by the individual. Generally, CHOP has fewer side effects than m-BACOD.

For the treatment of advanced KS, a number of drugs have been used, including vinblastine, vincristine, etoposide, doxorubicin, liposomal doxorubicin, and alpha interferon. In general, the effectiveness of the treatment has less to do with the drugs or combination of drugs used than to differences in the CD4+ counts and the history of opportunistic infections of the people treated.

**COMMENTS**

More progress is needed in the treatment of lymphoma and KS in people infected with HIV. A major problem in using chemotherapy is suppression of the immune system. Many of the drugs used in combination chemotherapy reduce the counts of white blood cells called neutrophils, which are essential to fighting infection. After chemotherapy, the immune system recovers slowly in people who already have low CD4+ counts. The lower the CD4+ count, the slower the recovery, which may require long periods of hospitalization. One approach that has proven successful in minimizing this problem is the use of colony-stimulating factors (G-CSF or GM-CSF) with the chemotherapy to maintain neutrophil counts and speed recovery after the chemotherapy is stopped. See the profiles on G-CSF and GM-CSF for more information on how these drugs work.

# CYCLOPHOSPHAMIDE

**BRAND NAME (MANUFACTURER)**
Cytoxan (Bristol-Myers Squibb Oncology); Neosar (Pharmacia & Upjohn)

**TYPE OF DRUG**
Anticancer agent

**USED FOR**
Cyclophosphamide is used to treat a wide variety of cancers, including Hodgkin's disease, lymphoma, leukemia, myeloma, mycosis fungoides, and cancers of the brain, eye, or breast. In people with HIV, cyclophosphamide is most commonly used in combination therapy for the treatment of AIDS-related lymphoma.

**GENERAL INFORMATION**
Cyclophosphamide is an alkylating agent, which means that it works by attaching to biologically important molecules such as DNA and RNA, interfering with cell growth and division. Alkylating agents are toxic to rapidly dividing cells, like those in a tumor or in the bone marrow (where blood cells are continually being replaced). Cyclophosphamide is one of the most widely

used chemotherapy drugs, in part because its toxicity is more specific to malignant cells and less likely to cause severe bone marrow toxicity than many other alkylating agents.

Although cyclophosphamide can be used by itself to treat cancers, it is used more frequently in combination with other chemotherapy drugs. The rationale is that different drugs have different ways of working and different side effects. By combining drugs, it is often possible to come up with a more effective treatment with reduced side effects and less risk of developing drug-resistant tumors.

For the treatment of AIDS-related lymphoma, cyclophosphamide is routinely used in a combination of drugs called CHOP, which consists of cyclophosphamide, doxorubicin, vincristine, and prednisone. It is also used in a combination of drugs called m-BACOD (methotrexate, bleomycin, doxorubicin, cyclophosphamide, vincristine, dexamethasone, and leucovorin). People with less progressive disease, no prior AIDS-defining illness, and no bone marrow or central nervous system involvement are more likely to respond to these treatments. The most important predictor of success is not the particular combination of drugs used, but the CD4+ count at the time the lymphoma is diagnosed. People with baseline CD4+ counts above 200 have the best response.

Cyclophosphamide is available as tablets for oral administration and as a solution for injection.

## TREATMENT

The dosage of cyclophosphamide varies widely depending on the cancer, the health of the individual, and other drugs being used at the same time. For most uses, the oral form of the drug is appropriate, but the intravenous form may be used by people with digestive problems that may make absorption problematic.

Although people with reduced kidney function may have increased levels of cyclophosphamide in their blood when taking the drug at recommended doses, there is no consistent evidence that dosage reductions are necessary with kidney disease.

## CAUTIONS AND WARNINGS

Cyclophosphamide should not be used by anyone with a known allergy to it. It should also not be used by people with severely depressed bone marrow function, which may occur in people with HIV after treatment with other drugs like AZT or ganciclovir.

Because cyclophosphamide is highly toxic, it should be used only in a setting where it is possible to have careful observation by health care professionals experienced in its use.

In some people with impaired immune function, treatment with cyclophosphamide has resulted in the development of secondary tumors, unrelated to the tumors originally treated. This possibility should be considered in any risk-benefit assessment of the drug.

Treatment with cyclophosphamide may cause significant suppression of immune responses, increasing the risk of serious, and potentially fatal, opportunistic infections. Cyclophosphamide treatment may need to be interrupted or the dose reduced in people who have developed opportunistic infections.

Because of the risk of serious, drug-related birth defects, women are encouraged to use effective birth control while using cyclophosphamide.

### SIDE EFFECTS

Cyclophosphamide may cause sterility in both sexes. In some people, this side effect has been irreversible. Menstrual irregularity commonly occurs in women using the drug. This is usually reversible after treatment stops.

Damage to the bladder, which can be severe, is a common side effect of cyclophosphamide. This side effect appears to be related to the dose and duration of therapy.

Heart damage has been reported in people using cyclophosphamide, primarily in people receiving high doses of the drug (ranging from 120 to 270 mg per kg of body weight, administered over a few days). In a few instances, severe and fatal congestive heart failure has occurred.

Nausea, vomiting, and temporary hair loss occur frequently with cyclophosphamide therapy. Less frequently, loss of appetite, abdominal discomfort, or diarrhea may occur.

Bone marrow toxicity that causes reductions in white blood cell counts are common with the use of cyclophosphamide. Reductions in the number of platelets (particles involved in blood clotting) and red blood cells develop occasionally, but are reversible after therapy stops.

Severe toxicity to the lungs or kidneys also occurs occasionally in people using the drug. Rarely, allergic reactions, such as anaphylactic shock, and death have been reported.

### PREGNANCY/BREAST-FEEDING

Cyclophosphamide can cause severe fetal harm when given to pregnant women. The drug should not be used by pregnant women if alternatives are available.

HIV may be passed from a woman to her child through breast milk. In areas where nutritionally sound alternatives are readily available, breast-feeding is discouraged for HIV-positive women. Cyclophosphamide is excreted

in human milk and can cause serious side effects in newborns. Women should discontinue nursing while using the drug.

**USE IN CHILDREN**

Cyclophosphamide has been used effectively in children at doses adjusted for weight or body surface area, with side effects similar to those seen in adults. However, some of these side effects may be severe or irreversible (such as sterility). The potential benefits and risks must be weighed for each child.

**USE IN THE ELDERLY**

Because kidney function generally declines with age, elderly or debilitated people may have greater variability in their blood levels of cyclophosphamide when taking the drug.

**DRUG INTERACTIONS**

Phenobarbital may increase the effect of cyclophosphamide. Cyclophosphamide may intensify the effect of succinyl choline. Use of cyclophosphamide with other drugs that are toxic to the kidneys (such as amphotericin B or foscarnet) may increase the risk of cyclophosphamide-related side effects.

**FOOD INTERACTIONS**

None reported.

**OTHER DRUGS USED FOR SIMILAR CONDITIONS**

For AIDS-related lymphoma, CHOP is a commonly used treatment. A number of other drug combinations, including m-BACOD, are also often used. There are no clinical studies directly comparing these different combinations, so it is not possible to say one is more effective than another. The choice of treatment often comes down to which combination is best tolerated by the individual. On average, CHOP has fewer side effects than m-BACOD for lymphoma.

**COMMENTS**

More progress is needed in the treatment of lymphoma and KS in people infected with HIV. A major problem in using chemotherapy is suppression of the immune system. Many of the drugs used in combination chemotherapy reduce the counts of white blood cells called neutrophils, which are essential to fighting infection. After chemotherapy, the immune system recovers slowly in people who already have low CD4+ counts. The lower the CD4+ count, the slower the recovery, which may require long periods of hospitalization. One approach that has proven successful in minimizing this problem is the use of colony-stimulating factors (G-CSF or GM-CSF) with the chemotherapy to maintain neutrophil counts and speed recovery after the chemotherapy is stopped. See the profiles on G-CSF and GM-CSF for more information on how these drugs work.

# CYTARABINE

**BRAND NAME (MANUFACTURER)**
Cytosar-U (Pharmacia & Upjohn)

**OTHER NAMES**
ara-C; cytosine arabinoside

**TYPE OF DRUG**
Anticancer agent

**USED FOR**
Cytarabine is approved for the treatment of leukemia in children and adults, usually in combination with other anticancer drugs. In HIV-infected people it was studied as an anti-HIV agent, but had no significant benefit. It is sometimes used to treat progressive multifocal leukoencephalopathy (PML), a disease of the central nervous system, in people with HIV. However, recent clinical information showed no activity for this indication.

**GENERAL INFORMATION**
Cytarabine is a synthetic chemical that mimics one of the building blocks in DNA. In cancer cells, cytarabine slows down DNA synthesis, which eventually kills the cells. Because cytarabine acts on any rapidly dividing cell, it is highly toxic to the cells in the bone marrow that produce blood cells and components of the immune system.

Cytarabine is used most frequently in combination with other chemotherapy drugs to treat cancers. The rationale is that different drugs have different ways of working and different side effects. By combining drugs, it is often possible to come up with a more effective treatment with reduced side effects and less risk of developing drug-resistant tumors.

Cytarabine is available as a sterile powder for injection.

**TREATMENT**
Cytarabine may be injected into a vein, under the skin, or into a large muscle. It may also be delivered intrathecally (through a tube) directly into the fluid surrounding the brain or spinal cord. Dosages vary depending on the condition of the patient, the other drugs also being administered, and the type of cancer treated.

Ondansetron or granisetron are often used along with cytarabine to reduce or prevent the nausea and vomiting caused by the drug.

**CAUTIONS AND WARNINGS**
Cytarabine should not be used by people with a known allergy to it. Treatment is generally started slowly and cautiously in people with preexisting bone marrow suppression caused by drugs. AZT or ganciclovir may be stopped for the period cytarabine is used to prevent additive bone marrow toxicity.

Because of the risk of serious, drug-related birth defects, women are encouraged to use effective birth control while using cytarabine.

### SIDE EFFECTS

The most significant side effect of cytarabine is bone marrow suppression, which results in reduced lymphocyte, platelet, and red blood cell counts. In severe cases, these reductions can increase the risk of opportunistic infection, severe bleeding, and anemia. Less serious side effects of cytarabine include nausea, vomiting, diarrhea, abdominal pain, oral sores, and abnormal liver function.

In a few people, the drug has caused a side effect called the cytarabine syndrome, symptoms of which include fever, bone pain, chest pain, rash, inflammation in the eyes, and malaise. It usually occurs six to twelve hours after injection. Corticosteroids have been shown to be effective in treating or preventing the syndrome.

Allergic reactions have occurred in some people receiving the drug. These reactions have been severe and sometimes fatal. When used at high doses, the drug may cause toxicity to the central nervous system, digestive tract, and lungs.

### PREGNANCY/BREAST-FEEDING

Cytarabine is toxic to rapidly dividing cells, like those in a malignant tumor or in a fetus. Birth defects have been reported in children whose mothers took the drug during the first trimester of pregnancy. The risk is still significant, but lower, during the last two trimesters. Pregnant women are encouraged to discuss the benefits and potential risks of cytarabine with their physician before deciding whether or not to use the drug.

HIV can be passed from a woman to her child through breast milk. In areas where nutritionally sound alternatives are readily available, breast-feeding is discouraged for HIV-positive women. It is not known if cytarabine is excreted in human milk, but because of the potential toxicity of the drug, women should consider alternatives to breast-feeding while using it.

### USE IN CHILDREN

Cytarabine has been effectively used in children with leukemia without additional side effects from those expected for adults.

### USE IN THE ELDERLY

No alterations in dosage or administration are recommended for older adults with normal liver and kidney function.

### DRUG INTERACTIONS

Cytarabine may reduce the effectiveness of gentamicin or flucytosine. The use of cyclophosphamide with cytarabine may increase the risk of damage to the heart.

**FOOD INTERACTIONS**
None reported.

**OTHER DRUGS USED FOR SIMILAR CONDITIONS**
For AIDS-related lymphoma, a commonly used treatment is a combination called CHOP, which consists of cyclophosphamide, doxorubicin, vincristine, and prednisone. There have been no studies to directly compare CHOP against cytarabine-containing drug regimens for AIDS-related lymphoma, so it is not possible to say one would be more effective than the other. The choice of therapy is often determined by which drugs or combinations the individual can tolerate.

**COMMENTS**
More progress is needed in the treatment of lymphoma and KS in people infected with HIV. A major problem in using chemotherapy is suppression of the immune system. Many of the drugs used in combination chemotherapy reduce the counts of white blood cells called neutrophils, which are essential to fighting infection. After chemotherapy, the immune system recovers slowly in people who already have low CD4+ counts. The lower the CD4+ count, the slower the recovery, which may require long periods of hospitalization. One approach that has proven successful in minimizing this problem is the use of colony-stimulating factors (G-CSF or GM-CSF) with the chemotherapy to maintain neutrophil counts and speed recovery after the chemotherapy is stopped. See the profiles on G-CSF and GM-CSF for more information on how these drugs work.

# DAUNORUBICIN

**BRAND NAME (MANUFACTURER)**
Cerubidine (Bedford)

**TYPE OF DRUG**
Anticancer agent

**USED FOR**
Daunorubicin is used primarily for the treatment of leukemias in adults and children. In people with HIV, a new formulation, called liposomal daunorubicin, is now available for the treatment of AIDS-related Kaposi's sarcoma (KS).

**GENERAL INFORMATION**
Daunorubicin is a modified form of an antibiotic isolated from a species of fungus-like bacteria called *Streptomyces coeruleorubidus*. The drug inhibits the synthesis of nucleic acids, which prevents cancer cells from dividing. Daunorubicin has an almost identical chemical structure to the more widely

used anticancer agent doxorubicin, but the two drugs work against different types of tumors.

Standard intravenous daunorubicin is rarely used in people infected with HIV. Liposomal daunorubicin (DaunoXome) was recently approved for the treatment of KS. In a mechanism that is not completely understood, encapsulating daunorubicin in liposomes increases the concentration of the drug at the tumor site without increasing the concentration of the drug in the blood or other healthy tissues. In theory, it should target more drug against the cancer while limiting the drug's side effects. As yet, large clinical trials have not produced conclusive evidence of the effectiveness of this formulation.

### TREATMENT

For the treatment of leukemia, daunorubicin is usually combined with cytarabine or vincristine/prednisone. Eradication of the leukemic cells requires a profound suppression of the bone marrow. The dosing schedules vary depending on the disease and the combination of drugs used.

In clinical trials, the dosing of liposomal daunorubicin varied from 40 to 60 mg per square meter of body surface injected every two weeks for the duration of the study.

Granisetron or ondansetron are often used along with daunorubicin to reduce or prevent the nausea or vomiting caused by the drug.

### CAUTIONS AND WARNINGS

The dosage of standard intravenous daunorubicin should be reduced for people with reduced liver or kidney function to avoid increased toxicity that results from increased blood levels of the drug.

Daunorubicin is a potent bone marrow suppressant (suppression will occur in virtually all people given a therapeutic dose of the drug) and increases the risk of opportunistic infection or bleeding. When used by people taking AZT or ganciclovir, drugs called colony-stimulating factors (e.g., G-CSF) are often used as well to limit bone marrow suppression.

People with heart disease or who have previously been treated with doxorubicin have an increased risk of heart damage when using daunorubicin.

Daunorubicin may cause high levels of uric acid in the blood as a result of its effects on destroying cancerous cells. As a precaution, allopurinol is often given before daunorubicin is injected.

Because of the risk of serious, drug-related birth defects, women are encouraged to use effective birth control while using daunorubicin.

### SIDE EFFECTS

For standard intravenous daunorubicin, fatal congestive heart failure may occur either during therapy or months to years after the drug was used. The risk of heart failure increases based upon the total cumulative dose of drug

taken. The risk increases with a cumulative dose exceeding 400 to 550 mg per square meter of body surface area in adults, 300 mg per square meter of body surface area in children over age two, or 10 mg/kg in chilldren under two years of age.

Daunorubicin can cause severe bone marrow suppression in either its standard intravenous form or when encapsulated by liposomes.

Reversible hair loss occurs in most people treated with standard daunorubicin. Nausea and vomiting can occur but are usually mild. Diarrhea has occasionally been reported. Rarely, allergic reactions including fever, chills, and skin rash occur.

Daunorubicin may temporarily make the urine turn red.

**PREGNANCY/BREAST-FEEDING**

Daunorubicin has not been formally studied in pregnant women, but it is highly toxic to rapidly dividing cells, such as those in a malignant tumor or in a fetus. Pregnant women are encouraged to discuss the benefits and potential risks of daunorubicin with their physician before deciding to use the drug.

HIV can be passed from a woman to her child through breast milk. In areas where nutritionally sound alternatives are readily available, breast-feeding is discouraged for HIV-positive women. Daunorubicin may be excreted in human milk, and because of the potential toxicity to newborns, women should consider alternatives to breast-feeding while using the drug.

**USE IN CHILDREN**

Standard intravenous daunorubicin has successfully been used in children, but in infants and children the drug is more likely to be toxic to the heart. In a number of children, daunorubicin has severely impaired heart function, resulting in congestive heart failure and death.

**USE IN THE ELDERLY**

Older adults may be more susceptible to the side effects of the drug and may require reduced doses.

**DRUG INTERACTIONS**

None reported.

**FOOD INTERACTIONS**

None reported.

**OTHER DRUGS USED FOR SIMILAR CONDITIONS**

For the treatment of advanced KS, a number of drugs and combinations of them have been used, including bleomycin, vinblastine, vincristine, etoposide, doxorubicin, liposomal doxorubicin, and alpha interferon. In general, the response to treatment is influenced by the CD4+ counts when therapy is initiated, the general health status of the people treated, and the opportunistic infections and treatments they've received.

**COMMENTS**

More progress is needed in the treatment of lymphoma and KS in people infected with HIV. A major problem in using chemotherapy is suppression of the immune system. Many of the drugs used in combination chemotherapy reduce the counts of white blood cells called neutrophils, which are essential to fighting infection. After chemotherapy, the immune system recovers slowly in people who already have low CD4+ counts. The lower the CD4+ count, the slower the recovery, which may require long periods of hospitalization. One approach that has proven successful in minimizing this problem is the use of colony-stimulating factors (G-CSF or GM-CSF) with the chemotherapy to maintain neutrophil counts and speed recovery after the chemotherapy is stopped. See the profiles on G-CSF and GM-CSF for more information on how these drugs work.

# DAUNORUBICIN-LIPOSOMAL

**BRAND NAME (MANUFACTURER)**
DaunoXome (NexStar)

**TYPE OF DRUG**
Anticancer agent

**USED FOR**
Liposomal daunorubicin has been approved by the FDA for the treatment of advanced Kaposi's sarcoma (KS) in people living with HIV.

**GENERAL INFORMATION**
Daunorubicin is a modified form of an antibiotic isolated from a species of fungus-like bacteria called *Streptomyces coeruleorubidus*. The drug inhibits the synthesis of nucleic acids, which prevents cancer cells from multiplying. Daunorubicin has an almost identical chemical structure to the more widely used anticancer agent doxorubicin, but the two drugs work against different types of tumors.

In liposomal daunorubicin, the drug is encapsulated in a fatty membrane to make tiny "bubbles" called liposomes. The rationale for encapsulating the drug is to improve the specificity of its effects while reducing its toxicity to healthy cells. In a process that is not completely understood, liposomes deposit more of the active drug in tumors than in the bloodstream while limiting the drug's side effects.

**TREATMENT**
Liposomal daunorubicin is usually given by intravenous injection over a 60-minute period at a dose of 40 mg per square meter of body surface area.

Granisetron or ondansetron are often used concomitantly with liposomal daunorubicin to reduce or prevent the nausea or vomiting caused by the drug.

## CAUTIONS AND WARNINGS

The dosage of liposomal daunorubicin should be reduced for people with reduced liver or kidney function to avoid increased toxicity that results from increased blood levels of the drug.

Liposomal daunorubicin is a bone marrow suppressant and increases the risk of opportunistic infection or bleeding. When used by people also taking AZT or ganciclovir, drugs called colony-stimulating factors (e.g., G-CSF) are often used as well to limit bone marrow suppression.

People with heart disease or who have previously been treated with a class of drugs known as anthracyclines have an increased risk of heart damage when using daunorubicin. Careful monitoring of the heart is recommended.

Because of the risk of serious, drug-related birth defects, women are encouraged to use effective birth control while using liposomal daunorubicin.

## SIDE EFFECTS

Liposomal daunorubicin can cause fatal congestive heart failure which may occur either during therapy or months to years after the drug was used.

Severe bone marrow suppression can occur with liposomal daunorubicin.

Other side effects reported were hair loss, vomiting, nausea, fatigue, fever, diarrhea, difficulty breathing, headache, abdominal or back pain, and anorexia.

## PREGNANCY/BREAST-FEEDING

Liposomal daunorubicin has not been formally studied in pregnant women, but it is highly toxic to rapidly dividing cells, such as those in a malignant tumor or in a fetus. Pregnant women are encouraged to discuss the benefits and potential risks of liposomal daunorubicin with their physician before deciding to use the drug.

HIV can be passed from a woman to her child through breast milk. In areas where nutritionally sound alternatives are readily available, breast-feeding is discouraged for HIV-positive women. Liposomal daunorubicin may be excreted in human milk, and because of the potential toxicity to newborns, women should consider alternatives to breast-feeding while using the drug.

## USE IN CHILDREN

The safety and effectiveness of the drug for children has not been studied.

## USE IN THE ELDERLY

The safety and effectiveness of the drug for the elderly has not been studied.

## DRUG INTERACTIONS

None reported.

**FOOD INTERACTIONS**
None reported.

**OTHER DRUGS USED FOR SIMILAR CONDITIONS**
For the treatment of advanced KS, a number of drugs and combinations of them have been used, including bleomycin, vinblastine, vincristine, etoposide, doxorubicin, liposomal doxorubicin, and alpha interferon. In general, the response to treatment is influenced by the CD4+ counts when therapy is initiated, the general health status of the people treated, and the opportunistic infections and treatments they have received.

**COMMENTS**
More progress is needed in the treatment of lymphoma and KS in people infected with HIV. A major problem in using chemotherapy is suppression of the immune system. Many of the drugs used in combination chemotherapy reduce the counts of white blood cells called neutrophils, which are essential to fighting infection. After chemotherapy, the immune system recovers more slowly in people who already have low CD4+ counts. This may require long periods of hospitalization. One approach that has proven successful in minimizing this problem is the use of colony-stimulating factors (G-CSF or GM-CSF) with the chemotherapy to maintain neutrophil counts and speed recovery after the chemotherapy is stopped. See the profiles on G-CSF and GM-CSF for more information on how these drugs work.

# DOCETAXEL

**BRAND NAME (MANUFACTURER)**
Taxotere (Rhone-Poulenc Rorer)

**TYPE OF DRUG**
Anticancer agent

**USED FOR**
Docetaxel is used primarily to treat breast cancer that has not responded to conventional treatment with less toxic chemotherapy drugs.

**GENERAL INFORMATION**
Docetaxel is a drug originally derived from the Pacific yew tree. It works by interfering with structures inside cells necessary for cell division. Consequently, it is highly toxic to rapidly dividing cells, such as those in tumors or in normal bone marrow.

In people with HIV, docetaxel may be a potential treatment for KS.

Docetaxel is available as a solution for intravenous injection.

## TREATMENT

For the treatment of breast cancer, docetaxel is usually injected intravenously at 60-100 mg per square meter of body surface area over 1 hour every three weeks. The optimal dose for KS has not yet been determined.

Because docetaxel can cause serious allergic reactions, people using the drug are given dexamethasone before treatment.

## CAUTIONS AND WARNINGS

Docetaxel is highly toxic. It should not be used by people with a known allergy to it or to other drugs made with polysorbate 80. It should be used only with careful observation by health care professionals experienced in its use.

Docetaxel is not recommended for people whose neutrophil counts are lower than 1,500 because of the risk of infection. People with very high bilirubin levels or very high liver enzymes (SGOT and/or SGPT) and very high alkaline phosphatase levels should not use docetaxel.

Docetaxel should be used with caution by people with liver impairment because of an increased risk of side effects.

## SIDE EFFECTS

The most serious side effect of docetaxel observed during clinical trials was severe allergic reactions, which occurred in about 1% of the people using the drug. Bone marrow toxicity, resulting in deficiency of white blood cells called neutrophils, was common in clinical trials, but was manageable and reversible. Fluid retention and weakness were the most common side effects reported.

Other side effects include muscle ache, skin disease, nerve sensation, and inflammation of the mouth.

## PREGNANCY/BREAST-FEEDING

Docetaxel has not been formally studied in pregnant women, but the drug is highly toxic to rapidly dividing cells, like those in a fetus. In animal studies, the drug caused birth defects, and it is likely that similar birth defects may occur in humans. Pregnant women are encouraged to discuss the benefits and potential risks of docetaxel with their physician before deciding to use the drug.

HIV may be passed from a woman to her child through breast milk. In areas where nutritionally sound alternatives are readily available, breast-feeding is discouraged for HIV-positive women. It is not known whether docetaxel is excreted in human milk. However, because of the potential toxicity of the drug, women are encouraged to consider alternatives to breast-feeding while using it.

## USE IN CHILDREN

Docetaxel has not been formally studied in children and is not recommended for pediatric use.

**USE IN THE ELDERLY**

No changes in dosage or administration are required for older adults.

**DRUG INTERACTIONS**

Docetaxel and cisplatin used together may result in increased risk of bone marrow toxicity. Ketoconazole may inhibit metabolism of docetaxel, potentially increasing blood levels of the drug.

Although no formal drug-interaction studies have been performed, it is reasonable to assume that docetaxel may intensify the bone marrow toxicity of drugs such as AZT or ganciclovir.

**FOOD INTERACTIONS**

Because docetaxel is administered intravenously, food does not affect its absorption into the body.

**OTHER DRUGS USED FOR SIMILAR CONDITIONS**

For the treatment of advanced KS, a number of other drugs have been used, including bleomycin, vinblastine, vincristine, etoposide, doxorubicin, liposomal doxorubicin, liposomal daunorubicin, and alpha interferon. In general, the effectiveness of the treatment has less to do with the drugs or combinations used than with differences in the CD4+ counts and history of opportunistic infections of the people treated. People with more extensive disease, other opportunistic infections, prior treatment with chemotherapy, or lower CD4+ counts are less likely to respond to treatment.

# DOXORUBICIN

**BRAND NAME (MANUFACTURER)**

Adriamycin (Pharmacia & Upjohn); Rubex (Bristol-Myers Squibb)

**TYPE OF DRUG**

Anticancer agent

**USED FOR**

Doxorubicin is widely used to treat leukemia, lymphoma, and cancers of the brain, skin, breast, ovaries, bladder, thyroid, and lungs. In people infected with HIV, it is used primarily in combination with other drugs to treat AIDS-related lymphoma and Kaposi's sarcoma (KS).

**GENERAL INFORMATION**

Doxorubicin is a modified form of an antibiotic isolated from the genus *Streptomyces*. The drug inhibits the synthesis of nucleic acids, which prevents cancer cells from multiplying. It is a highly effective drug, but also very toxic. A number of new formulations of doxorubicin have been developed to minimize its toxicity. See the profile "Doxorubicin-liposomal" (Doxil) for more information.

Although doxorubicin can be used by itself to treat cancers, it is used more frequently in combination with other chemotherapy drugs. The rationale is that different drugs have different ways of working and different side effects. By combining drugs, it is often possible to come up with a more effective treatment with reduced side effects and less risk of developing drug-resistant tumors.

For the treatment of AIDS-related lymphoma, doxorubicin is routinely used in a combination of drugs called CHOP, which consists of cyclophosphamide, doxorubicin, vincristine, and prednisone. Less frequently, it is used in a combination of drugs called m-BACOD (methotrexate, bleomycin, doxorubicin, cyclophosphamide, vincristine, dexamethasone, and leucovorin). People with less invasive disease, no prior AIDS-defining illness, and no bone marrow or central nervous system involvement are more likely to respond. People with baseline CD4+ counts above 200 have the best chance of success.

For the treatment of KS in people infected with HIV, doxorubicin is used alone or in combination with bleomycin and vincristine or vinblastine in a regimen called ABV. In clinical studies, the effectiveness of treatment strongly depended on the condition and medical history of the people treated. People with more extensive disease, other opportunistic infections, prior treatment with chemotherapy, or lower CD4+ counts were less likely to respond. A recent study showed that a liposomal formulation of doxorubicin (Doxil) when used alone is more effective in treating KS and less toxic than the BV combination. Doxil alone was also significantly less toxic than a combination of Doxil, bleomycin and vincristine.

Doxorubicin is available as a solution for intravenous injection.

## TREATMENT

The dosage of doxorubicin varies widely depending on the cancer, the health of the individual, and other drugs being used at the same time. Lower doses may be used in people with inadequate bone marrow reserves as a result of AIDS, age, prior chemotherapy, or infiltration of the cancer into the bone marrow.

Granisetron or ondansetron are often used along with doxorubicin to reduce or prevent the nausea and vomiting caused by the drug.

## CAUTIONS AND WARNINGS

Doxorubicin should be used with caution by people whose bone marrow function is suppressed because of previous chemotherapy or radiation.

People with heart disease may be at increased risk of heart damage caused by the drug. Heart damage, potentially leading to heart failure, is more common in people who have received a total cumulative dose of the drug exceeding 400 to 500 mg per square meter of body surface area. Daunorubicin and

doxorubicin are structurally similar and have cumulative toxicity to the heart, so when calculating the total cumulative dose of doxorubicin, any treatment with daunorubicin should be included as well. Heart failure can occur during treatment or even several weeks after the drug is stopped.

Because doxorubicin is metabolized in the liver, its side effects may occur more frequently in people with impaired liver function.

Doxorubicin causes a red color in the urine for one to two days after the drug is administered.

## SIDE EFFECTS

Doxorubicin is a highly toxic drug when administered in its standard intravenous form. Potentially fatal damage to the bone marrow and heart are its most serious side effects. Heart failure that occurs after high cumulative doses of the drug can result in death. Bone marrow suppression, common in people using the drug, may increase the risk of opportunistic infections or bleeding.

Reversible, complete hair loss occurs in most people taking the drug. Excessive pigmentation under the nails or in the creases of the skin also occurs, primarily in treated children. The drug commonly causes acute nausea and vomiting, which may be severe. Inflammation of the stomach or esophagus may occur five to ten days after administration and may cause ulcers. Ulceration and necrosis of the colon may occur, leading to bleeding or severe infections that can be fatal.

## PREGNANCY/BREAST-FEEDING

Doxorubicin has not been formally studied in pregnant women, but it is highly toxic to rapidly dividing cells, such as those in a malignant tumor or in a fetus. Pregnant women are encouraged to discuss the benefits and potential risks of doxorubicin with their physician before deciding to use the drug. Women using the drug are encouraged to use effective contraception.

HIV can be passed from a woman to her child through breast milk. In areas where nutritionally sound alternatives are readily available, breast-feeding is discouraged for HIV-positive women. Doxorubicin may be excreted in human milk, and because of the potential toxicity to newborns, women should consider alternatives to breast-feeding while using the drug.

## USE IN CHILDREN

Doxorubicin is not recommended for use in children because its safety and effectiveness for them has not yet been established in clinical trials.

## USE IN THE ELDERLY

Older adults may be more susceptible to the side effects of the drug and may require reduced doses.

**DRUG INTERACTIONS**
Doxorubicin may increase the toxicity of radiation and other anticancer drugs, including cyclophosphamide and 6-mercaptopurine.

**FOOD INTERACTIONS**
None reported.

**OTHER DRUGS USED FOR SIMILAR CONDITIONS**
For the treatment of advanced KS, a number of drugs have been used, including bleomycin, vinblastine, vincristine, etoposide, liposomal doxorubicin, and alpha interferon. In general, the effectiveness of treatment depends on the health status of the individual, his or her CD4+ counts, prior treatment history, and history of opportunistic infections. The choice of treatment is often determined by which drugs can be best tolerated by the individual.

**COMMENTS**
More progress is needed in treatment of HIV-related lymphoma and KS. A major problem in using chemotherapy is suppression of the immune system. Many of the drugs used in combination chemotherapy reduce the counts of white blood cells called neutrophils, which are essential to fighting infection. After chemotherapy, the immune system recovers slowly in people who already have low CD4+ counts and may require long periods of hospitalization. One approach that has proven successful in getting around this problem is the use of colony-stimulating factors (G-CSF or GM-CSF) with the chemotherapy to maintain neutrophil counts and speed recovery after the chemotherapy is stopped.

# DOXORUBICIN – LIPOSOMAL

**BRAND NAME (MANUFACTURER)**
Doxil (Sequus)

**OTHER NAMES**
Stealth doxorubicin; DOX-SL

**TYPE OF DRUG**
Anticancer agent

**USED FOR**
Liposomal doxorubicin has been approved by the FDA for the treatment of Kaposi's sarcoma (KS) in people living with HIV.

**GENERAL INFORMATION**
Doxorubicin is a highly effective drug used to treat cancers, but is also highly toxic. The drug inhibits the synthesis of nucleic acids, which prevents cancer cells from dividing. Unfortunately, it is also toxic to rapidly dividing non-

cancerous cells in the body, including the bone marrow and the lining of the stomach and intestines. In liposomal doxorubicin, the drug is encapsulated in a fatty membrane to make tiny "bubbles" called liposomes. The rationale for delivering the drug inside liposomes is to improve its effects while reducing its toxicity to healthy cells. In a process that is not completely understood, liposomes deposit more of the active drug in tumors than in the bloodstream.

Because the liver also breaks down liposomes, releasing the doxorubicin, it is also subject to the toxicity of the drug. To counter this toxicity, the liposomes used in Doxil are coated with a layer of polyethylene glycol, a substance that allows them to pass through the liver undetected. These "stealth" liposomes survive in the circulation far longer than doxorubicin alone or traditional liposomes, allowing more time for the drug to reach its target.

In U.S. clinical trials, liposomal doxorubicin has been tested as a treatment for KS in people with HIV who have failed other therapies. The results have shown promise. The drug is available for treating KS that does not respond to standard therapy. There is some indication that it may also be a superior, first-line treatment for KS. In fact, a recent study showed that a liposomal doxorubicin (Doxil), when used alone, is more effective in treating KS and less toxic than a combination of bleomycin and vincristine. Doxil alone was also significantly less toxic than a combination of Doxil, bleomycin, and vincristine.

### TREATMENT
In clinical trials, liposomal doxorubicin was started at a dose of 10 to 20 mg per square meter of body surface area, injected intravenously every two weeks. If the disease failed to respond, the dosage was increased.

### CAUTIONS AND WARNINGS
Liposomal doxorubicin, like standard intravenous doxorubicin, should be used with caution by people who have suppressed bone marrow function.

People with heart disease may be at increased risk of heart damage caused by the drug.

Because liposomal doxorubicin is metabolized by the liver, its side effects may occur more frequently in people with impaired liver function.

### SIDE EFFECTS
Side effects reported (and the percentages of people who reported them) in clinical trials included nausea (25%), diarrhea (25%), vomiting (14%), stomach upset (12%), hair loss (12%), and constipation (8%). Significant bone marrow toxicity was associated with the drug's use.

### PREGNANCY/BREAST-FEEDING
Liposomal doxorubicin has not been formally studied in pregnant women, but it is highly toxic to rapidly dividing cells, like those in a fetus. Pregnant

women are encouraged to discuss the benefits and potential risks of the drug with their physician before trying to enter a clinical trial to use the drug.

HIV may be passed from a woman to her child through breast milk. In areas where nutritionally sound alternatives are readily available, breast-feeding is discouraged for HIV-positive women. Doxorubicin may be excreted in human milk, and because of the potential toxicity of the drug to newborns, women should consider alternatives to breast-feeding while using it.

**USE IN CHILDREN**
Liposomal doxorubicin has not been studied or used in children, and no information is available.

**USE IN THE ELDERLY**
The kidneys and liver often function less effectively as people age. Consequently, the dosage of liposomal doxorubicin may need to be reduced in the elderly.

**DRUG INTERACTIONS**
Doxorubicin may increase the toxicity of radiation and other anticancer drugs, including cyclophosphamide and 6-mercaptopurine.

**FOOD INTERACTIONS**
Because liposomal doxorubicin is administered intravenously, food does not affect absorption of the drug into the body.

**OTHER DRUGS USED FOR SIMILAR CONDITIONS**
For treatment of advanced KS, a number of drugs have been used, including bleomycin, vinblastine, vincristine, etoposide, doxorubicin, and alpha interferon. In general, the effectiveness of the treatment has had less to do with the drugs used than to differences in the CD4+ counts and the history of opportunistic infections of the people treated. The choice of treatment is often determined by which drugs can best be tolerated by the individual.

**COMMENTS**
More progress is needed in the treatment of lymphoma and KS in people infected with HIV. A major problem in using chemotherapy is suppression of the immune system. Many of the drugs used in combination chemotherapy reduce the counts of white blood cells called neutrophils, which are essential to fighting infection. After chemotherapy, the immune system recovers slowly in people who already have low CD4+ counts. The lower the CD4+ count, the slower the recovery, which may require long periods of hospitalization. One approach that has proven successful in minimizing this problem is the use of colony-stimulating factors (G-CSF or GM-CSF) with the chemotherapy to maintain neutrophil counts and speed recovery after the chemotherapy is stopped. See the profiles on G-CSF and GM-CSF for more information on how these drugs work.

# ETOPOSIDE

**BRAND NAME (MANUFACTURER)**
VePesid (Bristol-Myers Squibb Oncology)

**OTHER NAME**
VP-16

**TYPE OF DRUG**
Anticancer agent

**USED FOR**
Etoposide has been approved by the FDA for treatment of small-cell lung cancer and testicular cancer that has failed other treatment. In clinical trials, the drug has also been used by people infected with HIV for the treatment of advanced Kaposi's sarcoma (KS), AIDS-related lymphoma, and cytomegalovirus (CMV) infection.

**GENERAL INFORMATION**
Etoposide is a derivative of a naturally occurring plant toxin. It works by interfering with DNA production in actively dividing cells. The drug is available as capsules or as a solution for injection. The capsules have been used regularly in studies of KS, while the solution for injection is the form most often used in studies of AIDS-related lymphoma.

Some clinical evidence supports the use of etoposide for advanced KS, but in clinical trials, the drug's effect was short-lived. Like most other chemotherapy drugs, etoposide can be toxic to bone marrow and has a number of other severe side effects. The major advantage of etoposide for KS is that it can be taken orally. Most other treatments require intravenous injections.

For the treatment of AIDS-related lymphoma, etoposide has been tested in clinical trials in a number of different combinations of chemotherapy drugs. Examples include CDE (cyclophosphamide, doxorubicin, and etoposide) and ACVB-LNH84 (doxorubicin, cyclophosphamide, vindesine, bleomycin, prednisone, methotrexate, leucovorin, ifosfamide, etoposide, asparaginase, and cytarabine).

Duration of response and impact on survival depends more on the disease state of the people taking the drugs than the drugs themselves. People with less progressive disease, no prior AIDS-defining illness, and no bone marrow or central nervous system involvement are more likely to respond to treatment. The most important predictor of treatment success is the CD4+ count at the time the cancer is diagnosed. Generally, people with higher CD4+ counts are more likely to respond to treatment.

**TREATMENT**

The typical dose of etoposide injected intravenously is 50 to 100 mg per square meter of body surface area, administered with other chemotherapy drugs for three to five days, repeated in three- to four-week intervals. The dose of the oral drug is generally twice that of the intravenous drug, because less is absorbed.

When used for AIDS-related lymphoma, the dose of intravenous etoposide varies widely depending on the combination of drugs.

**CAUTIONS AND WARNINGS**

Etoposide should not be used by anyone with a known allergy to it. Bone marrow toxicity may occur during or after treatment, so most physicians will carefully monitor the blood counts of people taking the drug.

Etoposide is a toxic drug that can have serious side effects. The dose may need to be reduced or discontinued if severe reactions occur. Most of the side effects are reversible if detected early.

**SIDE EFFECTS**

Bone marrow toxicity is the most serious side effect of etoposide and occurs to some extent in most people who take the drug. The risk of the side effect and its severity depends on the dose of the drug. Bone marrow recovery is usually complete within three weeks after treatment, and no cumulative toxicity has been reported. Drugs that stimulate the bone marrow to produce white blood cells (e.g., G-CSF) are often used to counteract the bone marrow toxicity of etoposide.

About two-thirds of people taking etoposide lose their hair during therapy, but it grows back once the drug is stopped.

Peripheral neuropathy, nerve damage characterized by numbness, tingling, or pain in the extremities, occurs in 1% to 2% of people using etoposide.

Nausea and vomiting are the major digestive tract side effects of the drug. About 1% of people stop taking the drug because of it. Nausea and vomiting are slightly more frequent when using the oral drug. Ondansetron or granisetron may be used concomitantly with etoposide to reduce or prevent the nausea and vomiting caused by the drug.

Allergic reactions to etoposide, which may include fever, rash, itching, etc., occur in less than 2% of the people who take the drug. Reversible low blood pressure affects 1% to 2% of people taking the drug.

**PREGNANCY/BREAST-FEEDING**

Etoposide has not been formally studied in pregnant women. The drug is highly toxic to rapidly dividing cells, such as those in a malignant tumor or in a fetus. Etoposide can cause birth defects when taken during pregnancy. In animal studies, the drug caused fetal tumors and death of embryos when as little as

1% of the human dose was administered. Pregnant women are encouraged to discuss the benefits and potential risks of the drug with their physician before deciding to use it.

HIV can be passed from a woman to her child through breast milk. In areas where nutritionally sound alternatives are readily available, breast-feeding is discouraged for HIV-positive women. It is not known whether etoposide is excreted in human milk. Because of the potential toxicity of the drug, women are encouraged to consider alternatives to breast-feeding while using it.

### USE IN CHILDREN
Etoposide is not recommended for children. The drug is metabolized differently in children than adults, which makes them at higher risk for side effects, especially when using higher doses.

### USE IN THE ELDERLY
Older adults may be more susceptible to the side effects of the drug and may require reduced doses.

### DRUG INTERACTIONS
When used with other anticancer agents, etoposide has on rare occasions caused acute leukemia. Etoposide may intensify the bone marrow toxicity of AZT or ganciclovir. The combination of etoposide and ddI, ddC, or d4T may increase the risk of peripheral neuropathy.

### FOOD INTERACTIONS
None reported.

### OTHER DRUGS USED FOR SIMILAR CONDITIONS
For the treatment of advanced KS, a number of drugs have been used, including bleomycin, vinblastine, vincristine, doxorubicin, liposomal doxorubicin, and alpha interferon. In general, the effectiveness of treatment depends on the health of the individual, his or her CD4+ counts, prior treatment history, and history of opportunistic infections. The choice of treatment is often determined by which drugs can best be tolerated by the individual.

For lymphoma, a commonly used treatment is a chemotherapy combination called CHOP, which consists of cyclophosphamide, doxorubicin, vincristine, and prednisone. No clinical studies have directly compared CHOP and etoposide-containing regimens for the treatment of AIDS-related lymphoma, so it is not possible to say one is more effective than another. The choice of treatment is often determined by which combination is best tolerated by the individual.

### COMMENTS
More progress is needed in the treatment of lymphoma and KS in people infected with HIV. A major problem in using chemotherapy is suppression of the immune system. Many of the drugs used in combination chemotherapy reduce the counts

of white blood cells called neutrophils, which are essential to fighting infection. After chemotherapy, the immune system recovers slowly in people who already have low CD4+ counts. The lower the CD4+ count, the slower the recovery, which may require long periods of hospitalization. One approach that has proven successful in minimizing this problem is the use of colony-stimulating factors (G-CSF or GM-CSF) with the chemotherapy to maintain neutrophil counts and speed recovery after the chemotherapy is stopped. See the profiles on G-CSF and GM-CSF for more information on how these drugs work.

# HUMAN CHORIONIC GONADOTROPIN

**BRAND NAME (MANUFACTURER)**
A.P.L. (Wyeth-Ayerst); Pregnyl (Organon); Profasi (Serono)

**OTHER NAME**
HCG

**TYPE OF DRUG**
Hormone

**USED FOR**
Human chorionic gonadotropin (HCG) is used to induce ovulation and pregnancy in women with poorly functioning ovaries. It is also used in men whose pituitary glands do not produce enough of the hormones necessary to cause development of secondary sex characteristics, and in boys to correct for a condition where the testicles do not descend into the scrotum.

Some preliminary evidence suggests that HCG—or some factor found in it—may be useful as a treatment for Kaposi's sarcoma (KS) in people with HIV. In some small programs in France and southern California, physicians are using the drug experimentally.

HCG is sometimes used, but not approved, to treat HIV-related wasting syndrome, although no clinical studies and little anecdotal evidence at this time supports this use.

**GENERAL INFORMATION**
HCG is a naturally occurring hormone produced by the human placenta and excreted in the urine of pregnant women. HCG inhibits the mother's immune system from rejecting the fetus as "foreign" tissue. HCG also supports continued secretion of the hormones estrogen and progesterone, which prevent menstruation during pregnancy. In men, HCG stimulates the testes to produce male hormones (such as testosterone).

In 1993, a few European women with KS were reported to have had "spontaneous resolution" of their lesions after becoming pregnant. These initial reports generated interest in HCG as a treatment for KS, and animal studies were started. Investigators at the National Cancer Institute found that KS cell lines implanted into mice did not develop into tumors during early pregnancy. Because many other physiological changes besides production of HCG occur in pregnancy, it was not possible to determine whether the effect was due to HCG alone. Other animal studies confirmed the anti-KS effects of HCG, and initial clinical studies in volunteers with HIV have shown that HCG can be active in the treatment for KS in humans. More recent presentations suggest HCG itself may not be the active ingredient affecting KS, but rather another as yet unidentified substance with appears sporadically in commercial HCG.

HCG is available for injection only.

### TREATMENT

The dosage used depends on the disorder, the person's age, and the person's weight.

Both the French group and the southern California group are directly injecting KS skin lesions with the hormone. Various dosages and schedules are being tested, and, as yet, the data are too preliminary to make recommendations. However, this approach cannot treat KS in other organs in the body (e.g., lungs).

### CAUTIONS AND WARNINGS

HCG should not be used in people with precocious puberty, prostate cancer, or any other cancer that is worsened by male hormones. HCG should not be used in people who know they are allergic to it. When used to treat boys whose testicles have not descended, the drug may induce precocious puberty. Since the drug stimulates the production of androgens, and androgens cause fluid retention, the drug should be used with caution in people with heart or kidney disease, epilepsy, history of migraine headaches, or asthma.

### SIDE EFFECTS

HCG can cause headache, irritability, restlessness, depression, fatigue, swelling, precocious puberty, breast enlargement in men, and pain at the site of injection. It can also cause ovarian hyperstimulation, a syndrome of sudden ovarian enlargement. In women, it may cause rupture of ovarian cysts, multiple births, or blood clots.

### PREGNANCY/BREAST-FEEDING

Although HCG is naturally produced by women during pregnancy, it has not been formally studied in pregnant women as a drug. HCG did cause birth defects in mice, but it is not known whether this would also occur in humans.

Pregnant women are encouraged to discuss the benefits and potential risks of HCG with their physician before deciding to use the drug.

HIV can be passed from a woman to her child through breast milk. In areas where nutritionally sound alternatives are readily available, breast-feeding is discouraged for HIV-positive women. It is not known if HCG is excreted in milk. Because of the potential toxicity of the drug, women are encouraged to consider alternatives to breast-feeding while using it.

**USE IN CHILDREN**
The safety and effectiveness of the drug for children under age four have not been studied.

**USE IN THE ELDERLY**
No available information.

**DRUG INTERACTIONS**
None reported.

**FOOD INTERACTIONS**
Because HCG is administered by injection, it is unlikely that food would affect the absorption or activity of the drug in the body.

**OTHER DRUGS USED FOR SIMILAR CONDITIONS**
For treatment of advanced KS, a number of drugs have been used, including bleomycin, vinblastine, vincristine, etoposide, doxorubicin, and alpha interferon. In general, the effectiveness of the treatment has had less to do with the drugs used than to differences in the CD4+ counts and history of opportunistic infections of the people treated. The choice of treatment is often determined by which drugs can best be tolerated by the individual.

**COMMENTS**
For the treatment of KS, early evidence suggested that the beta chain of HCG is necessary to produce the desired response, an unusual finding since all other activity of HCG has been associated with its alpha chain. More recent laboratory studies have begun to question whether the beta chain of HCG is really the active compound. Instead, researchers now believe that a previously unidentified factor, present in inconsistent amounts in commercial HCG, may be the active ingredient. Consequently, commercially available preparations of HCG may or may not contain the active ingredient and thus may cause typical toxicity with no potential for benefit. People with KS who are interested in pursuing HCG as a therapy are encouraged to seek out clinical trials, where the most active formulation is being used.

The majority of information on the use of HCG as part of a regimen for wasting comes from anecdotal reports from body-builders, where HCG is sometimes used as part of a regimen with anabolic steroids. After a course of anabolic steroids, some body-builders will use HCG in the belief that it helps

"kick start" their body's production of testosterone, since anabolic steroids can cause the body to stop its natural testosterone production. The safety of using either anabolic steroids or HCG has not been fully evaluated in people with HIV, and either drug should be used only under the guidance of a physician.

# INTERFERON ALPHA-2

**BRAND NAME (MANUFACTURER)**
Intron A (Schering); Roferon-A (Roche)

**OTHER NAMES**
IFN-a; interferon alpha-2a; interferon alpha-2b

**TYPE OF DRUG**
Biological response modifier/antiviral agent

**USED FOR**
Alpha interferon is used for the treatment of chronic hepatitis B and C, certain types of leukemia, and some types of viral warts. In people with HIV, it is sometimes used to treat AIDS-related Kaposi's sarcoma (KS). In clinical trials, it has also been tested alone and in combination with other antivirals as a potential treatment for HIV infection.

**GENERAL INFORMATION**
Alpha interferon is a small protein naturally produced by the immune system. It has antiviral, anticancer, and immune-modulating activities, although how it works is not completely understood. Two genetically engineered forms of alpha interferon are available. Interferon alpha-2a is available under the brand name Roferon-A. Interferon alpha-2b is available as Intron A. The two drugs have minor differences in chemical structure, but no evidence suggests that one is more effective than the other.

Alpha interferon is sometimes used to treat KS. A number of clinical trials have shown that the drug is beneficial in people with early-stage KS who have CD4+ counts greater than 400 when treatment started. Much lower response rates are observed in people with lower CD4+ counts. People who have had other opportunistic infections, weight loss of more than 10% or fifteen pounds, or fever greater than 100°F without an identifiable source of infection are less likely to respond to treatment.

For the treatment of chronic hepatitis B, alpha interferon is the only FDA-approved therapy available in the United States. The drug was approved based on studies of non-HIV-infected people. Hepatitis B was cleared from approximately 37% of people taking alpha interferon for three to six months, com-

pared to 17% of people who received a placebo. Alpha interferon is less effective in treating hepatitis in people who are co-infected with HIV.

Alpha interferon has been tested alone and in combination with other antivirals as a possible treatment for HIV infection. Because high doses of interferon cause severe toxicity in people infected with HIV, several approaches have been attempted to find an effective, well-tolerated dose. Test-tube studies showed that interferon seems to improve the antiviral activity of AZT, ddI, ddC, and d4T. Consequently, a number of studies were started that combined AZT and alpha interferon. The largest study included 402 volunteers with CD4+ counts between 150 and 500. They received either a combination of AZT (500 mg daily) and alpha interferon (3 million units, three times a week) or AZT alone for forty-eight weeks. At the end of the study, there was no evidence that the addition of alpha interferon conferred any additional benefit compared to AZT alone. Other studies of interferon in other combinations (with ddI or with ddI and AZT) are being performed to determine the clinical value of alpha interferon for the treatment of HIV infection.

Alpha interferon is available as a solution for injection.

**TREATMENT**

For the treatment of KS, the recommended dose for interferon alpha-2a is 36 million units injected under the skin (subcutaneous injection) or into a large muscle (intramuscular injection) daily for ten to twelve weeks. The recommended dose for interferon alpha-2b is 30 million units injected three times a week. These high doses are rarely tolerated by most people infected with HIV, so dose reductions are common.

The recommended dose of interferon alpha-2b for the treatment of chronic hepatitis B is 30 to 35 million units per week, either 5 million units injected per day or 10 million units injected three times a week for sixteen weeks. Usually, dose reductions are required because of serious side effects.

**CAUTIONS AND WARNINGS**

Alpha interferon should not be used by anyone with a known allergy to it, mouse immunoglobulins, or any other component in the products. It should not be used for the treatment of rapidly progressing KS that has spread to the internal organs.

The drug should be used with caution by people with heart, kidney, or liver disease and by those with seizure disorders or other reduced central nervous system function. People taking alpha interferon may have an impaired ability to operate automobiles or other dangerous machinery.

**SIDE EFFECTS**

Most people who take alpha interferon experience side effects. Generally, the side effects are more severe when taking higher doses. In HIV-infected people treated for KS, nearly everyone taking alpha interferon at the recommended dose will experience "flu-like" symptoms that may include fatigue, fever, muscle weakness, headache, chills, and bone pain. Loss of appetite, nausea, and diarrhea occur in about half of the people taking the drug. Vomiting and abdominal pain occur less frequently.

The most common central nervous system side effect of alpha interferon is dizziness, which occurs in about half of the people taking the drug. Decreased alertness and depression occur less frequently.

About one-quarter of people taking the drug experience coughing. Fewer people have difficulty breathing or chest pain. Slightly more than one in five people taking the drug experience some hair loss.

**PREGNANCY/BREAST-FEEDING**

Alpha interferon has not been formally studied in pregnant women. In animal studies, the drug caused an increased rate of spontaneous abortions. A similar drug, called human leukocyte interferon, has caused altered levels of reproductive hormones in women. Pregnant women are encouraged to discuss the benefits and potential risks of alpha interferon with their physician before deciding to use the drug.

HIV can be passed from a woman to her child through breast milk. In areas where nutritionally sound alternatives are readily available, breast-feeding is discouraged for HIV-positive women. It is not known whether alpha interferon is excreted in human milk. Because of the potential toxicity of the drug to newborns, women are encouraged to consider alternatives to breast-feeding while using it.

**USE IN CHILDREN**

Clinical experience with the use of alpha interferon in HIV-infected children is limited. Over the years, there have been scattered reports of children treated with alpha interferon, but little concrete information about the safety and efficacy of the drug was available. In late 1994, results were published from a controlled trial of alpha interferon and AZT in children who were HIV-positive but without symptoms of the disease. The study was designed primarily to determine whether the combination of drugs was safe, but the investigators also tried to get a preliminary indication as to whether it slowed the progression of HIV disease. In general, alpha interferon was well tolerated. Only two of forty-five children had to stop therapy because of flu-like side effects. Other severe side effects were avoided when the dose of alpha interferon was equal to or less than 10 million units per square meter of body

surface area, three times a week, combined with AZT at 180 mg per square meter of body surface area, taken every six hours. The study also suggested, but was not designed to prove, that the combination of alpha interferon and AZT may be more effective in slowing disease progression than AZT alone in children who have not previously received anti-HIV therapy.

**USE IN THE ELDERLY**
Older adults may be more susceptible to the side effects of the drug and may require reduced doses.

**DRUG INTERACTIONS**
Alpha interferon may increase the bone marrow toxicity of AZT, flucytosine, ganciclovir, pentamidine, pyrimethamine, and anticancer drugs.

**FOOD INTERACTIONS**
None reported.

**OTHER DRUGS USED FOR SIMILAR CONDITIONS**
For the treatment of advanced KS, a number of drugs have been used, including bleomycin, vinblastine, vincristine, etoposide, doxorubicin, and liposomal doxorubicin. In general, the effectiveness of treatment depends on the health of the individual, his or her CD4+ counts, prior treatment history, and history of opportunistic infections. The choice of treatment is often determined by which drugs can best be tolerated by the individual.

For the treatment of HIV, standard therapy with AZT in combination with other antivirals is still the preferred treatment. There is no conclusive evidence at this time that alpha interferon is a valuable addition to standard therapy.

**COMMENTS**
Several years ago, a study out of Kenya reported tiny doses of alpha interferon (a few hundred units) taken orally (called Kemron) could bring about a stunning reversal of AIDS. Since then, more than eighteen other studies have failed to confirm this result, and the general consensus is that oral alpha interferon has no value as a treatment for HIV other than as a placebo.

# IRINOTECAN

**BRAND NAME (MANUFACTURER)**
Camptosar (Pharmacia & Upjohn)

**OTHER NAMES**
CPT-11

**TYPE OF DRUG**
Anticancer agent

**USED FOR**
Irinotecan is used primarily to treat colon or rectal cancer that has not responded or has recurred on conventional chemotherapy drugs. It is also being tested in clinical trials as a potential treatment for Kaposi's sarcoma (KS), lymphoma, and progressive multifocal leukoencephalopathy (PML) in people living with HIV.

**GENERAL INFORMATION**
Irinotecan belongs to a class of drugs known as topoisomerase inhibitors. Irinotecan is highly toxic to rapidly dividing cells, such as those in tumors or in normal bone marrow.

Irinotecan is available for intravenous injection.

**TREATMENT**
The recommended dose of irinotecan for treating ovarian cancer is 125 mg per square meter of body surface area, administered intravenously once weekly over a 90-minute period for 4 weeks. After a 2-week rest period, the course of treatment may be repeated every 6 weeks. People with significantly reduced neutrophil levels and/or severe diarrhea should reduce the dose of irinotecan. It is recommended that dexamethasone and antinausea drugs such as ondansetron and granisetron be given 30 minutes prior to irinotecan infusions.

People with profuse sweating, abdominal cramping, or diarrhea within 24 hours of starting irinotecan should consider intravenous atropine to relieve some of these side effects.

**CAUTIONS AND WARNINGS**
Irinotecan is highly toxic. It should not be used by people who know they are allergic to it, and it should be used only with careful observation by health care professionals.

Irinotecan is not recommended for people whose neutrophil counts are lower than 1,500 or whose platelet counts are lower than 100,000 because of the risk of infection or bleeding.

**SIDE EFFECTS**
The most serious side effects reported in the clinical studies were diarrhea, vomiting, fever, nausea, and decreased neutrophil counts. Other commonly reported side effects were anorexia, constipation, abdominal pain, loss of strength, chills, headache, hair loss, sweating, rash, insomnia, dizziness, and difficulty in breathing.

**PREGNANCY/BREAST-FEEDING**
Irinotecan has not been formally studied in pregnant women, but the drug is highly toxic to rapidly dividing cells, like those in a fetus. In animal studies, the drug caused fetal damage and it is likely that similar fetal damage may

occur in humans. Pregnant women are encouraged to discuss the benefits and potential risks of irinotecan with their physician before deciding to use the drug.

HIV may be passed from a woman to her child through breast milk. In areas where nutritionally sound alternatives are readily available, breast-feeding is discouraged for HIV-positive women. It is not known whether irinotecan is excreted in human milk. However, because of the potential toxicity of the drug, women are encouraged to consider alternatives to breast-feeding while using it.

**USE IN CHILDREN**
Irinotecan has not been formally studied in children and is not recommended for pediatric use.

**USE IN THE ELDERLY**
No changes in dosage or administration are required for older adults.

**DRUG INTERACTIONS**
Although no formal drug-interaction studies have been performed, it is reasonable to assume that irinotecan may add to the bone marrow toxicity of drugs such as AZT or ganciclovir.

**FOOD INTERACTIONS**
Because irinotecan is administered intravenously, food does not affect its absorption into the body.

**OTHER DRUGS USED FOR SIMILAR CONDITIONS**
For the treatment of colon or rectal cancer, a number of other drugs and combinations are used. For the treatment of advanced KS, a number of other drugs have been used, including bleomycin, vinblastine, vincristine, etoposide, doxorubicin, liposomal doxorubicin, and alpha interferon. In general, the effectiveness of the treatment has less to do with the drugs or combinations used than to differences in the CD4+ counts and history of opportunistic infections of the people treated. People with more extensive disease, other opportunistic infections, prior treatment with chemotherapy, or lower CD4+ counts are less likely to respond to treatment. For the treatment of PML, no therapy has been shown to be effective.

# METHOTREXATE

**BRAND NAME (MANUFACTURER)**
Methotrexate USP (Lederle); Rheumatrex (Lederle)

**OTHER NAME**
MTX

**TYPE OF DRUG**
Anticancer agent

**USED FOR**
Methotrexate is used to treat severe psoriasis, rheumatoid arthritis, and certain cancers, including some leukemias, breast cancer, certain skin cancers, and some lymphomas. In people living with HIV, methotrexate is often used in combination chemotherapy for the treatment of AIDS-related lymphoma.

**GENERAL INFORMATION**
Methotrexate is chemically similar to the B vitamin folic acid. In cells, the drug interferes with the normal action of the vitamin, stopping synthesis of DNA and preventing the cells from multiplying. Consequently, the drug is highly toxic against rapidly dividing cells, such as those found in tumors, skin plaques common in psoriasis, and normal bone marrow. Leucovorin (folinic acid) is usually used with methotrexate to reduce the toxicity of the chemotherapy to normal tissues.

Although methotrexate can be used by itself to treat cancers, it is used more frequently in combination with other chemotherapy drugs. The rationale is that different drugs have different ways of working and different side effects. By combining drugs, it is often possible to come up with a more effective treatment with reduced side effects and less risk of developing drug-resistant tumors.

For the treatment of AIDS-related lymphoma, methotrexate is often used in a combination of drugs called m-BACOD. The combination consists of methotrexate, bleomycin, doxorubicin (Adriamycin), cyclophosphamide, vincristine (Oncovin), dexamethasone, and leucovorin. About half of the people using this combination of drugs experience a remission of their disease, but the effect is usually short-lived. People with less disease, no prior AIDS-defining illness, and no bone marrow or central nervous system involvement are more likely to respond to treatment. The most important predictor of success is the CD4+ count at the time the cancer is diagnosed. People with higher CD4+ counts are more likely to respond to treatment.

Methotrexate is available as a solution for injection and as tablets for oral administration.

**TREATMENT**
A wide variety of dosing schedules are used for methotrexate, depending on the condition, the overall health of the individual, and other drugs being used. In general, the oral form of the drug is preferred when low doses are necessary, because absorption is rapid and effective blood levels can quickly be achieved. When higher doses are necessary or when the individual has problems in the gut (diarrhea, etc.) that may interfere with absorption, the inject-

able form of the drug may be used. In people with impaired kidney function, the dose of the drug may need to be reduced or delayed and increased dosages of leucovorin may be necessary to counteract the toxicity.

## CAUTIONS AND WARNINGS

Methotrexate is highly toxic. People with a known allergy to the drug should not use it, and it should be used only in a setting where careful observation by health care professionals experienced in its use is possible. Because of the potential for serious liver or kidney damage, people with a history of alcohol abuse or alcoholic liver disease should not use the drug.

For the treatment of psoriasis or rheumatoid arthritis, the drug should only be used by people with severe, disabling disease that is unresponsive to other, less toxic therapy.

Because of the drug's significant potential for liver and kidney damage, physicians will generally monitor the liver and kidney function of people taking the drug.

Nonsteroidal anti-inflammatory drugs (NSAIDs: aspirin, ibuprofen, naproxen, etc.) used with high-dose methotrexate may cause severe and potentially fatal toxicity to the bone marrow or gut. Despite this potential interaction, studies of methotrexate and NSAIDs in people with rheumatoid arthritis showed that low doses of the two types of drug could be used together, but careful monitoring by a physician is required.

Because of the risk of serious drug-related birth defects, women and men using the drug are encouraged to use effective contraception.

## SIDE EFFECTS

The frequency and severity of side effects with methotrexate are related to the dose and frequency that the drug is used. Methotrexate can cause severe liver damage, generally only after prolonged use. Methotrexate-induced lung damage may occur at any time during therapy, even when relatively low doses of the drug are used. This damage may not be reversible. Anyone experiencing a dry, nonproductive cough when using the drug should contact a physician immediately.

Methotrexate may cause severe bone marrow toxicity, resulting in anemia, reduced white blood cell counts, or reduced platelet counts (particles involved in blood clotting).

Diarrhea, stomach ulcers, and other gastrointestinal toxicity may occur while using methotrexate. In some cases, the drug has caused fatal perforation of the intestines.

The most frequently reported side effects of methotrexate include stomach ulceration, reduced white blood cell counts, nausea, and abdominal distress.

Other frequently reported side effects include malaise, fatigue, chills, fever, dizziness, and increased susceptibility to infection.

A wide range of additional side effects, affecting virtually every organ system in the body, have been reported after using methotrexate.

### PREGNANCY/BREAST-FEEDING

Methotrexate can cause fetal death or birth defects when taken by pregnant women. It can also cause mutations in sperm that result in birth defects in the children of fathers using the drug when conception occurs. The drug should not be used in pregnancy unless the condition is life-threatening and justifies the risk to the fetus. Pregnant women are encouraged to discuss the benefits and potential risks of methotrexate with their physician before deciding to use the drug.

HIV may be passed from a woman to her child through breast milk. In areas where nutritionally sound alternatives are readily available, breast-feeding is discouraged for HIV-positive women. Methotrexate is excreted in human milk and can cause serious and potentially fatal side effects in newborns. The drug should not be used by nursing mothers. When use of the drug is necessary, women should use alternatives to breast-feeding.

### USE IN CHILDREN

Methotrexate is used in children at dosages adjusted for weight to treat a number of different cancers. The side effects in children are generally the same as in adults. Because of the potential toxicity of the drug, however, it should not be used for psoriasis or arthritis in children.

### USE IN THE ELDERLY

Older adults may be more susceptible to the side effects of the drug and may require reduced doses.

### DRUG INTERACTIONS

As described above, nonsteroidal anti-inflammatory drugs (NSAIDs: aspirin, ibuprofen, naproxen, etc.) used with high-dose methotrexate may cause severe and potentially fatal toxicity to the bone marrow or gut.

Oral antibiotics such as tetracycline and chloramphenicol may decrease intestinal absorption of methotrexate taken orally and interfere with the metabolism of the drug by bacteria in the gut.

Vitamin preparations containing folic acid or its derivatives may decrease the effectiveness of intravenously injected methotrexate. People with folate deficiencies may be at increased risk of methotrexate toxicity.

Trimethoprim/sulfamethoxazole has been reported rarely to increase bone marrow suppression in people receiving methotrexate. Other drugs that suppress bone marrow (e.g., AZT or ganciclovir) may intensify the bone marrow toxicity of methotrexate.

The use of methotrexate with other drugs with kidney toxicity (e.g., amphotericin B or foscarnet) may increase the risk of drug-related side effects.

**FOOD INTERACTIONS**
Food interferes with methotrexate taken orally. The tablets should be used one hour before or two hours after meals. Food should not affect absorption of methotrexate injected into the body.

**OTHER DRUGS USED FOR SIMILAR CONDITIONS**
For the treatment of AIDS-related lymphoma, a commonly used therapy is a combination of drugs called CHOP (cyclophosphamide, doxorubicin, vincristine, and prednisone). No studies have directly compared CHOP to methotrexate-containing combinations, so it is not possible to say one combination would be more effective than another. The choice of treatment is often determined by which combination is best tolerated by the individual. On average, CHOP has fewer side effects than methotrexate-containing combinations such as m-BACOD.

**COMMENTS**
More progress is needed in the treatment of lymphoma and KS in people infected with HIV. A major problem in using chemotherapy is suppression of the immune system. Many of the drugs used in combination chemotherapy reduce the counts of white blood cells called neutrophils, which are essential to fighting infection. After chemotherapy, the immune system recovers slowly in people who already have low CD4+ counts. The lower the CD4+ count, the slower the recovery, which may require long periods of hospitalization. One approach that has proven successful in minimizing this problem is the use of colony-stimulating factors (G-CSF or GM-CSF) with the chemotherapy to maintain neutrophil counts and speed recovery after the chemotherapy is stopped. See the profiles on G-CSF and GM-CSF for more information on how these drugs work.

# PACLITAXEL

**BRAND NAME (MANUFACTURER)**
Taxol (Bristol-Myers Squibb Oncology)

**TYPE OF DRUG**
Anticancer agent

**USED FOR**
Paclitaxel is used primarily to treat ovarian and breast cancers that have not responded to conventional treatment with less toxic chemotherapy drugs. It

is also being tested in clinical trials as a potential treatment for Kaposi's sarcoma (KS) in people living with HIV.

### GENERAL INFORMATION

Paclitaxel is a drug originally derived from the Pacific yew tree. It works by interfering with structures inside cells necessary for cell division. Consequently, it is highly toxic to rapidly dividing cells, such as those in tumors or in normal bone marrow.

In people with HIV, paclitaxel is being tested as a potential treatment for KS. The studies are in their early stages, and although the results have been encouraging, it is too early to tell whether the drug will be a useful addition to the available KS therapies.

Paclitaxel is available as a solution for intravenous injection.

### TREATMENT

Because paclitaxel can cause serious allergic reactions, people using the drug are premedicated with dexamethasone, antihistamines (such as diphenhydramine), or cimetidine, ranitidine, or other histamine blockers.

The optimal dosing schedules of paclitaxel for ovarian cancer, breast cancer, or KS have not yet been determined. The dosages tested range from 135 to 175 mg per square meter of body surface area, administered intravenously over the course of three hours. People with reduced neutrophil counts (white blood cells involved in fighting infection) or who experience peripheral neuropathy should receive reduced dosages.

### CAUTIONS AND WARNINGS

Paclitaxel is highly toxic. It should not be used by people who know they are allergic to it, and it should be used only with careful observation by health care professionals experienced in its use.

Paclitaxel injectable solution contains polyoxyethylated castor oil, which is also found in a number of other injectable drug solutions, including cyclosporine and teniposide. People with known allergies to these other injectable solutions should not use paclitaxel.

Paclitaxel is not recommended for people whose neutrophil counts are lower than 1,500 or whose platelet counts are lower than 100,000 because of the risk of infection or bleeding.

Paclitaxel should be used with caution by people with liver impairment because of an increased risk of side effects.

### SIDE EFFECTS

The most serious side effect of paclitaxel observed during clinical trials was severe and potentially fatal allergic reactions, which occurred in about 2% of the people using the drug. Bone marrow toxicity, resulting in deficiency of white blood cells called neutrophils, was common in clinical trials, but was

manageable and reversible. Peripheral neuropathy, a condition characterized by numbness, tingling, or pain in the extremities, was the most common neurological side effect in clinical trials. The neuropathy was generally cumulative with repeated doses, and more likely to occur in people at risk for developing the side effect, such as people who had experienced neuropathy as a side effect of other therapy.

Other side effects include irregular heart rhythm, hair loss, diarrhea, skin rashes, nausea, vomiting, stomach irritation, and seizures.

### PREGNANCY/BREAST-FEEDING
Paclitaxel has not been formally studied in pregnant women, but the drug is highly toxic to rapidly dividing cells, like those in a fetus. In animal studies, the drug caused spontaneous abortions and birth defects, and it is likely that similar birth defects may occur in humans. Pregnant women are encouraged to discuss the benefits and potential risks of paclitaxel with their physician before deciding to use the drug.

HIV may be passed from a woman to her child through breast milk. In areas where nutritionally sound alternatives are readily available, breast-feeding is discouraged for HIV-positive women. It is not known whether paclitaxel is excreted in human milk. However, because of the potential toxicity of the drug, women are encouraged to consider alternatives to breast-feeding while using it.

### USE IN CHILDREN
Paclitaxel has not been formally studied in children and is not recommended for pediatric use.

### USE IN THE ELDERLY
Older adults may be more susceptible to the side effects of the drug and may require reduced doses.

### DRUG INTERACTIONS
Paclitaxel and cisplatin used together may result in increased risk of bone marrow toxicity. Ketoconazole may inhibit metabolism of paclitaxel, potentially increasing blood levels of the drug.

Although no formal drug-interaction studies have been performed, it is reasonable to assume that paclitaxel may intensify the bone marrow toxicity of drugs such as AZT or ganciclovir and increase the risk of peripheral neuropathy when used with other neuropathy-inducing drugs such as ddI, ddC, and d4T.

### FOOD INTERACTIONS
Because paclitaxel is administered intravenously, food does not affect its absorption into the body.

**OTHER DRUGS USED FOR SIMILAR CONDITIONS**

For the treatment of ovarian and breast cancers, a number of other drugs and combinations are used. For the treatment of advanced KS, a number of other drugs have been used, including bleomycin, vinblastine, vincristine, etoposide, doxorubicin, liposomal doxorubicin, and alpha interferon. In general, the effectiveness of the treatment has less to do with the drugs or combinations used than to differences in the CD4+ counts and history of opportunistic infections of the people treated. People with more extensive disease, other opportunistic infections, prior treatment with chemotherapy, or lower CD4+ counts are less likely to respond to treatment.

# TOPOTECAN

**BRAND NAME (MANUFACTURER)**
Hycamtin (SmithKline Beecham)

**TYPE OF DRUG**
Anticancer agent

**USED FOR**
Topotecan is used primarily to treat ovarian cancer that has not responded to conventional chemotherapy drugs. It is also being tested in clinical trials as a potential treatment for Kaposi's sarcoma (KS), lymphoma, and progressive multifocal leukoencephalopathy (PML) in people living with HIV. Additionally, in laboratory studies, topotecan has anti-HIV activity.

**GENERAL INFORMATION**
Topotecan belongs to a class of drugs known as topoisomerase inhibitors. Topotecan is highly toxic to rapidly dividing cells, such as those in tumors or in normal bone marrow.

In people with HIV, topotecan is being tested as a potential treatment for KS, lymphoma, and PML. The studies are in their early stages and no results have been reported.

Topotecan is available for intravenous injection.

**TREATMENT**
The recommended dose of topotecan for treating ovarian cancer is 1.5 mg per square meter of body surface area, administered intravenously once daily over a 30-minute period for 5 consecutive days. A typical course of therapy is 21 days (5 days on drug and 16 days off drug). A minimum of four courses of treatment are required. People with significantly reduced neutrophil levels should either reduce the dose of topotecan to 0.25 mg per square meter of body surface area or add G-CSF to counteract the low neutrophil levels. People

with moderate kidney function impairment should reduce the dose of topotecan to 0.75 mg per square meter of surface area.

## CAUTIONS AND WARNINGS

Topotecan is highly toxic. It should not be used by people who know they are allergic to it, and it should be used only with careful observation by health care professionals.

Topotecan is not recommended for people whose neutrophil counts are lower than 1,500 or whose platelet counts are lower than 100,000 because of the risk of infection or bleeding.

## SIDE EFFECTS

Bone marrow toxicity, resulting in deficiency of white blood cells called neutrophils, was the most common serious side effect in clinical trials, but was manageable and reversible. Other commonly reported side effects include nausea, vomiting, diarrhea, constipation, abdominal pain, headache, and difficulty in breathing.

## PREGNANCY/BREAST-FEEDING

Topotecan has not been formally studied in pregnant women, but the drug is highly toxic to rapidly dividing cells, like those in a fetus. In animal studies, the drug caused spontaneous abortions and birth defects, and it is likely that similar birth defects may occur in humans. Pregnant women are encouraged to discuss the benefits and potential risks of topotecan with their physician before deciding to use the drug.

HIV may be passed from a woman to her child through breast milk. In areas where nutritionally sound alternatives are readily available, breast-feeding is discouraged for HIV-positive women. It is not known whether topotecan is excreted in human milk. However, because of the potential toxicity of the drug, women are encouraged to consider alternatives to breast-feeding while using it.

## USE IN CHILDREN

Topotecan has not been formally studied in children and is not recommended for pediatric use.

## USE IN THE ELDERLY

No changes in dosage or administration are required for older adults.

## DRUG INTERACTIONS

Although no formal drug-interaction studies have been performed, it is reasonable to assume that topotecan may intensify the bone marrow toxicity of drugs such as AZT or ganciclovir.

## FOOD INTERACTIONS

Because topotecan is administered intravenously, food does not affect its absorption into the body.

**OTHER DRUGS USED FOR SIMILAR CONDITIONS**

A number of other drugs have been used for the treatment of advanced KS, including bleomycin, vinblastine, vincristine, etoposide, doxorubicin, liposomal doxorubicin, and alpha interferon. In general, the effectiveness of the treatment has less to do with the drugs or combinations used than to differences in the CD4+ counts and history of opportunistic infections of the people treated. People with more extensive disease, other opportunistic infections, prior treatment with chemotherapy, or lower CD4+ counts are less likely to respond to treatment. For the treatment of PML, no therapy has been shown to be effective.

# VINBLASTINE

**BRAND NAME (MANUFACTURER)**
Velban (Lilly)

**TYPE OF DRUG**
Anticancer agent

**USED FOR**
Vinblastine is used for the treatment of Hodgkin's disease, lymphoma, testicular cancer, and breast cancer. In people with HIV, it used for the treatment of Kaposi's sarcoma (KS).

**GENERAL INFORMATION**
Vinblastine belongs to a class of cancer drugs called vinca alkyloids, which are naturally occurring chemicals isolated from the periwinkle plant. Vinca alkyloids stop the growth of tumors by preventing cells from dividing.

Another commonly used vinca alkyloid is vincristine. The two drugs have similar chemical structures but different potency against different types of cells. For example, vincristine has a relatively low toxicity to normal cells in the bone marrow when compared to vinblastine and is often the drug of choice in people with impaired bone marrow function.

Although vinblastine can be used by itself to treat cancers, it is used more frequently in combination with other chemotherapy drugs. The rationale is that different drugs have different ways of working and different side effects. By combining drugs, it is often possible to come up with a more effective treatment with reduced side effects and less risk of developing drug-resistant tumors.

For the treatment of KS in people infected with HIV, vinblastine has been used alone, but more frequently is used in combination with bleomycin. It is also used in a two-drug combination with vincristine and a three-drug com-

bination with bleomycin and doxorubicin. When vinblastine was used by itself to treat KS in a clinical trial, the results were disappointing. When combined with other drugs, the response rates improved. As with all HIV-related anticancer treatments, people with more extensive disease, other opportunistic infections, prior treatment with chemotherapy, or lower CD4+ counts were less likely to respond well to treatment.

Vinblastine is available as a solution for intravenous injection.

## TREATMENT

The dose and schedule of administration of vinblastine varies depending on the disease and the other drugs being administered concurrently.

Vinblastine is generally injected no more than once per week to avoid serious reductions in white blood cell counts. Dose reductions may be required for people who have impaired liver function, but no reductions are necessary for those with impaired kidney function.

## CAUTIONS AND WARNINGS

Vinblastine should not be used by anyone with a known allergy to it. It should also not be used by people with low counts of the white blood cells called neutrophils, because the drug will worsen this condition, leading to increased risk of infection or severe bleeding.

Because of the risk of serious drug-related birth defects, women are encouraged to use effective contraception while using vinblastine.

## SIDE EFFECTS

In general, side effects occur most frequently when large doses of the drug are used. The most common side effect is reduction in the number of white blood cells, which occurs, to some extent, in virtually everyone using the drug. Hair loss occurs commonly. Constipation, loss of appetite, nausea, vomiting, abdominal pain, sore mouth, jaw pain, diarrhea, stomach bleeding, and rectal bleeding may occur. Nerve damage that may result in numbness, loss of reflexes, depression, headache, convulsions, tingling, or pain in the extremities occurs infrequently.

## PREGNANCY/BREAST-FEEDING

Vinblastine has not been formally studied in pregnant women, but it is highly toxic to rapidly dividing cells, like those in a malignant tumor or in a fetus. Consequently, it has significant potential for causing fetal harm. Pregnant women are encouraged to discuss the benefits and potential risks of vinblastine with their physician before deciding whether to use the drug.

HIV can be passed from a woman to her child through breast milk. In areas where nutritionally sound alternatives are readily available, breast-feeding is discouraged for HIV-positive women. Vinblastine may be excreted in

human milk, and given the drug's potential toxicity to infants, women should consider alternatives to breast-feeding while using it.

### USE IN CHILDREN
Vinblastine has been effectively used in children at reduced dosages. The recommended starting dose for children is 2.5 mg per square meter of body surface area, increased as necessary and tolerated to a maximum dose of 12.5 mg per square meter of body surface area.

### USE IN THE ELDERLY
Older adults may be more susceptible to the side effects of the drug and may require reduced doses.

### DRUG INTERACTIONS
Vinblastine may reduce drug levels of phenytoin, potentially increasing the risk of seizures in people taking the combination. Vinblastine should not be used with AZT or ganciclovir because the combinations may cause additive bone marrow toxicity.

### FOOD INTERACTIONS
None reported.

### OTHER DRUGS USED FOR SIMILAR CONDITIONS
For the treatment of advanced KS, a number of drugs have been used, including bleomycin, vincristine, etoposide, doxorubicin, liposomal doxorubicin, and alpha interferon. In general, the effectiveness of the treatment has less to do with the drugs or combination of drugs used than to differences in the CD4+ counts and history of opportunistic infections of the people treated. The choice of treatment is often determined by which drugs are tolerated by the individual.

# VINCRISTINE

### BRAND NAME (MANUFACTURER)
Oncovin (Lilly)

### TYPE OF DRUG
Anticancer agent

### USED FOR
Vincristine is used for the treatment of a wide variety of cancers including leukemia and Hodgkin's disease. In people with HIV, it is used primarily as part of combination therapy for non-Hodgkin's lymphoma and Kaposi's sarcoma (KS).

**GENERAL INFORMATION**

Vincristine belongs to a class of anti-cancer drugs called vinca alkyloids, which are naturally occurring chemicals isolated from the periwinkle plant. Vinca alkyloids stop the growth of tumors by preventing cells from dividing.

Another commonly used vinca alkyloid is vinblastine. The two drugs have similar chemical structures but different potencies against different types of cells. For example, vincristine has a relatively low toxicity to normal cells in the bone marrow when compared to vinblastine and is often the drug of choice in people with impaired bone marrow function.

Although vincristine can be used by itself to treat cancers, it is used more frequently in combination with other chemotherapy drugs. The rationale is that different drugs have different ways of working and different side effects. By combining drugs, it is often possible to come up with a more effective treatment with reduced side effects and less risk of developing drug-resistant tumors.

For the treatment of KS in people infected with HIV, vincristine has been used alone, but more frequently is used in a combination with bleomycin called BV. It is also used in a two-drug combination with vinblastine (VV) and a three-drug combination with bleomycin and doxorubicin (ABV). In clinical trials, the number of people whose KS was suppressed by treatment varied from study to study. These differences in response rates probably have less to do with the drugs themselves than to differences in the people treated. People with more extensive disease, other opportunistic infections, prior treatment with chemotherapy, or lower CD4+ counts were less likely to respond to treatment. A recent study showed that a liposomal formulation of doxorubicin (Doxil) when used alone is more effective in treating KS and less toxic than the BV combination. Doxil alone was also significantly less toxic than a combination of Doxorubicin, bleomycin, and vincristine.

For the treatment of AIDS-related lymphoma, vincristine is used in two different combinations. The first, called m-BACOD, consists of methotrexate, bleomycin, doxorubicin, cyclophosphamide, vincristine, dexamethasone, and leucovorin. M-BACOD is toxic to bone marrow, and many HIV-positive individuals cannot tolerate it. In response, a lower-dose version of the combination was tested in a group of people with AIDS. The results were similar to those achieved with the full-dose version of the combination, but with fewer dose-related side effects. The second combination therapy used for lymphoma that includes vincristine is called CHOP. CHOP consists of cyclophosphamide, doxorubicin, vincristine, and prednisone. The response rates for CHOP and m-BACOD are similar. About half the people using the

chemotherapy experience a remission of their disease, but the effect is short-lived.

People with less disease, no prior AIDS-defining illness, and no bone marrow or central nervous system involvement are more likely to respond to treatment. The most important predictor of success is not the drugs used, but the CD4+ count at the time the cancer is diagnosed.

## TREATMENT

Vincristine is available for intravenous injection only. The dose and schedule of administration of the drug vary depending on the disease and the other drugs being administered concurrently.

## CAUTIONS AND WARNINGS

Vincristine should not be used by anyone with a known allergy to it. Because of the risk of liver toxicity, the drug should not be administered to anyone receiving radiation therapy of the liver.

Vincristine should be used with caution in people with neurological disorders or when other drugs that can cause nerve damage are also being used.

Because of the risk of serious drug-related birth defects, women are encouraged to use effective contraception while using vincristine.

## SIDE EFFECTS

The most common side effect of vincristine is hair loss. When injected weekly, reduced white blood cell counts, pain, and constipation occur, but usually last less than a week. Reducing the dose of the drug will often reduce or eliminate these symptoms.

The most serious side effects of vincristine are neurological, and they are often progressive. Peripheral neuropathy, a condition characterized by tingling numbness or pain in the extremities, is the most common. With continued treatment, pain, loss of coordination, loss of reflexes, and eventual paralysis may occur. Convulsions, frequently with hypertension, have occurred in a number of people taking the drug. Several instances of convulsions followed by coma have occurred in treated children. Rarely, short-term blindness has occurred.

Other side effects of vincristine include abdominal cramps, weight loss, vomiting, mouth sores, diarrhea, bleeding in the gut, elevated uric acid in the urine, loss of bladder tone, hypertension, low blood pressure, rash, fever, and headache.

## PREGNANCY/BREAST-FEEDING

Vincristine has not been formally studied in pregnant women, but it is highly toxic to rapidly dividing cells, like those in a malignant tumor or in a fetus. Consequently, it has significant potential for causing fetal harm. Pregnant

women are encouraged to discuss the benefits and potential risks of vincristine with their physician before deciding whether or not to use the drug.

HIV can be passed from a woman to her child through breast milk. In areas where nutritionally sound alternatives are readily available, breast-feeding is discouraged for HIV-positive women. Vincristine may be excreted in human milk, and given the drug's potential toxicity, women should consider alternatives to breast-feeding while using it.

**USE IN CHILDREN**
For children, the most commonly used dose of vincristine is 2 mg per square meter of body surface area injected weekly. For children weighing 10 kg or less (22 lb.), the recommended starting dose is 0.05 mg per kg of body weight, administered once per week.

**USE IN THE ELDERLY**
Older adults may be more susceptible to the side effects of the drug and may require reduced doses.

**DRUG INTERACTIONS**
Vincristine used with mitomycin-C may cause severe breathing problems. Like other anticancer drugs, vincristine may reduce the blood levels of the anticonvulsant phenytoin, potentially increasing the risk of seizures in people who take the combination.

Vincristine may increase the risk of peripheral neuropathy when used with ddI, ddC, and d4T.

**FOOD INTERACTIONS**
None reported.

**OTHER DRUGS USED FOR SIMILAR CONDITIONS**
For the treatment of advanced KS, a number of drugs have been used, including bleomycin, vinblastine, etoposide, doxorubicin, liposomal doxorubicin, and alpha interferon. In general, the effectiveness of the treatment has less to do with the drugs or combination of drugs used than to differences in the CD4+ counts and history of opportunistic infections of the people treated.

For lymphoma, CHOP is a commonly used treatment. No clinical studies have directly compared CHOP and m-BACOD for the treatment of AIDS-related lymphoma, so it is not possible to say one is more effective than the other. The choice of treatment often comes down to which combination is best tolerated by the individual. On average, CHOP has fewer side effects than m-BACOD.

# ANTICANCER EXPERIMENTAL DRUGS

The following drugs are being tested for the treatment of cancers associated with HIV, primarily Kaposi's sarcoma and AIDS-related lymphoma. Generally, they are not widely available; most can be obtained only when participating in clinical trials.

## KAPOSI'S SARCOMA

Some evidence has been reported that angiogenesis (the formation of new blood vessels) may be an important factor in the development of Kaposi's sarcoma (KS). On its own, a tumor cannot grow larger than the size of a pea. Therefore, it relies on a process called angiogenesis, where blood vessels grow into the tumor in order to "feed" them. Antiangiogenesis drugs, also called angiogenesis inhibitors, block blood vessels from growing into the tumor. The antiangiogenic compounds rPF4, SP-PG, and TNP-470 are being studied as potential treatments of Kaposi's sarcoma.

New research suggests that human herpes virus-8 (HHV-8) may play a major role in the development of KS. Compounds which inhibit HHV-8 including cidofovir and foscarnet are being studied as potential treatments of Kaposi's sarcoma. As yet, no anti-herpes drug has been shown to have a significant effect on KS. Some scientists believe that the role of HHV-8 may be important primarily in the initial development of tumors, and that once a KS tumor forms, the KS may be self-sustaining, independent of HHV-8. If this proves correct, anti-HHV-8 drugs may play a significant role as preventive therapy against KS, but perhaps not be as important after KS has already developed.

Other treatments being studied for external KS lesions include cryotherapy (freezing with liquid nitrogen) and phototherapy (with polyporphyrin and 9-cis-retinoic acid). For KS lesions in the mouth and throat, radiation therapy is being investigated. While radiation therapy has been used to reduce tumor size, the side effects can be severe and life-threatening, and lesions can recur even in areas that have been irradiated. Other KS drugs being studied include OPC-8212 (Arkin-Z, Vesnarinone), Liarozole, and thalidomide.

### RPF4

rPF4 (recombinant platelet factor 4) is a synthetic, genetically engineered version of a naturally occurring blood protein, platelet factor 4, which inhibits angiogenesis (blood-vessel formation). It is available only in clinical trials and is given by injection directly into exposed lesions.

### SP-PG

SP-PG (Tecogalan, DS-4152) is an experimental antiangiogenic drug that has been shown to inhibit the formation of new blood vessels in laboratory animals. Tested as an intravenous treatment of KS, it is only available in clinical trials.

### TNP-470

TNP-470 (AGM-1470) is an analogue of fumagillin, a naturally secreted antibiotic of the fungus *Aspergillus fumigatus fresenius*. A potent inhibitor of blood-vessel formation, it is being tested as a treatment for KS as well as for solid tumors. Preliminary results have not shown substantial single-agent anti-KS activity.

### OPC-8212

OPC-8212 (Arkin-Z, Vesnarinone) is a quinolinone derivative used in Japan to treat congestive heart failure and is being tested in the United States as a treatment for KS.

### TRETINOIN

Tretinoin (all-trans retinoic acid; ATRA) is a derivative of vitamin A being tested as a topical and oral treatment for KS. Although the oral form appears to have an effect on the disease, it also has serious side effects, including severe nausea and vomiting, intolerable headaches, malaise, altered blood calcium levels, and inflammation of the pancreas. A liposomal formulation of tretinoin (AR-623) is currently being studied.

### CIDOFOVIR

Cidofovir (Vistide) is approved for the treatment of CMV retinitis. In laboratory studies, cidofovir is active against HHV-8 and is being tested as a treatment for KS.

### FOSCARNET

Foscarnet (Foscavir) is approved for the treatment of CMV retinitis and herpes simplex virus, which is refractory to acyclovir. Similar to cidofovir, in laboratory studies, foscarnet is active against HHV-8.

## AIDS-RELATED LYMPHOMA

### MITOGUAZONE

Mitoguazone (MGBG, Methyl GAG, methyl-glyoxalbisguanylhydrazone) is a cancer drug originally synthesized in 1898 that has been resurrected as a potential treatment for non-Hodgkin's lymphoma (NHL). The drug has a number of effects, including suppressing a biochemical pathway required for DNA synthesis. In a small clinical trial in non-HIV-infected people, a mitoguazone-containing drug combination was highly active in suppressing

NHL. The drug is being tested in clinical trials of AIDS-related NHL because it has little bone marrow toxicity (so it can be used with antiretrovirals), it crosses the blood-brain barrier (so it may be effective against lymphomas in the brain), and it is active in test-tube studies against many lymphoma cell lines.

Other drugs under investigation for the treatment of lymphoma include OK-B7 with radioactive iodine, immunotoxin therapy, anti-CD19, anti-CD22, and anti-B4 attached to an immunotoxin, ricin. Studies are also looking at using IL-2 and IL-4, which have been shown to inhibit tumor growth in laboratory studies.

# ANTIDIARRHEAL DRUGS

Diarrhea is a common problem for many people living with HIV. It occurs when bowel movements are loose (unformed) or watery. Diarrhea can be dangerous as it can result in severe dehydration, weight loss, weakness and malnutrition. It can also result in poor absorption of drugs, leading to decreased blood levels. This results in the same effect as taking too small a dose of drug, which hastens the development of drug resistance. Since many different factors can contribute to diarrhea, it is crucial that the causes be properly identified and treated and that plenty of fluids are taken right away to avoid dehydration. The treatment of diarrhea may involve nutritional and dietary intervention as well as the use of drugs to treat the underlying causes and to treat the symptoms. This section covers drugs primarily used to treat the symptoms of diarrhea, but not the causes, along with some other important suggestions for managing diarrhea.

The first step in managing diarrhea is to start drinking more fluids right away to prevent dehydration. Because diarrhea can result in significant water loss and dehydration, it is *very* important that fluids are restored immediately. Drinking Gatorade or other electrolyte-rich fluids can help restore nutrient levels and replace lost water.

## DETERMINE THE CAUSE

There are many potential causes of diarrhea, and several may be occurring at once. It's important to identify all the causes and treat them appropriately. These may include infections in the gut (e.g., parasitic, bacterial, fungal, and viral infections), side effects of medications, lactose intolerance, diet and/or HIV itself.

If a person has blood in the stool (i.e., feces) and/or has a fever, there may be an infection causing the diarrhea. A physician should be seen right away. Physicians will take a stool sample, test for the possible infections, and recommend appropriate treatment. Some common infections include *cryptosporidium, microsporidium, Mycobacterium avium* complex (MAC), *cytomegalovirus* (CMV), *giardia,* and *salmonella.* When diarrhea is caused by a known infection, physicians may prescribe the appropriate antibiotic, antifungal, antiparasitic, or antiviral medication. It is important to remember that an infection may exist even without bloody stool or a fever.

Many antiviral drugs, such as nelfinavir and ddI, list diarrhea as a common side effect. A number of antibiotics like clarithromycin, azithromycin, and ciprofloxacin can also cause diarrhea. Treating the symptoms may help in such cases.

Lactose intolerance can also result in diarrhea. Many people with HIV cannot properly digest lactose, a sugar found in milk, cheese, and other dairy products. Some medications come in capsules that contain lactose, such as the current formulation of saquinavir. If lactose intolerance is suspected, try eliminating dairy products to see if this improves the condition. It is often possible to correct the problem by using over-the-counter products designed to help digest lactose.

A person's diet may inadvertently also contribute to the problem. High levels of fat in the diet are particularly difficult for the body to deal with during times of intestinal distress. In general, a low fat diet is easier to digest and puts less strain on the digestive system and liver.

Finally, chronic diarrhea may simply be a direct result of HIV infection of the lymphatic tissues lining the intestinal tract. This is particularly difficult to combat since the best solution is potent antiviral therapy, yet diarrhea and poor absorption directly interfere with the uptake of these drugs. In this case, controlling the symptoms of diarrhea may help correct the underlying cause by simply forcing the body to do a better job absorbing and retaining antiviral therapies. If no other causes can be identified, people should assess their antiviral regimen, as failing therapies may add to increased HIV infection in the gut.

Unfortunately, it is often difficult to determine the cause of diarrhea. Sometimes, repeated diagnostic tests must be run before a clear cause is identified. When diarrhea is short-term and goes away on its own, it may not matter much. But when it is continuing and chronic, it is very important to keep searching for the cause, however unpleasant it may be.

### TREAT THE SYMPTOMS

A number of over-the-counter medications and certain foods can temporarily help slow the diarrhea. However, these may just mask the problem without solving it. Identifying the cause(s) of diarrhea is critical to successful treatment, and symptom management should generally be considered only a "Band-Aid" solution.

- **Antidiarrheal medications:** Imodium (loperamide), Kaopectate and Pepto-Bismol are over-the-counter drugs that can offer some relief for mild-to-moderate diarrhea. Lomotil (diphenoxylate) can help with moderate diarrhea, but must be prescribed by a physician. In the most severe cases, physicians may prescribe tincture of opium or other narcotics. These drugs reduce muscle contractions in the intestines, thereby slowing the movement of food and liquid through the gut. Still another option is octreotide (Sandostatin), a synthetic hormone that also slows movement through the intestines. These drugs are covered in this section.

However, if there is an infection causing the diarrhea, antidiarrheal drugs may prevent it from being cleared and may actually worsen the problem, resulting in a potentially life-threatening situation. Therefore, they should be used with the utmost care. If the diarrhea does not go away in a few days despite using these medications, consult a physician.

- Bulking Agents (like Metamucil) and *soluble fiber* sources can help slow diarrhea by helping absorb liquids in the intestinal tract and causing bulking of stools. This approach is particularly useful with some drug-induced diarrhea. In general, soluble fiber is found in the "inside" or pulp parts of fruits and vegetables. Foods high in soluble fiber include oatmeal, white rice, grits, cream of wheat, bananas, soft breads (not whole grain), and applesauce, among others.

- Avoid insoluble fiber: Insoluble fiber is generally found in the outer skin of fruits and vegetables. This type of fiber doesn't absorb water and prompts the intestines to move it along as quickly as possible, thus intensifying diarrhea. It is also best to avoid typical "roughage" like lettuce, whole grain rice or wheat, and the skins of fruits or vegetables as these help clean out the intestines and can aggravate the bowels and intensify diarrhea.

- Restoring the "friendly flora": Certain "friendly" bacteria and yeast (meaning that they don't cause infections) may help restore the environment of the gut. These natural bacteria—Acidophilus, various digestive enzymes, and *S. Boulardii*—are often destroyed by commonly used antibiotics.

Other treatments in development include thalidomide, DEHOP (diethylhomospermene) and Bovine Colostrum (Sporidin-G is currently in phase II/III clinical trials).

Although antidiarrheal medications are helpful, people should be cautious because these drugs may prevent infection-causing agents from leaving the body, thereby prolonging the problem if it is infectious in nature.

The following antidiarrheal drugs are covered in this section:

- bismuth subsalicylate
- diphenoxylate
- loperamide
- octreotide
- opium (tincture)

# BISMUTH SUBSALICYLATE

**BRAND NAME (MANUFACTURER)**
Pepto-Bismol (Procter & Gamble)

**TYPE OF DRUG**
Antidiarrheal

**USED FOR**
Bismuth subsalicylate is used to treat heartburn, indigestion, upset stomach, and nausea. In people with HIV, it is also widely used for diarrhea.

**GENERAL INFORMATION**
Bismuth subsalicylate relieves heartburn, indigestion, nausea, and other symptoms of upset stomach by coating the lining in the stomach. It is thought to work against diarrhea by binding to bacteria and their toxins and by slowing down fluid flowing through the gut. However, the drug does not affect the underlying causes of the condition, which may be infection, anxiety, cancers, or drug-related side effects.

Bismuth subsalicylate is available over the counter (without a prescription) as tablets, caplets, and two different-strength liquids.

**TREATMENT**
The recommended adult dosage of the regular-strength liquid is two tablespoons, repeated every half hour to one hour, if needed, to a maximum of eight doses in a twenty-four-hour period. Two tablets or caplets are equivalent to two tablespoons of the liquid. Diarrhea is usually controlled within twenty-four hours.

The maximum-strength liquid has twice the drug concentration of the regular form. The recommended volume per dose of the maximum-strength liquid is the same, but it should be repeated only every hour, if needed, for a maximum of four doses in any twenty-four-hour period.

**CAUTIONS AND WARNINGS**
Bismuth subsalicylate should not be used by anyone with a known allergy to it or to aspirin. Because of the additional risk of side effects, people taking blood thinners or drugs for diabetes or gout should use bismuth subsalicylate with caution.

People using the drug should drink plenty of fluids to replace those lost because of diarrhea. Severe dehydration or imbalance in the electrolytes in the blood should be treated as well. In addition, potential nutritional deficiencies associated with diarrhea should be addressed with a trained health care professional or nutritionist who specializes in HIV disease.

If the diarrhea is bloody, accompanied by a high fever, or continues for more than two days, a physician should be contacted.

**SIDE EFFECTS**

Bismuth subsalicylate is generally well tolerated. It may cause a temporary darkening of the tongue or stools.

**PREGNANCY/BREAST-FEEDING**

Bismuth subsalicylate is generally considered safe during pregnancy, but as with all medications, pregnant women should use it with caution.

HIV may be passed from a woman to her child through breast milk. In areas where nutritionally sound alternatives are readily available, breast-feeding is discouraged for HIV-positive women. In general, however, bismuth subsalicylate is considered safe for infants of breast-feeding women.

**USE IN CHILDREN**

Children can safely and effectively use bismuth subsalicylate at doses adjusted for weight and age. Children and teenagers who have or are recovering from chicken pox or the flu should not use the drug to treat nausea or vomiting. These symptoms could be an early sign of Reye's syndrome, a rare but serious illness.

**USE IN THE ELDERLY**

No changes in dosage or administration are recommended for older adults.

**DRUG INTERACTIONS**

Bismuth subsalicylate is chemically similar to aspirin and may intensify the effects of aspirin. If ringing in the ears occurs while taking the two drugs simultaneously, bismuth subsalicylate should be stopped.

**FOOD INTERACTIONS**

None reported.

**OTHER DRUGS USED FOR SIMILAR CONDITIONS**

For relatively mild diarrhea, bismuth subsalicylate or bulk-forming agents and adsorbents such as kaolin pectin (Kaopectate) may be appropriate. Loperamide (Imodium) is another over-the-counter drug useful as first-line therapy against mild-to-moderate diarrhea. For treatment of chronic diarrhea, stronger agents may be necessary, including diphenoxylate plus atropine, codeine, morphine, or methadone. When these fail to work or are not appropriate, hormone therapy with octreotide acetate may be useful.

# DIPHENOXYLATE

**BRAND NAME (MANUFACTURER)**

Diphenoxylate + Atropine: Lomotil (Searle)

**TYPE OF DRUG**

Antidiarrheal

**USED FOR**

Diphenoxylate combined with atropine is used to treat the symptoms of diarrhea. In people with HIV, it is often used to treat diarrhea caused by infections of the gut or diarrhea that is a side effect of other drugs.

**GENERAL INFORMATION**

The combination of diphenoxylate and atropine is available as tablets and liquid in a brand name called Lomotil. It is also available in generic form. Diphenoxylate is the ingredient that reduces the symptoms of diarrhea. Although its exact mechanism of action is unknown, it probably works by increasing the amount of time food or liquid takes to go through the intestines. However, the drug does not affect the underlying causes of the condition, which may be infection, anxiety, cancers, or drug-related side effects.

Diphenoxylate is chemically similar to the narcotic pain reliever meperidine (Demerol). Consequently, it is potentially addictive. Atropine is added in small amounts to reduce the potential for abuse of diphenoxylate.

**TREATMENT**

Prescription antidiarrheal medications should be used only under the guidance of a physician. Inappropriate dosing may not only result in discomfort, but serious medical complications.

The recommended initial dose of diphenoxylate is two 2.5 mg tablets or 10 ml of the liquid, taken four times daily, with dose reductions as prescribed when the diarrhea stabilizes.

Improvement of the diarrhea usually occurs within forty-eight hours of taking the drug. If improvement does not occur within ten days, the drug is unlikely to be effective no matter how long it is taken.

**CAUTIONS AND WARNINGS**

This product should not be used by anyone with a known allergy to diphenoxylate or atropine or anyone with a liver disease called obstructive jaundice. It should also not be used to treat diarrhea caused by bacteria in the gut that produce toxins.

Diphenoxylate may impair the mental and physical abilities necessary to operate dangerous machinery or to drive an automobile.

People using the drug should drink plenty of fluids to replace those lost because of diarrhea. Severe dehydration or imbalance in the electrolytes in the blood should be treated as well. In addition, potential nutritional deficiencies associated with diarrhea should be addressed with a trained health care professional or nutritionist who specializes in HIV disease.

Diphenoxylate may prolong or worsen diarrhea caused by toxic bacteria that invade the lining of the gut. These bacteria include some strains of *E. coli, Shigella, and Salmonella.* Similarly, diphenoxylate may prolong or worsen

the diarrhea that results from the use of broad-spectrum antibiotics that disrupt the normal mix of microorganisms in the gut.

Diphenoxylate may cause serious enlargement of the colon in some people with colon disease. If bloating or abdominal pain occurs while taking the drug, treatment should be stopped and a physician contacted immediately.

Diphenoxylate should be used with caution in people with liver or kidney disease, because they have a higher risk of serious side effects, including drug-induced coma.

## SIDE EFFECTS

At recommended doses of diphenoxylate, its side effects include headache, dizziness, restlessness, vomiting, nausea, loss of appetite, drowsiness, confusion, lethargy, allergic reactions, abdominal pain, numbness in the extremities, euphoria, depression, inflammation of the pancreas, and toxic inflammation of the colon. Overdose of the drug may result in severe lethargy, coma, and potentially fatal breathing difficulties.

Side effects of atropine include fever, abnormal heart rhythm, difficulty urinating, flushing, and dryness of the skin and mouth.

## PREGNANCY/BREAST-FEEDING

Diphenoxylate has not been formally studied in pregnant women. In animal studies it reduced fertility and resulted in low birth weights when given at a dose equivalent to fifty times the human dose. It is not known whether these effects would also occur in humans. Pregnant women are encouraged to discuss the benefits and potential risks of diphenoxylate with their physician before deciding to use the drug.

HIV may be passed from a woman to her child through breast milk. In areas where nutritionally sound alternatives are readily available, breast-feeding is discouraged for HIV-positive women. Diphenoxylate is excreted into human milk and can cause serious sedation in infants. Because of the potential toxicity of the drug, women should consider alternatives to breast-feeding while taking it.

## USE IN CHILDREN

Lomotil is not recommended for children under the age of two because they vary widely in their ability to metabolize the drug, and accidental overdose may result in coma, severe and potentially fatal breathing difficulties, or permanent brain damage. The drug may be used for older children with caution, after careful consideration of their nutritional status and extent of dehydration.

The liquid form of the drug is recommended for children under the age of thirteen. The recommended starting dosage for children is 0.3 to 0.4 mg per kg of body weight, divided into four equal doses during the day. The dosage

is often decreased for children with poor nutritional status or severe dehydration. After the condition stabilizes, a maintenance dose, as low as one-fourth the initial dose, may be used to prevent recurrence of symptoms.

If no response to the drug is seen within forty-eight hours, it is unlikely the drug will be effective.

### USE IN THE ELDERLY
Older adults may be more susceptible to the side effects of the drug and may require reduced doses.

### DRUG INTERACTIONS
Use of diphenoxylate with antidepressants of the monoamine oxidase (MAO) inhibitor class (e.g., tranylcypromine, phenelzine, isocarboxazid) may result in severe and unpredictable side effects. Diphenoxylate may intensify the effect of central nervous system depressants, including barbiturates, alcohol, tranquilizers, muscle relaxants, and narcotic pain medications.

The side effects of atropine may be increased by amantadine, haloperidol, tranquilizers, procainamide, and quinidine.

### FOOD INTERACTIONS
None reported.

### OTHER DRUGS USED FOR SIMILAR CONDITIONS
For relatively mild diarrhea, bismuth subsalicylate or bulk-forming agents and adsorbents such as kaolin pectin (Kaopectate) may be appropriate. Loperamide (Imodium) is another over-the-counter drug useful as first-line therapy against mild-to-moderate diarrhea. For treatment of chronic diarrhea, stronger agents may be necessary, including morphine or methadone. When these fail or are not appropriate, hormone therapy with octreotide acetate may be useful.

# LOPERAMIDE

### BRAND NAME (MANUFACTURER)
Imodium A-D (McNeil); Imodium (Janssen); Pepto Diarrheal Control (Procter & Gamble)

### TYPE OF DRUG
Antidiarrheal

### USED FOR
Loperamide is used to treat the symptoms of diarrhea. In people with HIV, it is often used to treat the symptoms of diarrhea caused by infections of the gut or diarrhea that is a side effect of other drugs.

## GENERAL INFORMATION

Loperamide slows the movement of food and fluid through the gut, which reduces the symptoms of diarrhea. However, the drug does not affect the underlying causes of the condition, which may be infection, anxiety, cancers, or drug-related side effects.

Loperamide is available both by prescription and over the counter as a liquid and tablets for oral administration.

## TREATMENT

For symptomatic treatment of acute diarrhea in adults, the over-the-counter medication can be taken at a dose of four teaspoonfuls or two caplets (4 mg of active drug) after the first loose bowel movement. If needed, two teaspoonfuls or one caplet may be taken after each additional loose bowel movement. No more than eight teaspoonfuls or four caplets should be taken in any twenty-four-hour period. If improvement is not seen in forty-eight hours, the drug should be discontinued.

The prescription form of the drug should only be used under the guidance of a physician. It is used for acute diarrhea and for cases where the diarrhea becomes chronic. The recommended initial dose of loperamide is 4 mg followed by 2 mg after each unformed stool until the diarrhea is controlled. The dosage is then lowered and individualized for each person to prevent the symptoms from recurring. The average daily maintenance dosage in clinical trials was 4 to 8 mg, but dosages as high as 16 mg per day were used. If clinical improvement is not observed after ten days at 16 mg per day, it is unlikely the drug will ever be effective.

## CAUTIONS AND WARNINGS

Loperamide should not be used by anyone with a known allergy to it. The drug can cause constipation and should not be used by anyone for whom this would cause serious medical complications.

People using the drug should drink plenty of fluids to replace those lost because of diarrhea. Severe dehydration or imbalance in the electrolytes in the blood should be treated as well. In addition, potential nutritional deficiencies associated with diarrhea should be addressed with a trained health care professional or nutritionist who specializes in HIV disease.

Loperamide may prolong or worsen diarrhea caused by toxic bacteria that invade the lining of the gut. These bacteria include some strains of *E. coli, Shigella, and Salmonella.* Similarly, loperamide may prolong or worsen the diarrhea that results from the use of broad-spectrum antibiotics that disrupt the normal mix of microorganisms in the gut.

Loperamide may cause serious enlargement of the colon in some people with colon disease. If bloating or abdominal pain occurs while taking the drug, treatment should be stopped and a physician contacted immediately.

Loperamide should be used with caution in people with liver disease, because they have a higher risk of serious side effects, including central nervous system depression (sedation, lethargy, reduced breathing rate, etc.).

### SIDE EFFECTS

At over-the-counter and prescribed doses, loperamide is generally well tolerated. Side effects that have been reported by people taking the drug include allergic reactions, abdominal pain or discomfort, nausea, vomiting, constipation, tiredness, drowsiness or dizziness, and dry mouth.

### PREGNANCY/BREAST-FEEDING

Loperamide has not been formally studied in pregnant women. In animal studies, it did not cause fetal harm, but it is not known whether the same would be true for humans. Pregnant women are encouraged to discuss the benefits and potential risks of loperamide with their physician before deciding to use the drug.

HIV may be passed from a woman to her child through breast milk. In areas where nutritionally sound alternatives are readily available, breast-feeding is discouraged for HIV-positive women. It is not known whether loperamide is excreted in human milk.

### USE IN CHILDREN

Diarrhea in children is usually an acute, self-limiting infection, best controlled by diet and fluids. Loperamide should not be used by children under the age of two since they metabolize the drug variably, particularly those who are dehydrated. In children aged two to five, the nonprescription liquid form of the drug is used, but only under the guidance of a physician. For older children, the prescription drug may be used, but at reduced dosages, and again under the guidance of a physician.

### USE IN THE ELDERLY

Elderly people with diarrhea have a greater risk of complications than younger people, and they are often more susceptible to the side effects of drugs used to treat the condition. Because liver function often declines with age, elderly people may need to take reduced dosages of loperamide.

### DRUG INTERACTIONS

Loperamide reduces the rate at which ddI is absorbed into the body, but not the total amount absorbed. Because loperamide is a central nervous system depressant, it may intensify the effect of other depressants, including alcohol, tranquilizers, and narcotic pain relievers.

**FOOD INTERACTIONS**

Loperamide may be taken with or without food.

**OTHER DRUGS USED FOR SIMILAR CONDITIONS**

For relatively mild diarrhea, bismuth subsalicylate or bulk-forming agents and adsorbents such as kaolin pectin (Kaopectate) may be appropriate. Loperamide is useful as first-line therapy against mild-to-moderate diarrhea. For treatment of chronic diarrhea, stronger agents may be necessary, including diphenoxylate plus atropine, codeine, morphine, or methadone. When these fail or are not appropriate, hormone therapy with octreotide acetate may be useful.

# OCTREOTIDE

**BRAND NAME (MANUFACTURER)**

Sandostatin (Sandoz)

**OTHER NAME**

Somatostatin analogue

**TYPE OF DRUG**

Antidiarrheal-synthetic hormone

**USED FOR**

Octreotide has been approved by the FDA to treat elevated growth-hormone levels associated with a condition called acromegaly (characterized by abnormal enlargement of the skeleton) and to treat the symptoms of diarrhea caused by certain types of tumors. In people with HIV, octreotide is used to treat persistent diarrhea that is not attributable to a specific or otherwise treatable cause.

**GENERAL INFORMATION**

Octreotide is a synthetic version of the natural hormone somatostatin. It regulates the blood levels of a number of other hormones in the body and has a wide range of effects. Specifically, for diarrhea it inhibits gastrointestinal hormones, which slows the time it takes for food or liquids to pass through the gut. Octreotide improves only the symptoms of diarrhea. However, the drug does not affect the underlying causes of the condition, which may be infection, anxiety, cancers, or drug-related side effects.

Octreotide has been tested in a number of clinical studies of people living with HIV. The response rates varied from study to study, but roughly half of the people taking the drug had some improvement in their diarrhea.

Octreotide is available as a solution for injection.

### TREATMENT

Octreotide is usually administered subcutaneously (by injection under the surface of the skin). It can be administered intravenously for those who have intravenous access lines, but it is more likely to cause nausea when given by this route.

For most indications, the drug is initially given at a dose of 50 microgram (mcg), injected three times a day and increased as needed and tolerated. It may also be effective when used twice daily.

In clinical trials for AIDS-related chronic diarrhea, octreotide has been tested in a wide range of doses, from 150 mcg per day up to 1,500 mcg per day. The appropriate dose depends on the severity of the condition, the health of the individual, and how well the drug is tolerated.

### CAUTIONS AND WARNINGS

Octreotide is eliminated from the body by the kidneys. In people with impaired kidney function, the dosage of the drug may need to be reduced.

Octreotide may alter the absorption of dietary fats in some people. The drug may also reduce vitamin B12 levels in some people, who may require supplements.

People using the drug should drink plenty of fluids to replace those being lost. Severe dehydration or imbalance in the electrolytes in the blood should be treated as well. In addition, potential nutritional deficiencies associated with diarrhea should be addressed with a trained health care professional or nutritionist who specializes in HIV disease.

### SIDE EFFECTS

The side effects of octreotide are most completely known for people who took the drug to treat abnormal growth-hormone levels. However, because of their underlying condition and other drugs used, this group of people is highly susceptible to certain side effects. For many of the adverse effects listed below, it is not known whether the drug itself was responsible for the effect or how frequently the side effects can be expected for people using the drug for AIDS-related diarrhea.

Thirty to 58% of acromegalics using octreotide in clinical trials experienced diarrhea, loose stools, nausea, and abdominal discomfort. Vomiting, gas, and constipation were experienced by fewer than 10% of them.

About half of the acromegalics who took the drug had altered gallbladder function, which often resulted in gallstones. About one in five experienced abnormal heart rate or rhythm.

Abnormal blood sugar levels occurred in 18% of acromegalics, but only in 1.5% of other people taking the drug.

Other adverse effects associated with the drug include pain on injection, headache, dizziness, fatigue, weakness, itching, joint pain, backache, urinary-tract infection, cold symptoms, flu symptoms, bruising, swelling, flushing, blurred vision, and hair loss.

### PREGNANCY/BREAST-FEEDING

Octreotide has not been formally studied in pregnant women. In animal studies, the drug did not cause fetal harm, but it is not known whether the same would be true for humans. Pregnant women are encouraged to discuss the benefits and potential risks of octreotide with their physician before deciding to use the drug.

HIV may be passed from a woman to her child through breast milk. In areas where nutritionally sound alternatives are readily available, breast-feeding is discouraged for HIV-positive women. It is not known whether octreotide is excreted in breast milk.

### USE IN CHILDREN

There has been limited use of octreotide in children. Doses of 1 to 10 mcg per kg of body weight have been well tolerated in the small number of children who have used it, but too little information is available to make recommendations.

### USE IN THE ELDERLY

No alterations in dosage or administration are recommended for elderly people with normal liver and kidney function.

### DRUG INTERACTIONS

Octreotide can cause alterations in nutrient absorption, so it may have an effect on orally administered drugs. Administration of octreotide along with cyclosporine may decrease blood levels of cyclosporine.

People receiving insulin or other drugs used to control blood sugar levels, heart medications, or drugs used to control fluid or electrolyte balances may need to adjust their dosages of these drugs.

### FOOD INTERACTIONS

Food does not affect the absorption of octreotide.

### OTHER DRUGS USED FOR SIMILAR CONDITIONS

For relatively mild diarrhea, bismuth subsalicylate or bulk-forming agents and adsorbents such as kaolin pectin (Kaopectate) may be appropriate. Loperamide (Imodium) is another over-the-counter drug useful as first-line therapy against mild-to-moderate diarrhea. For treatment of chronic diarrhea, stronger agents may be necessary, including diphenoxylate plus atropine, codeine, morphine, or methadone. When these fail or are not appropriate, hormone therapy with octreotide acetate may be useful.

# OPIUM (TINCTURE)

**TYPE OF DRUG**
Narcotic analgesic - antidiarrheal

**USED FOR**
Tincture of opium is used to treat the symptoms of severe diarrhea. In people with HIV, it is often used to treat the symptoms of diarrhea caused by infections of the gut or diarrhea that is a side effect of other drugs.

**GENERAL INFORMATION**
Tincture of opium is a liquid extract of the opium poppy. It contains more than twenty different compounds called alkaloids, many of which have potent effects on the central nervous system. Morphine is the most abundant alkaloid found in opium, but numerous others contribute to its effects.

Narcotics block the transmission of nerve signals from the brain to the muscles in the intestines, reducing muscle contraction. Consequently, food and liquids spend more time moving through the gut. However, the drug does not affect the underlying causes of the condition, which may be infection, anxiety, cancers, or drug-related side effects.

**TREATMENT**
Tincture of opium is taken orally. The recommended dosage varies depending on the severity of the condition, the health of the individual, and the other drugs being used concurrently. The effect of the drug lasts approximately four hours, so doses must be repeated approximately six times a day.

**CAUTIONS AND WARNINGS**
Tincture of opium should not be used by anyone with a known allergy to it or any other opiate. The drug can be addictive on extended use and can cause severe withdrawal symptoms when it is stopped. However, this is seldom if ever a problem for people who use the drug correctly and only for short periods. Because of its addictive potential, tincture of opium may not be appropriate therapy for people with a history of drug abuse, alcoholism, or marked personality disorders.

Opium reduces the mental and physical abilities to drive an automobile or operate dangerous machinery.

Tincture of opium should be used with caution by people with a history of breathing difficulties, kidney impairment, or liver impairment because they have a higher risk of side effects caused by the drug.

Tincture of opium may prolong or worsen diarrhea caused by toxic bacteria that invade the lining of the gut. These bacteria include some strains of *E. coli, Shigella, and Salmonella.*

People using the drug should drink plenty of fluids to replace those lost because of diarrhea. Severe dehydration or imbalance in the electrolytes in the blood should be treated as well. In addition, potential nutritional deficiencies associated with diarrhea should be addressed with a trained health care professional or nutritionist who specializes in HIV disease.

### SIDE EFFECTS
The most common side effects of opium are related to its depressive effects. They include sedation, dizziness, slow heartbeat, confusion, nausea, vomiting, and constipation. At high doses, the drug can cause slow or irregular breathing, severe drowsiness, loss of consciousness, or coma.

### PREGNANCY/BREAST-FEEDING
Tincture of opium has not been formally studied in pregnant women. It is usually not used during pregnancy, especially in the third trimester or during delivery because it can cause sedation or breathing difficulties in newborns. Pregnant women are encouraged to discuss the benefits and potential risks of the drug with their physician before deciding to use it.

HIV may be passed from a woman to her child through breast milk. In areas where nutritionally sound alternatives are readily available, breast-feeding is discouraged for HIV-positive women. Many of the narcotic compounds found in tincture of opium pass into breast milk and can cause serious side effects in newborns. Women are encouraged to consider alternatives to breast-feeding while using the drug.

### USE IN CHILDREN
Because infants have immature kidney and liver function, they are at increased risk for side effects of the drug. Generally, the drug is not appropriate for young children.

### USE IN THE ELDERLY
Older adults may be more susceptible to the side effects of the drug, especially disorientation and confusion, and often require reduced doses.

### DRUG INTERACTIONS
Tincture of opium may intensify the effects of other central nervous system depressants, including narcotic pain relievers, antihistamines, tranquilizers, sleeping pills, and alcohol.

The use of opium in combination with monoamine oxidase (MAO) inhibitors such as phenelzine may cause extremely high blood pressure.

### FOOD INTERACTIONS
The drug may be taken with or without food.

### OTHER DRUGS USED FOR SIMILAR CONDITIONS
For relatively mild diarrhea, bismuth subsalicylate or bulk-forming agents and adsorbents such as kaolin pectin (Kaopectate) may be appropriate.

Loperamide (Imodium) is another over-the-counter drug useful as first-line therapy against mild-to-moderate diarrhea. For treatment of chronic diarrhea, stronger agents may be necessary, including diphenoxylate plus atropine, codeine, morphine, or methadone. When these fail or are not appropriate, hormone therapy with octreotide acetate may be useful.

# ANTIFUNGAL DRUGS

Although serious fungal infections are rare in the general population, they are more common in people living with HIV. These infections may affect only the surface of the skin or mucous membranes, or they may be systemic, spreading throughout the body. Candidiasis, cryptococcosis, and histoplasmosis are three types of fungal infections that frequently occur in people infected with HIV.

Most antifungal drugs work by altering the permeability of fungal cell walls. The chemicals necessary for the fungus to live leak out of the cell and the fungus dies. The following antifungal drugs are profiled in this section:

- amphotericin B

- amphotericin B colloidal dispersion

- amphotericin B lipid complex

- clotrimazole

- fluconazole

- flucytosine

- itraconazole

- ketoconazole

- metronidazole

- miconazole

- nystatin

- terbinafine


In addition, brief descriptions of experimental therapies for fungal infection are included at the end of this section. They include:

- ZD0870

- voriconazole

- SCH 56592

- L-743,872

- LY303366

- Liposomal amphotericin B

# AMPHOTERICIN B

**BRAND NAME (MANUFACTURER)**
Fungizone (Apothecon, Bristol-Myers Squibb)

**TYPE OF DRUG**
Antifungal agent

**USED FOR**
Intravenous (IV) amphotericin B is used and approved for the treatment of progressive, potentially life-threatening fungal infections. In people with HIV, IV amphotericin B is routinely used to initially treat severe cryptococcosis, histoplasmosis, aspergillosis, blastomycosis, and coccidioidomycosis. An oral suspension formulation is approved for the treatment of candidal infection in the mouth.

**GENERAL INFORMATION**
IV amphotericin B is a potent, but highly toxic, drug that is effective against a wide range of fungi. IV amphotericin B was the only available treatment for many fungal diseases until the development of oral azole antifungal drugs such as ketoconazole, itraconazole, and fluconazole. Amphotericin B remains the initial therapy of choice for severe histoplasmosis and cryptococcal meningitis, although use of the azoles is gaining wider acceptance for mild-to-moderate disease. The oral suspension amphotericin B is commonly used to treat fluconazole-resistant oral candidiasis.

A number of new formulations of amphotericin B have been developed to minimize the drug's toxicity. See the profiles on Amphotericin B Colloidal Dispersion and Amphotericin B Lipid Complex for more information on these drugs. A third liposomal formulation, Ambisome, will soon be approved in the United States. See the section on experimental antifungal drugs for more information.

Amphotericin B is slowly metabolized and excreted from the body and can be found in urine up to seven weeks after treatment. The drug works by attacking the cell membranes of fungi. Because human and fungal cell membranes contain similar compounds, amphotericin B's side effects may be a result of the drug attacking human cell membranes as well.

Standard amphotericin B must be injected intravenously.

**TREATMENT**
The usual dose of amphotericin B is 0.7 mg per kg of body weight per day. Therapy is continued until the person stabilizes or improves, usually no longer than two to three weeks. Afterward, some type of lifelong maintenance therapy is recommended to prevent the recurrence of the disease.

Amphotericin B is occasionally used as maintenance therapy, but fluconazole is generally the maintenance drug of choice because it is as effective, has fewer side effects, and can be taken orally.

Because amphotericin B is toxic, a test dose is often injected. Temperature, respiration, and blood pressure are monitored for two to four hours after injection.

Amphotericin B is administered by slow intravenous injection over a period of two to six hours. In people with good heart and kidney function, the drug is usually started at 0.25 mg per kg of body weight, which is increased as tolerated. People with severe infections may receive higher initial doses. Those with impaired kidney or heart function may receive smaller initial doses. The maximum daily dose should not exceed 1.5 mg per kg of body weight per day.

Steroids are sometimes given in addition to amphotericin B for people with high pressure inside the skull.

Oral suspension amphotericin B should be taken between meals to ensure prolonged contact with the lesions. The dose of the oral drug is 100 mg (1mL) given four times daily (total daily dose of 400 mg) and the duration of treatment is usually two weeks. The drug is placed on the tongue and should be swished around for as long as possible before swallowing.

### CAUTIONS AND WARNINGS

Amphotericin B should not be used by anyone with a known allergy to it. IV amphotericin B must be injected slowly to avoid serious side effects, which may include shock, irregular heart rhythms, and altered blood pressure.

IV amphotericin B is excreted from the body by the kidneys and can cause severe damage to them. The drug should be used with caution by people with impaired kidney function. Physicians should closely monitor kidney function and provide additional intravenous hydration to reduce the risk of amphotericin to the kidneys.

### SIDE EFFECTS

IV amphotericin B has potentially severe side effects, which appear to occur more frequently in people with HIV than in the general population. The major side effects are kidney toxicity and anemia. Other reactions include fever, shaking, chills, altered blood pressure, changes in appetite, nausea, vomiting, and headache, which occur one to three hours after starting an intravenous infusion. These reactions are usually most severe with the first few doses and usually diminish with subsequent treatment.

The serious kidney toxicity caused by IV amphotericin B is most evident when people take the drugs for long periods of time (six to ten weeks or longer). With azole drugs being used more frequently for maintenance therapy, IV

amphotericin B is often used for much shorter periods of time, and severe kidney side effects occur less frequently. However, most people who take IV amphotericin B will experience some side effects, even at less than full dose. The minor side effects can be reduced by taking acetaminophen (Tylenol) and diphenhydramine (Benadryl) one half to one hour before using amphotericin B. Meperidine has been shown in some people to decrease the duration of shaking, chills, and fever that may accompany the infusion of amphotericin B.

### PREGNANCY/BREAST-FEEDING

Although no formal studies have been performed, amphotericin B has been used by a small number of pregnant women without apparent harm to their unborn children. Pregnant women are encouraged to discuss the benefits and potential risks of amphotericin B with their physician before deciding to use the drug.

HIV can be passed from a woman to her child through breast milk. In areas where nutritionally sound alternatives are readily available, breast-feeding is discouraged for HIV-positive women. It is not known whether amphotericin B passes into human milk, but because of the potential toxicity to infants, pregnant women should consider alternatives to breast-feeding while taking it.

### USE IN CHILDREN

Although there have been no formal studies, amphotericin B has been given to a small number of children without unusual side effects. In general, it is advisable to use the lowest effective dose when giving the drug to children.

### USE IN THE ELDERLY

In otherwise healthy older adults with normal kidney function, no dose reduction is recommended. However, kidney function often declines with age, and older people with reduced kidney function may not be able to tolerate full doses of the drug.

### DRUG INTERACTIONS

Anticancer drugs may increase the risk of kidney damage and low blood pressure when given with amphotericin B. When used with amikacin, pentamidine, cyclosporine, or foscarnet, amphotericin B may increase the risk of kidney damage. Similarly, the use of amphotericin B with AZT, flucytosine, or ganciclovir may result in increased risk of bone marrow damage.

Ketoconazole, itraconazole, or fluconazole may interfere with the activity of amphotericin B or cause fungal resistance, potentially reducing the drug's effectiveness. The use of high-dose corticosteroids with amphotericin B may decrease potassium levels and increase the risk of cardiovascular side effects. Flucytosine may increase the toxicity of amphotericin B. Acute pulmonary

toxicity has been reported in people receiving amphotericin B and leukocyte (white blood cell) transfusions.

**FOOD INTERACTIONS**

Oral suspension amphotericin B should be administered between meals. There are no reported food interactions with IV amphotericin B.

**OTHER DRUGS USED FOR SIMILAR CONDITIONS**

IV amphotericin B with or without flucytosine is the treatment of choice for severe cryptococcal infections. As the infection comes under control, usually within two weeks, therapy is often switched to fluconazole. Fluconazole is also used for long-term maintenance therapy to prevent recurrent infection. For less severe cryptococcal infections, fluconazole may be used from the start. Itraconazole is a newer antifungal drug. It does not cross the blood/brain barrier as well as fluconazole, but in small studies it has been as effective in treating cryptococcal infections. Liposomal amphotericin B is an experimental treatment used in clinical trials for cryptococcal infections.

Itraconazole and liposomal amphotericin B are alternatives to standard amphotericin B for the treatment of histoplasmosis. Recent studies have shown that itraconazole is nearly as effective as IV amphotericin B in treating histoplasmosis in people infected with HIV. Those studies, however, often excluded people with very severe disease, people with infections of the central nervous system, and people receiving medications that interfere with the uptake of itraconazole. Fluconazole has been less effective than IV amphotericin B in clinical trials of histoplasmosis, but it can be administered orally and has fewer side effects. The proper role of IV amphotericin B and the azoles (itraconazole or fluconazole) in the treatment of histoplasmosis has yet to be determined.

**COMMENTS**

There is considerable debate whether it is worthwhile to use azoles (or any antifungal drugs) to prevent disease. Fungal infections in AIDS are generally so responsive to treatment that it may not be necessary to continually take drugs to try to prevent them, especially since it adds another, perhaps unnecessary, drug to a person's daily regimen. In addition, prolonged use of azole antifungals may cause the spread of strains resistant to them. For example, fluconazole-resistant candida and cryptococcus have been a growing concern in recent years. Once the drug loses its effectiveness against these fungi, a person may have to rely on the highly toxic IV amphotericin B. Because of this concern many physicians recommend using azole antifungals only for treatment and maintenance, but not for prevention of fungal disease in people with HIV.

# AMPHOTERICIN B
## COLLOIDAL DISPERSION

**BRAND NAME (MANUFACTURER)**
Amphotec (Sequus)

**OTHER NAMES**
ABCD

**TYPE OF DRUG**
Antifungal agent

**USED FOR**
Amphotericin B colloidal dispersion (ABCD) is approved for the treatment of aspergillosis in people who are no longer responding to or are intolerant of intravenous amphotericin B.

For people with HIV, ABCD is also sometimes used to treat cryptococcal meningitis and histoplasmosis.

**GENERAL INFORMATION**
Standard intravenous amphotericin B is an effective, but highly toxic, antifungal drug. The drug works by attacking the cell membranes of fungi. The toxic effects of amphotericin B can include fever, chills, muscle pain, inflammation of veins, vomiting, potassium loss, kidney toxicity, and anemia.

Liposomal forms of amphotericin, such as ABCD and ABLC (amphotericin B Lipid Complex), have been developed to reduce the drug's toxicity. In these forms, the active drug is encapsulated in or attached to tiny fatty bubbles called liposomes. The rationale is that the liposomes may deliver the drug preferentially to diseased organs while keeping levels low in the blood and sensitive organs such as the kidneys.

ABCD is available for intravenous injection.

**TREATMENT**
The usual dose of ABCD is 3 to 4 mg per kg of body weight per day. The dose is usually increased to 6 mg per kg if there is no therapeutic response at the lower dose. ABCD is usually infused at a rate of one mg per kg per hour. People should be closely monitored during the first infusion.

**CAUTIONS AND WARNINGS**
ABCD should not be used by anyone with a known allergy to it. ABCD must be injected slowly to avoid serious side effects, which may include shock, irregular heart rhythms, and altered blood pressure.

People with kidney dysfunction can use ABCD. However, it is recommended that people monitor kidney function while on ABCD.

## SIDE EFFECTS

ABCD has potentially severe side effects. The most common side effects are fever, shaking, chills, altered blood pressure, nausea, vomiting, and headache, which usually occur one to three hours after starting an intravenous infusion. These reactions are usually most severe with the first few doses and usually diminish with subsequent treatment.

Meperidine may be useful in some people to decrease the duration of shaking, chills, and fever that may accompany the infusion of ABCD.

## PREGNANCY/BREAST-FEEDING

No formal studies have been conducted in pregnant women with ABCD. However, IV amphotericin B has been used by a small number of pregnant women without apparent harm to their unborn children. Pregnant women are encouraged to discuss the benefits and potential risks of ABCD with their physician before deciding to use the drug.

HIV can be passed from a woman to her child through breast milk. In areas where nutritionally sound alternatives are readily available, breast-feeding is discouraged for HIV-positive women. It is not known whether ABCD passes into human milk, but because of the potential toxicity to infants, pregnant women should consider alternatives to breast-feeding while taking it.

## USE IN CHILDREN

ABCD has been used in children at the same daily dose as in adults.

## USE IN THE ELDERLY

No dose modifications are necessary.

## DRUG INTERACTIONS

Anticancer drugs may increase the risk of kidney damage and low blood pressure when given with ABCD. When used with amikacin, pentamidine, cyclosporine, flucytosine or foscarnet, ABCD may increase the risk of kidney damage.

Ketoconazole, itraconazole, or fluconazole may interfere with the activity of ABCD or cause fungal resistance, potentially reducing the drug's effectiveness. The use of high-dose corticosteroids with ABCD may decrease potassium levels and increase the risk of cardiovascular side effects.

## FOOD INTERACTIONS

ABCD may be taken with or without food.

## OTHER DRUGS USED FOR SIMILAR CONDITIONS

IV amphotericin B with or without flucytosine is the treatment of choice for severe cryptococcal infections. As the infection comes under control, usually within two weeks, therapy is often switched to fluconazole. Fluconazole is also used for long-term maintenance therapy to prevent recurrent infection. For less severe cryptococcal infections, fluconazole may be used from the start. Itraconazole is a newer antifungal drug. It does not cross the blood/brain barrier

as well as fluconazole, but in small studies it has been as effective in treating cryptococcal infections.

For the treatment of histoplasmosis, itraconazole and IV amphotericin B are alternatives to standard ABCD. Recent studies have shown that itraconazole is nearly as effective as IV amphotericin B in treating histoplasmosis in people infected with HIV. Fluconazole has been less effective than IV amphotericin B in clinical trials of histoplasmosis, but it can be administered orally and has fewer side effects. The proper role of IV amphotericin B and the azoles (itraconazole or fluconazole) in the treatment of histoplasmosis has yet to be determined.

# AMPHOTERICIN B
## LIPID COMPLEX

**BRAND NAME (MANUFACTURER)**
Abelcet (The Liposome Company)

**OTHER NAMES**
ABLC

**TYPE OF DRUG**
Antifungal agent

**USED FOR**
Amphotericin B Lipid Complex (ABLC) is approved for the treatment of invasive fungal infections in people who are no longer responding to or are intolerant of intravenous amphotericin B.

For people with HIV, ABLC is also sometimes used to treat cryptococcal meningitis and histoplasmosis.

**GENERAL INFORMATION**
Standard intravenous amphotericin B is an effective, but highly toxic, antifungal drug. The drug works by attacking the cell membranes of fungi. The toxic effects of amphotericin B can include fever, chills, muscle pain, inflammation of veins, vomiting, potassium loss, kidney toxicity, and anemia.

Liposomal forms of amphotericin, such as ABCD (amphotericin B Colloidal Dispersion) and ABLC, have been developed to reduce the drug's toxicity. In these forms, the active drug is encapsulated in or attached to tiny fatty bubbles called liposomes. The rationale is that the liposomes may deliver the drug preferentially to diseased organs while keeping levels in the blood and sensitive organs such as the kidneys low.

ABLC is available for intravenous injection.

## TREATMENT
The usual dose of ABLC is 5 mg per kg of body weight per day. ABLC is usually infused at a rate of 2.5 mg per kg per hour. People should be closely monitored during the first infusion.

## CAUTIONS AND WARNINGS
ABLC should not be used by anyone with a known allergy to it. ABLC should be injected slowly to avoid serious side effects, which may include shock, irregular heart rhythms, and altered blood pressure.

ABLC is excreted from the body by the kidneys and can cause severe kidney damage. The drug should be used with caution by people with impaired kidney function. Physicians should closely monitor kidney function and provide additional intravenous hydration to reduce the risk of amphotericin to the kidneys.

## SIDE EFFECTS
ABLC has potentially severe side effects. The most common side effects are fever, shaking, chills, altered blood pressure, nausea, vomiting, and headache, which usually occur one to three hours after starting an intravenous infusion. These reactions are usually most severe with the first few doses and usually diminish with subsequent treatment.

Meperidine may be useful in some people to decrease the duration of shaking, chills, and fever that may accompany the infusion of ABLC.

## PREGNANCY/BREAST-FEEDING
No formal studies have been conducted in pregnant women with ABLC. However, IV amphotericin B has been used by a small number of pregnant women without apparent harm to their unborn children. Pregnant women are encouraged to discuss the benefits and potential risks of ABLC with their physician before deciding to use the drug.

HIV can be passed from a woman to her child through breast milk. In areas where nutritionally sound alternatives are readily available, breast-feeding is discouraged for HIV-positive women. It is not known whether ABLC passes into human milk, but because of the potential toxicity to infants, pregnant women should consider alternatives to breast-feeding while taking it.

## USE IN CHILDREN
ABLC has been successfully used to treat children under 16 years of age. The usual dose of ABLC for children is 5 mg per kg of body weight daily.

## USE IN THE ELDERLY
No dose modifications are necessary.

**DRUG INTERACTIONS**

Anticancer drugs may increase the risk of kidney damage and low blood pressure when given with ABLC. When used with amikacin, pentamidine, cyclosporine, flucytosine or foscarnet, ABLC may increase the risk of kidney damage.

Ketoconazole, itraconazole, or fluconazole may interfere with the activity of ABLC or cause fungal resistance, potentially reducing the drug's effectiveness. The use of high-dose corticosteroids with ABLC may decrease potassium levels and increase the risk of cardiovascular side effects.

**FOOD INTERACTIONS**

ABLC may be taken with or without food.

**OTHER DRUGS USED FOR SIMILAR CONDITIONS**

IV amphotericin B with or without flucytosine is the treatment of choice for severe cryptococcal infections. As the infection comes under control, usually within two weeks, therapy is often switched to fluconazole. Fluconazole is also used for long-term maintenance therapy to prevent recurrent infection. For less severe cryptococcal infections, fluconazole may be used from the start. Itraconazole is a newer antifungal drug. It does not cross the blood/brain barrier as well as fluconazole, but in small studies it has been as effective in treating cryptococcal infections.

For the treatment of histoplasmosis, itraconazole and IV amphotericin B are alternatives to standard ABLC. Recent studies have shown that itraconazole is nearly as effective as IV amphotericin B in treating histoplasmosis in people infected with HIV. Fluconazole has been less effective than IV amphotericin B in clinical trials of histoplasmosis, but it can be administered orally and has fewer side effects. The proper role of IV amphotericin B and the azoles (itraconazole or fluconazole) in the treatment of histoplasmosis has yet to be determined.

# CLOTRIMAZOLE

**BRAND NAME (MANUFACTURER)**

Lotrimin (Schering); Mycelex (Bayer)

**TYPE OF DRUG**

Antifungal agent

**USED FOR**

Clotrimazole is used to treat mild fungal infections of the mouth, skin, and vagina. In people with HIV, it is usually used to treat infections caused by Candida albicans.

## GENERAL INFORMATION

Clotrimazole is a broad-spectrum antifungal agent of the azole class. It is available by prescription and sold in less-concentrated forms over the counter in drugstores. Lotions, creams, solutions, vaginal tablets, and troches (lozenges) are the various forms of clotrimazole. The drug works locally by penetrating into the affected area and preventing multiplication of the fungus. It has no systemic action. Using clotrimazole on one area of the body will have no effect on fungal infections elsewhere in the body.

## TREATMENT

The topical cream or solution should be massaged into the affected area in the morning and evening. If the infection does not improve within a week, it may not be caused by Candida.

The vaginal cream should be used once daily with the applicator for seven to fourteen days. If the vaginal tablet is used instead, the recommended dose is one tablet at bedtime for seven days or two tablets inserted each day for three days.

The troche is routinely taken five times per day for two weeks or more for the treatment of candidiasis in the mouth or esophagus. It should be allowed to dissolve in the mouth, not swallowed or chewed.

## CAUTIONS AND WARNINGS

Clotrimazole should not be used by anyone with a known allergy to it. If itching, rashes, or other allergic reactions develop, the drug should be stopped. As with all antibiotics, the drug should be used for the entire time prescribed even though the symptoms may have disappeared. Inform the physician if the area of application shows increased irritation.

## SIDE EFFECTS

Clotrimazole has relatively few side effects. The most common involve irritation of the skin, including redness, stinging, blistering, peeling, swelling, itching, and burning.

## PREGNANCY/BREAST-FEEDING

Topical use of clotrimazole has not been associated with harm to the fetus in women who used the drug during their second and third trimesters. It has not been studied in pregnant women during the first trimester. Pregnant women are encouraged to discuss the benefits and potential risks of clotrimazole with their physician before deciding to use the drug.

HIV can be passed from a woman to her child through breast milk. In areas where nutritionally sound alternatives are readily available, breast-feeding is discouraged for HIV-positive women. Clotrimazole is unlikely to cause harm to the breast-fed infants of nursing mothers who use it.

**USE IN CHILDREN**

Clotrimazole is safe and effective in children when used topically at the recommended doses.

**USE IN THE ELDERLY**

No changes in dose or administration are necessary for elderly people.

**DRUG INTERACTIONS**

None reported.

**FOOD INTERACTIONS**

Food does not affect the topical administration of clotrimazole.

**OTHER DRUGS USED FOR SIMILAR CONDITIONS**

For candida infections, a number of other topical and systemic antifungal agents are available. Minor or localized infections may be effectively treated with topical medications such as nystatin or miconazole. Mild-to-moderate infections may require a systemic azole such as fluconazole, ketoconazole, or itraconazole. In a comparative study of oral candida infections in 334 HIV-positive volunteers, systemic fluconazole was more effective than clotrimazole in eradicating the fungus. In addition, volunteers who took fluconazole were more likely to remain disease-free through the second week of follow-up. When choosing a treatment for candida infections, the improved efficacy of the systemic agents should be weighed against the increased risk of systemic side effects.

# F L U C O N A Z O L E

**BRAND NAME (MANUFACTURER)**

Diflucan (Roerig/Pfizer)

**TYPE OF DRUG**

Antifungal agent

**USED FOR**

Fluconazole has been approved and is used in people with HIV for the treatment of cryptococcal meningitis, candidal infections of the esophagus, mouth, and throat (thrush), and vaginal candidiasis.

In people with HIV, fluconazole is also used, but not approved, to treat histoplasmosis and to prevent candidiasis, cryptococcosis, and histoplasmosis. It is also being studied for the treatment of coccidioidomycosis.

**GENERAL INFORMATION**

Fluconazole is a systemic antifungal drug that circulates through the blood, so it is useful for fungal infections that can't be treated with topical creams or lotions. Fluconazole works by selectively interfering with the metabolism of the fungus, preventing it from building its cell walls.

Fluconazole is provided both as tablets and solution for intravenous injection. Since oral administration is rapid and effective, most people will be able to take the tablets. The intravenous solution is generally used by people who have difficulty absorbing the drug.

Fluconazole is used three ways: to treat initial fungal infections, to maintain or suppress fungi so that symptoms don't return, and to prevent initial infection.

### TREATMENT OF ACUTE INFECTION

Several different doses of fluconazole are being studied for the treatment of active infections. A commonly used dosage for treatment of mouth or throat candidiasis is 200 mg on the first day, followed by 100 mg once daily. For systemic candidiasis, a dosage of 400 mg on the first day, followed by 200 mg once daily, is often used. Treatment is continued for a minimum of four weeks and for at least two weeks after symptoms disappear.

A commonly used dosage for treatment of cryptococcal meningitis is 400 mg on the first day, followed by 200 mg once daily. If the lower dose is not effective, 400 to 800 mg daily may be used. The recommended duration of treatment for cryptococcal meningitis is ten to twelve weeks after the cerebrospinal fluid culture becomes negative. In HIV infection, however, it is recommended that all people who have undergone initial treatment for cryptococcal meningitis be placed on maintenance therapy for life to prevent recurrence of the disease.

### MAINTENANCE

Fluconazole can be used at 50 to 200 mg per day to prevent recurrence of candidiasis. For maintenance of cryptococcal meningitis, a number of doses are being studied, including 200 mg three times a week and 400 mg three times a week.

### PREVENTION

Fluconazole is relatively safe and is often recommended to prevent initial fungal infection in people whose CD4+ counts have dropped below 50. A number of different dosages of fluconazole are currently being studied for the prevention of fungal infection, although there is no formal consensus on the best prophylactic dose.

One dosage used for prevention of relapse of cryptococcal meningitis in people with AIDS is 200 mg once daily. For prevention of candidiasis, 100 to 200 mg once daily is sometimes used.

### CAUTIONS AND WARNINGS

Fluconazole should not be used by anyone with a known allergy to it. It is not known whether people who are allergic to other azole antifungal agents will be allergic to fluconazole, so caution should be used when taking flu-

conazole by people who have had an allergic reaction to clotrimazole, keto-conazole, itraconazole, or other azole compounds.

People who develop a skin rash during therapy should notify their physi-cians. The rash may be an indication that the person is developing exfolia-tive skin disorder, a potentially fatal skin disease.

## SIDE EFFECTS

Sixteen percent of people treated with fluconazole in clinical trials experi-enced side effects. These side effects were reported more frequently in people infected with HIV. The most common side effects were nausea, headache, skin rash, vomiting, abdominal pain, and diarrhea.

## PREGNANCY/BREAST-FEEDING

There have been no well-controlled studies of fluconazole in pregnant women. In animal testing, embryo death and birth defects were observed in rats whose mothers were given high doses of fluconazole, but it is not known whether the same would be true in humans. Pregnant women are encouraged to dis-cuss the benefits and potential risks of fluconazole with their physician be-fore deciding to use the drug.

HIV can be passed from a woman to her child through breast milk. In ar-eas where nutritionally sound alternatives are readily available, breast-feed-ing is discouraged for HIV-positive women. Fluconazole is also excreted in breast milk and may cause serious side effects in infants. Because of the po-tential toxicity of the drug, women should consider alternatives to breast-feeding while taking it.

## USE IN CHILDREN

Fluconazole has been approved by the FDA for treatment of systemic candidal infections of the mouth, throat, and esophagus in children. The recommended dose for children three to thirteen years of age is 2 to 8 mg per kg of body weight daily.

## USE IN THE ELDERLY

Older adults may be more susceptible to the side effects of fluconazole and may require reduced doses.

## DRUG INTERACTIONS

Cimetidine, ranitidine, and rifampin may decrease fluconazole levels and reduce its effectiveness. Hydrochlorothiazide may increase fluconazole levels. Flu-conazole may increase the levels of atovaquone, AZT, cyclosporine, and phenytoin, potentially increasing the risk of side effects from these drugs.

Fluconazole (at doses of 400 mg a day or higher) should not be taken with astemizole or terfenadine because of possible increased risks of serious heart disease. People that must take fluconazole with astemizole or cisapride should be carefully monitored for possible cardiac toxicity. Fluconazole intensifies

the blood-thinning effect of warfarin. When used together, the warfarin dose may need to be adjusted.

Fluconazole increases the levels of rifabutin in the body, which may increase the risk of inflammation of the eye.

Fluconazole may decrease the effectiveness of oral contraceptives. Fluconazole used in combination with sulfonylurea oral hypoglycemic drugs may increase the risk of low blood sugar levels.

**FOOD INTERACTIONS**
None reported.

**OTHER DRUGS USED FOR SIMILAR CONDITIONS**
Fluconazole is the treatment of choice for active esophageal candidiasis, mild cases of cryptococcal meningitis, and maintenance of cryptococcal meningitis. For severe cases of cryptococcal meningitis, amphotericin B with or without flucytosine is often used initially, followed by fluconazole. Nystatin, clotrimazole, itraconazole, and ketoconazole are other therapies used for candidiasis. Fluconazole is recommended as secondary treatment for histoplasmosis after itraconazole or amphotericin B.

In general, fungal disease that is resistant to fluconazole will also be resistant to the other oral azoles, including ketoconazole and itraconazole. In these cases, amphotericin B may be the only effective alternative.

**COMMENTS**
For decades, standard therapy for serious fungal disease has been amphotericin B. However, it is potentially toxic and must be given intravenously. Fluconazole is a member of a relatively new class of antifungal drugs called azole compounds. These drugs are less toxic than amphotericin B and can be administered orally. Fluconazole is effective against fewer fungal pathogens than amphotericin B, but it is significantly less toxic and can penetrate into spinal fluid where the fungi that cause meningitis multiply.

There is considerable debate whether it is worthwhile to use fluconazole (or any antifungal drug) to prevent disease. Fluconazole clearly works for this purpose, but it is cost prohibitive for many people and may not be cost-effective for anyone. Fungal infections in AIDS are generally so responsive to treatment that it may not be necessary to take drugs to try to prevent them, especially since it adds another, perhaps unnecessary and certainly expensive, drug to a person's daily regimen. In addition, prolonged use of fluconazole may cause the spread of strains resistant to the drug. Because of this concern and the risk of azole-related drug interactions, many physicians recommend azole antifungals only for treatment and maintenance, but not for prevention of fungal disease in people with HIV. Other physicians, however, argue that the sporadic, on/off use of such drugs for frequently recurring fun-

gal infections may itself lead more quickly to drug resistance than using the drugs preventively. Until a definitive clinical trial is conducted, the choice between these two points of view will largely be a matter of opinion.

# FLUCYTOSINE

**BRAND NAME (MANUFACTURER)**
Ancobon (Roche)

**OTHER NAMES**
5-FC; 5-fluorocytosine

**TYPE OF DRUG**
Antifungal agent

**USED FOR**
Flucytosine is used to treat serious, blood-borne fungal infections caused by Candida and Cryptococcus.

In people infected with HIV, flucytosine is also used in combination with amphotericin B or fluconazole for the treatment of serious cryptococcal meningitis.

**GENERAL INFORMATION**
Flucytosine is an antifungal agent thought to work by inhibiting DNA and RNA synthesis in fungal cells. The result is unbalanced growth that causes the death of the fungus. The drug readily penetrates the blood-brain barrier and is an effective treatment for infections of the central nervous system. Flucytosine is available as 250- and 500 mg capsules for oral administration.

For treatment of cryptococcal meningitis, flucytosine is often combined with amphotericin B, because test-tube studies show the two to have a synergistic effect against Cryptococcus. Studies in people have had mixed results, but the combination may be superior in effectiveness to amphotericin B alone. Steroids may be added to the combination for people with high cranial pressure (pressure inside the skull).

**TREATMENT**
The usual dose of flucytosine when used in combination with amphotericin B is 75 mg per kg of body weight per day, taken in four equal doses at six-hour intervals. Nausea and vomiting may be reduced or avoided if the capsules are taken a few at a time over a fifteen-minute period. In cases of reduced kidney function, the dose may need to be lowered.

After treatment of acute infection, some type of maintenance therapy must be used for life to prevent the recurrence of cryptococcal disease. Amphotericin B is used occasionally as maintenance therapy, but fluconazole is gener-

ally the drug of choice because it is effective, has fewer side effects, and can be taken orally.

## CAUTIONS AND WARNINGS

Flucytosine should not be used by anyone with a known allergy to it. The drug should be used with extreme caution in people with reduced kidney function, because of the increased risk of serious side effects. Similarly, the drug should be used with caution by people with bone marrow suppression.

Before people take flucytosine, their doctors will almost certainly check their blood cell counts, levels of electrolytes, and kidney function.

## SIDE EFFECTS

The most common side effects of flucytosine are weakness, malaise, inflammation of the liver, yellowing of the eyes or skin, abdominal pain, diarrhea, loss of appetite, nausea, vomiting, skin rashes, redness, itching, sore throat, bruising, or unusual bleeding.

Less common side effects include heart attack, difficulty breathing, chest pain, sensitivity to the sun, dry mouth, liver damage, development of ulcers, hearing loss, headache, vertigo, sleepiness, confusion, hallucination, fever, and bone marrow toxicity. In HIV infection, especially in individuals taking other drugs toxic to bone marrow (AZT, ganciclovir, etc.), flucytosine can be particularly problematic.

## PREGNANCY/BREAST-FEEDING

Flucytosine has not been formally studied in pregnant women. In animal studies, it caused fetal tumors when given at approximately one-quarter of the human dose, but it is not known whether the drug would cause similar tumors in humans. Pregnant women are encouraged to discuss the benefits and potential risks of flucytosine with their physician before deciding to use the drug.

HIV can be passed from a woman to her child through breast milk. In areas where nutritionally sound alternatives are readily available, breast-feeding is discouraged for HIV-positive women. It is not known whether flucytosine is excreted in human milk. Because of the drug's potential toxicity, women are encouraged to consider alternatives to breast-feeding while using it.

## USE IN CHILDREN

Little information is available regarding the use of flucytosine for candidal or cryptococcal infections in HIV-positive children. In one survey of thirty-eight hospitals in the United States, pediatricians reported that amphotericin B with or without flucytosine was an effective treatment for severe cryptococcal infections in children. For treatment of candidal infections or less severe cryptococcal infections, many physicians recommend fluconazole because it is less toxic than amphotericin B and is approved by the FDA specifically for use in children.

**USE IN THE ELDERLY**
Older adults may be more susceptible to the side effects of the drug and may require reduced doses.

**DRUG INTERACTIONS**
Cytarabine may reduce the effectiveness of flucytosine. Combinations of flucytosine and amphotericin B, ganciclovir, or alpha interferon may increase the risk of bone marrow toxicity. To be effective, flucytosine should be used two hours before or after taking antacids; otherwise flucytosine will have no effect.

**FOOD INTERACTIONS**
Flucytosine may be taken with food if it causes stomach upset.

**OTHER DRUGS USED FOR SIMILAR CONDITIONS**
Amphotericin B with or without flucytosine is the treatment of choice for severe cryptococcal infections. As the infection comes under control, therapy is often switched to fluconazole. Fluconazole is also used for long-term maintenance therapy to prevent recurrent infection. For less severe cryptococcal infections, fluconazole may be used from the start. Itraconazole is an antifungal drug that does not enter the cerebrospinal fluid as well as fluconazole, but in small studies it has been as effective as fluconazole in treating cryptococcal infections. Liposomal amphotericin B is a new treatment used to treat cryptococcal infections.

# I T R A C O N A Z O L E

**BRAND NAME (MANUFACTURER)**
Sporanox (Janssen)

**TYPE OF DRUG**
Antifungal agent

**USED FOR**
Itraconazole is approved and used by people with HIV for the treatment of blastomycosis, histoplasmosis, aspergillosis, onychomycosis (toenail fungus) and oral and esophageal candida (thrush), all of which are infections due to various fungi. It is also being tested as a treatment for cryptococcal meningitis in people with HIV.

**GENERAL INFORMATION**
Itraconazole is a broad-spectrum antifungal drug. It is available as an oral solution and as capsules for oral administration. The oral solution is used for thrush and the oral capsule is generally used for systemic infections. Itra-

conazole works by interfering with the metabolism of the fungus, preventing it from building its cell walls.

## TREATMENT

The normal dose of itraconazole in capsules is 100 to 200 mg taken twice per day. If the infection is life threatening, a total dose of 600 mg may be used the first day, followed by the lower dose thereafter. Itraconazole is often used after clearing of infection at a maintenance dose of 400 mg a day to prevent recurrence of histoplasmosis and 200 mg a day to prevent recurrence of cryptococcal infections. Dose reductions may be necessary in people with reduced liver function. The normal dose of itraconazole oral solution is 100-200 mg once a day.

## CAUTIONS AND WARNINGS

Itraconazole should not be used by anyone with a known allergy to it. People allergic to other azole antifungal drugs (fluconazole, ketoconazole, etc.) may also be allergic to itraconazole.

## SIDE EFFECTS

In clinical trials, nausea and vomiting occurred in 5% to 10% of people who took itraconazole. Rashes occurred in 8% of people taking the drug, more frequently in those infected with HIV. Swelling, itching, fever, headache, diarrhea, and high blood pressure were reported by 2.5% to 5%. Between 1% and 2% reported fatigue, malaise, dizziness, sleepiness, changes in sex drive, or impotence.

## PREGNANCY/BREAST-FEEDING

Itraconazole has not been formally studied in pregnant women. In animal studies, it caused birth defects, but it is not known whether this would be true for humans. Pregnant women are encouraged to discuss the benefits and potential risks of itraconazole with their physician before deciding to use the drug.

HIV can be passed from a woman to her child through breast milk. In areas where nutritionally sound alternatives are readily available, breast-feeding is discouraged for HIV-positive women. Itraconazole is excreted in human milk. Because of the potential toxicity of the drug to newborns, women are encouraged to consider alternatives to breast-feeding while using it.

## USE IN CHILDREN

Itraconazole has not been formally studied in children. A small number of children from three to sixteen years of age have been treated at 100 mg per day without reported serious side effects. In animal studies, the drug caused bone defects in young animals. The long-term effect in children is unknown.

## USE IN THE ELDERLY

Older adults may be more susceptible to the side effects of the drug and may require reduced doses.

**DRUG INTERACTIONS**

Itraconazole should not be used in combination with terfenadine, astemizole, cisapride, triazolam, midazolam, lovastatin, or simvastatin because of the risk of potentially fatal side effects.

Itraconazole may lead to increased blood levels of cyclosporine, digitalis, rifabutin, or phenytoin, potentially increasing the risk of their side effects.

Phenytoin, rifampin, cimetidine, isoniazid, and amphotericin B may lower blood levels of itraconazole, potentially interfering with its activity.

Itraconazole may enhance the anticoagulant effect of warfarin-like drugs.

Severe low blood sugar has been reported in people receiving azole anti-fungal agents like itraconazole and oral sulfonylurea hypoglycemic drugs.

Ritonavir can significantly increase itraconazole blood levels. In addition, itraconazole can increase levels of saquinavir in the blood. Combinations of itraconazole with indinavir, delavirdine, or nevirapine may affect the levels of all these drugs in the blood.

**FOOD INTERACTIONS**

Itraconazole should be taken with food.

**OTHER DRUGS USED FOR SIMILAR CONDITIONS**

For the treatment of histoplasmosis, alternatives to itraconazole are flucona-zole and amphotericin B. Amphotericin B has been the treatment of choice for many years, but recent studies have shown itraconazole is nearly as ef-fective in treating histoplasmosis in people infected with HIV. In addition, itraconazole has been shown to be more effective than fluconazole in treat-ing histoplasmosis.

Amphotericin B with or without flucytosine is the treatment of choice for severe cryptococcal infections. As the infection is controlled, therapy is often switched to fluconazole. Fluconazole is also used for long-term maintenance therapy to prevent recurrent infection. For less severe cryptococcal infections, fluconazole may be used initially. Itraconazole is an antifungal drug that does not enter the cerebrospinal fluid as well as fluconazole, but in small studies it has been as effective in treating cryptococcal infections. Liposomal am-photericin B is an experimental treatment used in clinical trials for the treat-ment of cryptococcal infections.

Amphotericin B is the treatment of choice for blastomycosis in people in-fected with HIV. Fluconazole and itraconazole are effective alternatives for people with mild-to-moderate disease.

**COMMENTS**

There is considerable debate whether it is worthwhile to use azoles (or any antifungal drugs) to prevent disease. Fungal infections in AIDS are generally so responsive to treatment that it may not be necessary to continually take

drugs to try to prevent them, especially since it adds another, perhaps unnecessary, drug to a person's daily regimen. In addition, prolonged use of azole antifungals may cause the spread of strains resistant to them. For example, fluconazole-resistant candida and cryptococcus have been a growing concern in recent years. If the drug loses its effectiveness against these fungi, it will not be useful to treat active infection should it occur, and a person may have to rely on the highly toxic amphotericin B. Consequently, many physicians recommend azole antifungals for treatment and maintenance, but not for prevention of fungal disease in people with HIV. However, in a small study of people with fluconazole-resistant thrush, 55% of people receiving itraconazole oral solution had complete resolution of their lesions.

# KETOCONAZOLE

**BRAND NAME (MANUFACTURER)**
Nizoral (Janssen)

**TYPE OF DRUG**
Antifungal agent

**USED FOR**
Ketoconazole is used to treat fungal infections, including candidiasis, blastomycosis, and histoplasmosis.

For people infected with HIV, ketoconazole is used primarily to treat oral thrush and vaginal yeast infections caused by Candida.

**GENERAL INFORMATION**
Ketoconazole is a triazole antifungal drug. It works by selectively interfering with the metabolism of susceptible fungi, preventing them from building their cell walls.

Only a small percentage of ketoconazole taken orally passes through the blood-brain barrier. Consequently, the drug is not useful for fungal infections of the brain, such as cryptococcal meningitis.

Ketoconazole is available in 200 mg tablets, 2% cream, and 2% shampoo. The shampoo and topical cream are used to treat localized infections. The oral drug is used to fight fungal infections that are more severe or widespread in the body.

**TREATMENT**
The recommended dose of ketoconazole is generally 200 mg once a day. In serious infections, the dose may be increased to 400 mg once a day. In a small number of children, a single daily dose of 3.3 to 7 mg per kg of body weight has been used effectively.

The minimum duration of treatment for candidal infections is one or two weeks. People with chronic candidal infections may require long-term maintenance therapy to prevent recurrence of symptoms. In clinical trials, ketoconazole at a dose of 200 mg per day has proven effective in preventing recurrence of candidal infections in HIV-positive volunteers.

## CAUTIONS AND WARNINGS

Ketoconazole should not be used by anyone with a known allergy to it. It should also not be used in combination with terfenadine or astemizole, because of the potential for serious and potentially fatal drug interactions.

## SIDE EFFECTS

The most common side effects of ketoconazole are nausea, vomiting, abdominal pain, and itching. Less frequently, headache, dizziness, sleepiness, fever and chills, fear of light, diarrhea, impotence, and reduced blood cell or platelet counts may occur. Rarely, ketoconazole has caused severe liver damage, anaphylactic shock, suicidal tendencies, and severe depression.

## PREGNANCY/BREAST-FEEDING

Ketoconazole has not been formally studied in pregnant women. In animal studies, it caused birth defects, but it is not known whether this would be true for humans. Pregnant women are encouraged to discuss the benefits and potential risks of ketoconazole with their physician before deciding to use the drug.

HIV can be passed from a woman to her child through breast milk. In areas where nutritionally sound alternatives are readily available, breast-feeding is discouraged for HIV-positive women. When taken orally, ketoconazole may be excreted in human milk. Because of the potential toxicity of the drug to newborns, women are encouraged to consider alternatives to breast-feeding while using it. It is unlikely that ketoconazole used topically by nursing women would cause side effects in their newborns.

## USE IN CHILDREN

Ketoconazole has not been studied formally in children under two years of age. In older children, the drug has been used in dosages ranging from 3.3 to 7.0 mg per kg of body weight per day. In a clinical trial comparing ketoconazole and fluconazole for the treatment of oral thrush in children with HIV, each drug was effective in suppressing the infection in about 80% to 90% of the participants. After treatment was stopped, the infection returned in a large percentage of the children, regardless of which drug they used initially.

## USE IN THE ELDERLY

Elderly people may take this drug without special restrictions.

**DRUG INTERACTIONS**
Ketaconazole increases indinavir levels in the blood by 68%, nelfinavir levels by 35%, and saquinavir levels by 3-fold. Ritonavir may increase levels of ketaconazole in the blood. In addition, ketaconazole increases delavirdine levels by 50% and may affect nevirapine levels as well.

Ketoconazole increases terfenadine and astemizole concentrations in the blood and has resulted in serious and sometimes fatal heart damage. Ketoconazole may also increase the blood levels of cyclosporine, prednisone, and methylprednisolone, potentially increasing the risk of side effects from these drugs.

Phenytoin, rifampin, and isoniazid may reduce the blood concentration of ketoconazole, potentially reducing its antifungal effectiveness.

Ketoconazole may enhance the anticoagulant effect of warfarin-like drugs and cause severe low blood sugar when taken with sulfonylurea oral hypoglycemic drugs. Alcohol may increase the risk of nausea, vomiting, and low blood pressure when taken with ketoconazole.

Ketoconazole tablets require an acidic stomach in order to properly dissolve. Antacids, cimetidine, ddI, and ranitidine should be taken either two hours before or after ketoconazole to ensure adequate drug levels. Drinking a carbonated cola while taking ketoconazole may increase drug absorption.

**FOOD INTERACTIONS**
Ketoconazole is absorbed most effectively into the body when taken with food.

**OTHER DRUGS USED FOR SIMILAR CONDITIONS**
For candidal infections, a number of other topical and systemic antifungal agents are available. Minor or localized infections may be effectively treated with topical medications such as nystatin, miconazole, or clotrimazole. More severe or widespread infections may require a systemic azole such as fluconazole, ketoconazole, or itraconazole. Clinical trials suggest that fluconazole may be slightly more effective than ketoconazole at treating candidal infections, but it is also significantly more expensive.

# METRONIDAZOLE

**BRAND NAME (MANUFACTURER)**
Femazole (Major); Flagyl (Searle); Metezol (Glenwood); MetroGel (Galderma); Protostat (Ortho); Satric (Savage)

**TYPE OF DRUG**
Antibiotic/antiprotozoal/antifungal agent

**USED FOR**

Metronidazole is used to treat acute amoebic dysentery, infections of the vagina, bone, brain, nervous system, gums, urinary tract, abdomen, and skin. The drug may also be used to treat pneumonia and inflammation of the colon. In people with HIV, the drug is also being tested as a treatment for microsporidiosis.

**GENERAL INFORMATION**

Metronidazole is a broad-spectrum antibiotic used to treat a number of bacterial, amoebic, fungal, and protozoal infections. The drug interferes with the DNA in susceptible organisms, preventing them from multiplying.

It is available as tablets, a solution for intravenous injection, and as a gel for topical use.

**TREATMENT**

The dosing schedule for metronidazole varies depending on the infection and the formulation of the drug used. For treatment of serious anaerobic infections (including gynecological infections), the intravenous form of the drug is usually used first. For adults, an initial dose of 15 mg per kg of body weight is recommended, followed by maintenance doses of 7.5 mg per kg of body weight every six hours. After the infection has been controlled, therapy may be switched to oral tablets, at a recommended dose of 7.5 mg per kg of body weight, taken every six hours, not to exceed 4 g during any twenty-four-hour period.

For vaginal infections, the drug may be used as a gel that is administered into the vagina with an applicator. The recommended dose is one applicator-full (approximately 37.5 mg of active drug) twice daily for five days.

For infectious lesions on the skin caused by susceptible microorganisms, the drug may be used as a topical gel, applied in a thin film twice daily to the entire affected area. The area to be treated should be thoroughly washed before application.

**CAUTIONS AND WARNINGS**

Metronidazole should not be used by anyone with a known allergy to it. People with central nervous system diseases should use the drug with caution because of the risk of convulsions or peripheral neuropathy, a condition characterized by numbness, tingling, or pain in the extremities.

People with severe impairment of liver function may accumulate metronidazole and its metabolites in their bodies, possibly necessitating dose reductions.

Alcohol should be avoided while using metronidazole and for one day after stopping it because of the potential for serious drug interactions (see below).

## SIDE EFFECTS

The most serious side effects of metronidazole are convulsions and peripheral neuropathy. The most common side effect is nausea, which occurs in roughly 10% of people using the drug. Nausea may be accompanied by headache, loss of appetite, vomiting, diarrhea, heartburn, constipation, or cramping.

Other side effects reported less frequently include metallic taste, reversible bone marrow toxicity, dizziness, vertigo, loss of coordination, confusion, irritability, depression, insomnia, allergic reactions, dry mouth, fever, incontinence, darkened urine, and infection by Candida.

## PREGNANCY/BREAST-FEEDING

Metronidazole has not been formally studied in pregnant women. The drug crosses the placenta and freely enters fetal circulation. In animal studies, the drug caused fetal toxicity when administered by injection but not when administered orally. It is not known whether the same would be true in humans. Pregnant women are encouraged to discuss the benefits and potential risks of metronidazole with their physician before deciding to use the drug.

HIV may be passed from a woman to her child through breast milk. In areas where nutritionally sound alternatives are readily available, breast-feeding is discouraged for HIV-positive women. Metronidazole is excreted in human milk. Because of the potential toxicity of the drug, women are encouraged to consider alternatives to breast-feeding while using it.

## USE IN CHILDREN

Metronidazole has been used in children for the treatment of amoebic dysentery without unexpected side effects at dosages adjusted for weight. The drug has not been studied or widely used for other types of infections in children.

## USE IN THE ELDERLY

Older adults may be more susceptible to the side effects of the drug and may require reduced doses.

## DRUG INTERACTIONS

Metronidazole may intensify the effect of blood thinners such as warfarin, possibly requiring adjustment of the blood-thinner dose.

Phenytoin or phenobarbital may reduce blood levels of metronidazole, possibly reducing the drug's effectiveness. Metronidazole may increase blood levels of phenytoin or lithium, potentially increasing the risk of their side effects. Cimetidine may increase metronidazole blood levels.

Alcohol used in combination with metronidazole may cause severe abdominal cramps, nausea, vomiting, headaches, and flushing.

Psychotic reactions have been reported in alcoholics using metronidazole and disulfiram in combination. Metronidazole should not be used within two weeks of using disulfiram.

Although specific drug interaction studies have not been performed, it is reasonable to assume that metronidazole may increase the risk of peripheral neuropathy in people taking other neuropathy-inducing drugs (such as ddI, ddC or d4T).

**FOOD INTERACTIONS**
Oral metronidazole may be taken with food to avoid stomach upset.

**OTHER DRUGS USED FOR SIMILAR CONDITIONS**
For treatment of bacterial infections, metronidazole is generally reserved for use when other less toxic alternatives, such as the penicillins or cephalosporins, are not effective. For treatment of microsporidiosis, there is no standard treatment. Albendazole is another drug being tested for the condition in people with HIV.

# MICONAZOLE

**BRAND NAME (MANUFACTURER)**
Monistat (Ortho)

**TYPE OF DRUG**
Antifungal agent

**USED FOR**
Miconazole is used by people with HIV for treatment of fungal infections of the vagina and skin, primarily those caused by Candida. An intravenous form of the drug is sometimes used in hospitals for fungal infections of the blood.

**GENERAL INFORMATION**
Miconazole is a topical antifungal drug available in prescription and non-prescription strengths. Miconazole powder or cream is applied directly to the skin to treat common infections including athlete's foot, ringworm, or jock itch. Miconazole cream or suppositories are used to treat candidal infections of the vagina.

**TREATMENT**
The usual amount of the cream for vaginal use is one applicator-full used at bedtime for three to seven days. The topical creams or powders are applied to the affected area twice a day for up to a month.

**CAUTIONS AND WARNINGS**
Miconazole should not be used by anyone with a known allergy to it. The cream or suppositories may interact with the latex in condoms or diaphragms, potentially weakening their structure and protective value.

If a rash or other sign of allergic reaction occurs during treatment, the drug should be stopped. If the infection has not cleared within seven days of treat-

ment, the fungus may be resistant to miconazole, and other therapies should be considered.

## SIDE EFFECTS

When used vaginally, miconazole may cause burning, itching, cramping, or irritation. In clinical trials these side effects were observed in about 2% of women taking the drug. Other less common side effects included headache, hives, and skin rash.

## PREGNANCY/BREAST-FEEDING

Miconazole can be absorbed into the body in small amounts when used vaginally. Because of the potential harm of the drug to the fetus, the drug is not recommended for use during the first trimester of pregnancy, although no birth defects were noted in 514 pregnant women who used the drug in clinical trials. Pregnant women are encouraged to discuss the benefits and potential risks of miconazole with their physician before deciding to use the drug.

HIV can be passed from a woman to her child through breast milk. In areas where nutritionally sound alternatives are readily available, breast-feeding is discouraged for HIV-positive women. When used topically, miconazole enters the bloodstream in only small amounts, so the drug is unlikely to cause side effects in breast-fed infants of nursing mothers.

## USE IN CHILDREN

Miconazole is generally considered safe and effective for children when used topically.

## USE IN THE ELDERLY

No alterations in dosage or administration are necessary for elderly people.

## DRUG INTERACTIONS

None reported.

## FOOD INTERACTIONS

None reported.

## OTHER DRUGS USED FOR SIMILAR CONDITIONS

For candida infections, a number of other topical and systemic antifungal agents are available. Minor or localized infections may be effectively treated with other topical medications such as nystatin or clotrimazole. More severe or widespread infections may require a systemic drug such as fluconazole, ketoconazole, or itraconazole.

# NYSTATIN

## BRAND NAME (MANUFACTURER)

Mycostatin (Bristol-Myers Squibb Oncology); Pedi-Dri (Pedinol)

**TYPE OF DRUG**
Antifungal agent

**USED FOR**
Nystatin is used by people with HIV for the topical treatment of fungal infections, especially candida infections of the mouth (thrush) and vagina.

In test-tube studies, very high doses of nystatin have been effective in slowing HIV multiplication in cells. Clinical trials of the safety and effectiveness of intravenous nystatin as a treatment for HIV infection are under way.

**GENERAL INFORMATION**
Nystatin is a broad-spectrum antifungal drug that works by interfering with the ability of fungi to build their cell walls. It is available as cream and ointment for topical application, vaginal troches, oral tablets designed to be dissolved in the mouth, and as a solution for intravenous administration. An extended-release formulation and a formulation in which the drug is enclosed within fatty particles called liposomes are currently under development.

**TREATMENT**
For vaginal candida infections, one vaginal troche should be inserted daily for fourteen days. For candida infections in the mouth, one to two oral tablets should be dissolved in the mouth per day for as long as fourteen days. Treatment should continue for forty-eight hours after symptoms disappear. The oral tablets should not be chewed or swallowed. The oral suspension should be swished around the mouth and then swallowed.

**CAUTIONS AND WARNINGS**
Nystatin should not be used by anyone with a known allergy to it. If a rash or other sign of allergic reaction occurs during treatment, the drug should be stopped.

**SIDE EFFECTS**
Nystatin rarely causes side effects. Nausea or irritation of the mouth or vagina are occasionally reported. Large oral doses may cause diarrhea, stomach upset, vomiting, or rashes.

**PREGNANCY/BREAST-FEEDING**
Nystatin has not been formally studied in pregnant women. When used topically, nystatin enters the bloodstream in only small amounts, and fetal harm is unlikely. An increase in birth defects was found in one study where a combination of nystatin and tetracycline was used orally before the thirteenth week of pregnancy. Pregnant women are encouraged to discuss the benefits and potential risks of nystatin with their physician before deciding to use the drug.

HIV can be passed from a woman to her child through breast milk. In areas where nutritionally sound alternatives are readily available, breast-feed-

ing is discouraged for HIV-positive women. Nystatin used topically is generally considered safe for use while nursing.

**USE IN CHILDREN**
Nystatin is used safely and effectively by children. It is important that children taking the oral tablets understand that they should not be swallowed or chewed.

**USE IN THE ELDERLY**
No changes in dose or administration are necessary in elderly people.

**DRUG INTERACTIONS**
None reported.

**FOOD INTERACTIONS**
None reported.

**OTHER DRUGS USED FOR SIMILAR CONDITIONS**
For candida infections, a number of other topical and systemic antifungal agents are available. Minor or localized infections may be effectively treated with other topical, over-the-counter medications such as miconazole or clotrimazole. More severe or widespread infections may require a systemic drug such as fluconazole, ketoconazole, or itraconazole.

# T E R B I N A F I N E

**BRAND NAME (MANUFACTURER)**
Lamisil (Novartis)

**TYPE OF DRUG**
Antifungal agent

**USED FOR**
Terbinafine tablets are used by people with HIV for the treatment of onychomycosis (toenail and fingernail fungus). Terbinafine cream is used to treat athlete's foot, jock itch, and ringworm.

**GENERAL INFORMATION**
Terbinafine is an antifungal drug that works by selectively interfering with the metabolism of susceptible fungi, preventing them from building their cell walls. It is available as a cream for topical application and as tablets for oral administration.

**TREATMENT**
For fingernail fungus infection, 250 mg of terbinafine is usually given once a day for 6 weeks. For toenail fungus infections, the dose is usually 250 mg of terbinafine once a day for 12 weeks. For the treatment of athlete's foot, jock

itch, and ringworm, terbinafine cream is usually applied twice a day on the affected area until clinical signs and symptoms are significantly improved.

**CAUTIONS AND WARNINGS**
Terbinafine should not be used by anyone with a known allergy to it.

**SIDE EFFECTS**
In clinical trials, headache, rash, and diarrhea occurred in 6–13% of people who took terbinafine. Abdominal pain, nausea, and taste changes occurred in about 3% of people.

**PREGNANCY/BREAST-FEEDING**
Terbinafine has not been formally studied in pregnant women. In animal studies, it did not cause fetal harm, but it is not known whether this would be true for humans. Pregnant women are encouraged to discuss the benefits and potential risks of terbinafine with their physician before deciding to use the drug.

HIV can be passed from a woman to her child through breast milk. In areas where nutritionally sound alternatives are readily available, breast-feeding is discouraged for HIV-positive women. Terbinafine is excreted in human milk. Because of the potential toxicity of the drug to newborns, women are encouraged to consider alternatives to breast-feeding while taking it.

**USE IN CHILDREN**
Terbinafine has not been formally studied in children.

**USE IN THE ELDERLY**
No changes in dose or administration are necessary in elderly people.

**DRUG INTERACTIONS**
Rifampin will significantly lower blood levels of terbinafine, resulting in substantial decrease in activity.

Terfenadine and cimetidine will increase blood levels of terbinafine.

Terbinafine will decrease blood levels of cyclosporine.

**FOOD INTERACTIONS**
None reported.

**OTHER DRUGS USED FOR SIMILAR CONDITIONS**
For toenail fungus infection, itraconazole is an alternative to terbinafine. More severe or widespread infections may require a systemic drug such as fluconazole, ketoconazole, or itraconazole.

# ANTIFUNGAL
## EXPERIMENTAL DRUGS

The following drugs are being tested for the treatment of fungal infections associated with HIV. Generally, they are not widely available; most can be obtained only when participating in clinical trials.

### ZDO870, VORICONAZOLE, SCH 56592, L-743,872, LY303366

A number of drugs are highly effective in the treatment and prevention of many of the fungal infections commonly seen in people with HIV. Once successful treatment is completed, lifelong maintenance therapy is sometimes required to prevent a relapse of severe or life-threatening fungal infections. A growing problem for people with HIV is the emergence of infections resistant to standard treatment. ZDO870, voriconazole, SCH 56592 (all are new azole drugs) and L-743,872 and LY303366 (which belong to a new class of antifungal drugs known as echinocandins) are being tested in both the lab and in the clinic as possible treatments for people with resistant fungal infections.

### LIPOSOMAL AMPHOTERICIN B (AMBISOME)

AmBisome (Fujisawa) is a liposomal form of amphotericin B that is approved for use in Europe and in Latin America. It has been recommended for approval in the United States and is likely to be approved soon by the FDA. AmBisome has been shown to be at least as safe or safer than the traditional formulation of amphotericin B. It also causes fewer kidney-related side effects and injection-related toxicity. The drug is as effective as amphotericin B for the treatment of candidiasis, aspergillosis, cryptococcal meningitis, and other fungal infections. In clinical studies, AmBisome was used at doses from 1 to 5 mg per kg of body weight per day.

AmBisome has also been tested in a small clinical trial of immune compromised children ages 1.8 to 16 years. Although the most effective dosage has not been determined, doses up to 6 mg per kg of body weight per day were tolerated without serious kidney toxicity.

# ANTIHISTAMINES

Histamine is one of the chemicals secreted by specialized cells during an allergic reaction. Histamine causes inflammation, accelerates the heart rate, and increases secretion of acid in the stomach. Antihistamines block the action of histamine, reducing inflammation. They also pass into the brain, causing sedation and depression of various brain functions, including vomiting and coughing.

Antihistamines are most frequently used to reduce inflammation of the nose and upper respiratory tract resulting from an allergic reaction to pollen, house dust, animal fur, or other similar substances. They are also used to reduce certain drug-induced allergic side effects, including skin rashes, redness, swelling, hives, and breathing difficulties.

The following drugs are covered in this section:
- astemizole
- brompheniramine
- cetirizine
- chlorpheniramine
- cromolyn
- diphenhydramine
- fexofenadine
- loratadine
- phenindamine
- terfenadine

# ASTEMIZOLE

**BRAND NAME (MANUFACTURER)**
Hismanal (Janssen)

**TYPE OF DRUG**
Antihistamine

**USED FOR**
Astemizole is used to treat the symptoms of seasonal allergies, including sneezing and irritation of the eyes and nose.

**GENERAL INFORMATION**
Astemizole is a relatively new and long-acting antihistamine. The main difference between this drug and the older antihistamines is that it causes less drowsiness and is more suitable for people who need to stay alert.

Astemizole is available in tablet form for oral administration.

**TREATMENT**

The recommended dosage of astemizole for adults and children over the age of twelve is one 10 mg tablet, taken once daily. Because of the risk of serious heart toxicity, this dosage should not be exceeded.

**CAUTIONS AND WARNINGS**

Astemizole should not be used by anyone with a known allergy to it. Because astemizole may rarely cause severe heart toxicity, it should be used with caution by people with cardiac disease. It should also not be used in combination with quinine, ketoconazole, itraconazole, or erythromycin because of the risk of serious, potentially fatal cardiac side effects. Similarly, because astemizole is metabolized by the liver, it should not be used by people with impaired liver function.

**SIDE EFFECTS**

Common side effects of astemizole include drowsiness, headache, and fatigue. Other side effects are rare, but include cardiac toxicity, muscle ache, depression, palpitation, rash, and swelling.

**PREGNANCY/BREAST-FEEDING**

Astemizole has not been formally studied in pregnant women. In animal studies it caused fetal damage when administered at doses up to 100 times the human dose, but the relevance of these results to humans is unknown. Pregnant women are encouraged to discuss the benefits and potential risks of astemizole with their physician before deciding to use the drug.

HIV can be passed from a woman to her child through breast milk. In areas where nutritionally sound alternatives are readily available, breast-feeding is discouraged for HIV-positive women. Because of the potential toxicity of astemizole to newborns, women are encouraged to consider alternatives to breast-feeding while using it.

**USE IN CHILDREN**

Astemizole is used in children over twelve years of age at the dosages described above. Its safety and effectiveness in younger children has not yet been demonstrated in clinical trials.

**USE IN THE ELDERLY**

Older adults, especially those with significantly reduced liver function, may be more susceptible to the side effects of astemizole and usually require reduced dosages of the drug.

**DRUG INTERACTIONS**

Severe cardiac toxicity has been reported (rarely) in people taking astemizole with the azole antifungal drugs itraconazole or ketoconazole. Because other azole-type drugs (e.g., fluconazole, metronidazole, miconazole) are chemi-

cally similar to itraconazole and ketoconazole, they may also result in serious side effects when used with astemizole.

Drug-interaction studies have shown that the macrolide antibiotic erythromycin also increases astemizole blood levels, and a few instances of serious heart toxicity have occurred in people using these combinations. Because other macrolide antibiotics, including azithromycin and clarithromycin, are similar to erythromycin, they may also cause serious side effects when used with astemizole.

Astemizole should not be taken together with delavirdine, indinavir, nelfinavir, ritonavir, and saquinavir because of the risk of increased side effects. In addition, astemizole should not be taken with any quinine drugs.

Astemizole may intensify the effect of other central nervous system depressants, including alcohol, barbiturates, narcotic pain relievers, and sedatives.

**FOOD INTERACTIONS**
Astemizole should be taken at least one hour before or two hours after a meal.

**OTHER DRUGS USED FOR SIMILAR CONDITIONS**
A number of other antihistamines are available both over the counter and by prescription. A partial list includes chlorpheniramine, diphenhydramine, hydroxyzine, loratadine, phenindamine, and brompheniramine. They vary in their effects and the amount of drowsiness they produce. In general, there is no perfect antihistamine. The choice usually depends on which is most effective and has the fewest or least significant side effects for the individual.

# BROMPHENIRAMINE

**BRAND NAME (MANUFACTURER)**
Bromfed (Muro); Dimetane (Robins)

**TYPE OF DRUG**
Antihistamine

**USED FOR**
Brompheniramine is used to treat allergic reactions such as hay fever, hives, and inflammation of the eye. It is also used to prevent or treat allergic reactions to blood transfusions or compounds taken to enhance X-ray images. Occasionally it is used as a supplementary therapy to epinephrine for the treatment of anaphylactic shock.

In people with HIV, the drug is also used to reduce certain drug-induced allergic side effects, including skin rashes, redness, swelling, hives, and breathing difficulties.

Brompheniramine is also a common ingredient in many over-the-counter medications used to treat the symptoms of colds or flu.

**GENERAL INFORMATION**

Brompheniramine belongs to a group of antihistamines called alkylamines. They are among the most active antihistamines and are generally effective at low doses. They are less likely than many other antihistamines to produce drowsiness and are often appropriate for use during the day. However, many people taking these drugs still experience drowsiness.

Like other antihistamines, brompheniramine relieves allergic skin reactions such as itching, swelling, and redness. It also reduces the sneezing and running nose associated with hay fever.

The drug is available in a wide variety of formulations, including capsules, tablets, cough syrup, and a solution for injection.

**TREATMENT**

The appropriate dose of brompheniramine varies widely depending on the formulation used, the condition treated, and other drugs being used at the same time.

**CAUTIONS AND WARNINGS**

Brompheniramine should not be used by anyone with a known allergy to it. It should also not be used by anyone with severe high blood pressure, severe coronary-artery disease, urinary retention, stomach ulcers, narrow-angle glaucoma, or people receiving monoamine oxidase (MAO) inhibitor drugs (e.g., phenelzine, isocarboxazid).

Because of the risk of serious side effects, brompheniramine should be used with caution in people with heart disease, high blood pressure, diabetes, thyroid disease, glaucoma, or prostate disease.

Brompheniramine may impair the mental and physical abilities necessary to operate dangerous machinery or to drive an automobile.

**SIDE EFFECTS**

Drowsiness is the most common side effect of brompheniramine. Less often, fatigue, nausea, giddiness, dry mouth, blurred vision, heart palpitations, flushing, and increased irritability or excitement (especially in children) may occur.

**PREGNANCY/BREAST-FEEDING**

Brompheniramine has not been formally studied in pregnant women. The available clinical evidence suggests that the drug may cause an increased incidence of birth defects when used during the first four months of pregnancy. Pregnant women are encouraged to discuss the benefits and potential risks of the drug with their physician before deciding to use it.

HIV may be passed from a woman to her child through breast milk. In areas where nutritionally sound alternatives are readily available, breast-feeding is discouraged for HIV-positive women. Brompheniramine is excreted in human milk and may cause side effects in newborns. The drug also sup-

presses the production of breast milk and can prevent it completely if administered during the first twelve hours after delivery.

### USE IN CHILDREN

Children over the age of six may use brompheniramine at doses adjusted for weight and age. The drug is not recommended for younger children because they are more likely to experience side effects while taking it.

### USE IN THE ELDERLY

Older adults are especially susceptible to the side effects of this drug. If it is necessary to use the drug, they generally receive reduced doses.

### DRUG INTERACTIONS

Brompheniramine may intensify the effect of other central nervous system depressants, including alcohol, narcotic pain relievers, tranquilizers, and sleeping pills. When brompheniramine is taken with MAO inhibitors, there is an increased risk of a dangerous rise in blood pressure.

Brompheniramine may intensify the drying effect of other antihistamines.

### FOOD INTERACTIONS

None reported.

### OTHER DRUGS USED FOR SIMILAR CONDITIONS

A number of other antihistamines are available both over the counter and by prescription. A partial list includes chlorpheniramine, diphenhydramine, hydroxyzine, loratadine, phenindamine, and terfenadine. In general, there is no perfect antihistamine. The choice usually depends on which is most effective and has the fewest or least significant side effects for the individual.

# CETIRIZINE

### BRAND NAME (MANUFACTURER)

Zyrtec (Pfizer)

### TYPE OF DRUG

Antihistamine

### USED FOR

Cetirizine is used for the relief of seasonal and perennial allergies, stuffy and runny nose, itching of the eyes, scratchy throat, allergic skin reactions, and asthma triggered by allergic reactions.

In people with HIV, the drug is also used to reduce some drug-induced allergic effects, including skin rashes, redness, swelling, hives, and breathing difficulties.

### GENERAL INFORMATION

Cetirizine is a long-acting antihistamine that causes less sedation than most other antihistamines available in the United States.

Cetirizine is available as tablets for oral administration.

**TREATMENT**

The most commonly used dosage for adults and children over the age of twelve is one 10 mg tablet taken daily on an empty stomach. A dose of 5 mg is recommended for people with impaired kidney function.

**CAUTIONS AND WARNINGS**

Cetirizine should not be used by anyone with a known allergy to it. Cetirizine should not be use together with alcohol and other antidepressants because of increased likelihood of drowsiness.

**SIDE EFFECTS**

Cetirizine is generally well tolerated. In clinical trials, approximately 3% of people taking cetirizine stopped treatment prematurely because of side effects. The most common side effects were drowsiness, fatigue, and dry mouth.

**PREGNANCY/BREAST-FEEDING**

Cetirizine has not been formally studied in pregnant women. In animal studies, the drug did not cause fetal harm, but it is not known whether the same would be true in humans. Pregnant women are encouraged to discuss the benefits and potential risks of cetirizine with their physician before deciding to use the drug.

HIV can be passed from a woman to her child through breast milk. In areas where nutritionally sound alternatives are readily available, breast-feeding is discouraged for HIV-positive women. Cetirizine is excreted in breast milk. Because of the potential toxicity of the drug to nursing infants, women are encouraged to consider alternatives to breast-feeding while using it.

**USE IN CHILDREN**

Cetirizine is used in children over the age of twelve at the dosage described above. It is not recommended for younger children because its safety and effectiveness in them has not yet been demonstrated in clinical trials.

**USE IN THE ELDERLY**

Older adults, especially those with reduced kidney function, may require reduced dosages of the drug.

**DRUG INTERACTIONS**

Theophylline slightly increased blood levels of cetirizine.

**FOOD INTERACTIONS**

Cetirizine may be taken with or without food.

**OTHER DRUGS USED FOR SIMILAR CONDITIONS**

A number of other antihistamines are available both over the counter and by prescription. A partial list includes chlorpheniramine, diphenhydramine, hydroxyzine, brompheniramine, loratadine, and terfenadine. They vary in their effects and the amount of drowsiness they produce. In general, there is

no perfect antihistamine. The choice usually depends on which is most effective and has the fewest or least significant side effects for the individual.

# CHLORPHENIRAMINE

**BRAND NAME (MANUFACTURER)**
Alermine; Aller-Chlor; Chlor-Trimeton; Comtrex; Histex; Teldrin (various manufacturers)

**TYPE OF DRUG**
Antihistamine

**USED FOR**
Chlorpheniramine is used to treat allergic reactions such as hay fever, hives, and inflammation of the eye, among others. It is also used to prevent or treat allergic reactions to blood transfusions or compounds taken to enhance X-ray images. Occasionally it is used as a supplementary therapy to epinephrine for the treatment of anaphylactic shock.

In people with HIV, the drug is also used to reduce certain drug-induced allergic side effects, including skin rashes, redness, swelling, hives, and breathing difficulties.

Chlorpheniramine is also a common ingredient in many over-the-counter medications used to treat the symptoms of colds or flu.

**GENERAL INFORMATION**
Chlorpheniramine is an antihistamine that has been widely used for more than thirty years. Like other antihistamines, it relieves allergic skin reactions such as itching, swelling, and redness. It also reduces the sneezing and running nose associated with hay fever.

The drug is available in a wide variety of formulations, including capsules, tablets, syrup, and oral suspension.

**TREATMENT**
The appropriate dose of chlorpheniramine varies widely depending on the formulation used, the condition treated, and other drugs being used at the same time. The usual dosage for people over thirteen years of age is 4 mg, taken every four to six hours up to a maximum of 24 mg per day. Children and elderly adults generally use lower doses.

**CAUTIONS AND WARNINGS**
Chlorpheniramine should not be used by anyone with a known allergy to it. It should also not be used by anyone with severe high blood pressure, severe coronary-artery disease, difficulty urinating, stomach ulcers, narrow-angle glaucoma, or people receiving monoamine oxidase (MAO) inhibitor drugs (e.g., phenelzine, isocarboxazid).

Because of the risk of serious side effects, the drug should be used with caution in people with heart disease, high blood pressure, diabetes, thyroid disease, glaucoma, or prostate disease.

Chlorpheniramine may impair the mental and physical abilities necessary to operate dangerous machinery or to drive an automobile.

## SIDE EFFECTS

Drowsiness is the most common side effect of chlorpheniramine. Less often allergic skin reactions, sensitivity to bright light, increased perspiration, chills, reduced blood pressure, headache, altered heartbeat, insomnia, dizziness, loss of coordination, confusion, restlessness, nervousness, euphoria, tingling in the extremities, blurred vision, ringing in the ears, stomach upset, loss of appetite, nausea, vomiting, constipation, diarrhea, difficulty urinating, difficulty breathing, dry mouth, and irritability or excitement (especially in children) may occur.

## PREGNANCY/BREAST-FEEDING

Chlorpheniramine has not been formally studied in pregnant women. In general, antihistamines used at prescribed doses do not pose a significant risk of birth defects, but there are exceptions. In addition, antihistamines taken during the last three months of pregnancy may cause severe allergic reactions in newborns or premature infants. Pregnant women are encouraged to discuss the benefits and potential risks of chlorpheniramine with their physician before deciding to use the drug.

HIV can be passed from a woman to her child through breast milk. In areas where nutritionally sound alternatives are readily available, breast-feeding is discouraged for HIV-positive women. Chlorpheniramine is excreted in human milk. Because of the potential toxicity of the drug, women are encouraged to consider alternatives to breast-feeding while using it.

## USE IN CHILDREN

Chlorpheniramine is not recommended for children under the age of seven because of the risk of serious side effects. Older children can use the drug at dosages adjusted for age and weight.

## USE IN THE ELDERLY

Older adults are more sensitive to the side effects of chlorpheniramine, especially confusion, difficulty urinating, dizziness, drowsiness, nightmares, excitability, nervousness, restlessness, irritability, and dry mouth. Generally, dose reductions are necessary for the elderly.

## DRUG INTERACTIONS

The combination of chlorpheniramine and MAO inhibitors may cause severe rises in blood pressure. Chlorpheniramine may intensify the effects of

other central nervous system depressants, including alcohol, narcotic pain relievers, barbiturates, sedatives, and tranquilizers.

### FOOD INTERACTIONS
Chlorpheniramine may be taken with or without food.

### OTHER DRUGS USED FOR SIMILAR CONDITIONS
A number of other antihistamines are available both over the counter and by prescription. A partial list includes brompheniramine, diphenhydramine, hydroxyzine, loratadine, phenindamine, and terfenadine. They vary in their effects and the amount of drowsiness they produce. In general, there is no perfect antihistamine. The choice usually depends on which is most effective and has the fewest and least significant side effects for the individual.

# CROMOLYN

### BRAND NAME (MANUFACTURER)
Intal (Fisons); Nasalcrom (Fisons); Gastrocrom (Fisons)

### TYPE OF DRUG
Antihistamine

### USED FOR
Cromolyn is used primarily to prevent asthma and allergic reactions. In people living with HIV, it is also used to prevent breathing difficulties (bronchoconstriction) caused by aerosol pentamidine.

### GENERAL INFORMATION
Cromolyn is an anti-allergy drug developed in the early 1970s. It works by inhibiting the release of histamine and certain other inflammatory compounds from specialized cells called mast cells.

As a drug to prevent asthma, cromolyn is slow to act. Although some people respond quickly to the drug, it usually takes weeks of regular dosing with an inhaler before the drug has any effect.

Cromolyn is also available as a nasal spray to prevent hay fever and as eye drops to prevent allergic inflammation of the eye. The oral version of the drug is used to treat intestinal food allergies or diarrhea caused by a rare disease called systemic mastocytosis.

### TREATMENT
For management of bronchial asthma in adults and children five years of age and older, the usual starting dose is two metered inhalations four times daily at regular intervals. This dose should not be exceeded, but not everyone will respond to this dose. For cromolyn to be effective against asthma, the drug must be taken consistently at regular intervals. Dose reductions may be necessary for people with liver or kidney disease.

The nasal spray is recommended for adults and children above six years of age. One spray in each nostril, three to four times a day, is the usual dose. Similarly, the eye drops are used at a recommended dose of one drop in each eye, four to six times a day.

The adult dosage of the oral form of cromolyn is usually two capsules, taken four times a day, half an hour before meals and at bedtime. Infants and children receive reduced dosages based on age and weight.

### CAUTIONS AND WARNINGS
Cromolyn should not be used by anyone with a known allergy to it.

Because it may take weeks of treatment before its full effect is felt, cromolyn is not appropriate treatment for acute attacks of asthma or allergies.

The inhaler should be used with caution by people with heart disease because the propellants may affect heart rhythms.

### SIDE EFFECTS
In general, the side effects of cromolyn are mild. Coughing, wheezing, irritation of the throat, nose or eyes, bad taste, and nausea were the most frequent side effects reported in clinical trials. Less commonly, allergic reactions, dizziness, frequent urination, joint swelling or pain, discharge of tears, headache, rash, fluid in the lungs, burning in the chest, and muscle weakness have been reported.

### PREGNANCY/BREAST-FEEDING
Cromolyn has not been formally studied in pregnant women. In animal studies, it caused spontaneous abortions and low birth weights in animals given high doses of the drug, but it is not known whether the same would occur in humans. Pregnant women are encouraged to discuss the benefits and potential risks of cromolyn with their physician before deciding to use the drug.

HIV can be passed from a woman to her child through breast milk. In areas where nutritionally sound alternatives are readily available, breast-feeding is discouraged for HIV-positive women. It is not known whether cromolyn is excreted in human milk. Because of the potential toxicity of the drug, women are encouraged to consider alternatives to breast-feeding while using it.

### USE IN CHILDREN
The inhaler form of cromolyn is used at the doses described above for children over five. The nasal form is recommended for children six years of age and older. These formulations are not recommended for younger children because of the risk of side effects.

The oral form of cromolyn is recommended for full-term infants and children at dosages adjusted for weight and age. It is not recommended for premature infants.

**USE IN THE ELDERLY**

No changes in dosage or administration are recommended for older adults.

**DRUG INTERACTIONS**

Cromolyn used in combination with isoproterenol during pregnancy may increase the risk of birth defects.

**FOOD INTERACTIONS**

When cromolyn is administered to the lungs, nose, or eyes, food does not affect absorption of the drug. The oral form of the drug should be taken half an hour before meals and at bedtime. It should not be taken with fruit juice, milk, or food.

**OTHER DRUGS USED FOR SIMILAR CONDITIONS**

For treatment of asthma or allergic reactions, a number of antihistamines or bronchodilators may be used. The choice of drug depends on the age and condition of the individual, the specific allergy and its intensity, and other drugs being used at the same time.

# DIPHENHYDRAMINE

**BRAND NAME (MANUFACTURER)**

Benadryl (Warner Wellcome); DPH-Elixir (Alra)

**TYPE OF DRUG**

Antihistamine

**USED FOR**

Diphenhydramine is used to treat the symptoms of a wide variety of conditions, including allergies, hay fever, and motion sickness. It has also been used as a sleep aid and a treatment for the involuntary muscle movements caused by psychoactive drugs or Parkinson's disease. The drug is occasionally used to prevent nausea and vomiting in pregnancy. In people living with HIV, diphenhydramine is commonly used to suppress the allergic symptoms caused by certain drugs, including trimethoprim/sulfamethoxazole, amphotericin B, alpha interferon, and pentamidine.

**GENERAL INFORMATION**

Diphenhydramine was originally released in 1945, and since then it has become one of the most widely used antihistamines. It is available in numerous forms both over the counter and by prescription. It is often combined with decongestants, pain relievers, and cough medications for the treatment of cold and flu symptoms. It relieves sore throats, runny noses, and sneezing caused by allergic reactions. In most people it causes drowsiness.

**TREATMENT**

The recommended dosage varies depending on the condition and form of the drug. For most uses, the usual adult dosage is 50 to 200 mg per day, split into equal doses taken every four to six hours. Children receive lower doses, adjusted for their weight and age. Generally, the drug begins to act within twenty minutes when injected or sixty minutes when used orally.

The effect of diphenhydramine may become weaker with prolonged use as the body develops a tolerance to it. As it loses its effectiveness, it may be necessary to switch to an antihistamine of a different class.

**CAUTIONS AND WARNINGS**

Diphenhydramine should not be used by anyone with a known allergy to it. Because of the potential for severe side effects, the drug should be used with caution in people with narrow-angle glaucoma, peptic ulcers, enlarged prostate, bladder-neck obstructions, asthma, high blood pressure, heart disease, or thyroid disease.

Diphenhydramine may cause drowsiness and impair the mental and physical abilities to operate dangerous machinery or to drive an automobile.

**SIDE EFFECTS**

The most common side effects of diphenhydramine are sedation, dizziness, loss of coordination, heartburn, dry mouth, and thickening of secretions in the lungs. Other side effects that occur less frequently include nausea, vomiting, blurred vision, difficulty urinating, disorientation, excitement, loss of appetite, diarrhea, tightness in the chest, wheezing, ringing in the ears, and convulsions.

**PREGNANCY/BREAST-FEEDING**

Diphenhydramine has not been formally studied in pregnant women. Women are encouraged to discuss the benefits and potential risks of diphenhydramine with their physician before deciding to use the drug.

HIV may be passed from a woman to her child through breast milk. In areas where nutritionally sound alternatives are readily available, breast-feeding is discouraged for HIV-positive women. Diphenhydramine passes into breast milk and can cause sedation or other serious side effects in newborns. The drug is not recommended for nursing mothers.

**USE IN CHILDREN**

Diphenhydramine is not recommended for newborn children, especially those born prematurely, because their immature kidney function leaves them at high risk for the side effects of the drug. In infants and older children, a physician's dosing recommendation should be followed carefully, because overdose may cause hallucinations, convulsions, and death.

**USE IN THE ELDERLY**

People over the age of sixty have a greater risk of side effects from antihistamines, including diphenhydramine. At recommended dosages, dizziness, sedation, or low blood pressure may occur. Elderly people may require lower doses.

**DRUG INTERACTIONS**

Diphenhydramine may intensify the effects of other central nervous system depressants, including tranquilizers, sleeping pills, some antipsychotic drugs, alcohol, and narcotic pain relievers.

Monoamine oxidase (MAO) inhibitors (e.g., phenelzine, tranylcypromine) may prolong and intensify the drying effects of antihistamines.

**FOOD INTERACTIONS**

Diphenhydramine may be taken with or without food.

**OTHER DRUGS USED FOR SIMILAR CONDITIONS**

A number of other antihistamines are available both over the counter and by prescription. A partial list includes brompheniramine, chlorpheniramine, hydroxyzine, loratadine, phenindamine, and terfenadine. They vary in their effects and the amount of drowsiness they produce. In general, there is no perfect antihistamine. The choice usually depends on which is most effective and has the fewest and least significant side effects for the individual.

# F E X O F E N A D I N E

**BRAND NAME (MANUFACTURER)**

Allegra (Hoechst Marion Roussel)

**TYPE OF DRUG**

Antihistamine

**USED FOR**

Fexofenadine is used for the relief of seasonal allergies, stuffy and runny nose, itching of the eyes, scratchy throat, allergic skin reactions, and asthma triggered by allergic reactions.

**GENERAL INFORMATION**

Fexofenadine is a relatively long-acting antihistamine that causes less sedation than most other antihistamines available in the United States. Consequently, it is often used by people who experience drowsiness while taking other antihistamines.

Fexofenadine is available as tablets for oral administration.

**TREATMENT**

A commonly used dosage for adults and children over the age of twelve is one 60 mg tablet, taken twice daily. A dose of 60 mg once daily is recommended for people with impaired kidney function.

**CAUTIONS AND WARNINGS**

Fexofenadine should not be used by anyone with a known allergy to it.

**SIDE EFFECTS**

Fexofenadine is generally well tolerated. In clinical trials, approximately 2% of people taking fexofenadine stopped treatment prematurely because of side effects. The most common side effects were nausea, drowsiness, fatigue, and difficulty in breathing.

**PREGNANCY/BREAST-FEEDING**

Fexofenadine has not been formally studied in pregnant women. In animal studies, the drug did not cause fetal harm, but it is not known whether the same would be true in humans. Pregnant women are encouraged to discuss the benefits and potential risks of fexofenadine with their physician before deciding to use the drug.

HIV can be passed from a woman to her child through breast milk. In areas where nutritionally sound alternatives are readily available, breast-feeding is discouraged for HIV-positive women. It is not known whether fexofenadine is excreted in breast milk. Because of the potential toxicity of the drug to nursing infants, women are encouraged to consider alternatives to breast-feeding while using it.

**USE IN CHILDREN**

Fexofenadine is used in children over the age of twelve at the dosage described above. It is not recommended for younger children because its safety and effectiveness in them has not yet been demonstrated in clinical trials.

**USE IN THE ELDERLY**

In healthy elderly adults taking fexofenadine in a clinical trial, the blood levels of the drug were significantly higher than in younger subjects. Dose reductions may be required for this population to reduce the risk of side effects.

**DRUG INTERACTIONS**

Ketoconazole and erythromycin may increase blood levels of fexofenadine, but in a clinical trial, people taking fexofenadine with or without ketoconazole or erythromycin had no difference in the rate of side effects.

**FOOD INTERACTIONS**

Not known.

**OTHER DRUGS USED FOR SIMILAR CONDITIONS**

A number of other antihistamines are available both over the counter and by prescription. A partial list includes chlorpheniramine, diphenhydramine, hydroxyzine, brompheniramine, and terfenadine. They vary in their effects and the amount of drowsiness they produce. In general, there is no perfect antihistamine. The choice usually depends on which is most effective and has the fewest and least significant side effects for the individual.

# LORATADINE

**BRAND NAME (MANUFACTURER)**
Claritin (Schering)

**TYPE OF DRUG**
Antihistamine

**USED FOR**
Loratadine is used for the relief of seasonal allergies, stuffy and runny nose, itching of the eyes, scratchy throat, allergic skin reactions, and asthma triggered by allergic reactions.

In people with HIV, the drug is also used to reduce certain drug-induced allergic side effects, including skin rashes, redness, swelling, hives, and breathing difficulties.

**GENERAL INFORMATION**
Loratadine is a long-acting antihistamine that causes less sedation than most other antihistamines available in the United States. Consequently, it is often used by people who experience drowsiness while taking other antihistamines.

Loratadine is available as tablets for oral administration.

**TREATMENT**
The commonly used dosage for adults and children over the age of twelve is one 10 mg tablet, taken once daily on an empty stomach. Because loratadine is metabolized by the liver, people with impaired liver function may have difficulty clearing the drug from their bodies. For them, the recommended starting dose is one 10 mg tablet taken every other day.

**CAUTIONS AND WARNINGS**
Loratadine should not be used by anyone with a known allergy to it. The drug should be used with caution by people with liver disease, because of the risk of serious side effects.

**SIDE EFFECTS**
Loratadine is generally well tolerated. In clinical trials, approximately 2% of people taking loratadine stopped treatment prematurely because of side effects. The most common side effects were headache, drowsiness, fatigue, and dry mouth.

**PREGNANCY/BREAST-FEEDING**
Loratadine has not been formally studied in pregnant women. In animal studies, the drug did not cause fetal harm, but it is not known whether the same would be true in humans. Pregnant women are encouraged to discuss the benefits and potential risks of loratadine with their physician before deciding to use the drug.

HIV can be passed from a woman to her child through breast milk. In areas where nutritionally sound alternatives are readily available, breast-feeding is discouraged for HIV-positive women. Loratadine is excreted in breast milk. Because of the potential toxicity of the drug to nursing infants, women are encouraged to consider alternatives to breast-feeding while using it.

**USE IN CHILDREN**
Loratadine is used in children over the age of twelve at the dosage described above. It is not recommended for younger children because its safety and effectiveness in them has not yet been demonstrated in clinical trials.

**USE IN THE ELDERLY**
In healthy elderly adults taking loratadine in a clinical trial, the blood levels of the drug were significantly higher than in younger subjects. Dose reductions may be required for this population to reduce the risk of side effects.

**DRUG INTERACTIONS**
Ketoconazole may increase blood levels of loratadine, but in a clinical trial, people taking loratadine with or without ketoconazole had no difference in the rate of side effects. However, there were rare reports of serious and potentially fatal heart toxicity when loratadine was taken with ketoconazole or itraconazole.

Although formal drug interaction studies have not been performed, macrolide antibiotics (azithromycin, clarithromycin, erythromycin, etc.), cimetidine, ranitidine, or theophylline may cause drug interactions when used with loratadine.

Unlike other antihistamines, loratadine does not intensify the effect of alcohol or other central nervous system depressants.

**FOOD INTERACTIONS**
Food delays absorption of loratadine but increases the total amount absorbed. Although the effect of food is not expected to have clinical consequences, the manufacturer recommends taking the drug on an empty stomach.

**OTHER DRUGS USED FOR SIMILAR CONDITIONS**
A number of other antihistamines are available both over the counter and by prescription. A partial list includes chlorpheniramine, diphenhydramine, hydroxyzine, brompheniramine, and terfenadine. They vary in their effects and the amount of drowsiness they produce. In general, there is no perfect antihistamine. The choice usually depends on which is most effective and has the fewest and least significant side effects for the individual.

# PHENINDAMINE

**BRAND NAME (MANUFACTURER)**
Nolahist (Carnrick)
Phenindamine + Chlorpheniramine + Phenylpropanolamine: Nolamine (Carnrick)

**TYPE OF DRUG**
Antihistamine

**USED FOR**
Phenindamine is used to temporarily relieve runny nose, sneezing, itching of the nose or throat, and itchy, watery eyes due to hay fever or other upper respiratory allergies.

In people with HIV, the drug is also used to reduce certain drug-induced allergic side effects, including skin rashes, redness, swelling, hives, and breathing difficulties.

**GENERAL INFORMATION**
Phenindamine is an antihistamine available over the counter and by prescription. It is used alone to treat symptoms of allergic reactions and in combination with decongestants in cold or flu medications.

Phenindamine is available as tablets for oral administration.

**TREATMENT**
The usual dose of phenindamine for adults and children over the age of twelve is one 25 mg tablet taken every four to six hours, not to exceed six tablets in any twenty-four-hour period. Younger children receive reduced dosages based on age and weight.

**CAUTIONS AND WARNINGS**
Phenindamine should not be used by anyone with a known allergy to it. It should also not be used by anyone with breathing problems such as emphysema or bronchitis, glaucoma, difficulty urinating, or prostate disease.

Because of the risk of serious side effects, the drug should be used with caution in people with heart disease, high blood pressure, diabetes, or thyroid disease.

Phenindamine may impair the mental and physical abilities necessary to operate dangerous machinery or to drive an automobile.

**SIDE EFFECTS**
Drowsiness is the most common side effect of phenindamine. Less often, dry mouth, nervousness, insomnia, and increased irritability or excitement (especially in children) may occur.

**PREGNANCY/BREAST-FEEDING**
Phenindamine has not been formally studied in pregnant women. In general, antihistamines at commonly used doses do not pose a significant risk of birth

defects, but there are exceptions. Pregnant women are encouraged to discuss the benefits and potential risks of phenindamine with their physician before deciding to use the drug.

HIV can be passed from a woman to her child through breast milk. In areas where nutritionally sound alternatives are readily available, breast-feeding is discouraged for HIV-positive women. Phenindamine may be excreted in human milk. Because of the potential toxicity of the drug, women are encouraged to consider alternatives to breast-feeding while using it.

**USE IN CHILDREN**
Children may be more susceptible to the side effects of phenindamine, and they are usually given reduced doses of the drug.

**USE IN THE ELDERLY**
No changes in dosage or administration are recommended for older adults.

**DRUG INTERACTIONS**
Phenindamine may intensify the effects of other central nervous system depressants, including alcohol, narcotic pain relievers, barbiturates, sedatives, and tranquilizers.

**FOOD INTERACTIONS**
None reported.

**OTHER DRUGS USED FOR SIMILAR CONDITIONS**
A number of other antihistamines are available both over the counter and by prescription. A partial list includes brompheniramine, chlorpheniramine, diphenhydramine, hydroxyzine, loratadine, and terfenadine. They vary in their effects and the amount of drowsiness they produce. In general, there is no perfect antihistamine. The choice usually depends on which is most effective and has the fewest and least significant side effects for the individual.

# TERFENADINE

**BRAND NAME (MANUFACTURER)**
Seldane (Hoechst Marion Roussel)

**TYPE OF DRUG**
Antihistamine

**USED FOR**
Terfenadine is used to treat the symptoms of seasonal allergies, including sneezing and irritation of the eyes and nose. In people with HIV, the drug is also used to reduce certain drug-induced allergic side effects, including skin rashes, redness, swelling, hives, and breathing difficulties.

**GENERAL INFORMATION**

Terfenadine is a relatively new long-acting antihistamine. The main difference between this drug and the older antihistamines is that it causes less drowsiness and is often suitable for people who need to stay alert.

Terfenadine is available as regular and extended-release tablets for oral administration.

**TREATMENT**

The recommended dosage of terfenadine for adults and children over the age of twelve is one 60 mg tablet, taken twice daily. Because of the risk (rare) of serious heart toxicity, this dose should not be exceeded.

**CAUTIONS AND WARNINGS**

Terfenadine should not be used by anyone with a known allergy to it. It should also not be used in combination with ketoconazole, itraconazole, or macrolide antibiotics (e.g., erythromycin, clarithromycin, azithromycin, or troleandomycin) because of the risk of serious, potentially fatal cardiac side effects. Similarly, because terfenadine is metabolized by the liver, it should not be used by people with impaired liver function.

Because terfenadine may rarely cause severe heart toxicity, it should be used with caution by people with cardiac disease.

**SIDE EFFECTS**

Common side effects of terfenadine include nausea and loss of appetite. Other side effects are rare and include cardiac toxicity, rapid heartbeat, low blood pressure, palpitations, fainting, dizziness, allergic skin reactions, headache, hair loss, anaphylactic shock, difficulty breathing, confusion, depression, insomnia, menstrual disorders, muscle or bone pain, nightmares, sensitivity to light, acute psoriasis, seizures, sweating, reduced platelet counts (increasing the risk of bleeding), urinary disturbances, and visual disturbances.

**PREGNANCY/BREAST-FEEDING**

Terfenadine has not been formally studied in pregnant women. In animal studies it caused reduced survival and weight gain when administered at doses up to 125 times the human dose, but the relevance of these results to humans is unknown. Pregnant women are encouraged to discuss the benefits and potential risks of terfenadine with their physician before deciding to use the drug.

HIV can be passed from a woman to her child through breast milk. In areas where nutritionally sound alternatives are readily available, breast-feeding is discouraged for HIV-positive women. Because of the potential toxicity of terfenadine to newborns, women are encouraged to consider alternatives to breast-feeding while using it.

## USE IN CHILDREN

Terfenadine is used in children over twelve years of age at the dosages described above. It is not recommended for younger children because its safety and effectiveness in them has not yet been demonstrated in clinical trials.

## USE IN THE ELDERLY

Older adults, especially those with significantly reduced liver function, may be more susceptible to the side effects of terfenadine and usually require reduced dosages of the drug.

## DRUG INTERACTIONS

Severe cardiac toxicity has been reported in people taking terfenadine with the azole antifungal drugs itraconazole or ketoconazole. Because of the chemical similarity of other azole-type drugs (e.g., fluconazole, metronidazole, miconazole) to itraconazole and ketoconazole, use of these other drugs together with terfenadine may also result in serious side effects.

Terfenadine should not be used together with delavirdine, indinavir, nelfinavir, ritonavir, or saquinavir because of the increased risk of serious side effects.

Drug interaction studies have shown that the macrolide antibiotics erythromycin and clarithromycin also increase terfenadine blood levels, and a few instances of serious heart toxicity have occurred in people using these combinations. Because other macrolide antibiotics, including azithromycin, are chemically similar to clarithromycin, they may also cause serious side effects when used with terfenadine.

Combinations of monoamine oxidase (MAO) inhibitors (isocarboxazid, tranylcypromine, etc.) or some common antidepressants with terfenadine may cause dangerous increases in blood pressure.

Terfenadine may intensify the effect of other central nervous system depressants, including alcohol, barbiturates, narcotic pain relievers, sedatives, and tranquilizers.

## FOOD INTERACTIONS

None reported.

## OTHER DRUGS USED FOR SIMILAR CONDITIONS

A number of other antihistamines are available both over the counter and by prescription. A partial list includes chlorpheniramine, diphenhydramine, hydroxyzine, loratadine, phenindamine, and brompheniramine. They vary in their effects and the amount of drowsiness they produce. In general, there is no perfect antihistamine. The choice usually depends on which is most effective and has the fewest and least significant side effects for the individual.

# ANTINAUSEA/
# ANTIVOMITING DRUGS

Nausea and vomiting have many causes, including digestive tract infection, pregnancy, motion sickness, and central nervous system problems. They can also occur as a side effect of drugs, particularly antivirals and those used to treat cancer.

Nausea and vomiting occur when the brain receives signals from other parts of the body, including the inner ear and the part of the brain that monitors the blood. If the signals indicate that something is wrong, such as toxic chemicals being found in the blood, the brain sends another signal to the muscles of the stomach to contract and expel its contents.

Drugs used to treat the process may act at any (or all) of the steps in the process. Three main types of antiemetics (antivomiting drugs) are commonly used in people with HIV. The phenothiazines, which include prochlorperazine and thiethylperazine, prevent the brain from triggering the stomach muscles. Antihistamines, including hydroxyzine, reduce the sensitivity of the brain to incoming signals from other parts of the body. Other compounds work at numerous steps in the process.

The following drugs are covered in this section:

- granisetron
- hydroxyzine
- metoclopramide
- ondansetron
- prochlorperazine
- promethazine
- scopolamine
- thiethylperazine
- trimethobenzamide

In addition, a brief description of marijuana, a controlled substance used (but not FDA-approved) to treat nausea and vomiting, is included at the end of this section.

# GRANISETRON

**BRAND NAME (MANUFACTURER)**
Kytril (SmithKline Beecham)

**TYPE OF DRUG**
Antinausea/antivomiting agent

**USED FOR**
Granisetron is approved to prevent nausea and vomiting caused by drugs used to treat cancer. In people with HIV, it is used to treat nausea and vomiting caused by some of the drugs used to treat AIDS-related opportunistic infections or malignancies.

**GENERAL INFORMATION**
Granisetron blocks nerve signals carried by a chemical messenger called serotonin. Receptors for serotonin are found on the nerve endings in the gut and in the area of the brain that triggers vomiting. Stopping these signals reduces the nausea and vomiting in a way that is not completely understood.

Granisetron is available as a solution for intravenous (IV) injection and as tablets for oral administration.

**TREATMENT**
The recommended dose of IV granisetron is 10 micrograms (mcg) per kg of body weight per day, injected intravenously within thirty minutes before chemotherapy begins. The recommended dose of granisetron tablets is 1 mg twice daily. The first dose of granisetron should be taken 1 hour before chemotherapy begins with the subsequent dose taken 12 hours after the first.

**CAUTIONS AND WARNINGS**
Granisetron should not be used by anyone with a known allergy to it.

Because granisetron is metabolized by the liver, people who have impaired liver function may have elevated levels of the drug in their blood when taking recommended doses. However, dose reductions are usually not necessary.

**SIDE EFFECTS**
Headache is the most common side effect, occurring in 14-21% of people using the drug in clinical trials. Other common side effects (and the percentage of people affected) include muscle weakness (5-14%), drowsiness (4%), diarrhea (4-8%), fever (3-5%), and constipation (3-18%). High blood pressure, low blood pressure, irregular heart rhythms, agitation, anxiety, and abnormal taste were reported less frequently.

**PREGNANCY/BREAST-FEEDING**
Granisetron has not been formally studied in pregnant women. In animal studies it did not cause fetal harm, but it is not known whether this would be true for

humans. Pregnant women are encouraged to discuss the benefits and potential risks of granisetron with their physician before deciding to use the drug.

HIV may be passed from a woman to her child through breast milk. In areas where nutritionally sound alternatives are readily available, breast-feeding is discouraged for HIV-positive women. It is not known whether granisetron is excreted in human milk. Because of the potential toxicity of the drug to newborns, women are encouraged to consider alternatives to breast-feeding while taking it.

### USE IN CHILDREN
Little information regarding the use of granisetron for children under the age of two is available. Consequently, it is not recommended for this age group.

In clinical studies, children between the ages of two and sixteen were given granisetron at a wide range of dosages for the prevention of vomiting caused by chemotherapy. The studies showed that granisetron prevented vomiting as well in children as in adults, without unexpected or increased frequency of side effects.

### USE IN THE ELDERLY
During clinical trials, 713 people and 325 people aged sixty-five or over took the recommended dosage of IV granisetron and granisetron tablets respectively. The effectiveness and safety of the drug were similar in this age group to that in younger people.

### DRUG INTERACTIONS
No significant drug interactions have yet been identified.

### FOOD INTERACTIONS
Because granisetron is intravenously injected, food does not affect its absorption.

### OTHER DRUGS USED FOR SIMILAR CONDITIONS
For treatment or prevention of nausea and vomiting, a number of different types of drugs are available. Drugs used include metoclopramide, antihistamines (e.g., dimenhydrinate, meclizine, and promethazine), phenothiazines (e.g., prochlorperazine or thiethylperazine), and ondansetron. The different types of drugs differ significantly in their side effects, and the choice of therapy is often determined by the side effects for which an individual is at risk.

# HYDROXYZINE

### BRAND NAME (MANUFACTURER)
Atarax (Roerig/Pfizer); Marax (Roerig/Pfizer); Vistaril (Pfizer)

### TYPE OF DRUG
Psychoactive–antihistamine, antianxiety agent, sedative

## USED FOR

Hydroxyzine is used for symptomatic relief of anxiety and tension. It is also used to treat nausea and vomiting, itching caused by allergies, and as a sedative before surgery.

## GENERAL INFORMATION

Hydroxyzine inhibits the action of histamine, a substance secreted by specialized cells called mast cells. Histamine has a number of effects, including accelerating the heart rate, causing inflammation, and increasing the secretion of acid in the stomach. How hydroxyzine achieves its psychoactive effects is not clearly understood.

Hydroxyzine is available in tablets, syrup, and a solution for injection into muscles.

## TREATMENT

The dose of hydroxyzine varies by age, condition treated, and the form of the drug used. The usual adult dose is 50 to 100 mg taken four times daily. Children under age six receive lower doses, routinely 50 mg daily divided into four equal doses. Children over the age of six often receive 50 to 100 mg daily, divided into four equal doses.

## CAUTIONS AND WARNINGS

Hydroxyzine should not be used by anyone with a known allergy to it. The drug may cause drowsiness and interfere with the ability to operate an automobile or dangerous machinery.

## SIDE EFFECTS

The side effects of hydroxyzine are usually mild and of short duration. They include dry mouth; drowsiness, which often disappears after a few days of continued use; and muscle twitching. In rare cases, the drug may cause tremors or convulsions, but this usually occurs only at substantially higher-than-normal doses.

## PREGNANCY/BREAST-FEEDING

Hydroxyzine is not approved by the FDA for use in early pregnancy because it caused fetal harm in animal studies. However, the effects of the medication in pregnant women have not been formally studied in clinical trials. Women are encouraged to discuss the benefits and potential risks of hydroxyzine with their physician before deciding to use the drug during pregnancy.

HIV can be passed from a woman to her child through breast milk. In areas where nutritionally sound alternatives are readily available, breast-feeding is discouraged for HIV-positive women. It is not known whether hydroxyzine is excreted in human milk. Because of the potential toxicity of the drug to newborns, women are encouraged to consider alternatives to breast-feeding while using it.

**USE IN CHILDREN**

The drug has been used safely and effectively in children without unexpected side effects.

**USE IN THE ELDERLY**

Elderly people may be more susceptible to some of the side effects of hydroxyzine, and may require a lower dose.

**DRUG INTERACTIONS**

Hydroxyzine may exacerbate the effects of central nervous system depressants, such as narcotics, barbiturates, sedatives, tranquilizers, antihistamines, and alcohol.

**FOOD INTERACTIONS**

Hydroxyzine may be taken with food if it causes stomach upset.

**OTHER DRUGS USED FOR SIMILAR CONDITIONS**

For the treatment of anxiety, the most commonly used drugs are the benzodiazepines, which include diazepam, lorazepam, chlordiazepoxide, alprazolam, oxazepam, temazepam, flurazepam, and triazolam, among others. These drugs all act by similar mechanisms, but vary somewhat in how quickly they act and the side effects they produce.

Diphenhydramine (Benadryl) and terfenadine are antihistamines that can be substituted for hydroxyzine in the treatment of allergic reactions. Diphenhydramine may also be substituted for hydroxyzine when a sedative is necessary. A number of drugs can be used in place of hydroxyzine to treat nausea and vomiting.

# METOCLOPRAMIDE

**BRAND NAME (MANUFACTURER)**

Clopra (Quantum); Reglan (Robins)

**TYPE OF DRUG**

Antinausea/antivomiting agent

**USED FOR**

Metoclopramide is used for a wide variety of conditions. It is used to treat gastroesophageal reflux disease, a condition in which the stomach contents flow back up the esophagus causing heartburn and fullness after meals. Nursing mothers are occasionally given metoclopramide to increase milk production. In people with HIV, the drug is perhaps most frequently used to prevent nausea and vomiting associated with HIV disease or drug treatment and to relieve loss of appetite.

## GENERAL INFORMATION

It is not entirely known how metoclopramide works. It has a number of activities, including stimulating the movement of food and liquids through the upper gastrointestinal tract and interfering with certain transmitters of nerve signals. It also affects secretion of a number of hormones in the body.

Metoclopramide is available as tablets, oral solution, and solution for injection.

## TREATMENT

For most of its uses, metoclopramide is taken at a dose of 10 to 15 mg, four times a day. It is usually taken thirty minutes before each meal and at bedtime. For prevention of nausea and vomiting associated with cancer therapy, the injectable solution is used. The initial two doses are usually 1 to 2 mg, depending on the type of chemotherapy used and its potential to cause nausea or vomiting. The first intravenous injection is usually done thirty minutes before receiving chemotherapy and repeated every two hours for two doses and then every three hours for three doses.

The dosages are usually reduced for people with impaired kidney or liver function.

## CAUTIONS AND WARNINGS

Metoclopramide should not be used by anyone with a known allergy to it. It should also not be used in cases where stimulating movement in the gut may be dangerous, including cases where the gut is perforated, bleeding, or blocked by an obstruction.

People with high blood pressure, Parkinson's disease, asthma, liver or kidney disease, or a history of seizures should not take metoclopramide because of the increased risk of side effects.

Metoclopramide may impair the mental or physical abilities needed to drive an automobile or operate dangerous machinery.

## SIDE EFFECTS

The side effects of metoclopramide are usually related to the size of the dose taken. About 20% to 30% of people who take the drug experience side effects. Most side effects disappear when the drug is stopped.

About 10% of people taking 10 mg four times a day experience restlessness, drowsiness, fatigue, and lethargy. Insomnia, headache, confusion, dizziness, or mental depression occur less frequently. In people taking the higher doses recommended for treatment of nausea associated with cancer drugs, the incidence of drowsiness is about 70%. In people with HIV disease, diarrhea is a common side effect of metoclopramide.

About 0.2% of people taking 30 to 40 mg per day of the drug experience restlessness and involuntary movements of the arms and legs, face, tongue, lips, or other parts of the body. In people taking higher doses, the incidence

is about 2% of adults over the age of thirty and 25% or higher in children and young adults. These symptoms can be reversed with a drug called diphenhydramine.

Rarely, people taking the drug may experience neuroleptic malignant syndrome, a potentially fatal condition characterized by high fever, altered consciousness, and muscle rigidity.

**PREGNANCY/BREAST-FEEDING**

Metoclopramide has not been formally studied in pregnant women. In animals, it did not cause birth defects, but it is not known whether this would also be true for humans. Pregnant women are encouraged to discuss the benefits and potential risks of metoclopramide with their physician before deciding to use the drug.

HIV may be passed from a woman to her child through breast milk. In areas where nutritionally sound alternatives are readily available, breastfeeding is discouraged for HIV-positive women. Metoclopramide is excreted in human milk and can cause side effects in infants. When taken by women who have just given birth, the drug increases milk production. Because of the potential toxicity of the drug, lactating women should use the drug only after thorough discussion with their physician.

**USE IN CHILDREN**

Insufficient clinical data are available to recommend using metoclopramide for children under the age of eighteen.

**USE IN THE ELDERLY**

Older adults may be more susceptible to the side effects of the drug and may require reduced doses.

**DRUG INTERACTIONS**

Metoclopramide may intensify the effect of central nervous system depressants, including alcohol, tranquilizers, and narcotic pain relievers. The use of metoclopramide with monoamine oxidase (MAO) inhibitors (e.g., phenelzine or tranylcypromine) may result in unpredictable side effects.

Absorption of drugs from the stomach may be diminished by metoclopramide, while the speed and extent of absorption of drugs in the small intestine may be increased. Consequently, metoclopramide may reduce absorption of digoxin and increase the absorption of acetaminophen, tetracycline, levodopa, ethanol, and cyclosporine.

Metoclopramide may influence the effects of insulin on blood sugar. Adjustment of the timing and dose of insulin may be required when using metoclopramide.

**FOOD INTERACTIONS**

Metoclopramide should be taken thirty minutes before meals and at bedtime.

**OTHER DRUGS USED FOR SIMILAR CONDITIONS**

For treatment or prevention of nausea and vomiting, a number of different types of drugs are available. In addition to metoclopramide, other drugs used include antihistamines (e.g., meclizine and promethazine), phenothiazines (e.g., prochlorperazine or thiethylperazine), granisetron, and ondansetron. The different types of drugs differ significantly in their side effects, and the choice of therapy often is determined by the side effects for which an individual is at risk.

# ONDANSETRON

**BRAND NAME (MANUFACTURER)**
Zofran (Glaxo Wellcome)

**TYPE OF DRUG**
Antinausea/antivomiting agent

**USED FOR**
Ondansetron is approved to prevent nausea and vomiting caused by surgery or drugs used to treat cancer. In people with HIV, it is used to treat nausea and vomiting caused by some of the drugs used to treat AIDS-related opportunistic infections or malignancies.

**GENERAL INFORMATION**
Ondansetron blocks nerve signals carried by a chemical messenger called serotonin. Receptors for serotonin are found on the nerve endings in the gut and in the area of the brain that triggers vomiting. Stopping the signals reduces the nausea and vomiting in a way that is not completely understood.

Ondansetron has been tested in a number of small clinical trials that included volunteers infected with HIV. The results of these studies suggest the drug may help with some HIV, cancer, or opportunistic infection therapies.

Ondansetron is available as tablets for oral administration and in a solution for intravenous injection.

**TREATMENT**
The recommended dose of ondansetron tablets is 8 mg, taken twice daily. For prevention of nausea and vomiting associated with chemotherapy, the first dose of ondansetron should be taken thirty minutes before treatment begins, with the subsequent dose taken eight hours after the first dose.

The recommended dose of IV ondansetron is a single 32 mg dose or three 0.15 mg/kg doses. For the single dose regimen, ondansetron is given over a 15-minute infusion a half hour before starting chemotherapy. For the three-dose regimen, the first dose is given over a fifteen-minute infusion a half hour

before starting chemotherapy with the subsequent doses taken four and eight hours after the first dose.

In clinical trials of people infected with HIV, ondansetron was used at the same dosage as above.

### CAUTIONS AND WARNINGS

Ondansetron should not be used by anyone with a known allergy to it.

Because ondansetron is metabolized by the liver, people who have impaired liver function may have elevated levels of the drug in their bodies when taking recommended doses. Dose reductions are usually necessary for this group of people.

Women absorb ondansetron faster than men, and it leaves their bodies more slowly. As a result, the drug accumulates to higher levels in women than men, but no clinical evidence suggests that it is more effective or more likely to cause side effects in women.

### SIDE EFFECTS

Headache is the most common side effect of ondansetron, occurring in between 17% to 25% of people using the drug in clinical trials. Other common side effects in clinical trials (and the percentage of people affected) included constipation (9% to 11%), fever (7% to 8%), fatigue (5% to 13%), diarrhea (6% to 16%), and dizziness (5% to 12%). Serious allergic reactions, including anaphylactic shock and chest spasms, have been reported but are rare.

### PREGNANCY/BREAST-FEEDING

Ondansetron has not been formally studied in pregnant women. In animal studies it did not cause fetal harm, but it is not known whether this would be true for humans as well. Pregnant women are encouraged to discuss the benefits and potential risks of ondansetron with their physician before deciding to use the drug.

HIV may be passed from a woman to her child through breast milk. In areas where nutritionally sound alternatives are readily available, breast-feeding is discouraged for HIV-positive women. Ondansetron is excreted in the milk of laboratory animals, but it is not known if this is the case in human milk.

### USE IN CHILDREN

In clinical studies, 182 children between the ages of four and eighteen were given IV ondansetron at a wide range of dosages for the prevention of vomiting caused by the chemotherapy drug cisplatin. In general, ondansetron prevented vomiting as well in children as in adults, without unexpected or increased levels of side effects. Ondansetron tablets have not been formally studied in children.

For children two to twelve years of age, the recommended dose of IV ondansetron is 0.1 mg/kg for children weighing 40 kg (88 pounds) or less, or a single 4 mg dose for children over 40 kg. For children between four and twelve years of age, the recommended oral dosage is one 4 mg tablet three times a day. For children twelve years of age or older, the recommended oral dosage is 8 mg twice daily.

**USE IN THE ELDERLY**
One hundred and thirty-seven elderly people participated in the pre-marketing clinical trials for ondansetron. The drug accumulated to slightly higher levels in older people, but there was no significant difference in effectiveness or frequency of side effects in people over or under the age of sixty-five. No changes in dosage or administration are recommended for elderly people.

**DRUG INTERACTIONS**
No significant drug interactions have yet been identified for ondansetron.

**FOOD INTERACTIONS**
Ondansetron is absorbed into the body at higher levels when taken with food, but this effect does not affect the efficacy or safety of the drug. Ondansetron may be taken with or without food.

**OTHER DRUGS USED FOR SIMILAR CONDITIONS**
For treatment or prevention of nausea and vomiting, a number of different types of drugs are available. Drugs used include antihistamines (e.g., meclizine or promethazine), phenothiazines (e.g., prochlorperazine or thiethylperazine), or granisetron. The different types of drugs differ significantly in their side effects, and the choice of therapy is often determined by the side effects for which an individual is at risk.

# PROCHLORPERAZINE

**BRAND NAME (MANUFACTURER)**
Compazine (SmithKline Beecham)

**TYPE OF DRUG**
Antinausea/antivomiting agent

**USED FOR**
Prochlorperazine is used to treat severe nausea and vomiting. It may also be used for the short-term treatment of anxiety when other medications with fewer serious side effects are inappropriate.

**GENERAL INFORMATION**
Prochlorperazine belongs to a class of psychoactive drugs called phenothiazines. Although the mechanism by which they work is unknown, they have potent

effects on the central nervous system and other organs. They can reduce blood pressure, stop seizures, and control nausea and vomiting.

Prochlorperazine is available in tablets, extended-release capsules, suppositories, syrup, and solution for injection.

### TREATMENT

When nausea and vomiting are severe and the person cannot keep oral medications down, the 25 mg suppositories are used. A typical dose is one suppository taken twice a day. For the tablets, the adult dose is usually 5 or 10 mg, taken three or four times a day. Daily dosages over 40 mg should be used only in cases where the symptoms are resistant to treatment. The extended-release capsules are usually used once or twice a day.

Similar dosages are used when the drug is used to treat anxiety, but no more than 20 mg per day should be administered for this purpose, and the drug should not be taken for longer than twelve weeks.

### CAUTIONS AND WARNINGS

Prochlorperazine should not be used by anyone with a known allergy to it. It should also not be used by people receiving large doses of other depressants (e.g., alcohol, tranquilizers, etc.) or those in severely depressed states.

People who are allergic to other phenothiazines may also be allergic to prochlorperazine and should use the drug with caution. Similarly, people who are exposed to extreme heat or phosphorus pesticides and people with a history of seizures or heart disease should use the drug with caution because of the increased risk of side effects.

Prochlorperazine may impair the mental and physical abilities necessary to operate dangerous machinery or to drive an automobile.

### SIDE EFFECTS

Drowsiness, dizziness, missed periods, blurred vision, and skin reactions are common side effects of prochlorperazine.

Tardive dyskinesia is a special neuromuscular side effect of phenothiazines. It is characterized by potentially irreversible, involuntary muscle movements that usually involve the tongue, face, mouth, lips, jaw, torso, and extremities. Although the side effect occurs most frequently among the elderly (especially elderly women), it is not possible to predict whether an individual will develop the disorder. The risk of the side effect and the likelihood it will be irreversible are believed to be increased with increased duration of treatment and cumulative dose.

Other neuromuscular side effects of phenothiazines include agitation, jitteriness, insomnia, muscle spasm, difficulty swallowing, tremors, and shuffling gait, among others.

Antipsychotic drugs, including prochlorperazine, can cause a potentially fatal side effect called neuroleptic malignant syndrome. The syndrome is characterized by high fever, muscle rigidity, altered mental status, irregular pulse or blood pressure, and abnormal heart rhythms. If these symptoms occur, the drug should be stopped and a physician contacted immediately.

Other side effects of prochlorperazine include low blood pressure or fluctuations in blood pressure, weight change, swelling in the extremities, allergic reactions, and liver damage. In some cases, the drug has caused deficiencies in white blood cell counts.

**PREGNANCY/BREAST-FEEDING**

Prochlorperazine has not been formally studied in pregnant women. In clinical practice, there have been reported instances of prolonged jaundice, involuntary muscle movements, and altered reflexes in newborn infants whose mothers received phenothiazines. Pregnant women are encouraged to discuss the benefits and potential risks of prochlorperazine with their physician before deciding to use the drug.

HIV may be passed from a woman to her child through breast milk. In areas where nutritionally sound alternatives are readily available, breast-feeding is discouraged for HIV-positive women. Phenothiazines are excreted in human milk. Because of its potential toxicity to newborns, women are encouraged to consider alternatives to breast-feeding while using it.

**USE IN CHILDREN**

Children are more susceptible to the side effects of prochlorperazine than adults, even at moderate doses. If signs of restlessness or excitement occur in children taking the drug, it should be stopped and a physician should be contacted.

Prochlorperazine should not be used in pediatric surgery or in children under the age of two years or those who weigh less than twenty pounds. For older children with severe nausea or vomiting, the dose of the drug should be adjusted according to the severity of the symptoms and the response of the individual. The recommended starting dose is 2.5 mg, taken one to three times per day, depending on the child's weight.

**USE IN THE ELDERLY**

Older adults may be more susceptible to the side effects of the drug and may require reduced doses.

**DRUG INTERACTIONS**

Prochlorperazine may intensify the effect of other central nervous system depressants, including alcohol, antihistamines, tranquilizers, narcotic pain relievers, and sedatives.

Phenothiazines can diminish the effect of oral anticoagulants such as warfarin. Thiazide diuretics may accentuate the low blood pressure that occurs as a side effect of prochlorperazine.

Prochlorperazine may reduce the effectiveness of guanethidine and other blood-pressure medications. Concomitant administration of propranolol with phenothiazines results in increased blood levels of both drugs, potentially increasing the risk of side effects.

Phenothiazines may increase the risk of seizures and require dose adjustments in people taking anticonvulsants.

## FOOD INTERACTIONS

Foods with caffeine may interfere with the effects of prochlorperazine and should be avoided while taking the drug.

## OTHER DRUGS USED FOR SIMILAR CONDITIONS

For treatment or prevention of nausea and vomiting, a number of different types of drugs are available. Drugs used include metoclopramide, antihistamines (e.g., dimenhydrinate, meclizine, and promethazine), phenothiazines (e.g., thiethylperazine), granisetron, and ondansetron. The different types of drugs differ significantly in their side effects, and the choice of therapy is often determined by the side effects for which an individual is at risk.

# PROMETHAZINE

## BRAND NAME (MANUFACTURER)

Mepergan (Wyeth-Ayerst); Phenergan (Wyeth-Ayerst); Prometh (Barre-National)

## TYPE OF DRUG

Antihistamine/antivomiting/sedative

## USED FOR

Promethazine is used to treat allergic reactions, to prevent or control drug-induced nausea or vomiting, and to lightly sedate both adults and children. It is also used to treat motion sickness and for post-surgical pain relief when prescribed with narcotic pain relievers.

## GENERAL INFORMATION

Promethazine belongs to a class of psychoactive drugs called phenothiazines, which are usually used to treat psychosis. Promethazine has little of the central nervous system activity of other phenothiazines. Instead, it is a potent antihistamine, which is thought to be responsible for its antinausea, antivomiting, and sedative effects.

Promethazine is available in a wide variety of forms, including syrups, tablets, suppositories, and liquids. It is often combined with cough suppressants,

pain relievers, or decongestants as a treatment for the symptoms of infection by cold or flu viruses.

## TREATMENT

For the treatment of nausea and vomiting, the average effective dose of promethazine in adults is 25 mg, taken as necessary at four- to six-hour intervals. The usual dose for children over the age of two is 0.5 mg per pound of body weight up to the adult dose, adjusted for the severity of the condition being treated. When the oral medication cannot be tolerated, the injectable form of the drug or suppositories may be used.

To produce light sedation, 25 to 50 mg taken at bedtime is effective for most adults. Children are generally given 12.5 to 25 mg at bedtime.

For motion sickness, the usual adult dose is 25 mg, taken twice daily. The initial dose should be taken one-half to one hour before travel is intended.

For the treatment of allergic reactions, either due to environmental allergens (pollen, etc.) or caused by medications, the average oral dose of promethazine is 25 mg, taken before bedtime. After treatment is started, the dose should be adjusted to the smallest effective amount.

## CAUTIONS AND WARNINGS

Promethazine should not be used by anyone with an allergy to it or to other phenothiazine psychoactive drugs.

Promethazine may cause drowsiness and impair the ability to operate an automobile or dangerous machinery. The drug may increase the risk of seizures in people with a history of seizures.

Promethazine should be used with caution in people with heart or liver disease, because of the risk of serious side effects.

People experiencing involuntary muscle movements or sensitivity to sunlight while taking the drug should notify their doctors.

## SIDE EFFECTS

Common side effects of promethazine include sedation, drowsiness, and thickening of the mucus. Less frequently, blurred vision, dry mouth, dizziness, confusion, disorientation, sore throat, fever, fatigue, impaired motor coordination, muscle spasms, trembling, difficulty urinating, sensitivity to sunlight, sweating, loss of appetite, hallucinations, and seizures occur.

## PREGNANCY/BREAST-FEEDING

Promethazine has not been formally studied in pregnant women. However, most clinical evidence indicates that the risk of birth defects with this class of drugs is low. Pregnant women are encouraged to discuss the benefits and potential risks of promethazine with their physician before using the drug.

Pregnant women are often at risk for low blood iron levels, which can result in anemia. This is especially true for women using promethazine alone or in

combination with AZT. Women using promethazine during pregnancy should closely follow their physician's recommendations for use of vitamin and mineral supplements.

HIV can be passed from a woman to her child through breast milk. In areas where nutritionally sound alternatives are readily available, breast-feeding is discouraged for HIV-positive women. It is not known whether promethazine is excreted in human milk. Because of the potential toxicity of the drug, women are encouraged to consider alternatives to breast-feeding while taking it.

### USE IN CHILDREN
In children older than two, promethazine has been used safely and effectively. Because there is limited experience, the drug is not recommended in children under two.

### USE IN THE ELDERLY
Older adults may be more susceptible to the side effects of the drug and may require reduced doses.

### DRUG INTERACTIONS
Promethazine may intensify the central nervous system depressive effects of alcohol, narcotic pain relievers, barbiturates, sedatives, hypnotics, tricyclic antidepressants, and tranquilizers. These drug combinations should be avoided.

Use of monoamine oxidase (MAO) inhibitors together with promethazine may cause low blood pressure and involuntary or uncoordinated movements.

Promethazine may interfere with the effects of amphetamines or appetite stimulants. The combination of promethazine and oral antithyroid drugs may increase the risk of low white blood cell counts.

Use of promethazine and quinidine may increase the effects and side effects of both drugs on the heart.

### FOOD INTERACTIONS
Promethazine may be taken with food or milk if it causes stomach upset.

### OTHER DRUGS USED FOR SIMILAR CONDITIONS
For treatment or prevention of nausea and vomiting, a number of different types of drugs are available. Drugs used include metoclopramide, antihistamines (e.g., dimenhydrinate or meclizine), phenothiazines (e.g., prochlorperazine or thiethylperazine), granisetron, and ondansetron. The different types of drugs differ significantly in their side effects, and the choice of therapy is often determined by the side effects for which an individual is at risk.

# SCOPOLAMINE

**BRAND NAME (MANUFACTURER)**
Transderm Scop (Novartis)

**OTHER NAME**
Transdermal-V

**TYPE OF DRUG**
Antinausea/antivomiting agent

**USED FOR**
Scopolamine is used primarily to prevent nausea and vomiting associated with motion sickness in adults, but it is also used to prevent nausea and vomiting from other causes as well.

**GENERAL INFORMATION**
Scopolamine is a naturally occurring chemical purified from plants of the nightshade family. It is classified as an alkaloid and has similar effects as the related drug atropine. Scopolamine relaxes smooth muscles, lessens tremors and convulsions, increases heart rates, and counteracts the toxicity of phosphorus-containing drugs and pesticides. It is not known exactly how scopolamine prevents nausea and vomiting, but the drug is thought to act on the vomiting center of the brain, inhibiting the transmission of the vomiting signals to the gut.

Scopolamine is administered through a transdermal disc that is applied to an area of intact, thin skin, such as behind the ear. Over the course of three days, the drug is released and absorbed through the skin and into the bloodstream at a roughly constant rate.

**TREATMENT**
Only one transdermal disc should be used at a time. It should be applied to a hairless area of skin behind the ear four hours before the antivomiting effect is needed (when used to prevent motion sickness). After the disc is applied on dry skin, the hands should be washed thoroughly with soap and water and dried. If residual drug gets into the eyes, it may cause stinging and blurred vision.

Upon removal, the disc should be discarded, and the hands and the area where the disc was attached should be thoroughly cleaned with soap and water. If treatment longer than three days is required, the old disc should be discarded and a new disc should be applied behind the other ear.

**CAUTIONS AND WARNINGS**
Scopolamine should not be used by anyone with a known allergy to it. Drowsiness, disorientation, and confusion may result from using the drug, which

may impair the mental and physical abilities to operate dangerous machinery or drive an automobile.

Because of the risk of serious side effects, the drug should be used with caution in people suspected of having intestinal or bladder obstructions. People with impaired liver or kidney function are at higher risk of central nervous system side effects from scopolamine than healthy individuals.

If pain, reddening of the eyes, and dilated pupils occur while using the drug, the disc should be removed and a physician contacted. These symptoms may indicate the drug is causing narrow-angle glaucoma.

**SIDE EFFECTS**

The most common side effect of scopolamine is dryness of the mouth, which occurs in about two-thirds of people using the drug. A less frequent side effect is drowsiness. Infrequently, disorientation; memory loss; dizziness; restlessness; hallucinations; confusion; difficulty urinating; skin rashes; and dry, itchy, or red eyes; and pain have been reported.

**PREGNANCY/BREAST-FEEDING**

Scopolamine has not been formally tested in pregnant women. In animal studies, it caused spontaneous abortions, but it is not known whether the same would be true for humans. Pregnant women are encouraged to discuss the benefits and potential risks of scopolamine with their physician before deciding to use the drug.

HIV may be passed from a woman to her child through breast milk. In areas where nutritionally sound alternatives are readily available, breast-feeding is discouraged for HIV-positive women. It is not known whether scopolamine is excreted in milk. Because of the potential toxicity of the drug, women are encouraged to consider alternatives to breast-feeding while using it.

**USE IN CHILDREN**

Children are particularly susceptible to the side effects of alkaloids. The scopolamine disc should not be used in children because it may produce serious side effects in them.

**USE IN THE ELDERLY**

Older adults may be more susceptible to the side effects of the drug and may require reduced doses.

**DRUG INTERACTIONS**

Scopolamine may intensify the effects of other central nervous system depressants, including alcohol, tranquilizers, sleeping pills, narcotic pain relievers, other alkaloids (e.g., atropine), antihistamines, and antidepressants.

**FOOD INTERACTIONS**

Because scopolamine is administered directly through the skin, food does not affect the absorption of the drug.

**OTHER DRUGS USED FOR SIMILAR CONDITIONS**
For treatment or prevention of nausea and vomiting, a number of different types of drugs are available. Drugs used include metoclopramide, antihistamines (e.g., dimenhydrinate, meclizine, and promethazine), phenothiazines (e.g., prochlorperazine or thiethylperazine), granisetron, and ondansetron. The different types of drugs differ significantly in their side effects, and the choice of therapy is often determined by the side effects for which an individual is at risk.

# THIETHYLPERAZINE

**BRAND NAME (MANUFACTURER)**
Torecan (Roxane)

**TYPE OF DRUG**
Antinausea/antivomiting agent

**USED FOR**
Thiethylperazine is used for the treatment of nausea and vomiting.

**GENERAL INFORMATION**
Thiethylperazine belongs to a class of psychoactive drugs called phenothiazines. Although the mechanism by which they work is unknown, they have potent effects on the central nervous system and other organs. They can reduce blood pressure, stop seizures, and control nausea and vomiting.

Thiethylperazine is available as tablets for oral administration and as a solution for intramuscular injection.

**TREATMENT**
For adults, the usual daily dose is 10 mg, taken one to three times daily as necessary.

**CAUTIONS AND WARNINGS**
Thiethylperazine should not be used by anyone with a known allergy to it. It should also not be used by people receiving large doses of other depressants (e.g., alcohol, tranquilizers, etc.) or those in comatose or severely depressed states.

People who are allergic to other phenothiazines may also be allergic to thiethylperazine and should use the drug with caution. Similarly, people who are exposed to extreme heat or phosphorus pesticides and people with a history of seizures or heart disease should use the drug with caution because of the increased risk of side effects.

Thiethylperazine may impair the mental and physical abilities necessary to operate dangerous machinery or to drive an automobile.

The injectable solution of thiethylperazine contains sulfites and should not be used by people with sulfite allergies.

Phenothiazine drugs may cause increased levels of prolactin in the body. About one-third of human breast cancers are prolactin-dependent, meaning that elevated levels of prolactin may cause the cancer to worsen. Consequently, phenothiazines may not be appropriate for people with breast cancer, although there is no evidence that the drugs can cause breast cancer.

## SIDE EFFECTS

Some cases of drowsiness, dizziness, headache, fever, and restlessness have been reported in people using the drug. Dry mouth, blurred vision, ringing in the ears, and swelling in the extremities have also occurred as side effects.

Serious side effects, such as convulsions and involuntary muscle movements, are uncommon, but they have occurred.

Phenothiazines, including thiethylperazine, can cause a potentially fatal side effect called neuroleptic malignant syndrome. The syndrome is characterized by high fever, muscle rigidity, altered mental status, irregular pulse or blood pressure, and abnormal heart rhythms. If these symptoms occur, the drug should be stopped and a physician contacted immediately.

## PREGNANCY/BREAST-FEEDING

Because of the risk of serious fetal harm, thiethylperazine should not be used in pregnant women.

HIV may be passed from a woman to her child through breast milk. In areas where nutritionally sound alternatives are readily available, breast-feeding is discouraged for HIV-positive women. It is not known whether thiethylperazine is excreted in human milk. Because of the potential toxicity of the drug for newborns, women are encouraged to consider alternatives to breast-feeding while using it.

## USE IN CHILDREN

Thiethylperazine has not been studied formally in young children. Consequently there are no recommendations for its use in them.

## USE IN THE ELDERLY

No changes in dosage or administration are usually necessary for elderly people taking thiethylperazine.

## DRUG INTERACTIONS

Thiethylperazine may intensify the effects of other central nervous system depressants, including alcohol, barbiturates, and narcotic analgesics. The drug may also intensify the neurological effects of atropine and phosphorus-containing pesticides.

## FOOD INTERACTIONS

None reported.

**OTHER DRUGS USED FOR SIMILAR CONDITIONS**

For treatment or prevention of nausea and vomiting, a number of different types of drugs are available. Drugs used include metoclopramide, antihistamines (e.g., dimenhydrinate, meclizine, and promethazine), phenothiazines (e.g., prochlorperazine), granisetron, and ondansetron. The different types of drugs differ significantly in their side effects, and the choice of therapy is often determined by the side effects for which an individual is at risk.

# TRIMETHOBENZAMIDE

**BRAND NAME (MANUFACTURER)**

Tigan (SmithKline Beecham)

**TYPE OF DRUG**

Antinausea/antivomiting agent

**USED FOR**

Trimethobenzamide is used for the treatment of nausea and vomiting.

**GENERAL INFORMATION**

Trimethobenzamide is chemically unrelated to most other drugs used to treat nausea and vomiting. Although its mechanism of action is not clearly understood, it is thought that the drug acts on the part of the brain that controls vomiting. By blocking the signals from that part of the brain to the gut, the drug suppresses the urge to vomit. Trimethobenzamide treats the symptoms of nausea and vomiting only, not the underlying cause, which may be infection, malignancy, or a side effect of another drug being taken.

Trimethobenzamide is available in capsules, suppositories, and a solution for injection.

**TREATMENT**

The recommended dosage of trimethobenzamide varies depending on the severity of the symptoms and the response of the individual. For most adults, the tablets are used at a dose of 250 mg, taken three or four times a day. For children between thirty and ninety pounds, the commonly used dose is 100 mg, taken three or four times a day.

The adult suppositories contain 200 mg of the drug. There is also a pediatric suppository that contains 100 mg of the drug. The adult dose is generally 200 mg (one adult suppository) taken three or four times a day. For children thirty pounds and under, the usual dose is one-half of an adult suppository or one pediatric suppository (100 mg) taken three or four times a day. Children between thirty and ninety pounds are usually given one-half to one adult suppository or one to two pediatric suppositories (100 to 200 mg) three or four times a day.

## CAUTIONS AND WARNINGS

Trimethobenzamide should not be used by anyone with a known allergy to it. The injectable form of the drug should not be used in children, and the suppositories should not be used in premature or newborn infants.

The suppositories contain benzocaine and should not be used by anyone with a known allergy to this local anesthetic.

Trimethobenzamide may interfere with the mental or physical abilities necessary to operate dangerous machinery or drive an automobile.

## SIDE EFFECTS

The most common side effect of the drug is drowsiness. Other side effects include allergic skin reactions, involuntary muscle movements, tremors, low blood pressure, blurred vision, coma, convulsions, depression of mood, diarrhea, disorientation, dizziness, headache, jaundice, and muscle cramps. Most of these side effects disappear after the drug is stopped, but some may require additional treatment.

## PREGNANCY/BREAST-FEEDING

Trimethobenzamide has not been formally studied in pregnant women. In animal studies, it caused stillbirths and spontaneous abortions, but it is not known whether the same would be true in humans. Pregnant women are encouraged to discuss the benefits and potential risks of trimethobenzamide with their physician before deciding to use the drug.

HIV may be passed from a woman to her child through breast milk. In areas where nutritionally sound alternatives are readily available, breast-feeding is discouraged for HIV-positive women. It is not known whether trimethobenzamide is excreted in breast milk. Because of the potential toxicity of the drug to newborns, women are encouraged to consider alternatives to breast-feeding while using it.

## USE IN CHILDREN

Trimethobenzamide should be used with caution in children to treat vomiting. In general, children should be given the drug only when the vomiting is persistent and there is a known cause. There are two reasons for this limitation. First, centrally acting drugs like trimethobenzamide have been implicated in Reye's syndrome in children with viral infections. Reye's syndrome is a potentially fatal disorder characterized by high fever, persistent and severe vomiting, lethargy, and irrational behavior. The disorder may progress to coma, convulsions, and death. Although the connection between the drug and the syndrome is not proven, it is prudent to be cautious about giving the drug to children. Secondly, the side effects of trimethobenzamide may be confused with neurological disorders that may be causing the vomiting, making diagnosis and treatment of these underlying causes difficult.

**USE IN THE ELDERLY**

Elderly people may be more susceptible to the side effects of trimethobenzamide, but no changes in dosage or administration are usually recommended for them.

**DRUG INTERACTIONS**

Trimethobenzamide may intensify the effects of other central nervous system depressants, including alcohol, narcotic pain relievers, tranquilizers, antihistamines, and sleeping pills.

**FOOD INTERACTIONS**

Trimethobenzamide may be taken with or without food.

**OTHER DRUGS USED FOR SIMILAR CONDITIONS**

For treatment or prevention of nausea and vomiting, a number of different types of drugs are available. In addition to trimethobenzamide, drugs used include metoclopramide, antihistamines (e.g., dimenhydrinate, meclizine, and promethazine), phenothiazines (e.g., prochlorperazine or thiethylperazine), granisetron, and ondansetron. The different types of drugs differ significantly in their side effects, and the choice of therapy is often determined by the side effects for which an individual is at risk.

# ANTINAUSEA/ANTIVOMITING
## EXPERIMENTAL DRUGS

**MARIJUANA**

Marijuana, a preparation of leaves or flower buds of Cannabis Sativa, is a controlled substance that has been used for thousands of years for its medicinal and psychoactive properties. Medicinally, marijuana has been used to treat a variety of conditions, including nausea, vomiting, and glaucoma. It has also been used to stimulate appetite. A synthetic form of the active drug found in marijuana (THC; dronabinol) has been approved for use as an appetite stimulant (see the antiwasting treatments). It is also used to treat nausea and vomiting. However, because marijuana contains a complex combination of chemicals, some users argue that the synthetic form is not as effective as the herb. Similarly, the relative balance of chemical compounds in the natural form of the drug varies widely from crop to crop, making it difficult to generalize about the properties of marijuana. Several cities now permit, or at least tolerate, the activity of groups that provide marijuana for medicinal use by people with serious illnesses. Because marijuana is a controlled substance, few studies on its use in people with HIV have been performed, and its safety has not yet been established. Smoking marijuana may increase the risk of lung infections associated with HIV disease, but people continue to smoke the drug or bake it in food, based on anecdotal reports of its effectiveness.

# ANTIPROTOZOAL DRUGS

Protozoa are single-celled organisms that are present in the soil. They can be transmitted to or between humans through contaminated food or water, sexual contact, or bites from insects. There are many different types of protozoal infections. In people with HIV, toxoplasmosis and cryptosporidiosis are among the most common. Pneumocystis carinii pneumonia (PCP) was thought to be caused by a protozoa, but is now believed to be caused by fungi. The risk for PCP or toxoplasmosis increases as CD4+ counts drop below 200. Cryptosporidiosis usually occurs in people with CD4+ counts below 75.

Good hygiene and safe food-handling practices are essential parts of any effort to control protozoal infection. In addition, a variety of drugs are used to prevent or treat these diseases. Some, such as dapsone or trimethoprim/sulfamethoxazole, are also used for their antibacterial action. Others are rarely used except in specific protozoal infections. Certain antifungal drugs, such as amphotericin B, may also be used for specific protozoal diseases.

The drugs profiled in this section include:
- albendazole
- atovaquone
- dapsone
- ivermectin
- paromomycin
- pentamidine
- primaquine
- pyrimethamine
- quinacrine
- sulfadiazine
- trimethoprim/sulfamethoxazole
- trimetrexate

In addition, a brief description of tinidazole and NTZ, experimental therapies for protozoal infections, are included at the end of this section.

# ALBENDAZOLE

**BRAND NAME**
Albenza, Eskazole, Zentel (SmithKline Beecham)

**TYPE OF DRUG**
Antiprotozoal agent

## USED FOR

Albendazole is used primarily as a treatment for tapeworm. In people living with HIV, it is sometimes used to treat microsporidiosis.

## GENERAL INFORMATION

Albendazole has been used to treat microsporidiosis with some anecdotal success. No results from clinical studies have been reported.

## TREATMENT

For the treatment of tapeworm, albendazole is normally taken at a daily dose of 400 mg twice daily with meals. For people less than 60 kg (132 pounds), a dose of 15 mg/kg is used twice a day with meals.

For the treatment of microsporidiosis in clinical trials, the dosage of albendazole was 800 mg twice daily for 28 days.

## CAUTIONS AND WARNINGS

Albendazole should not be used by anyone with a known allergy to it or to the benzimidazole class of drugs.

## SIDE EFFECTS

Albendazole can cause bone marrow suppression and blood counts should be routinely monitored while on the drug. Other side effects reported were abnormal liver function tests, abdominal pain, nausea, and vomiting.

## PREGNANCY/BREAST-FEEDING

Albendazole has not been formally studied in pregnant women. In animal studies, the drug caused fetal defects. Pregnant women are encouraged to discuss the benefits and potential risks of albendazole with their physician before deciding to use the drug.

HIV can be passed from a woman to her child through breast milk. In areas where nutritionally sound alternatives are readily available, breast-feeding is discouraged for HIV-positive women. Albendazole is excreted in breast milk and can cause serious side effects in nursing infants. Women are encouraged to consider alternatives to nursing while using the drug.

## USE IN CHILDREN

Children may use albendazole at dosages adjusted for weight.

## USE IN THE ELDERLY

No changes in dosage or administration are recommended for older adults.

## DRUG INTERACTIONS

Dexamethasone, praziquantel, and cimetidine will raise albendazole levels in blood.

## FOOD INTERACTIONS

Albendazole should be taken with food.

**OTHER DRUGS USED FOR SIMILAR CONDITIONS**
There is no proven treatment for microsporidiosis.

# ATOVAQUONE

**BRAND NAME (MANUFACTURER)**
Mepron (Glaxo Wellcome)

**OTHER NAMES**
BW 566C80; 566; Acuvel

**TYPE OF DRUG**
Antiprotozoal agent

**USED FOR**
Atovaquone is used for the treatment of mild-to-moderate *Pneumocystis carinii* pneumonia (PCP) when other drugs more commonly used for the infection cannot be tolerated. It is used less frequently as a treatment for protozoal infections caused by *Toxoplasma gondii*.

**GENERAL INFORMATION**
Atovaquone is a drug that was originally developed to treat malaria and later found to be effective in the treatment of PCP and infections of the brain and digestive tract caused by other protozoal pathogens.

Atovaquone has been shown to be effective for mild-to-moderate PCP, but less effective than TMP/SMX. In one study of 322 volunteers with PCP, more people treated with atovaquone had progressive disease than those treated with TMP/SMX, and more people taking atovaquone died within four weeks of treatment. However, fewer people treated with atovaquone stopped taking the drug because of side effects than those treated with TMP/SMX.

Atovaquone must bind to fat to be absorbed in the small intestine to be effective. Problems with absorption may be one reason the drug is not effective in more people. Unfortunately, many people with HIV have difficulty absorbing the drug, so adequate therapeutic levels are not achieved. The FDA has now approved a new liquid formulation of Atovaquone that may be better absorbed.

Atovaquone has also been compared to pentamidine for the treatment of mild-to-moderate PCP. In one study of 109 patients, oral atovaquone and intravenous pentamidine had roughly the same effectiveness. Fewer people on atovaquone stopped therapy because of side effects.

Atovaquone is available as tablets and liquid for oral administration.

## TREATMENT

The standard dose of the original formulation of atovaquone has been 750 mg taken three times a day with food for twenty-one days. Food, especially fatty food, dramatically improves the absorption of the drug and improves the likelihood of successful treatment and survival. The standard dose of the new, liquid formulation is 10 ml (1500 mg) either two or four times a day.

## PREVENTION

Atovaquone is being studied in the prevention of PCP and toxoplasmosis. There is also some evidence that atovaquone may also have activity against certain species of *Microsporidia*. Because of the wide variability in how atovaquone is absorbed from person to person, the drug is used for prevention primarily by people who cannot tolerate standard preventive agents. These uses of the drug are not approved by the FDA or supported by extensive clinical data.

## CAUTIONS AND WARNINGS

Atovaquone should not be taken by people who know they are allergic to it. The drug has been studied only in mild-to-moderate PCP. It is not known if it would be effective in people who are failing therapy with TMP/SMX.

Disorders of the digestive tract, especially diarrhea, may interfere with uptake of atovaquone. People with serious problems of the gut may not gain any benefit from using atovaquone and should consider other therapies.

## SIDE EFFECTS

It is often difficult to distinguish HIV symptoms from side effects caused by atovaquone. In a comparative trial, volunteers using atovaquone stopped therapy because of side effects less often than those using TMP/SMX. In a comparative trial with pentamidine, volunteers taking atovaquone had more cases of fever, rash, cough, and sweating.

## PREGNANCY/BREAST-FEEDING

Atovaquone has not been formally studied in pregnant women. In animal studies, the drug caused early abortions, but it is not known if the same would be true for humans. Pregnant women are encouraged to discuss the benefits and potential risks of atovaquone with their physician before deciding to use the drug.

HIV can be passed from a woman to her child through breast milk. In areas where nutritionally sound alternatives are readily available, breast-feeding is discouraged for HIV-positive women. It is not known if atovaquone is excreted in human milk, but it is excreted in animal milk. Because of its potential toxicity, women should consider alternatives to breast-feeding while taking the drug.

### USE IN CHILDREN

Atovaquone has been used to a limited extent in children with HIV. In a formal study of its safety and metabolism in children, a dosage of 40 mg per kg of body weight per day was well tolerated in children between the ages of four months and twelve years. This dosage is slightly higher by weight than the adult dose but did not result in any serious toxicities or side effects. As with adults, atovaquone can be used as an alternative therapy for PCP when other less toxic or better-absorbed drugs have failed or are not tolerated.

### USE IN THE ELDERLY

Older adults may be more susceptible to the side effects of the drug and may require reduced doses.

### DRUG INTERACTIONS

Acetaminophen, acyclovir, benzodiazepines, cephalosporin antibiotics, laxatives, and rifampin may decrease atovaquone levels in the blood, potentially making it less effective. AZT, fluconazole, and prednisone may increase atovaquone levels in the blood, increasing the risk of side effects.

### FOOD INTERACTIONS

The absorption of atovaquone is increased three times when taken with food. It is important to take food, especially fatty food, to ensure the drug is absorbed sufficiently to be effective.

### OTHER DRUGS USED FOR SIMILAR CONDITIONS

The drug of choice for treatment of PCP is TMP/SMX. For people who cannot tolerate it, dapsone or intravenous pentamidine may be appropriate. Many physicians prescribe dapsone when TMP/SMX is not tolerated and reserve pentamidine for when neither TMP/SMX nor dapsone can be used. Because the original version of the drug was poorly absorbed by people with HIV, atovaquone is normally used only when these drugs are ineffective or not tolerated. It is less clear what the appropriate role should be for the newer improved version of atovaquone.

For the treatment of toxoplasmosis, pyrimethamine with sulfadiazine, clindamycin, or azithromycin are the preferred therapies.

### COMMENTS

Intravenous and oral suspension forms of atovaquone are currently being tested in clinical trials. If they are effective in increasing levels of the drug in the blood, atovaquone may become a more attractive treatment and preventive agent for PCP.

# DAPSONE

**BRAND NAME (MANUFACTURER)**
Dapsone USP (Jacobus)

**TYPE OF DRUG**
Antibiotic/antiprotozoal agent

**USED FOR**
Dapsone is approved for treatment of certain skin infections and leprosy. It is also used, but not approved, for the treatment and prevention of *Pneumocystis carinii* pneumonia (PCP) and occasionally for the treatment of mycobacterial or other protozoal infections in people living with HIV.

**GENERAL INFORMATION**
Dapsone is a sulfone antibiotic that stops certain bacteria from multiplying, but does not kill them. It is usually considered backup therapy for the treatment of mild-to-moderate PCP in people who cannot tolerate the preferred drugs such as trimethoprim/sulfamethoxazole (TMP/SMX) or intravenous pentamidine. Similarly, dapsone is considered second-line therapy for the prevention of PCP.

**TREATMENT**
For treatment of mild-to-moderate PCP, dapsone is generally taken at a dose of 100 mg per day, combined with a dose of trimethoprim (TMP) of 20 mg per kg of body weight per day. While this combination has not been studied as extensively as TMP/SMX, it appears to be quite effective.

Dapsone is occasionally used as a treatment for toxoplasmosis in people who cannot tolerate pyrimethamine. The recommended dosage of dapsone for this infection is 100 mg per day.

**PREVENTION**
All HIV-positive people develop some level of risk for PCP if their CD4+ counts fall to dangerously low levels. This includes anyone who has already had PCP or any other AIDS-related condition and asymptomatic HIV-infected people with consistent CD4+ counts below 200 or whose percentage of CD4+ cells is 15% or below. In addition, many physicians recommend PCP prophylaxis for HIV-infected individuals with CD4+ counts greater than 200 if they also have symptoms of oral thrush or HIV-related infections. Since many people who once had CD4+ counts below the 200 threshold level have seen their counts rise in response to antiviral therapy, it is tempting for them to abandon preventive medicines. However, most experts discourage any discontinuance of preventive therapies and believe it is safest to use only the lowest sustained CD4+ a person experienced as the basis for making decisions about preven-

tive treatment. This view may or may not change as researchers gain more experience with the people who have regained large numbers of CD4+ cells.

There is no clear consensus on the best dose of dapsone to use to prevent PCP. The drug is given in various doses, including 100 mg tablets twice weekly, 50 mg once daily, and 100 mg once daily. Some studies suggest the lower doses may not be as effective as the higher doses in preventing PCP. The use of TMP with dapsone has been discussed by AIDS experts as a prophylactic alternative, but it has not been well studied. The combination of dapsone with pyrimethamine may be comparable to standard therapies.

HIV-infected people with a history of toxoplasmosis and who have CD4+ counts under 200 should consider preventive therapy for toxoplasma gondii. For this use, dapsone is prescribed at 100 mg twice a week.

### CAUTIONS AND WARNINGS

Dapsone should not be used by people who know they are allergic to it. Dapsone should not be used by people with a deficiency of glucose-6-phosphate dehydrogenase (G6PD). The deficiency is found primarily in men. About 10% to 15% of African-American men have it, and it is also widespread in men of eastern-Mediterranean ancestry. When dapsone is used with people who have the deficiency, it can cause blood cells to burst, resulting in severe anemia. Deaths have been associated with this use.

People taking dapsone should tell their doctors if they have loss of color or jaundice. Blood counts should be done frequently on people taking dapsone for extended periods.

### SIDE EFFECTS

The most serious side effect of dapsone is anemia, accompanied by shortened red-blood-cell life span and a rise in abnormal hemoglobin. These side effects are dose related and occur to some extent in almost all people taking the drug, but it is uncommon for them to be severe enough to stop therapy. Peripheral neuropathy, a condition whose symptoms include numbness, tingling, and pain in the extremities, is an unusual side effect of dapsone. Other side effects of dapsone include muscle weakness, nausea, vomiting, abdominal pain, inflammation of the pancreas, vertigo, and blurred vision.

### PREGNANCY/BREAST-FEEDING

Dapsone has not been formally studied in pregnant women or laboratory animals. However, it has been used extensively by pregnant women in all trimesters of pregnancy without reported birth effects. Pregnant women are encouraged to discuss the benefits and potential risks of dapsone with their physician before deciding to use the drug.

HIV can be passed from a woman to her child through breast milk. In areas where nutritionally sound alternatives are readily available, breast-feeding is discouraged for HIV-positive women. Dapsone is excreted in human

milk in substantial amounts and can cause anemia or liver toxicity in newborns. Because of the potential toxicity of the drug, women should consider alternatives to breast-feeding while taking it.

**USE IN CHILDREN**
Dapsone can be used in children at reduced doses, generally at 2 mg per kg of body weight per day. The drug is generally considered not to affect the later growth or development of the child.

**USE IN THE ELDERLY**
Older adults may be more susceptible to the side effects of the drug and may require reduced doses.

**DRUG INTERACTIONS**
Dapsone used with AZT or ganciclovir may increase the risk of bone marrow toxicity. Dapsone may decrease the effectiveness of clofazimine and increase the risk of peripheral neuropathy when used with ddC, ddI, or d4T. Probenecid or trimethoprim may increase dapsone levels in the blood. Similarly, dapsone may increase trimethoprim levels. Dapsone should be taken either two hours before or two hours after ddI, because ddI tablets contain a buffer that reduces dapsone absorption into the body. Taking pyrimethamine with dapsone may increase the risk of side effects of the blood, including anemia. Rifampin reduces the levels of dapsone in the blood and may make higher doses necessary to maintain the effect of dapsone.

**FOOD INTERACTIONS**
None reported.

**OTHER DRUGS USED FOR SIMILAR CONDITIONS**
For treatment of PCP, the therapy of choice is TMP/SMX. However, a significant number of adults infected with HIV cannot tolerate TMP/SMX. In these cases, dapsone or intravenous pentamidine may be appropriate. Atovaquone is sometimes used when these alternatives fail or are not tolerated. Other therapies used less frequently include trimetrexate, primaquine, and clindamycin.

For prevention of PCP, TMP/SMX is the drug of choice. For people who cannot tolerate it, dapsone or aerosol pentamidine may be appropriate. Most physicians prescribe dapsone if TMP/SMX is not tolerated and reserve aerosol pentamidine when neither TMP/SMX or dapsone can be taken.

For treatment of toxoplasmosis, pyrimethamine with sulfadiazine or clindamycin is standard therapy. For prevention of toxoplasmosis, TMP/SMX is the drug of choice, with dapsone used less frequently.

# IVERMECTIN

**BRAND NAME**
Stromectol (Merck)

**TYPE OF DRUG**
Antiprotozoal agent

**USED FOR**
Ivermectin is used to treat intestinal parasitic infections caused by *Strongyloides stercoralis* or *Onchocerca volvulus*. In people living with HIV, it is sometimes used to treat scabies.

**GENERAL INFORMATION**
Ivermectin is a broad-spectrum antiparisitic drug. It binds to the nerve and muscle cells causing them to 'break down' and results in paralyzing or killing the parasite.

Ivermectin is available as a tablet for oral administration.

**TREATMENT**
The dose of ivermectin is usually 150-250 micrograms of ivermectin per kg of body weight. A single dose is usually sufficient to cure people from these parasites.

**CAUTIONS AND WARNINGS**
Ivermectin should not be used by anyone with a known allergy to it. Ivermectin must be taken with water.

**SIDE EFFECTS**
Dizziness, rash, joint pain, and abnormal sensation in the eyelids are reported side effects of ivermectin. Less commonly, decreased blood pressure, muscle ache, and headaches may occur when using ivermectin.

**PREGNANCY/BREAST-FEEDING**
Ivermectin has not been formally studied in pregnant women. Pregnant women should discuss the benefits and potential risks of the drug with their physician before deciding to use it.

HIV can be passed from a woman to her child through breast milk. In areas where nutritionally sound alternatives are readily available, breast-feeding is discouraged for HIV-positive women. Ivermectin is excreted in breast milk and can cause serious side effects in nursing infants. Women are encouraged to consider alternatives to nursing while using the drug.

**USE IN CHILDREN**
The safety and effectiveness of ivermectin has not been established for children weighing under 15 kg (33 pounds).

**USE IN THE ELDERLY**
No changes in dosage or administration are recommended for older adults.

**DRUG INTERACTIONS**
None reported.

**FOOD INTERACTIONS**
Ivermectin may be taken with or without food.

**OTHER DRUGS USED FOR SIMILAR CONDITIONS**
For the treatment of *Strongyloides stercoralis,* thiabendizole is another option. The treatment of choice for *Onchocerca volvulus* is ivermectin.

For scabies, other treatment options include permethrin cream or Lindane (gamma benzene hexachloride) cream.

# PAROMOMYCIN

**BRAND NAME (MANUFACTURER)**
Humatin (Parke-Davis)

**OTHER NAMES**
Aminosidine; AMS

**TYPE OF DRUG**
Antibiotic/antiprotozoal agent

**USED FOR**
Paromomycin has been approved by the FDA to treat amoebic infections of the intestines. It is also used occasionally in people living with HIV to treat cryptosporidiosis.

**GENERAL INFORMATION**
Paromomycin is an antibiotic of the aminoglycoside class, similar in its action to neomycin, streptomycin, erythromycin, and others. It is poorly absorbed in humans, so high concentrations stay in the gut where many parasites that cause diarrhea multiply.

A number of small clinical trials have suggested that paromomycin may reduce the symptoms of diarrhea and reduce the numbers of cryptosporidia in the intestines of people infected with HIV. Larger clinical trials are currently ongoing to determine if these promising results can be confirmed. It is too early to know whether the drug will be effective for many people with HIV.

Paromomycin is available as tablets for oral administration.

**TREATMENT**
The dosage and administration of paromomycin varies depending on the organism causing the infection. For amoebic infections, the usual dose is 650 mg taken three times a day for twenty-one days. In clinical trials to treat

cryptosporidiosis in people with HIV, the adult dosage was 2,000 mg per day, split into four equal doses, taken for fourteen to thirty days.

**CAUTIONS AND WARNINGS**

Paromomycin should not be used by anyone with a known allergy to it. It should also not be used by anyone with an obstruction in the intestines.

**SIDE EFFECTS**

Paromomycin taken orally is absorbed poorly into the bloodstream, so it generally causes few side effects. Nausea, abdominal cramps, and diarrhea have been reported in people taking more than 3 g of the drug a day. Rarely, kidney toxicity and hearing loss have been reported.

**PREGNANCY/BREAST-FEEDING**

Paromomycin has not been formally studied in pregnant women. Other aminoglycosides can cause severe fetal hearing loss when taken during pregnancy. Pregnant women are encouraged to discuss the benefits and potential risks of paromomycin with their physician before using the drug.

HIV may be passed from a woman to her child through breast milk. In areas where nutritionally sound alternatives are readily available, breast-feeding is discouraged for HIV-positive women. Aminoglycoside antibiotics pass into breast milk, but the small amounts excreted when normal doses are used should pose little risk to breast-fed infants.

**USE IN CHILDREN**

Paromomycin has been used at dosages adjusted for weight in children to treat amoebic infections. There is little experience with the drug in HIV-positive children with cryptosporidiosis.

**USE IN THE ELDERLY**

No changes in dosage or administration are recommended for elderly people.

**DRUG INTERACTIONS**

Although specific information about paromomycin is not available, a wide range of drugs increase the risk of hearing loss and/or kidney failure when taken with aminoglycosides. These drugs include other aminoglycosides, furosemide, polymyxins, amphotericin B, cisplatin, and cyclosporine.

**FOOD INTERACTIONS**

Paromomycin should be taken with food.

**OTHER DRUGS USED FOR SIMILAR CONDITIONS**

For treatment of cryptosporidiosis, there is no standard, proven therapy. Azithromycin and atovaquone are sometimes used to control the infection. For symptomatic relief of the diarrhea, octreotide or other antidiarrheals may be used.

# PENTAMIDINE

**BRAND NAME (MANUFACTURER)**
NebuPent (Fujisawa); Pentam (Fujisawa); Pentacarinat (Armour)

**TYPE OF DRUG**
Antiprotozoal agent

**USED FOR**
Pentamidine is used for the treatment of *Pneumocystis carinii* pneumonia (PCP) in people for whom trimethoprim/sulfamethoxazole (TMP/SMX) is ineffective or intolerable.

**GENERAL INFORMATION**
Pentamidine is an antiprotozoal drug administered either by injection or as an aerosol. The injectable drug is highly effective against severe PCP. In clinical trials, it has been roughly equivalent to TMP/SMX in its effectiveness, but because some side effects of pentamidine such as inflammation of the pancreas are irreversible, TMP/SMX remains the therapy of choice for PCP.

Aerosolized pentamidine was developed to target the drug directly to the lungs, where the pneumocystis organism causes the most damage. Because it doesn't directly get into the bloodstream, aerosolized pentamidine causes fewer severe side effects. However, the aerosolized form does not affect Pneumocystis infections in parts of the body other than the lungs. Also, it is often difficult to make sure the drug is adequately distributed throughout the lungs.

**TREATMENT**
For treatment of active PCP infection, pentamidine is used intravenously or injected into a muscle. The recommended dose for adults and children is 4 mg per kg of body weight injected once a day for twenty-one days. When used intravenously, pentamidine should be injected over a period of one hour or more to reduce the chance of drug-related toxicity.

**PREVENTION**
The aerosolized form of the drug is used primarily for prevention of PCP infection. Pentamidine for aerosolized use is provided in 300 mg vials. The contents of the vials must be dissolved in 6 ml of sterile water and placed into a nebulizer. The nebulizer should be used until all the liquid is gone, which takes thirty to forty-five minutes at a flow rate of five to seven liters per minute at forty to fifty pounds per square inch of pressure. The solution should be used immediately after mixing and should not be stored. Effective treatment often requires the patient to sit or lie in unusual positions for part of the treatment regimen to aide in the distribution of the drug.

In clinical trials, aerosolized pentamidine effectively reduced the incidence of initial or recurrent PCP as compared to no treatment, but was less effec-

tive than standard oral therapies such as TMP/SMX or dapsone. Its use today is primarily limited to people who cannot tolerate TMP/SMX or dapsone, although some physicians also used it as supplemental therapy in patients who suffer breakthroughs on oral therapy.

### CAUTIONS AND WARNINGS

Pentamidine should not be used by anyone with a known allergy to it.

Aerosolized pentamidine is not completely effective in preventing PCP. People taking the drug should be vigilant for symptoms such as difficulty breathing, coughing, or fever, which may indicate a medical evaluation and more aggressive treatment is necessary. Aerosolized pentamidine does not affect pneumocystis infections outside the lungs. Pentamidine should not be mixed with any other drugs in the nebulizer.

Pentamidine should be used with caution by people with abnormal blood pressure, blood sugar, or blood electrolyte (calcium, potassium, etc.) levels.

Because of the risk of increased side effects, people with reduced kidney or liver function should use the drug with caution.

### SIDE EFFECTS

The most frequent side effects of aerosolized pentamidine are coughing and tightening of the chest that interferes with breathing. These side effects occurred in 38% and 15%, respectively, of people using the drug in clinical trials. Fatigue, metallic taste in the mouth, shortness of breath, decreased appetite, dizziness, rashes, nausea, irritation of mouth or nasal cavities, chest pain, congestion, night sweats, chills, and vomiting also occur frequently.

Of the people taking injectable pentamidine in clinical trials, more than 58% experienced some side effects. The most frequently reported (occurring in more than 2% of volunteers) were pain or hardness at the injection site, nausea, loss of appetite, low blood pressure, reduced white blood cell counts, fever, low blood sugar, rash, and metallic taste. Less frequently, confusion, hallucinations, and anemia were observed. In some cases, pentamidine caused death due to severe low blood pressure, low blood sugar, acute inflammation of the pancreas, or irregular heart rhythms.

### PREGNANCY/BREAST-FEEDING

Pentamidine has not been formally studied in pregnant women or animals. Women are encouraged to discuss the benefits and potential risks of the drug with their physician before deciding to use it during pregnancy.

HIV can be passed from a woman to her child through breast milk. In areas where nutritionally sound alternatives are readily available, breast-feeding is discouraged for HIV-positive women. It is not known whether pentamidine is excreted in human milk. Because of the potential toxicity of the drug,

women are encouraged to consider alternatives to breast-feeding while using it.

**USE IN CHILDREN**

Aerosolized pentamidine to prevent PCP has been tested in HIV-positive children older than 3.5 months. In a study specifically designed to examine the drug's pulmonary side effects, there was no significant difference in these children in heart rate, respiratory rate, blood pressure, or breathing before or after treatment. In another study of older children (ages three to fifteen), the drug caused a bitter taste and short periods of coughing in about 75% of the participants. In a number of studies performed by groups around the world, aerosolized pentamidine was effective in preventing PCP, both in infants under one year of age and in older children. However, because of its potentially serious side effects and because it has not been as effective as standard oral prophylaxis in adults, the drug is still considered appropriate for children only after TMP/SMX has failed or is not tolerated. Dapsone is the third-line drug for use after both of these fail.

For the treatment of PCP, intravenous and intramuscular pentamidine were shown to be effective in children greater than four months of age.

**USE IN THE ELDERLY**

No specific limitations are recommended for aerosolized pentamidine. Injectable pentamidine is metabolized by the kidneys. People with reduced kidney function may have high levels of the drug in their blood when taking recommended doses. Because kidney function often declines with age, elderly people may need to use reduced doses of the injectable drug.

**DRUG INTERACTIONS**

When used with AZT, alpha interferon, or anticancer drugs, pentamidine may increase the risk of the damage they cause to bone marrow. People who use ddI in combination with pentamidine may have an increased risk of inflammation of the pancreas. Foscarnet may intensify the effects of pentamidine on blood sugar levels and kidney function, potentially increasing the risk of these side effects.

**FOOD INTERACTIONS**

None reported.

**OTHER DRUGS USED FOR SIMILAR CONDITIONS**

TMP/SMX is the drug of choice for the treatment PCP. It has been well studied and effectively used by large numbers of people. Unfortunately, more than half of the people with AIDS cannot tolerate its side effects. In these cases, intravenous pentamidine, dapsone with or without trimethoprim, or atovaquone may be appropriate. Trimetrexate with leucovorin and primaquine with clindamycin are experimental treatments that are also used.

TMP/SMX is also the drug of choice for the prevention of initial or recurrent PCP infection. If the drug is not effective or well tolerated, dapsone or aerosolized pentamidine may be used. Most physicians prescribe dapsone if TMP/SMX is not tolerated and reserve aerosolized pentamidine when neither TMP/SMX or dapsone can be used.

# PRIMAQUINE

**BRAND NAME**
Primaquine USP (Sanofi Winthrop)

**TYPE OF DRUG**
Antiprotozoal agent

**USED FOR**
Primaquine is used primarily as a treatment for malaria. In people living with HIV, it is sometimes used with clindamycin to treat or prevent *Pneumocystis carinii* pneumonia (PCP).

**GENERAL INFORMATION**
Primaquine was introduced in 1952. It is highly effective in eliminating certain types of malarial protozoa from all parts of the body. It is often used after initial treatment with chloroquine, a faster-acting drug that suppresses the chills and fever of malaria.

For treatment of mild-to-moderate PCP in people with HIV, primaquine has been combined with clindamycin. In perhaps the largest study to date, sixty volunteers were treated with intravenous or oral clindamycin and oral primaquine. Fifty-five of the sixty responded to treatment, and forty-six of the sixty completed a full course of therapy. The side effects were generally mild. The authors concluded that the combination was effective and well tolerated.

**TREATMENT**
For treatment of malaria, primaquine is normally taken at a daily dose of 15 mg or a weekly dose of 30 to 45 mg.

For treatment of PCP in clinical trials, the dosage of primaquine was 30 mg per day for 21 days.

**CAUTIONS AND WARNINGS**
Primaquine should not be used by anyone with a known allergy to it. It should also not be used by people who have recently received quinacrine, because the combination may be toxic.

People with glucose-6-phosphate dehydrogenase (G6PD) deficiency should use primaquine with caution because of the risk of severe anemia. G6PD is a

genetic disorder found most frequently in African-American men and men of eastern-Mediterranean ancestry.

### SIDE EFFECTS

Nausea, vomiting, loss of appetite, and abdominal discomfort are common side effects of primaquine. Less commonly, blurred vision, allergic skin reactions, dizziness, headache, darkening of the urine, and anemia may occur. In rare cases, bone marrow toxicity may occur when using primaquine.

### PREGNANCY/BREAST-FEEDING

Primaquine has not been formally studied in pregnant women. Pregnant women should discuss the benefits and potential risks of the drug with their physician before deciding to use it.

HIV can be passed from a woman to her child through breast milk. In areas where nutritionally sound alternatives are readily available, breast-feeding is discouraged for HIV-positive women. Primaquine is excreted in breast milk and can cause serious side effects in nursing infants. Women are encouraged to consider alternatives to nursing while using the drug.

### USE IN CHILDREN

Children may use primaquine at dosages adjusted for age and weight. However, they may be more susceptible to the side effects of the drug than adults.

### USE IN THE ELDERLY

No changes in dosage or administration are recommended for older adults.

### DRUG INTERACTIONS

Drugs which suppress bone marrow activity (AZT, ganciclovir, alpha interferon, etc.) may intensify the bone marrow toxicity of primaquine.

### FOOD INTERACTIONS

Primaquine may be taken with or without food.

### OTHER DRUGS USED FOR SIMILAR CONDITIONS

For the treatment of PCP, the therapy of choice is TMP/SMX. When the drug is not tolerated, dapsone or intravenous pentamidine may be appropriate. For prevention of PCP, TMP/SMX is also the drug of choice. When it is not tolerated, dapsone or aerosol pentamidine may be appropriate. Most physicians prescribe dapsone as second-line therapy and reserve aerosol pentamidine when neither TMP/SMX or dapsone can be used. Clindamycin plus primaquine is generally reserved for cases where none of these other treatments is effective or tolerated.

# PYRIMETHAMINE

### BRAND NAME (MANUFACTURER)
Daraprim (Glaxo Wellcome)

**TYPE OF DRUG**
Antiprotozoal agent

**USED FOR**
Pyrimethamine is used as part of combination drug therapy to treat toxoplasmosis. It is also used alone and in combination with other drugs to prevent malaria or recurrent toxoplasmosis.

**GENERAL INFORMATION**
Pyrimethamine is a folic acid antagonist. It interferes with the uptake of this essential B vitamin in susceptible parasites, including those that cause malaria and toxoplasmosis, thus weakening and eventually killing these organisms.

Because parasites can rapidly develop resistance to pyrimethamine, the drug is usually used in combination with sulfa drugs. The activity of the combination when used against parasites greatly exceeds that of either drug used alone.

For the treatment of toxoplasmosis, pyrimethamine is usually combined with sulfadiazine. Because both drugs cross the blood-brain barrier, the combination is effective against toxoplasmosis encephalitis, a serious and potentially fatal infection of the brain.

Pyrimethamine is available as tablets for oral administration.

**TREATMENT**
The combination of pyrimethamine (50 to 75 mg per day) and sulfadiazine taken for at least six weeks is the standard approved treatment for toxoplasmosis. Folinic acid is usually added to protect against the bone marrow toxicity of the combination. Response to therapy is high, with 80% to 90% of the people using the combination showing clinical improvement within three weeks. But the relapse rate is also high when therapy is stopped, so lifelong maintenance therapy is usually necessary.

The dosage of pyrimethamine required for the treatment of toxoplasmosis is ten to twenty times higher than that used for malaria and approaches a toxic level. Many of the people with HIV taking this combination experience either pyrimethamine toxicity or allergic reactions to sulfadiazine. In some cases it may be possible to desensitize individuals to sulfadiazine by restarting the drug at very small doses and gradually building up to therapeutic levels.

**MAINTENANCE/PREVENTION**
To prevent recurrent toxoplasmosis in people with HIV, pyrimethamine in combination with sulfadiazine is generally used for life.

Pyrimethamine is being studied to prevent the initial occurrence of toxoplasmosis. One large clinical study of pyrimethamine used alone for toxoplasmosis prophylaxis in 264 people with CD4+ counts lower than 200 failed

to show any significant benefit from the drug, possibly because so few cases of toxoplasmosis occurred in the study population whether the drug was used or not. Of more concern, the study revealed a significantly higher death rate for people taking the drug than for those taking a placebo. Another larger study also failed to show any benefit from pyrimethamine prophylaxis, but did not confirm an increased mortality in people using it.

Many physicians recommend prophylaxis for initial occurrence of toxoplasmosis for people with CD4+ counts below 200 who have antibodies to the parasite (indicating they have been infected), but the drug of choice is usually trimethoprim/sulfamethoxazole.

**CAUTIONS AND WARNINGS**

Pyrimethamine should not be used by anyone with a known allergy to it. It should also not be used in people with blood disorders caused by folate (vitamin B) deficiencies.

**SIDE EFFECTS**

Allergic reactions, particularly when pyrimethamine is administered with sulfa drugs, can occur at any dose. In rare cases, a severe and life-threatening form of allergic reaction known as Stevens-Johnson Syndrome, has been associated with pyrimethamine plus sulfadiazine. At doses of pyrimethamine used to treat toxoplasmosis, loss of appetite or vomiting may occur.

Other side effects include anemia, reduced white blood cell or platelet counts, blood in the urine, or abnormal heart rhythms. Rarely, the drug may cause insomnia, diarrhea, headache, light-headedness, dry mouth, fever, malaise, skin discoloration, depression, seizures, and breathing disorders.

**PREGNANCY/BREAST-FEEDING**

Pyrimethamine has not been formally studied in pregnant women. In animal studies it caused spontaneous abortions and birth defects, but it is not known if the same would be true in humans. Pregnant women are encouraged to discuss the benefits and potential risks of the drug with their physician before deciding to use it.

HIV may be passed from a woman to her child through breast milk. In areas where nutritionally sound alternatives are available, breast-feeding is discouraged for HIV-positive women. Pyrimethamine is excreted in human milk and can cause serious side effects in infants. Women are encouraged to consider alternatives to breast-feeding while using the drug.

**USE IN CHILDREN**

The pediatric dose of pyrimethamine for toxoplasmosis is 1 mg per kg of body weight, divided into two equal daily doses. After two to four days, this dose may be reduced by half.

**USE IN THE ELDERLY**

No changes in dosage or administration are necessary for people older than sixty years of age.

**DRUG INTERACTIONS**

Use of pyrimethamine with other drugs that cause bone marrow toxicity (e.g., AZT, ganciclovir, chloroquine, alpha interferon, TMP/SMX, dapsone, and some sulfa drugs) may increase the risk of bone marrow suppression. Use of pyrimethamine with lorazepam may increase the risk of liver toxicity. Para-aminobenzoic acid may reduce pyrimethamine levels, potentially reducing its effectiveness.

**FOOD INTERACTIONS**

Pyrimethamine may be taken with food to prevent stomach upset, loss of appetite, or vomiting.

**OTHER DRUGS USED FOR SIMILAR CONDITIONS**

For treatment of toxoplasmosis, the standard therapy is pyrimethamine in combination with sulfadiazine. In place of or in addition to sulfadiazine in combination therapy, clindamycin, azithromycin, or gamma interferon may be used. Atovaquone is a newer drug that has shown potential as a treatment for toxoplasmosis.

For prevention of toxoplasmosis in people with CD4+ counts less than 200 who have been exposed to the microorganism, TMP/SMX is the drug of choice, with dapsone or atovaquone as alternatives. Pyrimethamine in combination with sulfadiazine is the combination of choice for maintenance therapy.

For treatment of malaria, a number of drugs are generally used before trying pyrimethamine. They include chloroquine, primaquine, and quinine. Pyrimethamine is usually used when these drugs are not effective or tolerated.

# QUINACRINE

**BRAND NAME (MANUFACTURER)**

Atabrine (Sanofi Winthrop)

**TYPE OF DRUG**

Antiprotozoal agent

**USED FOR**

Quinacrine is used to treat giardiasis and tapeworm. It is occasionally used for the treatment of malaria.

### GENERAL INFORMATION

Quinacrine was first developed and widely used during World War II to prevent malaria. Since then, more effective drugs have been developed for malaria. Quinacrine is now used primarily to treat the intestinal infection giardiasis. This disease, caused by a protozoan, is characterized by diarrhea, gas, and abdominal pain.

Quinacrine is available as tablets for oral administration.

### TREATMENT

For treatment of giardiasis, the recommended adult dose is 100 mg, taken three times a day for five to seven days. For children, the recommended dose is 7 mg per kg of body weight daily, split into three equal doses, not to exceed the adult dose. If necessary, the course of treatment can be repeated after a break of two weeks if the protozoan is not completely eradicated.

For treatment of tapeworm, higher doses are generally required, but for a shorter period.

### CAUTIONS AND WARNINGS

Quinacrine should not be used by anyone with a known allergy to it. Because quinacrine increases the toxicity of a related drug, primaquine, the two drugs should not be used together.

Quinacrine should be used with caution in people with psoriasis because the drug may precipitate a severe attack of the disease. Quinacrine is known to concentrate in the liver; it should be used with caution in people with liver disease or a history of alcoholism.

A physician should be contacted if blurred vision or any other visual disturbances occur while using quinacrine.

### SIDE EFFECTS

Quinacrine may cause a temporary yellow color of the skin or urine. Commonly, headache, dizziness, diarrhea, loss of appetite, nausea, and abdominal cramps may occur when taking the drug. Infrequent side effects include vomiting, allergic skin reactions, nervousness, vertigo, irritability, emotional changes, and nightmares. Rarely, convulsions or psychotic episodes, difficulty focusing, and blurred vision have been described in people who have taken the drug for long periods to suppress malaria.

### PREGNANCY/BREAST-FEEDING

Quinacrine has not been formally studied in pregnant women. There is some evidence that the drug may cause birth defects, so it is usually not used during pregnancy for treatment of tapeworm or giardiasis because these infections are not life-threatening. In some cases, it is used during pregnancy for treating malaria when the risk of the disease to the mother outweighs the risk of the drug to the fetus. Pregnant women are encouraged to discuss the

benefits and potential risks of quinacrine with their physician before deciding to use the drug.

HIV may be passed from a woman to her child through breast milk. In areas where nutritionally sound alternatives are readily available, breast-feeding is discouraged for HIV-positive women. Generally, quinacrine used by breast-feeding women is not considered dangerous for their infants.

**USE IN CHILDREN**
Quinacrine is used in children older than age four, at doses adjusted for age and weight. Younger children, especially newborns, are not given the drug because of the risk of its side effects.

**USE IN THE ELDERLY**
Quinacrine should be used with special caution in elderly people because they may be at higher risk for the side effects of the drug, especially disorientation or mental disturbances. Dose reductions are often necessary.

**DRUG INTERACTIONS**
Quinacrine increases blood levels of primaquine, increasing the risk of side effects of this drug. The two drugs should not be used together.

Alcohol taken in combination with quinacrine may cause flushing, nausea, vomiting, abdominal pain, and headache.

**FOOD INTERACTIONS**
Quinacrine should be taken after meals to reduce the potential for stomach upset. For children who cannot easily swallow the tablets, the drug may be pulverized and the bitter taste masked with jam or honey.

**OTHER DRUGS USED FOR SIMILAR CONDITIONS**
Other commonly used drugs for giardiasis are metronidazole or furazolidone. For tapeworms, niclosamide or praziquantel may be used. For treatment of malaria, a number of drugs are more effective than quinacrine, including chloroquine, primaquine, pyrimethamine, and quinine.

# S U L F A D I A Z I N E

**BRAND NAME (MANUFACTURER)**
Sulfadiazine Tablets USP (Eon)

**TYPE OF DRUG**
Antibiotic/antiprotozoal agent

**USED FOR**
Sulfadiazine is used to treat urinary-tract infections, chancroid (vaginal ulcers), and trachoma. Sulfadiazine is used along with pyrimethamine to treat toxoplasmosis. It is also occasionally used to treat malaria resistant to chlo-

roquine, meningitis when used with streptomycin, and ear infections when used with penicillin.

## GENERAL INFORMATION

Sulfadiazine is one of a number of sulfa drugs. They work by interfering with folic acid (vitamin B) metabolism in susceptible organisms, which prevents them from multiplying. Sulfa drugs are particularly useful in urinary-tract infections because the drugs tend to concentrate in the urine before they pass out of the body.

Because parasites can rapidly develop resistance to sulfadiazine, the drug is usually used in combination with pyrimethamine for toxoplasmosis. The activity of the combination against the parasite greatly exceeds that of either drug alone. Because both drugs cross the blood-brain barrier, the combination is effective against toxoplasmosis encephalitis, a serious and potentially fatal infection of the brain.

ulfadiazine is available as tablets for oral administration.

## TREATMENT

The combination of sulfadiazine (2 to 4 g per day) and pyrimethamine taken for at least six weeks is the standard approved treatment for toxoplasmosis. Folinic acid is usually added to protect against the bone marrow toxicity of the combination. Response to therapy is high, with 80% to 90% of the people using the combination showing clinical improvement within three weeks. But the relapse rate is also high when therapy is stopped, so lifelong maintenance therapy is usually necessary.

The combination of sulfadiazine and pyrimethamine is often toxic. More than half of the people with HIV taking the combination experience either pyrimethamine toxicity or allergic reactions to sulfadiazine. In some cases it may be possible to desensitize individuals to the sulfadiazine by starting the drug at small doses and gradually building up to therapeutic levels.

## MAINTENANCE

To prevent recurrent toxoplasmosis in people with HIV, pyrimethamine in combination with sulfadiazine is generally used for life. The recommended dosage of both drugs is half the dosage used to suppress the active infection.

## CAUTIONS AND WARNINGS

Sulfadiazine should not be used by anyone with a known allergy to any sulfa drug, thiazide-type diuretics, or oral antidiabetes medications. It should also not be used by anyone with the condition porphyria, a disorder in the metabolism of certain chemicals in the body, including hemoglobin.

Because of the risk of serious side effects, sulfadiazine should not be used by anyone with severe kidney or liver disease.

The presence of a sore throat, jaundice, or loss of color while taking sulfadiazine may be an early sign of a serious blood disorder. A physician should be contacted if these symptoms occur.

People with a metabolic disorder called glucose-6-phosphate dehydrogenase (G6PD) deficiency should use sulfadiazine with caution because of the risk of severe anemia. This deficiency is genetic and is found most frequently in men of African-American and eastern-Mediterranean ancestry.

Because sulfa drugs often cause photosensitivity, people taking the drug should avoid bright light or sunlight. People using sulfadiazine should drink plenty of fluids to reduce the risk of kidney damage.

### SIDE EFFECTS

The most common side effects of sulfadiazine are allergic reactions, including skin rashes, itching, anaphylactic shock, swelling, sensitivity to light, joint pain, fever, and chills. The most serious side effects of the drug are blood disorders, including reduced counts of red blood cells, white blood cells, and platelets (particles involved in blood clotting).

Other side effects of the drug include headache, peripheral neuropathy, mental depression, convulsion, weakness, hallucinations, ringing in the ears, vertigo, insomnia, and kidney toxicity. Rarely, goiter production, changes in urination, and low blood sugar levels have occurred in people taking the drug.

### PREGNANCY/BREAST-FEEDING

Sulfadiazine has not been formally studied in pregnant women. In animal studies, the drug caused fetal defects. Other sulfa drugs pass through the placenta, but rarely affect the developing fetus. Pregnant women are encouraged to discuss the benefits and potential risks of sulfadiazine with their physician before deciding to use the drug.

HIV may be passed from a woman to her child through breast milk. In areas where nutritionally sound alternatives are readily available, breast-feeding is discouraged for HIV-positive women. Sulfadiazine is excreted in breast milk. Because of the potential toxicity of the drug to newborns, women are encouraged to consider alternatives to breast-feeding while using it.

### USE IN CHILDREN

For children over two months of age, sulfadiazine is used at an initial dose of 150 mg per kg of body weight per day, divided into four to six equal doses, with a maximum of 6 g used in any single day.

Children under the age of two months can be treated with sulfadiazine in combination with pyrimethamine for the treatment of congenital toxoplasmosis. The appropriate dosage is determined by a physician experienced in this use.

**USE IN THE ELDERLY**
Older adults may be more susceptible to the side effects of the drug and may require reduced doses.

**DRUG INTERACTIONS**
Sulfadiazine used in combination with oral antidiabetes medications (sulfonylureas) or thiazide diuretics may increase the risk of low blood sugar levels. Sulfadiazine may increase the blood concentrations of methotrexate or blood thinners like warfarin, potentially increasing the risk of side effects from these drugs.

Indomethacin, probenecid, and salicylates (including aspirin) increase blood levels of sulfadiazine, potentially increasing the risk of sulfadiazine-related side effects.

Sulfadiazine may increase the risk of ddI- or ddC-induced peripheral neuropathy.

**FOOD INTERACTIONS**
For best absorption into the body, sulfadiazine should be taken with a full glass of water and on an empty stomach.

**OTHER DRUGS USED FOR SIMILAR CONDITIONS**
For treatment of toxoplasmosis, the standard therapy is pyrimethamine in combination with sulfadiazine. In place of or in addition to sulfadiazine in combination therapy, clindamycin, azithromycin, or gamma interferon may be useful. Atovaquone is a newer drug that has shown potential as a treatment for toxoplasmosis.

# TRIMETHOPRIM/ SULFAMETHOXAZOLE

**BRAND NAME (MANUFACTURER)**
Bactrim (Roche); Septra (Glaxo Wellcome)

**OTHER NAMES**
Cotrimoxazole; TMP/SMX

**TYPE OF DRUG**
Antibiotic/antiprotozoal agent

**USED FOR**
Trimethoprim/sulfamethoxazole (TMP/SMX) is an antibiotic used to treat and prevent a wide variety of bacterial and protozoal infections. In people with HIV, it is used primarily to treat or prevent *Pneumocystis carinii* pneumonia

(PCP). It is also used for toxoplasmosis, urinary-tract infections, sinus infections, ear infections, bronchitis, and diarrhea caused by *Shigella* or other bacteria.

### GENERAL INFORMATION

TMP/SMX is a combination product containing two antibiotics—trimethoprim and sulfamethoxazole. It is used for many bacterial infections because it is effective, inexpensive, and easily administered. Because it is so widely used in the general population, its side effects are well understood and most physicians are experienced with its use.

Unfortunately, up to half of the people living with HIV are allergic to the drug and experience high fever and skin rash when taking it. If the allergic reaction is not too severe, it is often possible to continue using the drug while using antihistamines like diphenhydramine (Benadryl) or corticosteroids (e.g., dexamethasone or prednisone) to treat the allergic symptoms. In most cases it is possible to desensitize individuals to the drug by starting the drug again at small doses and gradually building back up to therapeutic levels. Desensitization carries some risk of causing a second allergic reaction, which in some cases can be severe.

Despite these limitations, TMP/SMX is the antibiotic of choice to treat or prevent PCP in people with HIV, because clinical studies have shown that it is more effective than other antibiotics or combinations used for this infection. A number of studies have shown that TMP/SMX used in people with CD4+ counts below 200 results in fewer episodes of the infection and increased survival for the people who take the drug. In addition, because TMP/SMX is effective against a broad range of microorganisms, using the drug may prevent other bacterial or protozoal infections as well, such as toxoplasmosis.

TMP/SMX is available as a solution for injection, an oral suspension, and as single-strength and double-strength tablets for oral administration.

### TREATMENT

Most people use the double-strength tablets because they are easy to take and fewer are required than when taking the single-strength tablets. For most infections, one double-strength tablet taken twice a day is the normal adult dose. For treatment of active PCP, the dose for adults and children is 15 to 20 mg of trimethoprim per kg of body weight plus 75 to 100 mg of sulfamethoxazole per kg of body weight per day, divided into three or four equal doses. For a 140 lb. (64 kg) adult, this translates to two double-strength tablets taken every six hours.

### MAINTENANCE/PREVENTION

For prevention of initial or recurrent PCP infection, the recommended dose of TMP/SMX for adults is one double-strength tablet taken once a day. Some clinical evidence suggests a double-strength tablet taken three times a week

may prevent PCP, but it may not be as effective as daily dosing. For children, the recommended dosage is 75 mg of trimethoprim per square meter of body surface area plus 375 mg of sulfamethoxazole per square meter of surface area taken twice a day on three consecutive days each week.

For prevention of toxoplasmosis in adults, TMP/SMX is used at a similar dosing schedule, one double-strength tablet taken daily.

### CAUTIONS AND WARNINGS

TMP/SMX should not be used by anyone with a known allergy to trimethoprim or the sulfa drugs. It should also not be used by anyone with anemia caused by folate (vitamin B) deficiency.

TMP/SMX should be discontinued at the first sign of an allergic reaction, such as the appearance of a skin rash, sore throat, high fever, muscle pain, shortness of breath, loss of color, or jaundice.

Because of the risk of serious side effects, TMP/SMX should be used with caution in people with impaired liver or kidney function, those with vitamin B deficiencies, people receiving anticonvulsant therapy, people who are malnourished or unable to absorb nutrients, and those with severe allergies or asthma.

Like other sulfa drugs, TMP/SMX may cause sensitivity to bright light or sunlight.

### SIDE EFFECTS

The most common side effects of the drug are nausea, vomiting, loss of appetite, and allergic skin reactions (primarily rashes).

Other, less common side effects of TMP/SMX include hepatitis, inflammation of the pancreas, abdominal pain, diarrhea, kidney toxicity, meningitis, convulsions, peripheral neuropathy, vertigo, ringing in the ears, headache, hallucinations, depression, apathy, nervousness, muscle pain or weakness, fatigue, and insomnia.

Severe and fatal allergic reactions, although rare, have occurred when using the drug.

### PREGNANCY/BREAST-FEEDING

In animal studies, TMP/SMX caused spontaneous abortions and fetal defects. In a retrospective study of 120 human pregnancies during which the mother was treated with TMP/SMX, there was no increase in birth defects in women who took the active drug when compared to those who took a placebo. Pregnant women are encouraged to discuss the benefits and potential risks of TMP/SMX with their physician before deciding to use the drug.

HIV may be passed from a woman to her child through breast milk. In areas where nutritionally sound alternatives are readily available, breast-feeding is discouraged for HIV-positive women. TMP/SMX is excreted in human

milk and may cause side effects in newborns. Women are encouraged to consider alternatives to breast-feeding while using the drug.

### USE IN CHILDREN
TMP/SMX is used in children at the dosages described above. It should be used with caution in children less than one month of age, because newborns have immature kidney and liver function. Current federal guidelines for PCP prophylaxis recommend that all babies born to HIV-positive women should start TMP/SMX at four to six weeks of age.

### USE IN THE ELDERLY
Older adults may be more susceptible to the side effects of the drug and may require reduced doses. Severe skin reactions and bone marrow toxicity are the most frequently reported severe side effects in elderly people.

### DRUG INTERACTIONS
Concurrent use of TMP/SMX with diuretics, especially thiazides, increases the risk of hemorrhaging in the skin or other bleeding disorders. TMP/SMX may increase the blood levels of phenytoin, AZT, and theophylline, potentially increasing the risk of side effects from these drugs.

When used with AZT or ganciclovir, TMP/SMX may cause increased bone marrow toxicity resulting in reduced levels of red blood cells and certain white blood cells called neutrophils. TMP/SMX used with pyrimethamine may cause reduced levels of red blood cells. TMP/SMX may also increase the effect of blood thinners such as warfarin and increase bleeding in people taking both drugs.

### FOOD INTERACTIONS
People using TMP/SMX should drink plenty of fluids to decrease the risk of kidney toxicity or the development of kidney stones.

### OTHER DRUGS USED FOR SIMILAR CONDITIONS
For the treatment of PCP, the therapy of choice is TMP/SMX. When the drug is not tolerated, dapsone with trimethoprim, intravenous pentamidine, clindamycin with primaquine, or atovaquone may be appropriate. For prevention of PCP, TMP/SMX is also the drug of choice. When it is not tolerated, dapsone or aerosol pentamidine may be appropriate. Most physicians prescribe dapsone as second-line therapy and reserve aerosol pentamidine for when neither TMP/SMX nor dapsone can be used.

For prevention of toxoplasmosis in people whose CD4+ count is less than 200, TMP/SMX is the therapy of choice, with dapsone used less frequently. Atovaquone, a newer antibiotic, is being evaluated in clinical trials for prevention of PCP and toxoplasmosis.

For treatment of toxoplasmosis, pyrimethamine with sulfadiazine or clindamycin is standard therapy.

# TRIMETREXATE

**BRAND NAME (MANUFACTURER)**
Neutrexin (U.S. Bioscience)

**TYPE OF DRUG**
Antibiotic/antiprotozoal agent

**USED FOR**
Trimetrexate is used to treat *Pneumocystis carinii* pneumonia (PCP) in immuno-compromised people for whom trimethoprim/sulfamethoxazole (TMP/SMX) has failed or cannot be tolerated.

**GENERAL INFORMATION**
Trimetrexate interferes with the metabolism of folic acid (vitamin B) in bacteria, protozoa, and mammalian cells (including human cells). This action disrupts DNA, RNA, and protein synthesis, preventing the cells from multiplying. Trimetrexate is normally used in combination with leucovorin (folinic acid), another B vitamin. In humans and other mammals, leucovorin is taken up into cells and converted to folic acid, where it can counteract the toxicity of trimetrexate. Susceptible bacteria and protozoa cannot take leucovorin into their cells, so in the presence of trimetrexate, they die.

In a large clinical trial, trimetrexate plus leucovorin was compared to TMP/SMX for the treatment of PCP in people with AIDS. The observed mortality in the trimetrexate group was approximately twice that in the TMP/SMX group, demonstrating that TMP/SMX is a much more effective treatment. However, almost half of HIV-positive people with PCP cannot tolerate full doses of TMP/SMX and require alternatives.

Trimetrexate is available as a solution for injection.

**TREATMENT**
Trimetrexate must be administered in combination with leucovorin. When administered alone, trimetrexate is toxic to human cells. Leucovorin therapy generally continues for seventy-two hours after the last dose of trimetrexate.

Trimetrexate is usually administered at a dose of 45 mg per square meter of body surface area as a single daily intravenous injection. The recommended duration of therapy is twenty-one days for trimetrexate and twenty-four days for leucovorin.

The dosages may be reduced in people with liver or kidney disease and those who experience significant bone marrow toxicity while taking the drug.

**CAUTIONS AND WARNINGS**
Trimetrexate should not be used by anyone with a known allergy to it, leucovorin, or methotrexate. Failure to take leucovorin with trimetrexate may

result in severe bone marrow or gastrointestinal toxicity and could result in death.

The drug should be used with caution in people with kidney or liver disease, because they may be at higher risk for side effects.

**SIDE EFFECTS**

In clinical studies, the most common side effects of trimetrexate were bone marrow toxicity, liver toxicity, fever, rash, nausea/vomiting, electrolyte imbalances, confusion, and fatigue. Approximately 10% of people taking trimetrexate during clinical trials stopped the drug because of side effects.

**PREGNANCY/BREAST-FEEDING**

Trimetrexate has not been formally studied in pregnant women. In animal studies, the drug caused significant fetal harm. Pregnant women are encouraged to discuss the benefits and potential risks of the drug with their physician before using it. Women taking the drug are encouraged to use effective contraception.

HIV may be passed from a woman to her child through breast milk. In areas where nutritionally sound alternatives are readily available, breast-feeding is discouraged for HIV-positive women. It is not known whether trimetrexate is excreted in human milk. Because of the potential toxicity of the drug, women are encouraged to consider alternatives to breast-feeding while using it.

**USE IN CHILDREN**

There is limited clinical experience with trimetrexate in children under eighteen years of age. No recommendations can be made at this time.

**USE IN THE ELDERLY**

Older adults may be more susceptible to the side effects of the drug and may require reduced doses.

**DRUG INTERACTIONS**

The following drugs may affect trimetrexate levels in the blood or have their blood levels affected by trimetrexate: acetaminophen, cimetidine, clarithromycin, delavirdine, erythromycin, fluconazole, itraconazole, ketoconazole, nevirapine, protease inhibitors, ranitidine, rifabutin, and rifampin.

Trimetrexate can caused additive bone marrow toxicity when used with AZT or ganciclovir. These may have to be stopped or colony-stimulating factors (e.g., G-CSF) may be needed to counteract the toxicity of the combination.

**FOOD INTERACTIONS**

Trimetrexate is administered intravenously, so food does not affect its absorption into the body.

**OTHER DRUGS USED FOR SIMILAR CONDITIONS**

TMP/SMX is the drug of choice for PCP. In cases where it is ineffective or intolerable, dapsone with trimethoprim, clindamycin with primaquine, intravenous pentamidine, or atovaquone may be used. Trimetrexate is used in people with moderate-to-severe PCP only when none of these other drugs is appropriate.

# ANTIPROTOZOAL
## EXPERIMENTAL DRUGS

**TINIDAZOLE**

Tinidazole (Fasigyn), manufactured by Pfizer, is a drug used as a first-line therapy for a variety of parasitic and amoebic infections. In the United States, tinidazole is used experimentally as an alternative to the standard therapy for amoebic infection, metronidazole.

**NTZ (NITAZOXANIDE)**

NTZ is an experimental antiprotozoal therapy currently being studied as a therapy for cryptosporidiosis and other parasitic infections.

# ANTISEIZURE DRUGS

This section contains profiles of drugs used to prevent seizures (convulsions).

Seizures are caused by abnormal electrical activity in the brain. Normally, a relatively low level of electricity travels through the brain, but excessive or dysregulated electrical signals build up in a seizure and trigger chaotic muscle contractions, accompanied by severe confusion or eventual loss of consciousness. Most often a condition known as epilepsy is the cause, but injury, certain drugs, extreme stress, or HIV-related neurological damage can also cause seizures.

Antiseizure drugs suppress electrical activity in the brain, which prevents the spread of uncontrolled electrical stimulation. Unfortunately, normal brain activity may also be affected, resulting in difficulty remembering, inability to concentrate, loss of coordination, or lethargy. The key is to find the dosage that prevents seizures without causing serious side effects. This dosage is different for each individual.

The following drugs are covered in this section:
- carbamazepine
- clonazepam
- fosphenytoin
- gabapentin
- lamotrigine
- phenobarbital
- phenytoin
- topiramate
- valproic acid

Diazepam (Valium) is also used to prevent seizures. It is covered in the psychoactive drugs section.

# CARBAMAZEPINE

**BRAND NAME (MANUFACTURER)**
Tegretol (Novartis)

**TYPE OF DRUG**
Antiseizure drug

**USED FOR**
Carbamazepine is used primarily to prevent seizures. It is also used to treat trigeminal neuralgia, which is excruciating pain of the face, teeth, mouth,

and nasal cavity. Similarly, in people living with HIV, carbamazepine is occasionally used to treat the painful symptoms of peripheral neuropathy, a neurological disorder characterized by numbness, tingling, or pain in the arms, legs, hands, or feet.

## GENERAL INFORMATION

Carbamazepine is chemically related to the tricyclic antidepressants, such as amitriptyline. It was first developed to treat trigeminal neuralgia, but it has gained widespread use as therapy to reduce the likelihood of seizures caused by abnormal nerve signals in the brain. It is particularly suitable for children because it does not have a sedative effect. In some but not all people with HIV, the drug is effective in eliminating the painful symptoms of peripheral neuropathy.

Seizures may be caused by any of the central nervous system disorders or infections associated with HIV infection. Toxoplasmosis is the most common cause of seizures in people with AIDS. Between 15% and 30% of people with toxoplasmosis experience seizures. Carbamazepine treats the symptoms of the neurological disorders, not the underlying causes. When the seizures are caused by an opportunistic infection of the central nervous system, therapy should also include appropriate antibiotic, antifungal, or antiparasitic treatment.

Carbamazepine is available as tablets to be chewed or swallowed and as an oral suspension.

## TREATMENT

To prevent seizures, the recommended starting dose of carbamazepine for adults and children over 12 years of age is 400 mg per day, split into two or four equal doses. The dosage may be increased gradually as necessary and tolerated up to a maximum of 1,000 mg per day for children between the ages of twelve and fifteen, and 1,200 mg per day for older adolescents and adults. After the person stabilizes, the minimum effective maintenance dose, usually 800 to 1,200 mg per day, is used to prevent seizures from recurring.

For treatment of neuralgia, the recommended starting dose for adults is 200 mg per day, split into two or four equal doses. The dosage may be increased as necessary and tolerated up to a maximum of 1,200 mg per day. Control of pain can be maintained in most people with 400 to 800 mg daily, but the dosage required ranges from 200 to 1,200 mg per day.

Using the oral suspension of the drug results in higher peak blood levels of carbamazepine than when using the tablets. Consequently, the total daily dosage is generally split into two equal doses when using the tablets and four equal doses when using the oral suspension.

## CAUTIONS AND WARNINGS

Carbamazepine should not be used by anyone with a known allergy to it or to any tricyclic antidepressant, including amitriptyline, desipramine, imipramine, nortriptyline, protriptyline, etc. Because of the risk of serious side effects, it should not be used in combination with monoamine oxidase (MAO) inhibitor antidepressants such as isocarboxazid or tranylcypromine.

Carbamazepine should be used with caution in people with a history of bone marrow suppression because the drug can cause bone marrow toxicity. Carbamazepine may also increase pressure within the eye and should be used with caution in people with glaucoma.

Stopping the drug abruptly in people using it to control seizures may, by itself, trigger seizures.

Carbamazepine may interfere with the mental and physical abilities necessary to operate dangerous machinery or to drive an automobile.

## SIDE EFFECTS

Common side effects of carbamazepine are dizziness, unsteadiness, drowsiness, nausea, vomiting, blurred vision, confusion, hostility, headache, and severe water retention. Less common side effects are mood changes and excitability (especially in children). Allergic skin reactions may also occur.

## PREGNANCY/BREAST-FEEDING

The use of drugs that prevent seizures, including carbamazepine, during pregnancy is associated with an increased risk of birth defects. About 10% of children exposed to anticonvulsant medication before birth experience malformations. The abnormalities may be minor, including wide nasal bridge, low-set ears or forehead, small or absent nails, or skin folds in the corners of the eyes, but they may be serious as well, including malformations of the heart, lungs, brain, or gastrointestinal tract. In addition, some children exposed to carbamazepine in the womb develop childhood cancers.

The risk of birth defects or cancers caused by anticonvulsants must be balanced against the risk of seizures during pregnancy. Prolonged or frequent seizures may cause brain damage or death in the mother and decreased oxygen supply in the fetus, which may also cause birth defects. The risk of fetal harm from carbamazepine may be higher when combinations of anticonvulsants are used. If after discussion with her physician, a pregnant woman decides to use an anticonvulsant, single-agent therapy is usually preferable to combination drug therapy.

HIV can be passed from a woman to her child through breast milk. In areas where nutritionally sound alternatives are readily available, breast-feeding is discouraged for HIV-positive women. Carbamazepine is excreted in

human milk. Because of the potential toxicity of the drug to newborns, women are encouraged to consider alternatives to breast-feeding while using the drug.

## USE IN CHILDREN

Children older than six years of age are given carbamazepine at dosages adjusted for age and weight. The drug is not recommended for younger children because its safety and effectiveness for them has not yet been established in clinical trials.

## USE IN THE ELDERLY

Older adults may be more susceptible to the side effects of carbamazepine, especially confusion or agitation. Dose reductions may be necessary to reduce the risk of these side effects.

## DRUG INTERACTIONS

Phenobarbital, phenytoin, and primidone may reduce blood levels of carbamazepine. Carbamazepine may reduce blood levels of delavirdine, warfarin, doxycycline, haloperidol, valproic acid, and theophylline.

Erythromycin, clarithromycin, cimetidine, propoxyphene, terfenadine, isoniazid, fluoxetine, or calcium channel blockers (e.g., diltiazem, nifedipine) may elevate blood levels of carbamazepine, potentially increasing the risk of its side effects.

Carbamazepine may reduce the effectiveness of oral contraceptives or quinidine. Lithium taken in combination with carbamazepine may increase the risk of neurological side effects.

## FOOD INTERACTIONS

Carbamazepine should be taken with meals to avoid stomach upset and to ensure proper absorption of the drug into the body.

## OTHER DRUGS USED FOR SIMILAR CONDITIONS

Seizures may be treated with barbiturates such as phenobarbital, benzodiazepines such as clonazepam or diazepam, hydantoin derivatives such as phenytoin, mephenytoin, or ethotoin, as well as other classes of drugs. The drug of choice depends on the age and health of the individual, the cause of the seizures, and the tolerability of specific drugs.

For peripheral neuropathy, there is no standard therapy. Amitriptyline, nortriptyline, or analgesics (such as ibuprofen, acetaminophen, codeine, hydrocodone, oxycodone, methadone, or morphine) may be used to treat the pain associated with neuropathy. Various other new drugs are being tested in clinical trials for their ability to reverse nerve damage, but none of them have received FDA approval for this use or are widely available.

# CLONAZEPAM

## BRAND NAME (MANUFACTURER)
Klonopin (Roche)

## OTHER NAME
Clonopin

## TYPE OF DRUG
Antiseizure drug

## USED FOR
Clonazepam is used alone or in combination drug therapy to prevent and treat epileptic seizures.

## GENERAL INFORMATION
Clonazepam belongs to a group of psychoactive drugs known as benzodiazepines. In general, the benzodiazepines are used to treat anxiety and insomnia, but clonazepam is used almost exclusively as an anticonvulsant in people who have not responded to standard therapy.

Unfortunately, many people develop a tolerance for clonazepam, and the drug often loses its effectiveness after a few months of therapy. To counter this effect, the drug's dosage may be increased or therapy switched to a different anticonvulsant.

Seizures may be caused by any of the central nervous system disorders or infections associated with HIV infection. Toxoplasmosis is the most common cause of seizures in people with AIDS. Between 15% and 30% of people with toxoplasmosis experience seizures. Clonazepam treats the symptoms of the neurological disorders, not the underlying causes. When the seizures are caused by an opportunistic infection of the central nervous system, therapy should also include appropriate antibiotic, antifungal, or antiparasitic treatment.

Clonazepam is available as tablets for oral administration.

## TREATMENT
The recommended initial dosage for adults is 1.5 mg per day, divided into three equal doses. The dosage may be increased in increments of 0.5 to 1.0 mg every three days until seizures are adequately controlled or until side effects become serious. The maximum recommended daily dose is 20 mg.

## CAUTIONS AND WARNINGS
Clonazepam should not be used by anyone with a known allergy to it or the other benzodiazepines (including alprazolam, diazepam, chlordiazepoxide, flurazepam, and triazolam). It should also not be used by people with an eye disease called acute narrow-angle glaucoma.

Clonazepam may interfere with the mental or physical abilities necessary to operate dangerous machinery or to drive an automobile.

When used in people with several concurrent types of seizure disorders, clonazepam may increase the risk or precipitate the onset of major seizures.

The abrupt withdrawal of clonazepam, particularly in those taking large doses of the drug over longer periods of time, may precipitate seizures. Consequently, gradual withdrawal from the drug is necessary.

Because clonazepam is excreted by the kidneys, it should be used with caution in people with kidney disease. Similarly, because of the risk of serious side effects, clonazepam should be used with caution in people with respiratory (breathing) disease.

**SIDE EFFECTS**
The most common side effects of clonazepam are drowsiness, dizziness, unsteadiness, increased salivation, and altered behavior.

**PREGNANCY/BREAST-FEEDING**
The use of drugs that prevent seizures during pregnancy is associated with an increased risk of birth defects. Most information regarding birth defects caused by anticonvulsants comes from studies of phenytoin, phenobarbital, and diphenylhydantoin, but anecdotal reports suggest all known anticonvulsants cause birth defects.

About 10% of children exposed to anticonvulsant medication before birth experience malformations. The abnormalities may be minor, including wide nasal bridge, low-set ears or forehead, small or absent nails, or skin folds in the corners of the eyes, but they may be serious as well, including malformations of the heart, lungs, brain, or gastrointestinal tract.

This risk of birth defects must be balanced against the risk of seizures during pregnancy. Prolonged or frequent seizures may cause brain damage or death in the mother and decreased oxygen supply in the fetus, which may also cause birth defects. Pregnant women are encouraged to discuss the benefits and potential risks of clonazepam with their physician before using the drug.

HIV can be passed from a woman to her child through breast milk. In areas where nutritionally sound alternatives are readily available, breast-feeding is discouraged for HIV-positive women. Clonazepam is excreted in human milk. Because of the potential toxicity of the drug to newborns, women are encouraged to consider alternatives to breast-feeding while using it.

**USE IN CHILDREN**
Infants and children are prescribed clonazepam at dosages adjusted for age and weight. However, the drug should be used with caution in children because long-term use may affect their physical or mental development.

## USE IN THE ELDERLY
Older adults may be more susceptible to the side effects of the drug and may require reduced doses.

## DRUG INTERACTIONS
Clonazepam may intensify the effects of other central nervous system depressants, including alcohol, antihistamines, tranquilizers, sedatives, monoamine oxidase (MAO) inhibitor antidepressants (such as tranylcypromine or isocarboxazid), tricyclic antidepressants (such as amitriptyline or chlordiazepoxide), and other anticonvulsants (such as phenytoin or phenobarbital).

Phenobarbital or phenytoin may reduce blood levels of clonazepam. The effects of clonazepam may be prolonged when taken with cimetidine, oral contraceptives, disulfiram, fluoxetine, isoniazid, ketoconazole, metoprolol, probenecid, propoxyphene, propranolol, rifampin, and valproic acid.

Antacids, including the one in ddI tablets and powder, may reduce absorption of clonazepam in the body. Clonazepam should be taken an hour before or an hour after taking antacids.

Cigarette smoking may counter the effects of clonazepam. Theophylline may reduce the sedative effects of the drug.

Clonazepam may increase blood levels of digoxin, potentially increasing the risk of digoxin-related toxicity. Clonazepam may reduce blood levels of levodopa.

## FOOD INTERACTIONS
Clonazepam may be taken with or without food.

## OTHER DRUGS USED FOR SIMILAR CONDITIONS
Seizures may be treated with barbiturates such as phenobarbital, benzodiazepines such as clonazepam or diazepam, hydantoin derivatives such as phenytoin, mephenytoin, or ethotoin, as well as other classes of drugs. The drug of choice depends on the age and health of the individual, the cause of the seizures, and the tolerability of specific drugs.

# FOSPHENYTOIN

## BRAND NAME (MANUFACTURER)
Cerebyx (Parke-Davis)

## TYPE OF DRUG
Antiseizure drug

## USED FOR
Fosphenytoin is used to control and prevent seizures.

## GENERAL INFORMATION

Fosphenytoin is an antiseizure drug used in the treatment of epilepsy. The drug probably works by stabilizing nerves in the motor cortex of the brain, making them less responsive to the excessive stimulation or environmental changes that may trigger seizures.

Seizures may be caused by any of the central nervous system disorders or infections associated with HIV infection. Toxoplasmosis is the most common cause of seizures in people with AIDS. Between 15% and 30% of people with toxoplasmosis experience seizures. Fosphenytoin treats the symptoms of the neurological disorders, not the underlying causes. When the seizures are caused by an opportunistic infection of the central nervous system, therapy should also include appropriate antibiotic, antifungal, or antiparasitic treatment.

Fosphenytoin is a pro-drug of another antiseizure drug, phenytoin. This means that the body's chemical response to fosphenytoin changes it into phenytoin. Therefore, every 75 mg of fosphenytoin is equal to 50 mg of phenytoin after it is metabolized by the body. The dosages are correspondingly given in phenytoin equivalent doses (PE) so that people do not have to convert between the doses of the active and inactive drugs.

Fosphenytoin is available as a solution for intravenous injection.

## TREATMENT

The usual loading dose of fosphenytoin is 15 to 20 mg PE/kg administered at 100 to 150 mg PE/min. Fosphenytoin should not be given faster than 150 mg PE/min. Following the loading dose, fosphenytoin or phenytoin (either intravenously or orally by tablet) is given at a maintenance dose.

## CAUTIONS AND WARNINGS

Fosphenytoin should not be used by anyone with a known allergy to it, to phenytoin, or to any of the other hydantoin antiseizure medications. If fosphenytoin is stopped abruptly, it may cause severe seizures. The dosage should be tapered off slowly under the direction of a physician.

People with low blood pressure, impaired heart function, or slow heart rate should not use fosphenytoin. In these cases, other antiseizure medications should be used.

Fosphenytoin can cause low blood pressure if the drug is administered too quickly. Blood pressure, heart rate and respiratory function should be continuously monitored during the infusion.

People with reduced liver function may accumulate the drug in their bodies, potentially increasing their risk of side effects.

## SIDE EFFECTS

The most common side effects include rapid or unusual growth of the gums, slurred speech, confusion, uncontrolled eye movements, dizziness, insomnia,

twitching, double vision, fatigue, irritability, depression, and headaches. These side effects usually disappear over time if the drug is taken continuously.

Less common side effects include nausea, vomiting, diarrhea, constipation, fever, rashes, hair loss, weight gain, numbness in the extremities, chest pains, sensitivity to sunlight, joint pain, and high blood pressure.

Rarely, fosphenytoin can cause fatal allergic reactions or liver damage.

### PREGNANCY/BREAST-FEEDING

During pregnancy, the use of antiseizure drugs, including fosphenytoin, is associated with an increased risk of birth defects. About 10% of children exposed to anticonvulsant medication before birth experience malformations. The abnormalities may be minor, such as wide nasal bridge, low-set ears or forehead, small or absent nails, and skin folds in the corners of the eyes, or more serious, such as defects of the heart, lungs, brain, or gastrointestinal tract. This risk of birth defects must be balanced against the risk of seizures during pregnancy. Prolonged or frequent seizures may cause brain damage or death in the mother and decreased oxygen supply, which may also cause birth defects. Pregnant women are encouraged to discuss the benefits and potential risks of fosphenytoin with their physician before using the drug.

HIV can be passed from a woman to her child through breast milk. In areas where nutritionally sound alternatives are readily available, breast-feeding is discouraged for HIV-positive women. Fosphenytoin may be excreted in human milk, but is generally considered safe for use during nursing.

### USE IN CHILDREN

The safety and effectiveness of fosphenytoin has not yet been established for children.

### USE IN THE ELDERLY

Older adults may be more susceptible to the side effects of the drug and may require reduced doses.

### DRUG INTERACTIONS

Fosphenytoin interacts with a large number of other drugs. The following drugs increase the blood levels of fosphenytoin, potentially increasing the risk of its side effects: alcohol, allopurinol, amiodarone, aspirin, azithromycin, benzodiazepines, chloramphenicol, chlorpheniramine, cimetidine, clarithromycin, disulfiram, fluconazole, ibuprofen, isoniazid, itraconazole, ketoconazole, metronidazole, miconazole, omeprazole, phenacemide, phenothiazine antipsychotics, phenylbutazone, succinimide antiseizure medications, sulfa drugs, tricyclic antidepressants, trimethoprim, valproic acid.

The following drugs may reduce blood levels of fosphenytoin, potentially reducing its effectiveness: alcohol, antacids, anticancer drugs, barbiturates,

carbamazepine, charcoal, diazoxide, folic acid, influenza virus vaccine, loxapine succinate, nitrofurantoin, pyridoxine, rifampin, sucralfate, and theophylline.

Fosphenytoin may decrease the effectiveness of the following drugs: corticosteroids, coumarin-type anticoagulants (warfarin), digitoxin, doxycycline, estrogens, furosemide, itraconazole, ketoconazole, oral contraceptives, quinidine, rifampin, theophylline, and vitamin D.

Fosphenytoin affects the following drugs in an unpredictable manner: clonazepam, cyclosporine, dopamine, furosemide, levodopa, levonorgestrel, mebendazole, oral antidiabetes medications, and phenothiazines.

Lithium toxicity may be increased by fosphenytoin. Corticosteroids may mask the effects of allergic reactions to fosphenytoin. The pain-relieving effect of meperidine may be decreased by fosphenytoin while increasing the risk of opioid-related side effects.

**FOOD INTERACTIONS**
None reported.

**OTHER DRUGS USED FOR SIMILAR CONDITIONS**
Seizures may be treated with barbiturates such as phenobarbital, benzodiazepines such as clonazepam or diazepam, hydantoin derivatives such as mephenytoin or ethotoin, as well as other classes of drugs. The drug of choice depends on the age and health of the individual, the cause of the seizures, and the tolerability of specific drugs.

**COMMENTS**
Different brands of phenytoin may not be identical and may require dose adjustments. A physician should be consulted before changing brands.

# GABAPENTIN

**BRAND NAME (MANUFACTURER)**
Neurontin (Parke-Davis)

**TYPE OF DRUG**
Antiseizure drug

**USED FOR**
Gabapentin is used primarily as supplementary therapy for the treatment of partial seizures in people with epilepsy. In people who are infected with HIV, gabapentin is sometimes used as a treatment for AIDS dementia complex (ADC) and less often for peripheral neuropathy. Peripheral neuropathy is nerve damage that may be a direct or indirect result of HIV infection, toxicity of certain drugs, or other unrelated causes. The symptoms include numbness, tingling, or pain in the hands, arms, legs, or feet.

### GENERAL INFORMATION

The exact mechanism by which gabapentin exerts its activity is unknown.

Seizures may be caused by any of the central nervous system disorders or infections associated with HIV infection. Toxoplasmosis is the most common cause of seizures in people with AIDS. Between 15% and 30% of people with toxoplasmosis experience seizures. Phenobarbital treats the symptoms of the neurological disorders, not the underlying causes. When the seizures are caused by an opportunistic infection of the central nervous system, therapy should also include appropriate antibiotic, antifungal, or antiparasitic treatment.

Gabapentin is available as tablets for oral administration.

### TREATMENT

The dose of gabapentin is usually 300–600 mg every 8 hours. To minimize potential side effects from gabapentin, the dose is usually increased over a few days. On the first day of starting gabapentin, it is usually given at 300 mg once a day at bedtime, followed by 300 mg twice a day on the second day and finally 300 mg three times a day on the third day. The dose of gabapentin can be further increased up to a total dose of 1,800 mg per day.

### CAUTIONS AND WARNINGS

Gabapentin should not be taken by anyone with a known allergy to it. People with abnormal kidney function may need to take reduced doses of the drug.

### SIDE EFFECTS

The most common side effects of gabapentin are fatigue, drowsiness, dizziness, and abnormal muscle coordination. Less common side effects include abdominal pain, tremors, double vision, and reduction in vision.

### PREGNANCY/BREAST-FEEDING

Gabapentin has not been formally studied in pregnant women. In animal studies, the drug caused birth defects, but it is not known whether this would be true for humans. Pregnant women are encouraged to discuss the benefits and potential risks of gabapentin with their physician before deciding to use the drug.

HIV can be passed from a woman to her child through breast milk. In areas where nutritionally sound alternatives are readily available, breast-feeding is discouraged for HIV-positive women. It is not known whether gabapentin is excreted in human milk. Because of the potential toxicity of the drug, women are encouraged to consider alternatives to breast-feeding while using it.

### USE IN CHILDREN

Gabapentin has not been formally studied in children under 12 and little clinical information is available to make recommendations about its use.

### USE IN THE ELDERLY

Older adults may be more susceptible to the side effects of the drug and may require reduced doses.

**DRUG INTERACTIONS**

Cimetidine increases gabapentin levels in blood, whereas antacids decrease gabapentin levels in blood.

**FOOD INTERACTIONS**

Gabapentin can be taken with or without food.

**OTHER DRUGS USED FOR SIMILAR CONDITIONS**

Seizures may be treated with barbiturates such as phenobarbital, benzodiazepines such as clonazepam or diazepam, hydantoin derivatives such as mephenytoin or ethotoin, as well as other classes of drugs. The drug of choice depends on the age and health of the individual, the cause of the seizures, and the tolerability of specific drugs. The most effective currently available treatments for AIDS-related dementia are the antiviral drugs. To date, AZT is the most widely used treatment for dementia, though recent evidence suggests that a number of other antiviral drugs may be equally effective for this purpose. The usual dose of AZT for HIV infection is 600 mg per day. Treatment of dementia may require higher doses of AZT, up to 1,000 mg per day, a dose many people with AIDS are unable to tolerate. Other antiviral drugs known to cross the blood-brain barrier are d4T, 3TC, and nevirapine. Psychoactive drugs, including antidepressants, stimulants, anticonvulsants, and antipsychotics, are used to treat the symptoms of dementia, but they do not affect the underlying causes of the disease.

Treatment of peripheral neuropathy is currently aimed at reducing painful symptoms. Research is being done on therapies to regenerate nerves, but at this time, no effective therapy to halt or reverse the damage associated with peripheral neuropathy is available.

The choice of medication is usually based on the severity of the symptoms. Mild symptoms without functional impairment are often treated with nonnarcotic pain relievers such as ibuprofen. Moderate symptoms with some functional limitation are often treated with tricyclic antidepressants such as amitriptyline or nortriptyline. Severe symptoms with severe functional limitation may require narcotic pain relievers such as methadone or the fentanyl patch.

# LAMOTRIGINE

**BRAND NAME (MANUFACTURER)**

Lamictal (Glaxo Wellcome)

**TYPE OF DRUG**

Antiseizure drug

**USED FOR**

Lamotrigine is used as supplementary therapy for the treatment of partial seizures in people with epilepsy.

In people with HIV, it is occasionally used to treat peripheral neuropathy (nerve damage that may be a direct or indirect result of HIV infection, toxicity of certain drugs, or other unrelated causes. The symptoms include numbness, tingling, or pain in the hands, arms, legs, or feet.

**GENERAL INFORMATION**

The exact mechanism by which lamotrigine exerts antiseizure activity is not known.

Seizures may be caused by any of the central nervous system disorders or infections associated with HIV infection. Toxoplasmosis is the most common cause of seizures in people with AIDS. Between 15% and 30% of people with toxoplasmosis experience seizures. Phenobarbital treats the symptoms of the neurological disorders, not the underlying causes. When the seizures are caused by an opportunistic infection of the central nervous system, therapy should also include appropriate antibiotic, antifungal, or antiparasitic treatment.

Lamotrigine is available as tablets for oral administration.

**TREATMENT**

The recommended dose of lamotrigine is 50 mg once a day for 2 weeks for people not taking valproic acid. The dose is then increased to 50 mg every 8 hours for two weeks and finally to 150-250 mg every 8 hours. For people who are receiving valproic acid, the above mentioned dose of lamotrigine should be halved.

In people with impaired kidney function, the dosage of lamotrigine is generally reduced because these people may be more susceptible to the drug's side effects.

**CAUTIONS AND WARNINGS**

Lamotrigine should not be used by anyone with a known allergy to it.

Stopping the drug abruptly in people using it to control seizures may, by itself, trigger seizures. A stepwise reduction in dose over two weeks (about 50% each week) is recommended.

Lamotrigine can cause severe and potentially life-threatening rashes, including Stevens-Johnson Syndrome. Life-threatening rashes are more likely in children taking the drug than in adults. In general, these rashes occur 2-8 weeks after starting lamotrigine.

**SIDE EFFECTS**

The most common side effects of lamotrigine include headache, nausea, vomiting, dizziness, loss of muscular coordination, drowsiness, rash, double vision, and blurred vision. Other side effects include fever, abdominal pain,

diarrhea, painful digestion, lack of coordination, and insomnia. Lamotrigine can also cause potentially life-threatening rashes, including Stevens-Johnson Syndrome.

### PREGNANCY/BREAST-FEEDING

Lamotrigine has not been formally studied in pregnant women. However, pregnant women are encouraged to discuss the benefits and potential risks of lamotrigine with their physician before using the drug.

HIV can be passed from a woman to her child through breast milk. In areas where nutritionally sound alternatives are readily available, breast-feeding is discouraged for HIV-positive women. Lamotrigine is excreted in breast milk and because of the potential toxicity of the drug to newborns, women are encouraged to consider alternatives to breast-feeding while using it.

### USE IN CHILDREN

The safety and effectiveness of lamotrigine has not been established for children under 16 years of age.

### USE IN THE ELDERLY

Older adults with impaired kidney or liver function may be more susceptible to the side effects of the drug and may require reduced doses.

### DRUG INTERACTIONS

Lamotrigine decreases valproic acid levels in blood. Phenytoin and carbamazepine decrease lamotrigine levels in blood, whereas valproic acid increases lamotrigine levels in blood.

### FOOD INTERACTIONS

None reported.

### OTHER DRUGS USED FOR SIMILAR CONDITIONS

Seizures may be treated with barbiturates, benzodiazepines such as clonazepam or diazepam, hydantoin derivatives such as phenytoin, mephenytoin, or ethotoin, as well as other classes of drugs. The drug of choice depends on the age and health of the individual, the cause of the seizures, and the tolerability of specific drugs.

# PHENOBARBITAL

### BRAND NAME (MANUFACTURER)

Belladonna + Phenobarbital: Bellatal (Richwood)
Phenobarbital + Hyoscyamine + Atropine +Scopolamine: Donnatal (A.H. Robbins)

### TYPE OF DRUG

Antiseizure drug

**USED FOR**

Phenobarbital is used primarily for the prevention and treatment of epileptic seizures, but it is also occasionally used as a sedative.

**GENERAL INFORMATION**

Phenobarbital is a barbiturate, a group of central nervous system (CNS) depressants that are prescribed primarily for insomnia. Barbiturates are capable of producing all levels of CNS mood alteration, from excitation to mild sedation, hypnosis, and deep coma. By suppressing electrical activity in the brain, phenobarbital prevents the uncontrolled stimulation of the brain that occurs during seizures.

Seizures may be caused by any of the central nervous system disorders or infections associated with HIV infection. Toxoplasmosis is the most common cause of seizures in people with AIDS. Between 15% and 30% of people with toxoplasmosis experience seizures. Phenobarbital treats the symptoms of the neurological disorders, not the underlying causes. When the seizures are caused by an opportunistic infection of the central nervous system, therapy should also include appropriate antibiotic, antifungal, or antiparasitic treatment.

Phenobarbital is available as an elixir, tablets, and a solution for injection. It is also available in a number of combination products.

**TREATMENT**

As with all psychoactive drugs, the dosage of phenobarbital must be adjusted for the individual's age, weight, condition, and other drugs being used concurrently. In general, the lowest effective dosage of the drug is used. Depending on the use, phenobarbital dosages range from 30 to 400 mg per day.

In elderly or debilitated people and in those with impaired liver or kidney function, the dosage of phenobarbital is generally reduced because these people may be more susceptible to the drug's side effects.

**CAUTIONS AND WARNINGS**

Phenobarbital should not be used by anyone with a known allergy to it or to any other barbiturate, those with a history of high fevers, severely impaired liver function, or those with severe respiratory disease.

Phenobarbital is habit forming and may not be appropriate for people with a history of chronic drug or alcohol use or in those with mental depression or suicidal tendencies. The drug may also interfere with the mental and physical abilities needed to drive an automobile or operate dangerous machinery.

**SIDE EFFECTS**

The most common side effects of phenobarbital include drowsiness, clumsiness, unsteadiness, dizziness, lethargy, drug "hangover," breathing difficulty, and allergic reactions. Less common effects include nausea, vomiting, con-

stipation, agitation, confusion, nightmares, nervousness, hallucinations, insomnia, anxiety, low blood pressure, headache, fever, anemia, and jaundice.

## PREGNANCY/BREAST-FEEDING

The use of drugs that prevent seizures, including phenobarbital, during pregnancy is associated with an increased risk of birth defects. About 10% of children exposed to anticonvulsant medication before birth experience malformations. The abnormalities may be minor, including wide nasal bridge, low-set ears or forehead, small or absent nails, or skin folds in the corners of the eyes, but they may be serious as well, including malformations of the heart, lungs, brain, or gastrointestinal tract. This risk of birth defects must be balanced against the risk of seizures during pregnancy. Prolonged or frequent seizures may cause brain damage or death in the mother and decreased oxygen supply in the fetus, which may also cause birth defects. Pregnant women are encouraged to discuss the benefits and potential risks of phenobarbital with their physician before using the drug.

HIV can be passed from a woman to her child through breast milk. In areas where nutritionally sound alternatives are readily available, breast-feeding is discouraged for HIV-positive women. Phenobarbital is excreted in breast milk. Because of the potential toxicity of the drug to newborns, women are encouraged to consider alternatives to breast-feeding while using it.

## USE IN CHILDREN

Phenobarbital is used in children at dosages adjusted for age and weight. Even at reduced dosages, the drug is more likely to cause excitability in children than adults. In addition, phenobarbital has been reported to cause difficulty in thinking in children.

## USE IN THE ELDERLY

In elderly or debilitated people, phenobarbital is more likely to cause excitability, depression, or confusion than in younger, healthy people. Consequently, dose reductions are generally necessary.

## DRUG INTERACTIONS

Phenobarbital may intensify the effect of other CNS depressants, including alcohol, antihistamines, benzodiazepines (alprazolam, diazepam, chlordiazepoxide, triazolam, etc.), narcotic pain relievers, other sedatives, anticonvulsants, and tranquilizers.

Phenobarbital may reduce the effectiveness of drug thinners such as warfarin and acenocoumarol. Barbiturates appear to reduce the blood levels of corticosteroids (hydrocortisone, prednisone, etc.), doxycycline, and estradiol. Phenobarbital may reduce the effectiveness of oral contraceptives.

Monoamine oxidase (MAO) inhibitors increase blood levels and prolong the action of barbiturates. Valproic acid and sodium valproate increase blood levels of phenobarbital, possibly increasing the risk of side effects of the drug.

When phenytoin and phenobarbital are used in combination, the blood levels of each drug may be raised or lowered by the other in an unpredictable manner.

**FOOD INTERACTIONS**
Phenobarbital may be taken with or without food.

**OTHER DRUGS USED FOR SIMILAR CONDITIONS**
Seizures may be treated with barbiturates, benzodiazepines such as clonazepam or diazepam, hydantoin derivatives such as phenytoin, mephenytoin, or ethotoin, as well as other classes of drugs. The drug of choice depends on the age and health of the individual, the cause of the seizures, and the tolerability of specific drugs.

# PHENYTOIN

**BRAND NAME (MANUFACTURER)**
Dilantin (Parke-Davis)

**TYPE OF DRUG**
Antiseizure drug

**USED FOR**
Phenytoin is used to control and prevent seizures.

**GENERAL INFORMATION**
Phenytoin is an antiseizure drug that is often used in the treatment of epilepsy. The drug probably works by stabilizing nerves in the motor cortex of the brain, making them less responsive to the excessive stimulation or environmental changes that may trigger seizures.

Seizures may be caused by any of the central nervous system disorders or infections associated with HIV infection. Toxoplasmosis is the most common cause of seizures in people with AIDS. Between 15% and 30% of people with toxoplasmosis experience seizures. Phenytoin treats the symptoms of the neurological disorders, not the underlying causes. When the seizures are caused by an opportunistic infection of the central nervous system, therapy should also include appropriate antibiotic, antifungal, or antiparasitic treatment.

Phenytoin is available as tablets, extended-release tablets, oral suspension, and as a solution for injection.

**TREATMENT**
Phenytoin tablets must be taken several times a day. The extended-release tablets need to be taken only once a day, but the total daily dose should remain the same. The recommended initial dose is 300 mg per day, which may

be increased up to 600 mg per day if necessary. The recommended dose for children is 5 mg per kg of body weight per day, split into two or three equal doses to a maximum of 300 mg per day.

## CAUTIONS AND WARNINGS

Phenytoin should not be used by anyone with a known allergy to it or any of the other hydantoin antiseizure medications. If phenytoin is stopped abruptly, it may cause severe seizures. The dosage should be tapered off slowly under the direction of a physician.

Phenytoin should not be used by people with low blood pressure, impaired heart function, or slow heart rate. In these cases, other antiseizure medications should be used.

People with reduced liver function may accumulate the drug in their bodies, potentially increasing the risk of side effects.

## SIDE EFFECTS

The most common side effects include rapid or unusual growth of the gums, slurred speech, confusion, uncontrolled eye movements, dizziness, insomnia, twitching, double vision, fatigue, irritability, depression, and headaches. These side effects usually disappear over time if the drug is taken continuously.

Less common side effects include nausea, vomiting, diarrhea, constipation, fever, rashes, hair loss, weight gain, numbness in the extremities, chest pains, sensitivity to sunlight, joint pain, and high blood pressure.

Rarely, phenytoin can cause fatal allergic reactions or liver damage.

## PREGNANCY/BREAST-FEEDING

During pregnancy, the use of drugs that prevent seizures, including phenytoin, is associated with an increased risk of birth defects. About 10% of children exposed to anticonvulsant medication before birth experience malformations. The abnormalities may be minor, including wide nasal bridge, low-set ears or forehead, small or absent nails, or skin folds in the corners of the eyes, but they may be serious as well, including malformations of the heart, lungs, brain, or gastrointestinal tract. This risk of birth defects must be balanced against the risk of seizures during pregnancy. Prolonged or frequent seizures may cause brain damage or death in the mother and decreased oxygen supply, which may cause birth defects in the fetus. Pregnant women are encouraged to discuss the benefits and potential risks of phenytoin with their physician before using the drug.

HIV can be passed from a woman to her child through breast milk. In areas where nutritionally sound alternatives are readily available, breast-feeding is discouraged for HIV-positive women. Phenytoin may be excreted in human milk, but the drug is generally considered safe for use during nursing.

**USE IN CHILDREN**
Children have effectively used phenytoin at the dosages described above.

**USE IN THE ELDERLY**
Older adults may be more susceptible to the side effects of the drug and may require reduced doses.

**DRUG INTERACTIONS**
Phenytoin interacts with a large number of other drugs. The following drugs increase the blood levels of phenytoin, potentially increasing the risk of its side effects: alcohol, allopurinol, amiodarone, aspirin, azithromycin, benzodiazepines, chloramphenicol, chlorpheniramine, cimetidine, clarithromycin, disulfiram, fluconazole, ibuprofen, isoniazid, itraconazole, ketoconazole, metronidazole, miconazole, omeprazole, phenacemide, phenothiazine antipsychotics, phenylbutazone, succinimide antiseizure medications, sulfa drugs, tricyclic antidepressants, trimethoprim, valproic acid.

The following drugs may reduce blood levels of phenytoin, potentially reducing its effectiveness: alcohol, antacids, anticancer drugs, barbiturates, carbamazepine, charcoal, diazoxide, folic acid, influenza virus vaccine, loxapine succinate, nitrofurantoin, pyridoxine, rifampin, sucralfate, and theophylline.

Phenytoin may decrease the effectiveness of the following drugs: corticosteroids, coumarin-type anticoagulants (warfarin), digitoxin, doxycycline, estrogens, furosemide, itraconazole, ketoconazole, oral contraceptives, quinidine, rifampin, theophylline, and vitamin D.

Phenytoin affects the following drugs in an unpredictable manner: clonazepam, cyclosporine, dopamine, furosemide, levodopa, levonorgestrel, mebendazole, oral antidiabetes medications, and phenothiazines.

Phenytoin may increase lithium toxicity. Corticosteroids may mask the effects of allergic reactions to phenytoin. Phenytoin may decrease the pain-relieving effect of meperidine, but may increase the risk of opioid-related side effects.

**FOOD INTERACTIONS**
Phenytoin should not be taken with foods high in calcium (milk, cheese, nuts, etc.) because calcium reduces the absorption of the drug into the body.

**OTHER DRUGS USED FOR SIMILAR CONDITIONS**
Seizures may be treated with barbiturates such as phenobarbital, benzodiazepines such as clonazepam or diazepam, hydantoin derivatives such as mephenytoin or ethotoin, as well as other classes of drugs. The drug of choice depends on the age and health of the individual, the cause of the seizures, and the tolerability of specific drugs.

**COMMENTS**

Different brands of phenytoin may not be identical and may require dose adjustments. A physician should be consulted before changing brands.

# TOPIRAMATE

**BRAND NAME (MANUFACTURER)**
Topamax (McNeil/Ortho)

**TYPE OF DRUG**
Antiseizure drug

**USED FOR**
Topiramate is used as supplementary therapy for the treatment of people with partial onset seizures.

**GENERAL INFORMATION**
The exact mechanism by which topiramate exerts antiseizure activity is not known.

Seizures may be caused by any of the central nervous system disorders or infections associated with HIV infection. Toxoplasmosis is the most common cause of seizures in people with AIDS. Between 15% and 30% of people with toxoplasmosis experience seizures. Phenobarbital treats the symptoms of the neurological disorders, not the underlying causes. When the seizures are caused by an opportunistic infection of the central nervous system, therapy should also include appropriate antibiotic, antifungal, or antiparasitic treatment.

Topiramate is available as tablets for oral administration.

**TREATMENT**
The recommended dose of topiramate is 200 mg twice a day. Topiramate should be started at lower doses and gradually increased over 8 weeks until the 200 mg twice a day dose is reached.

In people with impaired liver or kidney function, the dosage of topiramate is generally reduced because these people may be more susceptible to the drug's side effects.

**CAUTIONS AND WARNINGS**
Topiramate should not be used by anyone with a known allergy to it.

Stopping the drug abruptly in people using it to control seizures may, by itself, trigger seizures.

People on topiramate should drink a lot of water to reduce the risk of developing kidney stones.

## SIDE EFFECTS

The most common side effects of topiramate include drowsiness, dizziness, speech disorders, difficulty with memory or concentration, depression and confusion. Rarely, topiramate can cause serious side effects, including kidney stones and numbness.

## PREGNANCY/BREAST-FEEDING

Topiramate has not been formally studied in pregnant women. In animal studies, topiramate did cause harm to the fetus. Pregnant women are encouraged to discuss the benefits and potential risks of topiramate with their physician before using the drug.

HIV can be passed from a woman to her child through breast milk. In areas where nutritionally sound alternatives are readily available, breast-feeding is discouraged for HIV-positive women. It is not known if topiramate is excreted in breast milk. Because of the potential toxicity of the drug to newborns, women are encouraged to consider alternatives to breast-feeding while using it.

## USE IN CHILDREN

The safety and effectiveness of topiramate has not been established for children.

## USE IN THE ELDERLY

Elderly people with normal kidney and liver function should be able to take topiramate without dosage modification. Older adults with impaired kidney or liver function may require reduced doses.

## DRUG INTERACTIONS

Topiramate levels in blood are decreased by phenytoin, carbamazepine, and valproic acid. Topiramate will increase phenytoin levels in blood.

## FOOD INTERACTIONS

Topiramate may be taken with or without food.

## OTHER DRUGS USED FOR SIMILAR CONDITIONS

Seizures may be treated with barbiturates, benzodiazepines such as clonazepam or diazepam, hydantoin derivatives such as phenytoin, mephenytoin, or ethotoin, as well as other classes of drugs. The drug of choice depends on the age and health of the individual, the cause of the seizures, and the tolerability of specific drugs.

# VALPROIC ACID

## BRAND NAME (MANUFACTURER)

Depakene (Abbott); Depakote (Abbott)

**OTHER NAMES**
Dipropylacetic acid; valproate

**TYPE OF DRUG**
Antiseizure drug

**USED FOR**
Valproic acid is used to prevent and treat epileptic seizures.

**GENERAL INFORMATION**
Valproic acid is an anticonvulsant used primarily when other anticonvulsants have failed to control seizures. By suppressing electrical activity in the brain, valproic acid prevents the uncontrolled stimulation of the brain that triggers seizures. Because valproic acid is less sedating than some other anticonvulsants, it is often used in children with various seizure disorders.

Seizures may be caused by any of the central nervous system disorders or infections associated with HIV infection. Toxoplasmosis is the most common cause of seizures in people with AIDS. Between 15% and 30% of people with toxoplasmosis experience seizures. Valproic acid treats the symptoms of the neurological disorders, not the underlying causes. When the seizures are caused by an opportunistic infection of the central nervous system, therapy should also include appropriate antibiotic, antifungal, or antiparasitic treatment.

Valproic acid is available as capsules and syrup for oral administration.

**TREATMENT**
As with all psychoactive drugs, the lowest effective dosage of valproic acid should be used. The recommended starting dose for adults is 15 mg per kg of body weight per day, gradually increased as necessary and tolerated. The maximum recommended dose is 60 mg per kg of body weight per day. The capsules should be swallowed without chewing to avoid irritation of the mouth and throat.

**CAUTIONS AND WARNINGS**
Valproic acid should not be used by anyone with a known allergy to it.

Because of the risk of serious and potentially fatal side effects, valproic acid should be used with caution in people with liver disease. People taking other anticonvulsants, children, those with inherited metabolic disorders, those with severe seizure disorders accompanied by mental retardation, and people with brain disease are at the highest risk for liver toxicity caused by valproic acid.

A physician should be contacted immediately if symptoms of liver toxicity (yellowing in the eyes or skin, for example) develop while taking valproic acid. If the drug is stopped abruptly, it may trigger new seizures.

Valproic acid may interfere with the mental and physical abilities necessary to drive an automobile or to operate dangerous machinery.

## SIDE EFFECTS

The most common side effects of the drug are nausea, vomiting, indigestion, drowsiness, weakness, allergic skin reactions, emotional upset, depression, abnormal thinking, aggression, and hyperactivity.

Less common side effects include diarrhea, stomach cramps, constipation, changes in appetite, headache, abnormal eye movements, double vision, loss of coordination, tremors, and reduced platelet counts (increasing the risk of bleeding).

## PREGNANCY/BREAST-FEEDING

Like other drugs used to prevent seizures, valproic acid may cause severe birth defects. About 10% of children exposed to anticonvulsant medication before birth experience malformations. The abnormalities may be minor, including wide nasal bridge, low-set ears or forehead, small or absent nails, or skin folds in the corners of the eyes, but they may be serious as well, including malformations of the heart, lungs, brain, or gastrointestinal tract. This risk of birth defects must be balanced against the risk of seizures during pregnancy. Prolonged or frequent seizures may cause brain damage or death in the mother and decreased oxygen supply, which may cause birth defects in the fetus. Pregnant women are encouraged to discuss the benefits and potential risks of valproic acid with their physician before using the drug.

HIV can be passed from a woman to her child through breast milk. In areas where nutritionally sound alternatives are readily available, breast-feeding is discouraged for HIV-positive women. Valproic acid is excreted in human milk. Because of the potential toxicity of the drug to newborns, women are encouraged to consider alternatives to breast-feeding while using it.

## USE IN CHILDREN

Children over the age of two are given valproic acid at dosages adjusted for age and weight. The drug is not recommended for children under age two because they are more susceptible to the severe, potentially fatal liver toxicity of the drug.

## USE IN THE ELDERLY

Older adults may be more susceptible to the side effects of the drug and may require reduced doses.

## DRUG INTERACTIONS

Valproic acid may intensify the effects of other central nervous system (CNS) depressants, including alcohol, antihistamines, barbiturates, monoamine oxidase (MAO) inhibitors (isocarboxazid, tranylcypromine, etc.), narcotic pain relievers, sedatives, and tranquilizers.

Valproic acid may increase blood levels of phenobarbital or primidone, potentially resulting in severe CNS depression when the drugs are taken to-

gether. When used with aspirin, carbamazepine, dicumarol, and phenytoin, valproic acid may raise or lower blood concentrations of these drugs.

Valproic acid may reduce phenytoin blood levels, potentially resulting in "breakthrough" seizures. Use of valproic acid together with clonazepam may induce absence seizures (during which the person appears to be daydreaming) in people with a history of absence seizures.

Valproic acid may increase the blood-thinning effect of aspirin or warfarin. It may also reduce the effectiveness of oral contraceptives.

### FOOD INTERACTIONS

Valproic acid may be taken with or without food. Depakote sprinkle capsules can be taken whole or mixed with a small amount of pudding, applesauce, or other food. The mixture should be swallowed (not chewed) as soon as it is prepared.

### OTHER DRUGS USED FOR SIMILAR CONDITIONS

Seizures may be treated with barbiturates such as phenobarbital, benzodiazepines such as clonazepam or diazepam, hydantoin derivatives such as phenytoin, mephenytoin, or ethotoin, as well as other classes of drugs. The drug of choice depends on the age and health of the individual, the cause of the seizures, and the tolerability of specific drugs.

# ANTIULCER DRUGS

This section contains profiles of drugs used to relieve symptoms and promote the healing of ulcers.

The lining of the gut is normally covered with a layer of thick mucus, which protects it from stomach acid. If something damages this layer, the acid can attack the lining, destroy the tissues, and cause ulcers. These ulcers may be accompanied by severe abdominal pain, vomiting, or loss of appetite.

Recent studies report that a bacteria, *Helicobacter pylori,* is associated with certain ulcers. People who smoke heavily, routinely take nonsteroidal anti-inflammatory drugs like aspirin or ibuprofen, overuse alcohol or coffee, or experience chronic stress are predisposed to developing ulcers.

Sucralfate and drugs called histamine blockers are commonly used to treat the symptoms of ulcers. Sucralfate forms a coating over the ulcer, protecting it from stomach acid and allowing it to heal. The histamine blockers (e.g., cimetidine or ranitidine) reduce the amount of stomach acid secreted, which also reduces the irritation and allows the ulcer to heal. Because neither type of drug affects the underlying causes of ulcers, the ulcers often return after the drugs are stopped and treatment must be repeated.

The following drugs are covered in this section:

- antacids
- cimetidine
- famotidine
- nizatidine
- omeprazole
- ranitidine
- sucralfate

# ANTACIDS

**BRAND NAMES**
Aluminum and magnesium antacids: Algicon; Aludrox; Alumid; Di-Gel; Gaviscon; Gelusil; Maalox; Mintox; Mylanta; Riopan; Rolaids; Tralmag; WinGel
Calcium antacids: Amitone; Calcilac; Dicarbosil; Genalac; Pama; Titracid; Tums

**USED FOR**

Antacids are used to neutralize stomach acid and relieve heartburn, acid indigestion, esophageal reflux disease (acid backing up into the esophagus from the stomach), and other conditions related to stomach upset.

**GENERAL INFORMATION**

Aluminum hydroxide is the ingredient most commonly used in antacids. Because it may cause constipation, aluminum hydroxide is often combined with magnesium, which has a balancing laxative effect. Calcium-containing antacids have become more popular recently, in part because their manufacturers have marketed them as calcium supplements to prevent osteoporosis in women, a condition in which bones become brittle with age. Some antacids (Maalox Plus and Mylanta, among others) also contain a chemical called simethicone, which is used to reduce the gas that may be caused by the reaction of the aluminum or magnesium salts with the stomach acid.

In HIV disease, antacids should be used carefully because they reduce the absorption of a number of drugs used to combat HIV or to treat opportunistic infections. For a list of possible drug interactions, see the "Drug interactions" section on page 298.

**TREATMENT**

The dosing of the antacids depends on the particular drug used and the condition being treated. More severe conditions, such as stomach ulcers, often require substantially higher doses, which should only be used with the guidance of a physician.

In general, to neutralize stomach acid, most of the drugs are taken four to six times daily as needed. Most are available as tablets or liquid. Liquids are often preferable for their superior coating effect. Tablets should be completely chewed before swallowing.

**CAUTIONS AND WARNINGS**

Antacids should not be used by anyone with a known allergy to them. As over-the-counter medications, they are indicated for short-term use. Stomach acid problems that do not improve after short-term treatment may be symptoms of serious gastrointestinal disease.

Because of the increased potential for aluminum toxicity, aluminum antacids should be used with caution by people who have had bleeding in the stomach or intestines.

Calcium antacids may have a rebound effect. After the drugs are stopped, the problem may return worse than it was initially.

**SIDE EFFECTS**

The most common side effect of aluminum-containing antacids is constipation. Nausea and vomiting may infrequently occur. Bone pain and muscle

weakness may occur when large doses have regularly been taken for long periods of time.

Magnesium antacids may cause diarrhea. In people with kidney disease, magnesium antacids may cause magnesium toxicity. Some magnesium-containing antacids taken regularly over long periods may cause kidney stones.

Calcium antacids may cause milk-alkali syndrome, a condition characterized by headache, nausea, irritability, and muscle weakness. When the antacid is continued despite these symptoms, it may cause severe kidney toxicity and kidney failure.

### PREGNANCY/BREAST-FEEDING
Short-term use of antacids during pregnancy usually does not cause fetal harm. Long-term use of high doses is not recommended. Pregnant women should discuss the benefits and potential risks of antacids with their physician before deciding to use the drugs.

HIV may be passed from a woman to her child through breast milk. In areas where nutritionally sound alternatives are readily available, breast-feeding is discouraged for HIV-positive women. However, antacids are generally considered safe to take while breast-feeding.

### USE IN CHILDREN
Children can effectively use antacids at dosages reduced for age and body weight. Newborns have immature kidneys and may be more susceptible to side effects of the drugs than adults. In general, antacids are not recommended for children under the age of six.

### USE IN THE ELDERLY
Elderly people can generally use antacids without special restrictions. Older people with metabolic bone diseases should not take antacids that contain aluminum. Anyone with severe kidney disease should not use magnesium or aluminum antacids.

### DRUG INTERACTIONS
Antacids reduce the absorption of drugs that require acidity in the stomach. A partial lists of drugs poorly absorbed with antacids includes azithromycin, ciprofloxacin, ddC, delavirdine, flucytosine, isoniazid, itraconazole, ketoconazole, corticosteroids, quinolone antibiotics, aspirin, tetracyclines, quinidine, benzodiazepine tranquilizers, phenothiazine tranquilizers, warfarin, digitalis, phenytoin, allopurinol, calcitriol, captopril, cimetidine, dicoumarol, diflunisal, flecainide, iron supplements, levodopa, lithium, nitrofurantoin, ranitidine, tolmetin, and valproic acid. These drugs should be taken an hour before or an hour after antacids for proper absorption.

Antacids may increase absorption of famotidine, metronidazole, pyrimethamine, and theophylline.

Taking antacids with sodium polystyrene sulfonate may result in kidney failure.

**FOOD INTERACTIONS**
Antacids may be taken with or without food.

**OTHER DRUGS USED FOR SIMILAR CONDITIONS**
A large number of antacid products are available. Generally, they differ in their acid-neutralizing capability and the side effects they cause. The neutralizing capacity depends not only on the chemicals used in the antacid, but also on how it is formulated, and how much antacid is put into the tablet or liquid. Generally, liquid antacids have greater neutralizing capacity than either powders or tablets.

For more serious conditions than can be treated with antacids that chemically neutralize stomach acid, antiulcer drugs such as cimetidine or ranitidine, which prevent secretion of stomach acid in the first place, may be appropriate.

# CIMETIDINE

**BRAND NAME (MANUFACTURER)**
Tagamet (SmithKline Beecham)

**TYPE OF DRUG**
Antiulcer agent

**USED FOR**
Cimetidine is primarily used for the treatment of ulcers. It is also used for the prevention of recurrent ulcers and upper digestive tract bleeding in the critically ill.

The drug has also been shown to have some effects on the immune system and has been proposed as a possible treatment for the immune suppression associated with HIV infection, based on the results of a small German study that suggested the drug has some anti-HIV activity.

**GENERAL INFORMATION**
Cimetidine inhibits the action of histamine, a substance secreted by specialized cells called mast cells. Histamine has a number of effects, including accelerating the heart rate, causing inflammation, and increasing the secretion of acid in the stomach. Recent studies suggest, however, that many, if not most, peptic ulcers are caused by a bacteria, *Helicobacter pylori,* and may most effectively be treated by a combination of antibiotics and antiulcer medications. In this model, cimetidine treats only the symptoms of ulcers without affecting the underlying disease.

Cimetidine prevents the action of histamine by blocking the surface receptors that bring the compound into cells. Histamine receptors can also be found on the surface of lymphocytes, and histamine may impair lymphocyte function and reduce CD4+ counts in people infected with HIV. Recent studies indicate that cimetidine does not significantly increase CD4+ counts or decrease the amount of HIV in the blood.

Cimetidine is available as tablets for oral administration.

## TREATMENT

For treatment of ulcers, cimetidine is usually taken at a dose of 800 mg at bedtime. For prevention of recurrent ulcers, the drug is usually taken at 400 mg at bedtime. The doses are reduced for people with reduced kidney function.

## CAUTIONS AND WARNINGS

Cimetidine should not be used by people who know they are allergic to it. It may also mask the symptoms of stomach cancer.

## SIDE EFFECTS

Cimetidine has few side effects. The most common are headache, diarrhea, sleepiness, and dizziness. Mental confusion, agitation, depression, anxiety, and hallucinations have rarely been reported, primarily in severely ill people who take the drug. An overdose of the drug may cause excessively rapid heartbeat or respiratory failure.

The drug has a slight inhibitory effect on male hormones, which may explain why some people experience painful, swollen breasts after taking the drug for a month or more.

## PREGNANCY/BREAST-FEEDING

Cimetidine has not been formally studied in pregnant women. In animal studies, the drug did not cause fetal harm, but it is not known whether the same would be true for humans. Pregnant women are encouraged to discuss the benefits and potential risks of cimetidine with their physician before deciding to use the drug.

HIV can be passed from a woman to her child through breast milk. In areas where nutritionally sound alternatives are readily available, breast-feeding is discouraged for HIV-positive women. Cimetidine is excreted in high concentrations in human milk. Because of the potential toxicity of the drug, women are encouraged to consider alternatives to breast-feeding while using it.

## USE IN CHILDREN

Cimetidine has not been studied formally in children under the age of sixteen. In limited clinical experience, it has been used at doses of 20 to 40 mg per kg of body weight per day without unexpected side effects.

**USE IN THE ELDERLY**
Older people generally respond well to cimetidine, but they may be more susceptible to the side effects of the drug and often require reduced doses.

**DRUG INTERACTIONS**
Cimetidine may increase the blood concentrations of warfarin-type anticoagulants, phenytoin, propranolol, nifedipine, chlordiazepoxide, diazepam, certain tricyclic antidepressants, lidocaine, theophylline, and metronidazole, potentially increasing the risk of side effects of these drugs.

Cimetidine may decrease fluconazole, itraconazole, or delavirdine levels in the body, potentially reducing the activity of these drugs. Cimetidine and nevirapine should be used with caution as cimetidine may decrease nevirapine levels and render the drug ineffective.

Cimetidine and ddI or ketoconazole should be taken at least two hours apart in order to ensure proper absorption of the drugs.

**FOOD INTERACTIONS**
Cimetidine may be taken with or without food.

**OTHER DRUGS USED FOR SIMILAR CONDITIONS**
Nizatidine, famotidine, and ranitidine are histamine blockers that are also used to treat ulcers. The drugs have similar side effects and work by a similar mechanism. It is unlikely that people who don't respond to one would respond to another.

# FAMOTIDINE

**BRAND NAME (MANUFACTURER)**
Pepcid (Merck)

**TYPE OF DRUG**
Antiulcer agent

**USED FOR**
Famotidine is used primarily for the treatment of ulcers. It is also used for the prevention of recurrent ulcers, treatment of excessive secretion of stomach acid, and treatment of gastric reflux disease, a condition where stomach acid backs up into the esophagus.

**GENERAL INFORMATION**
Famotidine inhibits the action of histamine, which is secreted by specialized cells called mast cells. Histamine has a number of effects, including accelerating the heart rate, causing inflammation, and increasing the secretion of acid in the stomach. Famotidine prevents the action of histamine by blocking the surface receptors that bring the compound into cells.

Recent studies suggest, however, that many, if not most, peptic ulcers are caused by a bacteria, *Helicobacter pylori,* and may most effectively be treated by a combination of antibiotics and antiulcer medications. In this model, famotidine treats the symptoms of ulcers without affecting the underlying disease.

Famotidine is available as tablets, as a suspension for oral administration, and as an injectable solution.

## TREATMENT

Most people will use the tablets or oral suspension. For treatment of acute ulcer, the recommended adult dosage is 40 mg, taken once a day at bedtime. Most ulcers will heal within four weeks of treatment, and there is rarely any reason to continue the full dose of the drug beyond six to eight weeks. After the ulcer is healed, the drug may be continued at a dosage of 20 mg a day to prevent recurrence of the condition.

For gastroesophageal reflux disease, the recommended dosage is 20 mg, taken twice daily, for up to six weeks. If the condition has caused ulceration of the esophagus, a dose of 40 mg twice a day may be used.

In people with severe impairment of kidney function, the dosages may need to be reduced.

## CAUTIONS AND WARNINGS

Famotidine should not be used by anyone with a known allergy to it.

Famotidine does not affect the underlying cause of ulcers. If the drug is stopped, the condition may return. In addition, famotidine may mask the symptoms of stomach cancer.

## SIDE EFFECTS

The most common side effect of famotidine is headache. Less common side effects include dizziness, diarrhea, and constipation.

## PREGNANCY/BREAST-FEEDING

Famotidine has not been formally studied in pregnant women. In animal studies, the drug did not cause fetal harm, but it is unknown whether the same would be true for humans. Pregnant women are encouraged to discuss the benefits and potential risks of famotidine with their physician before deciding to use the drug.

HIV can be passed from a woman to her child through breast milk. In areas where nutritionally sound alternatives are readily available, breast-feeding is discouraged for HIV-positive women. It is not known whether famotidine is excreted in human milk. Because of the potential toxicity of the drug, women are encouraged to consider alternatives to breast-feeding while using it.

## USE IN CHILDREN

The safety and effectiveness of famotidine for children have not yet been established in clinical trials.

**USE IN THE ELDERLY**
Older adults may be more susceptible to the side effects of the drug and may require reduced doses.

**DRUG INTERACTIONS**
Famotidine may inhibit the absorption of ketoconazole or vitamin B12. Cigarette smoking may reverse the effect of famotidine on stomach acid.

**FOOD INTERACTIONS**
Famotidine may be taken with or without food.

**OTHER DRUGS USED FOR SIMILAR CONDITIONS**
Nizatidine, cimetidine, and ranitidine are histamine blockers that are also used to treat ulcers. They have similar side effects and work by a similar mechanism. People who don't respond to one are unlikely to respond to another.

# NIZATIDINE

**BRAND NAME (MANUFACTURER)**
Axid (Lilly)

**TYPE OF DRUG**
Antiulcer agent

**USED FOR**
Nizatidine is primarily used for the treatment of ulcers. It is also used for the prevention of recurrent ulcers and gastroesophageal reflux disease, a condition where stomach acid backs up into the esophagus.

**GENERAL INFORMATION**
Nizatidine inhibits the action of histamine, a substance secreted by specialized cells called mast cells. Histamine has a number of effects, including accelerating heart rate, causing inflammation, and increasing secretion of acid in the stomach. Nizatidine prevents the action of histamine by blocking the surface receptors that bring the compound into cells.

Recent studies suggest, however, that many, if not most, peptic ulcers are caused by a bacteria, *Helicobacter pylori,* and may most effectively be treated by a combination of antibiotics and antiulcer medications. In this model, nizatidine treats only the symptoms of ulcers without affecting the underlying disease.

Nizatidine is available as capsules for oral administration.

**TREATMENT**
The recommended adult dosage for active ulcer is 300 mg taken once daily at bedtime. After the ulcer heals, a maintenance dose of 150 mg per day taken at bedtime may be used to prevent recurrence of the disorder.

For gastroesophageal reflux disease, the recommended dosage is 150 mg, taken twice a day.

These dosages may need to be reduced for people with severely impaired kidney function.

## CAUTIONS AND WARNINGS

Nizatidine should not be used by anyone with a known allergy to it or other similar histamine receptor antagonists, including famotidine, cimetidine, or ranitidine.

Nizatidine does not affect the underlying cause of ulcers. If the drug is stopped, the condition may return. In addition, nizatidine may mask the symptoms of stomach cancer.

## SIDE EFFECTS

The most common side effects of nizatidine are fatigue and increased perspiration. Less commonly, headache, abdominal pain, diarrhea, nausea, and dizziness are reported by people taking the drug.

## PREGNANCY/BREAST-FEEDING

Nizatidine has not been formally studied in pregnant women. In animal studies, the drug caused spontaneous abortions and reduced birth weights, but it is not known whether the same would be true for humans. Pregnant women are encouraged to discuss the benefits and potential risks of nizatidine with their physician before deciding to use the drug.

HIV can be passed from a woman to her child through breast milk. In areas where nutritionally sound alternatives are readily available, breast-feeding is discouraged for HIV-positive women. Small amounts of nizatidine are excreted in human milk. Because of the potential toxicity of the drug, women are encouraged to consider alternatives to breast-feeding while using it.

## USE IN CHILDREN

The safety and effectiveness of nizatidine for children have not yet been established in clinical trials.

## USE IN THE ELDERLY

Older adults may be more susceptible to the side effects of the drug and may require reduced doses.

## DRUG INTERACTIONS

Nizatidine may increase blood levels of aspirin in people taking high doses of the pain reliever. No other drug interactions have been detected in clinical trials. Drugs tested include theophylline, chlordiazepoxide, lorazepam, lidocaine, phenytoin, and warfarin.

## FOOD INTERACTIONS

Nizatidine may be taken with or without food.

**OTHER DRUGS USED FOR SIMILAR CONDITIONS**
Famotidine, cimetidine, and ranitidine are histamine blockers that are also used to treat ulcers. The drugs have similar side effects and work by a similar mechanism. People who don't respond to one are unlikely to respond to another.

# OMEPRAZOLE

**BRAND NAME (MANUFACTURER)**
Prilosec (Astra Merck)

**TYPE OF DRUG**
Antiulcer agent

**USED FOR**
Omeprazole is primarily used for short-term treatment of stomach and intestinal ulcers. It is also used to treat gastroesophageal reflux disease, a condition where stomach acid backs up into the esophagus.

A combination of omeprazole and clarithromycin, an antibiotic, is used to treat and clear duodenal ulcers caused by bacterial infection.

**GENERAL INFORMATION**
Omeprazole suppresses the secretion of acid in the stomach by a different mechanism than other antiulcer drugs such as ranitidine and cimetidine. Omeprazole prevents the release of acid by blocking the surface enzymes that allow the secretion of acid. Recent studies suggest, however, that many, if not most, peptic ulcers are caused by a bacteria, *Helicobacter pylori,* and may most effectively be treated by a combination of antibiotics and antiulcer medications. In this model, omeprazole treats only the symptoms of ulcers without affecting the underlying disease.

Omeprazole is available as tablets for oral administration.

**TREATMENT**
For treatment of duodenal ulcers, omeprazole is usually taken at a dose of 20 mg once daily for four weeks or more. To prevent recurrence of ulcers, omeprazole (40 mg once daily) is given with clarithromycin (500 mg three times daily) for 14 days and then given alone at 20 mg once daily for another 14 days.

To treat stomach ulcers and gastroesophageal reflux disease, the recommended dose is 20 mg daily for 4-8 weeks.

Omeprazole tablets should not be opened, chewed, or crushed, but should be swallowed whole.

### CAUTIONS AND WARNINGS

Omeprazole should not be used by people who know they are allergic to it. It should not be used with clarithromycin in people who have a known allergy to clarithromycin. Clarithromycin should also not be used in pregnant women because of the potential toxicity to the fetus.

### SIDE EFFECTS

Omeprazole is generally well tolerated and has few side effects. The most common are headache, diarrhea, abdominal pain, and nausea. Other side effects include dizziness, rash, constipation, cough, and back pain.

### PREGNANCY/BREAST-FEEDING

Omeprazole has not been formally studied in pregnant women. In animal studies, the drug caused some fetal harm and developmental problems at doses almost 100 times higher than the average human dose. It is not known whether the same would be true for humans. Pregnant women are encouraged to discuss the benefits and potential risks of omeprazole with their physician before deciding to use the drug.

HIV can be passed from a woman to her child through breast milk. In areas where nutritionally sound alternatives are readily available, breast-feeding is discouraged for HIV-positive women. It is not known whether omeprazole is excreted in human milk. Because of the potential toxicity of the drug, women are encouraged to consider alternatives to breast-feeding while using it.

### USE IN CHILDREN

Safety and effectiveness in children has not been established.

### USE IN THE ELDERLY

Older people may be more susceptible to the side effects of the drug and often require reduced doses.

### DRUG INTERACTIONS

Omeprazole may prolong the clearing of warfarin-type anticoagulants, phenytoin, diazepam, propranolol, benzodiazepines, cyclosporine, and disulfiram, potentially increasing the risk of side effects of these drugs.

Because omeprazole prevents secretion of stomach acid, it theoretically may inhibit the activity of drugs that require an acidic stomach environment, such as ketaconazole, ampicillin, and iron salts.

### FOOD INTERACTIONS

No information available.

### OTHER DRUGS USED FOR SIMILAR CONDITIONS

Nizatidine, cimetidine, famotidine, and ranitidine are histamine blockers that are also used to treat ulcers. The drugs have similar side effects and work by a similar mechanism. It is unlikely that people who don't respond to one would

respond to another. Sucralfate is another antiulcer medication that works by a different mechanism.

# RANITIDINE

**BRAND NAME (MANUFACTURER)**
Zantac (Glaxo Wellcome); Tritec (Glaxo Wellcome)

**TYPE OF DRUG**
Antiulcer agent

**USED FOR**
Ranitidine is used for the short-term treatment of stomach and intestinal ulcers. It is also used to prevent stress ulcers, bleeding in the stomach or intestines, and stomach irritation caused by aspirin and other nonsteroidal anti-inflammatory drugs.

Ranitidine is used in combination with clarithromycin, an antibiotic, to treat duodenal ulcers.

**GENERAL INFORMATION**
Ranitidine inhibits the action of histamine, a substance secreted by specialized cells called mast cells. Histamine has a number of effects, including accelerating the heart rate, causing inflammation, and increasing the secretion of acid in the stomach. Ranitidine prevents the action of histamine by blocking the surface receptors that bring the compound into cells.

Recent studies suggest, however, that many, if not most, peptic ulcers are caused by a bacteria, *Helicobacter pylori*, and may most effectively be treated by a combination of antibiotics and antiulcer medications. In this model, ranitidine treats only the symptoms of ulcers without affecting the underlying disease.

Ranitidine is available in tablets, capsules, effervescent tablets and granules, syrup, and solution for injection. The tablets and capsules come in 150, 300, and 400 mg strengths. The effervescent forms, which must be dissolved in water before taken, are available in single doses of 150 mg.

**TREATMENT**
The usual dose of ranitidine is 150 to 300 mg a day. In severe cases, a dose of 600 mg may be used. When ranitidine is used in combination with clarithromycin, the usual dose of ranitidine is 400 mg twice daily for 4 weeks. Clarithromycin is taken for the first two weeks at a dose of 500 mg three times daily. People with severe reductions in kidney function may require reduced doses.

It may take several days of treatment before blood levels of ranitidine stabilize and the drug begins to have an effect.

### CAUTIONS AND WARNINGS
Ranitidine should not be taken by anyone with a known allergy to it. The drug should be taken with caution by people with liver or kidney disease because it is broken down by the liver and excreted from the body by the kidneys.

### SIDE EFFECTS
In general, ranitidine is well tolerated and side effects occur infrequently. The most common side effects include headache, nausea, vomiting, agitation, constipation, diarrhea, abdominal pain, rash, swollen breasts, impotence, and reduced sex drive. Less frequently, ranitidine may cause fatigue, dizziness, confusion, hallucinations, depression, sleeplessness, inflammation of the pancreas, hair loss, and joint pain. In rare cases, ranitidine may be toxic to bone marrow and cause reductions in white blood cell counts or platelets.

### PREGNANCY/BREAST-FEEDING
Ranitidine has not been formally studied in pregnant women. In animal studies, the drug did not cause fetal harm, but it is not known whether this would be true for humans. Pregnant women are encouraged to discuss the benefits and potential risks of ranitidine with their physician before deciding to use the drug.

HIV can be passed from a woman to her child through breast milk. In areas where nutritionally sound alternatives are readily available, breast-feeding is discouraged for HIV-positive women. Very high levels of ranitidine pass through breast milk. Because of the potential toxicity of the drug to newborns, ranitidine is not recommended for use by nursing women.

### USE IN CHILDREN
Ranitidine is not recommended for children because its safety and effectiveness have not been formally studied or established for them.

### USE IN THE ELDERLY
Older adults may be more susceptible to the side effects of the drug and may require reduced doses.

### DRUG INTERACTIONS
Antacids may reduce the absorption of ranitidine into the body, potentially lowering the drug's effectiveness. When taken with ddI, ranitidine slightly elevates ddI blood levels, and ddI reduces the blood levels of ranitidine. These drug interactions can be avoided if the two drugs are taken at least two hours apart.

Ranitidine may increase blood levels of glipizide, glyburide, theophylline, and procainamide. It may also decrease absorption of diazepam. Smoking cigarettes may reverse the effects of ranitidine on stomach acid.

There have been some reports that ranitidine may increase or decrease the effect of warfarin on blood clotting.

**FOOD INTERACTIONS**
Ranitidine may be taken with or without meals.

**OTHER DRUGS USED FOR SIMILAR CONDITIONS**
Nizatidine and cimetidine are histamine blockers that are also used to treat ulcers. The drugs have similar side effects and work by a similar mechanism. It is unlikely that people who don't respond to one would respond to the other.

# SUCRALFATE

**BRAND NAME (MANUFACTURER)**
Carafate (Hoechst Marion Roussel)

**TYPE OF DRUG**
Antiulcer agent

**USED FOR**
Sucralfate is used to treat and prevent the recurrence of stomach and intestinal ulcers.

**GENERAL INFORMATION**
Sucralfate accelerates healing of stomach and intestinal disorders. It is not well absorbed from the gut into the body. Rather, it stays intact in the gastrointestinal tract. Sucralfate does not neutralize stomach acid (as antacids do) and it does not systemically reduce stomach acid production (like cimetidine or ranitidine). Instead, it forms a protective barrier over the ulcer that protects it from further attack by digestive acids and enzymes, thus giving the ulcer time to heal.

Sucralfate is available as tablets or suspension for oral administration.

**TREATMENT**
In treating active ulcers, the recommended dosage for adults is 1 g of sucralfate taken four times a day on an empty stomach.

Although healing may occur within the first week or two, treatment should continue for four to eight weeks, unless the healing has been confirmed by X rays or endoscopy.

To prevent recurrence of ulcers, sucralfate is used at a dose of 1 g taken twice a day.

**CAUTIONS AND WARNINGS**
Sucralfate should not be used by anyone with a known allergy to it.

Sucralfate accelerates healing of ulcers, but it does not affect the underlying causes. After the drug is stopped, the ulcers may return if the underlying cause is not addressed.

People with impaired kidney function who use sucralfate in combination with aluminum-containing antacids may be at increased risk for aluminum toxicity.

## SIDE EFFECTS

Sucralfate is well tolerated and only rarely must the drug be stopped because of side effects. In clinical trials, the most common side effect of the drug was constipation, which was reported in 2% of volunteers taking the drug. Other side effects, which occurred in fewer than 0.5% of volunteers, included diarrhea, nausea, vomiting, indigestion, gas, dry mouth, itching, rash, dizziness, insomnia, sleepiness, vertigo, back pain, headache, or allergic reactions.

## PREGNANCY/BREAST-FEEDING

Sucralfate has not been formally studied in pregnant women. In animal studies, the drug did not cause fetal harm, but it is not known whether the same would be true for humans. Pregnant women are encouraged to discuss the benefits and potential risks of sucralfate with their physician before deciding to use the drug.

HIV may be passed from a woman to her child through breast milk. In areas where nutritionally sound alternatives are readily available, breast-feeding is discouraged for HIV-positive women. However, because sucralfate is so poorly absorbed into the bloodstream, the drug is unlikely to cause harm to breast-fed infants whose mothers take it.

## USE IN CHILDREN

There is little clinical experience with sucralfate in children. Generally it is not prescribed for them. When it is used, the dose is adjusted for age and weight.

## USE IN THE ELDERLY

No changes in dosage or administration are recommended for older adults.

## DRUG INTERACTIONS

Sucralfate may reduce absorption of the following drugs: cimetidine, ciprofloxacin, digoxin, ketoconazole, norfloxacin, phenytoin, ranitidine, tetracycline, and theophylline. Sucralfate may also alter the effectiveness of blood-thinning drugs, such as warfarin.

Antacids should not be used within one-half hour before or after taking sucralfate because they affect absorption of the drug.

## FOOD INTERACTIONS

Food interferes with the activity of sucralfate. The drug should be used an hour before meals and at bedtime. Prolonged treatment with sucralfate may

interfere with uptake of certain vitamins, including vitamins A, D, E, and K. A physician will advise when supplements are necessary.

## OTHER DRUGS USED FOR SIMILAR CONDITIONS

For simple stomach upset, a wide variety of antacids are available. When antacids are not enough, a number of drugs that reduce acid secretion in the stomach may be used. They include cimetidine, ranitidine, and famotidine. Sucralfate works by a different mechanism, but it has the same clinical effect—healing or preventing ulcers. The choice of therapy depends on the severity of the condition, the age and health of the individual, the response to the different drugs, and other drugs being used at the same time.

# ANTIVIRAL DRUGS

This section contains profiles of antiviral drugs, both those used to treat HIV infection itself and those targeted at viruses that cause opportunistic infections in people who are positive for HIV.

## ANTI-HIV DRUGS

Once HIV was identified as the underlying cause of AIDS, a major scientific effort was started to find drugs capable of stopping or slowing the virus. The effort has not identified a "magic bullet" to cure the disease, but meaningful progress has been made, especially since the introduction of protease inhibitors. A balanced approach to understanding and making decisions about anti-HIV therapy must include knowledge of the benefits, risks, and limitations of existing drugs, as well as the prospects for improvement offered by rational combinations and newer drugs.

Anti-HIV drugs can be categorized into groups based on which step in the virus's life cycle they target or how they do it. The first drugs to be approved are called nucleoside analogue reverse transcriptase inhibitors (NARTIs, including AZT, ddI, ddC, d4T, 3TC). They work by mimicking one of the naturally occurring building blocks of DNA in the cell, thereby interfering with reverse transcription, a process essential for HIV to reproduce itself. Another class of drugs, called non-nucleoside reverse transcriptase inhibitors, targets the same process, but uses a different chemical approach. This class includes the drugs nevirapine and delavirdine. Another class of drugs called protease inhibitors works at a later stage in the viral life cycle, after the virus has successfully infected the cell and is attempting to make new copies of itself. This class include such drugs as indinavir, nelfinavir, ritonavir, and saquinavir. Other drugs that target different steps in the viral life cycle are being tested in clinical trials, along with new drugs in each of the previously studied classes.

Despite the large amount of clinical information available regarding anti-HIV drugs, a good deal of uncertainty remains about certain key questions, such as when to start treatment, which drugs to use or combine, and when to switch.

Current federal guidelines recommend anti-HIV therapy for people who have been diagnosed with AIDS, people who are experiencing symptoms associated with HIV disease, and people who have any significant loss of CD4+ cells and moderate or higher levels of HIV viral load. The effects of treatment are most easily seen in people suffering the most rapid decline. This does not mean, however, that it is necessarily best to wait until disease progression is obvious before beginning treatment. It is simply the time where the clinical data supporting treatment are strongest. Newer, more sensitive diag-

nostic tests have been developed to chart the progression of HIV disease. As more experience is gained with them, it may be possible to make very specific statements about when to begin treatment. For now, these tests only add to the information that can be considered when making a decision.

The choice of treatment is also a matter of some controversy. New Federal Guidelines recommend using a combination of two of the older class of drugs, nucleoside analogues, along with one protease inhibitor as the optimum approach to therapy. This recommendation is based upon new information which shows that treatment is most effective and lasts the longest when it reduces the level of HIV viral load below the limit of detection on the currently available viral load tests. Early approaches using any single drug, or combinations of two of the older drugs, are now considered inadequate. Single drug or two-drug combination therapy have been shown to have very little chance of reducing levels of below the limit of detection and are thus unlikely to produce long-lasting effects. Some two-drug combinations, such as AZT + ddI or AZT + 3TC have been shown to delay disease progression and prolong survival. But today, this is no longer good enough. Instead, effective treatment must also produce results that last as long as possible. Today, this means using three-drug combinations.

For more complete information on how to use the drugs listed in this section, be sure to read the chapter of this book entitled "Antiviral Strategies."

The following anti-HIV drugs are described in this section:

**NUCLEOSIDE ANALOGUES REVERSE TRANSCRIPTASE INHIBITORS (NARTIS)**

- AZT
- ddC
- ddI
- d4T
- 3TC

**NON-NUCLEOSIDE REVERSE TRANSCRIPTASE INHIBITORS (NNRTIS)**

- nevirapine
- delavirdine

**PROTEASE INHIBITORS**

- indinavir
- nelfinavir
- ritonavir
- saquinavir

In addition, brief descriptions of experimental therapies for HIV are included at the end of this section.

## OTHER ANTIVIRAL DRUGS

A number of other viruses can cause serious or fatal infections in people whose immune systems are already weakened by HIV. Some of them (like cytomegalovirus) rarely cause complications in people with healthy immune systems. Others (like hepatitis B) are serious health threats for the general population and even more dangerous for people with weakened immune systems. The following drugs, listed by the viral infection they are used to treat, are covered in this section:

### ANTICYTOMEGALOVIRUS DRUGS
- cidofovir
- foscarnet
- ganciclovir

### ANTIHERPES/VARICELLA DRUGS
- acyclovir
- famciclovir
- trifluridine
- valacyclovir

### ANTIGENITAL HERPES DRUGS
- imiquimod
- podofilox

Brief descriptions of experimental therapies for viral infection are also included at the end of this section. Another strategy for treating viral infection attempts to modulate the immune system's antiviral activity. See the "Immune-based therapy" and "Vaccines" sections for information about such drugs.

# 3TC

## BRAND NAME (MANUFACTURER)
Epivir (Glaxo Wellcome)
AZT + 3TC: Combivir (Glaxo Wellcome)

## OTHER NAME
Lamivudine

## TYPE OF DRUG
Antiviral—anti-HIV

## USED FOR
3TC is approved for combination use with AZT for the treatment of HIV infection where antiviral therapy is warranted. It is most effective when used in a combination therapy regimen with at least two other antiviral medications. 3TC is also being studied for the treatment of hepatitis B infection.

**GENERAL INFORMATION**

3TC is an orally administered anti-HIV drug known as a nucleoside analogue, similar in effect to AZT, ddI, d4T and ddC. The drug mimics a naturally occurring building block of DNA and works by interfering with HIV replication, thus reducing the production of new virus and slowing disease progression.

3TC has been shown to have significant antiviral activity when used in triple combinations including a potent protease inhibitor (indinavir, ritonavir, or nelfinavir). A number of recent studies have also proven the value of an AZT + 3TC + indinavir combination, and 3TC is used as the primary drug of its class in a number of other combination therapies.

3TC is a potent drug, but must be used very carefully. Used by itself for HIV infection, 3TC has a very potent, but very short-lived benefit because resistance to the drug develops rapidly. Once resistance sets in, the drug remains useful only because the mutation that causes resistance to it is believed by some to increase the effectiveness of AZT (and perhaps some other nucleoside analogue drugs). Resistance can be avoided or greatly delayed if 3TC is initiated along with a potent protease inhibitor. Studies of 3TC plus AZT have shown that this combination can delay progression to AIDS and improve survival. However, the collective weight of all recent research indicates that the most effective use of 3TC is in three-drug combination therapies because these are most likely to reduce viral load below the limit of detection, prevent the development of drug resistance, and provide the greatest delay in disease progression and death.

**TREATMENT**

The recommended dosage for adults and adolescents (ages 12–16) is 150 mg twice daily in combination with other antiviral therapies. The recommended dose for children 3 months of age to 12 years is 4 mg/kg twice daily (up to a maximum of 150 mg twice daily).

**CAUTIONS AND WARNINGS**

3TC should not be used by anyone with a known allergy to it. It is not known whether people who are allergic to any of the other nucleoside analogues will also be allergic to 3TC. In addition, use of 3TC in children increases the risk of pancreatitis, an inflammation of the pancreas.

**SIDE EFFECTS**

3TC appears to be relatively well tolerated with few side effects. The most common side effects include nausea, headaches, fatigue, diarrhea, peripheral neuropathy, low white blood cell count, and anemia (low red blood cell count), although very few of the reported side effects have caused people to discon-

tinue the drug. Adults using 3TC may also experience some hair loss. Children using 3TC may develop pancreatitis.

### PREGNANCY/BREAST-FEEDING
3TC has not been formally studied in pregnant women. In animal studies, it did not cause fetal harm, but it is not known whether the same would be true in humans. 3TC should be used during pregnancy only if the potential benefits justify the risks involved.

HIV can be passed from a woman to her child through breast milk. In areas where nutritionally sound alternatives are readily available, breast-feeding is discouraged for HIV-positive women. It is not known whether 3TC is secreted in human milk. Because of the potential toxicity, women should consider alternatives to breast-feeding while taking the drug.

### USE IN CHILDREN
3TC has been shown to be safe and effective in children and is approved for their use. In one study, thirty-one children between three months and seventeen years of age received doses of 3TC up to 6 mg per kg of body weight twice a day. Little significant drug-related toxicity was observed. However, children using 3TC have an increased risk of developing pancreatitis.

### USE IN THE ELDERLY
The safety and effectiveness of 3TC in people over age 65 has not been established, therefore no recommendations are available at this time.

### DRUG INTERACTIONS
TMP/SMX (Bactrim/Septra) and nelfinavir have been shown to increase 3TC levels in the blood. Levels of amantadine, cimetidine, ethambutol, and ranitidine may be effected when taken with 3TC.

### FOOD INTERACTIONS
3TC can be taken with or without food.

### OTHER DRUGS USED FOR SIMILAR CONDITIONS
Anti-HIV drugs in the same class as 3TC include ddI, ddC, d4T, and AZT. Other anti-HIV drugs of other types include indinavir, ritonavir, nelfinavir, saquinavir, nevirapine, and delavirdine. The most effective use of these antiretroviral agents is three or four drug combinations with at least one highly active antiviral (indinavir, ritonavir, nelfinavir, nevirapine, or 3TC).

### COMMENTS
3TC is considered a highly active antiviral therapy, but only when used in combination with other antiviral medications. Used alone or in a mediocre combination or with previously used drugs, drug resistance can develop rapidly. When used in a triple combination with another nucleoside analogue like AZT or D4T and a potent protease inhibitor, 3TC is a very strong and important antiviral therapy.

In considering the optimum combination of drugs, it is important to weigh immediate benefit and long-term benefit as well as preservation of future options. The best use of 3TC is most likely in triple combination regimens with two other antiviral therapies.

# ACYCLOVIR

**BRAND NAME (MANUFACTURER)**
Zovirax (Glaxo Wellcome)

**OTHER NAME**
ACV

**TYPE OF DRUG**
Antiviral

**USED FOR**
Acyclovir has been approved by the FDA for:
- treatment of initial infection of genital herpes
- prevention of recurring genital herpes
- treatment of herpes zoster (shingles) and chicken pox

In people with HIV, acyclovir is also used as a possible control of unidentified herpesviruses that may contribute to HIV disease.

**GENERAL INFORMATION**
Genital herpes is caused by herpes simplex virus (HSV). Shingles and chicken pox are caused by varicella zoster virus (VZV). Both HSV and VZV belong to a family of viruses called herpes viruses. Once a person is infected with a herpes virus, he or she will remain infected for life. Periodic reactivation of the virus will cause the symptoms to recur.

Acyclovir is a synthetic chemical that mimics one of the building blocks of DNA. In cells that are infected with certain herpes viruses (including HSV and VZV), acyclovir slows down the replication of viral DNA. Like other antiviral drugs, it does not rid the body of the virus, but merely acts to reduce the severity and slow the development of the infection.

In people with HIV, acyclovir may need to be used at higher doses or for longer duration than in the general population to effectively treat or suppress genital herpes or shingles.

Some physicians have prescribed acyclovir to treat or prevent other conditions, such as hairy leukoplakia or cytomegalovirus (CMV) infection, but there is little evidence that acyclovir is effective for these conditions. Well-controlled clinical trials have shown that acyclovir has no effect in treating or preventing CMV disease.

Acyclovir is available in capsules, tablets, and suspension for oral use, ointment for topical use, and powder for intravenous injection.

## TREATMENT

The oral forms and the ointment are the most widely used, because of ease of administration. Common oral dosages for adults for the treatment of genital herpes are 600 to 1,000 mg daily, and treatment generally continues for at least seven days. Lower doses are usually used to suppress reactivation of herpes symptoms.

Treatment of VZV infection requires higher doses, on the order of 2,000 to 4,000 mg per day. Since acyclovir is excreted from the body by the kidneys, the dosages should be reduced for people with reduced kidney function.

Acyclovir is sometimes administered intravenously for more severe varicella virus infections or for people who cannot use the tablets. The intravenous form of the drug is also approved for herpes simplex encephalitis, a rare, but potentially fatal inflammation of the brain.

## CAUTIONS AND WARNINGS

Acyclovir should not be used by anyone with a known allergy to it.

Strains of herpes simplex virus resistant to treatment with acyclovir are becoming more common, though they are still found relatively infrequently. Resistant strains appear to arise in people taking the drug intermittently over a long period of time, especially in those with weakened immune systems. Taking acyclovir erratically or in doses too low to suppress herpes simplex promotes this resistance.

## SIDE EFFECTS

Standard doses of acyclovir seldom result in significant side effects. Some people experience short-term side effects such as nausea, vomiting, and headaches. Diarrhea, dizziness, loss of appetite, fatigue, or a medicinal taste in the mouth can occur, but this is uncommon.

A few people using the intravenous form of the drug have had kidney damage when the drug was injected too quickly, but this side effect is extremely rare when the individual is given adequate fluids and the injection proceeds slowly. Furthermore, the damage is reversible if acyclovir is discontinued.

Even with chronic use (which is common in HIV-positive people), acyclovir causes few side effects. Rarely, side effects such as headaches, diarrhea, bone marrow toxicity, nausea, rashes, insomnia, fatigue, fever, and muscle cramps are reported. Long-term, high-dose users on occasion report neuropathy, a tingling or pain in the fingers and toes that, if drug-related, usually disappears when the dose is lowered or the drug is stopped.

## PREGNANCY/BREAST-FEEDING
Acyclovir has not been formally tested in pregnant women. In animal stud-ies, it did not cause fetal harm, but it is not known whether the same would be true for humans. Pregnant women are encouraged to discuss the benefits and potential risks of acyclovir with their physician before deciding to use it.

HIV can be passed from a woman to her child through breast milk. In areas where nutritionally sound alternatives are readily available, breast-feeding is discouraged for HIV-positive women. Acyclovir also passes through breast milk. Because of the potential toxicity of the drug, women should consider alternatives to breast-feeding while taking the drug.

## USE IN CHILDREN
Acyclovir may be used in children to treat herpes or chicken pox at dosages prescribed by a physician. For the treatment of chicken pox, however, some physicians feel that acyclovir use may dampen the immune response to the virus and increase the likelihood of shingles (reactivation of VZV infection) later in life. Until more data are available, some physicians may choose not to treat mild cases of chicken pox in children.

## USE IN THE ELDERLY
Older adults may be more susceptible to the side effects of the drug and may require reduced doses.

## DRUG INTERACTIONS
Using probenecid and acyclovir together may increase acyclovir levels in the blood, potentially increasing the risk of side effects. In test tubes, AZT and alpha interferon have increased antiviral activity when either is combined with acyclovir. Whether or not this effect occurs in the body is unknown.

## FOOD INTERACTIONS
Acyclovir may be taken with or without food.

## OTHER DRUGS USED FOR SIMILAR CONDITIONS
For HSV and VZV infections, acyclovir is the treatment of choice. Other drugs are used primarily when a person cannot tolerate acyclovir or when the in-fection is caused by acyclovir-resistant strains of the virus. Famciclovir and valacyclovir are relatively new antiviral drugs approved by the FDA for VZV and HSV. They require less frequent dosing compared to acyclovir. Intrave-nously administered ganciclovir and foscarnet are effective against both HSV and VZV, but they have significant toxicities. Vidarabine is active against most strains of HSV that are resistant to acyclovir, but comparative studies have shown that foscarnet is more effective and less toxic. Vidarabine was previ-ously used to treat herpes simplex infections of the brain, but acyclovir is more effective and better tolerated. Trifluridine is a topical agent that is effective against HSV. Valacyclovir is an anti-herpes drug that is converted to acyclovir

in the body. Consequently, viruses that are resistant to acyclovir are likely to be resistant to valacyclovir as well.

**COMMENTS**
There is some, but not compelling, evidence that acyclovir may help people with advanced stages of AIDS survive longer. Analysis of one large study showed that using acyclovir (600 or 800 mg daily) with AZT resulted in an increased survival of about one year when compared to using AZT alone. Using the drug for longer periods seemed to increase the survival benefit. Since the information comes from a largely uncontrolled trial and represents a secondary, unplanned analysis of the data, it cannot be given the same weight as evidence from a well controlled clinical trial.

In clinical trials, acyclovir had no apparent impact on HIV levels or CD4+ counts, so how it may be increasing survival isn't really known. Some herpes-viruses (other than herpes simplex) may act as cofactors in AIDS pathogenesis, and by suppressing herpes viruses, acyclovir may slow progression of the disease and increase survival. As other studies have failed to confirm this benefit, some researchers consider this an interesting but unproven use of acyclovir.

# A Z T

**BRAND NAME (MANUFACTURER)**
Retrovir (Glaxo Wellcome)

**OTHER NAMES**
Zidovudine; ZDV; azido-deoxythymidine

**TYPE OF DRUG**
Antiviral–anti-HIV

**USED FOR**
AZT was originally approved for the treatment of HIV infection in adults with CD4+ counts less than 500. The most common and effective use of the drug today is in combination therapy regimens with two other antiretroviral therapies.

AZT is also used to reduce the risk of mother-to-child transmission of the virus during pregnancy and birth and to treat HIV-infected children over three months of age who have HIV-related symptoms or who are asymptomatic with significant HIV-related suppression of their immune systems.

**GENERAL INFORMATION**
AZT is an antiretroviral drug known as a nucleoside analogue. It mimics a naturally occurring building block of DNA and works by interfering with

HIV replication, thus reducing production of new virus and slowing the progression of the disease.

Although AZT was used alone for many years as single-agent therapy, research has clearly shown that combination therapy with two or more additional drugs is superior in reducing viral load below the limit of detection and in delaying disease progression and death. A number of studies have proven the efficacy of AZT in combination therapy. Two large studies, ACTG 175 and the European/Australian Delta study, both showed that combinations of AZT + ddI and AZT + ddC were both more effective than use of AZT alone. A number of studies have also shown that AZT + 3TC is a very effective combination and is often used as the cornerstone of combinations with other drugs.

More recently, a number of studies have shown the effectiveness of AZT in three-drug combinations. ACTG 320 showed that the combination of AZT + 3TC + indinavir (Crixivan) was more potent than any two of these drugs used alone. The three-drug regimen is more effective because it is able to prevent the development of resistance to 3TC which occurs almost universally in people who use it for 2 months or longer. Once resistance sets in, the drug remains useful only because the mutation which causes 3TC resistance has a beneficial side effect in that it may increase the effectiveness of AZT (and perhaps other nucleoside analogue drugs). Once resistance is present though, 3TC loses its ability to directly produce large reductions in viral load. As a result, many researchers believe that AZT + 3TC should not be used as first-line therapy and that this combination should only be used as part of a three-drug regimen so as not to lose the beneficial antiviral effects of 3TC.

AZT is available as capsules, syrup, and as sterile solution for intravenous injection.

### TREATMENT

The recommended dose for adults is 500 to 600 mg per day (100 mg capsules taken approximately every 3/4 hours for 500 mg/day, or 2 x 100 mg capsules taken every 8 hours for 600 mg/day). The recommended dose of AZT for adults is 500 to 600 mg per day. For the 500 mg per day dose, a 100 mg capsule can be taken five times a day (approximately every 3-4 hours), or the total amount may be split into three unequal doses (200 mg, 100 mg, 200 mg) taken every eight hours. For the 600 mg per day dose, two 100 mg capsules can be taken every eight hours.

AZT is also available in a 300 mg tablet that can be taken twice daily (total daily dose of 600 mg). However, it remains to be seen if this twice daily dosing is truly equivalent to three times daily dosing, or whether the less frequent dosing will hasten the development of resistance.

Because AZT is known to cross the blood-brain barrier, high doses of the drug have sometimes been used to treat AIDS-related dementia. The dose used to treat dementia is 1,000 mg per day. Because the causes of dementia may vary, diagnosing and treating the cause (whenever possible) is important. Possible causes include HIV, CMV, toxoplasmosis, and B-vitamin deficiencies.

**CAUTIONS AND WARNINGS**

AZT should not be used by anyone with a known allergy to it.

AZT is metabolized by the liver and eliminated from the body primarily through the kidneys. Consequently, the drug should be used with caution by people with kidney or liver disease.

**SIDE EFFECTS**

Side effects occur more frequently in people taking high doses of AZT (greater than 600 mg per day) or in people with more advanced disease at the time therapy is started. The most common side effects of AZT are headaches, nausea, hypertension, and a general sense of feeling ill. These side effects may be due to the drug itself or to the person's anxiety about taking it. Often, these common side effects disappear after a few weeks of therapy.

The most serious side effects of AZT are anemia, granulocytopenia, and myopathy. Anemia is a deficiency in the red blood cells caused by suppression of the bone marrow. AZT-induced anemia can be treated by reducing the dose, switching to another antiretroviral drug, providing a transfusion, or by using a drug called erythropoietin (EPO), which stimulates production of red blood cells. Transfusions are recommended only for severe anemia. EPO cannot replace a transfusion if the anemia is severe.

Granulocytopenia is a lowering of the white blood cell counts, particularly cells called neutrophils, which are active in fighting bacterial infection. Like anemia, it is caused by suppression of the bone marrow. AZT-caused granulocytopenia can be treated with a colony-stimulating factor (G-CSF), which stimulates the production of white blood cells. G-CSF is preferred over the other commonly available colony-stimulating factor (GM-CSF) because it is better tolerated and is less likely to cause an increase in HIV replication (which has been reported after the use of GM-CSF).

Myopathy is a weakness or degeneration of the muscle tissue. It can be caused by HIV infection itself or by long-term treatment with AZT.

**PREGNANCY/BREAST-FEEDING**

AZT is recommended for pregnant, HIV-positive women to reduce the risk of transferring HIV to their newborn children. The majority of children born to HIV-positive women are not infected with HIV, but an estimated seven thousand HIV-infected women deliver infants annually in the United States, and 15% to 30% of the children (approximately eighteen hundred) will be in-

fected with HIV if AZT is not used. Newer, more potent drugs are now being studied to prevent transmission of HIV from mother to child. It is likely that stronger combinations of drugs will be more effective than AZT alone.

A landmark study showed that the risk of transmitting HIV from infected women to their newborn children was reduced by two-thirds if the mothers were given AZT during the second and third trimesters of pregnancy and labor and the babies were given AZT after birth. The mothers were given 500 mg AZT per day, starting from week fourteen to thirty-four of pregnancy. The minimum length of treatment was six weeks, but most received AZT for a longer duration. Intravenous treatment was continued during delivery, and the child received AZT for six weeks after delivery.

In animal studies, extremely high doses of AZT have been shown to cause cancer. However, at doses equivalent to those given to humans, no cancers were found except in animals given AZT over their entire life span. An NIH panel has concluded that the risks do not outweigh the potential benefit in preventing mother-to-child transmission and that AZT should continue to be used in this fashion.

HIV can be passed from a woman to her child through breast milk. In areas where nutritionally sound alternatives are readily available, breast-feeding is discouraged for HIV-positive women. It is not known if AZT is secreted in human milk. Because of the potential toxicity, women should consider alternatives to breast-feeding while taking the drug.

**USE IN CHILDREN**

AZT is approved for use in immunodeficient children aged three months and older. The current recommended dosage is 90 to 180 mg per square meter of body surface area, not to exceed 200 mg every six hours. In an ongoing study of AZT in children, there have been no significant differences in efficacy between the 90 and 180 mg doses. Children appear to tolerate AZT better than adults, even at the higher dose, so researchers continue to recommend the higher dose, especially in combating neurological complications of HIV infection, which are common in children.

A long-term study of 839 children compared AZT, ddI, and a combination of AZT and ddI for treatment of HIV infection. AZT alone was discontinued midway through the study when researchers found that it was the least effective of the three therapies. Children taking AZT + ddI or ddI alone had significantly less risk of developing an opportunistic infection, nerve deterioration, and death. In addition, the group treated with AZT had unexpectedly high rates of side effects such as bleeding. Before the study, AZT had been the first drug usually given to HIV-infected children This study has thrown the older recommendations into doubt, and, as yet, no new consensus has

been developed on the most appropriate treatment for children with HIV. It is very likely, however, that the three-drug regimens now routinely recommended for adults will become the norm for children as well. Parents of HIV-positive children are encouraged to discuss the benefits and risks of available antiretroviral therapies with their physician before choosing a treatment strategy.

For children under three months of age, there is less clinical data on the best dosage of AZT. In newborn children, the kidneys are not fully developed, and this low kidney function may result in elevated levels of AZT if the normal dose for children is administered. In these cases, the physician should closely monitor the blood levels of the drug.

**USE IN THE ELDERLY**
Older adults may be more susceptible to the side effects of the drug and may require reduced doses.

**DRUG INTERACTIONS**
Because AZT is primarily excreted through the kidneys, using other drugs that are toxic to the kidneys may increase the risk of side effects with AZT. Also, because AZT can cause decreased white blood cell levels (granulocytopenia), any drugs which have similar effects should be used with caution. Examples of these include dapsone, ganciclovir, rifabutin, clarithromycin, pentamidine, pentoxifylline, amphotericin B, flucytosine, vincristine, vinblastine, adriamycin, antineoplastics, and interferon. Many of these drugs are used to treat or prevent opportunistic infections associated with HIV infection, so it is likely that people taking AZT will also be taking one or more of them. Drugs that stimulate blood production (EPO and G-CSF, for example) may be used to treat the anemia or granulocytopenia caused by certain drugs or drug interactions.

When AZT is used in combination with clarithromycin, rifabutin, or rifampin, the levels of AZT may be reduced in the blood. Probenecid and pyrimethamine/sulfadiazine may increase AZT levels in the blood. When used in combination with these drugs, the AZT dose may need to be adjusted.

Combinations of AZT and acyclovir, ddI, ddC, delavirdine, foscarnet, alpha interferon, 3TC, or protease inhibitors may increase the anti-HIV activity of AZT or extend the duration of its effectiveness.

**FOOD INTERACTIONS**
Food may reduce the absorption of AZT taken orally; however, it does not appear to affect its antiviral activity. Therefore, AZT can be taken with or without food.

**OTHER DRUGS USED FOR SIMILAR CONDITIONS**
Other anti-HIV drugs in the same class include ddI, ddC, d4T, and 3TC. Other types of anti-HIV drugs include indinavir, ritonavir, nelfinavir, saquinavir,

nevirapine, and delavirdine. The most effective use of these antiretroviral agents is three- or four-drug combinations with at least one highly active antiviral (indinavir, ritonavir, nelfinavir, nevirapine, or 3TC).

**COMMENTS**
Although AZT was long used as first-line therapy for the treatment of HIV, the development of more potent drugs has changed the standard of care. The most effective use of AZT is now known to be in three- or four-drug combination therapy regimens including a potent antiviral therapy.

AZT produces modest increases in CD4+ counts and reduces the number of opportunistic infections and other symptoms of HIV infection in people with CD4+ counts lower than 200 and in people with higher counts who are symptomatic. These benefits generally last six to eighteen months, although this varies widely. However, the drug has not shown a clear survival benefit in long-term use in clinical studies.

Studies show that, over time, AZT used alone results in the development of drug resistance and loss of effectiveness. In considering the optimum combination of drugs, it is important to weigh immediate benefit and long-term benefit as well as preservation of future options. The best use of AZT is most likely in triple combination regimens with two other antiviral therapies.

# CIDOFOVIR

**BRAND NAME (MANUFACTURER)**
Vistide (Gilead)

**TYPE OF DRUG**
Antiviral

**USED FOR**
Cidofovir is a new antiviral given intravenously to treat cytomegalovirus (CMV) retinitis in people with AIDS. Cidofovir is not approved to treat other types of CMV infection or CMV in non-HIV-infected people. The drug is sometimes used, but not approved, for the treatment of herpes simplex virus (HSV) and for a certain type of genital warts.

**GENERAL INFORMATION**
CMV is a virus that can cause serious infection in many different organs, including the eyes, intestines, stomach, lungs, kidneys, and esophagus. Cidofovir slows, but does not permanently stop, the progression of CMV retinitis, an opportunistic infection that can cause blindness in people with weakened immune systems. It may also act against CMV disease in other parts of the body, but there is less clinical evidence to support its use in these cases.

Cidofovir interferes with the multiplication of CMV, thereby slowing the destruction of the retina (the light-sensitive tissue at the back of the eye) and loss of vision. However, cidofovir is not a cure for CMV retinitis. People taking the drug may continue to lose their vision and should have regular eye examinations at least every six weeks to determine whether a change in treatment is required.

Cidofovir is available as a solution for intravenous injection.

## TREATMENT

The recommended dose, frequency, and rate of infusion of cidofovir should not be exceeded in order to prevent increased toxicity. The initial dose is 5 mg per kg body weight given over 1 hour once weekly for two weeks. For maintenance therapy, cidofovir should be given at 5 mg per kg given over 1 hour once every two weeks. People should receive at least one liter of saline solution during the 1-2 hour period before the injection.

Cidofovir should be given along with probenecid to minimize kidney problems. The usual dose of probenecid is 2 grams given orally 3 hours before injection with cidofovir. Another 1 gram of probenecid should be given 2 hours and 8 hours after the injection is completed.

## CAUTIONS AND WARNINGS

Cidofovir should not be used by anyone with a known allergy to it, probenecid, or other sulfa-containing drugs.

Cidofovir should only be injected into a vein and not directly into the eye (intraocular injection).

Cidofovir can cause serious kidney toxicity. Therefore, the drug should only be given together with probenecid and with prior infusion of saline solution for adequate kidney hydration. Dose adjustment or discontinuation of the drug may be required for people with impaired kidney function.

In animal studies, cidofovir was also shown to have some cancer-causing effects.

## SIDE EFFECTS

The most serious side effect of cidofovir is kidney toxicity, seen in almost 50% of people receiving the drug at a maintenance dose (without probenecid). Other side effects include neutropenia (20%), fever (15%), nausea and vomiting, headache and diarrhea. In clinical trials, almost 25% of people taking the maintenance dose discontinued the drug due to side effects.

The side effects of probenecid include headache, nausea, vomiting, and allergic reactions (including rash, fever, and chills). Taking probenecid after a meal can help reduce nausea.

**PREGNANCY/BREAST-FEEDING**
Cidofovir has not been formally studied in pregnant women. In animal studies, the drug did cause some toxicity to the fetus, but it is not known whether the same would be true in humans. Pregnant women are encouraged to discuss the benefits and potential risks of using cidofovir with their physician before deciding whether or not to use the drug.

HIV can be passed from a woman to her child through breast milk. In areas where nutritionally sound alternatives are readily available, breast-feeding is discouraged for HIV-positive women. It is not known if cidofovir is excreted in human milk. Because of the potential toxicity, women should consider alternatives to breast-feeding while taking the drug.

**USE IN CHILDREN**
The safety and effectiveness in children has not been established, but the drug in children may cause increased cancer and reproductive problems.

**USE IN THE ELDERLY**
Older adults may be more susceptible to the side effects of the drug and may require reduced doses. Elderly people with reduced kidney function may require reduced doses and should use the drug with caution.

**DRUG INTERACTIONS**
Cidofovir should not be given together with other drugs known to cause kidney toxicity, such as amphotericin B, aminoglycosides (amikacin, gentamicin, streptomycin, erythromycin), foscarnet, and intravenous pentamidine.

In addition, probenecid can interfere with the metabolism or clearance of a number of drugs, including acetaminophen, acyclovir, aminosalicyclic acid, barbiturates, benzodiazepines, bumetanide, clofibrate, methotrexate, famotidine, furosemide, nonsteroidal anti-inflammatory agents, theophylline, and AZT. People taking AZT are suggested to stop AZT or reduce the dose by 50% when taking probenecid.

**FOOD INTERACTIONS**
Food prior to each dose of probenecid can help reduce drug-related nausea and vomiting.

**OTHER DRUGS USED FOR SIMILAR CONDITIONS**
Foscarnet, ganciclovir, cidofovir, and ganciclovir implants are the drugs approved for the treatment of CMV retinitis. Although they are all effective in slowing CMV, they have different side effects, drug interactions, dosages, and route of administration. Depending on the circumstances, one may be a better choice than the other. Some of these therapies can be used to treat CMV throughout the body (and possibly prevent CMV from spreading throughout the rest of the body) whereas others will only treat a specific organ (i.e., the eye) and may allow CMV to spread to other parts of the body.

# D 4 T

**BRAND NAME (MANUFACTURER)**
Zerit (Bristol-Myers Squibb Oncology)

**OTHER NAMES**
Stavudine; didehydro-deoxythymidine

**TYPE OF DRUG**
Antiviral–anti-HIV

**USED FOR**
d4T is approved for use in people with advanced HIV disease who are intolerant of or have failed other approved antiretroviral therapies. It is also commonly used but not formally approved for the treatment of HIV infection in combination with other antiviral agents.

**GENERAL INFORMATION**
d4T is an orally administered antiviral drug, similar to AZT, ddI, 3TC, and ddC. It mimics a naturally occurring building block of DNA to interfere with HIV replication, thus reducing production of new virus and slowing the progression of the disease. However, like other available anti-HIV drugs, d4T is not a cure for HIV infection, and people who take it may continue to progress, develop symptoms, and experience opportunistic infections.

The most effective use of d4T is now in triple combination therapy regimens. Combinations of d4T + 3TC and d4T + 3TC along with another drug, generally a potent protease inhibitor or nevirapine, are believed to be effective in delaying disease progression and death, reducing viral load, and increasing CD4+ cell counts. The French ALTIS study showed that the combination of d4T + 3TC is as effective as AZT + 3TC. Another study showed that d4T + ddI may be an effective option for people unable to tolerate AZT. Very few three-drug combinations including d4T have yet been completed, but its performance in two-drug regimens is at least as strong as any other combination of nucleoside analogue drugs. Thus, most researchers believe it can be a good partner in three-drug combinations.

It should be noted, however, that d4T should probably not be combined with AZT. The two drugs compete for the same elements in the body, and one study has shown that people receiving the combination fared worse than those on other regimens. However, another study found that people using this combination experienced no adverse effects.

**TREATMENT**
Clinical trials of d4T suggest that the optimum dose of the drug is 40 mg twice daily. However, volunteers in an expanded access program for d4T received either a 20 mg dose or 40 mg, and the 20 mg twice daily was shown to be as

effective as the higher dose and associated with significantly less peripheral neuropathy and other side effects. This lower dosage is currently being tested in clinical trials. d4T is available in four different dosage tablets 40 mg, 30 mg, 20 mg, and 15 mg.

## CAUTIONS AND WARNINGS

People who know they are allergic to d4T should not take the drug. It is not known at this time if people who are allergic to other nucleoside analogues (AZT, ddI, ddC, and 3TC) will also be allergic to d4T.

Since d4T is metabolized by the liver, people with a history of liver problems should inform their doctors and have their liver function monitored closely when taking d4T.

## SIDE EFFECTS

One serious side effect of d4T is peripheral neuropathy, a condition characterized by numbness, tingling, or sharp, burning pain in the feet, legs, or hands. Fifteen percent to 21% of people in the clinical studies of d4T reported this side effect.

Like AZT, d4T seems to interfere with the ability of the bone marrow to produce certain white blood cells called neutrophils. However, this side effect (neutropenia) occurs rarely, apparently less frequently with d4T than with AZT.

Other side effects of d4T reported in clinical trials include fungal infections of the skin, dry skin, and elevated liver enzymes (indicating possible liver toxicity).

## PREGNANCY/BREAST-FEEDING

d4T has not been formally studied in pregnant women. It did cause fetal harm when given to pregnant laboratory animals, but it is not known whether the same would be true for humans. Pregnant women are encouraged to discuss the benefits and potential risks of d4T with their physician before deciding to use the drug.

HIV can be passed from a woman to her child through breast milk. In areas where nutritionally sound alternatives are readily available, breast-feeding is discouraged for HIV-positive women. It is not known if d4T is excreted in human milk, but because of the potential toxicity of the drug, women should consider alternatives to breast-feeding while taking it.

## USE IN CHILDREN

Studies of d4T in children are still ongoing, and early results show that the drug is relatively safe, causing the same side effects as in adults taking the drug. One study compared AZT to d4T in children and showed that children taking d4T gained more weight and lost fewer CD4+ cells than those receiving AZT.

**USE IN THE ELDERLY**

Older adults may be more susceptible to the side effects of d4T and may require reduced doses.

**DRUG INTERACTIONS**

Drug interaction studies continue, but any drugs that cause peripheral neuropathy should be used with caution when taken with d4T. When d4T is used in combination with such drugs, the risk of these side effects may be higher. These drugs include ddI, ddC, foscarnet, amphotericin B, and dapsone.

Use of ganciclovir or intravenous pentamidine with d4T may increase the risk of pancreatic disease.

AZT and d4T are activated by the same enzymatic system in cells, and the drugs may interfere with the other's activity.

**FOOD INTERACTIONS**

d4T can be taken with or without food.

**OTHER DRUGS USED FOR SIMILAR CONDITIONS**

Other anti-HIV drugs in the same class include ddI, ddC, d4T, and 3TC. Other types of anti-HIV drugs include indinavir, ritonavir, nelfinavir, saquinavir, nevirapine, and delavirdine. The most effective use of these antiretroviral agents is three- or four-drug combinations with at least one highly active antiviral (indinavir, ritonavir, nelfinavir, nevirapine, or 3TC).

**COMMENTS**

Many questions remain regarding the appropriate use of d4T. Questions include when to switch from other antiretrovirals to d4T, when or if it should be used instead of other antivirals, what is the best dose, what are the potential drug interactions, what are the most effective combinations, and how quickly resistance to d4T develops. However, the drug's high level of performance when combined with ddI or 3TC speaks well for its ability to play an important role in three-drug combinations. For many people, d4T offers an important and attractive alternative to AZT in combination therapy, especially for people who have already exhausted AZT or who cannot tolerate it.

The optimal use of d4T along with other antiviral drugs remains to be seen. However, it is clear that the best use of any antiviral is in combination with at least two other potent antiviral therapies.

# D D C

**BRAND NAME (MANUFACTURER)**

Hivid (Roche)

**OTHER NAMES**

Dideoxycytidine; zalcitabine

**TYPE OF DRUG**
Antiviral–anti-HIV

**USED FOR**
ddC was originally approved for the treatment of HIV infection in adults with advanced HIV disease who either are intolerant to AZT or have disease progression while receiving AZT. The most common use of the drug now is in triple combination regimens including at least one potent antiviral therapy.

**GENERAL INFORMATION**
ddC is an orally administered antiviral, similar in effect to other nucleoside analogues such as AZT, ddI, d4T, and 3TC. It mimics a naturally occurring building block of DNA and slows down the progression of HIV replication by interfering with reverse transcription, a process necessary for HIV to multiply. However, like other available anti-HIV drugs, ddC is not a cure for HIV infection, and people who take it may continue to progress, developing HIV symptoms and opportunistic infections.

Results from two large studies comparing single drug antiviral treatment to combination therapies confirm that combination therapy is superior to AZT alone. They also suggest that in most cases another combination, AZT + ddI, is more effective than AZT + ddC.

The most common use of ddC today is to serve as one element in a three-drug combination, typically made up of two of the older, nucleoside analogue drugs (AZT, ddI, ddC, d4T, 3TC) and either a protease inhibitor or a non-nucleoside reverse transcriptase inhibitor (nevirapine or delavirdine). The drug is indicated primarily when it hasn't been used before by the patient.

ddC is available as tablets for oral administration.

**TREATMENT**
Available clinical information suggests that the optimum dose is 2.25 mg per day divided into three equal doses of 0.75 mg. The dose may need to be reduced for people with impaired kidney or liver function.

**CAUTIONS AND WARNINGS**
People who know they are allergic to ddC or any of the ingredients in the tablets should not use the drug.

Peripheral neuropathy—nerve damage that typically includes numbness, tingling, or sharp burning pain in the feet, legs, or hands—is the most serious side effect of ddC. People taking the drug who experience these symptoms should contact their doctors. Use of ddC is discouraged for people with a previous history of peripheral neuropathy. In addition, ddC should not be combined with ddI, as this may increase the risk of developing neuropathy.

ddC may cause severe disease of the pancreas (pancreatitis), which has been fatal in some cases. People who are taking ddC and start having abdominal

pain and vomiting should discontinue use of the drug and call their doctor immediately because they may be experiencing symptoms of pancreatitis. The drug should be used with caution by people who have had pancreatic disease, a history of heavy alcohol consumption, or poor kidney function.

## SIDE EFFECTS

Peripheral neuropathy is a common, dose-related side effect that occurred in 22% to 35% of volunteers taking ddC as single-agent therapy in clinical studies. If caught early, the symptoms are usually temporary and reversible after discontinuing the drug, but in a few cases, the symptoms have continued or worsened after the drug was stopped.

Pancreatic disease is another serious, but rare, side effect of ddC. Slightly more than 1% of people taking the drug experience this potentially fatal inflammation of the pancreas. For those with a previous history of pancreatitis, the risk of the side effect may be more than five times higher. However, the risk of pancreatic disease is lower when using ddC than when using ddI.

Other significant, but rare, side effects of ddC include ulcers in the mouth or esophagus and congestive heart failure.

## PREGNANCY/BREAST-FEEDING

ddC has not been formally studied in pregnant women. In animal studies, the drug caused birth defects and an increased rate of spontaneous abortions, but it is not known whether the same would be true in humans. Pregnant women are encouraged to discuss the benefits and potential risks of ddC with their physician before deciding to use the drug.

HIV can be passed from a woman to her child through breast milk. In areas where nutritionally sound alternatives are readily available, breast-feeding is discouraged for HIV-positive women. It is not known whether ddC is excreted in human milk. Because of the potential toxicity of the drug, women should consider alternatives to breast-feeding while taking it.

## USE IN CHILDREN

ddC has been used to a limited extent in children living with HIV, but clinical trials are still ongoing to determine the appropriate role and standard dosing for the drug. In children, ddC has been studied alone, in combination with AZT, and in regimens where ddC and AZT are alternated every few weeks. In general, the drug has worked in children similar to the way it works in adults. There have been no unexpected side effects or increases in known side effects of the drug when used in children at doses lower than 0.04 mg per kg of body weight, taken every six hours.

## USE IN THE ELDERLY

Older adults may be more susceptible to the side effects of the drug and may require reduced doses.

**DRUG INTERACTIONS**
Aminoglycoside antibiotics, amphotericin B, anticancer drugs, antineoplastics, chloramphenicol, cisplatin, dapsone, disulfiram, ethionamide, foscarnet, hydralazine, iodoquinol, isoniazid, metronidazole, intravenous pentamidine, phenytoin, probenecid, or ribavirin may increase the risk of peripheral neuropathy when used with ddC. The combination of ddI and ddC significantly increases the risk of peripheral neuropathy and should be avoided. AZT may increase the antiviral effectiveness of ddC, but it may also increase the risk of pancreatic disease.

Antacids, metoclopramide, or cimetidine may decrease ddC levels in the body, potentially reducing its effectiveness. Intravenous pentamidine may increase the risk of pancreatic disease when used with ddC.

**FOOD INTERACTIONS**
ddC can be taken with or without food.

**OTHER DRUGS USED FOR SIMILAR CONDITIONS**
Other anti-HIV drugs in the same class include AZT, ddI, d4T, and 3TC. Other types of anti-HIV drugs include indinavir, ritonavir, nelfinavir, saquinavir, nevirapine, and delavirdine. The most effective use of these antiretroviral agents is three- or four-drug combinations with at least one highly active antiviral (indinavir, ritonavir, nelfinavir, nevirapine, or 3TC).

**COMMENTS**
The available clinical information suggests that ddC is not as effective as AZT when used alone to treat HIV infection, although in the current standard of care, single-agent therapy should always be avoided to prevent the development of drug resistance. The most effective use of the drug is probably in combination regimens, although ddC is one of the least active of the currently approved antiviral drugs. Studies have shown that for people who have not previously received antiviral therapy, AZT + ddC may be effective, but even then, the two drugs should be added to a third, highly active agent, like a protease inhibitor.

Individuals should contact their physician and discuss different combination regimens for treatment of their HIV infection.

# DDI

**BRAND NAME (MANUFACTURER)**
Videx (Bristol-Myers Squibb Oncology)

**OTHER NAMES**
Didanosine; dideoxyinosine

**TYPE OF DRUG**
Antiviral–anti-HIV

**USED FOR**

ddI is approved for the treatment of adults with advanced HIV infection who have received prolonged AZT therapy. It is also approved for children (over six months of age) with advanced HIV infection who cannot tolerate AZT or who have experienced disease progression while on AZT.

Today the most common use of ddI is in combination regimens including two other potent antiviral therapies.

**GENERAL INFORMATION**

ddI is an antiviral drug known as a nucleoside analogue, similar in effect to AZT, ddC, 3TC, and d4T. It mimics a naturally occurring building block of DNA and works by interfering with HIV replication, thus reducing the production of new virus and slowing the progression of infection.

Despite the effectiveness of ddI over AZT monotherapy, research indicates that the best use of antivirals is in combination. Results from two large studies comparing single drug antiviral treatment to combination therapies confirm that combination therapy is superior to AZT alone.

A combination of ddI and d4T has also been shown to be effective, and the combination has also shown efficacy when combined with ritonavir, a protease inhibitor. Many combinations of ddI with AZT and other protease inhibitors or non-nucleosides have shown promising results.

The most common use of ddI today is to serve as one element in a three-drug combination, typically made up of two of the older, nucleoside analogue drugs (AZT, ddC, d4T, 3TC) and either a protease inhibitor or a non-nucleoside reverse transcriptase inhibitor (nevirapine or delavirdine). The drug is indicated primarily when it hasn't been used before by the patient.

ddI is available as tablets, chewable tablets, or as a powder that can be dissolved in water.

**TREATMENT**

ddI should be taken every 12 hours, either one hour before or two hours after eating. Adults should take two tablets at a time to provide the proper buffering. The recommended starting dose of tablets for adults is 200 mg twice daily for people weighing more than 132 pounds, and 125 mg twice daily for people weighing less than 132 pounds.

The doses for the buffered powder are slightly higher. The dose is 250 mg twice daily for people over 132 pounds, and 167 mg twice daily for people under 132 pounds.

Some people dissolve ddI in water, but it is rather chalk-like in taste. Mixing it with apple juice or milk can make ddI more palatable. Because the current "chewable" tablets are hard, some people put them in a coffee grinder.

A pediatric powder for oral solution is also available for children. It is usually mixed with a flavored antacid by the pharmacist and is administered in less volume than the adult buffered powder. Because the pediatric powder is more expensive, some pharmacists prescribe the adult powder to children, but have to divide the doses. Be aware that this may result in inaccurate dosing.

## CAUTIONS AND WARNINGS

ddI should not be used by anyone with a known allergy to it. Chewable ddI tablets contain the sweetener aspartame and should be used with caution by people with phenylketonuria, an inherited inability to metabolize phenylalanine.

ddI may cause severe disease of the pancreas (pancreatitis), which has been fatal in some cases. People who are taking ddI and start having abdominal pain and vomiting should discontinue use of the drug and call their doctor immediately because they may be experiencing symptoms of pancreatitis. The drug should be used with caution by people who have had pancreatic disease, a history of heavy alcohol consumption, or poor kidney function.

ddI may also cause peripheral neuropathy, which is nerve damage that may result in numbness, tingling, or pain in the feet or hands. Because of this potential toxicity, ddI use is discouraged for people with a history of neuropathy. In addition, the drug should not be combined with ddC, as this may increase the risk of neuropathy.

People who have impaired liver or kidney function have a higher risk of side effects when using ddI. In these cases, the dosage may need to be reduced.

## SIDE EFFECTS

Pancreatic disease (pancreatitis), which can be fatal, is the most serious side effect of ddI. In clinical trials, the disease occurred in 7% of volunteers given the recommended dose of ddI and 13% given a higher dose. In an expanded access program, about 30% of people who had pancreatic disease previously developed pancreatic disease again after treatment with ddI. Pancreatitis occurs more frequently in people with AIDS.

Peripheral neuropathy is another serious side effect that occurs in about 20% of all people taking the recommended dose of ddI. The side effect occurs more frequently in people in the later stages of AIDS and those taking higher doses. These symptoms appear to be related to the total dose of the drug taken over time as well as the overall health of the person and may require that the drug be discontinued or the dose be reduced. The symptoms are usually temporary and reversible when the dosage is lowered or the person stops taking

the drug. In some cases, after the drug is stopped, peripheral neuropathy may temporarily get worse before it gets better. If a person continues on the drug despite the neuropathy, it is possible to develop irreversible nerve damage. In other words, the longer one takes ddI in the presence of constant neuropathy, the more likely it is that the neuropathy will not go away.

Diarrhea is a common and often severe problem for people taking ddI due to the buffer in the ddI tablets or powder. Physicians may recommend an antacid that can induce constipation (Aldurox, Alternagel, Amphojel, for example) to counter the diarrhea.

ddI can increase the frequency of oral ulcers, especially if the tablets are chewed. Rinsing the mouth out with water after taking ddI may decrease the problem.

Other significant side effects that occur in more than 5% of people taking ddI include chills/fever, skin rashes, abdominal pain, headache, nausea/vomiting, and infection. In a small number of people, fatal liver failure has occurred.

### PREGNANCY/BREAST-FEEDING

Formal clinical trials of ddI in pregnant women are ongoing. In animal studies, ddI did not cause fetal harm, but it is not yet known whether the same would be true for humans. Pregnant women are encouraged to discuss the benefits and potential risks of ddI with their physician before deciding to use the drug.

HIV can be passed from a woman to her child through breast milk. In areas where nutritionally sound alternatives are readily available, breast-feeding is discouraged for HIV-positive women. It is not known whether ddI is excreted in human milk. Because of the potential toxicity of the drug, women should consider alternatives to breast-feeding while taking it.

### USE IN CHILDREN

ddI is approved for use in children older than six months who cannot effectively use AZT. Early stages of pancreatic disease, the major side effect of ddI, are often difficult to detect in children. In addition, absorption varies among children. If it appears a child is not benefiting from ddI use, or if the child is experiencing side effects, the physician should run absorption tests to determine if the dose should be adjusted.

An oral suspension (made from the pediatric buffered powder) is available for children. Pediatric dosing is dependent on the child's body surface area. The most commonly recommended dose is 200 mg per square meter of body surface area per day, divided into two equal doses taken every twelve hours.

A long-term study of 839 HIV-positive, symptomatic children compared AZT alone, ddI alone, and a combination of AZT and ddI. AZT alone was

discontinued midway through the study when researchers found that it was the least effective of the three therapies. Children taking AZT +ddI or ddI alone had significantly less risk of developing an opportunistic infection, nerve deterioration, and death. In addition, the group treated with AZT alone had unexpectedly high rates of side effects like bleeding and biochemical abnormalities. Before this study, AZT was the drug HIV-infected children were usually given first. This study has thrown the previous recommendations into doubt, and no new consensus has been developed on the most appropriate treatment for children with HIV. Parents of HIV-positive children are encouraged to discuss the benefits and potential risks of available antiviral therapies with their physician before choosing a treatment strategy for their children. Combination therapies including protease inhibitors are now being studied in children and are showing promising results.

**USE IN THE ELDERLY**
Older adults may be more susceptible to the side effects of ddI and may require reduced doses.

**DRUG INTERACTIONS**
When ddI is used in combination with other drugs that can cause pancreatic disease or peripheral neuropathy, the risk of these side effects may be higher. For example, ddI used in combination with pentamidine, alcohol, or ganciclovir may increase the risk of pancreatic disease, and ddI used in combination with zalcitabine (ddC) or some drugs used to treat other infections may significantly increase the risk of peripheral neuropathy.

Drugs that need an acidic stomach environment in order to work must be taken at least two hours before or after ddI. Dapsone, an antibiotic often used to treat bacterial infections in people with HIV, is one of these drugs. Others include cimetidine, ketoconazole, quinolone antibiotics, and ranitidine. Delavirdine, another anti-HIV drug, should be taken an hour before ddI. Indinavir, a protease inhibitor, can be difficult to take in combination with ddI because both cannot be taken with food, yet have to be taken one hour apart.

Ganciclovir, taken either orally or by intravenous injection, significantly increases ddI levels and may increase the risk of pancreatic disease. ddI decreases oral ganciclovir levels by up to 20% and may reduce its effectiveness.

**FOOD INTERACTIONS**
ddI must be taken on an empty stomach. Because ddI cannot be absorbed in an acidic stomach, a chemical buffer has been added to the tablets. Two tablets must be taken together to get the right amount of buffering. If the dose needs to be reduced, two lower-dose tablets must be used rather than taking one of the higher-dose tablets.

## OTHER DRUGS USED FOR SIMILAR CONDITIONS

Other anti-HIV drugs in the same class include AZT, ddC, d4T, and 3TC. Other types of anti-HIV drugs include indinavir, ritonavir, nelfinavir, saquinavir, nevirapine, and delavirdine. The most effective use of these antiretroviral agents is three- or four-drug combinations with at least one highly active antiviral (indinavir, ritonavir, nelfinavir, nevirapine, or 3TC).

## COMMENTS

Clinical studies determined that ddI is not as effective as AZT in adults who have not previously used antiviral drugs.

ddI does offer an option to people who can no longer tolerate AZT or whose disease has progressed despite AZT therapy. However, single agent therapy is no longer the standard of care, and the most effective use of any antiviral is in a three- or four-drug combination therapy regimen.

Questions still remain as to the appropriate use of ddI in combinations with other antiviral therapies. The combinations of AZT + ddI and d4T + ddI, along with a potent protease inhibitor non-nucleoside drug are likely the most effective uses of ddI in treating HIV.

# DELAVIRDINE

## BRAND NAME (MANUFACTURER)

Rescriptor (Pharmacia and Upjohn)

## TYPE OF DRUG

Antiviral–anti-HIV

## USED FOR

Delavirdine is approved for the treatment of adults with HIV infection when antiretroviral therapy is warranted. It should be used in a combination therapy regimen with at least two other antiviral medications.

## GENERAL INFORMATION

Delavirdine is an orally administered antiviral drug known as a non-nucleoside reverse transcriptase inhibitor (NNRTI), which attempts to slow or stop reproduction of the virus by inhibiting one of HIV's key enzymes, reverse transcriptase.

The optimal use of delavirdine remains to be seen. Combination therapies are most likely to reduce viral load, prevent the development of drug resistance, and delay disease progression. Studies with delavirdine show only modest anti-HIV activity. In addition, delavirdine has not been shown to significantly delay disease progression or prolong survival. Some of the apparent weakness of the drug may be due to the design of the particular clinical trials in which it was studied, none of which tested the drug in a truly optimal com-

bination. One potential but unproven use of delavirdine may be as a "companion drug" to boost levels of the protease inhibitors in people who are failing or not absorbing adequate levels of these drugs.

## TREATMENT
The recommended dose of delavirdine is 400 mg (four 100 mg tablets) three times a day for a total daily dose of 1,200 mg.

## CAUTIONS AND WARNINGS
Delavirdine should not be used by anyone with a known allergy to it. In addition, the drug should not be taken along with certain non-sedating antihistamines, sedative hypnotics, anti-arrhythmia drugs, calcium channel blockers, ergot alkaloid preparations, amphetamines, and cisapride. Use of these drugs with delavirdine can result in potential life-threatening side effects.

People with liver problems should be cautious about using delavirdine.

## SIDE EFFECTS
The most common side effects reported from studies of delavirdine include rash (18%), nausea (6.8%), headache (5.6%), fatigue (3.7%), diarrhea (4.2%), and increased liver function tests (5.8%). The rash primarily affects the upper body and is less intense on the rest of the body. The rash usually occurs within 1–3 weeks of starting delavirdine and lasts for about 2 weeks. Generally, the effects of the rash can be diminished with use of antihistamines or topical corticosteroids. However, if the rash becomes severe, contact a physician immediately.

## PREGNANCY/BREAST-FEEDING
Delavirdine has not been formally studied in pregnant women. However, in animal studies, the drug caused serious side effects to the mother and the fetus, including cancer and developmental problems. It is not known if the same would be true in humans. Delavirdine should be used during pregnancy only if the potential benefits justify the risks involved.

In addition, HIV can be passed from a woman to her child through breast milk. In areas where nutritionally sound alternatives are readily available, breast-feeding is discouraged for HIV-positive women. It is not known if delavirdine is excreted in human milk. Because of the potential toxicity, women should consider alternatives to breast-feeding while taking the drug.

## USE IN CHILDREN
Safety and effectiveness have not been established in children younger than 16 years, therefore no recommendations are available at this time.

## USE IN THE ELDERLY
Safety and effectiveness have not been established in adults over 65 years of age, therefore no recommendations are available at this time.

**DRUG INTERACTIONS**

There are a number of drug interactions between delavirdine and other commonly used therapies. Delavirdine should NOT be used with alprazolam, astemizole, cisapride, midazolam, rifampin, terfenadine, and triazolam as their use in combination with delavirdine may lead to serious and/or life-threatening side effects.

The following drugs may decrease delavirdine levels: antacids, carbamazepine, cimetidine, phenobarbital, phenytoin, ranitidine, and rifabutin. Delavirdine has also been shown to increase blood levels of the protease inhibitors.

**FOOD INTERACTIONS**

Delavirdine can be taken with or without food.

**OTHER DRUGS USED FOR SIMILAR CONDITIONS**

The other approved anti-HIV drug of the same class is nevirapine. Other antiviral therapies include indinavir, ritonavir, saquinavir, nelfinavir, AZT, 3TC, d4T, ddI, and ddC. The most effective use of these antiretroviral agents is three- or four-drug combinations with at least one highly active antiviral (indinavir, ritonavir, nelfinavir, nevirapine, or 3TC).

**COMMENTS**

The delavirdine studies conducted to date have shown only mediocre activity at best in reducing viral load and increasing CD4+ cell counts. Delavirdine has not been shown to delay disease progression or prolong survival. Therefore, it remains to be seen where the drug fits in among the mix of antiviral therapies. The best use of delavirdine may be as a "companion" drug as it is known to boost levels of the protease inhibitors. In addition, resistance to delavirdine can develop rapidly, and laboratory studies suggest that resistance to delavirdine will also result in resistance to other NNRTIs such as nevirapine and DMP-266 (an experimental drug). Because both of these drugs appear to be much more potent than delavirdine, it is important to use delavirdine properly or save it for later in order to preserve these options for future use.

Clearly, in considering the optimum combination of drugs, it is important to weigh immediate benefits *and* long-term benefits as well as preservation of future options. The best use of antivirals is most likely in triple combination regimens with two other antiviral therapies.

# FAMCICLOVIR

**BRAND NAME (MANUFACTURER)**

Famvir (SmithKline Beecham)

**TYPE OF DRUG**

Antiviral

**USED FOR**

Famciclovir is approved for the treatment of acute herpes zoster (shingles) caused by varicella zoster virus (VZV) and for the treatment of recurrent genital herpes (HSV).

**GENERAL INFORMATION**

Famciclovir is a synthetic chemical that mimics one of the building blocks of DNA. Inside the body, famciclovir is converted to the antiviral agent penciclovir. In cells infected with VZV or HSV, the drug slows down the replication of viral DNA. Like other antiviral drugs, it does not rid the body of the virus, but merely acts to reduce the severity and slow the growth of the infection.

Famciclovir is available as tablets for oral administration.

**TREATMENT**

For shingles, the recommended dose is 500 mg every eight hours for seven days. Therapy should be initiated as soon as herpes zoster is diagnosed. For genital herpes, the recommended dose is 125 mg every 12 hours for five days. The dosage may need to be adjusted in people with reduced kidney function. No dosage adjustment is necessary for reduced liver function.

**CAUTIONS AND WARNINGS**

Famciclovir should not be used by people who are allergic to it. Its effectiveness for other diseases caused by VZV (ophthalmic zoster or disseminated zoster, for example) has not been studied.

**SIDE EFFECTS**

In limited experience, famciclovir appears to have few side effects. In the clinical studies of famciclovir, the most frequent side effects were headache, nausea, and fatigue, which occurred in a similar frequency in people treated with a placebo.

**PREGNANCY/BREAST-FEEDING**

Famciclovir has not been formally studied in pregnant women. In animal studies, it did not cause fetal harm, but it is not known whether the same would be true for humans. Pregnant women are encouraged to discuss the benefits and potential risks of famciclovir with their physician before deciding to use the drug.

HIV can be passed from a woman to her child through breast milk. In areas where nutritionally sound alternatives are readily available, breast-feeding is discouraged for HIV-positive women. Famciclovir is excreted and concentrated in animal milk. It is not known if it is excreted in human milk, but because of the potential toxicity of the drug, women should consider alternatives to breast-feeding while taking it.

**USE IN CHILDREN**

The safety and efficacy of famciclovir in children is currently being studied; no recommendations are available at this time.

**USE IN THE ELDERLY**

No differences in side effects were seen in elderly participants in clinical trials when compared to younger volunteers. However, famiciclovir is cleared from the body more slowly in older adults and therefore older adults may be more susceptible to the side effects of the drug and may require reduced doses.

**DRUG INTERACTIONS**

Use with probenecid or other drugs eliminated primarily by the kidney may result in increased blood levels of famciclovir, which may increase the risk of side effects.

**FOOD INTERACTIONS**

Famciclovir may be taken with or without meals.

**OTHER DRUGS USED FOR SIMILAR CONDITIONS**

Famciclovir was developed as an alternative to acyclovir. Because acyclovir has a long history of safety and efficacy, it is still often the drug of choice for shingles. With viral resistance to acyclovir becoming more common, famciclovir may be an alternative. However, both acyclovir and famciclovir become activated by the same enzymatic pathway, and this pathway accounts for most resistance to acyclovir. Consequently, if a virus is resistant to acyclovir, it is often also resistant to famciclovir. Many physicians would use foscarnet rather than famciclovir for acyclovir-resistant HSV.

In a clinical trial comparing famciclovir to acyclovir for uncomplicated herpes zoster, famciclovir and acyclovir had similar response rates in healing lesions and relieving the pain associated with shingles. One distinct advantage for famciclovir is easier dosing. Famciclovir needs to be taken only three times a day.

**COMMENTS**

Famciclovir has not been tested for long periods in any group, and it has not been tested for prevention of herpesvirus diseases.

# FOSCARNET

**BRAND NAME (MANUFACTURER)**

Foscavir (Astra)

**TYPE OF DRUG**

Antiviral

**USED FOR**

Foscarnet is approved for the treatment of cytomegalovirus (CMV) retinitis in people with AIDS and for the treatment of acyclovir-resistant herpes in people with compromised immune systems. Additionally, foscarnet may be used in combination with ganciclovir for the treatment of CMV retinitis.

**GENERAL INFORMATION**

CMV infection can cause serious symptoms in many different organs, including the eyes, intestines, stomach, lungs, kidneys, and esophagus. Foscarnet slows, but does not stop, the progression of CMV retinitis, an opportunistic infection that can cause blindness in people with weakened immune systems. It may also act against CMV disease in other parts of the body, but there is less clinical evidence to support its use in these cases.

Foscarnet interferes with the multiplication of CMV, thereby slowing the destruction of the retina (the light-sensitive tissue at the back of the eye) and loss of vision. However, foscarnet is not a cure for CMV retinitis. People taking the drug may continue to lose their vision and should have regular eye examinations at least every six weeks to determine whether a change in treatment is required.

Foscarnet is available as a solution for injection.

**TREATMENT**

Foscarnet must be injected slowly into a vein. There is a significant risk of toxicity if the drug is injected too quickly, so an infusion pump must be used to control the amount of drug injected. The individual needs to be well hydrated before injection, which usually means that 500 ml to 1 liter of saline solution is injected before injecting foscarnet.

For initial treatment of CMV infection, the typical dose is 90 mg per kg of body weight given intravenously at a constant rate over a minimum of one hour every twelve hours for two to three weeks. After the initial treatment, the dose is usually 90 to 120 mg per kg of body weight per day. Most people receive the 90 mg dose because the higher dose hasn't been proven superior in clinical trials. Both the initial and maintenance dosages should be reduced for people with poor kidney function.

For varicella zoster virus or herpes simplex virus resistant to acyclovir, a dose of 40 mg of foscarnet per kg of body weight is commonly used. For herpes simplex, the injection is given once a day. For varicella zoster virus, the injection must be given every eight hours.

Because foscarnet can cause kidney damage and potentially fatal imbalances in certain body chemicals called electrolytes, physicians closely monitor people taking the drug. This includes monitoring kidney function two to three times a week during initial therapy and at least once every one to two

weeks during maintenance therapy. A similar schedule is recommended for monitoring calcium, magnesium, potassium, and phosphorus.

## CAUTIONS AND WARNINGS

Foscarnet should not be used by people with a known allergy to it.

Large doses or rapid injection of foscarnet can increase the toxicity of the drug. Recommended dosages should not be exceeded and infusions are usually administered over at least two hours.

## SIDE EFFECTS

Kidney toxicity is the major side effect of foscarnet and occurs to some degree in most people who take the drug. Approximately one-third of volunteers in clinical studies of foscarnet in people with AIDS developed serious kidney problems. Foscarnet has also been shown to cause changes in minerals and electrolytes in the blood that have led to seizures. Electrolyte imbalance is a serious and sometimes fatal side effect of foscarnet. Warning signs of these imbalances are numbness in the mouth, burning or prickling sensations, and seizures. People who experience them should contact their doctors immediately. Approximately 10% of 189 participants in five clinical trials of foscarnet had seizures.

Other side effects of foscarnet reported in 1% to 5% of people taking the drug include anemia, fever, fatigue, stiffness, muscle weakness, malaise, pain, infection, headache, prickling sensations, dizziness, involuntary muscle contractions, tingling, numbness, seizures, changes in appetite, nausea, diarrhea, vomiting, abdominal pain, depression, confusion, anxiety, coughing, difficulty breathing, rash, and increased sweating.

## PREGNANCY/BREAST-FEEDING

Foscarnet has not been formally studied in pregnant women. In animal studies it caused birth defects, but it is not known whether this would be true in humans as well. Pregnant women are encouraged to discuss the benefits and risks of foscarnet with their physician before deciding to use the drug.

HIV can be passed from a woman to her child through breast milk. In areas where nutritionally sound alternatives are readily available, breast-feeding is discouraged for HIV-positive women. It is not known if foscarnet is excreted in human milk, but because of the potential toxicity of the drug, women should consider alternatives to breast-feeding while taking it.

## USE IN CHILDREN

The safety and effectiveness of foscarnet have not been studied in children.

## USE IN THE ELDERLY

Older adults may be more susceptible to the side effects of the drug and may require reduced doses.

**DRUG INTERACTIONS**

Foscarnet may increase the risk of kidney toxicity when used with amino-glycoside antibiotics (amikacin, gentamicin, streptomycin, erythromycin), amphotericin B, ddC, and intravenous pentamidine. Use with intravenous pentamidine may also increase the risk of low blood sugar levels. Use of ddC along with foscarnet may increase the risk of peripheral neuropathy, a condition characterized by numbness, tingling, or pain in the extremities.

Use with imipenem-cilastin may increase the risk of seizures.

**FOOD INTERACTIONS**

Because foscarnet is administered by injection, food does not interfere with its absorption in the body.

**OTHER DRUGS USED FOR SIMILAR CONDITIONS**

Foscarnet, ganciclovir, cidofovir, and ganciclovir implants are the drugs approved for the treatment of CMV retinitis. Although they are all effective in slowing CMV, they have different side effects, drug interactions, dosages, and route of administration. Depending on the circumstances, one may be a better choice than the other. Some of these therapies can be used to treat CMV throughout the body (and possibly prevent CMV from spreading throughout the rest of the body) whereas others will only treat a specific organ (i.e., the eye) and may allow CMV to spread to other parts of the body.

# GANCICLOVIR

**BRAND NAME (MANUFACTURER)**
Cytovene (Roche), Vitrasert (Chiron)

**OTHER NAME**
DHPG, GCV

**TYPE OF DRUG**
Antiviral

**USED FOR**
Ganciclovir has been approved for treatment of cytomegalovirus (CMV) retinitis in people with weakened immune systems. It has also been approved for the prevention of a broader range of CMV diseases in people receiving organ or tissue transplants and for people with HIV. Ganciclovir is also approved for use in combination with foscarnet for the treatment of CMV retinitis. Additionally, a device containing ganciclovir that can be implanted directly into the eye is also approved for the treatment of CMV retinitis.

**GENERAL INFORMATION**

CMV infection can cause serious symptoms in many different organs, including the eyes, intestines, stomach, lungs, kidneys, and esophagus. Ganciclovir slows, but does not stop, the progression of CMV retinitis, an opportunistic infection that can cause blindness in people with weakened immune systems. It may also act against CMV disease in other parts of the body, but there is less clinical evidence to support its use in these cases.

Ganciclovir interferes with the multiplication of CMV, thereby slowing the destruction of the retina (the light-sensitive tissue at the back of the eye) and loss of vision. However, ganciclovir is not a cure for CMV retinitis. People taking the drug may continue to lose their vision and should have regular eye examinations at least every six weeks to determine whether a change in treatment is required.

Ganciclovir is available as tablets for oral administration, as a device for surgical implantation in the retina, and as powder for a solution for intravenous (IV) administration.

**TREATMENT**

Intravenously administered ganciclovir is provided as a sterile powder that must be reconstituted and infused into a vein. The rate of infusion should be carefully monitored so that toxic levels of the drug are not injected. No infusion pump is required.

The initial dosage for treatment of CMV retinitis is 5 mg per kg of body weight, used intravenously at a constant rate over one hour, every twelve hours, for fourteen to twenty-one days. Following this initial treatment, the recommended maintenance dose is 5 mg per kg of body weight, given intravenously over one hour, once per day. An alternate maintenance dose is 6 mg per kg of body weight given intravenously five days each week.

People with reduced kidney function and those who experience severe reductions in white blood cells (primarily those called neutrophils) or platelets (which are structures involved in blood clotting) may require a dosage reduction.

People receiving ganciclovir twice a day usually have their neutrophil and platelet counts measured at least twice a week. People with neutrophil counts less than 1,000 have their neutrophil and platelet counts measured as often as every day. Because of the possibility of kidney damage, a person's kidney function is usually tested at least every two weeks.

Studies with oral ganciclovir for maintenance of CMV have shown that it is not as effective as IV ganciclovir. However, there is a vast improvement in the quality of life for people on oral ganciclovir compared to the IV form.

Two studies comparing oral ganciclovir to placebo for the prevention of CMV disease have shown ambiguous results. One study showed that oral ganciclovir was able to significantly reduce the incidence of CMV while a second study failed to confirm this benefit. Consequently, the current Public Health Service guidelines do not recommend the use of oral ganciclovir for the prevention of CMV. Some researchers and physicians, however, disagree and elect to use the drug to prevent CMV. The recent success of combination therapy with protease inhibitors has also shown a significant reduction in new cases of CMV.

Studies with the ganciclovir implant have shown that it was able to greatly extend the durability of treatment compared to the IV form. Some researchers, however, remain concerned that this approach could lead to a greater incidence of CMV in the second eye or elsewhere in the body. Other researchers believe that the current optimal regimen for treating CMV retinitis is to use the ganciclovir implant in the affected eye with oral ganciclovir to prevent the spread of CMV into the other eye or elsewhere in the body.

## CAUTIONS AND WARNINGS

Ganciclovir should not be used by anyone with a known allergy to it or to acyclovir. Ganciclovir interferes with the ability of the bone marrow to make neutrophils and platelets. In people whose immune system is already severely suppressed, ganciclovir should be used only with great caution, though, unfortunately, this is also the population most likely to need the drug. In the past, people who had absolute neutrophil counts less than 500 or platelet counts less than 25,000 were not given the drug. Recently, new drugs, called colony-stimulating factors, have been developed that stimulate the production of white blood cells, but not platelets. Using them (e.g., G-CSF) allows these people to continue taking ganciclovir.

AZT (zidovudine) use also reduces neutrophil and platelet counts, and many people cannot tolerate AZT and ganciclovir simultaneously. When ganciclovir was first approved for use, most people with AIDS and CMV retinitis had to stop AZT therapy to take ganciclovir or use another anti-CMV drug. Now the use of G-CSF allows most people to use AZT and ganciclovir simultaneously.

## SIDE EFFECTS

The most frequent side effects of ganciclovir are reductions in the number of neutrophils and platelets. This increases the risk of infection and longer bleeding times. In an uncontrolled trial of 532 volunteers with AIDS receiving ganciclovir, 18% had severely reduced neutrophil counts and 4% had severely reduced platelet counts. The neutrophil and platelet counts generally returned to normal when the drug was stopped. Another significant side effect of ganciclovir

is kidney damage, which has been observed in as many as 20% of people who receive ganciclovir after organ or tissue transplants. Other side effects experienced less frequently include headache, confusion, anemia, fever, skin reactions, and abnormal liver function. More rarely, people experience chills, malaise, irregular heart rhythms, nausea, vomiting, loss of appetite, diarrhea, bleeding, abdominal pain, reduced red blood cell counts, difficulty breathing, itching, hair loss, inflammation, and pain.

### PREGNANCY/BREAST-FEEDING

Ganciclovir may cause infertility, birth defects, or tumors, so it should not be used during pregnancy. Effective contraception is recommended during treatment.

HIV can be passed from a woman to her child through breast milk. In areas where nutritionally sound alternatives are readily available, breast-feeding is discouraged for HIV-positive women. It is not known if ganciclovir passes through breast milk, but because of the potential toxicity of the drug, women should consider alternatives to breast-feeding while taking it.

### USE IN CHILDREN

Ganciclovir has been used in relatively few children. The limited information available suggests that ganciclovir acts the same way in children as in adults, with the same effectiveness and similar side effects.

There is some evidence that ganciclovir may have serious long-term consequences when used in children, but the life expectancy of HIV-positive children with CMV retinitis is relatively short, and the long-term safety of the drug in these children is usually less of a concern than preserving their eyesight. Children not infected with HIV who receive ganciclovir to prevent CMV disease after organ or tissue transplantation may be at a higher risk of developing cancers caused by the drug than adults.

### USE IN THE ELDERLY

Older adults may be more susceptible to the side effects of the drug and may require reduced doses.

### DRUG INTERACTIONS

AZT and ganciclovir both suppress neutrophil and platelet counts and may not be tolerated simultaneously. Ganciclovir increases ddI levels in the blood by up to 70%, possibly increasing the risk of pancreatic disease. ddI decreases ganciclovir levels by approximately 20%, possibly reducing its effectiveness. Ganciclovir may also increase the risk of pancreatic disease when used in combination with d4T.

Drugs that inhibit kidney function, such as probenecid, may increase the risk of kidney damage by ganciclovir. Other drugs that may have increased toxicity when used with ganciclovir include dapsone, pentamidine, flucytosine,

vincristine, vinblastine, adriamycin, amphotericin B, trimethoprim/sulfa combinations, and other nucleoside analogues (ddC, etc.).

Seizures have been reported in people who used ganciclovir in combination with imipenem-cilastin.

**FOOD INTERACTIONS**
None reported.

**OTHER DRUGS USED FOR SIMILAR CONDITIONS**
Foscarnet, ganciclovir, cidofovir, and ganciclovir implants are the drugs approved for the treatment of CMV retinitis. Although they are all effective in slowing CMV, they have different side effects, drug interactions, dosages, and route of administration. Depending on the circumstances, one may be a better choice than the other. Some of these therapies can be used to treat CMV throughout the body (and possibly prevent CMV from spreading throughout the rest of the body), whereas others will only treat a specific organ (i.e., the eye) and may allow CMV to spread to other parts of the body.

**COMMENTS**
A new version of oral ganciclovir is being developed which is able to achieve drug levels comparable to the intravenous formulation. As a result, it should prove to be more effective than the current formulation of oral ganciclovir and may serve as an effective alternative to IV therapy in all its current applications. It also offers the prospect of being more effective as a preventive agent than the current, poorly absorbed version of oral ganciclovir.

# IMIQUIMOD

**BRAND NAME (MANUFACTURER)**
Aldara (3M)

**TYPE OF DRUG**
Antiviral

**USED FOR**
Imiquimod is used to treat genital and anal warts in adults.

**GENERAL INFORMATION**
The exact mechanism by which imiquimod exerts antiviral activity is not known.
Imiquimod is administered as a cream.

**TREATMENT**
Imiquimod is usually applied to the wart area three times a week prior to sleeping. The cream should only be left on the skin for 6-10 hours and then washed off with soap and water.

**CAUTIONS AND WARNINGS**
It is not known whether imiquimod is effective for warts in the urethra, vagina, cervix, or rectum.

**SIDE EFFECTS**
In clinical trials, the most common side effects were inflammation and redness, ulceration, and flakiness of the skin.

**PREGNANCY/BREAST-FEEDING**
Imiquimod has not been formally studied in pregnant women. Because of the potential for birth defects, pregnant women are encouraged to discuss the benefits and potential risks of imiquimod with their physician before deciding to use the drug.

HIV can be passed from a woman to her child through breast milk. In areas where nutritionally sound alternatives are readily available, breast-feeding is discouraged for HIV-positive women. It is not known whether imiquimod is excreted in human milk. Because of the potential toxicity of the drug, women are encouraged to consider alternatives to breast-feeding while using it.

**USE IN CHILDREN**
The safety and effectiveness of imiquimod has not been established in children.

**USE IN THE ELDERLY**
No dose adjustments are necessary for older adults.

**DRUG INTERACTIONS**
None reported.

**FOOD INTERACTIONS**
Imiquimod is applied as a cream and will not be affected by food.

**OTHER DRUGS USED FOR SIMILAR CONDITIONS**
Genital warts are usually removed surgically, by laser, or frozen off. Other therapies used to treat genital warts include podofilox.

# INDINAVIR

**BRAND NAME (MANUFACTURER)**
Crixivan (Merck)

**TYPE OF DRUG**
Antiviral–anti-HIV

**USED FOR**
Indinavir is approved for treatment of HIV-infected adults when antiretroviral therapy is warranted. It should be used in a combination regimen with at least

two other antiviral medications, although the number of additional medications required may change as more potent therapies become available.

## GENERAL INFORMATION

Indinavir is an oral antiviral drug known as a protease inhibitor. Protease inhibitors work during a late stage of the HIV life cycle by inhibiting an enzyme that is crucial for the proper assembly of new virus particles. These virus particles are defective and non-functional and unable to infect more cells.

Research indicates that the most effective use of indinavir is in combination with other anti-HIV treatments. Combination therapies are most likely to produce lasting reduction in viral load, prevent the development of drug resistance, and delay disease progression. Two large studies have confirmed the benefit of indinavir when used in a triple combination along with AZT + 3TC. ACTG 320 and Merck 035 both demonstrated that in people with less than 400 CD4+ cells and prior use of antivirals, the combination could effectively decrease viral load below the limit of detection and significantly decrease the incidence of death and disease progression.

## TREATMENT

The recommended dose of indinavir is 800 mg every 8 hours and should be taken with a large glass of water. Indinavir is available in two different dosages, 400 mg and 200 mg capsules. It should be taken at least one hour before or two hours after a meal to increase the absorption of the drug. However, it can be taken with a low fat meal such as toast (no butter), corn flakes with skim milk, coffee, tea, or juices. Indinavir should NOT be taken with grapefruit juice as this will decrease the absorption of the drug.

## CAUTIONS AND WARNINGS

Indinavir should not be used by anyone with a known allergy to it. In addition, use of indinavir may result in the development of kidney stones or flank pain, especially in people suffering from dehydration for any reason. People taking indinavir should drink at least 8 glasses of water a day to reduce the risk of developing kidney stones. Additionally, people should not drink alcohol when taking indinavir as this creates temporary periods of dehydration that may increase the risk of kidney stones.

## SIDE EFFECTS

The most serious side effect noted in the clinical studies has been kidney stones including flank pain, which occurred in about 4% of people taking indinavir. Other side effects associated with indinavir reported in the clinical studies include: nausea (11.7%), elevated bilirubin levels (10%), abdominal pain (8.7%), headache (5.6%), diarrhea (4.6%), vomiting (4.1%), fatigue (3.6%), and insomnia (3.1%).

**PREGNANCY/BREAST-FEEDING**

Indinavir has not been formally studied in pregnant women. In animal studies, it did not cause fetal harm, but it is not known whether the same would be true in humans. Indinavir should be used during pregnancy only if the potential benefits justify the risks involved.

HIV can be passed from a woman to her child through breast milk. In areas where nutritionally sound alternatives are readily available, breast-feeding is discouraged for HIV-positive women. While indinavir is secreted in animal milk, it is not known if it is secreted in human milk. Because of the potential toxicity, women should consider alternatives to breast-feeding while taking the drug.

**USE IN CHILDREN**

The safety and effectiveness of indinavir in children has not been established, therefore no recommendations are available at this time.

**USE IN THE ELDERLY**

No information available.

**DRUG INTERACTIONS**

There are a number of significant drug interactions between indinavir and other common HIV therapies. Because ketoconazole (Nizoral) increases indinavir levels by 68%, the dose of indinavir should be reduced to 600 mg every 8 hours. The dose of rifabutin should be halved to 150 mg a day if it is taken with indinavir. Indinavir should NOT BE USED with terfenadine (Seldane), astemizole (Hismanal), cisapride (Propulsid), rifampin, triazolam (Halcion), or midazolam (Versed) as their use in combination may lead to serious and/or life-threatening side effects. Additionally, ddI should be taken at least an hour before or after taking indinavir. Indinavir has been shown to increase saquinavir (Invirase) levels 4.6–7.2 fold in the blood. If this combination is being considered, it should be used with the utmost care, and rigorous monitoring is recommended.

**FOOD INTERACTIONS**

Indinavir should not be taken with a full meal or fatty foods and should be taken at least one hour before or two hours after such a meal. However, indinavir can be taken with a low fat snack such as toast (no butter), corn flakes with skim milk, coffee, tea, or juices. It should NOT be taken with grapefruit juice as this will decrease the absorption of the drug.

**OTHER DRUGS USED FOR SIMILAR CONDITIONS**

Other approved anti-HIV drugs in this class include ritonavir, saquinavir, and nelfinavir. Other anti-HIV drugs in various other classes include AZT, 3TC, d4T, ddI, ddC, nevirapine, and delavirdine. The most effective use of these antiretroviral agents is in three- or four-drug combinations which in-

clude two highly active antivirals (indinavir, ritonavir, nelfinavir, nevirapine, or 3TC).

**COMMENTS**

The effect of indinavir on viral load and CD4+ cell counts is one of the most impressive seen to date. However, indinavir must be used correctly as improper use will speed the development of resistance. In addition, studies show that people who develop high level resistance to indinavir also become resistant (or "cross-resistant") to the other protease inhibitors, rendering these drugs ineffective in fighting HIV. This has been shown to occur when indinavir is used alone at lower doses and it is unknown whether the same pattern will develop at higher doses or when used in combination with nucleoside analogues. However, laboratory studies show that the changes (mutations) in HIV that cause resistance to indinavir are very similar to those for ritonavir, so it is likely that resistance to one indicates resistance to both. It is also established that resistance to saquinavir will hasten the development of resistance to indinavir. The resistance relationship between nelfinavir and indinavir is less well understood because adequate research has not yet been done.

Clearly, in considering the optimum combination of drugs, it is important to weigh immediate benefit *and* long-term benefit as well as preservation of future options. The best use of protease inhibitors is most likely in triple combination regimens with two other antiviral therapies. Indinavir's potent antiviral activity and relatively moderate side effect profile make it a good candidate for first-line therapy in combination with other antiretroviral treatments.

# NELFINAVIR

**BRAND NAME (MANUFACTURER)**
Viracept (Agouron)

**TYPE OF DRUG**
Antiviral–anti-HIV

**USED FOR**
Nelfinavir is approved for the treatment of adults and children with HIV infection when antiretroviral therapy is warranted. It should be used in a combination therapy regimen with at least two other antiviral medications.

**GENERAL INFORMATION**
Nelfinavir is an orally administered antiviral drug known as a protease inhibitor. Protease inhibitors work during a late stage of the HIV life cycle by inhibiting an enzyme that is crucial for the proper assembly of new virus particles.

These virus particles are defective and non-functional and unable to infect more cells.

Nelfinavir is a highly potent antiviral therapy and when used in combination therapies, it can effectively reduce viral load, prevent the development of drug resistance, and delay disease progression.

Nelfinavir is available as tablets or as a powder for oral suspension.

### TREATMENT

For adults, the recommended dose is 750 mg (three 250 mg tablets) taken three times daily with a meal or light snack. For children ages 2-13 years, the suggested dose is 20-30 mg/kg per dose, three times daily with food. For children unable to take tablets, an oral powder may be mixed with a small amount of water, milk, formula, soy formula, soy milk, or dietary supplements. The powder should not be mixed with acidic foods or juices (such as apple or orange juice).

### CAUTIONS AND WARNINGS

Nelfinavir should not be used by anyone with a known allergy to it. In addition, nelfinavir should not be taken with certain anti-arrhythmia drugs or sedatives. People with phenylketonuria (a congenital defect in metabolism which is often associated with mental problems) should be cautious about taking nelfinavir.

### SIDE EFFECTS

The most serious side effect reported in the clinical studies was diarrhea or loose stools of mild to moderate intensity that affected between 16%-32% of participants. Other side effects include nausea (7%), flatulence or gas (3%), and rash (3%).

### PREGNANCY/BREAST-FEEDING

Nelfinavir has not been formally studied in pregnant women, but it did not cause fetal harm when given to animals. Because it is not known whether the same would be true in humans, nelfinavir should be used during pregnancy only if clearly needed.

In addition, HIV can be passed from a woman to her child through breast milk. In areas where nutritionally sound alternatives are readily available, breast-feeding is discouraged for HIV-positive women. While nelfinavir is secreted in animal milk, it is not known if it is secreted in human milk. Because of the potential toxicity, women should consider alternatives to breast-feeding while taking the drug.

### USE IN CHILDREN

Nelfinavir has been shown to be safe and effective in children ages 2-13 years and is approved for pediatric use. Safety and effectiveness studies have not been performed in children less than 2 years old.

## USE IN THE ELDERLY
No information available.

## DRUG INTERACTIONS
Nelfinavir should NOT be used with terfenadine, astemizole, cisapride, triazolam, midazolam, or rifampin as their use in combination may lead to serious and/ or life-threatening side effects. Nelfinavir can also reduce blood levels of oral contraceptives (ethinyl estradiol) by nearly 50%. Nelfinavir can also increase blood levels of the other protease inhibitors (indinavir, ritonavir, and saquinavir).

## FOOD INTERACTIONS
Nelfinavir should be taken with a meal or a light snack. The main intent of this requirement is that the drug should not be taken after fasting or on an empty stomach.

## OTHER DRUGS USED FOR SIMILAR CONDITIONS
Other approved anti-HIV drugs of the same class include ritonavir, indinavir, and saquinavir. Other anti-HIV drugs in various other classes include AZT, 3TC, d4T, ddI, ddC, nevirapine, and delavirdine. The most effective use of these antiretroviral agents is in three- or four-drug combinations with at least one other highly active antiviral (indinavir, ritonavir, nelfinavir, nevirapine, or 3TC) not used previously by the patient.

## COMMENTS
Because of limited clinical trials with nelfinavir, it remains to be seen where the drug fits in the overall mix of antiretroviral therapies. Current information suggests that nelfinavir is a highly active antiviral that should be used in combination with other antiviral therapies. It appears to be more potent than the original, hard gel formulation of saquinavir, but since no comparative studies have been done, it is unclear whether it is fully equivalent in potency to indinavir and ritonavir. It is clear, however, that it is very potent when used in a three-drug combination therapy. Because nelfinavir has a slightly different resistance pattern than the other protease inhibitors, some researchers believe that development of resistance to nelfinavir may not result in direct resistance to other therapies, allowing them to still be effective in fighting HIV after a patient fails on nelfinavir. This has not been confirmed by meaningful clinical trials and other researchers dispute it. Prior use of other protease inhibitors may result in resistance to nelfinavir. Most researchers believe that there is a risk of cross-resistance between all currently available protease inhibitors, regardless of the order in which they are used.

Clearly, in considering the optimum combination of drugs, it is important to weigh immediate benefit *and* long-term benefit as well as preservation of future options. The best use of nelfinavir is most likely in triple combination regimens with two other antiviral therapies.

# NEVIRAPINE

**BRAND NAME (MANUFACTURER)**
Viracept (Boehringer Ingelheim)

**TYPE OF DRUG**
Antiviral–anti-HIV

**USED FOR**
Nevirapine is approved for the treatment of adults with HIV infection when antiretroviral therapy is warranted. It should be used in a combination therapy regimen with at least two other antiviral medications.

**GENERAL INFORMATION**
Nevirapine is an orally administered antiviral drug known as a non-nucleoside reverse transcriptase inhibitor (NNRTI), which attempts to slow or stop reproduction of the virus by inhibiting one of its key enzymes, reverse transcriptase.

Studies show that it can effectively decrease viral load in people regardless of whether they have previously used other antiviral therapies. Because resistance to nevirapine can develop very quickly when it is used alone, the drug should only be used in a potent combination therapy regimen. Combination therapies are most likely to produce long-lasting reductions in viral load, prevent the development of drug resistance, and delay disease progression.

**TREATMENT**
The recommended adult dosing schedule for nevirapine is a dose-escalated regimen in which one 200 mg is taken once daily for the first 14 days, followed by one 200 mg tablet twice daily, in combination with other antiviral therapies. Proper dosing for children has not yet been determined. The lead-in period is used to lessen the frequency of rash.

**CAUTIONS AND WARNINGS**
Nevirapine should not be used by anyone with a known allergy to it. In addition, use of nevirapine can result in severe and life-threatening skin reactions, including Stevens-Johnson syndrome.

**SIDE EFFECTS**
The most common side effects reported in studies include rash, fevers, nausea, headaches, and increases in liver enzymes. One rare but potentially life-threatening side effect is Stevens-Johnson syndrome, which is the result of severe skin rashes that may require a skin graft. The rashes usually occur during the first weeks of starting nevirapine and then gradually disappear. One approach to reduce the risk of rashes is to dose escalate nevirapine.

**PREGNANCY/BREAST-FEEDING**
Nevirapine is currently being studied in pregnant women as a way to prevent mother-to-child transmission of HIV. In animal studies, nevirapine did not cause fetal harm but did decrease fetal body weight. However, it is not known whether the same would be true in humans. Nevirapine should be used during pregnancy only if the potential benefits justify the risks involved.

In addition, HIV can be passed from a woman to her child through breast milk. In areas where nutritionally sound alternatives are readily available, breast-feeding is discouraged for HIV-positive women. One study shows that nevirapine is found in human breast milk. Because of the potential toxicity, women should consider alternatives to breast-feeding while taking the drug.

**USE IN CHILDREN**
The safety and effectiveness in children has not been established, therefore no recommendations are available at this time. However, nevirapine is being studied in combination regimens in a small number of children.

**USE IN THE ELDERLY**
Nevirapine has not been studied in people older than age 68, but dosing and administration most likely do not need to be altered for this group.

**DRUG INTERACTIONS**
There are a number of drug interactions between nevirapine and other commonly used therapies. Nevirapine appears to decrease drug levels of all the currently available protease inhibitors. Interaction studies with the protease inhibitors are ongoing and they should not be used in combination until more information becomes available.

Nevirapine should not be used with cimetidine, clavulanic acid, dicumarol, erythromycin, TMP/SMX (Bactrim/Septra), tolbutamide, and warfarin. There may also be interactions between nevirapine and common drugs such as clarithromycin, itraconazole, ketoconazole, rifabutin, and rifampin. For a complete list of drug interactions, see the Drug Interactions Chart.

**FOOD INTERACTIONS**
Nevirapine can be taken with or without food.

**OTHER DRUGS USED FOR SIMILAR CONDITIONS**
The other approved anti-HIV drug of the same class is delavirdine (Rescriptor). Other antiviral therapies include indinavir, ritonavir, saquinavir, nelfinavir, AZT, 3TC, d4T, ddI, and ddC. The most effective use of these antiretroviral agents is three- or four-drug combinations with at least one highly active antiviral (indinavir, ritonavir, nelfinavir, nevirapine, or 3TC).

**COMMENTS**
The most well-studied (though not necessarily the most potent) nevirapine combination, a triple-drug therapy of AZT + ddI + nevirapine, has shown

potent and sustained antiviral activity. The best use of nevirapine may be in people with early stage disease who have not previously used many other therapies, allowing them to save other potent therapies for later. In this context, some researchers believe it offers a viable alternative to three-drug combinations employing a protease inhibitor. The advantage of this approach is that it may offer a lengthy period of effective therapy while still preserving the protease inhibitor class of drugs for later use since it does not cause cross-resistance to protease inhibitors.

As with the anti-HIV therapies, it is important to maintain adequate blood levels of nevirapine to prevent the development of resistance. Nevirapine should be used in combination with at least two other antiviral drugs because resistance to nevirapine can develop rapidly when the drug is used alone. In addition, resistance to nevirapine results in cross-resistance to delavirdine rendering it inactive in fighting HIV.

In considering the optimum combination of drugs, it is important to weigh immediate benefit *and* long-term benefit as well as preservation of future options. The best use of nevirapine is most likely in triple combination regimens with two other antiviral therapies.

# PODOFILOX

**BRAND NAME (MANUFACTURER)**
Condylox (Oclassen)

**TYPE OF DRUG**
Antiviral

**USED FOR**
Podofilox is used to treat genital warts in adults.

**GENERAL INFORMATION**
The exact mechanism by which podofilox exerts antiviral activity is not known.
Podofilox is available as a solution for topical application.

**TREATMENT**
Podofilox is usually applied to the wart area twice daily for three consecutive days and then withheld for the next four days. This cycle should be repeated four times until the wart has disappeared.

**CAUTIONS AND WARNINGS**
Podofilox should not be used by people who know they are allergic to it. It is not known whether podofilox is effective for warts in the urethra, vagina, cervix, or rectum.

**SIDE EFFECTS**
In clinical trials, the most common side effects were burning sensation, pain, inflammation, and itching.

**PREGNANCY/BREAST-FEEDING**
Podofilox has not been formally studied in pregnant women. Because of the potential for birth defects, pregnant women are encouraged to discuss the benefits and potential risks of podofilox with their physician before deciding to use the drug.

HIV can be passed from a woman to her child through breast milk. In areas where nutritionally sound alternatives are readily available, breast-feeding is discouraged for HIV-positive women. It is not known whether podofilox is excreted in human milk and because of the potential toxicity of the drug, women are encouraged to consider alternatives to breast-feeding while using it.

**USE IN CHILDREN**
The safety and effectiveness of podofilox has not been established in children.

**USE IN THE ELDERLY**
No dose adjustments are necessary for older adults.

**DRUG INTERACTIONS**
None reported.

**FOOD INTERACTIONS**
Podofilox is applied as a cream and will not be effected by food.

**OTHER DRUGS USED FOR SIMILAR CONDITIONS**
Genital warts are usually removed surgically, by laser, or frozen off. Other therapies used to treat genital warts include imiquimod.

# RITONAVIR

**BRAND NAME (MANUFACTURER)**
Norvir (Abbott)

**TYPE OF DRUG**
Antiviral–anti-HIV

**USED FOR**
Ritonavir is approved for the treatment of adults and children with HIV infection when antiretroviral therapy is warranted. It should be used in a combination therapy regimen with at least two other reverse transcriptase inhibitor antiviral medications or one other protease inhibitor.

**GENERAL INFORMATION**

Ritonavir is an orally administered antiviral drug known as a protease inhibitor. Protease inhibitors work during a late stage of the HIV life cycle by inhibiting an enzyme that is crucial for the proper assembly of new virus particles. These virus particles are defective and unable to infect more cells.

Research indicates that the most effective use of ritonavir is in combination with other anti-HIV treatments. Combination therapies are most likely to reduce viral load, prevent the development of drug resistance, and delay disease progression. When used in combination therapies, ritonavir has been shown to significantly reduce viral load (1.7-2.5 log decrease) and thereby decrease the risk of disease progression and death. Studies have also shown that the two-drug combination of ritonavir and saquinavir is very effective in fighting HIV.

**TREATMENT**

The recommended dose of ritonavir is 600 mg twice daily with food. A brief period of dose escalation may help prevent some of the side effects associated with ritonavir. In these cases, ritonavir should be started at no less than 300 mg twice daily and increased in increments of 100 mg twice daily until the dose reaches 600 mg twice daily (total daily dose of 1,200 mg). Ritonavir is available in 100 mg capsules or as an oral liquid solution. The taste of the drug can be improved by mixing with chocolate milk or various nutritional supplements. In addition, it is necessary to refrigerate all forms of ritonavir.

The recommended dose in children is 400 mg per square meter body surface area. The dose should be started at 250 and should not exceed 600 mg per square meter.

**CAUTIONS AND WARNINGS**

Ritonavir should not be used by anyone with a known allergy to it. In addition, ritonavir should not be used in combination with certain non-sedating antihistamines, sedatives or hypnotics, anti-arrhythmia drugs, or ergot alkaloid preparations. Combination use of these drugs may result in potentially life-threatening side effects.

People who have either hepatitis B or C should be careful using ritonavir as these individuals may have a higher risk of increased transaminase levels. People with preexisting liver disease, liver enzyme abnormalities, or hepatitis should also exercise caution when taking ritonavir.

**SIDE EFFECTS**

The side effect profile of ritonavir is very extensive. Common side effects include mild tingling around the mouth, diarrhea, nausea, vomiting, fatigue, and flushing. Side effects can be severe at initiation of therapy, but may lessen over time. Many people discontinue ritonavir because of the side effects of the drug.

**PREGNANCY/BREAST-FEEDING**

Ritonavir has not been formally studied in pregnant women. In animal studies, it did cause some developmental problems in the fetus, but it is not known whether the same would be true in humans. Ritonavir should be used during pregnancy only if the potential benefits justify the risks involved.

HIV can be passed from a woman to her child through breast milk. In areas where nutritionally sound alternatives are readily available, breast-feeding is discouraged for HIV-positive women. It is not known whether ritonavir is secreted in human milk. Because of the potential toxicity, women should consider alternatives to breast-feeding while taking the drug.

**USE IN CHILDREN**

Ritonavir is approved for use in children ages 2-16. The recommended dose in children is 400 mg per square meter of body surface area, given twice daily. The dose should not exceed 600 mg per square meter. The starting dose in children is generally 250 mg per square meter and is then raised incrementally to 400 mg per square meter. Side effects in children are similar to those in adults. To minimize ritonavir taste problems in children, the child can be given peanut butter or a lifesaver to coat the mouth before taking the drug.

**USE IN THE ELDERLY**

Ritonavir has not been studied in people over 63 years of age.

**DRUG INTERACTIONS**

Ritonavir is known to interact with numerous antiviral therapies and treatments for opportunistic and other infections, too numerous to list here. For an extensive list of drug interactions, see the Drug Interactions Chart. On the positive side, it appears that ritonavir can be used safely with most or all other antiviral drugs, though dose adjustments might sometimes be required.

**FOOD INTERACTIONS**

Ritonavir should be taken with food.

**OTHER DRUGS USED FOR SIMILAR CONDITIONS**

Other approved anti-HIV drugs of the same class include indinavir, saquinavir, and nelfinavir. Other anti-HIV drugs in various other classes include AZT, 3TC, d4T, ddI, ddC, nevirapine, and delavirdine. The most effective use of these antiretroviral agents is three- or four-drug combinations with at least one highly active antiviral (indinavir, ritonavir, nelfinavir, nevirapine, or 3TC).

**COMMENTS**

Ritonavir has been shown to cause significant decreases in viral load and increases in CD4+ cell counts. It is an easier choice of drug for some people because it can be taken with meals and only has to be taken twice daily. However, ritonavir is associated with a high rate of initial side effects, including nausea, vomiting, and diarrhea, making the drug very difficult to tolerate. In

addition, studies show that people who develop resistance to ritonavir also become resistant (or "cross-resistant") to the other protease inhibitors, rendering these drugs ineffective in fighting HIV. Laboratory studies show that the changes (mutations) in HIV that cause resistance to indinavir can easily overlap those for ritonavir, so it is likely that resistance to one indicates resistance to both. It is also likely that resistance to saquinavir will hasten the development of resistance to ritonavir.

In considering the optimum combination of drugs, it is important to weigh immediate benefit *and* long-term benefit as well as preservation of future options. The best use of protease inhibitors is most likely in triple combination regimens with two other antiviral therapies.

# SAQUINAVIR

### BRAND NAME (MANUFACTURER)
Invirase (Hoffman-La Roche); improved formulation: Fortovase

### TYPE OF DRUG
Antiviral–anti-HIV

### USED FOR
Saquinavir is approved for the treatment of adults with advanced HIV infection. It should be used in a combination therapy regimen with at least two other antiviral medications.

### GENERAL INFORMATION
Saquinavir is an orally administered antiviral drug known as a protease inhibitor. Protease inhibitors work during a late stage of the HIV life cycle by inhibiting an enzyme that is crucial for the proper assembly of new virus particles. These virus particles are defective and unable to infect more cells.

Research indicates that the most effective use of saquinavir is in three- or four-drug combinations. Combination therapies are most likely to reduce viral load, prevent the development of drug resistance, and delay disease progression.

Because of a formulation problem with the original version of saquinavir, called the "hard gel capsule" (HGC) formulation, only about 4% of the drug reaches the bloodstream. Therefore, HGC saquinavir is not considered a potent antiviral therapy and presently should not be used as a first-line therapy for fighting HIV. Two- and three-drug combinations using HGC saquinavir have been shown to improve survival compared to single-drug therapies, but this is no longer an adequate standard of comparison. However, studies have shown that a combination regimen using saquinavir and ritonavir together is an effective use of the HGC formulation because ritonavir overcomes the mechanism

responsible for the poor absorption of HGC saquinavir. A new version of saquinavir, a soft gel formulation (also called the "soft gel capsule" or SGC), which will be sold under the brand name Fortovase, offers approximately a four-fold increase in absorption. This, plus a doubling of the standard daily dosage to 3,600 mg per day, provides a dosage roughly 8 to 10 times higher than offered by the earlier version. SGC saquinavir, Fortovase, is likely to be a reasonable competitor in the class of protease inhibitors.

## TREATMENT

The drug label recommends that saquinavir be used in combination with other antiviral medications at a dose of three 200 mg capsules (600 mg) taken three times daily (total daily dose of 1,800 mg). It should be taken within 2 hours after eating (preferably with a high-fat meal) to increase the absorption of the drug. Subsequent studies of the improved, SGC formulation of saquinavir, however, demonstrate that this dosing level is completely inadequate.

Studies of the new SGC saquinavir are using double the original dose of saquinavir, or six 200 mg soft gel capsules three times daily (total daily dose of 3,600 mg). Combined with the fact that the new formulation provides 4 times greater absorption, this should result in a total 8–10 times higher blood levels than the original version of saquinavir.

## CAUTIONS AND WARNINGS

Saquinavir should not be used by anyone with a known allergy to it. In addition, drug resistance can develop rapidly to saquinavir in its original formulation and can lead to cross resistance to the other protease inhibitors and to the improved HGC saquinavir.

## SIDE EFFECTS

The most commonly reported side effects in the clinical studies have been nausea, diarrhea, and abdominal pain. The majority of these side effects were considered to be of relatively mild intensity. Other reported side effects include weakness, confusion, and increased liver function tests.

## PREGNANCY/BREAST-FEEDING

Saquinavir has not been formally studied in pregnant women. In animal studies, it did not cause fetal harm, but it is not known whether the same would be true in humans. Saquinavir should be used during pregnancy only if the potential benefits justify the risks involved.

HIV can be passed from a woman to her child through breast milk. In areas where nutritionally sound alternatives are readily available, breast-feeding is discouraged for HIV-positive women. It is not known whether saquinavir is secreted in human milk. Because of the potential toxicity, women should consider alternatives to breast-feeding while taking the drug.

**USE IN CHILDREN**

The safety and effectiveness of saquinavir in children under 16 years has not been established, therefore no recommendations are available at this time.

**USE IN THE ELDERLY**

The safety and effectiveness of saquinavir in people over 65 years of age has not been studied, therefore no recommendations are available at this time.

**DRUG INTERACTIONS**

Saquinavir should not be taken together with astemizole, terfenadine, and rifampin. Ritonavir can increase saquinavir blood levels by 20-fold, and delavirdine increases saquinavir levels by 5-fold.

**FOOD INTERACTIONS**

Saquinavir should be taken with food. It should preferably be taken within two hours of a high-fat meal to increase absorption of the drug This should not be necessary, however, with the improved SGC formulation.

**OTHER DRUGS USED FOR SIMILAR CONDITIONS**

Other approved anti-HIV drugs of the same class include ritonavir, indinavir, and nelfinavir. Other anti-HIV drugs in various other classes include AZT, 3TC, d4T, ddI, ddC, nevirapine, and delavirdine. The most effective use of these antiretroviral agents is three- or four-drug combinations with at least one highly active antiviral (indinavir, ritonavir, nelfinavir, nevirapine, or 3TC).

**COMMENTS**

Saquinavir is the least effective of any of the current protease inhibitors and is not recommended for first-line therapy unless used in combination with ritonavir. Because of the formulation problem with the current saquinavir, using the drug is equivalent to using one of the other protease inhibitors at one-eighth to one-ninth of the recommended dosage. These low blood levels can hasten the development of drug resistance to all protease inhibitors.

Clearly, in considering the optimum combination of drugs, it is important to weigh immediate benefit *and* long-term benefit as well as preservation of future options. The best rule for the use of the original HGC saquinavir is not to use it at all or only use it in combination with ritonavir. This will result in the optimal antiviral activity and preserve a person's future options, including the option to use the improved SGC formulation.

The effectiveness of the new formulation of saquinavir is likely to be far better than the original version, but it is not yet clear how it compares to the other protease inhibitors.

# TRIFLURIDINE

**BRAND NAME (MANUFACTURER)**
Viroptic (Glaxo Wellcome)

**OTHER NAME**
Trifluorothymidine

**TYPE OF DRUG**
Antiviral

**USED FOR**
Trifluridine is used for topical treatment of infections caused by herpes simplex virus (HSV). In people infected with HIV, it has been used topically to treat skin, genital, and perianal HSV infections that have become resistant to acyclovir.

**GENERAL INFORMATION**
Trifluridine is an antiviral drug that works by interfering with DNA synthesis in infected cells. It has not been shown to be effective in preventing herpes virus infections, only for treating them. It is not effective against bacterial, fungal, or chlamydial infections.

In clinical trials of people with healthy immune systems, approximately 95% of people responded to topical trifluridine for HSV infections in the eye. On average, it took six to seven days to repair damage to the cornea caused by HSV. People with acyclovir-resistant herpes also responded well to trifluridine.

Trifluridine is available as a sterile solution for administration into the eyes.

**TREATMENT**
One drop should be administered every two hours while awake until the cornea has completely been repaired. The maximum daily dose is nine drops. If there are no signs of improvement after seven days, other therapies should be considered.

Other topical formulations are also available. In small clinical trials of trifluridine used topically for HSV infections in people with HIV, the drug was effective at completely healing lesions in more than half the people who used it. The mean time to healing was about thirty-two days, and no serious side effects were reported.

**CAUTIONS AND WARNINGS**
Trifluridine should not be used by people who know they are allergic to it. The drug may cause mild local irritation when administered, but these effects are usually only temporary.

Although it has not been reported, resistance to trifluridine is possible.

## SIDE EFFECTS

The most common side effect of the optical solution, occurring in approximately 5% of people in clinical trials, is a mild, temporary burning when dropping it into the eye. About 3% experienced some localized swelling.

## PREGNANCY/BREAST-FEEDING

Trifluridine has not been formally studied in pregnant women. In animals, it caused birth defects at high doses, but it is not known if this would occur in humans. Pregnant women are encouraged to discuss the benefits and potential risks of trifluridine with their physician before deciding to use the drug.

HIV can be passed from a woman to her child through breast milk. In areas where nutritionally sound alternatives are readily available, breast-feeding is discouraged for HIV-positive women. It is unlikely that trifluridine is excreted in human milk when the drug is used topically.

## USE IN CHILDREN

No information available.

## USE IN THE ELDERLY

No information available.

## DRUG INTERACTIONS

None reported.

## FOOD INTERACTIONS

None reported.

## OTHER DRUGS USED FOR SIMILAR CONDITIONS

Acyclovir, idoxuridine, and vidarabine are other anti-herpes drugs that can be applied topically. For most purposes, acyclovir is the drug of choice for HSV infections; however, acyclovir is not yet available in an eye-drop formula. Trifluridine has not only been effective as initial topical treatment for herpes, it has also shown some promise in treating infections where the virus is resistant to acyclovir, idoxuridine, and topical vidarabine.

# VALACYCLOVIR

## BRAND NAME (MANUFACTURER)

Valtrex (Glaxo Wellcome)

## TYPE OF DRUG

Antiviral

## USED FOR

Valacyclovir is used to treat herpes zoster (shingles), caused by the varicella zoster virus (VZV), and recurrent genital herpes, caused by herpes simplex virus (HSV).

**GENERAL INFORMATION**

Valacyclovir is a pro-drug of the anti-herpes drug acyclovir. In other words, when a person takes valacyclovir, the body chemically changes it into acyclovir in the body. The main advantage to taking a pro-drug like valacyclovir is that it provides much higher blood levels of the active drug than you can get by taking the active drug directly. Higher blood levels of the drug may mean more effective control of the infection. It also usually means that the drug can be taken less often.

Early clinical studies show that taking valacyclovir results in blood levels of acyclovir five times higher than similar doses of acyclovir itself. Other clinical studies suggest that valacyclovir treatment results in faster relief of the pain associated with herpes zoster attacks. However, in one study comparing valacyclovir and acyclovir for prevention against cytomegalovirus (CMV), valacyclovir was more toxic and more deaths occurred in people taking it than in those taking acyclovir. Consequently, administration of the drug was stopped in the study.

Valacyclovir is administered orally.

**TREATMENT**

For shingles, the recommended dose is 1 gram every eight hours for seven days. Therapy should be initiated as soon as herpes zoster is diagnosed. For genital herpes, the recommended dose is 500 mg every 12 hours for five days. The dosage may need to be adjusted in people with reduced kidney function. No dosage adjustment is necessary for reduced liver function.

**CAUTIONS AND WARNINGS**

Valacyclovir should not be taken by people who are allergic to it or to acyclovir. Its effectiveness for other diseases caused by VZV (ophthalmic zoster or disseminated zoster, for example) has not been studied.

**SIDE EFFECTS**

In clinical trials, the most common side effects were nausea, vomiting, or diarrhea. At high doses (8,000 mg daily) valacyclovir may affect the bone marrow, reducing levels of neutrophils, white blood cells involved in protecting from infection.

**PREGNANCY/BREAST-FEEDING**

Valacyclovir has not been formally studied in pregnant women. Because of the potential for birth defects, pregnant women are encouraged to discuss the benefits and potential risks of valacyclovir with their physician before deciding to use the drug.

HIV can be passed from a woman to her child through breast milk. In areas where nutritionally sound alternatives are readily available, breast-feeding is discouraged for HIV-positive women. Valacyclovir is excreted in hu-

man milk and because of the potential toxicity of the drug, women are encouraged to consider alternatives to breast-feeding while using it.

**USE IN CHILDREN**
The safety and effectiveness of valacyclovir has not been established in children.

**USE IN THE ELDERLY**
Older adults, especially those with impaired kidney function, may be more susceptible to the side effects of the drug and may require reduced doses.

**DRUG INTERACTIONS**
Probenecid and cimetidine will increase valacyclovir levels in blood.

**FOOD INTERACTIONS**
Valacyclovir can be taken with or without food.

**OTHER DRUGS USED FOR SIMILAR CONDITIONS**
For infections caused by HSV and VZV, acyclovir is usually the drug of choice because it is well tolerated and effective against most strains of the viruses. Other antiviral drugs that may be used when acyclovir is ineffective or not tolerated include foscarnet, trifluridine, and vidarabine. Famciclovir is another antiviral drug used for VZV and HSV. However, it works through the same cellular mechanism as acyclovir and is unlikely to be effective for viruses resistant to acyclovir.

# ANTIVIRAL DRUGS: EXPERIMENTAL AND SOON-TO-BE APPROVED

The following drugs are being tested for the treatment of HIV and other viral infections. Generally, they are not widely available; most can be obtained only when participating in clinical trials. Experimental anti-HIV drugs are described first, followed by drugs used to treat other viral infections.

## NUCLEOSIDE ANALOGUES

**ABACAVIR**
1592U89 (abacavir) is a nucleoside analogue with potent antiviral activity. Preliminary studies have shown dramatic decreases in HIV levels in blood and increases in CD4+ cell counts in people beginning therapy for the first time. Current studies are using a 300 mg twice daily dose. Future studies will determine its usefulness in combination with other antiviral drugs and in more advanced patient populations. So far, it has not been as effective in people who have used antivirals before, especially those who have developed resis-

tance to 3TC or ddI. Further studies are needed to show the resistance profile of 1592 and to better understand how and where 1592 will fit into the mix of antiretrovirals.

### MKC 442

Triangle Pharmaceuticals' MKC 442, a new nucleoside analogue compound, shows potent activity. MKC 442, although a nucleoside analogue, behaves very much like a non-nucleoside reverse transcriptase inhibitor. The highest dose group studied so far received 500 mg taken once a day, still a very modest dose level compared to most drugs. Participants in this dose group had a maximum 1 log drop in HIV RNA, which is quite impressive given that it was used as a single agent and it is unclear what the ideal dose will be. There has been no significant impact on CD4+ cell numbers seen to date. Higher doses of the drug are still being studied.

### LOBUCAVIR

Bristol-Myers Squibb is continuing to develop lobucavir (cyclobut-G). Although the drug is a nucleoside analogue like AZT, ddI, 3TC, etc., it mimics a different amino acid—called guanosine—than previous drugs of this category and appears to be active against a wide range of viruses, not just HIV. Lobucavir may inhibit hepatitis B, various herpes viruses, and cytomegalovirus (CMV). Phase II/III studies of an oral form of lobucavir have already shown that the drug does not have useful activity against HIV, though studies may continue to test its activity against other infections, such as CMV.

## NON-NUCLEOSIDE REVERSE TRANSCRIPTASE INHIBITORS

### DMP 266

DMP 266 (efavirenz, Sustiva) is the newest non-nucleoside reverse transcriptase inhibitor and is currently in clinical trials. Encouraging results have been reported in both treatment-naïve and experienced groups, especially when the drug is used together with indinavir (Crixivan). However, early studies suggest that the drug is cross-resistant with the other non-nucleoside analogues and therefore individuals who have become resistant to nevirapine or delavirdine are not likely to benefit from DMP 266. In addition, DMP 266 is likely to have the advantage of once daily dosing and may be powerful enough to be effective in two-drug combinations with a protease inhibitor.

## PROTEASE INHIBITORS

Protease inhibitors work during a late stage of the HIV life cycle by inhibiting an enzyme that is crucial to the proper assembly of viral parts necessary to produce a new viral particle. By inhibiting the protease enzyme, new HIV

particles released from an infected cell are structurally defective, nonfunctional, and cannot infect a new cell.

Reports from studies involving second generation protease inhibitors have been uniformly encouraging. Protease inhibitors in varying stages of development include ABT-378, PNU-140690, 141W94, BMS-234475, and BMS-232623.

## ABT-378

Abbott Laboratories' second generation protease inhibitor, currently called ABT-378, is just beginning clinical studies. The underlying compound in this drug is very potent but, like the original version of saquinavir, is very poorly absorbed by the body. Therefore, Abbott is blending it with approximately 50 mg of ritonavir, which in turn solves the problem of absorption, just as it does with saquinavir. The blend of the two compounds will be marketed as a single new drug. ABT-378 has some overlapping patterns of resistance with the available protease inhibitors, but the company hopes that the drug's high potency may allow it to work even against resistant virus. Initial animal studies suggest that once- or twice-daily dosing will be possible. As with any drug in an early stage of development, it's not yet possible to predict how well it will actually work in human use.

## PNU-140690

Pharmacia and Upjohn is developing PNU-140690, which is just beginning human studies. In a laboratory setting, this compound has a different resistance pattern from the currently approved drugs and so should be active against resistant virus.

## 141W94

Preliminary results show that 141W94 (the Glaxo Wellcome/Vertex protease inhibitor also known as VX-478) has potent antiviral activity when used in combination.

In laboratory studies, this drug has a long half life which may permit less frequent dosing. 141W94 may also penetrate into the brain and lymph nodes, widening its potential usefulness.

## BMS-234475 AND BMS-232623

Bristol-Myers Squibb is beginning research on two new protease inhibitors, BMS-234475 and BMS-232623. The first protease inhibitor, BMS-234475, will soon be entering phase II trials, while the second, BMS-232623, is still in early animal studies. It is too early to determine the effectiveness and potency of the two drugs.

## NUCLEOTIDE ANALOGUES

### PMEA / BIS-POM PMEA

PMEA (adefovir, Preveon) is a nucleotide analogue that inhibits HIV in the same way as does AZT and other nucleoside analogue drugs, but it has the advantage of acting on many viruses in addition to HIV. Bis-POM PMEA is an oral form of PMEA. Three studies of bis-POM PMEA, giving the drug alone or in combination with AZT, are ongoing in the United States. To date, studies have indicated a level of antiviral activity similar to that of the older approved nucleoside analogue drugs, such as AZT, ddI, or ddC.

### PMPA

Gilead Sciences is developing oral PMPA, a nucleotide analogue, which has shown good antiviral effect with few side effects. The intravenous form has been effective over a short period of time. However, with the availability of an oral formulation, the intravenous form will not be further developed. The oral form of the drug will soon be tested in clinical trials, and early studies show that the drug may only need once daily dosing, which may be very helpful in simplifying complex antiretroviral regimens. Long-term studies of the oral form of the drug are just beginning.

## ANTI-HIV DRUGS WITH DIFFERENT TARGETS

### FUSION INHIBITORS

Pentafuside (also known as T-20) is an inhibitor of HIV fusion that is currently in phase 1 human studies. This type of drug works by attempting to interfere with the ability of HIV to attach to cells. This drug is administered intravenously, and based on animal studies it readily penetrates tissue and the lymph nodes. Lack of an oral formulation may hinder development of this product.

Another drug, FP-21399, currently being developed by Fuji Immuno-Pharmaceuticals, appears to work similarly to T-20 and is currently in phase I studies. FP-21399 appears to interfere with HIV's ability to enter into the CD4+ cell. This drug also has to be administered intravenously and also appears to readily penetrate tissue and the lymph nodes.

A third drug, ISIS 5320, from ISIS Pharmaceuticals, works by a similar mechanism of action. Studies have shown that this drug specifically binds to HIV's envelope protein, gp120, and inhibits the binding of both infectious virus and virus-infected cells to both CD4+ expressing and non-CD4+ expressing cells. In laboratory studies, this drug also blocks cell to cell transmission of the virus. ISIS 5320 is expected to begin clinical studies in the near future.

A note of caution about all three of these drugs is the fact that all previous HIV drugs that attempted to work by blocking viral fusion have failed, pos-

sibly because the virus is capable of finding secondary attachment sites for any one that is blocked by a drug. It appears that it is fairly easy to create fusion inhibitors that work in isolated laboratory conditions, but very difficult to make them work in the body.

### INTEGRASE INHIBITORS

A new class of drugs called integrase inhibitors has attracted major attention in the pharmaceutical industry for the last few years. The role of the integrase enzyme is to integrate HIV's genetic material into the host cell's DNA. Integration is essential for HIV replication and effectively blocking this step would prevent HIV from making new virus. Only one drug of this type, zintevir (AR177) which is being developed by Aronex pharmaceuticals, is currently in phase I/II studies, but there have been no results released from these studies. Zintevir has to be administered intravenously. Many companies report that they have found making drugs of this type to be extremely difficult.

### ZINC FINGER INHIBITORS

Several groups are developing compounds to inhibit the "zinc finger" of HIV. Zinc finger activity is common to many viruses and thus it makes a good target for drug activity. Zinc fingers capture HIV's genetic material and help package it into newly formed virions (a whole virus particle). The zinc fingers may also play a role in an earlier stage of the HIV replication process. Parke-Davis' compound, CI-1012, is currently in phase I multiple dose studies at the NIH (National Institutes of Health) and a few other sites. A Dutch company is developing Azodicarbonamide (ADA) which is currently in phase I/II studies for people with advanced stage disease in Europe. Because these drugs operate at a different site, prior resistance or failure with protease inhibitors should not have any effect on their potency.


## OTHER TREATMENTS TARGETING HIV AND OTHER VIRUSES

### HYDROXYUREA

Hydroxyurea (Hydrea) is a prescription drug that has been used for more than thirty years to treat certain cancers and other human diseases. In laboratory studies, hydroxyurea has been found to stop or slow the reproduction of HIV by blocking the production of a protein in the infected cell that appears to play an important role in the ability of HIV to reproduce. Researchers hope that by giving hydroxyurea to people already taking nucleoside analogues such as AZT, ddI, d4T, or ddC, lower doses of the nucleoside analogue compounds may be given while enhancing their beneficial effects. A study looking at hydroxyurea in combination with ddI and d4T showed a

significant reduction in viral load in people who had not previously taken antiviral therapy. Two recent European studies have reported that a few patients treated early in the course of HIV disease with ddI+hydroxyurea combinations have been successfully taken off therapy and show no return of detectable viral RNA after one year. The patients involved had low viral levels to begin with, so it is unclear what their status would have been without treatment. However, they initially had measurable viral load and it became undetectable and has remained so for year after stopping treatment. In each case, the patients had been treated for approximately one year with the drug combination. Although there are many unaswered questions about these very preliminary reports, it is the first time that anyone has reported such findings.

### ISIS 2922

ISIS 2922 is an antisense compound being tested to treat cytomegalovirus (CMV) retinitis, a viral infection of the eye that can cause blindness, in people whose disease has progressed while using ganciclovir or foscarnet. ISIS 2922 inhibits CMV in the test tube by interfering with the RNA produced by a critical CMV gene. ISIS 2922 is injected into the eye for treatment of CMV retinitis.

### GEM 132

GEM 132 is an antisense compound being tested to treat CMV. It is being studied for the treatment of CMV outside of the eye as a systemic (body-wide) drug and also as a treatment for CMV retinitis as a drug that can be injected into the eye. In laboratory studies, GEM 132 seems to be much more potent than ISIS 2922 and may be effective against drug resistant strains of CMV. While the drug is well tolerated in humans, its antiviral effects remain to be seen.

# Antiwasting Treatments

Weight loss and malnutrition are common problems associated with HIV disease. AIDS-related wasting is defined as an unexplained loss of 10% or more of a person's normal lean body mass. Although weight loss can begin and become severe anywhere across the spectrum of CD4+ counts, the risk of wasting rises dramatically when CD4+ counts fall below 100.

There are many options to prevent or treat weight loss, and different approaches may be needed at different times during the progression of HIV disease. Nutritional and vitamin strategies, though often less well documented than drug strategies, may also be helpful in treating weight loss. For a discussion on developing a comprehensive weight maintenance program, see the chapter "Developing a Strategy for Weight Maintenance and Nutrition." Manipulation of certain cytokines (chemical messengers that are produced by immune system cells) is also used experimentally to treat wasting syndrome. Drugs used for this purpose, such as thalidomide, are addressed in the "Immune-based therapy" section.

This section contains profiles of appetite stimulants, hormone therapy, and intravenously administered nutrition used to treat wasting, as follows:

**APPETITE STIMULANTS**
- dronabinol
- megestrol

**HORMONE THERAPY**
- anabolic steroids
- human growth hormone

**INTRAVENOUS NUTRITION**
- total/partial parenteral nutrition

# Anabolic Steroids

**BRAND NAME (MANUFACTURER)**
Oral methyltestosterone: Android (ICN)
Oxandrolone: Oxandrin (BTG)
Testosterone injections: Delatestryl (BTG); Depo-testosterone (Upjohn); Virilon (Star); Nandrolone: Durabolin (Organon)
Testosterone patch: Testoderm (Alza); Androderm (SmithKline Beecham)

**USED FOR**
Anabolic steroids are used to treat deficiencies in testosterone that result in weight loss, reduced sex drive, and loss of energy. Oral testosterone is also used to treat inoperable breast cancer in postmenopausal women.

**GENERAL INFORMATION**

Weight loss is a common symptom in people with HIV that has many possible causes and solutions. It can be caused by opportunistic infections that interfere with the ability to absorb nutrients. It can be caused by inadequate intake of food—not eating enough due to lack of appetite or not being able to keep food down because of nausea or vomiting. Oral problems such as thrush or dry mouth may also contribute to decreased food intake. Weight loss can also be caused by a poorly understood condition called wasting, where lean muscle mass is lost in people with chronic diseases like HIV, tuberculosis, and certain cancers. Finally, weight loss and wasting can be caused by problems at the other end of the digestive process, such as chronic diarrhea (see the section of this book on antidiarrheal treatments). It is important, whenever possible, to diagnose and treat causes of unwanted weight loss while at the same time managing the symptoms.

Anabolic steroids are derivatives of testosterone, the natural male hormone produced primarily by the testes. Women also produce testosterone, but in smaller amounts than men. Testosterone is responsible for the masculinizing and tissue-building (anabolic) changes that occur in males during adolescence, including the growth of the reproductive tract and the development of secondary sexual characteristics.

Approximately half of the HIV-positive men with CD4+ counts below 200 have testosterone deficiencies, probably caused by HIV suppression of normal endocrine-gland function or by drugs (like ketoconazole) used to treat opportunistic infections. These deficiencies are associated with the weakness and loss of lean tissue mass in HIV-related weight loss.

Oral and injectable forms of testosterone have long been available to treat testosterone deficiencies. The oral form is metabolized by the liver and is infrequently used because it can cause serious liver toxicity. Injectable forms are used more commonly, but they can cause transient high levels ("peaks") of the drug in the blood, which may increase the risk of side effects.

Synthetic forms of anabolic steroids, including oxandrolone and nandrolone, are also available. Oxandrolone is available as tablets for oral administration. Nandrolone must be administered intravenously. The advantages of synthetic steroids include lower risk of liver toxicity and fewer of the "masculinizing" side effects common when injectable testosterone is used.

Two different daily-wear, non-adhesive testosterone patches are also available. The Testaderm patch is applied to the scrotum and provides serum testosterone levels that mimic the normal daily pattern in healthy adults. The Androderm patch can be worn anywhere, but must be moved upon new application in order to prevent skin irritation. Transdermal (through the skin) delivery also

avoids the peaks and troughs in blood levels that occur with testosterone injections.

## TREATMENT

For treatment of HIV-related weight loss, anabolic steroids are probably most effective for people with abnormally low testosterone levels. Consequently, before initiating treatment, physicians usually measure their patients' testosterone levels. Currently, anabolic agents are not FDA approved for treating HIV-related weight loss.

The injectable forms of testosterone are usually injected deep into a muscle once every two weeks. The testosterone patch is applied on a clean, dry area of the scrotum and should be replaced after twenty-two to twenty-four hours or, in the case of Androderm, applied to clean-shaven skin. These types of approaches are usually used when an individual has abnormally low testosterone levels (i.e., hypogonadism), as testosterone replacement therapy. Studies of the testosterone patch, Testoderm, in people with HIV-associated weight loss showed that those using the patch had increases in testosterone levels to normal. However, those receiving the patch experienced less weight gain compared to people receiving a placebo patch. Therefore testosterone patch therapy may only be useful in treating hypogonadism and is probably not a good option for treating the symptoms of weight loss associated with HIV.

Oxandrolone is an anabolic agent, though not potent enough to be used as testosterone replacement therapy. Unlike the other therapies mentioned here, oxandrolone is approved for treating weight loss when the cause of the weight loss is unknown (e.g., not associated with low testosterone or an infectious agent, such as parasites, etc.). HIV-associated weight loss falls into this category. Doses of oxandrolone being studied for the treatment of HIV-related weight loss are 20, 40, and 60 mg per day. Oxandrolone is currently available through prescription in 2.5 mg tablets.

For maximum effect against wasting, both adequate nutrition and exercise should be combined with anabolic steroid therapy. The drugs make cells ready to build tissue, but they have little effect without the proper building blocks (especially proteins) or exercise.

## CAUTIONS AND WARNINGS

Anabolic steroids should not be used by anyone with a known allergy to them. Men with known or suspected breast or prostate cancer should avoid them.

Because little is known about anabolic-replacement therapy in women, anabolic steroids for wasting should be used with extreme caution. When used in women, non-masculinizing anabolic steroids should be considered as a primary option. Oxandrolone, however, has been studied in women and shown to have some masculinizing affects, although far less than what is commonly seen

with testosterone therapy. In small studies some women reported irregular menstrual cycles and vaginal bleeding. If women are using anabolic agents and begin to show mild signs of virilization (e.g., facial hair growth, deepening of the voice), they should discontinue anabolic therapy as these side effects can become permanent.

Because of the risk of serious side effects, people with heart, kidney, or liver disease should use anabolic steroids with extreme caution.

### SIDE EFFECTS

Prolonged use of oral anabolic steroids has been associated with severe liver toxicity and liver cancer.

Other side effects of anabolic steroids include breast enlargement, acne, prostate/urinary-tract infections, abnormal hair growth, excessive frequency and duration of erections, fluid or salt retention, nausea, jaundice, changes in sex drive, reduced fertility, hardening of the arteries, headache, anxiety, depression, shrinking of the testicles, and allergic reactions. There are many women-specific side effects associated with therapy with anabolic agents. These include: clitoral enlargement, menstrual irregularities, deepening of voice, hair loss, acne, changes in sex drive. While these side effects may also be associated with oxandrolone, they are seemingly seen less frequently than with testosterone therapy.

The most common side effects of the testosterone patch in clinical trials were scrotal itching, discomfort, or irritation.

### PREGNANCY/BREAST-FEEDING

When used during pregnancy, anabolic steroids can cause "masculinization" of the female fetus, including enlargement of the clitoris, abnormal vaginal development, and fusion of genital folds to form a scrotum-like structure. Anabolic steroids should not be used by pregnant women.

HIV can be passed from a woman to her child through breast milk. In areas where nutritionally sound alternatives are readily available, breast-feeding is discouraged for HIV-positive women. It is not known whether anabolic steroids are excreted in breast milk. Because of the potential toxicity of the drugs to infants, women are encouraged to consider alternatives to breast-feeding while using them.

### USE IN CHILDREN

Anabolic steroids should be used with extreme caution in children. The drugs can prematurely stop bone growth.

### USE IN THE ELDERLY

Older men using anabolic steroids are at increased risk of enlarged prostate glands and prostate cancer. They should use the drug with extreme caution.

## DRUG INTERACTIONS

Anabolic steroids may increase the effectiveness of blood thinners, like warfarin, necessitating reductions in their dosage. Anabolic steroids may also increase blood levels of oxyphenbutazone.

In people with diabetes, anabolic steroids may decrease blood glucose levels and insulin requirements.

## FOOD INTERACTIONS

Anabolic steroids may be used with or without food.

## OTHER DRUGS USED FOR SIMILAR CONDITIONS

Megestrol, dronabinol, and recombinant human growth hormone are other drugs used to treat HIV-related appetite suppression or weight loss. Some people use marijuana to stimulate appetite. There is no consensus at this time which is the most appropriate treatment.

Various antibiotics or antifungal drugs may be used to treat intestinal infections that interfere with absorption in the gut. Adequate nutrition is also important. The appropriate therapy depends on the cause of the weight loss and may include all these different types of treatments, including anabolic steroids.

## COMMENTS

While anabolic steroids have routinely been prescribed to people who are hypogonadal (have low testosterone levels), little research has been done on the effects of anabolic steroids in people with HIV. Because many men who are HIV positive and have signs of wasting or fatigue also have low testosterone levels, physicians routinely prescribe anabolic steroids as part of replacement therapy. Some HIV positive people use anabolic steroids combined with exercise primarily for aesthetic reasons, to look stronger and healthier. The consequences of this are unclear. Not much is known about how the use of these drugs affects HIV replication, disease progression, or survival. Even less is known about the use of anabolic-steroid therapy in HIV-positive women. Testosterone is not only anabolic (facilitating the building of muscle), it is also masculinizing. Therefore, there is reason to believe men and women may not benefit equally from this approach to managing weight loss. Oxandrolone, however, has been studied in women, though not specifically in HIV, and appeared to be effective in promoting weight gain.

# DRONABINOL

## BRAND NAME (MANUFACTURER)

Marinol (Roxane)

**OTHER NAME**

Delta-9-THC

**TYPE OF DRUG**

Appetite stimulant–antiemetic

**USED FOR**

Dronabinol is used to treat weight loss caused by loss of appetite in people with AIDS. It is also used to treat nausea and vomiting as a result of cancer chemotherapy in people who have not responded to other antivomiting treatment.

**GENERAL INFORMATION**

Weight loss is a common symptom in people with HIV that has many possible causes and solutions. It can be caused by opportunistic infections that interfere with the ability to absorb nutrients. It can be caused by inadequate intake of food—not eating enough due to lack of appetite or not being able to keep food down because of nausea or vomiting. Oral problems such as thrush or dry mouth may also contribute to decreased food intake. Weight loss can also be caused by a poorly understood condition called wasting, where lean muscle mass is lost in people with chronic diseases like HIV, tuberculosis, and certain cancers. Finally, weight loss and wasting can be caused by problems at the other end of the digestive process, such as chronic diarrhea (see the section of this book on antidiarrheal treatments). It is important, whenever possible, to diagnose and treat causes of unwanted weight loss while at the same time managing the symptoms.

Dronabinol, also known as THC, is a naturally occurring substance found in marijuana. It has many effects on the central nervous system, including effects on appetite, mood, thinking, memory, and perception.

The appetite-stimulant effect of dronabinol in the treatment of HIV-related weight loss has been evaluated in a number of clinical trials. The largest trial included 139 volunteers who received either dronabinol or a placebo. The dosage given was 5 mg per day, 2.5 mg taken one hour before lunch and one hour before dinner. About 38% of those who took dronabinol had improved appetite. This was significantly higher than those who took the placebo. People taking dronabinol also gained weight, reported that they felt better, and had less nausea.

The people who were originally given dronabinol and stayed on the drug after the study ended were reexamined later. The improvement in appetite continued for six months or longer in some of them, and about one-third experienced a weight gain of about a pound within three months of being on the drug.

Other clinical trials of dronabinol at dosages ranging from 2.5 to 20 mg per day have confirmed the drug's ability to improve appetite. The higher dosages are not recommended because they tend to cause side effects in a higher percentage of people taking the drug.

## TREATMENT

The effects of dronabinol are dose-related, and the response varies from person to person. Consequently, the dose must be adjusted for each person. The recommended approach to stimulate appetite is as follows:

1. Begin with 2.5 mg before lunch and dinner. If side effects occur, they usually resolve in one to three days with continued use.
2. If side effects are persistent or severe, the dose should be reduced to 2.5 mg before dinner. Taking the single dose in the evening or at bedtime may reduce the severity of side effects.
3. For people who have minimal or no side effects, the dose may be increased to 2.5 mg before lunch and 5 mg before dinner or 5 mg before both meals.

To treat nausea or vomiting, most people responded to 5 mg three or four times a day. Some doctors prescribe dronabinol with other antivomiting drugs such as prochlorperazine, because in clinical trials the combination was more effective than either drug alone, without additional toxicity.

## CAUTIONS AND WARNINGS

Dronabinol should not be used by people who know they are allergic to it, marijuana, or sesame oil. The drug is a central nervous system depressant and may impair a person's ability to drive an automobile or operate dangerous machinery. It should not be used with alcohol or other depressants such as benzodiazepines (e.g., Valium) or barbiturates.

It should be used with caution in people with history of cardiac disease because it may cause low blood pressure, rapid heartbeat, or fainting.

Dronabinol affects the nervous system. It may worsen mania, depression, or schizophrenia. Mood shifts and, less frequently, hallucinations may occur. These effects are reversible and disappear when the drug is stopped, but a physician should be contacted immediately by anyone who experiences these side effects while taking the drug.

## SIDE EFFECTS

The most common side effects of dronabinol are of the central nervous system, including elation, easy laughing, dizziness, confusion, and drowsiness. These are generally dose-related and reversible when the drug is stopped.

## PREGNANCY/BREAST-FEEDING

Dronabinol has not been formally studied in pregnant women. In animal studies, it did not cause fetal harm, but it is not known whether the same would be

true for humans. Pregnant women are encouraged to discuss the benefits and potential risks of using dronabinol with their physician before deciding to take the drug.

HIV can be passed from a woman to her child through breast milk. In areas where nutritionally sound alternatives are readily available, breast-feeding is discouraged for HIV-positive women. Dronabinol is excreted and concentrated in human milk. Because of the potential toxicity of the drug, women should consider alternatives to breast-feeding while taking it.

**USE IN CHILDREN**

Dronabinol is not recommended for HIV-related loss of appetite in children because it has not been studied in this population. Pediatric dosage for treatment of chemotherapy-induced nausea and vomiting is the same as in adults.

**USE IN THE ELDERLY**

Dronabinol should be used with caution in elderly people because they are often more sensitive to the psychoactive effects of the drug. Dose reductions may be necessary.

**FOOD INTERACTIONS**

Dronabinol should be used before meals.

**DRUG INTERACTIONS**

Used together, dronabinol and amphetamines or cocaine can cause additive high blood pressure, rapid heartbeat, and possibly heart damage. Atropine, scopolamine, antihistamines, amitriptyline, amoxapine, desipramine, and other tricyclic antidepressants can cause rapid heartbeat, high blood pressure, or drowsiness when used with dronabinol.

When used with barbiturates, benzodiazepines, alcohol, lithium, opioids, buspirone, antihistamines, muscle relaxants, or other central nervous system depressants, dronabinol can cause additive drowsiness and central nervous system depression.

Disulfiram or fluoxetine used with dronabinol may cause hyperactivity, excitability, elation, or difficulty concentrating.

Dronabinol may cause lower levels of theophylline in the blood, possibly reducing its effectiveness.

**OTHER DRUGS USED FOR SIMILAR CONDITIONS**

Megestrol, oxandrolone, testosterone therapy, and recombinant human growth hormone are other drugs used to treat HIV-related appetite suppression or weight loss. Some people use marijuana to stimulate appetite. There is no consensus at this time which is the most appropriate treatment.

If the weight loss is being caused by opportunistic infections in the gut, antibiotic, antifungal, or antiparasitic therapy may be appropriate. Similarly, oral thrush or dry mouth may cause people to eat less and lose weight. In

these cases as well, appropriate treatment of the opportunistic infection may result in improved appetite and weight gain. If the weight loss is the result of poor nutrition, appropriate therapy may include dietary supplements.

**COMMENTS**

Before or when using dronabinol, it is recommended that people talk to their doctor and investigate for an identifiable cause of the weight loss. If caught early enough, many diseases that affect absorption of nutrients in the gut can be successfully treated. Dronabinol has been shown to be effective only in improving appetite. It may be used successfully to treat the symptoms of weight loss, regardless of the cause, but the most effective therapy is likely to include measures to address the underlying cause of the problem as well as the symptoms.

To stimulate appetite, marijuana has been used by some people with AIDS. Because smoking marijuana can irritate the lungs, some people prefer cooking it in their food. Dronabinol is a synthetic version of THC, the psychoactive chemical in marijuana. Consequently, it may not be appropriate for some people who are recovering from alcohol or other substance abuse.

Absorption of dronabinol is often problematic. It works in only about a third of the people who use it. In the rest it may not work at all or it may leave people too euphoric or dazed to participate in ordinary activities.

# HUMAN GROWTH HOR-MONE (rHGH)

**BRAND NAME (MANUFACTURER)**
Humatrope (Lilly); Protropin (Genentech); Serostim (Serono)

**OTHER NAMES**
HGH, rHGH; somatrem; somatropin

**TYPE OF DRUG**
Hormone

**USED FOR**
Recombinant human growth hormone (rHGH) is a synthetic version of natural human growth hormone the FDA has approved for treating children who do not grow normally because their bodies do not produce sufficient amounts of the growth hormone.

The drug has also been approved as a treatment for wasting syndrome in people living with HIV.

**GENERAL INFORMATION**
Weight loss is a common symptom in people with HIV that has many possible causes and solutions. It can be caused by opportunistic infections that

interfere with the ability to absorb nutrients. It can be caused by inadequate intake of food—not eating enough due to lack of appetite or not being able to keep food down because of nausea or vomiting. Oral problems such as thrush or dry mouth may also contribute to decreased food intake. Weight loss can also be caused by a poorly understood condition called wasting, where lean muscle mass is lost in people with chronic diseases like HIV, tuberculosis, and certain cancers. Finally, weight loss and wasting can be caused by problems at the other end of the digestive process, such as chronic diarrhea (see the section of this book on antidiarrheal treatments). It is important, whenever possible, to diagnose and treat causes of unwanted weight loss while at the same time managing the symptoms.

rHGH is a genetically engineered version of human growth hormone, a naturally occurring chemical that stimulates normal growth in children. It causes an increase in growth rate and protein synthesis, while reducing body fat stores.

In late 1994, the results of a large multicenter trial of rHGH demonstrated that the drug reverses lean tissue loss in HIV-infected people with wasting syndrome. In the study, 178 volunteers received either rHGH or a placebo for twelve weeks. Volunteers receiving rHGH demonstrated a decrease in body fat and an increase in lean body mass. This may indicate that rHGH helps to correct a metabolic abnormality and addresses one of the underlying causes of HIV-related wasting. People receiving rHGH had an average increase of 1.7 kg of lean body mass over the placebo group and demonstrated increases in treadmill endurance, suggesting that the quality of weight gained promoted increased energy.

**TREATMENT**

In clinical studies, the dose effective at increasing lean body mass in people infected with HIV was 6 mg of rHGH injected daily under the skin. Studies are ongoing to determine if lower doses are equally effective.

**CAUTIONS AND WARNINGS**

rHGH may stimulate the growth of active tumors, so it should not be used by people who have cancers that are not under control. The drug may also cause insulin resistance, glucose intolerance, and abnormal functioning of the thyroid gland.

rHGH should only be used after treatable causes of weight loss such as opportunistic infections in the gut or poor nutrition are ruled out or addressed. There is no evidence that the drug works to prevent weight loss.

In test-tube studies, rHGH stimulated the growth of Kaposi's sarcoma (KS) and increased the levels of HIV in cells, although this effect was not observed

in a large clinical trial. People who use rHGH should be monitored for drug-induced changes in KS or HIV viral load.

## SIDE EFFECTS

Treatment with rHGH may cause people to develop antibodies to growth hormone found naturally in the body. These antibodies don't seem to interfere with normal growth in children and are not harmful to adults.

In clinical trials of rHGH for wasting syndrome, the side effects included joint stiffness, swelling, nausea, and abnormal levels of sugars and triglycerides in the blood. These side effects were usually mild and reversible when the dose of the drug was reduced.

## PREGNANCY/BREAST-FEEDING

There have been no animal or human studies of rHGH in pregnancy. Pregnant women are encouraged to discuss the benefits and potential risks of rHGH with their physician before deciding to use the drug.

HIV can be passed from a woman to her child through breast milk. In areas where nutritionally sound alternatives are readily available, breast-feeding is discouraged for HIV-positive women. It is not known whether rHGH passes through human milk.

## USE IN CHILDREN

rHGH is used extensively in children to treat shortness due to a lack of growth hormone. There are no reports of its use in children for wasting syndrome, although a clinical trial is currently under way.

## USE IN THE ELDERLY

No changes in dosage or administration are recommended for elderly people.

## DRUG INTERACTIONS

Using rHGH with glucocorticoids may reduce the effect of rHGH.

## FOOD INTERACTIONS

Because rHGH is administered by injection, it is unlikely that food will affect the absorption or effectiveness of the drug.

## OTHER DRUGS USED FOR SIMILAR CONDITIONS

Dronabinol and megestrol may be appropriate if the weight loss is caused by lack of appetite. Some people also use marijuana to stimulate appetite. However, the weight increase caused by appetite stimulants is often only in fat. People treated with rHGH in clinical trials have a decrease in body fat and an increase in lean body mass, which is considered a healthier form of weight gain. Anabolic steroids, including testosterone therapy or therapy with oxandrolone, may also be useful in promoting weight gain in the form of lean body mass.

If the weight loss is caused by opportunistic infections in the gut, antibiotic, antifungal, or antiparasitic therapy is appropriate, rather than rHGH.

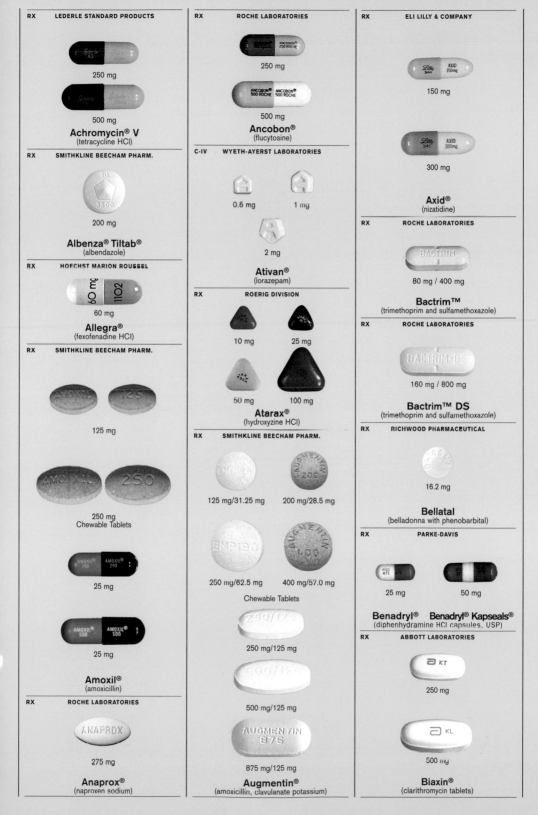


RX    LEDERLE STANDARD PRODUCTS

250 mg

500 mg

**Achromycin® V**
(tetracycline HCl)

RX    SMITHKLINE BEECHAM PHARM.

200 mg

**Albenza® Tiltab®**
(albendazole)

RX    HOECHST MARION ROUSSEL

60 mg

**Allegra®**
(fexofenadine HCl)

RX    SMITHKLINE BEECHAM PHARM.

125 mg

250 mg
Chewable Tablets

25 mg

25 mg

**Amoxil®**
(amoxicillin)

RX    ROCHE LABORATORIES

275 mg

**Anaprox®**
(naproxen sodium)


RX    ROCHE LABORATORIES

250 mg

500 mg

**Ancobon®**
(flucytosine)

C-IV    WYETH-AYERST LABORATORIES

0.5 mg      1 mg

2 mg

**Ativan®**
(lorazepam)

RX    ROERIG DIVISION

10 mg      25 mg

50 mg      100 mg

**Atarax®**
(hydroxyzine HCl)

RX    SMITHKLINE BEECHAM PHARM.

125 mg/31.25 mg      200 mg/28.5 mg

250 mg/62.5 mg      400 mg/57.0 mg

Chewable Tablets

250 mg/125 mg

500 mg/125 mg

875 mg/125 mg

**Augmentin®**
(amoxicillin, clavulanate potassium)


RX    ELI LILLY & COMPANY

150 mg

300 mg

**Axid®**
(nizatidine)

RX    ROCHE LABORATORIES

80 mg / 400 mg

**Bactrim™**
(trimethoprim and sulfamethoxazole)

RX    ROCHE LABORATORIES

160 mg / 800 mg

**Bactrim™ DS**
(trimethoprim and sulfamethoxazole)

RX    RICHWOOD PHARMACEUTICAL

16.2 mg

**Bellatal®**
(belladonna with phenobarbital)

RX    PARKE-DAVIS

25 mg      50 mg

**Benadryl®**    **Benadryl® Kapseals®**
(diphenhydramine HCl capsules, USP)

RX    ABBOTT LABORATORIES

250 mg

500 mg

**Biaxin®**
(clarithromycin tablets)

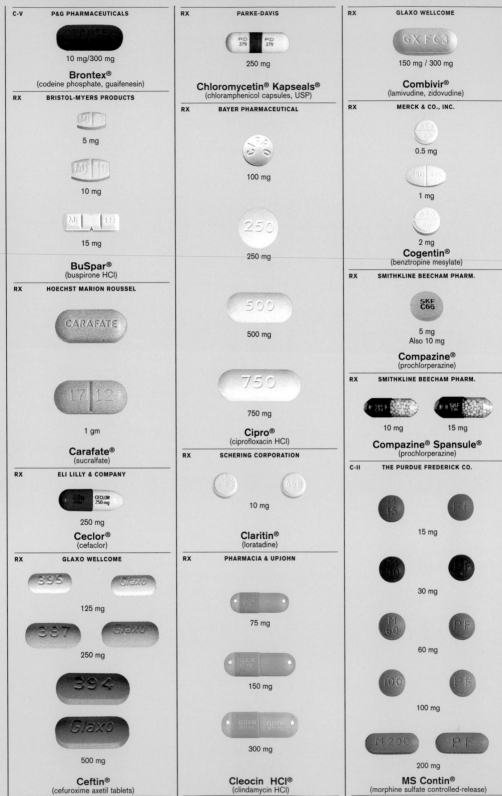

C-V  P&G PHARMACEUTICALS

10 mg/300 mg

**Brontex®**
(codeine phosphate, guaifenesin)

RX  BRISTOL-MYERS PRODUCTS

5 mg

10 mg

15 mg

**BuSpar®**
(buspirone HCl)

RX  HOECHST MARION ROUSSEL

CARAFATE

1 gm

**Carafate®**
(sucralfate)

RX  ELI LILLY & COMPANY

CECLOR 250 mg

250 mg

**Ceclor®**
(cefaclor)

RX  GLAXO WELLCOME

125 mg

250 mg

500 mg

**Ceftin®**
(cefuroxime axetil tablets)

RX  PARKE-DAVIS

PD 379  PD 379

250 mg

**Chloromycetin® Kapseals®**
(chloramphenicol capsules, USP)

RX  BAYER PHARMACEUTICAL

100 mg

250 mg

500 mg

750 mg

**Cipro®**
(ciprofloxacin HCl)

RX  SCHERING CORPORATION

10 mg

**Claritin®**
(loratadine)

RX  PHARMACIA & UPJOHN

75 mg

150 mg

300 mg

**Cleocin HCl®**
(clindamycin HCl)

RX  GLAXO WELLCOME

150 mg / 300 mg

**Combivir®**
(lamivudine, zidovudine)

RX  MERCK & CO., INC.

0.5 mg

1 mg

2 mg

**Cogentin®**
(benztropine mesylate)

RX  SMITHKLINE BEECHAM PHARM.

SKF C66

5 mg
Also 10 mg

**Compazine®**
(prochlorperazine)

RX  SMITHKLINE BEECHAM PHARM.

10 mg        15 mg

**Compazine® Spansule®**
(prochlorperazine)

C-II  THE PURDUE FREDERICK CO.

15 mg

30 mg

60 mg

100 mg

200 mg

**MS Contin®**
(morphine sulfate controlled-release)

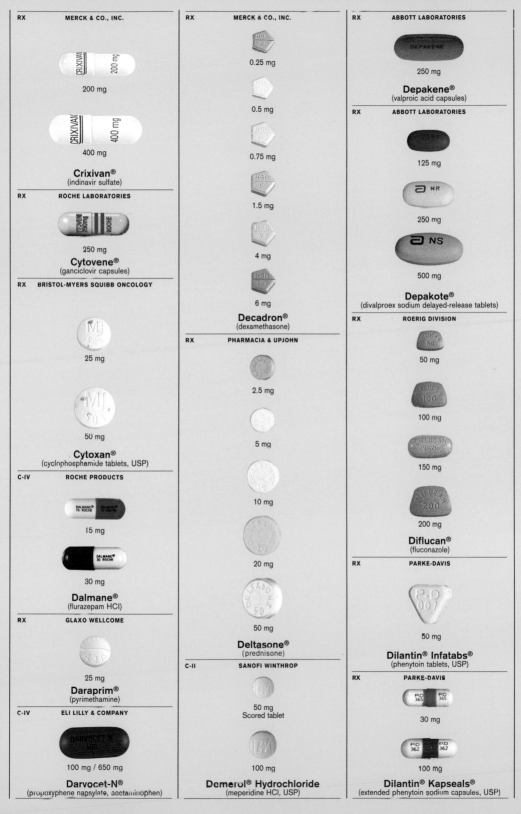

**RX — MERCK & CO., INC.**

200 mg

400 mg

**Crixivan®**
(indinavir sulfate)

**RX — ROCHE LABORATORIES**

250 mg

**Cytovene®**
(ganciclovir capsules)

**RX — BRISTOL-MYERS SQUIBB ONCOLOGY**

25 mg

50 mg

**Cytoxan®**
(cyclophosphamide tablets, USP)

**C-IV — ROCHE PRODUCTS**

15 mg

30 mg

**Dalmane®**
(flurazepam HCl)

**RX — GLAXO WELLCOME**

25 mg

**Daraprim®**
(pyrimethamine)

**C-IV — ELI LILLY & COMPANY**

100 mg / 650 mg

**Darvocet-N®**
(propoxyphene napsylate, acetaminophen)

**RX — MERCK & CO., INC.**

0.25 mg

0.5 mg

0.75 mg

1.5 mg

4 mg

6 mg

**Decadron®**
(dexamethasone)

**RX — PHARMACIA & UPJOHN**

2.5 mg

5 mg

10 mg

20 mg

50 mg

**Deltasone®**
(prednisone)

**C-II — SANOFI WINTHROP**

50 mg
Scored tablet

100 mg

**Demerol® Hydrochloride**
(meperidine HCl, USP)

**RX — ABBOTT LABORATORIES**

250 mg

**Depakene®**
(valproic acid capsules)

**RX — ABBOTT LABORATORIES**

125 mg

250 mg

500 mg

**Depakote®**
(divalproex sodium delayed-release tablets)

**RX — ROERIG DIVISION**

50 mg

100 mg

150 mg

200 mg

**Diflucan®**
(fluconazole)

**RX — PARKE-DAVIS**

50 mg

**Dilantin® Infatabs®**
(phenytoin tablets, USP)

**RX — PARKE-DAVIS**

30 mg

100 mg

**Dilantin® Kapseals®**
(extended phenytoin sodium capsules, USP)

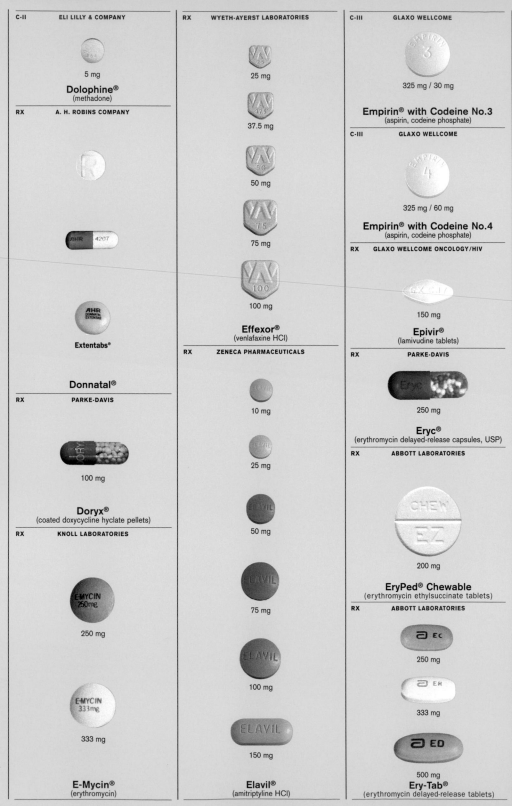

C-II    ELI LILLY & COMPANY

5 mg

**Dolophine®**
(methadone)

RX    A. H. ROBINS COMPANY

AHR    4207

AHR
DONNATAL
EXTENTABS

**Extentabs®**

**Donnatal®**

RX    PARKE-DAVIS

DORY

100 mg

**Doryx®**
(coated doxycycline hyclate pellets)

RX    KNOLL LABORATORIES

E-MYCIN
250mg

250 mg

E-MYCIN
333mg

333 mg

**E-Mycin®**
(erythromycin)

---

RX    WYETH-AYERST LABORATORIES

25 mg

37.5 mg

50 mg

75 mg

100 mg

**Effexor®**
(venlafaxine HCl)

RX    ZENECA PHARMACEUTICALS

10 mg

25 mg

50 mg

75 mg

100 mg

150 mg

**Elavil®**
(amitriptyline HCl)

---

C-III    GLAXO WELLCOME

EMPIRIN
3

325 mg / 30 mg

**Empirin® with Codeine No.3**
(aspirin, codeine phosphate)

C-III    GLAXO WELLCOME

EMPIRIN
4

325 mg / 60 mg

**Empirin® with Codeine No.4**
(aspirin, codeine phosphate)

RX    GLAXO WELLCOME ONCOLOGY/HIV

GX CJ7

150 mg

**Epivir®**
(lamivudine tablets)

RX    PARKE-DAVIS

Eryc

250 mg

**Eryc®**
(erythromycin delayed-release capsules, USP)

RX    ABBOTT LABORATORIES

CHEW
EZ

200 mg

**EryPed® Chewable**
(erythromycin ethylsuccinate tablets)

RX    ABBOTT LABORATORIES

a EC

250 mg

a ER

333 mg

a ED

500 mg
**Ery-Tab®**
(erythromycin delayed-release tablets)

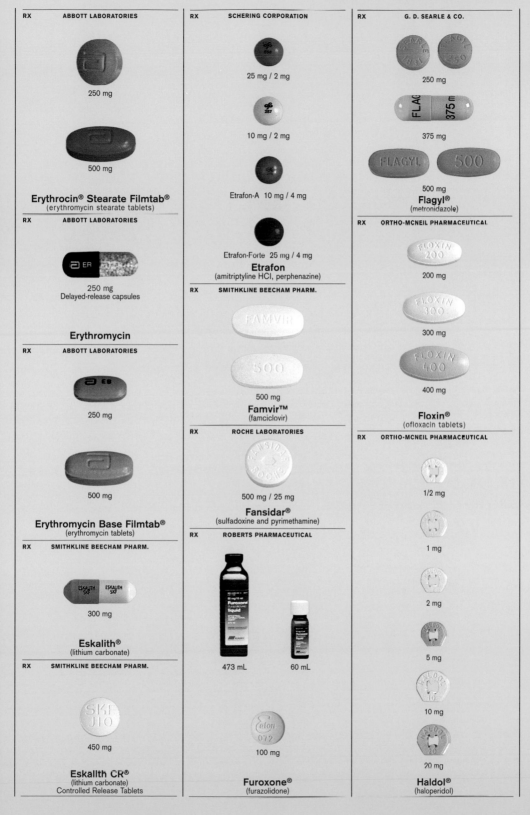

RX    ABBOTT LABORATORIES

250 mg

500 mg

**Erythrocin® Stearate Filmtab®**
(erythromycin stearate tablets)

RX    ABBOTT LABORATORIES

250 mg
Delayed-release capsules

**Erythromycin**

RX    ABBOTT LABORATORIES

250 mg

500 mg

**Erythromycin Base Filmtab®**
(erythromycin tablets)

RX    SMITHKLINE BEECHAM PHARM.

300 mg

**Eskalith®**
(lithium carbonate)

RX    SMITHKLINE BEECHAM PHARM.

450 mg

**Eskalith CR®**
(lithium carbonate)
Controlled Release Tablets

RX    SCHERING CORPORATION

25 mg / 2 mg

10 mg / 2 mg

Etrafon-A  10 mg / 4 mg

Etrafon-Forte  25 mg / 4 mg

**Etrafon**
(amitriptyline HCl, perphenazine)

RX    SMITHKLINE BEECHAM PHARM.

500 mg

**Famvir™**
(famciclovir)

RX    ROCHE LABORATORIES

500 mg / 25 mg

**Fansidar®**
(sulfadoxine and pyrimethamine)

RX    ROBERTS PHARMACEUTICAL

473 mL          60 mL

100 mg

**Furoxone®**
(furazolidone)

RX    G. D. SEARLE & CO.

250 mg

375 mg

500 mg

**Flagyl®**
(metronidazole)

RX    ORTHO-MCNEIL PHARMACEUTICAL

200 mg

300 mg

400 mg

**Floxin®**
(ofloxacin tablets)

RX    ORTHO-MCNEIL PHARMACEUTICAL

1/2 mg

1 mg

2 mg

5 mg

10 mg

20 mg

**Haldol®**
(haloperidol)

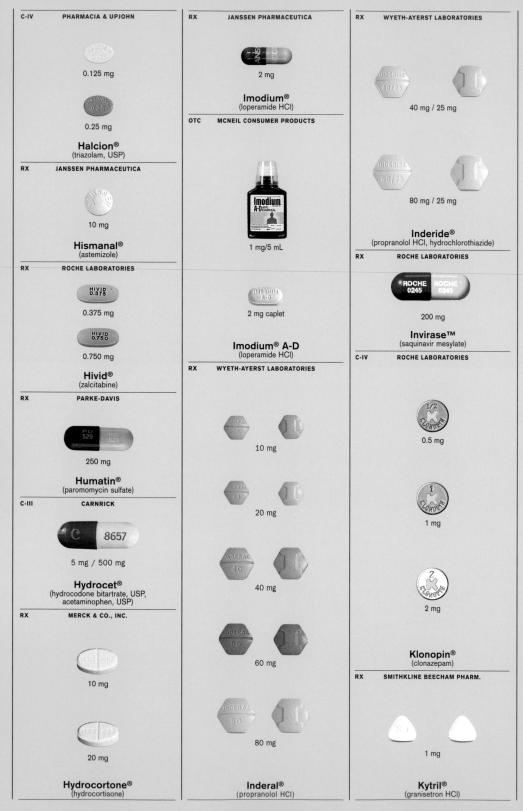

C-IV    PHARMACIA & UPJOHN

0.125 mg

0.25 mg

**Halcion®**
(triazolam, USP)

RX    JANSSEN PHARMACEUTICA

10 mg

**Hismanal®**
(astemizole)

RX    ROCHE LABORATORIES

0.375 mg

0.750 mg

**Hivid®**
(zalcitabine)

RX    PARKE-DAVIS

250 mg

**Humatin®**
(paromomycin sulfate)

C-III    CARNRICK

5 mg / 500 mg

**Hydrocet®**
(hydrocodone bitartrate, USP,
acetaminophen, USP)

RX    MERCK & CO., INC.

10 mg

20 mg

**Hydrocortone®**
(hydrocortisone)

---

RX    JANSSEN PHARMACEUTICA

2 mg

**Imodium®**
(loperamide HCl)

OTC    MCNEIL CONSUMER PRODUCTS

1 mg/5 mL

2 mg caplet

**Imodium® A-D**
(loperamide HCl)

RX    WYETH-AYERST LABORATORIES

10 mg

20 mg

40 mg

60 mg

80 mg

**Inderal®**
(propranolol HCl)

---

RX    WYETH-AYERST LABORATORIES

40 mg / 25 mg

80 mg / 25 mg

**Inderide®**
(propranolol HCl, hydrochlorothiazide)

RX    ROCHE LABORATORIES

200 mg

**Invirase™**
(saquinavir mesylate)

C-IV    ROCHE LABORATORIES

0.5 mg

1 mg

2 mg

**Klonopin®**
(clonazepam)

RX    SMITHKLINE BEECHAM PHARM.

1 mg

**Kytril®**
(granisetron HCl)

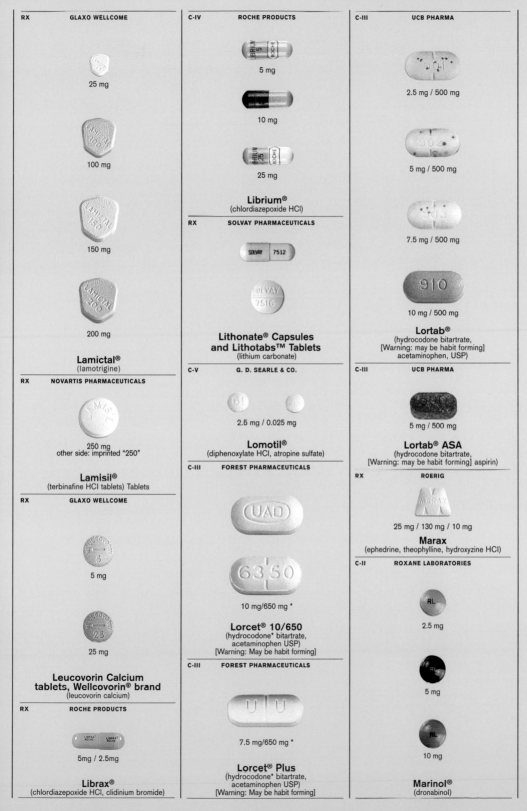

**RX  GLAXO WELLCOME**

25 mg

100 mg

150 mg

200 mg

**Lamictal®**
(lamotrigine)

**RX  NOVARTIS PHARMACEUTICALS**

250 mg
other side: imprinted "250"

**Lamisil®**
(terbinafine HCl tablets) Tablets

**RX  GLAXO WELLCOME**

5 mg

25 mg

**Leucovorin Calcium
tablets, Wellcovorin® brand**
(leucovorin calcium)

**RX  ROCHE PRODUCTS**

5mg / 2.5mg

**Librax®**
(chlordiazepoxide HCl, clidinium bromide)

**C-IV  ROCHE PRODUCTS**

5 mg

10 mg

25 mg

**Librium®**
(chlordiazepoxide HCl)

**RX  SOLVAY PHARMACEUTICALS**

SOLVAY 7512

SOLVAY 7516

**Lithonate® Capsules
and Lithotabs™ Tablets**
(lithium carbonate)

**C-V  G. D. SEARLE & CO.**

2.5 mg / 0.025 mg

**Lomotil®**
(diphenoxylate HCl, atropine sulfate)

**C-III  FOREST PHARMACEUTICALS**

UAD

63 50

10 mg/650 mg *

**Lorcet® 10/650**
(hydrocodone* bitartrate,
acetaminophen USP)
[Warning: May be habit forming]

**C-III  FOREST PHARMACEUTICALS**

U U

7.5 mg/650 mg *

**Lorcet® Plus**
(hydrocodone* bitartrate,
acetaminophen USP)
[Warning: May be habit forming]

**C-III  UCB PHARMA**

2.5 mg / 500 mg

5 mg / 500 mg

7.5 mg / 500 mg

910

10 mg / 500 mg

**Lortab®**
(hydrocodone bitartrate,
[Warning: may be habit forming]
acetaminophen, USP)

**C-III  UCB PHARMA**

5 mg / 500 mg

**Lortab® ASA**
(hydrocodone bitartrate,
[Warning: may be habit forming] aspirin)

**RX  ROERIG**

MARAX

25 mg / 130 mg / 10 mg

**Marax**
(ephedrine, theophylline, hydroxyzine HCl)

**C-II  ROXANE LABORATORIES**

RL
2.5 mg

RL
5 mg

RL
10 mg

**Marinol®**
(dronabinol)

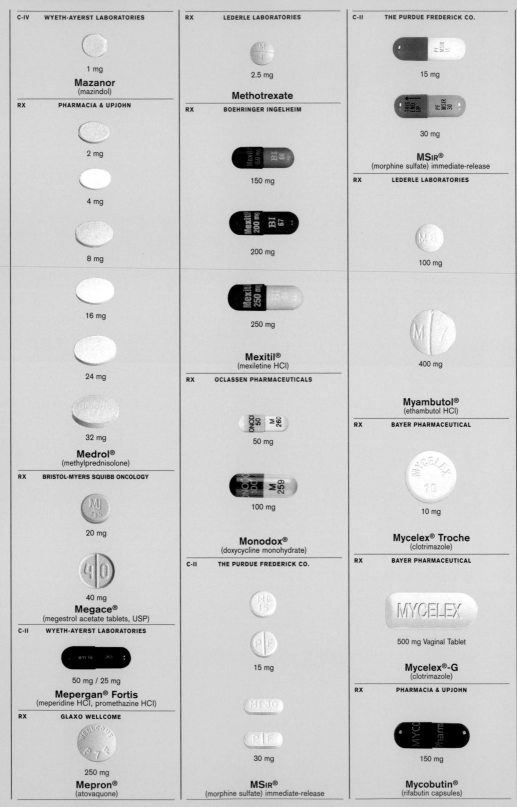

**C-IV**    WYETH-AYERST LABORATORIES

1 mg

## **Mazanor**
(mazindol)

**RX**    PHARMACIA & UPJOHN

2 mg

4 mg

8 mg

16 mg

24 mg

32 mg

## **Medrol®**
(methylprednisolone)

**RX**    BRISTOL-MYERS SQUIBB ONCOLOGY

20 mg

40 mg

## **Megace®**
(megestrol acetate tablets, USP)

**C-II**    WYETH-AYERST LABORATORIES

50 mg / 25 mg

## **Mepergan® Fortis**
(meperidine HCl, promethazine HCl)

**RX**    GLAXO WELLCOME

250 mg

## **Mepron®**
(atovaquone)

---

**RX**    LEDERLE LABORATORIES

2.5 mg

## **Methotrexate**

**RX**    BOEHRINGER INGELHEIM

150 mg

200 mg

250 mg

## **Mexitil®**
(mexiletine HCl)

**RX**    OCLASSEN PHARMACEUTICALS

50 mg

100 mg

## **Monodox®**
(doxycycline monohydrate)

**C-II**    THE PURDUE FREDERICK CO.

15 mg

30 mg

## **MSIR®**
(morphine sulfate) immediate-release

---

**C-II**    THE PURDUE FREDERICK CO.

15 mg

30 mg

## **MSIR®**
(morphine sulfate) immediate-release

**RX**    LEDERLE LABORATORIES

100 mg

400 mg

## **Myambutol®**
(ethambutol HCl)

**RX**    BAYER PHARMACEUTICAL

10 mg

## **Mycelex® Troche**
(clotrimazole)

**RX**    BAYER PHARMACEUTICAL

500 mg Vaginal Tablet

## **Mycelex®-G**
(clotrimazole)

**RX**    PHARMACIA & UPJOHN

150 mg

## **Mycobutin®**
(rifabutin capsules)

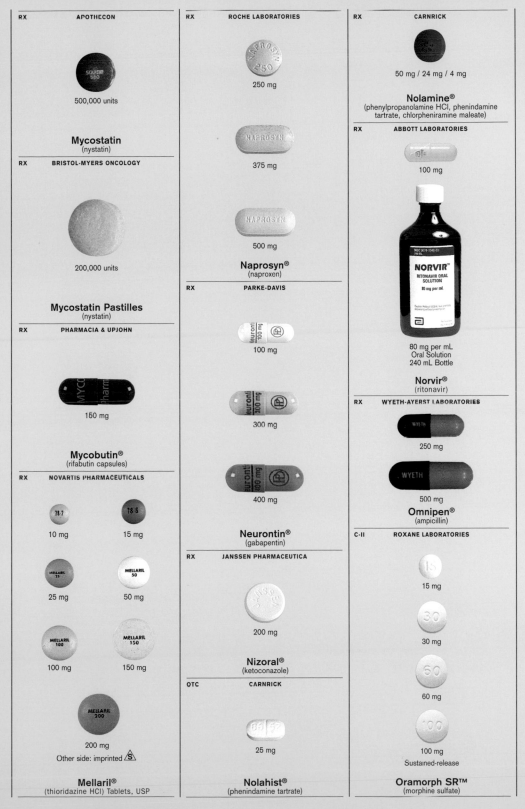

RX    APOTHECON

500,000 units

**Mycostatin**
(nystatin)

RX    BRISTOL-MYERS ONCOLOGY

200,000 units

**Mycostatin Pastilles**
(nystatin)

RX    PHARMACIA & UPJOHN

150 mg

**Mycobutin®**
(rifabutin capsules)

RX    NOVARTIS PHARMACEUTICALS

10 mg              15 mg

25 mg              50 mg

100 mg             150 mg

200 mg
Other side: imprinted

**Mellaril®**
(thioridazine HCl) Tablets, USP

---

RX    ROCHE LABORATORIES

250 mg

375 mg

500 mg

**Naprosyn®**
(naproxen)

RX    PARKE-DAVIS

100 mg

300 mg

400 mg

**Neurontin®**
(gabapentin)

RX    JANSSEN PHARMACEUTICA

200 mg

**Nizoral®**
(ketoconazole)

OTC    CARNRICK

25 mg

**Nolahist®**
(phenindamine tartrate)

---

RX    CARNRICK

50 mg / 24 mg / 4 mg

**Nolamine®**
(phenylpropanolamine HCl, phenindamine
tartrate, chlorpheniramine maleate)

RX    ABBOTT LABORATORIES

100 mg

80 mg per mL
Oral Solution
240 mL Bottle

**Norvir®**
(ritonavir)

RX    WYETH-AYERST LABORATORIES

250 mg

500 mg

**Omnipen®**
(ampicillin)

C-II    ROXANE LABORATORIES

15 mg

30 mg

60 mg

100 mg
Sustained-release

**Oramorph SR™**
(morphine sulfate)

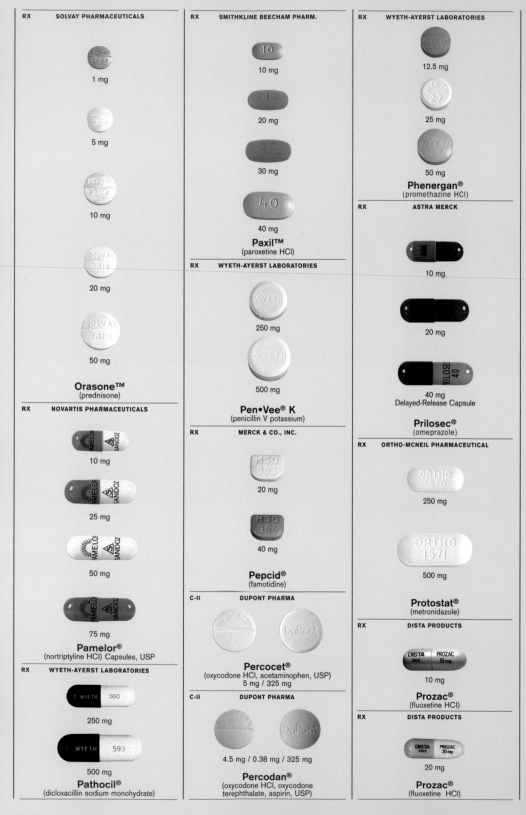

**RX** — SOLVAY PHARMACEUTICALS

1 mg

5 mg

10 mg

20 mg

50 mg

**Orasone™**
(prednisone)

**RX** — NOVARTIS PHARMACEUTICALS

10 mg

25 mg

50 mg

75 mg

**Pamelor®**
(nortriptyline HCl) Capsules, USP

**RX** — WYETH-AYERST LABORATORIES

250 mg

500 mg

**Pathocil®**
(dicloxacillin sodium monohydrate)

**RX** — SMITHKLINE BEECHAM PHARM.

10 mg

20 mg

30 mg

40 mg

**Paxil™**
(paroxetine HCl)

**RX** — WYETH-AYERST LABORATORIES

250 mg

500 mg

**Pen•Vee® K**
(penicillin V potassium)

**RX** — MERCK & CO., INC.

20 mg

40 mg

**Pepcid®**
(famotidine)

**C-II** — DUPONT PHARMA

**Percocet®**
(oxycodone HCl, acetaminophen, USP)
5 mg / 325 mg

**C-II** — DUPONT PHARMA

4.5 mg / 0.38 mg / 325 mg

**Percodan®**
(oxycodone HCl, oxycodone
terephthalate, aspirin, USP)

**RX** — WYETH-AYERST LABORATORIES

12.5 mg

25 mg

50 mg

**Phenergan®**
(promethazine HCl)

**RX** — ASTRA MERCK

10 mg

20 mg

40 mg
Delayed-Release Capsule

**Prilosec®**
(omeprazole)

**RX** — ORTHO-MCNEIL PHARMACEUTICAL

250 mg

500 mg

**Protostat®**
(metronidazole)

**RX** — DISTA PRODUCTS

10 mg

**Prozac®**
(fluoxetine HCl)

**RX** — DISTA PRODUCTS

20 mg

**Prozac®**
(fluoxetine HCl)

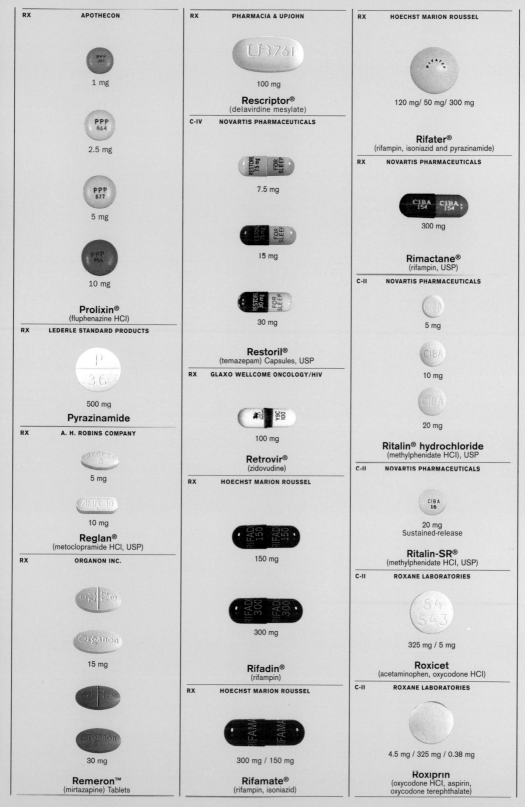

RX APOTHECON

1 mg

PPP 864
2.5 mg

PPP 877
5 mg

PPP 956
10 mg

**Prolixin®**
(fluphenazine HCl)

RX LEDERLE STANDARD PRODUCTS

P 36
500 mg
**Pyrazinamide**

RX A. H. ROBINS COMPANY

REGLAN 5
5 mg

10 mg
**Reglan®**
(metoclopramide HCl, USP)

RX ORGANON INC.

15 mg

30 mg
**Remeron™**
(mirtazapine) Tablets

---

RX PHARMACIA & UPJOHN

U 3761
100 mg
**Rescriptor®**
(delavirdine mesylate)

C-IV NOVARTIS PHARMACEUTICALS

RESTORIL 7.5 mg / FOR SLEEP
7.5 mg

RESTORIL 15 mg / FOR SLEEP
15 mg

RESTORIL 30 mg / FOR SLEEP
30 mg

**Restoril®**
(temazepam) Capsules, USP

RX GLAXO WELLCOME ONCOLOGY/HIV

Y9C 100
100 mg
**Retrovir®**
(zidovudine)

RX HOECHST MARION ROUSSEL

RIFADIN 150 / RIFADIN 150
150 mg

RIFADIN 300 / RIFADIN 300
300 mg

**Rifadin®**
(rifampin)

RX HOECHST MARION ROUSSEL

RIFAMATE / RIFAMATE
300 mg / 150 mg
**Rifamate®**
(rifampin, isoniazid)

---

RX HOECHST MARION ROUSSEL

RIFATER
120 mg/ 50 mg/ 300 mg
**Rifater®**
(rifampin, isoniazid and pyrazinamide)

RX NOVARTIS PHARMACEUTICALS

CIBA 154 / CIBA 154
300 mg
**Rimactane®**
(rifampin, USP)

C-II NOVARTIS PHARMACEUTICALS

CIBA
5 mg

CIBA
10 mg

CIBA
20 mg

**Ritalin® hydrochloride**
(methylphenidate HCl), USP

C-II NOVARTIS PHARMACEUTICALS

CIBA 16
20 mg
Sustained-release
**Ritalin-SR®**
(methylphenidate HCl, USP)

C-II ROXANE LABORATORIES

54 543
325 mg / 5 mg
**Roxicet**
(acetaminophen, oxycodone HCl)

C-II ROXANE LABORATORIES

4.5 mg / 325 mg / 0.38 mg
**Roxiprin**
(oxycodone HCl, aspirin,
oxycodone terephthalate)

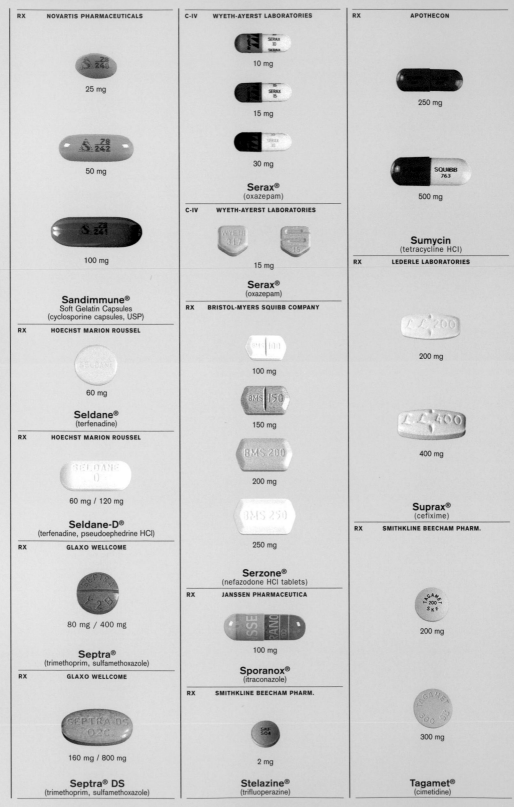

RX    NOVARTIS PHARMACEUTICALS

25 mg

50 mg

100 mg

**Sandimmune®**
Soft Gelatin Capsules
(cyclosporine capsules, USP)

RX    HOECHST MARION ROUSSEL

60 mg

**Seldane®**
(terfenadine)

RX    HOECHST MARION ROUSSEL

60 mg / 120 mg

**Seldane-D®**
(terfenadine, pseudoephedrine HCl)

RX    GLAXO WELLCOME

80 mg / 400 mg

**Septra®**
(trimethoprim, sulfamethoxazole)

RX    GLAXO WELLCOME

160 mg / 800 mg

**Septra® DS**
(trimethoprim, sulfamethoxazole)

C-IV    WYETH-AYERST LABORATORIES

10 mg

15 mg

30 mg

**Serax®**
(oxazepam)

C-IV    WYETH-AYERST LABORATORIES

15 mg

**Serax®**
(oxazepam)

RX    BRISTOL-MYERS SQUIBB COMPANY

100 mg

150 mg

200 mg

250 mg

**Serzone®**
(nefazodone HCl tablets)

RX    JANSSEN PHARMACEUTICA

100 mg

**Sporanox®**
(itraconazole)

RX    SMITHKLINE BEECHAM PHARM.

2 mg

**Stelazine®**
(trifluoperazine)

RX    APOTHECON

250 mg

500 mg

**Sumycin**
(tetracycline HCl)

RX    LEDERLE LABORATORIES

200 mg

400 mg

**Suprax®**
(cefixime)

RX    SMITHKLINE BEECHAM PHARM.

200 mg

300 mg

**Tagamet®**
(cimetidine)

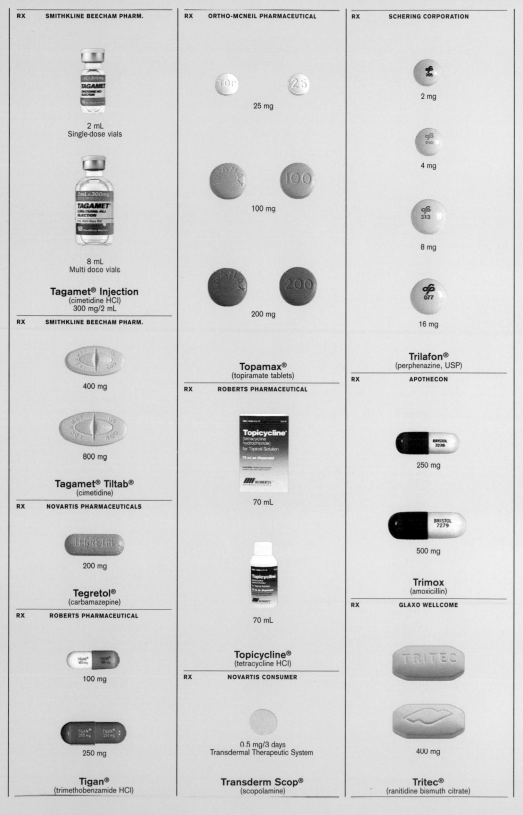

**RX**    SMITHKLINE BEECHAM PHARM.

2 mL
Single-dose vials

8 mL
Multi-dose vials

**Tagamet® Injection**
(cimetidine HCl)
300 mg/2 mL

**RX**    SMITHKLINE BEECHAM PHARM.

400 mg

800 mg

**Tagamet® Tiltab®**
(cimetidine)

**RX**    NOVARTIS PHARMACEUTICALS

200 mg

**Tegretol®**
(carbamazepine)

**RX**    ROBERTS PHARMACEUTICAL

100 mg

250 mg

**Tigan®**
(trimethobenzamide HCl)

**RX**    ORTHO-MCNEIL PHARMACEUTICAL

25 mg

100 mg

200 mg

**Topamax®**
(topiramate tablets)

**RX**    ROBERTS PHARMACEUTICAL

**Topicycline®**
(tetracycline
hydrochloride)
for Topical Solution
70 ml as dispensed

70 mL

70 mL

**Topicycline®**
(tetracycline HCl)

**RX**    NOVARTIS CONSUMER

0.5 mg/3 days
Transdermal Therapeutic System

**Transderm Scop®**
(scopolamine)

**RX**    SCHERING CORPORATION

2 mg

4 mg

8 mg

16 mg

**Trilafon®**
(perphenazine, USP)

**RX**    APOTHECON

250 mg

500 mg

**Trimox**
(amoxicillin)

**RX**    GLAXO WELLCOME

400 mg

**Tritec®**
(ranitidine bismuth citrate)

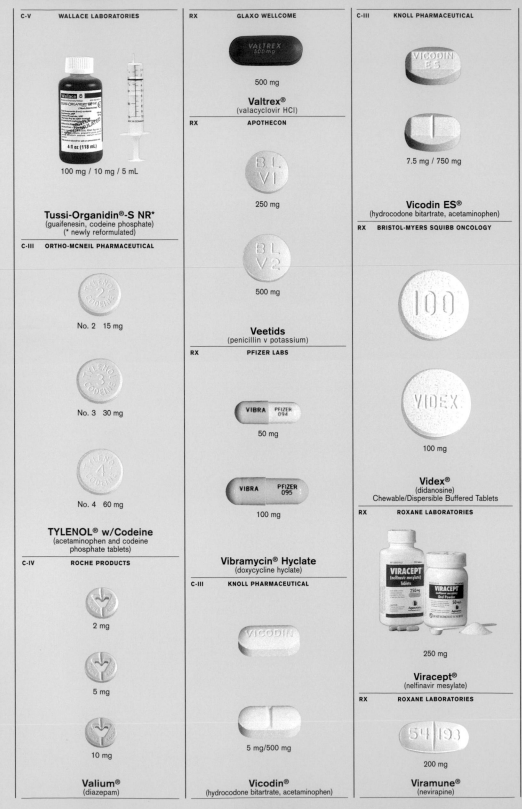

C-V     WALLACE LABORATORIES

100 mg / 10 mg / 5 mL

**Tussi-Organidin®-S NR\***
(guaifenesin, codeine phosphate)
(\* newly reformulated)

C-III     ORTHO-MCNEIL PHARMACEUTICAL

No. 2   15 mg

No. 3   30 mg

No. 4   60 mg

**TYLENOL® w/Codeine**
(acetaminophen and codeine
phosphate tablets)

C-IV     ROCHE PRODUCTS

2 mg

5 mg

10 mg

**Valium®**
(diazepam)

---

RX     GLAXO WELLCOME

500 mg

**Valtrex®**
(valacyclovir HCl)

RX     APOTHECON

250 mg

500 mg

**Veetids**
(penicillin v potassium)

RX     PFIZER LABS

50 mg

100 mg

**Vibramycin® Hyclate**
(doxycycline hyclate)

C-III     KNOLL PHARMACEUTICAL

5 mg/500 mg

**Vicodin®**
(hydrocodone bitartrate, acetaminophen)

---

C-III     KNOLL PHARMACEUTICAL

7.5 mg / 750 mg

**Vicodin ES®**
(hydrocodone bitartrate, acetaminophen)

RX     BRISTOL-MYERS SQUIBB ONCOLOGY

100 mg

**Videx®**
(didanosine)
Chewable/Dispersible Buffered Tablets

RX     ROXANE LABORATORIES

250 mg

**Viracept®**
(nelfinavir mesylate)

RX     ROXANE LABORATORIES

200 mg

**Viramune®**
(nevirapine)

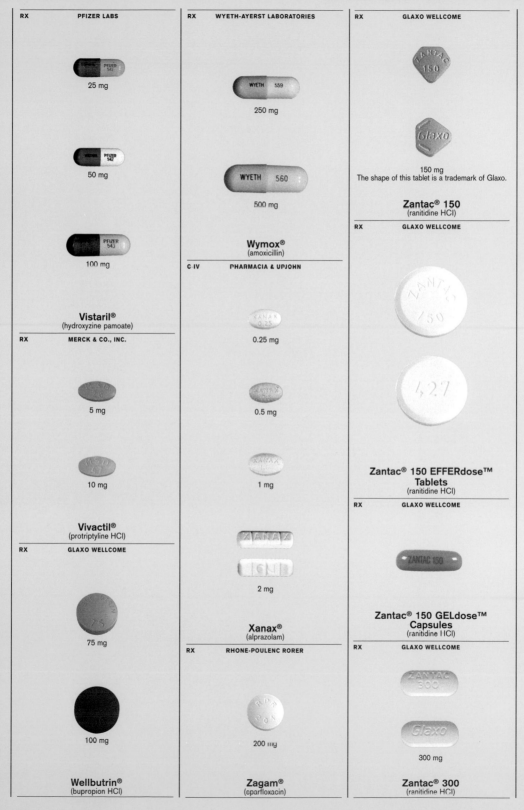

**RX**      PFIZER LABS

25 mg

50 mg

100 mg

**Vistaril®**
(hydroxyzine pamoate)

**RX**      MERCK & CO., INC.

5 mg

10 mg

**Vivactil®**
(protriptyline HCl)

**RX**      GLAXO WELLCOME

75 mg

100 mg

**Wellbutrin®**
(bupropion HCl)

**RX**      WYETH-AYERST LABORATORIES

250 mg

500 mg

**Wymox®**
(amoxicillin)

**C·IV**      PHARMACIA & UPJOHN

0.25 mg

0.5 mg

1 mg

2 mg

**Xanax®**
(alprazolam)

**RX**      RHONE-POULENC RORER

200 mg

**Zagam®**
(sparfloxacin)

**RX**      GLAXO WELLCOME

150 mg
The shape of this tablet is a trademark of Glaxo.

**Zantac® 150**
(ranitidine HCl)

**RX**      GLAXO WELLCOME

**Zantac® 150 EFFERdose™
Tablets**
(ranitidine HCl)

**RX**      GLAXO WELLCOME

**Zantac® 150 GELdose™
Capsules**
(ranitidine HCl)

**RX**      GLAXO WELLCOME

300 mg

**Zantac® 300**
(ranitidine HCl)

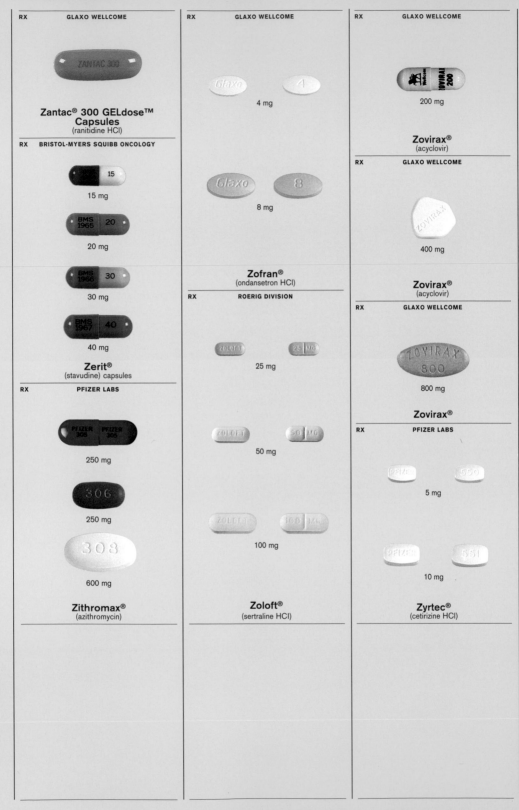

RX    GLAXO WELLCOME

**Zantac® 300 GELdose™
Capsules**
(ranitidine HCl)

RX    BRISTOL-MYERS SQUIBB ONCOLOGY

15 mg

20 mg

30 mg

40 mg

**Zerit®**
(stavudine) capsules

RX    PFIZER LABS

250 mg

250 mg

600 mg

**Zithromax®**
(azithromycin)

RX    GLAXO WELLCOME

4 mg

8 mg

**Zofran®**
(ondansetron HCl)

RX    ROERIG DIVISION

25 mg

50 mg

100 mg

**Zoloft®**
(sertraline HCl)

RX    GLAXO WELLCOME

200 mg

**Zovirax®**
(acyclovir)

RX    GLAXO WELLCOME

400 mg

**Zovirax®**
(acyclovir)

RX    GLAXO WELLCOME

800 mg

**Zovirax®**

RX    PFIZER LABS

5 mg

10 mg

**Zyrtec®**
(cetirizine HCl)

If the weight loss is being caused by poor nutrition or malabsorption not responsive to treatment, appropriate therapy may include dietary supplements or nutritional solutions administered intravenously.

**COMMENTS**
Before or when using rHGH, it is recommended that people talk to their doctor and investigate for an identifiable cause for the weight loss. If caught early, many diseases that affect absorption of nutrients in the gut can be successfully treated. rHGH may be used successfully to treat the symptoms of weight loss regardless of the cause, but the most effective therapy is likely to include measures to address the underlying problem as well as the symptoms.

Although rHGH appears effective in reversing wasting, it is expensive, even when obtained through expanded access programs. The cost should be compared to that of other methods for maintaining weight, some that can be even more costly, such as total parenteral nutrition (TPN).

Perhaps the best use of rHGH is in combination with good nutrition and exercise. Because studies show rHGH increases lean body mass and reduces fat, combining the drug with other appetite stimulants (such as megestrol) that primarily increase body fat may be useful. However, this combination has not been tested in clinical trials.

# MEGESTROL

**BRAND NAME (MANUFACTURER)**
Megace (Bristol-Myers Squibb Oncology)

**TYPE OF DRUG**
Synthetic hormone–appetite stimulant

**USED FOR**
Megestrol is available in two different forms. The oral suspension is prescribed for the treatment of anorexia and unexplained weight loss in people with HIV. The tablets are prescribed for treatment of symptoms of breast or endometrial cancer. Megestrol does not affect the course of breast cancer, endometrial cancer, or HIV; it simply alleviates the symptoms.

**GENERAL INFORMATION**
Weight loss is a common symptom in people with HIV that has many possible causes and solutions. It can be caused by opportunistic infections that interfere with the ability to absorb nutrients. It can be caused by inadequate intake of food—not eating enough due to lack of appetite or not being able to keep food down because of nausea or vomiting. Oral problems such as thrush or dry mouth may also contribute to decreased food intake. Weight loss can also be caused by a poorly understood condition called wasting, where lean

muscle mass is lost in people with chronic diseases like HIV, tuberculosis, and certain cancers. Finally, weight loss and wasting can be caused by problems at the other end of the digestive process, such as chronic diarrhea (see the section of this book on antidiarrheal treatments). It is important, whenever possible, to diagnose and treat causes of unwanted weight loss while at the same time managing the symptoms.

Megestrol is a synthetic derivative of the female sex hormone progesterone. It has been available for some time for the treatment of breast and endometrial cancers, but its use in HIV-infected people has been relatively recent.

In a number of clinical studies, megestrol improved appetite and increased the weight in people with HIV. In the largest trial, 270 volunteers received either megestrol acetate at doses of 10 mg, 400 mg, or 800 mg per day or a placebo. The volunteers had reduced appetite, malnutrition, substantial weight loss, and generally poor health before starting the study. Sixty-four percent taking 800 mg and 57% taking 400 mg of megestrol had statistically significant weight increases of five pounds or more compared to the placebo group. Most, if not all, of this weight gain was in the form of fat. People who gained weight also generally reported an improved overall sense of well-being.

## TREATMENT

For breast and endometrial cancer, the usual dose is 40 to 320 mg per day. For treatment of HIV-related weight loss, the usual dose is 800 mg per day to start, then reduced to 400 mg per day.

People with HIV taking megestrol for weight gain should continue taking the drug until they reach their desired weight. Then it may be discontinued until needed again, if ever.

## CAUTIONS AND WARNINGS

Megestrol should only be used after treatable causes of weight loss such as opportunistic infections in the gut or poor nutrition are ruled out or addressed. The drug should not be used to prevent weight loss, since there is no evidence it works for that purpose.

## SIDE EFFECTS

While significant numbers of volunteers in clinical trials reported diarrhea, impotence, rash, gas, high blood pressure, insomnia, and nausea, people receiving placebo reported these side effects as frequently as those receiving the drug. More rarely, megestrol causes serious blood clotting in the legs. It has also been reported to decrease testosterone levels and cause breast enlargement in men.

**PREGNANCY/BREAST-FEEDING**

Megestrol should not be used by pregnant women since it causes birth defects. Because of the possibility of birth defects, women taking megestrol are encouraged to use effective contraception.

HIV can be passed from a woman to her child through breast milk. In areas where nutritionally sound alternatives are readily available, breast-feeding is discouraged for HIV-positive women. Megestrol passes through breast milk, and although it has not been shown to cause problems in nursing infants, women should consider alternatives to breast-feeding while taking the drug.

**USE IN CHILDREN**

The safety and effectiveness of megestrol have not been studied in children.

**USE IN THE ELDERLY**

No changes in dosage or administration are recommended for elderly people.

**DRUG INTERACTIONS**

Megestrol may interfere with the effects of bromocriptine, so they should not be taken together. Rifampin may reduce the levels of megestrol in the body, possibly decreasing its effects.

**FOOD INTERACTIONS**

Megestrol may be taken with or without food.

**OTHER DRUGS USED FOR SIMILAR CONDITIONS**

Dronabinol, oxandrolone, testosterone therapy, and recombinant human growth hormone are other drugs used to treat HIV-related appetite suppression or weight loss. Some people use marijuana to stimulate appetite. There is no consensus at this time which is the most appropriate treatment.

If the weight loss is being caused by opportunistic infections in the gut, antibiotic, antifungal, or antiparasitic therapy may be appropriate. Similarly, oral thrush or dry mouth may cause people to eat less and lose weight. In these cases as well, appropriate treatment may result in improved appetite and weight gain. If the weight loss is caused by poor nutrition, appropriate therapy may include dietary supplements.

**COMMENTS**

Before or when using megestrol, it is recommended that people talk to their doctor to see if there is an identifiable cause for the weight loss. If caught early, many diseases that affect absorption of nutrients in the gut can be successfully treated. Megestrol may be used successfully to treat the symptoms of weight loss regardless of the cause, but the most effective therapy is likely to include measures to address the underlying problem as well as the symptoms.

The value of weight gain principally in the form of fat is unclear and disputed by many nutritionists. Ideally it would seem preferable to also restore

the lost lean muscle mass of people infected with HIV. For this reason, researchers are interested in studying megestrol in combination with therapies that improve lean muscle mass more effectively, such as anabolic steroids or rHGH.

Because megestrol has been shown to decrease testosterone levels, people taking the drug may want to have their testosterone levels monitored and utilize testosterone replacement therapy as appropriate. Low testosterone levels have been associated with unwanted weight loss.

# TOTAL PARENTERAL NUTRITION / PARTIAL PARENTERAL NUTRITION (TPN/PPN)

**TYPE OF DRUG**
Intravenous nutrient supplements

**USED FOR**
TPN and PPN are used to treat moderate-to-severe wasting in people with cancer and those living with HIV.

**GENERAL INFORMATION**
Weight loss is a common symptom in people with HIV that has many possible causes and solutions. It can be caused by opportunistic infections that interfere with the ability to absorb nutrients. It can be caused by inadequate intake of food—not eating enough due to lack of appetite or not being able to keep food down because of nausea or vomiting. Oral problems such as thrush or dry mouth may also contribute to decreased food intake. Weight loss can also be caused by a poorly understood condition called wasting, where lean muscle mass is lost in people with chronic diseases like HIV, tuberculosis, and certain cancers. Finally, weight loss and wasting can be caused by problems at the other end of the digestive process, such as chronic diarrhea (see the section of this book on antidiarrheal treatments). It is important, whenever possible, to diagnose and treat causes of unwanted weight loss while at the same time managing the symptoms.

TPN and PPN are liquid nutrients that are delivered intravenously through a thin flexible tube (catheter) that is surgically implanted in a major vein. PPN contains protein, carbohydrates, vitamins, minerals, and electrolytes. TPN contains these ingredients as well as essential lipids (fats). Some providers use PPN, in combination with solid-food nutrients, to treat moderate-to-severe wasting. When wasting becomes severe, TPN is used. Often, due to

expense (up to $13,000 per month), TPN is used too late to help restore body mass. As wasting increases in severity, it becomes more and more difficult to treat.

Relatively little information from clinical trials is available regarding the use of PPN or TPN in people with HIV. In small studies, TPN was most effective in people whose malnutrition was caused by problems with intake of food (such as difficulty swallowing) or malabsorption in the gut. In these people, TPN treatment resulted in increases in lean body mass as well as total body weight. In people whose malnutrition was caused by systemic infection, TPN treatment resulted in increased total body weight, but the weight gain was primarily in fat and water rather than muscle.

TPN has traditionally been regarded as a "last resort" when attempts at noninvasive dietary support and nutritional supplements have failed. Some physicians, however, take a more preventive approach and recommend using it temporarily after periods of weight loss to speed return to normal weight.

TPN and PPN are both administered intravenously.

**TREATMENT**
In PPN and TPN, the combination of nutrients is adjusted for each person's condition and requirements. An infusion pump is generally required, and the infusions can take from twelve to fourteen hours a day.

**CAUTIONS AND WARNINGS**
Because parenteral nutrition may cause metabolic imbalances, routine (generally weekly) screening of blood sugars and electrolytes must be performed on people receiving TPN or PPN.

The implanted surgical catheter must be kept clean and dry to prevent bacterial infections, which may be fatal.

**SIDE EFFECTS**
No definitive studies have been published on the side effects of TPN or PPN. Because the formulas consist primarily of ordinary nutrients, one might expect few side effects, provided the formula is properly balanced. As the length of treatment increases, the risk of bacterial infections through the catheter also increases. If not treated quickly, these infections can spread quickly to the blood and are sometimes fatal. If someone goes without eating solid food for any great length of time, it can become increasingly difficult to reinitiate oral food intake.

**PREGNANCY/BREAST-FEEDING**
HIV can be passed from a woman to her child through breast milk. In areas where nutritionally sound alternatives are readily available, breast-feeding is discouraged for HIV-positive women. Parenteral nutrition should be safe for use during pregnancy and breast-feeding.

**USE IN CHILDREN**

Parenteral nutrition can be used in children with compositions adjusted for their nutritional needs.

**USE IN THE ELDERLY**

No changes in dosage or administration are required for older adults.

**DRUG INTERACTIONS**

None reported.

**FOOD INTERACTIONS**

Parenteral nutrition may be used with or without solid food.

**OTHER DRUGS USED FOR SIMILAR CONDITIONS**

Adequate and balanced nutrition is the first step in maintaining lean body mass in people with HIV. Though their value is generally not proven by controlled clinical trials, vitamins and nutrient supplements may be helpful at all stages of HIV disease. Opportunistic infections of the gut should be treated aggressively to prevent malabsorption. Appetite stimulants, such as megestrol, dronabinol, or marijuana may be appropriate to treat symptomatic loss of appetite. Certain types of wasting may be treated with hormone therapy (e.g., human growth hormone and anabolic steroids), experimental cytokine manipulation, or parenteral nutrition. Each treatment for wasting has its advantages and disadvantages, but as with almost every aspect of HIV disease, preventing the problem is the best solution.

# CORTICOSTEROIDS

Corticosteroids are natural or synthetic versions of the hormones produced by the adrenal glands. They are generally immune-suppressive and affect a large number of biological processes in the body. They are used most often for their ability to reduce inflammation, especially when the inflammation is thought to be caused by excessive or inappropriate activity of the immune system. Arthritis, inflammatory bowel disease, and inflammation of the kidney are a few such conditions.

Some cancers, including a few types of leukemia and lymphoma, also respond to treatment with corticosteroids, and a number of corticosteroids are used in combination chemotherapy for Kaposi's sarcoma or AIDS-related lymphoma. Corticosteroids are sometimes used as supplementary therapy during treatment for Pneumocystis carinii pneumonia to suppress inflammation and the massive accumulation of white blood cells often seen with this disease. Corticosteroids are also widely used by people living with HIV to suppress the allergic reactions of certain drugs used to treat or prevent HIV-related opportunistic infections. They are also being studied for the treatment of HIV-related kidney toxicity. In a few instances, clinical trials have indicated corticosteroids may be useful in the general treatment of HIV disease, probably by suppressing excessive activation of cells in the immune system.

A wide variety of corticosteroids are available over the counter and by prescription. They have broadly similar actions, but they differ in their relative strength, duration of action, and form of administration.

The following corticosteroids are covered in this section:
- dexamethasone
- fluocinonide
- hydrocortisone
- methylprednisolone
- prednisone

# DEXAMETHASONE

**BRAND NAME (MANUFACTURER)**
Decadron (Merck), Dexameth (Major); Dexone (Reid-Rowell); Hexadrol (Organon)

**TYPE OF DRUG**
Corticosteroid

**USED FOR**

Dexamethasone is used to treat a wide variety of conditions including arthritis and other rheumatic diseases, connective tissue disease, skin disorders, allergic reactions, inflammation of the eyes, respiratory disease, certain blood disorders, inflammation of the brain, and to alleviate the pain of certain cancers. In people with HIV, it is commonly used alone to counteract allergic drug reactions and as part of combination chemotherapy for the treatment of AIDS-related lymphoma.

**GENERAL INFORMATION**

Dexamethasone is a synthetic steroid hormone, similar to those produced by the adrenal glands. Like other corticosteroids, dexamethasone has a wide range of biological actions. It is used most frequently for its anti-inflammatory effects, but it is also a potent inhibitor of certain immune responses.

Dexamethasone is available in a large number of different formulations, including tablets or liquid for oral administration, topical creams or lotions, ointments for administration to the eyes, inhalants, and as a solution for injection.

**TREATMENT**

The recommended dose of dexamethasone varies widely, depending on the condition, the formulation of the drug used, and the response of the individual. In general, a higher dose is used initially, followed by a lower maintenance dose.

Dexamethasone, like other corticosteroids, may cause severe side effects if stopped abruptly. In people who have used it chronically, the drug should be gradually tapered off under the supervision of a physician.

**CAUTIONS AND WARNINGS**

Dexamethasone should not be used by anyone with a known allergy to it or any of the other synthetic corticosteroids (including prednisone, methylprednisolone, hydrocortisone, and betamethasone). Injectable forms of dexamethasone include sulfites and should not be used by anyone with a known sulfite allergy.

Corticosteroids may suppress the immune response and worsen systemic fungal or bacterial infections (e.g., tuberculosis). Dexamethasone should not be used during active infections, unless it is being used to ameliorate the side effects of antifungal drugs like amphotericin B or as part of a comprehensive treatment strategy for bacterial sepsis.

Dexamethasone, like other corticosteroids, may mask some signs of infections, and because the drug suppresses some immune responses, other parasitic infections may occur while using it. Dexamethasone may also activate latent amoebic infections. It is recommended that amoebic infection be ruled out in people with unexplained diarrhea before starting dexamethasone therapy.

Because of the risk of serious side effects, people with liver or thyroid disease should use the drug with caution. Similarly, the drug should be used with caution in people with inflamed intestines, stomach infection, ulcers, kidney disease, high blood pressure, osteoporosis (bone thinning), and myasthenia gravis (a neuromuscular disease characterized by fatigue and exhaustion).

Dexamethasone can cause perforation of the cornea when used in people with herpes simplex infections of the eye.

### SIDE EFFECTS

Stomach upset, indigestion, and weight gain are common side effects of dexamethasone. More serious side effects usually occur only with high doses taken for prolonged periods. They may include abdominal enlargement or pain, weight gain, acne or other skin problems, bone pain or muscle weakness, bloody stools, sore throat, headaches, slow healing of cuts or bruises, increased urination, depression, mood changes, nightmares, shortness of breath, or unusual bleeding or bruising.

### PREGNANCY/BREAST-FEEDING

Large doses of corticosteroids taken over long periods during pregnancy can cause birth defects. Dexamethasone is usually not prescribed during pregnancy. Pregnant women are encouraged to discuss the benefits and potential risks of dexamethasone with their physician before deciding to use the drug.

HIV may be passed from a woman to her child through breast milk. In areas where nutritionally sound alternatives are readily available, breast-feeding is discouraged for HIV-positive women. Dexamethasone is excreted in human milk and can cause serious side effects in infants. Women are encouraged to consider alternatives to breast-feeding while using the drug.

### USE IN CHILDREN

Dexamethasone is used in children at dosages adjusted for age and weight. When taking the drug, children may be at increased risk of infection. Chicken pox and measles, for example, can be severe or even fatal in children taking dexamethasone who have not been exposed to or vaccinated for these diseases. Particular care should be taken to avoid exposing these children to the diseases while using dexamethasone.

### USE IN THE ELDERLY

Older adults are more likely to develop high blood pressure on long-term therapy with dexamethasone. Similarly, older women are especially susceptible to developing osteoporosis. Dose reductions may be necessary for elderly people on chronic therapy.

## DRUG INTERACTIONS

Use of dexamethasone together with insulin, oral antidiabetic medications, or digitalis may require increased doses of these drugs. Dexamethasone may alter the blood-thinning effect of warfarin, potentially requiring dose adjustments.

Oral contraceptives, estrogen, erythromycin, azithromycin, clarithromycin, and ketoconazole may increase blood levels of dexamethasone, potentially increasing the risk for the drug's side effects.

Barbiturates, aminoglutethimide, phenytoin, carbamazepine, rifampin, ephedrine, colestipol, and cholestyramine may reduce blood levels and the effectiveness of dexamethasone.

Dexamethasone may decrease the effects of aspirin, growth hormones, and isoniazid. Dexamethasone used with diuretics may cause severe loss of potassium from the blood.

Vaccination with live virus should not be done while taking dexamethasone, because the drug may interfere with the necessary immune response to the vaccine.

## FOOD INTERACTIONS

Oral dexamethasone, like other corticosteroids, may be taken with food to avoid stomach upset.

## OTHER DRUGS USED FOR SIMILAR CONDITIONS

A large number of synthetic steroids are currently available. They vary primarily in potency and in some side effects. Choosing one over another for a specific disease is usually a matter of preference and experience.

# FLUOCINONIDE

## BRAND NAME (MANUFACTURER)

Lidex (Roche)

## TYPE OF DRUG

Corticosteroid

## USED FOR

Fluocinonide is used for the topical treatment of redness, swelling, itching, and discomfort that occur as a result of allergy or inflammation.

## GENERAL INFORMATION

Fluocinonide is a synthetic corticosteroid, similar to the corticosteroids produced by the adrenal glands. Like other similar compounds, fluocinonide has a number of biological effects, but it is most widely used for the treatment of skin reactions caused by inflammation. Fluocinonide is not an appropriate

treatment for skin reactions caused by bacterial, fungal, or viral skin infection; the drug may make the infection and the symptoms worse.

Fluocinonide is available as cream, gel, ointment, and a topical solution.

### TREATMENT
Topical steroids are generally applied to the affected area as a thin film two to four times daily depending on the severity of the condition. In hairy areas, the hair should be parted to allow contact of the drug with the skin.

### CAUTIONS AND WARNINGS
Fluocinonide should not be used by anyone with a known allergy to it. It should also not be used in the external ear if the eardrum is perforated.

When fluocinonide is used topically and then covered with a waterproof dressing, significant amounts of the drug can be absorbed through the skin and into the bloodstream. These types of dressings should only be used with the guidance of a physician.

Like other corticosteroids, fluocinonide may worsen bacterial or fungal infections. If these infections occur during use of the drug, appropriate antibacterial or antifungal therapy should be started. If the infection does not improve, the steroid should be discontinued.

### SIDE EFFECTS
Infrequent side effects of fluocinonide include burning, itching, irritation, dryness, inflammation of hair follicles, rash, loss of pigmentation, thinning or weakening of the skin, secondary infection, and skin atrophy.

### PREGNANCY/BREAST-FEEDING
Corticosteroids taken internally may cause fetal harm. Topical corticosteroids are less likely to be absorbed well enough into the body to cause significant risk to developing babies, but there is some risk. Drugs in this class should not be used extensively on pregnant women, in large amounts, or for prolonged periods of time.

HIV can be passed from a woman to her child through breast milk. In areas where nutritionally sound alternatives are readily available, breast-feeding is discouraged for HIV-positive women. It is not likely that topical administration of fluocinonide will result in sufficient absorption to pose a significant risk to nursing infants. Nevertheless, caution should be observed by nursing women using the drug.

### USE IN CHILDREN
Children may absorb proportionally more topically administered corticosteroids and be more susceptible to their side effects. Administration of topical corticosteroids to children should be limited to the smallest effective amount to reduce the risk of side effects.

Parents should not use tight-fitting diapers or plastic pants on a child being treated for skin reactions in the diaper area. These garments may increase absorption of the drug to higher levels than was intended by the physician.

### USE IN THE ELDERLY
No changes in dosage or administration are required for older adults.

### DRUG INTERACTIONS
None reported after topical administration.

### FOOD INTERACTIONS
Fluocinonide may be used with or without food.

### OTHER DRUGS USED FOR SIMILAR CONDITIONS
Many other corticosteroids are currently available. They vary primarily in potency and in some side effects. Choosing one over another for a specific disease is usually a matter of preference and experience. Hydrocortisone is one of the least potent corticosteroids available, especially in concentrations available over the counter. It is also one of the safer corticosteroids and is unlikely to cause severe side effects when used as directed. Fluocinonide is more potent, requires a prescription, and has a greater risk of side effects.

# HYDROCORTISONE

### BRAND NAME (MANUFACTURER)
Anusol-HC (Parke-Davis); Cortef (Pharmacia & Upjohn); Hydrocortone (Merck); Hytone (Dermik); Cortaid (Pharmacia & Upjohn); Nutracort (Owen)

### OTHER NAME
Cortisol

### TYPE OF DRUG
Corticosteroid

### USED FOR
Hydrocortisone is used to treat various conditions including allergic skin reactions, Addison's disease, arthritis and other rheumatic diseases, adrenal hormone deficiencies, allergic drug reactions, asthma, some blood diseases, and inflammation.

Many people with advanced HIV disease have decreased adrenal gland function. Hydrocortisone is often used in these people as replacement therapy to correct the hormone level.

### GENERAL INFORMATION
Hydrocortisone is a synthetic steroid hormone, chemically identical to the hormone cortisol, which is naturally produced by the adrenal glands. Like other corticosteroids, hydrocortisone has a wide range of biological actions.

It is most frequently used for its anti-inflammatory effects, but it is also a potent inhibitor of certain immune responses.

Hydrocortisone is available in a number of formulations. Skin creams containing 0.5% to 1.0% hydrocortisone are available over the counter. More concentrated topical forms, injectable forms, suppositories, and oral forms are available by prescription. For most uses, the drug is applied topically.

**TREATMENT**

The recommended dose varies greatly depending on the formulation and the condition treated.

**CAUTIONS AND WARNINGS**

Hydrocortisone should not be used by anyone with a known allergy to it or any of the other synthetic corticosteroids (including prednisone, methylprednisolone, dexamethasone, and betamethasone).

When hydrocortisone is used topically and then covered with a waterproof dressing, significant amounts of the drug can be absorbed through the skin and into the bloodstream. This type of dressing should only be used under the supervision of a physician.

Bacterial or fungal infections may occur or worsen when hydrocortisone is used. Appropriate antibacterial or antifungal therapy should be used if these infections are present during use of the drug. If the infection does not improve, the steroid should be discontinued.

Because of the risk of serious side effects, people with liver or thyroid disease should use the oral or injectable forms of the drug with caution. Similarly, the drug should be used with caution in people with inflamed intestines, stomach infection, ulcers, kidney disease, high blood pressure, and osteoporosis.

Hydrocortisone, like other corticosteroids, may cause severe side effects if stopped abruptly. A gradual tapering off of the drug is necessary after prolonged use and should be done with the guidance of a physician. When the drug is used topically, tapering off is generally not required.

**SIDE EFFECTS**

The side effects of topically administered hydrocortisone are generally mild and may include burning, itching, irritation, dryness, thinning of the skin, slow growth of skin, or secondary infection.

The side effects of oral or injectable forms of the drug include dizziness, increased appetite, increased sweating, restlessness, sleep disorders, or weight gain. Serious, but rare, side effects include abdominal enlargement, acne, bone or muscle pain, blurred vision, black or tarry stools, convulsions, eye pain, fever, sore throat, headache, slow wound healing, mental depression, mood changes, muscle wasting, nightmares, unusual bleeding or bruising, and growth impairment in children.

**PREGNANCY/BREAST-FEEDING**

Oral doses of hydrocortisone taken during pregnancy may cause birth defects. Topical administration of the drug rarely results in blood levels high enough to harm the fetus. Pregnant women are encouraged to discuss the benefits and potential risks of hydrocortisone with their physician before deciding to use the drug.

HIV may be passed from a woman to her child through breast milk. In areas where nutritionally sound alternatives are readily available, breast-feeding is discouraged for HIV-positive women. Hydrocortisone taken orally or by injection passes into breast milk and may cause side effects in infants. Women are encouraged to consider alternatives to breast-feeding while taking the drug.

**USE IN CHILDREN**

Childrens' ydrocortisone dosages are routinely adjusted for weight and age. Young children may be more susceptible to side effects of the drug, including serious hormone deficiencies and pressure on the brain. Administration of hydrocortisone or any corticosteroids to children should be limited to the minimum effective amount to control the condition. Chronic administration of corticosteroids to children may interfere with their growth and development.

**USE IN THE ELDERLY**

Older adults may be more susceptible to the side effects of the drug and may require reduced doses.

**DRUG INTERACTIONS**

Most drug interactions occur with the injectable or oral forms of hydrocortisone. Generally, topical administration causes few drug interactions.

Aspirin and other nonsteroidal anti-inflammatory drugs (ibuprofen, naproxen, diflunisal, etc.) may aggravate the stomach upset caused by hydrocortisone. The dosage of blood thinners such as warfarin, oral antidiabetic drugs, or insulin may need to be adjusted when using hydrocortisone.

Hydrocortisone used with certain diuretics or digoxin may cause serious depletion of potassium in the body. Phenobarbital, phenytoin, rifampin, and ephedrine can reduce blood levels of hydrocortisone, potentially reducing its effectiveness as a systemic medication.

Oral contraceptives and estrogen may increase hydrocortisone levels in the blood, potentially increasing the risk of the drug's side effects.

Hydrocortisone may reduce blood levels of aspirin or isoniazid from the body, potentially reducing the effectiveness of these drugs. Cholestyramine and colestipol can reduce the absorption of hydrocortisone.

**FOOD INTERACTIONS**

Oral hydrocortisone may be taken with food to reduce stomach upset.

**OTHER DRUGS USED FOR SIMILAR CONDITIONS**

A large number of other corticosteroids are currently available. They vary primarily in potency and in side effects. Choosing one over another for a specific disease is usually a matter of preference and experience. Hydrocortisone is one of the least potent corticosteroids, especially in concentrations available over the counter. It is also one of the safer corticosteroids and is unlikely to cause severe side effects when used as directed.

# METHYLPREDNISOLONE

**BRAND NAME (MANUFACTURER)**

Medrol (Pharmacia & Upjohn); Solu-Medrol (Pharmacia & Upjohn); Depo-Medrol (Pharmacia & Upjohn)

**TYPE OF DRUG**

Corticosteroid

**USED FOR**

Methylprednisolone is used to treat a wide variety of conditions including hormone deficiencies, arthritis and other rheumatic diseases, connective tissue disease, skin disorders, allergic reactions, inflammation of the eyes, respiratory disease, certain blood disorders, inflammation of the brain, multiple sclerosis, certain kidney diseases, and palliative treatment of certain cancers.

**GENERAL INFORMATION**

Methylprednisolone is a synthetic steroid hormone, similar to those produced by the adrenal glands. Like other corticosteroids, it has a wide range of biological actions. It is used most frequently for its anti-inflammatory effects, but it is also a potent inhibitor of some other immune responses.

Methylprednisolone is available as tablets or liquid for oral administration, ointment for topical administration, and as a solution for injection.

**TREATMENT**

The initial dosage of oral methylprednisolone may vary from 4 to 48 mg per day depending on the condition being treated. Similarly, there is considerable variation in the dosages of the ointment prescribed for skin conditions.

Effective dosages vary from person to person and must be individualized on the basis of the disease and the response of the individual. If no response occurs after a reasonable period of time, another corticosteroid should be tried. After a response is obtained, the drug should gradually be tapered down to the lowest dose that is effective. Temporary increases in dosage may be required if the individual goes through stressful situations.

Methylprednisolone taken internally, like other corticosteroids, should not be stopped abruptly but should be gradually tapered off under the guidance of a physician.

## CAUTIONS AND WARNINGS

Methylprednisolone should not be used by anyone with a known allergy to it or by people with systemic (bodywide) fungal infections.

Corticosteroids, including methylprednisolone, may mask signs of infection, and new infections may appear during their use. There may be decreased resistance and difficulty localizing infections while taking corticosteroids.

Corticosteroid therapy should be stopped while undergoing vaccinations (especially smallpox), as it may prevent a sufficient response to provide immunity.

Methylprednisolone may reactivate latent tuberculosis. Treatment to prevent recurrent tuberculosis is recommended in people using corticosteroids.

People using systemic corticosteroids are more susceptible to infections. Chicken pox and measles, for example, can be more serious and potentially fatal in unvaccinated children or in adults using corticosteroids.

Corticosteroids should be used with caution in people with herpes simplex infections of the eye, because of the risk of perforation of the cornea.

Corticosteroids may aggravate existing emotional instability or psychosis.

## SIDE EFFECTS

At low doses, methylprednisolone rarely causes severe side effects. Common side effects include indigestion, weight gain, and salt or fluid retention. Prolonged use at higher doses may cause diabetes, glaucoma, muscle weakness, cataracts, seizures, thin or fragile skin, and fragile bones. The drug may retard the growth and development of children. It may also suppress immune function and cause opportunistic infections.

## PREGNANCY/BREAST-FEEDING

Methylprednisolone has not been formally studied in pregnant women. In clinical practice, topical use or injection into joints has not caused fetal harm. In low doses, the oral form of the drug is unlikely to cause harm to the baby. Pregnant women are encouraged to discuss the benefits and potential risks of methylprednisolone with their physician before deciding to use the drug.

HIV can be passed from a woman to her child through breast milk. In areas where nutritionally sound alternatives are readily available, breast-feeding is discouraged for HIV-positive women. There is no evidence that topical administration or injection of methylprednisolone into joints of breast-feeding women harms nursing infants. However, when the drug is taken orally, it may interfere with a nursing baby's growth. Women are encouraged to consider alternatives to breast-feeding while using the drug.

## USE IN CHILDREN

Dosage in infants and children should be adjusted for weight and age. Caution is advised, because the drug may affect their growth and development.

**USE IN THE ELDERLY**
Older adults may be more susceptible to the side effects of the drug and may require reduced doses.

**DRUG INTERACTIONS**
When cyclosporine is used with methylprednisolone, the blood levels of either drug may be increased, increasing the risk of drug-related side effects. Convulsions have been reported when the two drugs were used together.

Drugs that stimulate liver enzymes such as phenobarbital, phenytoin, and rifampin may reduce blood levels of methylprednisolone. Troleandomycin and ketoconazole may increase blood levels of methylprednisolone.

Methylprednisolone may decrease blood levels of chronic high-dose aspirin, which may reduce the effectiveness of the aspirin or increase the risk of aspirin toxicity when methylprednisolone is stopped.

Methylprednisolone may enhance or interfere with the effectiveness of oral blood thinners such as warfarin. Methylprednisolone taken orally or by injection may reduce blood levels of insulin, other antidiabetic drugs, or drugs used to control blood pressure.

Alcohol taken with oral methylprednisolone may increase the risk of peptic ulcers.

**FOOD INTERACTIONS**
A low-sodium and high-potassium diet is recommended when the oral or injectable forms of methylprednisolone are used for extended periods. Salt intake may need to be restricted when taking the drug orally, because the drug may cause salt retention.

**OTHER DRUGS USED FOR SIMILAR CONDITIONS**
A large number of synthetic steroids are currently available. They vary primarily in potency and in some side effects. Choosing one over another for a specific disease is usually a matter of preference and experience.

# PREDNISONE

**BRAND NAME (MANUFACTURER)**
Deltasone (Pharmacia & Upjohn); Liquid Pred (Muro); Meticorten (Schering); Orasone (Reid-Rowell)

**TYPE OF DRUG**
Corticosteroid

**USED FOR**
Prednisone is used to treat a wide variety of conditions including hormone deficiencies, arthritis and other rheumatic diseases, connective tissue disease, skin disorders, allergic reactions, inflammation of the eyes, respiratory dis-

ease, certain blood disorders, inflammation of the brain, multiple sclerosis, and to alleviate the pain of treatment of certain cancers. Less often, it is used in combination therapy to prevent organ or tissue transplant rejection.

In people with HIV, prednisone is commonly used to counteract allergic drug reactions and as part of combination chemotherapy for the treatment of AIDS-related lymphoma. It is also frequently used to treat people with severe *Pneumocystis carinii* pneumonia (PCP) and low blood oxygen to reduce lung inflammation and improve oxygenation of the blood. In recent studies, prednisone has been tested as a supplementary treatment used with general antiviral therapy. This approach uses the drug to counteract the overstimulation of immune system cells often seen in HIV disease. Results, while so far inconclusive, have been sufficiently positive to warrant further study.

## GENERAL INFORMATION

Prednisone is a synthetic steroid hormone, similar to those produced by the adrenal glands. Like other corticosteroids, prednisone has a wide range of biological actions. It is used most frequently for its anti-inflammatory effects, and as a potent inhibitor of certain immune responses.

Prednisone is available as tablets or liquid for oral administration.

## TREATMENT

The usual recommended dose of prednisone is about 1 mg per kg of body weight per day, depending on the specific condition being treated and the response of the individual.

Use of prednisone, like other corticosteroids, should not be stopped abruptly. The dosage should be gradually reduced under the guidance of a physician.

## CAUTIONS AND WARNINGS

Prednisone should not be used by anyone with a known allergy to it.

Corticosteroids, including prednisone, may mask some signs of infection, and new infections may appear during their use. Consequently, prednisone should be used with caution by people with systemic fungal infections.

Vaccinations should not be performed during prednisone or other corticosteroid therapy, because the drugs may interfere with the immune system's response to the vaccine.

Prednisone may reactivate latent tuberculosis. People with this condition who must use corticosteroids should use supplement drug treatment to prevent recurrent tuberculosis symptoms.

People using systemic corticosteroids are more susceptible to infections than healthy individuals. Chicken pox and measles, for example, can be more serious and potentially fatal in children who have not be vaccinated or in adults using corticosteroids.

Corticosteroids should be used with caution in people with herpes simplex infections of the eye, because of the risk of perforation of the cornea.

Prolonged use of prednisone may reduce potassium levels in the body to the point where supplements are needed.

## SIDE EFFECTS

When used at low doses, prednisone rarely causes serious side effects. Large doses, taken over prolonged periods, may cause indigestion, mood changes, bone or muscle weakness, fluid retention, acne, diabetes, facial rounding, abnormal hair growth, and high blood pressure.

## PREGNANCY/BREAST-FEEDING

Prednisone has not been formally studied in pregnant women, but other corticosteroids have caused serious fetal side effects when used during pregnancy. Pregnant women are encouraged to discuss the benefits and potential risks of the drug with their physician before deciding to use it.

HIV may be passed from a woman to her child through breast milk. In areas where nutritionally sound alternatives are readily available, breast-feeding is discouraged for HIV-positive women. Prednisone is excreted in human milk. Because of the potential toxicity of the drug, women are encouraged to consider alternatives to breast-feeding while using it.

## USE IN CHILDREN

Prednisone is used in children at dosages adjusted for age and weight.

## USE IN THE ELDERLY

Older adults may be more susceptible to the side effects of the drug and may require reduced doses.

## DRUG INTERACTIONS

Phenobarbital, phenytoin, and rifampin may reduce blood levels of prednisone, potentially reducing the drug's effectiveness. Ketoconazole may increase blood levels of prednisone, potentially increasing the risk of its side effects. Prednisone may decrease blood levels of aspirin or other salicylates. Prednisone may also increase or decrease the blood levels of oral blood thinners such as warfarin. Alcohol used with prednisone may increase the risk of ulcers.

## FOOD INTERACTIONS

Salt intake may need to be restricted when taking prednisone, because the drug may cause salt retention. The drug should be taken with food.

## OTHER DRUGS USED FOR SIMILAR CONDITIONS

A large number of synthetic steroids are currently available. They vary primarily in potency and in some side effects. Choosing one over another for a specific disease is usually a matter of preference and experience. For other anti-inflammatory purposes, a number of nonsteroidal anti-inflammatory drugs are available, including aspirin, ibuprofen, naproxen, and others.

# IMMUNE-BASED THERAPY

Immune-based therapies are treatments that have their effect by enhancing the general activity of the immune system or by specifically modulating the activity of some of its components. They may be used to help restore a person's general immune responsiveness, suppress specific viral infections, or counteract the bone marrow toxicity of some of the drugs used for HIV-related conditions.

In contrast to other sections in this book, the drugs described here are grouped together based on how they work (e.g., stimulating the immune system) rather than on their ultimate action (e.g., treating viral infection). The types of drugs listed include preparations of antibodies, drugs that stimulate production of red and white blood cells, cytokines (naturally occurring proteins that regulate the immune system), and other immune modulators.

Many of the drugs listed are used as treatments for viral infection. For other nonimmune-based antiviral therapies, see the "Antiviral drugs" section.

Vaccines, a special subset of immune-therapy drugs, are also described in their own section.

The following drugs are described in the profiles in this section:
- cyclosporine
- erythropoietin
- G-CSF
- GM-CSF
- immune globulin
- interleukin-2
- leucovorin

In addition, brief descriptions of experimental immune therapies used to treat HIV-related conditions are included at the end of this section.

# CYCLOSPORINE

**BRAND NAME (MANUFACTURER)**
Sandimmune (Novartis)

**OTHER NAMES**
Cyclosporin-A; CyA; CsA

**TYPE OF DRUG**
Immunosuppressant

**USED FOR**

Cyclosporine is used primarily to prevent rejection of organ or tissue transplants. It has also been studied as a treatment for HIV infection.

**GENERAL INFORMATION**

Cyclosporine is a naturally occurring chemical isolated from the fungus Tolypocladium. It has potent effects on the immune system, suppressing the body's natural defenses against infection and foreign cells. This is particularly useful after organ or tissue transplantation. If the donor and recipient do not have identical proteins on their cell surfaces (as is often the case), the recipient's immune system will try to reject the transplant. Cyclosporine stops the rejection, but in the transplant setting it must be taken for life, and it often leaves the body susceptible to opportunistic infections.

Cyclosporine has been tested in a number of small studies as a treatment for HIV infection in the hope that the drug's action on the immune system may inhibit HIV replication in CD4+ cells or suppress the harmful over-activation of the immune system caused by HIV infection. Studies of cyclosporine have yielded conflicting results. Some suggest there may be a benefit, while others have shown cyclosporine may actually worsen the disease.

In addition to ongoing research with cyclosporine, some researchers are working with drugs derived from cyclosporine. One, named SDZ 811, does not suppress the immune system but has potent anti-HIV activity in cells growing in test tubes. Test-tube studies also suggest that SDZ 811 works against HIV by a mechanism different from any of the commonly available antivirals.

Cyclosporine is generally taken in oral form. An injectable solution is available, but because it carries a higher risk of allergic reactions, it is used only when the oral forms cannot be effectively absorbed (e.g., in people with severe, chronic diarrhea).

**TREATMENT**

The dosage range and the frequency and timing of doses is adjusted for each individual, based on age and weight. Doses currently being studied in clinical trials of HIV range from 2 to 4 mg/kg per day.

Corticosteroids (primarily prednisone) are usually used in combination with cyclosporine, to reduce the severity of some of the drug's side effects. The dosage of the corticosteroids are adjusted on a case-by-case basis, according to the clinical situation.

The oral solution is not palatable. To improve its taste, it may be diluted with milk, chocolate milk, or orange juice, preferably at room temperature. After mixing, the liquid should be taken at once. After the liquid is gone, it is best to add more of the milk or juice to the glass to dissolve any remaining drug and drink it.

To achieve the most consistent blood levels of the drug, the dilutent should not be changed frequently, and the drug should be taken at a consistent time each day.

## CAUTIONS AND WARNINGS

Cyclosporine should not be used by anyone with a known allergy to it.

People taking other immunosuppressive drugs (except corticosteroids) should not take cyclosporine, because of the potential for infections or the development of lymphoma.

Cyclosporine should be used with caution in people with kidney or liver disease, because they may be at higher risk for the side effects of the drug.

## SIDE EFFECTS

The most common side effects of cyclosporine include high blood pressure, kidney toxicity, liver toxicity, tremors, abnormal hair growth, and gum disease. High blood pressure occurs in more than half the people who use the drug after organ transplantation. Similarly, kidney toxicity was reported in more than 25% and liver toxicity in more than 4% of people using the drug.

## PREGNANCY/BREAST-FEEDING

Cyclosporine has caused premature birth, low birth weight, and fetal death when used in pregnant women. Because cyclosporine is usually administered with other drugs in people with serious underlying disease, it is not known whether these effects were due to cyclosporine itself. Pregnant women are encouraged to discuss the benefits and potential risks of the drug with their physician before deciding to use it.

HIV may be passed from a woman to her child through breast milk. In areas where nutritionally sound alternatives are readily available, breast-feeding is discouraged for HIV-positive women. Cyclosporine is excreted in breast milk. Because of the potential toxicity of the drug, women should not breast-feed while using it.

## USE IN CHILDREN

Children as young as six months of age have used cyclosporine at dosages reduced for age and weight. There have been no unexpected side effects.

Premature infants and other newborns have immature kidneys and are susceptible to the side effects of the drug. It is not recommended for use in them.

## USE IN THE ELDERLY

Older adults may be more susceptible to the side effects of the drug and may require reduced doses.

## DRUG INTERACTIONS

The following drugs may intensify the kidney toxicity of cyclosporine: gentamicin, tobramycin, vancomycin, cimetidine, ranitidine, diclofenac, ampho-

tericin B, ketoconazole, melphalan, trimethoprim/sulfamethoxazole, and azapropazon. The following drugs may increase blood levels of cyclosporine, potentially increasing the risk of its side effects: diltiazem, nicardipine, verapamil, danazol, bromocriptine, metoclopramide, ketoconazole, fluconazole, itraconazole, erythromycin, and methylprednisolone. The following drugs decrease cyclosporine blood levels: rifampin and rifampin containing compounds (e.g., INH), rifabutin, phenytoin, phenobarbital, and carbamazepine.

Cyclosporine may increase blood levels of prednisolone, digoxin, lovastatin, and potassium-sparing diuretics, potentially increasing the risk of drug-related side effects. Cyclosporine may cause severe loss of potassium when used with certain diuretics.

Vaccinations may be less effective when taken while using cyclosporine.

**FOOD INTERACTIONS**
Cyclosporine may be taken with or without food. See above for additional information.

**OTHER DRUGS USED FOR SIMILAR CONDITIONS**
Other immunosuppressant drugs include azathioprine, chlorambucil, cyclophosphamide, methotrexate, as well as corticosteroids and some specific monoclonal antibodies. The choice of therapy depends on the organ or tissue being transplanted and the underlying condition of the recipient.

**COMMENTS**
Because of the potential for immune-suppressing drugs like cyclosporine to worsen immune suppression caused by HIV, cyclosporine should be used with great caution. Immune activation is also problematic in HIV disease, and immune-suppressing agents may prove to be useful in treating HIV disease. A small study examining the effect of cyclosporine on HIV replication and immune activation is currently being planned. Doses of cyclosporine being studied as a therapy for HIV (2 to 4 mg/kg per day) is three to four times lower than what is normally used in the transplant setting. Unlike the transplant setting, cyclosporine therapy in HIV would not have to be used as a lifetime therapy.

# ERYTHROPOIETIN

**BRAND NAME (MANUFACTURER)**
Epogen (Amgen); Procrit (Ortho Biotech)

**OTHER NAMES**
Epoetin alpha; EPO

**TYPE OF DRUG**
Immune-based therapy

**USED FOR**

Erythropoietin (EPO) is approved for use in the treatment of anemia caused by chronic kidney disease, AZT, and chemotherapy in people treated for cancer. The drug is routinely used, but not approved, to treat anemia caused by other drugs as well.

EPO should not be used to treat anemia caused by bleeding, iron deficiency, weakened red blood cell membranes, or severe anemia usually treated by transfusions.

**GENERAL INFORMATION**

Anemia, which is a deficiency in red blood cells, is frequently seen in people with HIV. It can be caused by HIV infection itself or as a side effect of treatment for HIV. EPO is a protein, made primarily by the kidney, that stimulates red blood cell production. A genetically engineered version of the drug is commercially available. It was tested in four placebo-controlled trials with a total of 297 HIV-infected anemic volunteers. The people who entered the studies with low EPO levels and who were treated with the genetically engineered drug required 40% less blood in transfusions than those given a placebo. As might be expected, volunteers who entered the studies already having high EPO levels did not respond to the drug.

EPO is available as a solution for intravenous injection.

**TREATMENT**

The recommended starting dose of EPO is 50 to 150 units per kg of body weight injected three times weekly. For people with HIV, the recommended dose is 100 units per kg of body weight as an intravenous injection or injection under the skin, three times per week for eight weeks. If the response is not satisfactory, the dose may be increased up to 300 units per kg. The response should be reevaluated every four weeks. If there is no response to a dose of 300 units per kg, it is unlikely that any dose of EPO will work.

EPO may be injected at a doctor's office or be self-administered at home.

**CAUTIONS AND WARNINGS**

EPO should not be used in people with uncontrolled high blood pressure, known allergy to mammalian-cell-derived products, or known allergy to human albumin.

Because EPO causes an increase in blood pressure, blood pressure must be closely monitored and controlled in those treated.

To reduce the risk of high blood pressure or seizures, the dose of EPO should be lowered if red blood cells accumulate too quickly. During hemodialysis, people treated with EPO may have an increased risk for blood clotting.

EPO will not be effective if the anemia is caused by iron deficiency, infection, cancer, blood loss, vitamin deficiency, aluminum poisoning, or inflammatory bone disease.

## SIDE EFFECTS

In two clinical trials of people with HIV treated with AZT, the most common side effects of EPO were fever, fatigue, headache, cough, diarrhea, rash, congestion, nausea, shortness of breath, muscle weakness, injection-site reactions, and dizziness. These side effects occurred in 9% to 38% of people given the drug, but similar side effects were reported by people given a placebo.

## PREGNANCY/BREAST-FEEDING

EPO has not been formally studied in pregnant women. In animal studies, EPO caused birth defects in rats whose mothers were given five times the human dose during pregnancy. It is not known whether the animal studies accurately reflect what would happen in humans. Pregnant women are encouraged to discuss the benefits and potential risks of EPO with their physician before deciding to take the drug.

HIV can be passed from a woman to her child through breast milk. In areas where nutritionally sound alternatives are readily available, breast-feeding is discouraged for HIV-positive women. It is not known whether EPO is excreted in human milk. High doses of the drug given to lactating rats resulted in some side effects in their offspring, but it is not known if this would be true for humans.

## USE IN CHILDREN

The safety and effectiveness of EPO have not been studied in children. The injection solution contains benzyl alcohol, which has been associated with sometimes fatal side effects when administered to premature infants.

## USE IN THE ELDERLY

No changes in dosage or administration are required for older adults.

## DRUG INTERACTIONS

There was no evidence of drug interactions with EPO in the clinical trials.

## FOOD INTERACTIONS

Because EPO is injected, it is unlikely that food would affect the absorption of the drug.

## OTHER THERAPIES USED FOR SIMILAR CONDITIONS

For treatment of anemia in HIV-infected people, transfusions are the only alternative routinely used. For treatment of AZT-induced anemia, people may choose to stay on AZT and have transfusions. They may also stop AZT therapy or decrease the dosage until their red blood cells recover. The problem with this option is that dose reductions may decrease AZT concentration in the

blood to levels that are ineffective in stopping HIV replication. Transfusions involve risks, such as infection and allergic reactions.

EPO is not an appropriate therapy for severe anemia and cannot replace the need for blood transfusions. However, early treatment of mild anemia with EPO may prevent the onset of severe anemia and the need for blood transfusions. Avoiding transfusions eliminates the risk of transfusion-related side effects and blood-borne diseases.

### COMMENTS

The availability of EPO has had a significant impact on treatment of HIV. It has reduced the need for transfusions and has allowed people to continue antiviral therapy, even though the drugs they are taking may cause severe anemia. Additionally, reducing the need for transfusions has reduced the risk of blood-borne disease.

# G - C S F

### BRAND NAME (MANUFACTURER)
Neupogen (Amgen)

### OTHER NAMES
Granulocyte–colony-stimulating factor; filgrastim

### TYPE OF DRUG
Immune-based therapy

### USED FOR
G-CSF is approved by the FDA for use in people with cancer receiving chemotherapy that causes bone marrow toxicity. It is also used by people living with HIV to counteract the bone marrow toxicity of certain drugs used to treat HIV and AIDS-related opportunistic infections. It is also commonly used to treat people with HIV with low neutrophil counts (neutropenia).

### GENERAL INFORMATION
G-CSF, a colony-stimulating factor, is a small, naturally occurring hormone that stimulates the production of certain white blood cells called neutrophils. Neutrophils play a critical role in fighting infection. Neutropenia is common among people with HIV, often the result of bone marrow toxicity caused by drugs such as AZT or ganciclovir.

Before the development of colony-stimulating factors, people would have to stop using drugs with bone marrow toxicity when their neutrophil counts dropped to dangerously low levels. In addition, drugs such as AZT and ganciclovir frequently couldn't be used together because their toxicity was

additive. Now it is common to use these and other drugs in combination with G-CSF, to prevent or reverse low neutrophil counts.

Drugs that can cause bone marrow toxicity usually also reduce the number of platelets circulating in the blood, called thrombocytopenia. Platelets are particles involved in the blood clotting process. When their numbers are reduced, blood clotting is less efficient and bleeding times are extended. G-CSF is not effective in increasing platelet count.

G-CSF is available as a solution for injection. It may be injected in the physician's office or at home by the patient.

## TREATMENT

The most widely prescribed dose of G-CSF is 5 micrograms (mcg) per kg of body weight per day, injected beneath the skin and sometimes injected directly into a vein. In some cases, such as bone marrow transplant, higher doses are used. The dose is usually adjusted for an individual's response to avoid overstimulating the production of neutrophils. The duration of therapy generally depends on how low the neutrophil counts are originally, how quickly the counts return to a normal range, and which drug(s) are responsible for the neutropenia. Frequency of dosing is also modified on the basis of need.

## CAUTIONS AND WARNINGS

G-CSF should not be used by anyone with a known sensitivity to it or with known allergies to proteins derived from the normal intestinal bacterium E. coli. Allergic reactions have been reported in less than one in four thousand people using the drug and may require administration of antihistamines (e.g., diphenhydramine), corticosteroids (e.g., dexamethasone), bronchodilators, or epinephrine.

Because G-CSF is a growth factor, it may stimulate the growth of malignant cells in tumors, particularly those of the bone marrow. The drug should be used with caution by people with cancers with myeloid characteristics (those involving the bone marrow).

## SIDE EFFECTS

In general G-CSF is well-tolerated. The most common side effect is bone pain, reported in about one-quarter of people using the drug in clinical trials. The pain was more severe in people using higher doses or in people who received the drug through intravenous rather than subcutaneous (under the skin) injection. Generally, the pain could be controlled with non-narcotic pain relievers.

Other side effects attributable to the drug in clinical trials included fever and elevated liver enzymes (potentially indicating some liver toxicity).

### PREGNANCY/BREAST-FEEDING

G-CSF has not been formally tested in pregnant women. In animal studies, it caused spontaneous abortions, bleeding, and birth defects when used at high doses. It is not known whether the same would be true in humans. Pregnant women are encouraged to discuss the benefits and potential risks of G-CSF with their physician before deciding to use the drug.

HIV may be passed from a woman to her child through breast milk. In areas where nutritionally sound alternatives are readily available, breast-feeding is discouraged for HIV-positive women. It is not known whether G-CSF is excreted in human milk. Because the drug is a protein that would probably be digested when taken orally, it is unlikely it would cause side effects in breast-fed infants of women taking it.

### USE IN CHILDREN

In clinical studies, G-CSF was no more toxic in children than in adults. In general, doses adjusted for body weight were well tolerated in children ranging from three months to eighteen years of age.

### USE IN THE ELDERLY

No changes in dosage or administration are required in elderly people.

### DRUG INTERACTIONS

None reported.

### FOOD INTERACTIONS

Because G-CSF is administered by injection, absorption of the drug is not affected by food.

### OTHER DRUGS USED FOR SIMILAR CONDITIONS

For treatment of reduction in neutrophil counts caused by HIV or drugs used to treat HIV-related infections, G-CSF is the drug of choice. Another colony-stimulating factor called GM-CSF is also commercially available. It is similar in its action to G-CSF, but there are some important differences. First, GM-CSF stimulates the production of a broader range of white blood cells, including macrophages (the M in GM-CSF) and the cells that produce platelets, while G-CSF does not. Second, GM-CSF has a broader range of side effects than G-CSF and may not be as well tolerated. Finally, there is some evidence that GM-CSF may stimulate the replication of HIV, because macrophages harbor the virus, though this has not been demonstrated in studies in humans.

# G M - C S F

### BRAND NAME (MANUFACTURER)

Leukine (Immunex); Prokine (Schering Plough)

**OTHER NAMES**

Granulocyte macrophage–colony-stimulating factor; sargramostim; molgramostim

**TYPE OF DRUG**

Immune-based therapy

**USED FOR**

GM-CSF is approved by the FDA to stimulate production of bone marrow cells after bone marrow transplantation. It has also been used in clinical trials of people living with HIV to counteract the bone marrow toxicity of antiviral drugs or other drugs used to treat opportunistic infections. It is currently in clinical trials in people with AIDS or cancer, and in children with low birth weight to evaluate its effectiveness in preventing opportunistic infections.

**GENERAL INFORMATION**

GM-CSF, a colony-stimulating factor, is a small, naturally occurring hormone that stimulates production of various white blood cells, including neutrophils, monocytes, and macrophages. Neutrophils play a critical role in fighting infection. People with HIV often have reduced neutrophil counts as a result of bone marrow toxicity caused by drugs such as AZT, alpha interferon, or ganciclovir. Reduced neutrophil counts are associated with increased risks of severe and life-threatening bacterial infections.

Drugs that cause bone marrow toxicity usually also reduce the number of platelets circulating in the blood. Platelets are particles involved in blood clotting. When their numbers are reduced, clotting is less efficient and bleeding times are extended. GM-CSF stimulates production of platelets.

Before the development of colony-stimulating factors, people would have to stop therapy with drugs that had bone marrow toxicity when their neutrophils or platelets dropped to dangerously low levels. In addition, drugs such as AZT and ganciclovir frequently couldn't be used together because their toxicity was additive. Now it is common to use these and other drugs in combination with colony-stimulating factors, to prevent or reverse reductions in neutrophil or platelet counts.

GM-CSF is generally not the drug of choice for this use, however. Because GM-CSF stimulates macrophages (which harbor HIV), the drug may also stimulate the replication of the virus. A few laboratory studies of GM-CSF demonstrated that it stimulated HIV replication. Studies in people, however, have not shown increased HIV levels as a consequence of GM-CSF therapy. Even still, G-CSF, a related drug, is usually used for treating and preventing neutropenia in people with HIV. G-CSF, however, is not effective in treating thrombocytopenia, a deficiency in the number of platelets.

GM-CSF is available as a solution for injection.

**TREATMENT**

The recommended dose of GM-CSF in adults is 250 micrograms (mcg) per square meter of body surface area per day. The dose is usually adjusted for each person to reduce risk of side effects and to avoid overstimulating white blood cell production. The duration of therapy depends on the initial white blood cell or neutrophil count, how quickly the bone marrow responds to therapy, and the drug(s) that originally caused the neutropenia. The frequency of dosing is adjusted according to the context it is being applied.

In laboratory studies, GM-CSF has been shown to enhance the ability of immune cells, called macrophages, to kill fungus, bacteria, mycobacteria, and protozoa, all of which can cause opportunistic infections in people with AIDS and cancer. Thus, large studies are ongoing to evaluate the ability of GM-CSF to enhance immune function and prevent disease. GM-CSF is also being studied in children with low birth weight, to evaluate its effectiveness in preventing the life-threatening infections common among these children. The dose of GM-CSF being used in the largest study in the context of AIDS is 250 mcg, three times weekly.

**CAUTIONS AND WARNINGS**

GM-CSF should not be used by anyone with a known sensitivity to it. One version of GM-CSF is grown in yeast, the other in E. coli. Therefore, people with known allergies to proteins derived from yeast should not use the sargamostim product, and people with allergies to components of the E. coli preparation should not use the malgromastim product. It should also not be used by people with high levels of malignant white blood cells in the bone marrow or blood (common in certain leukemias and bone marrow cancers).

GM-CSF may cause swelling in the extremities or in the tissue lining the inside of the chest. People with a history of pleurisy, fluid retention, fluid in the lungs, or congestive heart disease should use the drug with caution.

GM-CSF should be used with caution in people with breathing disorders.

Because GM-CSF is a growth factor, it may stimulate the growth of malignant cells in tumors, particularly those of the bone marrow. The drug should be used with caution by people with cancers with myeloid characteristics (those involving the bone marrow).

Because GM-CSF may stimulate HIV production, it should generally not be used by people with HIV unless they are also on antiretroviral therapies.

**SIDE EFFECTS**

GM-CSF is generally well tolerated. In clinical trials, the side effects that occurred most frequently were fever, weakness, headache, bone pain, chills, and muscle pain. Other side effects reported include diarrhea, rash, malaise, swelling, and elevated liver enzymes (potentially indicating liver toxicity).

**PREGNANCY/BREAST-FEEDING**

GM-CSF has not been formally studied in pregnant women or animals, and it is not known whether the drug has potential to cause fetal harm. Pregnant women should discuss the benefits and potential risks of GM-CSF with their physician before deciding to use the drug.

HIV may be passed from a woman to her child through breast milk. In areas where nutritionally sound alternatives are readily available, breast-feeding is discouraged for HIV-positive women. It is not known whether GM-CSF is excreted in human milk. Because the drug is a protein that would probably be digested when taken orally, it is unlikely it would cause side effects in breast-fed infants of women taking it.

**USE IN CHILDREN**

The available evidence suggests the drug is no more toxic in children than in adults. A large study of GM-CSF in children with low birth weight reveals that it may be useful in preventing infections.

**USE IN THE ELDERLY**

No changes in dosage or administration are recommended for elderly people.

**DRUG INTERACTIONS**

None reported.

**FOOD INTERACTIONS**

Because GM-CSF is administered by injection, absorption of the drug is not affected by food.

**OTHER DRUGS USED FOR SIMILAR CONDITIONS**

For reduction in neutrophil counts caused by HIV or drugs used to treat HIV-related infections, G-CSF is the treatment of choice. It is similar in its action to GM-CSF, but there are some important differences. First, GM-CSF stimulates the production of a broader range of white blood cells, including macrophages (the M in GM-CSF) and the cells that produce platelets, while G-CSF does not. Second, GM-CSF has a broader range of side effects than G-CSF and may not be as well tolerated. Finally, there is some evidence that GM-CSF may stimulate the replication of HIV, because macrophages harbor the virus, but this has not been seen in human studies.

# IMMUNE GLOBULIN (IVIG)

**BRAND NAME (MANUFACTURER)**

Gamimune N (Bayer); Gammagard (Baxter); Gammar (Armour); Polygam S/D (American Red Cross); Venoglobulin (Alpha Therapeutic); WinRho SD (Univax Biologics)

**OTHER NAMES**

Immune globulin intravenous (human); gamma globulin; IVIG; IGIV

**TYPE OF DRUG**

Immune-based therapy

**USED FOR**

Numerous brands of immune globulin are sold in the United States, and different brands have FDA approval for different conditions. Most are approved for the treatment of specific immune deficiencies such as primary immunodeficiency, a condition where babies are born without the ability to make antibodies. Similarly, most are approved for immune thrombocytopenia purpura (ITP), a condition characterized by bleeding lesions on the skin caused by an inadequate number of platelets in the blood. Some brands are indicated for the treatment of leukemia or the prevention of rejection reactions in bone marrow transplantation. Some are approved to reduce the frequency of bacterial infections in children infected with HIV.

IVIG is also used to prevent measles infection after exposure or to reduce the symptoms of hepatitis A and varicella zoster (shingles) infection.

**GENERAL INFORMATION**

IVIG is a collection of human antibodies made from large pools of human blood serum. It is used medically to provide antibodies to people whose bodies don't make enough or make antibodies that are not optimally functional. The process is called passive immunization and in essence means borrowing resistance to infection and disease from people with healthy immune systems.

Children are born before their immune systems are fully developed. They do carry their mother's antibodies, but they do not have a full range of their own. This can be a serious problem for children born with HIV infection. IVIG has been shown to be effective in reducing the number of bacterial infections in these children. The results of one large study also suggest that IVIG may improve CD4+ counts in some children, although another study found no such effect.

IVIG may also be beneficial for adults with AIDS, although there is less clinical evidence to support its use. Small studies of adults with AIDS suggest that IVIG may improve survival, decrease the frequency of fevers, reduce weight loss, and reduce the number of hospitalizations. Many investigators have seen at least temporary benefit from the use of IVIG, but because the clinical data are not conclusive, it is generally not recommended.

Some brands of IVIG, such as WinRho SD (also referred to as IGIV) have been proven effective and are approved for the treatment of immune thrombocytopenic purpura (ITP), a condition which occurs in 5% to 15% of HIV-infected people. ITP results in decreased levels of platelets in the blood, which

can lead to serious bleeding problems. One advantage of the WinRho product is that the infusion time required is far less than that of other approved products (3 to 5 minutes, versus several hours). It is significantly less expensive than the other IVIG preparations available on the market. Also, the WinRho product is the only immune globulin preparation that is pre-treated to disable and deactivate potential infectious agents, such as hepatitis C, which can be a danger in biologic products such as IVIG preparations. The spectrum of antibodies in the WinRho product is less than what is seen with many of the other products, however, and therefore its experimental use in treating conditions such as chronic sinusitis, is probably less desirable.

The different brands of IVIG are not all alike. They are prepared by different procedures and contain varying percentages of the different classes of antibodies. In clinical studies the different products were used at different dosages, so there is no way to know if all the different products would be equally effective in the treatment of AIDS.

It should be noted that IVIG therapy is generally quite expensive, and people considering its use may want to weigh the cost against the potential benefits.

IVIG is administered by intravenous injection.

### TREATMENT

The recommended dosages vary widely by brand and by condition treated. The recommended dose of IVIG for pediatric AIDS is 400 mg per kg of body weight once every four weeks. In one study that demonstrated a benefit of IVIG for HIV-positive adults, IVIG was used at a dose of 400 mg per kg of body weight for three consecutive days, followed by one treatment of 600 mg per kg of body weight every four weeks. AZT was concurrently used at a dose of 500 mg per day.

### CAUTIONS AND WARNINGS

IVIG should not be used by people who know they are allergic to immune globulin. People with a deficiency of IgA-type antibodies should not receive the drug, because they may develop antibodies against the immune globulin and experience severe allergic reactions the second time the immune globulin is injected.

Since IVIG is isolated from human blood serum, there is a low risk of being infected with viruses from the immune globulin preparations. Although the manufacturers treat IVIG to eliminate viruses there are known and suspected cases where individuals contracted hepatitis C from the drug. Recently the FDA removed a number of preparations of IVIG from sale because of contamination with hepatitis C. The WinRho product is the only preparation approved which is pre-treated to deactivate infectious agents.

### SIDE EFFECTS

Serious allergic reactions, including anaphylactic shock, are possible after treatment with IVIG. The most frequent side effects of the drug are headache, listlessness, a feeling of faintness, fever, chills, nausea, vomiting, chest tightening, difficulty breathing, and chest, back, or hip pain. In children with HIV who were studied in clinical trials, fever was the most common side effect.

### PREGNANCY/BREAST-FEEDING

IVIG is currently being tested in pregnant women in a clinical trial. From the early results, there is no reason to expect IVIG to cause fetal harm or side effects in nursing infants.

### USE IN CHILDREN

IVIG is used safely and effectively in children, without unexpected side effects. In one clinical study of 394 HIV-infected children, IVIG at a dose of 400 mg per kg of body weight administered every twenty-eight days significantly decreased the frequency of bacterial infections and decreased the frequency that the children were hospitalized. The children in the study were less than thirteen years of age and had an average CD4+ count of 937. The children were also receiving antibiotics. In the study, the drug was not effective for children with CD4+ counts less than 200. In addition, the drug had no effect on the frequency of viral opportunistic infection. Because of these limitations, IVIG is not recommended for routine use in children.

### USE IN THE ELDERLY

No changes in administration of IVIG are required for elderly people.

### DRUG INTERACTIONS

IVIG may interfere with successful immunization for measles, mumps, and rubella. Vaccines that use live microorganisms should not be used for six months after treatment with immune globulin.

### FOOD INTERACTIONS

Because IVIG is administered by injection, it is unlikely that food would interfere with the absorption or activity of the drug.

### OTHER DRUGS USED FOR SIMILAR CONDITIONS

IVIG is the only drug used in people with HIV to prevent such a broad range of bacterial infections. Specific antibiotics, such as trimethoprim/sulfamethoxazole, are used to prevent specific bacterial infections such as *Pneumocystis carinii* pneumonia. ITP is sometimes treated instead with steroids and, when other treatments fail, by removing the spleen. Studies have shown that AZT can sometimes be effective in treating ITP.

### COMMENTS

Special preparations of immune globulin that contain high levels of anti-HIV antibodies are currently being studied to prevent transmission of HIV from

infected mothers to their babies. Similarly, these HIV immune globulin are being tested to treat people in the late stages of AIDS, in an effort to reduce disease symptoms, especially of recurrent bacterial infections.

# INTERLEUKIN-2

**BRAND NAME (MANUFACTURER)**
Proleukin (Chiron)

**OTHER NAMES**
Aldesleukin; IL-2

**TYPE OF DRUG**
Immune-based therapy

**USED FOR**
Interleukin-2 (IL-2) is approved by the FDA for treatment of kidney cancer in adults. It is also being tested in clinical trials to boost the immune system in people living with HIV.

**GENERAL INFORMATION**
IL-2 is a small protein hormone, produced by the cells of the immune system. It plays an important role in the regulation of immune responses against infection or cancerous cells. In people living with HIV, IL-2 levels are abnormally low. It is thought that this deficiency contributes to the overall deterioration of the immune system in HIV disease.

IL-2 has been used in clinical trials of HIV disease and to stimulate the production of CD4+ and other cells vital to a healthy immune response.

A potentially serious concern with the drug is its effect on HIV replication. IL-2 activates resting immune cells, and active cells are where HIV multiplies. Both in laboratory studies and in people, IL-2 has caused increases in HIV replication. The benefit of boosting CD4+ cells must be weighed against the potential for stimulating the production of the virus. Because of this potential the drug should only be used in people receiving antiretroviral therapy.

The ability of IL-2 to stimulate the immune system has been tested in a number of small clinical trials. In one recent study, the drug increased CD4+ counts without increasing HIV levels (known as the viral load). This study included people with a mean CD4+ count of about 400, who received either IL-2 in combination with antivirals (AZT and/or ddI) or antivirals alone. At the end of one year, those receiving the IL-2 combination had mean CD4+ cell counts of about 900, whereas those receiving antiviral therapy alone had mean CD4+ cell counts of about 350. Viral levels were relatively stable in both groups. People with CD4+ cell counts below 200 are less likely to have

significant increases in CD4+ cell counts and the risk of increasing viral levels is higher. In a small study where IL-2 was used in conjunction with highly active antiviral therapy, including a potent protease inhibitor, however, people with low CD4+ cell counts, below 300, experienced increases in CD4+ cell counts without harmful affects on viral levels. While IL-2 therapy results in a significant increase in CD4+ cell counts, current and planned studies will answer the question as to the usefulness of this therapy in preserving and enhancing the immune system of people living with HIV.

IL-2 is administered by injection beneath the skin or into a vein.

**TREATMENT**

In clinical trials for HIV disease, IL-2 has been used in a wide variety of schedules. In the studies outlined above, IL-2 therapy was administered intravenously (IV) through continuous infusion, for five days every eight weeks (i.e., five-day course of therapy, every two months). Starting doses were 15 to 18 million International Units (MIU), daily for the five-day cycle. Most volunteers had dose reductions to manage side effects.

A number of small studies have proceeded trying to lessen the invasiveness of IL-2 therapy by delivering IL-2 through injections under the skin (subcutaneously). These studies show that it is possible to achieve substantial CD4+ cell increases, and lessen the side effects associated with IL-2, when it is delivered in this fashion. The regimens compared in the study were 7.5 MIU twice daily or 1.5 MIU twice daily (total daily doses of either 15 or 3 MIU). IL-2 therapy was delivered through injections, twice daily, under the skin, for five days. In both dose groups therapy was delivered either every 4 weeks or every 8 weeks. Those receiving the higher dose (7.5 MIU twice daily) were more likely to realize CD4+ cell increases and these increases were more robust than those receiving the 1.5 MIU twice daily dose. Many people in the 7.5 MIU twice daily group reduced their dosage of IL-2 to manage side effects. Most people reduced to a dose of 4.5 MIU twice daily (total daily dose of 9 MIU) for 5 days, every 8 weeks.

In another protocol, IL-2 was bound to polyethylene glycol (PEG) to permit less frequent infusions. For this protocol, PEG IL-2 was administered in doses ranging from 3 to 5 MIU once weekly for three weeks, then once every two weeks. In another protocol, PEG IL-2 was administered at 36,000 IU, injected into the skin twice a week for four months.

For treatment of kidney cancer, IL-2 is administered in two five-day treatment cycles, separated by a rest period. The recommended dosage is 600,000 IU per kg of body weight, administered every eight hours by intravenous infusion, for a total of fourteen doses. After a rest period of nine days, the treatment is

repeated. After four weeks the treatment is repeated if some benefit is observed.

**CAUTIONS AND WARNINGS**

IL-2 should not be used by anyone with abnormal heart or lung function. People who experience any of the following side effects during initial IL-2 therapy should suspend therapy: heartbeat or heart-rhythm disturbances, recurrent chest pain consistent with severe heart toxicity, severe suppression of breathing, severe kidney toxicity, coma or toxic psychosis, seizures, bleeding or perforation of the gut.

When severe side effects occur, the drug should be stopped rather than the dosage reduced.

IL-2 should be used with caution in people with a history of seizures, because it may increase their risk of experiencing additional seizures. Similarly, because IL-2 may increase HIV replication, it should not be used by people living with HIV unless viral levels are under control. It is perhaps safest and wisest to use IL-2 in combination with a highly active antiviral therapy regimen, one including a potent protease inhibitor.

**SIDE EFFECTS**

The side effects of IL-2 are frequent, often serious, and sometimes fatal. Common side effects, which may be severe, include fever, rash, and flu-like symptoms. Other side effects that occur in more than half the people who use the drug include low blood pressure, irregular heartbeat, congestion in the lungs, difficulty breathing, liver toxicity, bone marrow toxicity (anemia and reduced platelet counts), nausea and vomiting, diarrhea, changes in mental status, kidney toxicity, pain, fatigue, weakness, and malaise. Numerous other side effects, in virtually every organ or system in the body, occur less frequently. Most side effects associated with IL-2 are associated with the time of IL-2 administration, and typically resolve within 12 hours after IL-2 therapy is stopped. Clinicians and researchers studying IL-2 in HIV find that side effects can be lessened and made more manageable by pre-treating and preparing for them.

**PREGNANCY/BREAST-FEEDING**

IL-2 has not been formally studied in pregnant women. In view of its serious side effects, it should be used in pregnant women with extreme caution. Pregnant women are encouraged to discuss the benefits and potential risks of the drug with their physician before deciding to use it.

HIV may be passed from a woman to her child through breast milk. In areas where nutritionally sound alternatives are readily available, breast-feeding is discouraged for HIV-positive women. It is not known whether

IL-2 is excreted in breast milk. Because of IL-2's potential toxicity, women are encouraged to consider alternatives to breast-feeding while using it.

**USE IN CHILDREN**

The safety and efficacy of IL-2 have not been formally studied in children, and there is little clinical experience with the drug in this population.

**USE IN THE ELDERLY**

Older adults may be more susceptible to the side effects of the drug and may require reduced doses.

**DRUG INTERACTIONS**

Beta-blockers and other drugs used to control blood pressure may intensify the blood-pressure-lowering effect of IL-2. Because IL-2 may affect mental function, drug interactions may occur when it is used with psychoactive drugs such as narcotic analgesics, antivomiting drugs, sedatives, tranquilizers, or alcohol. IL-2 used with other drugs that can cause kidney toxicity (e.g., aminoglycoside antibiotics, indomethacin) may result in increased risk of kidney damage. Similarly, use of IL-2 with drugs with potential bone marrow toxicity (e.g., AZT, ganciclovir), heart toxicity (e.g., doxorubicin), or liver toxicity (e.g., methotrexate) may increase the risk of side effects in these organs.

Corticosteroids may reduce the effectiveness of IL-2.

**FOOD INTERACTIONS**

Because IL-2 is administered intravenously or through direct injection under the skin, food does not affect the drug's absorption into the body.

**OTHER DRUGS USED FOR SIMILAR CONDITIONS**

For treatment of HIV, the approved antiviral regimens remain the standard of care in people for whom therapy is warranted. IL-2 therapy, however, is not intended to have an anti-HIV effect, but rather is intended to maintain or enhance the immune system, particularly with regard to CD4+ cell number and function. At this point, immune-boosting drugs (such as IL-2) are still in the experimental stage. Another immune-boosting drug which may directly stimulate CD4+ cell growth is IL-15, which has not yet been studied in humans.

**COMMENTS**

IL-2 is an important immune-based therapy that warrants further study. Results from a number of studies demonstrate that IL-2 therapy, delivered either through continuous IV infusion or through twice daily injections under the skin, for five day cycles, every eight weeks, can profoundly impact CD4+ cell number. Studies also show that IL-2 therapy can enhance an existing repertoire of CD4+ cells, yet if certain classes of CD4+ cells are lost, they do not appear to return as a product of IL-2 therapy. While IL-2 also stimulates HIV replication, studies have shown that when administered to people who are taking

antiviral therapy, the effect on HIV replication can be controlled. There is still no clear understanding what periodic boosting of HIV replication, during the time of IL-2 cycles, will have on the overall HIV disease process. Analyses of the studies to date, however, do not suggest harmful overall effects, though clearly more research is needed to definitively answer this question. A number of studies of IL-2 therapy are ongoing and a large, international study of IL-2 therapy, administered through injection under the skin, is expected to begin in 1998.

# LEUCOVORIN

**BRAND NAME (MANUFACTURER)**
Wellcovorin (Glaxo Wellcome)

**OTHER NAMES**
Folinic acid; citrovorum factor

**TYPE OF DRUG**
Vitamin

**USED FOR**
Leucovorin is used to counteract the toxicity of certain antibiotics and anticancer drugs that cause anemia. It is also used to treat anemia due to other causes such as disease, nutritional deficiency, pregnancy, and infancy.

Leucovorin was initially developed to counteract the effects of the anticancer drug methotrexate. While that is still its primary use, it is now used by people with HIV to counteract the toxicity of drugs used for opportunistic infections. These drugs include pyrimethamine, sulfadiazine, clindamycin, and trimetrexate.

**GENERAL INFORMATION**
Folic acid is a B vitamin that is essential for a wide variety of biochemical reactions in the body, including the synthesis of components of proteins, DNA, and RNA. A number of antibiotics and anticancer drugs, called folic acid antagonists, interfere with the body's ability to use folic acid. When that happens, serious side effects, including life-threatening anemia, can occur. Leucovorin is another water-soluble B vitamin that counteracts the effects of folic acid antagonists.

Leucovorin is available as tablets or as a sterile powder for intravenous or intramuscular injection.

**TREATMENT**
The injectable form of leucovorin is primarily used when the person's digestive tract is not functioning well enough to absorb the oral drug. This condi-

tion often occurs after anticancer chemotherapy. When used to counteract the toxicity of methotrexate, a dose of 10 mg per square meter of body surface area is used every six hours until the serum levels of methotrexate are reduced to satisfactory levels.

The dose of oral leucovorin used to counter the toxicity of folic acid antagonists is approximately 5 to 15 mg per day.

### CAUTIONS AND WARNINGS

Leucovorin is only appropriate therapy for anemia caused by inhibition of the enzyme dihydrofolate reductase, which changes folic acid into the form utilized in DNA synthesis. It should not be used for other types of anemia.

Monitoring of serum methotrexate concentration is essential in determining the optimal dose and duration of treatment with leucovorin.

### SIDE EFFECTS

Some people who have been treated with oral or injectable leucovorin or folic acid may become allergic to the drug.

### PREGNANCY/BREAST-FEEDING

No animal or human studies have been done regarding the use of leucovorin during pregnancy. Pregnant women are encouraged to discuss the benefits and potential risks of leucovorin with their physician before deciding to use the drug.

HIV can be passed from a woman to her child through breast milk. In areas where nutritionally sound alternatives are readily available, breast-feeding is discouraged for HIV-positive women. It is not known whether leucovorin is excreted in breast milk.

### USE IN CHILDREN

Leucovorin can be used in children. Caution is required when antiseizure drugs and leucovorin are used simultaneously in children because of the possibility of drug interactions.

### USE IN THE ELDERLY

No changes in dosage or administration are recommended for elderly people.

### DRUG INTERACTIONS

Leucovorin may increase the toxicity of the anticancer drug fluorouracil. Deaths from severe digestive tract disease have been reported in elderly people receiving leucovorin and fluorouracil.

Leucovorin in high doses may counteract the antiseizure effect of epilepsy drugs, such as phenobarbital, phenytoin, and primidone, and increase the frequency of seizures in susceptible children.

### FOOD INTERACTIONS

None reported.

**OTHER DRUGS USED FOR SIMILAR CONDITIONS**

Simple deficiencies of folic acid may be reversed with folic acid supplements. When the deficiency is caused by the body's inability to utilize folic acid rather than a lack of folic acid, leucovorin is the drug of choice.

# IMMUNE-BASED THERAPY
## EXPERIMENTAL DRUGS

The following drugs are being tested as immune-based therapy for people with HIV. Generally, they are not widely available; most can be obtained only when participating in clinical trials.

**CYSTEINE PRECURSORS (N-ACETYL CYSTEINE [NAC] AND PROCYSTEINE)**

NAC and procysteine are derivatives of the amino acid cysteine. Not classified as true antivirals or immune modulators, they may indirectly inhibit HIV by raising the level of an antioxidant in blood cells called glutathione. As an antioxidant, glutathione plays an important role in protecting cells from the damaging effects of oxidizing agents. Laboratory research found that when cysteine precursors were added in certain cell types, glutathione levels increased and viral replication decreased.

Aerosolized NAC is commonly prescribed to treat bronchitis; intravenously, it's an antidote for acetaminophen (Tylenol) poisoning. Procysteine is only used experimentally for HIV. NAC is the more widely tested and better known of the two agents. In early human HIV trials with NAC, the drug was poorly absorbed. Currently, the biggest hurdle in clinical trials is to improve the absorption of the drug and to see if it raises glutathione levels in the blood. A study is under way in San Francisco.

**PENTOXIFYLLINE**

Pentoxifylline (Trental) is a drug prescribed since 1972 to treat a blood-circulation disease called intermittent claudication. For this condition it is essentially used to thin the blood. In the lab it was found that pentoxifylline exerts a broad anti-HIV effect by inhibiting several naturally occurring cytokines that, when present in abnormal levels in the blood, have been implicated in HIV disease progression. In one study in people with HIV who were receiving AZT or other antiviral drugs, a significant drop in the level of a specific cytokine, tumor necrosis factor, was found in many of the study volunteers. However, the level of HIV in the blood did not change. One major side effect reported was high fever. Results from other studies have been contradictory.

**THALIDOMIDE**

Thalidomide (Synovir) was widely used in Europe as a sedative prior to the discovery that it causes severe birth defects. Researchers have been looking at thalidomide as an immune modulator, an antiviral, as a treatment for HIV-related oral, esophageal, and vaginal ulcers, chronic diarrhea and for unwanted weight loss seen in people with HIV. In the test tube the drug inhibits levels of the cytokine tumor necrosis factor, which in high levels is believed to be implicated in increased HIV replication, HIV disease progression, KS progression, and wasting syndrome. In one clinical study, significant weight gain was seen in tuberculosis patients (some of whom were HIV-infected) treated with thalidomide. A study of thalidomide in people with HIV-associated oral ulcers demonstrated that 90% of those receiving thalidomide had resolution or improvement in these ulcers. Preliminary results from a study of thalidomide for the treatment of HIV-associated wasting syndrome showed those receiving the drug had improved weight gain over those receiving a placebo. In the wasting study the best tolerated dose was 100 mg daily. A number of other clinical trials of thalidomide are ongoing. Side effects associated with thalidomide include fatigue, rash, peripheral neuropathy (pain or tingling in the feet, legs, or hands). More recently there is some evidence that thalidomide may decrease neutrophil counts, causing neutropenia. Because thalidomide causes drowsiness, people should be cautious about drinking alcohol or taking other medications that may enhance this effect. Moreover, people should avoid driving or operating heavy machinery while this side effect persists. Caution should be used when taking thalidomide with other drugs that cause peripheral neuropathy or neutropenia. Recent data suggest that thalidomide may interfere with the metabolism of oral contraceptives. Because of the risk of serious and severe birth defects, women who have sex with men should use two forms of birth control if using thalidomide. If thalidomide is taken even once during the first trimester of pregnancy, the risk of harm to the fetus is near 100%. If a woman taking thalidomide thinks she may have become pregnant, it is best to discontinue thalidomide immediately and consult a health care provider.

**OTHER TNF INHIBITORS (OPC-8212, TNFR:FC, TNF MOAB, STNFR)**

Other drugs that work to inhibit tumor necrosis factor and are in various stages of development include OPC-8212, an oral agent used in Japan as a treatment for congestive heart failure; TNFR:Fc, a laboratory-produced molecule; TNF MoAb, specific single antibodies; sTNFr, and a soluble TNF receptor being studied at the National Institutes of Health.

## THYMIC PEPTIDES (THF GAMMA 2, THYMOPENTIN, THYMOSIN ALPHA, THYMODULIN, AND THYMOSTIMULIN)

Through years of research in the 1960s it was discovered that the thymus is a key immune-system organ, thought to be responsible, in part, for development and regulation of the immune system. Thymic peptides have been developed as immune-modulating treatments for HIV in hopes of stimulating a person's own immune system to fight HIV and diseases associated with HIV. These drugs include THF gamma 2, thymopentin, thymosin alpha, thymodulin, and thymostimulin. Presently there is little conclusive scientific evidence to support claims that thymic peptides are effective treatments for HIV. However, one study did show that people with no symptoms of HIV taking AZT with thymopentin had a lower incidence of oral thrush than those taking AZT alone. If the effect of thymopentin was solely as an antifungal, there may be less invasive ways to control candidiasis. If the effect was related to improved immune function, this could be an important new therapeutic approach. Unfortunately, the study, as with most studies of thymic peptides, was not designed well enough to draw definitive conclusions about the benefit of the drug.

## DEHSPM

DEHSPM is the acronym for diethylhomospermine, an intravenously given drug being tested to see if it will effectively reduce stool volume and frequency in people with AIDS and severe diarrhea.

## DNCB

DNCB is an industrial photochemical applied to the skin and believed to act as an immune modulator. It is theorized that by stimulating an immune response through the skin, a stronger immune-system reaction against HIV will be mounted. No data from well-controlled clinical trials suggest DNCB has any beneficial effect on HIV in humans. Studies in animals suggest DNCB may activate HIV. Anecdotal claims that DNCB raises CD8+ cells (suppressor T cells) in humans have yet to be confirmed.

## HIVIG

HIVIG is a preparation of HIV immunoglobulins enriched with specific antibodies to HIV. When injected in people, it is proposed that the preparation will neutralize HIV. A large multicenter study of HIVIG with AZT compared to IVIG with AZT is under way in HIV-infected pregnant women to see if HIVIG can augment the effect of AZT in preventing transmission of HIV to their children. Early studies of HIVIG in adults were encouraging and further study is warranted.

### CYTOKINES: IL-12, IL-4, GAMMA INTERFERON, IL-15, AND IL-10

IL-12, IL-4, and gamma interferon are immune-system messengers (cytokines) naturally present in the body. Synthetic versions are produced in the laboratory by genetic engineering. All have demonstrated a wide variety of biological activities. IL-12 is being clinically tested in people with HIV without symptoms and is believed to enhance the function of macrophages, as well as maintain or enhance cellular immune responses by preserving what is called a T-Helper type 1 balance of the immune system. IL-4 has been tested as an anti-KS treatment. Early results of the IL-4 study showed the drug had no apparent effect on KS progression, but appeared to have some anti-HIV activity. Gamma interferon is being tested to fight drug-resistant bacterial infections. Other cytokines, including IL-15 and IL-10, are still being investigated as potential therapies in HIV. IL-15 stimulates CD4+ cell growth, but is not thought to stimulate HIV replication to the extent of IL-2. IL-10 is a potent immune suppressing cytokine and is being evaluated for its ability to suppress immune activation associated with HIV. A small study showed that when IL-10 was administered in a single injection to people with HIV, HIV levels fell dramatically for a short period of time. Because of the potential harmful effects of IL-10 and its ability to immune suppress, great caution is being used as this study moves forward.

# Neuropathy drugs

Peripheral neuropathy (PN), or damage to the peripheral nerves (nerves outside the brain or spinal chord), is a potential side effect of many anti-HIV therapies or HIV itself and can greatly affect quality of life. It is often caused by a breakdown of the myelin sheath, the coating around nerve fibers that acts as an electrical insulator. Early signs of PN can include a sensation of burning, tingling, or numbness in the fingers or toes. Some people describe an electric shock sensation or a strange plastic or scab-like sensation when something touches their fingers or toes. In severe cases, touching the affected area can feel like touching an open wound. In some cases, there may be a deep soreness or shooting pains in the muscles of the legs and lower arms that may be transient but always affect the same general area. In more serious cases, severe pain and altered feedback in the nervous system may even interfere with walking.

Currently, there are no effective treatments that can stop or reverse this nerve damage. The most effective management of PN includes identifying the cause and, if possible, eliminating it. In many cases, the best treatment is simply pain management, and the type of medication used is generally determined by the severity of the PN.

Neuropathy can also be caused by HIV itself, and it's hard to know whether the disease or its treatment is causing the problem.

Neuropathy can be caused by certain drugs, most commonly ddC (Hivid), ddI (Videx), 3TC (Epivir), d4T (Zerit), isoniazid (INH), vincristine (Oncovin), dapsone, and vitamin $B_6$. Combination therapy with two or more of these drugs is believed to increase the risk of PN, though this is not well documented. PN will often go away if these drugs are changed, dose-reduced, or discontinued. It can sometimes take several months for PN to fully heal after removing the problematic drug, though some relief is often felt within a few weeks. In the most severe cases, peripheral neuropathy may never heal. It is critical to consult a physician before changing a drug regimen, as dose reduction of certain drugs can invite drug resistance. Be aware also that sometimes the symptoms of PN increase temporarily after a drug is stopped, but diminish soon thereafter. In some cases, if drugs are continued despite worsening PN, the nerve damage may become irreversible.

People with a history of diabetes or thyroid disease may have a greater likelihood of PN. Alcohol use or deficiency of vitamins B12 and E can also cause PN. In such cases, a physician can help design a treatment strategy for the condition. For vitamin B12 deficiency, vitamin B supplements may help, but too much vitamin B6 (over 200 mg per day) can worsen PN.

If the cause of PN can't be clearly identified (i.e., it may be due to HIV itself), or if the problem does not correct itself after stopping the drugs that may have caused it, chronic pain management may be required. Choice of treatment depends on the severity of symptoms. In the case of HIV-induced PN, some of the same drugs that potentially cause the problem may, in some cases, help relieve it.

For mild symptoms (tingling sensations but no problems walking, etc.), some people use a conservative strategy of simply observing the symptoms. Others find that mild pain can be relieved by using non-narcotic pain relievers such as ibuprofen (Advil) at doses of 600-800 mg 2-3 times daily.

For moderate symptoms (pain and can't walk as far as desired), people can take antidepressants such as amitriptyline or nortriptyline (mood elevators), combined with mild pain relievers. However, mood elevators are not approved for treating PN, and are believed to work best only when combined with traditional pain medications. Mexilitine, a drug used to treat irregular heart rhythms, is also sometimes used to treat PN, although in clinical trials it has shown little effect.

Severe symptoms include constant pain and the inability to walk or sleep at night. When experiencing this level of pain, it is recommended that you see a pain specialist. Specialists will have far more experience treating severe, chronic pain than most HIV physicians. They are also more experienced in managing high level narcotics and the associated problems. In severe cases, physicians may prescribe narcotic pain relievers such as methadone, a fentanyl patch, vicodin, morphine or codeine (see section on "Pain Relievers" for more information). Of these, methadone is least likely to be accompanied by the typical dulled sensations and euphoria associated with narcotics.

When the pain from PN is so great as to be seemingly untreatable (rarely), a pain specialist may recommend a "nerve block." In this procedure, a fluid, typically alcohol, is injected directly into a major nerve junction just above the sight of the worst pain. When they work, nerve blocks can be very effective and cause long-term reduction or elimination of pain. However, a major consideration is that they usually cause loss of sensation, and in worst-case scenarios, can be unpredictable. Clearly, nerve blocks should only be attempted by a specialist, and even then only after getting a second or third opinion.

**MANAGING NEUROPATHY**

None of the following suggestions have been formally studied, yet care providers and others offer them as suggestions for helping manage the symptoms of PN. For severe and prolonged pain, seeing a pain management specialist is key to developing a workable strategy.

- **Avoid tight-fitting shoes and socks.** People sometimes think that tight shoes can help with numbness and prevent rubbing, but they can actually exacerbate the pain and tingling. Many people find soft, loose cotton socks or loose, padded slippers to be helpful. Shoes should be neither tight nor excessively loose, and should offer good air circulation if possible.

- **Be sensitive to temperature.** Most people report that neuropathy feels worse in hot weather or when feet are heavily covered and don't have much opportunity for air circulation.

- **Keep feet uncovered in bed.** Bed sheets resting on your toes can also add to the problem. Some people use a semicircular hoop on which they rest their sheets to avoid contact. The important thing is to keep your feet uncovered at night. This helps keep the temperature down (which may help serious pain to "numb out") and also prevents friction between the sheets and toes.

- **Get up and walk around!** Although it may seem contradictory for people who are in pain and can't walk, getting blood to the feet by walking around can help relieve some of the pain. Too much walking, however, will only make the problem worse. A moderate amount of activity can distract a person from fixating on the pain, without adding to it.

- **Some people try acupuncture.** While this can often bring quick relief, many people report that the relief does not last for long and requires very frequent treatment.

- **Deep tissue massage.** Simply massaging sore feet helps improve circulation. Perhaps more importantly, it causes all the available neurons in that part of the nervous system to "fire." Once they "fire" or give off the chemical signal by which pain is transmitted, they must rest awhile before they can do so again. The result is that the pain is temporarily dulled. This is the same phenomenon as massaging any sore spot on the body.

- **Soaking feet in cool water.** When pain is severe, perhaps too strong to allow a person to sleep, water treatment can help. Put sore feet in a large dishpan (or special devices made for this purpose) and gradually fill with room-temperature water. Once filled, let the water keep running gently while you lower the temperature. The water will slowly become colder and eventually reach a point where most pain has stopped. Dry your feet off and go to bed, hopefully getting to sleep before the pain returns. This is also a good tactic to use while waiting for a pain medication to "kick-in."

- **Biofeedback.** Many people can be "trained" to deal with mild-to-moderate pain, largely by learning to divert their minds away from it. The pain from PN, after all, is not signaling any real harm to the body, as pain usually does. Some people ignore the pain and sensations of PN or live with them simply by learning to perceive them differently.

There are a few experimental therapies in clinical trials for the treatment of peripheral neuropathy. Nerve Growth Factor (NGF) may help repair damaged nerves. Early reports suggest that it may be useful in eliminating the most severe, shooting pains associated with neuropathy, but results will not be released until mid-1998. Lamictal (lamotrigine) and gabapentin are both approved antiseizure drugs that may be of use in treating neuropathy.

The following drugs are included in this section:
- amitriptyline
- mexiletine
- nortriptyline

# AMITRIPTYLINE

### BRAND NAME (MANUFACTURER)
Amitril (Parke-Davis); Elavil (Zeneca); Endep (Roche); Enovil (Hauk)

### TYPE OF DRUG
Psychoactive–tricyclic antidepressant

### USED FOR
Amitriptyline is used primarily for the relief of symptoms of mental depression. In HIV-positive people, amitriptyline is sometimes used (but not approved) to reduce the pain associated with peripheral neuropathy, a condition characterized by numbness, tingling, or pain in feet, legs, arms, or hands.

### GENERAL INFORMATION
Amitriptyline is a drug that belongs to a class known as tricyclic antidepressants. It is chemically unrelated to other classes of antidepressants, including monoamine oxidase (MAO) inhibitors. It is thought to work by increasing the concentrations of neurotransmitters called serotonin and norepinephrine in the brain. Some pain specialists believe that this class of drugs provides supplementary pain suppression indirectly, by changing the patient's mood and perception or attitude about the sensations interpreted as pain. They typically recommend its use in combination with another pain reliever rather than as a single agent.

Tricyclic antidepressants are usually taken over long periods. It takes weeks for steady levels of amitriptyline to build up in the blood, and it may take up

to a month for the drug to have an effect on depression. No clinical trial data is available to guide its use for treatment of neuropathy.

Amitriptyline is available as tablets and as a solution for injection.

**TREATMENT**

Most people will take the oral form of the drug. To prevent side effects, the dosage of amitriptyline should initially be low and increased as necessary until improvement, as long as there are no serious side effects.

The recommended initial dose for treatment of depression in adults is 75 mg a day and may be increased to 150 mg if necessary. A sedative effect may occur before the drug affects depression. Lower doses (50 mg per day) are recommended for adolescents and elderly people.

Once the drug has an effect on the depression, a maintenance dose of 50 to 100 mg per day is recommended for adults. This dose is continued for three months or longer to reduce the risk of relapse.

Doses used for the treatment of neuropathy are typically lower than those used for depression. Twenty-five to 50 mg per day is the most common range, though this dosage is based more on anecdote than clinical evidence.

**CAUTIONS AND WARNINGS**

Amitriptyline should not be used by people who know they are allergic to it. It should also not be taken by people who have HIV dementia or AIDS dementia complex, because it may cause acute delirium, a condition characterized by reduced attention span, rambling or incoherent speech, disorganized thinking, disorientation, or memory impairment.

Most antidepressants increase the risk of seizures in people susceptible to them. Because seizures are not uncommon in HIV disease, people who are infected with HIV should be cautious about taking antidepressants, including those in the tricyclic class.

Amitriptyline should not be taken with MAO inhibitor antidepressants. Extremely high fevers, severe convulsions, and death have occurred in people receiving tricyclic antidepressants and MAO-inhibiting drugs simultaneously.

When amitriptyline will be used to replace an MAO inhibitor for treatment of depression, a minimum of fourteen days should elapse after stopping the MAO inhibitor before starting therapy with amitriptyline. The amitriptyline should be started conservatively and cautiously with a gradual increase in dose until a response is achieved.

Amitriptyline should be used with caution in people with a history of seizures, difficulty urinating, or glaucoma. In people with angle-closure glaucoma, even average doses may cause severe side effects.

People with a history of heart disease should use amitriptyline with caution. It can produce rapid heartbeat, irregular rhythm, heart attack, and stroke.

Because of these effects, amitriptyline is not recommended for people recovering from heart attack. People with thyroid disease or people receiving thyroid medication should be closely monitored by their physician while taking the drug.

Amitriptyline may intensify the symptoms of psychosis or mania in people suffering from mental disorders. Amitriptyline may impair the mental or physical abilities required to operate heavy machinery or drive a car.

Abruptly stopping the medication may cause withdrawal symptoms, including nausea, headache, and a sickly feeling.

## SIDE EFFECTS

The most common side effects of the drug include chronic dry mouth (which can lead to serious problems of tooth decay), sleepiness, blurred vision; other less common effects include disorientation, confusion, hallucinations, muscle spasms, seizures, constipation, difficult urination, worsening glaucoma, and sensitivity to bright light or sunlight.

Rarely, amitriptyline can cause heart attack, stroke, irregular heartbeat or rhythm, vomiting, skin rashes, changes in appetite, diarrhea, swelling of the face and tongue, fluid retention, black discoloration of the tongue, jaundice, testicular swelling, breast enlargement in men or women, changes in sex drive, impotence, hair loss, weight change, increased perspiration, and suppression of the bone marrow (the site where cells of the blood and immune system are made).

## PREGNANCY/BREAST-FEEDING

Amitriptyline has not been formally studied in pregnant women. It does cross the placenta and there have been a few reports of deformities or delays in development in infants whose mothers took the drug during pregnancy. However, it is not known whether the drug itself caused these side effects. Pregnant women are encouraged to discuss the benefits and potential risks of using amitriptyline with their physician before making a decision whether or not to use the drug.

HIV can be passed from a woman to her child through breast milk. In areas where nutritionally sound alternatives are readily available, breast-feeding is discouraged for HIV-positive women. Amitriptyline is excreted in human milk and can cause sedation and other side effects in infants. Because of the potential toxicity of the drug, women should consider alternatives to breast-feeding while taking it.

## USE IN CHILDREN

Amitriptyline is not recommended for children under the age of twelve because the safety and effectiveness of the drug for them has not been formally studied.

**USE IN THE ELDERLY**

Older adults may be more susceptible to the side effects of the drug and may require reduced doses.

**DRUG INTERACTIONS**

Amitriptyline may reduce the effectiveness of some high blood pressure medications such as guanethidine. It may also intensify the effect of alcohol, barbiturates, and other central nervous system depressants.

Amitriptyline taken with MAO-inhibitor antidepressants can cause high fevers, convulsions, and occasionally death.

Delirium has been reported when amitriptyline was used with disulfiram or ethchlorvynol. Extremely high fevers have been reported when it was used with anticholingeric drugs or neuroleptic drugs, particularly during hot weather.

Cimetidine, quinidine, procainamide, acetazolamide, methylphenidate, thorazine, and compazine may increase blood levels of amitriptyline and increase the risk of side effects. Oral contraceptives reduce the effectiveness of amitriptyline.

**FOOD INTERACTIONS**

Amitriptyline may be taken with or without food.

**OTHER DRUGS USED FOR SIMILAR CONDITIONS**

For treatment of depression, there are many options, including other tricyclic antidepressants (desipramine, nortriptyline, protriptyline, amoxapine, maprotiline, imipramine, trimipramine, doxepin), MAO inhibitors (tranylcypromine, phenelzine, isocarboxazid), serotonin reuptake inhibitors (fluoxetine, paroxetine, and sertraline), and stimulants such as methylphenidate. The appropriate choice varies from person to person and depends on age, physical health and condition, and other drugs being concurrently used.

Desipramine is often the first choice among tricyclic antidepressants because it is effective and has relatively few side effects in most people. Amitriptyline is one of the more sedating tricyclics and perhaps causes the most severe dry mouth, constipation, blurred near vision, and difficulty urinating.

For peripheral neuropathy, there is no standard therapy. Analgesics, such as ibuprofen, acetaminophen, codeine, hydrocodone, oxycodone, or morphine, may be used to treat the pain associated with neuropathy. Acupuncture is an alternative therapy being studied for peripheral neuropathy, though like drugs, it is likely to require very frequent administration. Nimodipine has been used to prevent continued nerve damage associated with HIV infection, although conclusive evidence regarding its effectiveness is awaiting the results of clinical trials. Various other new drugs are being tested in clinical trials for their ability to reverse nerve damage, but none of them have received FDA approval for this use or are widely available.

# MEXILETINE

## BRAND NAME (MANUFACTURER)
Mexitil (Boehringer Ingelheim)

## TYPE OF DRUG
Antiarrhythmic–neuropathy treatment

## USED FOR
Mexiletine is approved by the FDA to treat irregular heart rhythms. The drug is sometimes used for the treatment of peripheral neuropathy in HIV-infected people. Peripheral neuropathy is nerve damage that may be a direct or indirect result of HIV infection, toxicity of certain drugs, or other unrelated causes. The symptoms include numbness, tingling, or pain in the hands, arms, legs, and feet.

## GENERAL INFORMATION
Mexiletine is a chemical derivative of the local anesthetic lidocaine. It is taken orally in capsules of 150, 200, and 250 mg.

Mexiletine slows the speed at which nerve impulses are carried through the heart, making the muscle less easily excitable, which helps maintain a steady heart rhythm.

There is little clinical evidence to support the use of mexiletine for peripheral neuropathy. The drug is being studied for neuropathy, but it is generally believed that mexiletine has no significant benefit for this condition.

## TREATMENT
The usual dosage of mexiletine to treat irregular heart rhythms is 600 to 1,200 mg per day split into two or three equal doses.

## CAUTIONS AND WARNINGS
People with liver disease should take the drug with caution because of the risk of increased side effects. Special monitoring may be required of people with a history of heart disease, low blood pressure, or seizure disorders who take the drug.

Like other drugs used to treat irregular heart rhythms, mexiletine may occasionally worsen heart-rhythm problems.

## SIDE EFFECTS
The most common side effects of mexiletine are nausea, vomiting, diarrhea, constipation, tremors, dizziness, light-headedness, nervousness, and loss of coordination. Less common side effects are rapid heartbeat, chest pains, reduced appetite, abdominal pains, stomach ulcers and bleeding, difficulty swallowing, dry mouth, weakness, fatigue, ringing or buzzing in the ears, depression, rash, swelling, or difficulty breathing. Peripheral neuropathy may also infrequently occur.

Rare side effects of the drug include abnormal heart rhythms, memory loss, hallucinations, fainting, low blood pressure, slow heartbeat, hot flashes, hair loss, impotence, decreased sex drive, malaise, and difficulty urinating.

### PREGNANCY/BREAST-FEEDING

Mexiletine has not been formally studied in pregnant women. In animal studies, the drug caused an increased rate of spontaneous abortions but did not cause observable birth defects. It is not known whether the same would be true for humans. Pregnant women are encouraged to discuss the benefits and potential risks of mexiletine with their physician before deciding to use the drug.

HIV can be passed from a woman to her child through breast milk. In areas where nutritionally sound alternatives are readily available, breast-feeding is discouraged for HIV-positive women. Mexiletine is excreted in breast milk. Because of the potential toxicity of the drug to newborns, women are encouraged to consider alternatives to breast-feeding while taking it.

### USE IN CHILDREN

Mexiletine has not been formally studied in children and few clinical data are available to make recommendations about its use in them.

### USE IN THE ELDERLY

Older adults may be more susceptible to the side effects of the drug and may require reduced doses.

### DRUG INTERACTIONS

Antacids, atropine, ammonium chloride, vitamin C, phenytoin, rifampin, phenobarbital, opioid analgesics, and tobacco may increase blood levels of mexiletine, potentially reducing its effectiveness. Bicarbonates and acetazolamide may increase blood levels of mexiletine, potentially increasing its side effects. Other drugs used to control heart rhythm may produce an additive effect on the heart. Mexiletine may increase blood levels of theophylline, potentially increasing its biochemical action and the risk of its side effects. Mexiletine may increase the blood levels of caffeine.

### FOOD INTERACTIONS

Mexiletine may be taken with food or milk if it causes stomach upset. The dose may need to be adjusted for the amount of acid in a person's diet. A high-acid diet (high in fruits, for example) may decrease mexiletine levels in the blood. A low-acid diet may cause the drug to accumulate in the body.

### OTHER DRUGS USED FOR SIMILAR CONDITIONS

Presently there is no effective therapy to halt or reverse the damage associated with peripheral neuropathy. The most practical approach is to identify the cause and, if possible, eliminate it.

Treatment of peripheral neuropathy is currently aimed at reducing painful symptoms. The choice of the medication is usually based on the severity of

the symptoms. People with mild symptoms and no functional impairment often take non-narcotic pain relievers such as ibuprofen. Moderate symptoms with some functional limitation are often treated with tricyclic antidepressants such as amitriptyline or nortriptyline. Severe symptoms with functional limitation may be treated with narcotic pain relievers such as methadone or the fentanyl patch. Acupuncture is an alternative therapy being studied for peripheral neuropathy, though like drugs, it is likely to require very frequent administration.

# NORTRIPTYLINE

**BRAND NAME (MANUFACTURER)**
Pamelor (Novartis)

**TYPE OF DRUG**
Psychoactive–tricyclic antidepressant

**USED FOR**
Nortriptyline is used for the relief of symptoms of mental depression. In HIV-positive people, it is occasionally used (but not approved) to reduce the pain associated with peripheral neuropathy, a condition characterized by numbness, tingling, or pain in feet, legs, arms, or hands.

**GENERAL INFORMATION**
Nortriptyline is a drug that belongs to a class known as tricyclic antidepressants. It is chemically unrelated to other classes of antidepressants, including monoamine oxidase (MAO) inhibitors. It is thought to work by increasing the concentrations of neurotransmitters called serotonin and norepinephrine in the brain.

Tricyclic antidepressants are usually taken over long periods. It takes weeks for steady levels of nortriptyline to build up in the blood, and it may take up to a month for the drug to have an effect on depression.

**TREATMENT**
Nortriptyline may be taken as capsules or liquid. To prevent side effects, the dosage of the drug should initially be low and increased as necessary until improvement, as long as there are no serious side effects.

The recommended initial dose for treatment of depression in adults is 75 to 100 mg a day. Doses above 150 mg per day are not recommended. Lower doses (30 to 50 mg per day) are recommended for adolescents and elderly people.

For treatment of neuropathy, lower doses may be prescribed.

**CAUTIONS AND WARNINGS**

Nortriptyline should not be used by anyone with a known allergy to it. It should also not be used by people recovering from heart attacks. Because of the risk of serious side effects, nortriptyline should not be used in combination with antidepressants of the monoamine oxidase (MAO) inhibitor class.

When nortriptyline will be used to replace an MAO inhibitor for treatment of depression, a minimum of fourteen days should elapse after stopping the MAO inhibitor before starting therapy with nortriptyline. Nortriptyline should be started conservatively and cautiously with a gradual increase in dose until a response is achieved.

Nortriptyline should be used with caution in people with a history of seizures, difficulty urinating, or glaucoma. People with thyroid disease or those receiving thyroid medication should use nortriptyline with caution because of the risk of heart toxicity.

Nortriptyline may impair the mental and physical abilities necessary to drive an automobile or operate dangerous machinery.

**SIDE EFFECTS**

The most common side effects of nortriptyline are sedation, dry mouth, constipation, confusion, blurred vision, disorientation, difficulty urinating, and sensitivity to bright light or sunlight. It may also cause hallucinations, muscle spasms, seizures, changes in blood pressure, altered heart rhythms, heart attack, anxiety, restlessness, excitement, loss of coordination, allergic reactions, nausea, vomiting, loss of appetite, diarrhea, enlargement of the breasts, changes in sex drive, and abnormal blood sugar levels.

Uncommon side effects include agitation, insomnia, nightmares, stomach cramps, black coloration of the tongue, jaundice, changes in weight, excessive perspiration, flushing, frequent urination, hair loss, and weakness.

**PREGNANCY/BREAST-FEEDING**

Nortriptyline has not been formally studied in pregnant women. Other tricyclic antidepressants have been associated with rare birth defects, but it is not known whether the same would be true for nortriptyline. Pregnant women are encouraged to discuss the benefits and potential risks of the drug with their physician before deciding to use it.

HIV can be passed from a woman to her child through breast milk. In areas where nutritionally sound alternatives are readily available, breast-feeding is discouraged for HIV-positive women. Nortriptyline is excreted in breast milk, but its effect on nursing infants is not known.

**USE IN CHILDREN**

Nortriptyline has not been studied in children. Consequently, it is not recommended for use in them.

**USE IN THE ELDERLY**
Older adults may be more susceptible to the side effects of the drug and may require reduced doses.

**DRUG INTERACTIONS**
Excessive alcohol consumption may increase the effects of nortriptyline, possibly leading to an overdose or an increased risk of suicide attempts, especially in people with a history of emotional disturbances or attempted suicide.

Quinidine or cimetidine may increase blood levels of nortriptyline, potentially increasing the risk of its side effects. Treatment with nortriptyline in combination with clonidine, debrisoquin, epinephrine, guanethidine, or methyldopa may result in increased blood pressure.

Nortriptyline increases blood levels of phenytoin, potentially increasing the risk of phenytoin side effects. It may also increase the risk of bleeding when taken with blood thinners such as warfarin.

**FOOD INTERACTIONS**
Nortriptyline may be taken with or without food.

**OTHER DRUGS USED FOR SIMILAR CONDITIONS**
For treatment of depression, there are many options, including other tricyclic antidepressants (desipramine, amitriptyline, protriptyline, amoxapine, maprotiline, imipramine, trimipramine, doxepin), MAO inhibitors (tranylcypromine, phenelzine, isocarboxazid), serotonin reuptake inhibitors (fluoxetine, paroxetine, and sertraline), and stimulants such as methylphenidate. The appropriate choice varies from person to person and depends on age, physical health and condition, and other drugs being concurrently used.

Desipramine is often the first choice among tricyclic antidepressants because it is effective and has relatively few side effects in most people.

For peripheral neuropathy, there is no standard therapy. Amitriptyline or analgesics (such as ibuprofen, acetaminophen, codeine, hydrocodone, oxycodone, or morphine) may be used to treat the pain associated with neuropathy. Nimodipine has been used to prevent continued nerve damage associated with HIV infection, although conclusive evidence regarding its effectiveness is awaiting the results of clinical trials. Various other new drugs are being tested in clinical trials for their ability to reverse nerve damage, but none of them have received FDA approval for this use or are widely available.

# Pain Relievers

Pain in HIV disease may be caused by various medications, medical procedures, opportunistic infections or malignancies, neurological complications of HIV infection, or stress. Treating pain usually means removing the underlying causes, when possible, and alleviating the symptoms. Appropriate antibiotic, antifungal, or antiparasitic drugs may be required to treat infectious causes of pain. (They are covered in their respective sections.) Pain relievers, also known as analgesics, are used for the symptomatic relief of pain.

Two different types of analgesics are commonly used: narcotics and non-narcotic pain relievers. For relief of minor pain, non-narcotic pain relievers such as acetaminophen and the nonsteroidal anti-inflammatory drugs (NSAIDs; e.g., aspirin, ibuprofen, and naproxen) are used. They are available both over the counter and by prescription. For more severe pain, narcotics such as codeine, meperidine, morphine, or fentanyl are prescribed. The non-narcotic drugs usually prevent stimulation of pain nerve endings so that pain signals do not pass to the brain. The narcotics prevent the transmission of pain signals within the brain and the rest of the central nervous system. Because the different types of analgesics work by different mechanisms, they are often used in combination to increase the pain relief and reduce the risk of side effects of high doses of either type used alone.

The following drugs, by drug type, are included in this section:

**NON-NARCOTIC PAIN RELIEVERS**

- acetaminophen
- aspirin
- ibuprofen
- naproxen

**NARCOTIC PAIN RELIEVERS**

- codeine
- fentanyl
- hydrocodone
- meperidine
- methadone
- morphine
- oxycodone

Tricyclic antidepressants (especially amitriptyline and nortriptyline) are sometimes used to reduce pain, especially the pain associated with peripheral neuropathy. See the section on neuropathy drugs for more details.

# ACETAMINOPHEN

**BRAND NAME (MANUFACTURER)**
Tylenol (McNeil)
Acetaminophen + Codeine: Tylenol #3 (McNeil)
Acetaminophen + Hydrocodone: Lortab (Whitby)
Acetaminophen + Oxycodone: Roxicet (Roxane)
Acetaminophen + Propoxyphene: Darvocet (Lilly)

**TYPE OF DRUG**
Analgesic

**USED FOR**
Acetaminophen is used for the temporary relief of fever and minor aches and pains.

**GENERAL INFORMATION**
Acetaminophen is a widely used pain reliever and fever reducer, available without a prescription. As a prescription medicine, it is used in combination with stronger pain relievers (such as oxycodone or propoxyphene) for the treatment of moderate-to-severe pain. Acetaminophen is also used in a number of cold and flu products in combination with antihistamines, decongestants, and sleeping medications. Used as indicated, acetaminophen is considered safe and effective.

Many forms and doses of acetaminophen are available. They are available as either tablets, caplets, or a solution for oral administration.

**TREATMENT**
For adults, one or two of the regular-strength over-the-counter Tylenol tablets (325 mg each) should be taken every three to four hours. Children six to twelve years old may take one-half to one tablet three to four times a day.

The extra-strength tablet (650 mg) is not meant for children under the age of twelve. Adults may take two tablets every eight hours, not to exceed six tablets in any twenty-four-hour period.

**CAUTIONS AND WARNINGS**
Acetaminophen should not be used by anyone with a known allergy to it. In massive overdoses, the drug may cause liver toxicity. The early symptoms are nausea, vomiting, perspiration, and general malaise. N-acetylcysteine (NAC) is commonly used to treat acetaminophen overdose.

**SIDE EFFECTS**
Acetaminophen is generally well tolerated. It causes much less stomach upset than pain relievers such as aspirin or compounds similar to aspirin. In long-term use, however, liver and kidney damage may occur, even by people who take recommended doses.

**PREGNANCY/BREAST-FEEDING**

Most evidence indicates that acetaminophen does not cause an increased risk of birth defects when used during pregnancy. Overdose during pregnancy has caused abortions or premature delivery in some cases. Early treatment of toxic overdoses is important for both the mother and fetus.

HIV can be passed from a woman to her child through breast milk. In areas where nutritionally sound alternatives are readily available, breast-feeding is discouraged for HIV-positive women. Acetaminophen is excreted in breast milk, but side effects caused by the drug in nursing infants are rare.

**USE IN CHILDREN**

Acetaminophen is routinely used in children at the doses listed above. In addition to the tablets, liquid drops are available for very young children. There tend to be fewer side effects or serious toxicity in children taking the drug when compared to adults, possibly because of differences in metabolism. In addition, compared to aspirin, acetaminophen is associated with a lower risk of Reye's syndrome, a serious and potentially fatal illness in children.

**USE IN THE ELDERLY**

No modifications in dose are necessary for elderly people.

**DRUG INTERACTIONS**

People who consume three or more alcohol-containing drinks a day are at a higher risk of kidney and liver damage due to acetaminophen.

The effect of acetaminophen may be reduced by the use of barbiturates, carbamazepine, phenytoin, rifampin, and sulfinpyrazone. These drugs also increase the risk of liver toxicity caused by acetaminophen.

**FOOD INTERACTIONS**

Acetaminophen may be taken with or without food.

**OTHER DRUGS USED FOR SIMILAR CONDITIONS**

An alternative to acetaminophen for the relief of minor pain are the NSAIDs (nonsteroidal anti-inflammatory drugs), such as aspirin, ibuprofen, and naproxen. NSAIDs reduce pain, fever, and inflammation. Acetaminophen generally works as well on pain and fever as the NSAIDs, but it has no effect on inflammation. On the other hand, acetaminophen generally causes less stomach upset than the NSAIDs.

# ASPIRIN

**BRAND NAME (MANUFACTURER)**

Bufferin (Bristol-Myers); Easprin (Parke-Davis); Ecotrin (SmithKline Beecham); Empirin (Glaxo Wellcome); Excedrin (Bristol-Myers); Equagesic (Wyeth-Ayerst); Gelprin (Alra)

**OTHER NAMES**
Acetylsalicylic acid; ASA

**TYPE OF DRUG**
Analgesic–nonsteroidal anti-inflammatory drug

**USED FOR**
Aspirin is used alone and in combination with other drugs for a wide variety of conditions, including mild-to-moderate pain, fever, inflammation, and arthritis. It is also used as a blood thinner to prevent heart attack or stroke. Aspirin has been tested in clinical trials as a treatment for HIV infection.

**GENERAL INFORMATION**
Aspirin is a nonsteroidal anti-inflammatory drug (NSAID). Although it has been used for over a century, exactly how it works is still unknown. It is thought to work to reduce fever by dilating (expanding) blood vessels, which increases blood flow to the skin, increasing evaporative cooling. Aspirin's anti-inflammatory properties are thought to be the result of its inhibition of the synthesis of prostaglandins, a group of complex hormones involved in inflammation, immune responses, and a number of other bodily functions.

Aspirin has been tested as a treatment for HIV infection. Certain prostaglandins induce HIV replication in cells in laboratory studies, so the rationale for using aspirin for HIV is to block prostaglandin-induced HIV replication. In small, preliminary laboratory studies of cells, there was some indication that an aspirin derivative inhibited the production of an HIV protein. A study of aspirin in people with HIV was stopped by an independent data safety monitoring board because of increased toxicity in the group receiving the drug.

Aspirin is available in a wide variety of forms, often combined with other drugs or antacids (to minimize stomach upset).

**TREATMENT**
The recommended dose of aspirin varies widely depending on the condition. For aches and pains, the usual adult dosage is 325 to 650 mg taken every four hours. Doses up to 5,200 mg per day may be used for arthritis or 7,800 mg per day for treatment of rheumatic fever.

**CAUTIONS AND WARNINGS**
Aspirin should not be used by anyone with a known allergy to it or any other salicylate. People who are allergic to aspirin may also be allergic to other NSAIDs, including indomethacin, sulindac, ibuprofen, naproxen, fenoprofen, ketoprofen, and tolmetin. Because of the risk of serious side effects, people with liver disease or a history of ulcers should not use aspirin.

Aspirin at doses over 1,000 mg per day has been associated with small increases in blood pressure, elevated nitrogen levels in the urine, and elevated

nitrogen levels in the blood. People taking aspirin over long periods will generally have the nitrogen in their blood periodically monitored.

Alcoholic beverages can worsen the stomach upset caused by aspirin and increase the risk of ulcers.

Aspirin is a blood thinner and can increase bleeding. For this reason, it is not recommended for use for one week before planned surgery.

High doses of aspirin (above 2,000 mg per day) may lower blood sugar and should be used with caution in diabetics who use insulin to control their condition.

## SIDE EFFECTS

The most common side effect of aspirin is stomach upset. At high doses of the drug, heartburn, nausea, and vomiting may also occur. More rarely, the drug may cause ulceration in the stomach or intestines, allergic reactions, hives, rashes, liver damage, and impaired vision.

## PREGNANCY/BREAST-FEEDING

Occasional use of aspirin during pregnancy has not been associated with fetal harm. Prolonged use during pregnancy has been associated with increased rates of stillbirths, birth defects, and slow growth of the fetus. Fetal death has been reported after an overdose of aspirin. When used during the last two weeks of pregnancy, aspirin may increase the risk of serious bleeding in the newborn. Pregnant women are encouraged to discuss the benefits and potential risks of aspirin with their physician before deciding to use the drug.

HIV may be passed from a woman to her child through breast milk. In areas where nutritionally sound alternatives are readily available, breast-feeding is discouraged for HIV-positive women. Aspirin used by nursing women, however, has not been associated with serious side effects in nursing infants.

## USE IN CHILDREN

Aspirin is not recommended for children under the age of sixteen because of the risk of Reye's syndrome. Reye's syndrome is a rare, potentially fatal disorder characterized by high fever, persistent and severe vomiting, lethargy, and irrational behavior. The disorder may progress to coma, convulsions, and death. The use of aspirin in children has been associated with Reye's syndrome.

## USE IN THE ELDERLY

Older adults may be more susceptible to the side effects of the drug and may require reduced doses.

## DRUG INTERACTIONS

Aspirin may intensify the effect of other blood thinners, such as warfarin. When used with aspirin, the dose of warfarin may need to be adjusted. Aspirin may increase the risk of stomach ulcers when taken with corticosteroids, phenylbutazone, or alcoholic beverages.

Aspirin counteracts the effects of probenecid and sulfinpyrazone. It may also reduce the effectiveness of medications taken for high blood pressure. Aspirin may increase blood levels of methotrexate or valproic acid, potentially increasing the risk of side effects from these drugs. Aspirin used with nitroglycerin tablets may cause severely reduced blood pressure.

### FOOD INTERACTIONS
Aspirin is generally taken with food or milk to reduce the risk of stomach upset.

### OTHER DRUGS USED FOR SIMILAR CONDITIONS
For treatment of mild-to-moderate pain or inflammation, a number of other NSAIDs may be used, including ibuprofen and naproxen, among others. Generally these other NSAIDs are as effective as aspirin but cause less stomach upset. Acetaminophen, because it is not an NSAID and does not cause Reye's syndrome, is the drug of choice to relieve pain or fever in children.

For the prevention of stroke in women, another NSAID called ticlopidine is occasionally used in place of aspirin. Other anticoagulants (blood thinners) used to prevent heart attack or stroke include warfarin and its derivatives.

# CODEINE

### BRAND NAME (MANUFACTURER)
Acetaminophen + Codeine: Phenaphen with codeine (Robins); Tylenol #3 (McNeil)
Aspirin + Codeine: Empirin with codeine (Glaxo Wellcome)
Guaifenesin + Codeine: Brontex (Procter & Gamble); Tussi-Organidin (Wallace)
Promethazine + Codeine: Phenergan with codeine (Wyeth-Ayerst)

### TYPE OF DRUG
Opioid analgesic

### USED FOR
Codeine is primarily used to relieve mild-to-moderate pain, often in combination with a non-narcotic pain reliever. It is also effective as a cough suppressant and is used as an ingredient in many nonprescription cold medicines and cough syrups.

### GENERAL INFORMATION
Codeine is a narcotic analgesic, derived from compounds isolated from opium poppies. It has been common in medical use since the beginning of the century. Like other opiates, it relieves pain by suppressing the transmission of pain signals in the central nervous system. By a similar mechanism, it suppresses the cough reflex, but it does not eliminate the cause of coughing.

Codeine is available in combination with analgesics (aspirin, acetaminophen, etc.) or other drugs in a number of formulations, including tablets, liquids, syrups, and as a solution for injection.

## TREATMENT

The dosage and administration of codeine varies widely depending on the condition, the health and weight of the individual, and other drugs being used at the same time.

## CAUTIONS AND WARNINGS

Codeine should not be used by anyone with a known allergy to it. Because of the risk of serious and potentially fatal side effects, it should be used with extreme caution in people with a history of asthma or other breathing disorders.

Codeine is habit-forming and may not be appropriate for people with a history of chronic alcohol or drug use. However, when taken as prescribed for short periods of time, addiction seldom occurs.

Codeine may interfere with the mental and physical abilities necessary to drive an automobile or operate dangerous machinery.

If slow or irregular breathing, severe drowsiness, or loss of consciousness occur when taking the drug, it should be stopped and a physician should be contacted.

## SIDE EFFECTS

The most frequent side effects of codeine are light-headedness, dizziness, sedation, nausea, vomiting, loss of appetite, and sweating. Less frequently, euphoria, headache, agitation, loss of coordination, minor hallucinations, disorientation, visual disturbances, dry mouth, constipation, flushing, rapid heartbeat, heart palpitations, difficulty urinating, reduced sex drive, impotence, allergic reactions, anemia, or jaundice may occur. Difficulty breathing is a rare but potentially serious side effect of the drug when used at recommended dosages.

## PREGNANCY/BREAST-FEEDING

Codeine has not been formally studied in pregnant women. In animal studies, it caused fetal harm, but it is not known whether the same would be true in humans. When taken during labor, codeine may cause suppression of the baby's breathing. Pregnant women are encouraged to discuss the benefits and potential risks of codeine with their physician before deciding to use the drug.

HIV can be passed from a woman to her child through breast milk. In areas where nutritionally sound alternatives are readily available, breast-feeding is discouraged for HIV-positive women. Codeine passes through breast milk. Because of the potential toxicity of the drug to newborns, women are encouraged to consider alternatives to breast-feeding while using it.

**USE IN CHILDREN**

Children may use codeine at dosages adjusted for age and weight.

**USE IN THE ELDERLY**

Older adults may be more susceptible to the side effects of the drug and may require reduced doses.

**DRUG INTERACTIONS**

The central nervous system (CNS) depression caused by codeine may intensify and be intensified by other CNS depressants, including alcohol, antihistamines, other narcotic pain relievers, sedatives, and tranquilizers.

**FOOD INTERACTIONS**

Codeine may be taken with or without food.

**OTHER DRUGS USED FOR SIMILAR CONDITIONS**

For treatment of mild-to-moderate pain, non-narcotic analgesics may be substituted for codeine, including aspirin, acetaminophen, ibuprofen, and naproxen. These drugs work by a different mechanism and have a different set of side effects, so they may be appropriate in instances where codeine should not be used (such as people with a history of breathing problems).

Hydrocodone, oxycodone, meperidine, and morphine are other narcotic analgesics that may be used instead of codeine for stronger pain. All of them work by a similar mechanism and have similar side effects. The choice of therapy is generally determined by the severity of pain.

# FENTANYL

**BRAND NAME (MANUFACTURER)**

Duragesic Transdermal System (Janssen)

**TYPE OF DRUG**

Opioid analgesic

**USED FOR**

The fentanyl patch is used for treatment of severe chronic pain in people who have malabsorption or otherwise cannot take oral medications. It is commonly used for cancer pain, but it is also used for the pain that may occur during advanced stages of HIV infection or for severe pain associated with peripheral neuropathy.

**GENERAL INFORMATION**

The fentanyl patch attaches to the skin and provides continuous systemic delivery of fentanyl, a potent and long-lasting opioid analgesic and sedative. The drug works by blocking pain signals in the central nervous system; this increases a person's tolerance for pain and decreases the perception of suffering.

## TREATMENT

As with all opioid analgesics, the dosage of fentanyl must be adjusted for an individual's response. Four different dosages of fentanyl are available with the patch. The lowest dosage is generally used first and increased as needed.

The patch is attached to a flat surface, such as the chest, back, flank, or upper arm. Hair in the area should be clipped, but not shaved. If the area needs to be cleaned, clean water should be used. Soap, oils, lotions, alcohol, or any other agent that might irritate the area should be avoided. The skin should be completely dry before application. When attaching the patch, pressure should be applied for thirty seconds, making sure contact is complete, especially around the edges. Each patch may be worn for seventy-two hours. The site of attachment should be changed each time the patch is changed.

## CAUTIONS AND WARNINGS

The fentanyl patch should not be used by people with a known allergy to the drug or to the patch's adhesive. The patch is also not appropriate for mild or intermittent pain than can be managed by other analgesics.

People using the patch should avoid exposing the application site to direct external heat sources such as electric blankets, heat lamps, saunas, hot tubs, etc. There is a potential for temperature-dependent increases in the drug's release from the patch.

Fentanyl may impair the mental or physical abilities necessary to operate dangerous machinery or to drive an automobile.

Fentanyl is addictive and may not be appropriate for people with a history of chronic alcohol or drug use.

Because of the risk of serious side effects, people with breathing disorders, heart disease, head injury, kidney or liver disease, or fever above 102.5°F should use the drug with caution.

Because residual fentanyl remains in the patch after use, it should be disposed of carefully, making sure that the patch is folded and the gel containing the drug is not exposed.

## SIDE EFFECTS

The side effects of fentanyl are similar to other narcotic pain relievers. Nausea, vomiting, constipation, dry mouth, drowsiness, confusion, and sweating are common. Respiratory depression, low blood pressure, high blood pressure, headache, loss of appetite, stomach upset, dizziness, nervousness, hallucinations, anxiety, depression, euphoria, allergic reactions, and difficulty urinating occur less frequently.

## PREGNANCY/BREAST-FEEDING

Fentanyl has not been formally studied in pregnant women. In animal studies, it caused spontaneous abortions. Pregnant women are encouraged to discuss

the benefits and potential risks of fentanyl with their physician before deciding to use the drug.

HIV may be passed from a woman to her child through breast milk. In areas where nutritionally sound alternatives are readily available, breast-feeding is discouraged for HIV-positive women. Fentanyl is excreted in breast milk and can cause serious sedation or depression of breathing in newborns. The drug is not recommended for use by nursing women.

### USE IN CHILDREN
Because of the risk of severe side effects, fentanyl should not be used by children under twelve years of age or children under the age of eighteen who weigh less than 110 pounds. Older, heavier children can use the drug at doses adjusted for weight.

### USE IN THE ELDERLY
Fentanyl is metabolized much slower in people over the age of sixty when compared to younger adults. Consequently, elderly people may be at increased risk for the drug's side effects. In general, the lowest effective dose of fentanyl should be used for elderly people.

### DRUG INTERACTIONS
Fentanyl, like other narcotic analgesics, may intensify the effect of other central nervous system depressants, including alcohol, antihistamines, sleeping pills, tranquilizers, antidepressants, and other narcotic analgesics.

### FOOD INTERACTIONS
Because fentanyl is delivered into the bloodstream from the skin, food does not affect absorption of the drug.

### OTHER DRUGS USED FOR SIMILAR CONDITIONS
A number of available narcotic analgesics are appropriate for severe, chronic pain. They differ primarily in their potency. For severe chronic pain, morphine or meperidine are often used. The disadvantage of these drugs is that their effect doesn't last long. They must be administered every few hours to maintain analgesia. The fentanyl patch provides longer-term relief. For people who hallucinate or become confused while using the fentanyl patch, extended-release morphine tablets (e.g., MS Contin) may be appropriate.

# HYDROCODONE

### BRAND NAME (MANUFACTURER)
Anexsia (Boehringer Mannheim); Hydrocet (Carnrick); Lorcet (UAD Labs); Lortab (Whitby)
Hydrocodone + Acetaminophen: Vicodin (Knoll)
Hydrocodone + Aspirin: Damason (Mason)

**TYPE OF DRUG**
Opioid analgesic

**USED FOR**
Hydrocodone is used to treat moderate to moderately severe pain. It is also used to suppress severe coughing.

**GENERAL INFORMATION**
Hydrocodone is a narcotic analgesic, derived from compounds isolated from the opium poppy. Like other narcotics, it works by suppressing the transmission of pain signals in the central nervous system. Like codeine, it also suppresses the cough reflex.

Hydrocodone is available in combination with non-narcotic analgesics such as aspirin or acetaminophen. Available formulations include tablets, syrup, and solution for injection.

**TREATMENT**
The dosage and administration of hydrocodone varies widely depending on the condition, the health of the individual, and other drugs being used at the same time.

**CAUTIONS AND WARNINGS**
Hydrocodone should not be used by anyone with a known allergy to it.

Hydrocodone is addictive and may cause drug dependence. Consequently, it may not be appropriate for people with a history of chronic alcohol or drug use. However, when used as directed for short periods, it rarely causes addiction.

People with head injuries are at higher risk for the side effects of narcotics. Hydrocodone should be used with extreme caution by people with chronic respiratory problems.

Hydrocodone may mask the symptoms and make diagnosis of acute abdominal disorders difficult. It may also impair the mental and physical abilities necessary to drive an automobile or operate dangerous machinery.

**SIDE EFFECTS**
The most frequently observed side effects of hydrocodone include light-headedness, dizziness, sedation, nausea, and vomiting. Less commonly, mental clouding, lethargy, anxiety, fear, mood changes, constipation, and difficulty urinating may occur. Difficult, irregular, or slow breathing are rare but potentially serious side effects of hydrocodone used at recommended dosages.

**PREGNANCY/BREAST-FEEDING**
Hydrocodone has not been formally studied in pregnant women. In animal studies it caused fetal harm, but it is not known whether the same would be true in humans. When administered during labor, the drug may cause severe suppression of breathing in newborns. Pregnant women are encouraged to

discuss the benefits and potential risks of the drug with their physician before deciding to use it.

HIV can be passed from a woman to her child through breast milk. In areas where nutritionally sound alternatives are readily available, breast-feeding is discouraged for HIV-positive women. Opioid narcotics can pass through breast milk. Because of the potential toxicity of the drug to newborns, women are encouraged to consider alternatives to breast-feeding while using hydrocodone.

**USE IN CHILDREN**
Hydrocodone is not recommended for use in children, because its safety and effectiveness for them has not yet been established in clinical trials.

**USE IN THE ELDERLY**
Older adults may be more susceptible to the side effects of the drug and may require reduced doses.

**DRUG INTERACTIONS**
Hydrocodone may intensify the effects of other central nervous system depressants, including alcohol, other narcotic pain relievers, antihistamines, sedatives, and tranquilizers.

**FOOD INTERACTIONS**
Hydrocodone may be taken with or without food.

**OTHER DRUGS USED FOR SIMILAR CONDITIONS**
Codeine, oxycodone, meperidine, and morphine are other narcotic analgesics that may be used instead of hydrocodone. All of them work by a similar mechanism and have similar side effects. The choice of therapy is generally determined by the severity of pain.

# IBUPROFEN

**BRAND NAME (MANUFACTURER)**
Advil (Whitehall); Motrin (Pharmacia & Upjohn)

**TYPE OF DRUG**
Analgesic–nonsteroidal anti-inflammatory drug

**USED FOR**
Ibuprofen is used for the relief of mild-to-moderate pain. It is also used for relief of the symptoms of rheumatoid arthritis, osteoarthritis, and primary dysmenorrhea.

**GENERAL INFORMATION**

Ibuprofen is a nonsteroidal anti-inflammatory drug (NSAID), like aspirin and naproxen. NSAIDs reduce pain, fever, and inflammation by a mechanism that is not fully understood. All NSAIDs also cause stomach upset to varying degrees.

Individuals' responses to NSAIDs vary greatly. One person may respond well to aspirin and gain little relief from ibuprofen, while another individual with similar pain or inflammation may have the reverse effect.

Ibuprofen is available in prescription and nonprescription strengths. The over-the-counter medication is sold as 200 mg tablets. Prescription strengths include 300, 400, 600, and 800 mg tablets.

**TREATMENT**

The recommended dose of ibuprofen varies depending on the intensity of the pain. For mild-to-moderate pain, the recommended dose is 400 mg every four to six hours. The inflammation that accompanies arthritis requires higher doses.

NSAIDs like ibuprofen have what is known as a therapeutic ceiling. Increasing the dose increases the pain relieving or anti-inflammatory effect up to a point. After that point, increasing doses increases the risk of side effects without additional therapeutic benefit. For this reason, using more ibuprofen than the 3,200 mg per day is not recommended.

**CAUTIONS AND WARNINGS**

Ibuprofen should not be used by anyone with a known allergy to it or to aspirin or other NSAIDs. By reducing fever and inflammation, ibuprofen may diminish the value of these symptoms in diagnosing other disorders.

Noninfectious meningitis with fever and coma has been observed on rare occasions in people treated with ibuprofen. Although it is probably more likely to occur in people with connective tissue diseases, it has been reported in some who do not have an underlying chronic disease.

As with other NSAIDs, long-term use of ibuprofen can cause kidney damage. People with reduced kidney function should be monitored closely.

**SIDE EFFECTS**

Minor stomach upset is common during the first few days of taking ibuprofen. Other common side effects include nausea, heartburn, diarrhea, constipation, and abdominal cramps.

Less common side effects include stomach ulcers, hepatitis, inflammation of the gallbladder, kidney inflammation, blood or protein in the urine, dizziness, fainting, nervousness, depression, hallucinations, disorientation, tingling in the hands and feet, light-headedness, itching, heart palpitations, chest pain, difficulty breathing, and muscle cramps.

Serious digestive tract toxicity such as bleeding, ulcers, and perforation of the gut can occur at any time, with or without warning symptoms, in people

who use NSAIDs chronically. The risk of these side effects increases with long-term chronic use.

### PREGNANCY/BREAST-FEEDING

Ibuprofen has not been formally studied in pregnant women. In animal studies, the drug did not cause fetal harm, but it is not known whether this would be true in humans. Certain other NSAIDs used in pregnant women can prematurely close the baby's ductus arteriosus, a duct that shunts fetal blood away from the baby's lungs before it is born. In addition, there have been a number of reports of serious side effects in infants whose mothers took ibuprofen during pregnancy. Consequently, ibuprofen should not be used during pregnancy.

HIV can be passed from a woman to her child through breast milk. In areas where nutritionally sound alternatives are readily available, breast-feeding is discouraged for HIV-positive women. In limited human studies, ibuprofen was found in low levels in human milk, but the drug is usually considered safe for use during nursing.

### USE IN CHILDREN

Ibuprofen is generally considered safe and effective for temporary use in children. The drug is not recommended for infants under the age of six months, because there are no formal clinical studies and little clinical experience with the drug for this group.

### USE IN THE ELDERLY

Older adults may be more susceptible to the side effects of the drug and may require reduced doses.

### DRUG INTERACTIONS

Ibuprofen may increase the blood levels and toxicity of methotrexate and lithium. It may also reduce the effect of furosemide and thiazides in some people.

### FOOD INTERACTIONS

Ibuprofen can be administered with food or milk if stomach upset occurs.

### OTHER DRUGS USED FOR SIMILAR CONDITIONS

Alternatives to ibuprofen for the relief of mild to moderate pain are acetaminophen and the other NSAIDs, including aspirin and naproxen. There are no hard and fast rules for choosing one of the drugs over another. All of them are effective in reducing minor pain. Acetaminophen generally causes less stomach upset than the NSAIDs, but it has no anti-inflammatory properties. Naproxen requires twice a day dosing compared to the four times a day necessary for ibuprofen or acetaminophen. For children and teenagers, acetaminophen is usually recommended for fever, to reduce the risk of Reye's syndrome, a potentially fatal illness associated with use of aspirin.

# MEPERIDINE

**BRAND NAME (MANUFACTURER)**
Demerol (Sanofi Winthrop); Mepergan (Wyeth-Ayerst)

**TYPE OF DRUG**
Opioid analgesic

**USED FOR**
Meperidine is used for relief of moderate-to-severe pain.

**GENERAL INFORMATION**
Meperidine is an opioid analgesic, similar in effect to morphine. Opioid analgesics relieve pain by blocking the transmission of pain signals in the central nervous system. Meperidine is available as a solution for injection, syrup, and 50 or 100 mg tablets.

**TREATMENT**
The dosage of meperidine varies depending on the cause of the pain and the age and health of the person taking the drug. The usual dosage range for adults is 50 to 150 mg, taken every three or four hours as necessary. Children receive a dose of 0.5 to 0.8 mg per pound of body weight, up to the adult dose, every three to four hours as necessary.

**CAUTIONS AND WARNINGS**
Meperidine should not be used by anyone with a known allergy to opioid analgesics. The drug should also not be used by anyone who is taking or has taken monoamine oxidase (MAO) inhibitors within fourteen days.

Meperidine is addictive and may cause drug dependence. Consequently, it may not be appropriate for people with a history of chronic alcohol or drug use. However, most people who use the drug for short periods at the recommended dosages do not become addicted and have little trouble stopping.

People with head injuries are at higher risk for the side effects of meperidine. Similarly, because of the risk of serious side effects, the drug should be used with extreme caution by people with chronic respiratory problems.

Meperidine may cause severe low blood pressure in people who have lost a significant amount of blood or those who are taking phenothiazine tranquilizers or anesthetics. Meperidine may cause drowsiness and impair the ability to operate automobiles or dangerous machinery.

**SIDE EFFECTS**
The most frequently observed side effects of meperidine include light-headedness, dizziness, sedation, nausea, vomiting, and sweating.

The most serious side effects of the drug are depression of breathing, low blood pressure, respiratory arrest, shock, and heart attack. The risk of these side effects increases as the dose of the drug is increased.

### PREGNANCY/BREAST-FEEDING

Meperidine crosses the placenta and can cause serious fetal side effects. The drug is not recommended for pregnant women.

HIV can be passed from a woman to her child through breast milk. In areas where nutritionally sound alternatives are available, breast-feeding is discouraged for HIV-positive women. Meperidine is excreted in human milk and can cause side effects in nursing infants. Because of this potential toxicity, women are encouraged to consider alternatives to breast-feeding while using the drug.

### USE IN CHILDREN

Meperidine is considered safe and effective for temporary use in children. Children who use the drug generally experience the same side effects as adults.

### USE IN THE ELDERLY

Older adults may be more susceptible to side effects and may require reduced doses.

### DRUG INTERACTIONS

Meperidine should be used with great caution and reduced dosage in people who are receiving other narcotic analgesics, general anesthetics, tranquilizers, sedatives, barbiturates, tricyclic antidepressants, or other central nervous system depressants, including alcohol. Severe depression of breathing, low blood pressure, or coma may result from combined use.

Taking cimetidine with a narcotic pain reliever may cause disorientation, depression of the nervous system, seizures, or difficulty breathing.

Meperidine taken with monoamine oxidase (MAO) inhibitors may cause potentially fatal side effects that include depression of breathing, blood pressure changes, and coma.

### FOOD INTERACTIONS

Meperidine may be used with food to prevent stomach upset.

### OTHER DRUGS USED FOR SIMILAR CONDITIONS

Codeine, hydrocodone, oxycodone, and morphine are other narcotic analgesics that may be used instead of meperidine. All of them work by a similar mechanism and have similar side effects. The choice of therapy is generally determined by the severity of pain.

# METHADONE

### BRAND NAME (MANUFACTURER)

Dolophine (Lilly); Methadone HCL (Roxane

### TYPE OF DRUG

Opioid analgesic

**USED FOR**

Methadone is used to treat severe pain. It is also used to treat addiction and reduce the withdrawal symptoms of other narcotics. In people living with HIV, methadone is sometimes used to treat the painful symptoms of peripheral neuropathy, a condition characterized by numbness, tingling, or pain in the arms, legs, hands, or feet.

**GENERAL INFORMATION**

Methadone is a long-acting synthetic narcotic analgesic with effects similar to morphine. Like all opioid analgesics, it works by suppressing the transmission of pain signals in the central nervous system. It is useful in the treatment of addiction because its withdrawal symptoms, although qualitatively similar to those of morphine or heroin, are less severe.

Methadone is a controlled substance. When used to treat narcotic addiction, it is subject to a number of regulations designed to limit access to the drug and reduce the risk of its being abused. When used as an analgesic, it may be dispensed by any licensed pharmacy.

Methadone is available as tablets and a solution for injection.

**TREATMENT**

When used to treat severe pain, the dosage of methadone is adjusted according to the severity of the pain and the response of the individual. The usual adult dosage is 2.5 to 10 mg taken every three to four hours as needed.

When used to treat addiction, a specific, detailed course of therapy is prescribed and administered by licensed health care professionals.

**CAUTIONS AND WARNINGS**

Methadone should not be used by anyone with a known allergy to it. Methadone is addictive and may cause drug dependence.

People with head injuries are at higher risk for the side effects of methadone. Similarly, because of the risk of serious side effects, the drug should be used with extreme caution by people with chronic respiratory problems.

Methadone may cause severe low blood pressure in people who have lost a significant amount of blood or those who are taking phenothiazine tranquilizers or certain anesthetics. Methadone may also cause drowsiness and impair the ability to operate automobiles or dangerous machinery.

Because of the risk of serious side effects, people with impaired liver or kidney function, thyroid disease, prostate disease, or difficulty urinating should use methadone with caution.

**SIDE EFFECTS**

The most serious side effects of methadone, as of other narcotic analgesics, are suppression of breathing, severe low blood pressure, respiratory arrest, shock, and heart attack. They occur more frequently with extended use at higher doses.

The most frequently observed side effects of methadone include light-headedness, dizziness, sedation, nausea, vomiting, sweating, and mood changes. Less frequently observed side effects include weakness, headache, insomnia, agitation, disorientation, visual disturbances, dry mouth, loss of appetite, constipation, diarrhea, flushing, chills, heart palpitations, fainting, difficulty urinating, changes in sex drive, impotence, and allergic skin reactions.

When using methadone or other high level narcotics, it may take several days to find the optimal dose that balances pain suppression and side effects.

### PREGNANCY/BREAST-FEEDING

Methadone has not been formally studied in pregnant women. Opioid analgesics have been associated with severe side effects in newborns when taken close to the time of delivery. Pregnant women are encouraged to discuss the benefits and potential risks of methadone with their physician before deciding to use the drug.

HIV can be passed from a woman to her child through breast milk. In areas where nutritionally sound alternatives are readily available, breast-feeding is discouraged for HIV-positive women. Opioid analgesics are excreted in human milk. Because of the potential toxicity of methadone to newborns, women are encouraged to consider alternatives to breast-feeding while using it.

### USE IN CHILDREN

Methadone is not recommended for use in children, because there has been too little experience in this population to determine the optimum dosing.

### USE IN THE ELDERLY

Older adults may be more susceptible to the side effects of the drug and may require reduced doses.

### DRUG INTERACTIONS

People who are addicted to heroin or who have received methadone for extended periods may experience withdrawal symptoms when using pentazocine or rifampin.

Therapeutic doses of meperidine (a similar narcotic analgesic) have caused severe reduced blood pressure in people taking monoamine oxidase (MAO) inhibitor drugs such as isocarboxazid or tranylcypromine. Similar reactions have not been reported by people using methadone, but the risk does exist.

Methadone may increase blood levels of desipramine, potentially increasing the risk of drug-related side effects.

### FOOD INTERACTIONS

Methadone may be taken with or without food.

### OTHER DRUGS USED FOR SIMILAR CONDITIONS

Codeine, hydrocodone, oxycodone, meperidine, and morphine are other narcotic analgesics that may be used instead of methadone. All of them work by a

similar mechanism and have similar side effects, although they have different analgesic strengths and side effect severity. The choice of therapy is generally determined by the severity of pain.

Treatment of peripheral neuropathy is currently aimed at reducing painful symptoms. The choice of the medication is usually based on the severity of the symptoms. People with mild symptoms and no functional impairment often take non-narcotic pain relievers such as ibuprofen. Moderate symptoms with some functional limitation are often treated with tricyclic antidepressants such as amitriptyline or nortriptyline. Severe symptoms with functional limitation may be treated with narcotic pain relievers such as methadone or the fentanyl patch.

# M O R P H I N E

**BRAND NAME (MANUFACTURER)**
Duramorph (Elkins-Sinn); MS Contin (Purdue Frederick); MSir (Purdue Frederick); Oramorph (Roxane); Roxanol (Roxane)

**TYPE OF DRUG**
Opioid analgesic

**USED FOR**
Morphine is used to treat moderate-to-severe pain.

**GENERAL INFORMATION**
Morphine is a narcotic pain reliever, derived from the opium poppy. It has been in widespread use since the nineteenth century. Like other narcotics, it works by suppressing the transmission of pain signals in the central nervous system. Compared to other analgesics, its effect wears off quickly and it must be administered frequently in order to continue relieving pain.

Morphine is available as tablets, suppositories, and a solution for injection.

**TREATMENT**
The dosage and administration of morphine varies depending on the cause of the pain, the severity of the pain, and the age and health of the person taking the drug. For most purposes, adults take 5 to 25 mg per dose, repeated every four hours. However, there is considerable variability in each individual's response to the drug. Some people with severe pain may require doses of 75 mg or more.

Unlike non-narcotic analgesics, morphine has no therapeutic ceiling, which is a dosage at which additional amounts of the drug do not result in additional pain relief. Increasing doses of morphine will continue to increase the

amount of pain relief, but serious side effects, such as sedation and suppression of breathing, become more common at higher doses.

### CAUTIONS AND WARNINGS

Morphine should not be used by anyone with a known allergy to opioid analgesics.

Because of the potential risk of severe high blood pressure, the drug should also not be used by anyone who is taking or has taken monoamine oxidase (MAO) inhibitors (e.g., phenelzine or tranylcypromine) within fourteen days or by people with a history of breathing difficulties, including severe asthma.

Because morphine may cause severe constipation, it should not be used by people with a condition called paralytic ileus, which is a chronic contraction of the intestines that obstructs the gut.

Morphine is addictive and may cause drug dependence. Consequently, it may not be appropriate for people with a history of chronic alcohol or drug use. However, most people who use the drug for short periods at the recommended dosages do not become addicted to it and have little trouble stopping the drug.

People with head injuries are at higher risk for the side effects of morphine. Similarly, because of the risk of serious side effects, the drug should be used with extreme caution by people with chronic respiratory problems.

Morphine may cause severe low blood pressure in people who have lost a significant amount of blood or those who are taking phenothiazine tranquilizers or certain anesthetics. Morphine may cause drowsiness and impair the ability to operate automobiles or dangerous machinery.

### SIDE EFFECTS

The most serious side effects of morphine, as of other narcotic analgesics, are suppression of breathing, severe low blood pressure, respiratory arrest, shock, and heart attack. They occur more frequently with extended use at higher doses.

The most frequently observed side effects of morphine include constipation, light-headedness, dizziness, sedation, nausea, vomiting, sweating, and mood changes. Less frequently observed side effects include weakness, headache, agitation, tremor, uncoordinated muscle movements, seizures, disorientation, visual disturbances, insomnia, dry mouth, loss of appetite, diarrhea, cramps, taste alterations, flushing, chills, rapid heartbeat, heart palpitations, fainting, changes in blood pressure, difficulty urinating, and allergic skin reactions.

### PREGNANCY/BREAST-FEEDING

Morphine has not been formally studied in pregnant women. Narcotics taken near the time of delivery may cause serious side effects (especially respira-

tory depression) in newborns. Pregnant women should discuss the benefits and risks of morphine with their physician before deciding to use it.

HIV can be passed from a woman to her child through breast milk. In areas where nutritionally sound alternatives are readily available, breast-feeding is discouraged for HIV-positive women. Morphine is excreted in human milk. Because of the potential toxicity of the drug for newborns, women are encouraged to consider alternatives to breast-feeding while using it.

### USE IN CHILDREN
Children may use morphine at dosages adjusted for age and weight. In general, they may be more susceptible to the side effects of the drug than adults.

### USE IN THE ELDERLY
Older adults may be more susceptible to the side effects of the drug and may require reduced doses.

### DRUG INTERACTIONS
Morphine may intensify the effect of other central nervous system depressants, including alcohol, antihistamines, other narcotic pain relievers, sedatives, and tranquilizers. Severe respiratory depression, low blood pressure, or sedation may occur when these combinations are used.

Narcotics, including morphine, may increase the action of muscle relaxants, potentially increasing the risk of serious respiratory depression.

Monoamine oxidase (MAO) inhibitors may cause severe rises in blood pressure when used with morphine.

### FOOD INTERACTIONS
Morphine may be taken with or without food.

### OTHER DRUGS USED FOR SIMILAR CONDITIONS
Codeine, hydrocodone, oxycodone, and meperidine are other narcotic analgesics that may be used instead of morphine. All of them work by a similar mechanism and have similar side effects, although their analgesic strength and the severity of their side effects differ significantly. The choice of therapy is generally determined by the severity of pain. Morphine is generally used for severe pain.

# NAPROXEN

### BRAND NAME (MANUFACTURER)
Naprosyn (Roche); Anaprox (Roche); Aleve (Procter & Gamble)

### TYPE OF DRUG
Analgesic–nonsteroidal anti-inflammatory drug

**USED FOR**

Naproxen is used for the relief of mild-to-moderate pain. It is also used to treat a number of inflammatory diseases, including rheumatoid arthritis, osteoarthritis, ankylosing spondylitis, tendinitis, bursitis, gout, fever, menstrual pain, and premenstrual headaches.

**GENERAL INFORMATION**

Naproxen is a nonsteroidal anti-inflammatory drug (NSAID), like aspirin and ibuprofen. In the United States, it is the most widely prescribed drug in its class.

NSAIDs reduce pain, fever, and inflammation by a mechanism that is not fully understood. A person's reaction to NSAIDs is highly individual. One may respond well to naproxen and gain little relief from ibuprofen. Another individual with identical pain or inflammation may react in exactly the opposite manner. All NSAIDs also cause stomach upset to varying degrees.

Naproxen is quickly absorbed into the bloodstream. Pain relief is usually evident within an hour after taking the first dose, but its maximum effect on arthritis or other inflammatory disorders may not be observed for up to a month of continual dosing.

NSAIDs like naproxen have what is known as a therapeutic ceiling. Increasing the dose increases the pain relieving or anti-inflammatory effect up to a point. After that point, increasing doses cause increased side effects without additional therapeutic benefit.

Naproxen is available in prescription and nonprescription tablets, enteric-coated tablets (to reduce stomach upset), and oral suspension.

**TREATMENT**

For treatment of inflammatory disorders such as arthritis, the usual adult starting dose is 250 to 500 mg, taken twice a day. This dose may be increased as necessary and tolerated up to 1,500 mg per day for limited periods. For treatment of mild-to-moderate pain, the recommended dosage is 200 to 275 mg every six to eight hours, up to a maximum daily dose of 1,250 mg.

**CAUTIONS AND WARNINGS**

Naproxen should not be used by anyone with a known allergy to it, aspirin, or other NSAIDs. By reducing fever and inflammation, the drug may diminish the value of these symptoms in diagnosing other disorders.

People with a history of ulcers or bleeding in the gut should use naproxen with caution. Minor stomach upset or gas is common during the first few days of treatment, but if persistent, they may be symptoms of serious drug toxicity.

As with other NSAIDs, long-term administration of naproxen can cause kidney or liver damage. People with reduced kidney or liver function should use the drug with caution, under the supervision of a physician.

**SIDE EFFECTS**
The most common side effects of naproxen include nausea, diarrhea, vomiting, constipation, stomach gas, stomach upset, and loss of appetite. Less common side effects include stomach ulcers, bleeding in the gut, hepatitis, inflammation of the gallbladder, painful urination, kidney toxicity, dizziness, fainting, nervousness, depression, hallucinations, confusion, disorientation, tingling in the hands or feet, light-headedness, itching, increased perspiration, dry mouth, heart palpitations, chest pain, difficulty breathing, and muscle cramps. Rare side effects include severe allergic reactions and kidney failure.

**PREGNANCY/BREAST-FEEDING**
Although NSAIDs can cross the placenta, they have not been shown to cause birth defects in humans. However, some NSAIDs used by pregnant women can prematurely close the baby's ductus arteriosus, a duct that shunts fetal blood away from the baby's lungs before it is born. In addition, there have been a number of reports of serious side effects in infants whose mothers took naproxen during pregnancy. Pregnant women are encouraged to discuss the benefits and potential risks of naproxen with their physician before deciding to use the drug.

HIV can be passed from a woman to her child through breast milk. In areas where nutritionally sound alternatives are readily available, breast-feeding is discouraged for HIV-positive women. Naproxen is excreted in human milk. Because of the drug's potential toxicity to newborns, women are encouraged to consider alternatives to breast-feeding if they need to use the drug.

**USE IN CHILDREN**
Naproxen is routinely used in children, especially for juvenile arthritis, at dosages adjusted for age and weight.

**USE IN THE ELDERLY**
Older adults may be more susceptible to the side effects of the drug and may require reduced doses.

**DRUG INTERACTIONS**
Although short-term studies showed no drug interaction between naproxen and coumarin-type blood thinners (e.g., warfarin), the drugs should be used together with caution, because other NSAIDs have been shown to alter the effectiveness of these drugs. Similarly, people using naproxen with hydantoin, sulfonamide, sulfonylurea, lithium, or methotrexate may be at increased risk of drug-induced toxicity.

Naproxen may reduce the effectiveness of beta-blockers (e.g., propranolol) used to treat high blood pressure. It may also reduce the effectiveness of furosemide.

Probenecid increases blood levels of naproxen, potentially increasing the risk of naproxen-related side effects.

Alcohol may increase the risk of naproxen-induced stomach irritation.

**FOOD INTERACTIONS**

Naproxen may be taken with or without food. If the drug causes stomach upset, it may be taken with an antacid.

**OTHER DRUGS USED FOR SIMILAR CONDITIONS**

Alternatives to naproxen for the relief of mild to moderate pain are acetaminophen and the other NSAIDs, including aspirin and ibuprofen. There are no hard and fast rules for choosing one of the drugs over another. All of them are effective in reducing minor pain. Acetaminophen generally causes less stomach upset than the NSAIDs, but it has no anti-inflammatory properties. Naproxen requires twice-a-day dosing compared to the four times a day necessary for ibuprofen or acetaminophen. For children and teenagers, acetaminophen is usually recommended for fever, to reduce the risk of Reye's syndrome, a potentially fatal illness associated with use of aspirin.

# OXYCODONE

**BRAND NAME (MANUFACTURER)**

Roxicodone (Roxane)

Oxycodone + acetaminophen: Percoset (DuPont); Roxicet (Roxane); Tylox (McNeil)

Oxycodone + aspirin: Percodan (Dupont); Roxiprin (Roxane)

**TYPE OF DRUG**

Opioid analgesic

**USED FOR**

Oxycodone is used to treat moderate to moderately severe pain.

**GENERAL INFORMATION**

Oxycodone is a narcotic analgesic, similar to morphine. Both relieve pain by blocking the transmission of pain signals in the central nervous system.

Oxycodone is available as tablets, caplets, and a solution for oral administration.

**TREATMENT**

The dosage and administration of oxycodone varies depending on the cause of the pain, the severity of the pain, and the age and health of the person taking the drug.

**CAUTIONS AND WARNINGS**

Oxycodone should not be used by anyone with a known allergy to it.

Oxycodone is addictive and may cause drug dependence. Consequently, it may not be appropriate for people with a history of chronic alcohol or drug use. However, when used for short periods at recommended doses, few people become addicted to the drug.

People with head injuries are at higher risk for the side effects of oxycodone. The drug should also be used with extreme caution by people with chronic respiratory problems.

Oxycodone may mask the symptoms and make diagnosis of acute abdominal disorders difficult. It may also cause drowsiness and impair the ability to operate automobiles or dangerous machinery.

**SIDE EFFECTS**

The most frequently observed side effects of oxycodone include light-headedness, dizziness, sedation, nausea, and vomiting. Other side effects include euphoria, depression, constipation, skin rash, and itching. At higher doses, the drug may cause irregular, slow, or suppressed breathing, which has been fatal in some instances.

**PREGNANCY/BREAST-FEEDING**

Oxycodone has not been formally studied in pregnant women. In animal studies it caused fetal harm, but it is not known whether the same would be true in humans. When administered during labor, the drug may cause severe suppression of breathing in newborns. Pregnant women are encouraged to discuss the benefits and potential risks of the drug with their physician before deciding to use it.

HIV can be passed from a woman to her child through breast milk. In areas where nutritionally sound alternatives are readily available, breast-feeding is discouraged for HIV-positive women. Narcotics can pass through breast milk. Because of the potential toxicity of the drug to newborns, women are encouraged to consider alternatives to breast-feeding while using oxycodone.

**USE IN CHILDREN**

Oxycodone is not recommended for children because its safety and effectiveness for them has not yet been demonstrated in clinical trials.

**USE IN THE ELDERLY**

Older adults may be more susceptible to the side effects of the drug and may require reduced doses.

**DRUG INTERACTIONS**

Oxycodone may intensify the effects of other central nervous system depressants, including alcohol, antihistamines, other narcotic pain relievers, sedatives, and tranquilizers.

The use of oxycodone in combination with monoamine oxidase (MAO) inhibitor antidepressants (such as tranylcypromine or isocarboxazid) or tricyclic antidepressants (such as amitriptyline or nortriptyline) may increase blood levels of either oxycodone or the antidepressant.

**FOOD INTERACTIONS**

Oxycodone may be taken with or without food.

**OTHER DRUGS USED FOR SIMILAR CONDITIONS**

Codeine, hydrocodone, meperidine, and morphine are other narcotic analgesics that may be used instead of oxycodone. All of them work by a similar mechanism and have similar side effects. The choice of therapy is generally determined by the severity of pain.

# Psychoactive Drugs

Psychological complications such as depression, anxiety, insomnia, psychosis, or mania can be the side effects or resulting symptoms of HIV infection. These conditions can have a significant effect on the quality of life of people with HIV, on disease progression, and on the ability to properly adhere to combination therapy regimens.

Because of the many issues that may influence a psychological condition, it is imperative to properly diagnose the condition to determine all the possible causes. The symptoms of depression and other conditions can be very difficult to assess in HIV-positive individuals. Psychological disorders can be the direct result of HIV infection, thought to be due to HIV-associated dementia or other HIV-associated neurological changes. Depression can also be a side effect of some anti-HIV medications (including AZT) or may be exacerbated by drug interactions. However, depression and other disorders may simply be side effects of HIV disease that manifest themselves as anxiety or as a lack of interest in activities because a person is bedridden or unable to socialize. During early stage infection, people with such symptoms likely have a true depressive disorder. However, in later stages of HIV disease, it becomes much more difficult to differentiate true symptoms of depression from symptoms such as lethargy and fatigue that may appear related to depression, but in fact are due to HIV infection itself. Therefore, it is important to effectively assess the underlying causes of the disorder before taking any medications.

The most effective method of treating people with psychological disorders includes a combination of counseling and medications. This section discusses the use of psychoactive medications, drugs that affect people psychologically, by examining various disorders and the medications used to treat them. The treatments described below are helpful in treating depression, anxiety, insomnia, and other psychological complications that may accompany HIV infection. Psychoactive drugs don't affect the underlying causes of these disorders, but they can provide symptomatic relief to allow people to live more normal lives.

Most of the drugs covered in this section have numerous effects on the nervous system, but each is usually reserved to treat one of the following conditions: anxiety, depression, insomnia, psychosis, or mania.

**ANXIETY**

Anxiety can be defined as persistent nervousness, tension, or panic caused by stress or other psychological causes. Antianxiety drugs (also known as minor tranquilizers) are used to promote relaxation or reduce the physical symptoms of anxiety. Benzodiazepines are a class of psychoactive drugs used to

treat anxiety and insomnia. They depress the central nervous system, causing relaxation and sedation. A class of drugs called beta-blockers reduces the shaking or palpitations that may occur when people panic in highly stressful situations, such as job interviews or speaking in public. Other drugs used to treat anxiety include buspirone, some antidepressants, and in special cases, barbiturates.

## DEPRESSION

Everyone feels depressed at times, but when it is prolonged and starts interfering with daily life, support, professional help, and/or psychoactive medications may be appropriate.

Depression is thought to be caused by a reduction in the level of certain chemicals, called neurotransmitters, in the brain. Antidepressants increase the levels of these chemicals in the spaces (called synapses) between nerve cells in the brain. Tricyclic antidepressants (e.g., amoxapine) and serotonin reuptake inhibitors (e.g., fluoxetine or sertraline) prevent cells from absorbing certain neurotransmitters, which increases their levels in the synapses. Monoamine oxidase (MAO) inhibitors increase neurotransmitter levels by interfering with the enzymes that break them down. It takes some time before antidepressants are effective. Ten to fourteen days may elapse after the initial dose before an effect is observable, and it may be six to eight weeks before they are fully effective.

Antidepressants often have severe side effects. MAO inhibitors in particular must be used with caution because they deactivate enzymes in the body that break down chemicals found in many foods, such as meat, cheese, yeast extracts, and red wine. Eating these foods while taking an MAO inhibitor can cause a dramatic rise in blood pressure.

## INSOMNIA

Insomnia has many causes, including anxiety and depression. When the cause is known and can be treated, sleep patterns generally return to normal. When the insomnia is persistent, sleeping drugs may be appropriate.

Most sleeping pills cause sedation by depressing the central nervous system. The most commonly used sleeping medications are the benzodiazepines, but barbiturates and some sedating antihistamines or antidepressant drugs are used as well.

The sleep induced by drugs is not the same as natural sleep. The drugs suppress brain activity and dreaming, and many have a "hangover" effect the next day. Because the drugs are often habit-forming and can cause withdrawal symptoms, they are usually recommended for short-term use only.

**PSYCHOSIS**

Psychosis is a condition in which a person may not be able to think clearly, recognize reality, or act rationally. The precise cause is often unknown, but stress, drug use, heredity, brain injury, or neurological disease may be involved. Drug treatment is usually reserved for when the psychosis is prolonged and interferes with normal life.

Most antipsychosis drugs, including a commonly used class called phenothiazines, work by inhibiting the activity of a neurotransmitter called dopamine. Dopamine is released in excess concentrations during psychosis. Antipsychotics reduce the effect of dopamine by blocking the nerve cell receptors that respond to the chemical.

Antipsychotics also interfere with the activity of another neurotransmitter, called acetylcholine, and after long-term use can cause involuntary muscle movements of the face and hands and other symptoms that resemble Parkinson's disease. These side effects may not be reversible when the drug is stopped.

**MANIA**

Mania (exaggerated euphoria or elation) is a type of psychosis that can be caused by a number of medical problems or as a side effect of certain drugs, such as the amphetamines, cocaine, and steroids. The most effective treatment is to remove the cause, if possible. Where the cause is unknown, drug treatment may be appropriate. Rapid or wild mood swings, with peaks of mania and troughs of depression, are usually treated with lithium, a drug that reduces the intensity of the mania and reduces the frequency of mood swings. Acute mania may be treated with haloperidol or phenothiazine drugs including thioridazine, fluphenazine, perphenazine, and trifluoperazine.

The following drugs, listed by class, are profiled in this section:

**BENZODIAZEPINES**
- alprazolam
- chlordiazepoxide
- diazepam
- flurazepam
- lorazepam
- midazolam
- oxazepam
- temazepam
- triazolam

**PHENOTHIAZINES**
- fluphenazine
- perphenazine
- thioridazine
- trifluoperazine

**TRICYCLIC ANTIDEPRESSANT**
- protriptyline

**SEROTONIN REUPTAKE INHIBITORS**
- fluoxetine

- paroxetine
- sertraline

**BETA-BLOCKER**
- propranolol

**OTHER**
- benztropine
- bupropion
- buspirone
- haloperidol
- lithium

- methylphenidate
- mirtazapine
- nefazodone
- venlafaxine

# ALPRAZOLAM

**BRAND NAME (MANUFACTURER)**
Xanax (Pharmacia & Upjohn)

**TYPE OF DRUG**
Psychoactive–antianxiety agent

**USED FOR**
Alprazolam is used primarily for short-term relief of anxiety. It is also effective for treating anxiety associated with depression and for treating panic disorders.

**GENERAL INFORMATION**
Alprazolam belongs to a class of psychoactive drugs called benzodiazepines. Benzodiazepines are the most commonly used antianxiety drugs because they are fairly safe, rapidly reduce the symptoms of anxiety, and don't have to be taken on an ongoing basis in order to be effective. All benzodiazepines cause dose-related suppression of the central nervous system, varying from slight impairment to hypnosis.

Alprazolam is available in tablets for oral administration.

**TREATMENT**
In general, the minimum effective dose of the drug should be used. The recommended starting dose for treatment of symptoms of anxiety is 0.25 to 0.5 mg taken three to four times a day. The dose may be increased, if necessary, at intervals of three to four days. The maximum daily dose is 4 mg.

When discontinuing the drug, it is recommended that the daily dose be decreased by no more than 0.5 mg every three days to avoid withdrawal symptoms. Some people may require an even slower dose reduction.

The suggested starting dose for the treatment of panic is 0.5 mg taken three times a day, but some people may require more than 4 mg per day. In clinical studies, participants have used dosages up to 10 mg per day, but the appropriate dose must be determined for each individual by starting at a low dose and slowly increasing until the desired effect is observed (as long as the drug is tolerated without serious side effects). After a period free of anxiety attacks, a carefully controlled dosage reduction and weaning may be attempted.

**CAUTIONS AND WARNINGS**

Alprazolam should not be used by people with glaucoma or a known allergy to the drug. It depresses the central nervous system, so it may not be appropriate to operate heavy machinery or drive a motor vehicle when taking it.

Like other benzodiazepines, alprazolam can be dangerous when taken with alcohol. Alcohol intensifies the depressive effect of benzodiazepines.

All benzodiazepines are habit-forming, and alprazolam is particularly likely to be addictive, even after relatively short-term use at the recommended doses. This usually means that, over time, increasing doses are needed to achieve the same effect. This differs from person to person, but in general, addiction is common after several months of use. The risk of dependency seems to be higher in people treated with relatively high doses (greater than 4 mg per day) and in those treated for more than eight to twelve weeks. Because treatment of panic disorder often requires doses over 4 mg per day, the risk of dependence among these people is greater than that for those treated for anxiety. Withdrawal reactions may occur when dosages of the drug are reduced for any reason.

Early morning anxiety, a type of withdrawal reaction that occurs in between doses, has been observed in people with panic disorder taking prescribed amounts of the drug.

**SIDE EFFECTS**

Side effects usually appear at the beginning of therapy and usually disappear over time. Most often the side effects include drowsiness, light-headedness, or dizziness. More serious side effects, although reported rarely, are seizures, hallucinations, taste alteration, double vision, liver toxicity, and jaundice.

Withdrawal symptoms include insomnia, headache, anxiety, fatigue, irritability, difficulty thinking or remembering, nausea, vomiting, diarrhea, weight loss, sweating, and rapid heartbeat.

**PREGNANCY/BREAST-FEEDING**

Benzodiazepines, including alprazolam, can cause birth defects when taken during pregnancy. Taken late in pregnancy, they may increase the risk that the baby will be born dependent on the drug. Pregnant women should avoid using alprazolam.

HIV can be passed from a woman to her child through breast milk. In areas where nutritionally sound alternatives are readily available, breast-feeding is discouraged for HIV-positive women. Benzodiazepines are excreted in human milk and can cause serious side effects in infants. Because of the potential toxicity of the drug, women should consider alternatives to breast-feeding while taking the drug.

**USE IN CHILDREN**
The safety and effectiveness of alprazolam in children under eighteen have not been studied.

**USE IN THE ELDERLY**
Elderly or debilitated people may be particularly susceptible to side effects of alprazolam. The starting dose for them is usually 0.25 mg two or three times a day. The dose may be gradually increased if needed and tolerated.

**DRUG INTERACTIONS**
Oral contraceptives and cimetidine may increase the concentration of alprazolam in the blood and potentially increase the risk of side effects. Benzodiazepines intensify the central nervous system depression caused by other psychoactive medications, anticonvulsants, antihistamines, and alcohol.

Alprazolam increases levels of imipramine and desipramine in the body, potentially increasing the risk of side effects.

**FOOD INTERACTIONS**
Alprazolam is absorbed into the body most effectively when taken on an empty stomach, but it can be taken with food if necessary.

**OTHER DRUGS USED FOR SIMILAR CONDITIONS**
Many different benzodiazepines are available by prescription. They include lorazepam, diazepam, chlordiazepoxide, oxazepam, temazepam, flurazepam, midazolam, and triazolam. They differ in their side effects, potencies, the time they take to work, and their tendency to cause withdrawal symptoms.

Buspirone is an antianxiety medication but not part of the benzodiazepine class. It is not addictive or sedating and has less tendency to slow down mental and physical reactions. On the other hand, it is not effective for many people.

# BENZTROPINE

**BRAND NAME (MANUFACTURER)**
Cogentin (Merck)

**TYPE OF DRUG**
Psychoactive–muscle relaxant

## USED FOR

Benztropine is used to treat the symptoms of Parkinson's disease. It is also used to prevent or treat the muscle spasms caused by certain drugs used to treat psychosis.

Benztropine can also be used to treat symptoms associated with Parkinson's disease, which is an uncommon manifestation of toxoplasmosis encephalitis in people infected with HIV.

## GENERAL INFORMATION

Benztropine is classified as an anticholinergic drug because it blocks the activity of a nerve-impulse transmitter called acetylcholine. Muscle rigidity is one of the primary symptoms of Parkinson's disease. Benztropine blocks the nerve signals that cause the rigidity, allowing the muscles to relax. By a similar mechanism, benztropine can prevent or counteract the muscle spasms that occur as a side effect of some psychoactive drugs.

Benztropine is available as a solution for injection and as tablets for oral administration. The injectable drug is used where rapid action is necessary and in cases where the muscle rigidity makes taking the tablets difficult or impossible.

## TREATMENT

As with all psychoactive drugs, the minimum effective dosage should be used. Therapy usually starts at a low dose and is increased gradually at five- or six-day intervals as necessary and as tolerated. For Parkinson's disease, the effective dosage ranges from 0.5 to 6.0 mg per day, with most adults using 1 to 2 mg per day. For treatment of muscle spasms caused by psychoactive drugs, benztropine is used at a dosage of 1 to 4 mg, once or twice a day, adjusted for the individual.

## CAUTIONS AND WARNINGS

Benztropine should not be used by anyone with a known allergy to it. It may impair the mental or physical abilities needed to operate dangerous machinery or drive an automobile.

Because benztropine may prevent sweating and interfere with the body's internal heat control, it should be used with caution by people with chronic illness, a history of alcoholism, central nervous system disease, and people with inability to sweat. Benztropine should also be used with caution by people doing manual labor in a hot environment. In these cases the drug can cause heatstroke, which on occasion has been fatal.

Benztropine should be used with caution in people with heart disease, prostate disorders, difficulty urinating, or glaucoma. Although the drug does not appear to affect simple glaucoma, it may worsen angle-closure glaucoma and should not be used by people with this condition.

**SIDE EFFECTS**

The most common side effects of benztropine include constipation, vomiting, nausea, dry mouth, and difficulty urinating. These can usually be eliminated or reduced in severity by lowering the dose of the drug.

Other side effects of benztropine include irregular heartbeat, confusion, disorientation, mental impairment, hallucinations, nervousness, depression, listlessness, numbness in the fingers, heatstroke, fever, and blurred vision. Occasionally, an allergic reaction such as a skin rash develops in people taking the drug.

**PREGNANCY/BREAST-FEEDING**

Benztropine has not been formally studied in pregnant women or animals, but in clinical practice, there has been no evidence that the drug causes fetal harm. Pregnant women are encouraged to discuss the benefits and potential risks of benztropine with their physician before deciding to take the drug.

HIV may be passed from a woman to her child through breast milk. In areas where nutritionally sound alternatives are readily available, breast-feeding is discouraged for HIV-positive women. Benztropine may reduce the amount of milk a woman can produce. In addition, infants are highly susceptible to the side effects of the drug. Women who must take the drug should discontinue breast-feeding.

**USE IN CHILDREN**

Because children are more sensitive than adults to the side effects of benztropine, the drug is not recommended for anyone under the age of three years. Older children who use the drug should be carefully monitored for side effects.

**USE IN THE ELDERLY**

Older adults may be more susceptible to the side effects of the drug and may require reduced doses.

**DRUG INTERACTIONS**

When benztropine is used with other psychoactive drugs, including phenothiazines (e.g., chlorpromazine), haloperidol, tricyclic antidepressants (e.g., amoxapine, amitriptyline, nortriptyline), or other anticholinergics (e.g., atropine), the risk of side effects is increased. In some cases, these combinations have been fatal.

**FOOD INTERACTIONS**

Oral benztropine is absorbed into the body most effectively when taken on an empty stomach, but it may be taken with food if it causes stomach upset.

**OTHER DRUGS USED FOR SIMILAR CONDITIONS**

Other drugs used to treat the symptoms of Parkinson's disease include diphenhydramine, levodopa, bromocriptine, and carbidopa. The choice of drug generally depends on the severity of the condition, the health of the individual,

and other drugs being used at the same time. In many cases, combinations of these drugs are more effective than using individual drugs alone.

# B U P R O P I O N

**BRAND NAME (MANUFACTURER)**
Wellbutrin (Glaxo Wellcome)

**TYPE OF DRUG**
Psychoactive–antidepressant

**USED FOR**
Bupropion is used to treat depression in people who cannot take other medications. The drug is also approved to assist smoking cessation.

**GENERAL INFORMATION**
Bupropion belongs to a class of drugs known as aminoketone antidepressants. It is chemically unrelated to tricyclic, tetracyclic, or other known classes of antidepressants. It is not known how bupropion works. It does not affect the cellular enzyme monoamine oxidase (MAO), which is the target of a class of antidepressants called MAO inhibitors. It raises brain levels of the neurotransmitters serotonin and norepinephrine only weakly, which is the mechanism of action of another class of antidepressants called serotonin reuptake inhibitors, such as fluoxetine (Prozac).

Bupropion is generally used only after other drugs have failed, because people taking it have a higher risk of seizures than those taking other antidepressants.

Antidepressant medications are usually taken over long periods. It may take three to four weeks for antidepressants, including bupropion, to have an effect on depression. Bupropion accumulates in the body's tissues with prolonged use, and after it is discontinued, the drug takes about two weeks to be completely cleared from the body.

Bupropion is available as tablets for oral administration.

**TREATMENT**
Bupropion is usually taken at a dosage of 300 to 400 mg per day, divided into three or four doses. The total dose is divided into these small amounts to reduce the risk of seizures.

**CAUTIONS AND WARNINGS**
Bupropion should not be used by anyone with a known allergy to it or people who have a history of seizures or eating disorders. The drug should also not be taken together with MAO inhibitors. At least fourteen days should elapse between discontinuing an MAO inhibitor and using bupropion.

In contrast to most other antidepressants, bupropion may cause weight loss. HIV-positive people who are already experiencing weight loss should consider using a different antidepressant.

Suddenly stopping bupropion may cause withdrawal symptoms or side effects.

## SIDE EFFECTS

The most serious side effect of bupropion is seizures. Approximately four out of every thousand people taking the drug experience seizures. The risk may be reduced if the total daily dose does not exceed 450 mg and if the drug is taken, as directed, in divided doses to reduce the maximum blood levels.

Other side effects of the drug include restlessness, agitation, anxiety, insomnia, confusion, hyperactivity, feelings of elation, delusions, hallucinations, or impaired mental function.

More than 28% of people treated with bupropion in clinical trials had loss of appetite and/or weight loss of more than five pounds.

## PREGNANCY/BREAST-FEEDING

Bupropion has not been formally studied in pregnant women. In animal studies it did not cause fetal harm, but it is not known whether the same would be true for humans. Pregnant women are encouraged to discuss the benefits and potential risks of bupropion with their physician before deciding whether or not to use the drug.

HIV may be passed from a woman to her child through breast milk. In areas where nutritionally sound alternatives are readily available, breast-feeding is discouraged for HIV-positive women. Bupropion may pass through human milk and cause serious side effects in nursing children. Because of the potential toxicity of the drug, women should consider alternatives to breast-feeding while taking it.

## USE IN CHILDREN

The safety and effectiveness of bupropion in people under eighteen have not been formally studied.

## USE IN THE ELDERLY

Older adults may be more susceptible to the side effects of the drug and may require reduced doses.

## DRUG INTERACTIONS

Bupropion is metabolized by the liver. Caution should be used when taking other drugs that affect the liver, including carbamazepine, cimetidine, phenobarbital, and phenytoin. There is some evidence of increased side effects when bupropion and L-dopa are used together.

Alcohol, tranquilizers, or other central nervous system depressants may intensify the effect of bupropion. Alcohol use also increases the risk of seizures caused by bupropion.

**FOOD INTERACTIONS**

Bupropion may be taken with or without food.

**OTHER DRUGS USED FOR SIMILAR CONDITIONS**

For treatment of depression, there are many options, including tricyclic anti-depressants (desipramine, nortriptyline, protriptyline, amoxapine, maprotiline, imipramine, trimipramine, doxepin), MAO inhibitors (tranylcypromine, phenelzine, isocarboxazid), serotonin reuptake inhibitors (fluoxetine, paroxetine, and sertraline), and stimulants such as methylphenidate. The appropriate choice varies from person to person and depends on age, physical health and condition, and other drugs being concurrently used.

# BUSPIRONE

**BRAND NAME (MANUFACTURER)**

BuSpar (Bristol-Myers Squibb)

**TYPE OF DRUG**

Psychoactive–antianxiety drug

**USED FOR**

Buspirone is used primarily for the short-term relief of anxiety. It is also occasionally used to treat the pain, fatigue, and cramps of premenstrual syndrome (PMS).

**GENERAL INFORMATION**

Buspirone is an antianxiety drug that is chemically different from and works by a completely different mechanism than most other antianxiety drugs. Buspirone is less sedating than a majority of antianxiety drugs and has no potential for addiction. It is also less likely to slow down mental and physical reactions in people who take it. It may be an appropriate choice for people who need to remain alert and for those with a potential for substance abuse.

Buspirone is available in tablets for oral administration.

**TREATMENT**

As with all psychoactive drugs, the lowest effective dosage of buspirone should be used. The recommended initial dose is 5 mg three times a day. The dose is usually increased gradually as necessary and as long as it is tolerated. Total daily doses of 20 to 30 mg are common after the condition has stabilized.

**CAUTIONS AND WARNINGS**

Buspirone should not be used by anyone with a known allergy to it. It is not recommended for people taking antidepressants of the monoamine oxidase (MAO) inhibitor class because of the potential for serious side effects.

People who are taking benzodiazepine antianxiety drugs (e.g., alprazolam, diazepam, chlordiazepoxide) and want to switch to buspirone should gradually reduce their dose under a doctor's supervision and stop taking the benzodiazepine before starting buspirone. This strategy reduces the risk of withdrawal symptoms from the benzodiazepines.

Although buspirone is less sedating than other antianxiety medications, drowsiness is still possible and there is no way to predict how an individual will react to the drug. People taking buspirone should be cautious about operating dangerous machinery or driving an automobile while on the drug.

### SIDE EFFECTS

Dizziness, nausea, headache, and nervousness were reported by 5% to 10% of people taking the drug in clinical trials. Light-headedness and excitability were reported by approximately 2% of people in clinical trials.

Other side effects that occur in more than 1% of people who use buspirone include chest pain, dream disturbances, ringing in the ears, sore throat, and nasal congestion. Side effects that were reported in fewer than 1% of people taking the drug included changes in blood pressure, redness and itching of the eyes, altered taste, altered smell, gas, changes in appetite, rectal bleeding, changes in urination patterns, menstrual irregularity, muscle cramps, muscle spasms, shortness of breath, changes in sex drive, allergic reactions, dry skin, weight changes (both gains and losses), and malaise.

### PREGNANCY/BREAST-FEEDING

Buspirone has not been formally studied in pregnant women. In animal studies, it did not cause fetal harm, but it is not known whether this would be true for humans. Pregnant women are encouraged to discuss the benefits and potential risks of buspirone with their physician before deciding to take the drug.

HIV may be passed from a woman to her child through breast milk. In areas where nutritionally sound alternatives are readily available, breast-feeding is discouraged for HIV-positive women. It is not known whether buspirone is excreted in human milk. However, it was excreted in the milk of laboratory animals. Because of the potential toxicity of the drug to their infants, women should consider alternatives to breast-feeding while taking it.

### USE IN CHILDREN

The safety and effectiveness of buspirone for children under the age of eighteen have not been formally studied in clinical trials.

### USE IN THE ELDERLY

Although buspirone has not been formally studied in the elderly, several hundred people over the age of sixty-five participated in studies of buspirone for the general population, and no unusual, age-related increase in side effects was identified.

**DRUG INTERACTIONS**

When used with MAO inhibitors (e.g., phenelzine or tranylcypromine), buspirone may increase the risk of serious elevations in blood pressure. Buspirone may increase haloperidol levels in the blood, potentially increasing the risk of side effects. The combination of buspirone and trazodone may cause liver toxicity.

**FOOD INTERACTIONS**

Food slows down the rate at which buspirone is absorbed into the body, but increases the total amount absorbed. Buspirone may be taken with or without food.

**OTHER DRUGS USED FOR SIMILAR CONDITIONS**

The benzodiazepines (e.g., alprazolam, diazepam, chlordiazepoxide) are the most frequently used antianxiety medications. They are fairly safe, they work rapidly, and they don't have to be taken on an ongoing basis to be effective. The drugs in the class differ somewhat in their side effects, potencies, the time they take to work, and their tendency to be addictive or cause withdrawal symptoms.

Buspirone is not addictive and is less likely to be sedating. On the other hand, it is not effective for many people, and in others it must be taken several times a day in order to be effective.

# CHLORDIAZEPOXIDE

**BRAND NAME (MANUFACTURER)**

Libritabs (Roche); Librax (Roche); Librium (Roche)

**TYPE OF DRUG**

Psychoactive–antianxiety agent

**USED FOR**

Chlordiazepoxide is used for the short-term relief of anxiety. It is also used to treat withdrawal symptoms of alcoholism and to prevent apprehension and anxiety.

**GENERAL INFORMATION**

Chlordiazepoxide was the first of a class of psychoactive drugs called benzodiazepines. Benzodiazepines are the most commonly used antianxiety drugs because they are fairly safe, they rapidly reduce symptoms of anxiety, and they don't have to be taken on an ongoing basis to be effective.

Chlordiazepoxide or other benzodiazepines are appropriate for short-term use in people experiencing extreme stress or anxiety.

Chlordiazepoxide is available as tablets for oral administration.

**TREATMENT**

The optimum dosage of chlordiazepoxide is determined by the diagnosis and the age and condition of the individual. For anxiety, the oral drug is generally used at 5 to 25 mg three or four times daily. The upper range is usually reserved for relief of severe anxiety disorders. Elderly people and children generally take lower doses: starting at 10 mg or less per day is common.

The injectable form of the drug is preferred for treating withdrawal symptoms of acute alcoholism. The adult dosage is 50 to 100 mg intramuscularly or intravenously, every two to four hours as necessary. When used for simple anxiety, the initial dose of the injectable is 50 to 100 mg initially, then reduced to 25 to 50 mg three or four times daily if necessary. Dose reductions are usually required for children and for elderly and/or debilitated people.

**CAUTIONS AND WARNINGS**

Chlordiazepoxide should not be used by anyone with a known allergy to it. The drug depresses the central nervous system, so it may not be appropriate to operate heavy machinery or drive a motor vehicle when taking it.

Like other benzodiazepines, chlordiazepoxide can be dangerous if taken with alcohol, which intensifies the depressive effect of benzodiazepines.

Taking chlordiazepoxide can be habit-forming. It appears that physical or psychological dependency may require several months of daily use, but dependency can sometimes occur much sooner. Rapid withdrawal after long-term use can lead to increased anxiety, insomnia, tremors, and in severe cases, seizures.

**SIDE EFFECTS**

The most common side effects of chlordiazepoxide include drowsiness, confusion, and loss of balance, especially among elderly or debilitated people. Less commonly, people experience constipation; depression; headache; low blood pressure; incontinence; jaundice; changes in sex drive; nausea; changes in salivation; skin rash; and in women, menstrual irregularities.

For people who use the drug routinely, periodic blood counts and liver function tests are recommended because both an increase or decrease in white blood cell count may occur after use of the drug.

**PREGNANCY/BREAST-FEEDING**

Chlordiazepoxide has not been formally studied in pregnant women. There is some evidence that it increases the risk of fetal deformities when used during the first trimester of pregnancy. Taken later in pregnancy, it may increase the risk that the baby will become addicted to it. Pregnant women are encouraged to discuss the benefits and potential risks of chlordiazepoxide with their physician before deciding whether or not to use the drug.

HIV can be passed from a woman to her child through breast milk. In areas where nutritionally sound alternatives are readily available, breast-feeding is discouraged for HIV-positive women. Chlordiazepoxide is excreted in human milk and can cause serious side effects in infants. Because of the potential toxicity of the drug, women should consider alternatives to breast-feeding while taking it.

**USE IN CHILDREN**
Because there is little information about the safety and effectiveness of the drug for children, the oral form of the drug is not recommended in children under six years of age, and the injectable form is not recommended for children under twelve.

**USE IN THE ELDERLY**
Elderly or debilitated people should receive the smallest effective dosage. Ten milligrams or less per day is recommended for initial treatment, only to be increased gradually as needed and tolerated.

**DRUG INTERACTIONS**
Chlordiazepoxide may decrease the effectiveness of carbamazepine, levodopa, and oral anticoagulants such as warfarin. It may increase the effects of phenytoin. Disulfiram, oral contraceptives, isoniazid, and cimetidine can increase the blood levels of chlordiazepoxide, potentially increasing the risk of side effects. Rifampin may decrease the effectiveness of chlordiazepoxide.

**FOOD INTERACTIONS**
Chlordiazepoxide is absorbed most effectively into the body when taken on an empty stomach, but if necessary, it can be taken with food to minimize stomach upset.

**OTHER DRUGS USED FOR SIMILAR CONDITIONS**
Many different benzodiazepines are available for prescription use. They include lorazepam, diazepam, alprazolam, oxazepam, temazepam, flurazepam, midzolam, and triazolam. The drugs differ somewhat in their side effects, potencies, the time they take to work, and their tendency to cause withdrawal symptoms.

Buspirone is an antianxiety medication that is not part of the benzodiazepine class. It is not addictive or sedating and has less tendency to slow down mental and physical reactions in people who take it. On the other hand, it is not effective for many people.

To treat anxiety accompanied by depression, a number of manufacturers market chlordiazepoxide/amitriptyline combinations.

# DIAZEPAM

**BRAND NAME (MANUFACTURER)**
Valium (Roche); Valrelease (Roche)

**TYPE OF DRUG**
Psychoactive–antianxiety agent

**USED FOR**
Diazepam is primarily used for the treatment of anxiety. It is also sometimes used to relax muscles, treat seizures, or to reduce the symptoms of acute alcohol withdrawal. Diazepam is also used to reduce anxiety before surgical procedures.

**GENERAL INFORMATION**
Diazepam belongs to a class of psychoactive drugs called benzodiazepines. Benzodiazepines are the most commonly used antianxiety drugs because they are fairly safe, they rapidly reduce the symptoms of anxiety, and they don't have to be taken on an ongoing basis to be effective.

Diazepam is available as tablets, capsules, and a solution for oral administration as well as a solution for intravenous administration.

**TREATMENT**
The usual dosage of diazepam for adults is 2 to 10 mg two to four times a day, depending on the severity of symptoms and the diagnosis.

Elderly people usually take reduced doses, starting at 2 to 2.5 mg once or twice a day, increasing the dosage as tolerated and only when necessary.

Diazepam is not for use in children under six years of age. Older children may receive 1 to 2.5 mg three to four times a day initially, increased gradually as needed and tolerated.

**CAUTIONS AND WARNINGS**
Diazepam should not be used by people who are allergic to the drug or people who have glaucoma unless they are receiving appropriate anti-glaucoma therapy. The drug depresses the central nervous system, so it may not be appropriate to operate heavy machinery or drive a motor vehicle when taking diazepam.

Like other benzodiazepines, diazepam can be dangerous when taken with alcohol. Alcohol intensifies the depressive effects of benzodiazepines.

Taking diazepam can be habit-forming. It appears that physical or psychological dependency may require several months of daily use, but dependency can sometimes occur much sooner. Rapid withdrawal after long-term use can lead to increased anxiety, insomnia, tremors, and in severe cases, seizures.

Abrupt withdrawal of diazepam when used with anticonvulsants may also cause a temporary increase in the frequency and/or severity of seizures.

**SIDE EFFECTS**

The most common side effects of diazepam include drowsiness, fatigue, and loss of balance. Less commonly, people taking the drug experience confusion, constipation, depression, headache, low blood pressure, incontinence, jaundice, changes in sex drive, nausea, changes in salivation, skin rash, slurred speech, tremor, difficulty urinating, vertigo, and blurred vision.

On rare occasion, individuals have experienced a deficiency in certain white blood cells called neutrophils after taking diazepam. For this reason, periodic blood counts and liver-function tests are recommended for people who use diazepam routinely.

**PREGNANCY/BREAST-FEEDING**

Diazepam may cause an increased risk for fetal deformities when used during the first trimester of pregnancy. Diazepam taken later in pregnancy may increase the risk that the baby will become dependent on it. Pregnant women should discontinue using the drug.

HIV can be passed from a woman to her child through breast milk. In areas where nutritionally sound alternatives are readily available, breast-feeding is discouraged for HIV-positive women. Diazepam is excreted in human milk and can cause serious side effects in infants. Because of the potential toxicity of the drug, women should consider alternatives to breast-feeding while taking it.

**USE IN CHILDREN**

Newborn infants have immature kidney and liver function and are often unable to metabolize drugs and excrete them from their bodies. In infants under thirty days of age, diazepam has caused prolonged central nervous system depression, possibly caused by the immature kidney function. The drug is not recommended for children under six months of age.

For older children, diazepam may effectively be used at lower doses than those given to adults. In general, the dose is started at 1 to 2.5 mg, taken three or four times daily, gradually increased as needed and tolerated.

**USE IN THE ELDERLY**

Older adults may be more susceptible to the side effects of the drug and may require reduced doses.

**DRUG INTERACTIONS**

Phenothiazines, cimetidine, oral contraceptives, narcotics, barbiturates, alcohol, monoamine oxidase (MAO) inhibitors, and other antidepressants may intensify the effect of diazepam and increase the risk of serious side effects.

Diazepam may decrease the effectiveness of carbamazepine, levodopa, and blood thinners (such as warfarin) and may increase the effects of phenytoin.

Concurrent use with rifampin may decrease the effectiveness of diazepam.

**FOOD INTERACTIONS**
Diazepam is absorbed most rapidly into the body when taken on an empty stomach, but it may be taken with food if it causes stomach upset.

**OTHER DRUGS USED FOR SIMILAR CONDITIONS**
Many different benzodiazepines are available for prescription use. They include lorazepam, chlordiazepoxide, alprazolam, oxazepam, temazepam, flurazepam, and triazolam, among others.

The drugs differ somewhat in their side effects, potencies, the time it takes for them to work, and their tendency to cause withdrawal symptoms.

Buspirone is an antianxiety medication that is not part of the benzodiazepine class. It is not addictive or sedating and has fewer tendencies to slow down mental and physical reactions in the people who take it. On the other hand, it is not effective for many people.

# FLUOXETINE

**BRAND NAME (MANUFACTURER)**
Prozac (Dista)

**TYPE OF DRUG**
Psychoactive–antidepressant

**USED FOR**
Fluoxetine is widely used to treat the symptoms of mental depression. It is less frequently used to treat obsessive-compulsive disorder, classic panic disorder, the eating disorder bulimia, and it can also be used as an appetite suppressant.

**GENERAL INFORMATION**
Fluoxetine is an antidepressant that belongs to a class known as serotonin reuptake inhibitors. It is chemically unrelated to tricyclic, tetracyclic, or other known classes of antidepressants. It has become widely used because it is effective and tends to have fewer side effects than older antidepressants (such as the monoamine oxidase inhibitors, for example). It does not cause sedation, weight gain, dry mouth, or constipation.

Antidepressant medications are usually taken over long periods. It takes four weeks or more before steady levels are built up in the blood, and it may take as long for the drug to have an effect on depression. Fluoxetine accumulates in the body's tissues with prolonged use, and the drug may stay in the body for weeks or months after discontinuing therapy. It is especially important that at least five weeks pass after stopping the drug before starting another drug that may interact with fluoxetine.

Fluoxetine has been studied in a number of small clinical trials in people with HIV infection. In general, it has been highly effective in reducing the symptoms of depression. People with low CD4+ counts (under 200) did as well on the drug as people with higher counts.

Fluoxetine is available as capsules for oral administration.

## TREATMENT

For depression, the recommended dose is 20 to 80 mg per day. As with all antidepressants, it is recommended that the lower dose be initially used and increased after several weeks as necessary if the person is not experiencing serious side effects. It may take up to four weeks to notice an effect. The dose may need to be reduced for people with poor liver or kidney function.

For obsessive-compulsive disorder, the recommended treatment is 20 mg per day taken in the morning. Full therapeutic effect may take five weeks or longer. A dose increase may be considered after several weeks if no improvement is seen, but the dose should not exceed 80 mg per day.

## CAUTIONS AND WARNINGS

Fluoxetine should not be used by anyone with a known allergy to it. It should not be used by people taking monoamine oxidase (MAO) inhibitor antidepressants. Because fluoxetine and MAO inhibitors remain in the body for a time after stopping therapy, fluoxetine should not be started within fourteen days of receiving an MAO inhibitor. MAO inhibitors should not be started within at least five weeks, and perhaps longer, after stopping fluoxetine.

People with diabetes should use fluoxetine with caution. The drug may alter control of sugar metabolism in the body.

## SIDE EFFECTS

Fluoxetine is relatively well tolerated. Its most common side effects (which were observed in more than 5% of people taking the drug in clinical trials) include anxiety, nervousness, insomnia, fatigue, tremors, sweating, changes in appetite, reduced sex drive, nausea, diarrhea, dizziness, or light-headedness.

## PREGNANCY/BREAST-FEEDING

There was no harm to the fetus when fluoxetine was given to pregnant laboratory animals, but there have been no studies of fluoxetine in pregnant women. Pregnant women are encouraged to discuss the benefits and potential risks of fluoxetine with their physician before deciding to use the drug.

HIV can be passed from a woman to her child through breast milk. In areas where nutritionally sound alternatives are readily available, breast-feeding is discouraged for HIV-positive women. Fluoxetine is excreted in human milk. Because of the potential toxicity of the drug, women should consider alternatives to breast-feeding while taking it.

### USE IN CHILDREN
The safety and effectiveness of fluoxetine for children have not been formally studied in clinical trials.

### USE IN THE ELDERLY
It is not known if fluoxetine is metabolized differently in elderly people than in younger people. No unexpected side effects have been seen in elderly people taking 20 mg daily.

### DRUG INTERACTIONS
Extreme drowsiness may occur when fluoxetine is taken with alcohol or other central nervous system depressants such as barbiturates, muscle relaxants, sleeping pills, antihistamines, or tranquilizers.

Fluoxetine increases the blood-thinning effect of warfarin, requiring adjustment of the warfarin dose. Similarly, fluoxetine may increase the effect of heart medicine such as digitoxin.

Serious side effects may occur if fluoxetine is taken with MAO inhibitors or by people with residual levels of MAO inhibitors in their blood.

Fluoxetine can increase the levels of tryptophan and increase the chance of tryptophan-related side effects, including anxiety, agitation, restlessness, and stomach irritation.

### FOOD INTERACTIONS
None reported.

### OTHER DRUGS USED FOR SIMILAR CONDITIONS
For treatment of depression, there are many options, including tricyclic antidepressants (desipramine, nortriptyline, protriptyline, amoxapine, maprotiline, imipramine, trimipramine, doxepin), MAO inhibitors (tranylcypromine, phenelzine, isocarboxazid), other serotonin reuptake inhibitors (paroxetine and sertraline), and stimulants such as methylphenidate. The appropriate drug varies from person to person and depends on age, physical health and condition, and other drugs being concurrently used.

# FLUPHENAZINE

### BRAND NAME (MANUFACTURER)
Prolixin (Apothecon)

### TYPE OF DRUG
Psychoactive–antipsychotic tranquilizer

### USED FOR
Fluphenazine is used for the management of psychosis, a mental disorder characterized by difficulty thinking, recognizing reality, and acting rationally.

## GENERAL INFORMATION

Fluphenazine belongs to a class of psychoactive drugs called phenothiazines. Although the mechanism by which they work is unknown, they have potent effects on the central nervous system and other organs. In addition to their effects on mental disorders, they also prolong the effects of anesthetics and other central nervous system depressants. They can reduce blood pressure, stop seizures, and prevent vomiting. Fluphenazine is more potent than most of the other phenothiazines and it is less likely to cause serious side effects.

Fluphenazine is available in a number of different chemical forms, which differ primarily in the duration of their action. The drug is available in tablets, as a solution for injection, and as an oral concentrate.

## TREATMENT

As with all psychoactive drugs, the minimum effective dosage should be taken. The oral forms of fluphenazine are usually initially used at a range of 2.5 to 10 mg per day, divided into equal doses given at six- to eight-hour intervals. Treatment usually starts at low initial dosages and is gradually increased as necessary and tolerated. Treatment is effective for most people with doses under 20 mg daily, but some people with severe disease may require up to 40 mg per day.

When the symptoms are controlled, the dosage can generally be reduced gradually to a daily dose of 1 to 5 mg, often given as a single daily dose. After stabilization on the short-acting forms of the drug, individuals may elect to switch to the longer-acting forms to make taking the drug easier. Once monthly intramuscular injections may be appropriate after control is achieved.

## CAUTIONS AND WARNINGS

Fluphenazine should not be used by anyone with a known allergy to it. It should also not be used by people with brain damage, those receiving large doses of other psychoactive drugs, or those in a coma or severely depressed states. The drug should also not be used by people with severe liver damage or blood disorders.

People who are allergic to other phenothiazines may also be allergic to fluphenazine and should use the drug with caution. Similarly, people who are exposed to extreme heat or phosphorus pesticides and people with a history of seizures or heart disease should use the drug with caution because of their increased risk of side effects.

Although phenothiazines are in general not addictive, some people have experienced withdrawal symptoms (including nausea, vomiting, dizziness, and tremors) when stopping therapy after receiving high doses. These symptoms may be reduced by taking an anti–Parkinson's disease drug like benztropine.

Fluphenazine may impair the mental and physical abilities necessary to operate dangerous machinery or to drive an automobile.

## SIDE EFFECTS

The side effects reported most frequently after using phenothiazines include loss of muscle coordination or tone, muscle rigidity, and other disorders of the nerve control of muscles. In general, the symptoms are reversible when treatment is stopped or benztropine is used, but in some cases they may persist.

Tardive dyskinesia is a special neuromuscular side effect of phenothiazines. It is characterized by potentially irreversible, involuntary muscle movements that usually involve the tongue, face, mouth, lips, jaw, torso, and extremities. Although the side effect occurs most frequently among the elderly (especially elderly women), it is not possible to predict whether an individual will develop the disorder. The risk of the side effect and the likelihood it will be irreversible are believed to be increased with increased duration of treatment and cumulative dose.

Antipsychotic drugs, including fluphenazine, can cause a potentially fatal side effect called neuroleptic malignant syndrome. The syndrome is characterized by high fever, muscle rigidity, altered mental status, irregular pulse or blood pressure, and abnormal heart rhythms. If these symptoms occur, the drug should be stopped and a physician contacted immediately.

Other side effects of fluphenazine include low blood pressure or fluctuations in blood pressure, weight change, swelling in the extremities, allergic reactions, and liver damage.

## PREGNANCY/BREAST-FEEDING

Fluphenazine has not been formally studied in pregnant women. Most evidence suggests, however, that phenothiazines have a low risk of causing birth defects or other fetal harm when used during pregnancy. Pregnant women are encouraged to discuss the benefits and potential risks of fluphenazine with their physician before deciding to use the drug.

HIV may be passed from a woman to her child through breast milk. In areas where nutritionally sound alternatives are readily available, breast-feeding is discouraged for HIV-positive women. It is not known whether fluphenazine is excreted in human milk. Other phenothiazines have not had serious adverse effects on nursing infants, but whether this would be true for fluphenazine is not known.

## USE IN CHILDREN

Fluphenazine has not been formally studied in children, and there are no recommendations regarding its use for them.

**USE IN THE ELDERLY**
Older adults may be more susceptible to the side effects of the drug and may require reduced doses.

**DRUG INTERACTIONS**
Fluphenazine may intensify the effects of alcohol, analgesics, narcotics, antihistamines, and barbiturates. Antacids may decrease absorption of fluphenazine. Phenobarbital or lithium may decrease the effect of fluphenazine. Guanethidine or methyldopa used with fluphenazine may cause increased blood pressure. Use of insulin with fluphenazine may result in increased blood sugar levels. Use of orphenadrine with fluphenazine may result in lowered blood sugar levels.

**FOOD INTERACTIONS**
None reported.

**OTHER DRUGS USED FOR SIMILAR CONDITIONS**
A number of different drugs are available for treating psychosis. They include chlorpromazine, thioridazine, trifluoperazine, haloperidol, loxapine, and thiothixene. They differ in their duration of action, side effects, dosage, and administration. Because different people respond differently to each of the drugs, the choice of therapy usually comes down to finding through trial and error a drug that is both effective and tolerable. In comparison to the others, fluphenazine has relatively mild effects on alertness and blood pressure, but it has a relatively high risk of causing neuromuscular side effects.

# FLURAZEPAM

**BRAND NAME (MANUFACTURER)**
Dalmane (Roche)

**TYPE OF DRUG**
Psychoactive–sedative

**USED FOR**
Flurazepam is used for the short-term treatment of insomnia.

**GENERAL INFORMATION**
Anxiety, depression, and many medications can cause sleep problems in people with HIV infection. Flurazepam, one of the most widely used sleeping pills in the United States, is a member of a class of psychoactive drugs called benzodiazepines. All of these drugs reduce anxiety or cause drowsiness to some degree. They differ mostly in the degree of their effects and the duration of their action. Flurazepam is one of the longer-acting benzodiazepines, so it may be more likely to cause a "hangover" effect.

Like other benzodiazepines, flurazepam can cause dependency. Withdrawal symptoms may include convulsions, tremors, abdominal pain, muscle cramps, vomiting, sweating, restlessness, perceptual disturbances, and insomnia. The risk of addiction is increased in people with a history of alcoholism, drug use, or marked personality disorders.

**TREATMENT**

The dose should be adjusted for the age, condition, and health of the individual. The usual adult dosage is 30 mg taken at bedtime. For some people, especially those who are elderly or debilitated, 15 mg may be sufficient. It may take one or two days of consecutive use before flurazepam is fully effective, and after stopping the drug, it may take a few days for its effects to wear off.

**CAUTIONS AND WARNINGS**

Flurazepam should not be used by anyone with a known allergy to it.

Sleep disorders may be symptoms of other physical or psychiatric problems. Eliminating the underlying cause of sleeplessness, if it can be determined, may be a better long-term solution to the problem.

Flurazepam, like other benzodiazepines, may be habit-forming if taken for more than three or four days in a row. Consequently, it is possible for a person taking the drug to develop withdrawal symptoms if the drug is suddenly discontinued, including convulsions, tremors, muscle cramps, insomnia, agitation, diarrhea, vomiting, and sweating.

As with all psychoactive drugs, the minimum effective dosage should be used because some of the drug's side effects are dose-related. Elderly people are especially susceptible to the dose-related side effects of the drug.

Flurazepam depresses the central nervous system. People taking the drug should not drive an automobile or operate heavy machinery. Because flurazepam is a relatively long-acting benzodiazepine, its effects on alertness may continue into the day after taking the drug when taken the previous night.

**SIDE EFFECTS**

The most common side effects of the drug include dizziness, drowsiness, lightheadedness, staggering, loss of muscle coordination, and falling.

Other less frequent side effects of the drug include headache, heartburn, upset stomach, nausea, vomiting, diarrhea, constipation, stomach pain, nervousness, talkativeness, apprehension, irritability, weakness, heart palpitations, body and joint pain, and difficulty urinating.

Severe sedation, lethargy, disorientation, and coma have been reported on rare occasions.

## PREGNANCY/BREAST-FEEDING

Flurazepam should not be used during pregnancy. Although flurazepam has not been formally studied in pregnant women, other benzodiazepines have caused birth defects when used during the first trimester of pregnancy. There have also been cases of severe side effects of flurazepam in infants whose mothers took the drug during pregnancy.

HIV may be passed from a woman to her child through breast milk. In areas where nutritionally sound alternatives are readily available, breast-feeding is discouraged for HIV-positive women. Flurazepam is excreted in breast milk and may cause serious side effects in newborn infants. Because of the potential toxicity of the drug, women should consider alternatives to breast-feeding while taking it.

## USE IN CHILDREN

The safety and effectiveness of flurazepam have not been studied in children under the age of fifteen, so there are no recommendations about pediatric use.

## USE IN THE ELDERLY

Older adults may be more susceptible to the side effects of the drug and may require reduced doses.

## DRUG INTERACTIONS

Flurazepam produces additive central nervous system depression when used with anticonvulsants, antihistamines, alcohol, and other drugs that produce central nervous system depression.

Oral contraceptives, cimetidine, disulfiram, probenecid, and isoniazid may increase the effects of flurazepam by increasing blood levels of the drug. Cigarette smoking, rifampin, and theophylline may reduce blood levels of flurazepam, potentially reducing the drug's effectiveness.

Flurazepam may increase the amount of phenytoin or digoxin in the blood, increasing the risk of side effects. Flurazepam used with clozapine has caused respiratory collapse in some people. Clozapine should not be used until at least one week after flurazepam is stopped.

## FOOD INTERACTIONS

None reported.

## OTHER DRUGS USED FOR SIMILAR CONDITIONS

A number of drugs are available for treatment of insomnia. Barbiturates such as secobarbital or phenobarbital are occasionally used. More commonly, sedatives such as lorazepam, diazepam, triazolam, or promethazine are used. There is no ideal treatment for insomnia. Choosing one depends primarily on which can be tolerated, which side effects a person is at risk for, and which proves to be the most effective for the individual.

# HALOPERIDOL

**BRAND NAME (MANUFACTURER)**
Haldol (McNeil)

**TYPE OF DRUG**
Psychoactive–tranquilizer

**USED FOR**
Haloperidol is used for management of the symptoms of psychotic disorders in children and adults. In children this may include treatment of hyperactivity, severe behavioral problems, inability to sustain attention, and an abnormally low tolerance for frustration. In adults, the treated disorders may include Tourette's syndrome, chronic schizophrenia, and phencyclidine psychosis.

**GENERAL INFORMATION**
Haloperidol affects a part of the brain called the hypothalamus. This part of the brain affects some of the automatic functions of the body, including temperature, metabolism levels, alertness, muscle tone, and hormone balance. It is not known exactly how the drug alleviates the symptoms of psychosis.

Haloperidol comes as tablets, a liquid concentrate, and injectable solution.

**TREATMENT**
Most adults and children use the tablet form unless they have difficulty swallowing it. The solution for injection is used for severely agitated people to achieve a rapid response. This formulation has not been tested in children.

The dose of haloperidol must be adjusted for a person's age, condition, severity of illness, previous response to other psychoactive drugs, and other medications taken at the same time. Children and elderly adults with impaired kidney function may require lower doses. The optimal response is usually obtained by starting with a low dose and gradually increasing it.

Haloperidol decanoate is a long-acting form of the drug and is administered by deep injection into a large muscle once a month. It is generally used only after a person has stabilized while taking the shorter-acting oral drug.

**CAUTIONS AND WARNINGS**
Haloperidol should not be used by people in severe central nervous system depression comatose states. It should also not be used by those with Parkinson's disease or who have a known allergy to the drug.

Tardive dyskinesia, a syndrome consisting of potentially irreversible, involuntary movements, may develop in people treated with haloperidol. The risk is correlated with length of therapy and total dose, but it is not possible to predict whether any individual will experience the side effect.

As with other central nervous system depressants, haloperidol may affect the mental and physical capacity to operate heavy machinery or drive an automobile.

Haloperidol should be used with caution in people with heart conditions because of the risk of low blood pressure and in those with a history of seizures or receiving anticonvulsant medication because haloperidol may increase the risk of seizures.

## SIDE EFFECTS

The most common side effect to haloperidol is drowsiness. Less commonly, haloperidol can cause jaundice, fever, bone marrow toxicity, alteration in blood pressure, abnormal heartbeat, heart attack, faintness, and dizziness.

Haloperidol can cause serious neurological side effects that include spasms of the neck muscles, severe stiffness of the back, rolling of the eyes, convulsions, difficulty swallowing, and symptoms associated with Parkinson's disease.

Haloperidol may cause an unusual increase in psychotic reactions, including paranoia, tiredness, lethargy, restlessness, confusion, bizarre dreams, insomnia, depression, or euphoria.

## PREGNANCY/BREAST-FEEDING

Haloperidol has not been formally studied in pregnant women. In animal studies, it did cause some evidence of fetal harm, but it is not known whether this would be true in humans. There have been reports of birth defects in women taking haloperidol with other drugs that have the potential to cause fetal harm, but it is not known whether haloperidol itself caused the birth defects. Pregnant women are encouraged to discuss the benefits and potential risks of haloperidol with their physician before deciding to use the drug.

HIV can be passed from a woman to her child through breast milk. In areas where nutritionally sound alternatives are readily available, breast-feeding is discouraged for HIV-positive women. Haloperidol is excreted at high concentrations in human milk. It is not recommended for nursing women.

## USE IN CHILDREN

Haloperidol has been used effectively in children without unexpected side effects.

## USE IN THE ELDERLY

Tardive dyskinesia is a haloperidol-related side effect that most commonly occurs in elderly people who take the drug, particularly elderly women.

Older adults may be more susceptible to the side effects of the drug and may require reduced doses.

**DRUG INTERACTIONS**

Irreversible brain damage has occurred in a small number of people treated with lithium and haloperidol. It is not known, however, whether the drugs actually caused the side effect.

The use of haloperidol with alcohol, sleeping pills, barbiturates, anesthetics, or narcotics may cause severe central nervous system depression and low blood pressure.

Haloperidol may reduce the blood pressure–lowering effect of guanethidine. Mixing haloperidol with propranolol may result in unusually low blood pressure. Blood concentrations of tricyclic antidepressants may be increased when they are used with haloperidol, increasing the risk of side effects.

**FOOD INTERACTIONS**

Haloperidol is absorbed most effectively when taken without food, but food may be used if the drug causes stomach upset.

**OTHER DRUGS USED FOR SIMILAR CONDITIONS**

Other drugs with antipsychotic and tranquilizing activity include thorazine, fluphenazine, mesoridazine, thioridazine, and trifluoperazine. In general, they are equally effective when given in therapeutically equivalent doses. The major differences are in the type and severity of side effects, which may be different from person to person.

# L I T H I U M

**BRAND NAME (MANUFACTURER)**

Eskalith (SmithKline Beecham); Lithonate (Reid-Rowell); Lithotabs (Reid-Rowell)

**TYPE OF DRUG**

Psychoactive–antimanic agent

**USED FOR**

Lithium is used to treat or prevent the manic phases of manic depression, a mental disorder in which a person's mood swings wildly from elation to depression.

Lithium has also been used but not approved to reduce or counteract the bone marrow toxicity of AZT in people with HIV, although there is little clinical evidence to support this use.

**GENERAL INFORMATION**

Lithium is the only effective drug available to treat mania. When ingested and absorbed into the body, lithium alters the way nerve cells transmit their

signals. This action effectively controls the symptoms of mania within one to three weeks after starting the drug.

Certain drugs commonly used by people infected with HIV, including AZT, can be toxic to bone marrow, often resulting in deficiencies in white blood cells. Because one side effect of lithium is an increase in white blood cells, the drug has been tested as a potential therapy to reverse the bone marrow toxicity of AZT. Encouraging results in studies in animals prompted the start of clinical trials in humans. In one study, twenty volunteers were randomly chosen to receive AZT and either lithium at a dose of 300 mg twice a day or a placebo, for an average of twenty-four weeks. While the group receiving lithium had a transient increase in neutrophil counts six weeks after starting therapy, by the end of twenty-four weeks of treatment there was no difference in the counts of neutrophils or CD4+ cells between groups. This lack of long-term effect dampened the interest in lithium as a treatment for AZT toxicity.

In the meantime, other drugs that stimulate white blood cell production have become available. One, called G-CSF, is now widely used for the condition.

Lithium is available in capsules, controlled-release tablets, and syrup.

**TREATMENT**
Lithium treatment is usually started with the immediate-release capsules and switched to the controlled-release tablets after the condition has stabilized. The immediate-release capsules are usually taken three or four times a day. The controlled-release tablets need to be taken only twice a day.

The optimal dose must be determined for each person, but most people take around 1,800 mg per day for acute episodes of mania. For long-term control after the condition has stabilized, the adult dose ranges from 600 to 1,200 mg per day.

When switching from the capsules to the tablets, it is important that the same total daily dose be given.

**CAUTIONS AND WARNINGS**
Lithium should not be used by anyone with a known allergy to it. In addition, it should generally not be used by people with significant kidney or heart disease, severe debilitation, or sodium deficiency because of the increased risk of side effects.

In most people, the effective dose of lithium is close to the dose that causes severe toxicity. In general, people taking the drug will be closely monitored by their physician to maintain appropriate levels of the drug in their blood.

People who experience diarrhea, nausea, vomiting, tremors, loss of coordination, drowsiness, or muscle weakness while taking lithium should contact their physicians as soon as possible. People with HIV may experience

these symptoms as a result of their disease or of other drugs being taken, but they may also be the early warning signs of lithium toxicity.

## SIDE EFFECTS

The side effects of lithium are generally dose-related, occurring more frequently and with greater severity when higher concentrations of lithium are in the blood. Hand tremors, frequent urination, mild nausea, general discomfort, and mild thirst may occur during initial therapy. These side effects usually subside with continued treatment or dose reductions. If they persist, the drug should be stopped.

Diarrhea, vomiting, drowsiness, muscle weakness, lack of coordination, giddiness, ringing in the ears, and blurred vision may occur at therapeutic levels of the drug. At dosages higher than recommended, severe side effects may occur.

## PREGNANCY/BREAST-FEEDING

Lithium can cause severe fetal harm and should not be taken during pregnancy, particularly during the first trimester. As many as 8% to 9% of babies exposed to lithium in the womb may develop heart defects. Other birth defects observed include brain and spine malformations. Women of childbearing age are encouraged to use effective contraception while taking the drug.

HIV may be passed from a woman to her child through breast milk. In areas where nutritionally sound alternatives are readily available, breast-feeding is discouraged for HIV-positive women. Lithium passes into breast milk. Because of the potential toxicity of the drug, women should consider alternatives to breast-feeding while using it.

## USE IN CHILDREN

Lithium has not been formally studied in children under the age of fifteen, so no recommendations regarding its pediatric use can be made.

## USE IN THE ELDERLY

Older adults may be more susceptible to the side effects of the drug and may require reduced doses. Even when lithium blood levels are within the recommended range, elderly people are at higher risk of the drug's side effects than the general population.

## DRUG INTERACTIONS

Haloperidol may increase the blood levels of lithium. This combination has caused weakness, fatigue, and confusion in some people, rarely resulting in permanent damage.

Lithium may reduce chlorpromazine levels in the blood, potentially reducing its effectiveness. Chlorpromazine may increase lithium levels in the blood, potentially resulting in increased side effects.

Sodium bicarbonate, acetazolamide, urea, mannitol, and theophylline neutralize the effect of lithium. Verapamil may reduce both the blood levels and toxicity of lithium.

Methyldopa, fluoxetine, carbamazepine, thiazide and loop diuretics, metronidazole, enalapril, captopril, and some arthritis medications like indomethacin or piroxicam may increase the effects of lithium.

Lithium may increase the blood levels of tricyclic antidepressants such as amoxapine, amitriptyline, desipramine, or maprotiline.

## FOOD INTERACTIONS

For best absorption, lithium should be taken immediately with food or milk. Because lithium can cause a reduction in body salt levels, it is important to maintain a well-balanced diet.

## OTHER DRUGS USED FOR SIMILAR CONDITIONS

Lithium is the only available drug treatment for mania. For AZT-induced white blood cell deficiencies, the colony-stimulating factor G-CSF is the drug of choice.

# LORAZEPAM

## BRAND NAME (MANUFACTURER)

Ativan (Wyeth-Ayerst)

## TYPE OF DRUG

Psychoactive–tranquilizer

## USED FOR

Lorazepam is used in adults for the treatment of anxiety. In addition, the injectable form of the drug is used as a sedative and as a pre-surgical medication for people who prefer not to remember the events of the day of their surgery.

## GENERAL INFORMATION

Lorazepam belongs to a class of psychoactive drugs called benzodiazepines. Benzodiazepines are the most commonly used antianxiety drugs because they are fairly safe, rapidly reduce the symptoms of anxiety, and don't have to be taken on an ongoing basis to be effective. All benzodiazepines cause dose-related suppression of the central nervous system, varying from slight impairment to deep sedation. Lorazepam is one of the more sedating benzodiazepines.

Like other benzodiazepines, lorazepam can cause dependency. Withdrawal symptoms may include convulsions, tremors, abdominal pain, muscle cramps, vomiting, sweating, restlessness, perceptual disturbances, and insomnia. The

risk of addiction is increased in people with a history of alcoholism, drug use, or marked personality disorders.

Lorazepam is available as tablets and a solution for intravenous injection.

## TREATMENT

The dose of lorazepam should be optimized for each individual. As with other psychoactive drugs, the minimum effective dosage should be used to minimize the risk of side effects. In general, treatment is started at a low dose and gradually increased as necessary and as tolerated.

The usual dosage range for healthy adults is 2 to 6 mg per day given in divided doses. For anxiety, most people require an initial dosage of 2 to 3 mg per day, split into two or three doses. Lorazepam tablets are used more commonly than the injection formulation.

Lower doses may be required for elderly people and people with kidney or liver impairment.

## CAUTIONS AND WARNINGS

Lorazepam should not be used by anyone with a known allergy to it. It should also not be used by people with acute narrow-angle glaucoma.

Lorazepam is metabolized in the liver and excreted by the kidney. Consequently, it should be used with caution by people with kidney or liver impairment.

Lorazepam depresses the central nervous system. People taking the drug should not drive an automobile or operate dangerous machinery.

## SIDE EFFECTS

Side effects of the drug usually occur early in treatment and disappear as treatment continues. The most frequent side effects in clinical trials were sedation (reported by about 16% of people taking the drug), dizziness (7%), weakness (4%), and unsteadiness (3%). Less frequent side effects include disorientation, depression, nausea, change in appetite, headache, sleep disturbance, agitation, and skin reactions. Transient amnesia or memory impairment has been reported after the use of other benzodiazepines.

## PREGNANCY/BREAST-FEEDING

Although lorazepam has not been formally studied in pregnant women, use of other benzodiazepines (chlordiazepoxide, diazepam, and meprobamate) during the first trimester of pregnancy has sometimes resulted in fetal malformations.

HIV may be passed from a woman to her child through breast milk. In areas where nutritionally sound alternatives are readily available, breast-feeding is discouraged for HIV-positive women. Lorazepam is excreted in breast milk and it may accumulate in nursing infants. Because of the potential toxicity

of the drug, women should consider alternatives to breast-feeding while taking it.

## USE IN CHILDREN
There is little clinical data regarding the use of lorazepam in children, therefore no recommendations about its use in this population can be made.

## USE IN THE ELDERLY
People over the age of fifty may have deeper and more prolonged sedation when using lorazepam. In addition, elderly people may be at increased risk for the drug's other side effects, which include unsteadiness and disorientation. In general, elderly people will use a reduced dosage of the drug to obtain the same therapeutic effects.

## DRUG INTERACTIONS
Lorazepam produces additive central nervous system depression when used with anticonvulsants, antihistamines, alcohol, and other drugs that produce central nervous system depression.

Smoking may reduce the effectiveness of lorazepam by reducing blood levels of the drug. The effects of lorazepam may be prolonged when taken with cimetidine, oral contraceptives, disulfiram, fluoxetine, isoniazid, ketoconazole, metoprolol, probenecid, propoxyphene, propranolol, rifampin, or valproic acid.

Theophylline may reduce lorazepam's sedative effects.

Antacids or ddI should be taken two hours before or after lorazepam, because they interfere with the drug's absorption into the body.

Phenytoin and digoxin blood levels are increased when taken with lorazepam, potentially increasing the risk of side effects from these drugs. Lorazepam may reduce blood levels of levodopa, potentially reducing its effectiveness.

## FOOD INTERACTIONS
Lorazepam is absorbed most effectively into the body when taken on an empty stomach, but it may be taken with food if it causes an upset stomach.

## OTHER DRUGS USED FOR SIMILAR CONDITIONS
Many different benzodiazepines are available for prescription use. They include alprazolam, diazepam, chlordiazepoxide, and flurazepam among others. The drugs differ somewhat in their side effects, potencies, the time they take to work, and their tendency to be addictive or cause withdrawal symptoms.

Buspirone is an antianxiety medication that is not part of the benzodiazepine class. It is not addictive and is less likely to be sedating. It also has fewer tendencies to slow down mental and physical reactions in the people who take it. On the other hand, it is not effective for many people.

# METHYLPHENIDATE

**BRAND NAME (MANUFACTURER)**
Ritalin (Novartis)

**TYPE OF DRUG**
Psychoactive–stimulant

**USED FOR**
Methylphenidate is a central nervous system stimulant used to treat attention-deficit disorders, primarily in children. It is also used in narcolepsy, a disorder involving uncontrollable sleep attacks or desire to sleep. It is also occasionally used to treat depression in people who do not respond to other medication.

Methylphenidate is also occasionally used but not approved for the treatment of AIDS dementia complex in people with HIV.

Methylphenidate is available as tablets for oral administration.

**GENERAL INFORMATION**
Attention-deficit disorder, which occurs primarily in young boys, involves moderate-to-severe distractability, short attention span, hyperactivity, wide emotional swings, and the tendency to be impulsive. A total treatment program for the disorder typically includes psychological, educational, and social measures as well as drug therapy.

Methylphenidate is a psychostimulant. It has proven useful in people who are withdrawn or apathetic. It works more rapidly than drugs in other classes of antidepressants.

**TREATMENT**
The dosage must be adjusted for each person. The standard dose for adults and adolescents is 20 to 30 mg per day. Some people may require up to 60 mg per day. The drug is also available in a slow-release (SR) form. The SR tablets must be swallowed whole, never crushed or chewed. The SR tablets can replace standard tablets when eight-hour dosing is necessary.

Children are generally given small initial doses with gradual weekly increments as necessary, if they don't experience serious side effects. The recommended dose for children is 5 mg twice daily before breakfast and lunch, with gradual dose increments of 5 to 10 mg each week. A daily dose over 60 mg is not recommended for children.

In treatment of symptoms of AIDS dementia complex, doses of 5 to 10 mg per day are often sufficient to alleviate apathy and to increase energy, concentration, and appetite.

## CAUTIONS AND WARNINGS

People with marked anxiety, tension, or agitation should not take the drug, since it may aggravate these symptoms. Methylphenidate should not be used by people who know they are allergic to it or those who have glaucoma, motor tics, or a family history of Tourette's syndrome.

There is some clinical evidence that suggests methylphenidate increases the likelihood of seizures in people with a prior history of seizures.

The drug should be used with caution in people with high blood pressure.

Chronic use of methylphenidate can cause dependency and psychosis.

## SIDE EFFECTS

Nervousness and insomnia are the most frequent side effects of the drug. Other observed side effects include hypersensitivity, anorexia, nausea, dizziness, heart palpitations, headache, drowsiness, high blood pressure and pulse changes, rapid heartbeat, angina, irregular heart rhythm, abdominal pain, and weight loss during prolonged therapy. There have also been rare reports of Tourette's syndrome and toxic psychosis.

## PREGNANCY/BREAST-FEEDING

Methylphenidate has not been formally studied in pregnant women. It passes through the placenta into the fetal blood circulation, but it has not been found to cause birth defects. Pregnant women are encouraged to discuss the benefits and potential risks of methylphenidate with their physician before deciding to use the drug.

HIV can be passed from a woman to her child through breast milk. In areas where nutritionally sound alternatives are readily available, breast-feeding is discouraged for HIV-positive women. It is not known if methylphenidate passes into human milk, but the drug has caused no significant problems among breast-fed infants.

## USE IN CHILDREN

Methylphenidate has not been studied in children under six. Children six and older are generally treated at the dosages listed above. The long-term effects in children have not been well established. Side effects in children may occur more frequently than in adults.

## USE IN THE ELDERLY

No changes in dosage or administration are recommended for elderly people.

## DRUG INTERACTIONS

Methylphenidate may decrease the effectiveness of the blood pressure medicine guanethidine. It may inhibit the metabolism of the blood-thinner warfarin, anticonvulsants (phenobarbital, diphenylhydantoin, primidone), phenylbutazone, and tricyclic antidepressants (imipramine, clomipramine, desipramine).

**FOOD INTERACTIONS**
Methylphenidate should be taken thirty to forty-five minutes before meals to maximize absorption of the drug into the body.

**OTHER DRUGS USED FOR SIMILAR CONDITIONS**
To alleviate symptoms of depression, a number of antidepressants, such as fluoxetine, are available. For treatment of AIDS dementia complex, haloperidol may be used. Amphetamines are sometimes prescribed to increase energy and improve concentration.

# MIDAZOLAM

**BRAND NAME (MANUFACTURER)**
Versed (Roche Laboratories)

**TYPE OF DRUG**
Psychoactive–sedative

**USED FOR**
Midazolam has a number of indications and effects depending on the dose and the route of administration. Midazolam is used intramuscularly prior to surgery as a sedative and to help people not remember the events of the day of their surgery. It is also administered intravenously for conscious sedation prior to short diagnostic, therapeutic, or endoscopic procedures, and for induction of general anesthesia, before administration of other anesthetic agents.

**GENERAL INFORMATION**
Midazolam is a member of a class of psychoactive drugs known as benzodiazepines. Benzodiazepines are the most commonly used antianxiety drugs because they are fairly safe, they rapidly reduce the symptoms of anxiety, and they don't have to be taken on an ongoing basis to be effective.

Midazolam is a short-acting central nervous system depressant and unlike other typical benzodiazepines, there is a significant risk of respiratory depression and respiratory arrest. Midazolam therefore should be used only in hospital or ambulatory care settings.

**TREATMENT**
Midazolam should be used only in hospital or ambulatory care settings, including physicians' offices that provide for continuous monitoring of respiratory and cardiac function. Dosage is to be administered very slowly by intravenous or intramuscular injection only by a doctor. The dose for conscious sedation may be as little as 1 mg, but should not exceed 2.5 mg. Lower doses are necessary for older (over 60 years) or debilitated people and in people also taking narcotics or other antidepressants. The dose for intramuscular

midazolam is 0.07 to 0.08 mg/kg and 0.2 to 0.05 mg/kg for adults older than 60 years.

**CAUTIONS AND WARNINGS**

Midazolam dosing should always be adjusted to the individual and should always be administered by skilled personnel. People should be continuously monitored for early signs of underventilation or apnea (lack of breathing), which can lead to hypoxia/cardiac arrest unless treated immediately.

**SIDE EFFECTS**

Fluctuations in vital signs were the most common side effects following perenteral administration of midazolam. Other side effects include apnea, variation in blood pressure, and pulse rate.

**PREGNANCY/BREAST-FEEDING**

Use of other benzodiazepines during the first trimester of pregnancy has sometimes resulted in fetal malformations. In animal studies, midazolam has not been found to cause cancers, but it is not known whether the same would be true in humans. Pregnant women are encouraged to discuss the benefits and potential risks of midazolam with their physician before deciding to use the drug.

HIV may be passed from a woman to her child though breast milk. In areas where nutritionally sound alternatives are readily available, breast-feeding is discouraged for HIV-positive women. Midazolam is excreted in human milk, and because of the potent toxicity of the drug, women should consider alternatives to breast-feeding while taking it.

**USE IN CHILDREN**

Safety and effectiveness of midazolam in children below the age of 18 years has not been established, therefore no recommendations about its pediatric use can be made.

**USE IN THE ELDERLY**

Because the danger of underventilation or apnea is greater in elderly patients and those with chronic diseases or decreased lung capacity, and because the peak effect may take longer in these people, increments should be smaller and the rate of injection slower.

**DRUG INTERACTIONS**

Narcotics (morphine, merperidine, and fentanyl), secobarbital and Innovar can increase the sedative effect of midazolam. Consequently, the dosage of midazolam should be adjusted according to the type and amount of other medications administered.

Midazolam should not be used with delavirdine, indinavir, itraconazole, ketoconazole, nelfinavir, ritonavir, or saquinavir as this may lead to serious side effects.

Caution is advised when midazolam is administered to people receiving erythromycin and clarithromycin since they may decrease the plasma clearance of midazolam.

## FOOD INTERACTIONS

There is little clinical data regarding the use of midazolam with food, therefore no recommendations about its use with food can be made. However, because the drug is given by injection, it is not likely that food would affect its activity.

## OTHER DRUGS USED FOR SIMILAR CONDITIONS

Other drugs to be used for conscious sedation prior to operative procedures should be discussed with your physician.

# MIRTAZAPINE

## BRAND NAME (MANUFACTURER)

Remeron (Organon)

## TYPE OF DRUG

Psychoactive–antidepressant

## USED FOR

Mirtazapine is used for the treatment of depression.

## GENERAL INFORMATION

Mirtazapine is an antidepressant that belongs to a class of drugs called piperazino-azepines. It has a tetracyclic chemical structure and is chemically unrelated to other classes of antidepressants such as serotonin reuptake inhibitors, tricyclics, or monoamine oxidase (MAO) inhibitors. As with other antidepressants, the mechanism of action of mirtazapine is unknown.

Mirtazapine is available as tablets for oral administration.

## TREATMENT

The recommended starting dose for mirtazapine is 15 mg/day. The dose should be administered as a single dose at bedtime. The effective dose range in clinical trials was generally 15-45 mg/day. People who do not respond to the initial 15 mg dose may benefit from dose increases up to a maximum of 45 mg/day, although the exact relationship between dose and response has not been fully studied. While people may notice improvement with mirtazapine therapy in 1 to 4 weeks, they should be advised to continue therapy as directed.

## CAUTIONS AND WARNINGS

Mirtazapine should not be used by anyone with a known allergy to it. Because mirtazapine can potentially affect physical performance, people should be careful engaging in activities requiring alertness until they have assessed

the drug's effect on their own physical activity. All people receiving antidepressants should be closely monitored during initial drug therapy. Prescriptions of mirtazapine should be written for the smallest quantity consistent with good patient management, in order to reduce the risk of overdose.

Mirtazapine should not be used by people taking monoamine oxidase (MAO) inhibitor antidepressants. Because MAO inhibitors remain in the body for a time after stopping therapy, mirtazapine should not be started within fourteen days of receiving or stopping an MAO inhibitor. In addition, people should allow at least fourteen days after stopping mirtazapine before starting an MAO inhibitor.

Suicidal tendencies are common with depression and may persist until significant remission occurs.

### SIDE EFFECTS

The most common side effects of mirtazapine are drowsiness, increased appetite, weight gain, dizziness, or flu-like symptoms. Mirtazapine may also impair judgment, thinking, and motor skills, because of its prominent sedative effect. The drowsiness associated with mirtazapine use may impair a patient's ability to drive, use machines, or perform tasks that require alertness.

### PREGNANCY/BREAST-FEEDING

Mirtazapine has not been formally studied in pregnant women. In animal studies, it did not cause any cancers, but resulted in some fetal deaths when given at 50 times the normal human dose. It is not known whether these effects would also occur in humans. Pregnant women are encouraged to discuss the benefits and potential risks of mirtazapine with their physician before deciding to use the drug.

HIV may be passed from a woman to her child through breast milk. In areas where nutritionally sound alternatives are readily available, breast-feeding is discouraged for HIV-positive women. It is not known whether mirtazapine is excreted in human milk. Because of the potential toxicity of the drug, women should consider alternatives to breast-feeding while taking it.

### USE IN CHILDREN

Safety and effectiveness of mirtazapine in children under the age of 18 years has not been established, therefore no recommendations about its use in this population can be made.

### USE IN THE ELDERLY

Although there were no unusual side effects seen in the elderly, mirtazapine should be administered to elderly patients with caution because of slower clearance from the body.

**DRUG INTERACTIONS**

Alcohol use has not been shown to affect blood levels of mirtazapine, but it can worsen the impairment of cognitive and motor skills produced by mirtazapine. Accordingly, people should be advised to avoid alcohol while taking mirtazapine. Diazepam has also been shown to worsen motor skills impaired by mirtazapine. Accordingly, patients should be advised to avoid diazepam and other similar drugs while taking mirtazapine.

**FOOD INTERACTIONS**

There is little clinical data regarding the use of mirtazapine with food.

**OTHER DRUGS USED FOR SIMILAR CONDITIONS**

For treatment of depression, there are many options, including tricyclic antidepressants (desipramine, nortriptyline, protriptyline, amoxapine, maprotiline, imipramine, trimipramine, doxepin), MAO inhibitors (tranylcypromine, phenelzine, isocarboxazid), other serotonin reuptake inhibitors (paroxetine and sertraline), and stimulants such as methylphenidate. The appropriate drug varies from person to person and depends on age, physical health and condition, and other drugs being concurrently used.

# NEFAZODONE

**BRAND NAME (MANUFACTURER)**

Serzone (Bristol-Myers Squibb)

**TYPE OF DRUG**

Psychoactive–antidepressant

**USED FOR**

Nefazodone is used for the treatment of depression.

**GENERAL INFORMATION**

Nefazodone is an orally administered antidepressant that belongs to a class of drugs known as phenylpiperazine antidepressants. Its chemical structure is unrelated to other classes of antidepressants such as seratonin reuptake inhibitors, tricyclics, tetracyclics, or monoamine oxidase (MAO) inhibitors.

As with all antidepressants, several weeks on treatment will be required to obtain the full antidepressant effect. As improvement is noted, it is important for a person to continue drug treatment as directed by their physician.

Nefazodone should not be used in combination with MAO inhibitors.

**TREATMENT**

The recommended starting dose is 200 mg/day, administered in two divided doses. The most effective dose range is generally 300-600 mg/day. Consequently, most people, depending on their tolerability and need for further clinical

effect, should gradually increase their dose as needed by 100 mg/day at intervals of no less than one week.

## CAUTIONS AND WARNINGS

Nefazodone should not be used by people taking monoamine oxidase (MAO) inhibitor antidepressants. Nor should it be used by people taking terfenadine or astemizole. Because nefazodone and MAO inhibitors remain in the body for a time after stopping therapy, nefazodone should not be started within fourteen days of receiving an MAO inhibitor. MAO inhibitors should not be started for at least five weeks, and perhaps longer, after stopping nefazodone.

Patients should be advised to notify their physician if they develop a rash, hives, or a related allergic phenomenon.

## SIDE EFFECTS

Since any psychoactive drug may impair judgment, thinking, or motor skills, patients should be cautioned about operating hazardous machinery, including automobiles, until they are reasonably certain that nefazodone therapy does not adversely affect their ability to engage in such activities.

The most common observed side effects associated with nefazodone are drowsiness, dry mouth, nausea, dizziness, constipation, asthenia, lightheadedness, blurred vision, confusion, and abnormal vision.

## PREGNANCY/BREAST-FEEDING

Nefazodone has not been formally studied in pregnant women. Pregnant women are encouraged to discuss the benefits and potential risks of nefazodone with their physician before deciding to use the drug.

HIV may be passed from a woman to her child through breast milk. In areas where nutritionally sound alternatives are readily available, breast-feeding is discouraged for HIV-positive women. It is not known whether nefazodone is excreted in human milk. Because of the potential toxicity of the drug, women should consider alternatives to breast-feeding while taking it.

## USE IN CHILDREN

Safety and effectiveness of nefazodone in children under the age of 18 years has not been established, therefore no recommendations about its use in this population can be made.

## USE IN THE ELDERLY

Due to higher blood levels of nefazodone seen in single dose studies in elderly patients, treatment should be initiated at half the usual dose. The usual precautions should be observed in elderly patients who have other medical illnesses or who are receiving other drugs at the same time.

## DRUG INTERACTIONS

Nefazodone should not be taken together with terfenadine or astemizole.

Nefazodone should not be used by people taking monoamine oxidase (MAO) inhibitor antidepressants or people with residual levels of MAO inhibitors in the blood. Nefazodone may also increase levels of digoxin and decrease levels of propranolol.

### FOOD INTERACTIONS
There is little clinical data regarding the use of nefazodone with food, therefore no recommendations about its use with food can be made.

### OTHER DRUGS USED FOR SIMILAR CONDITIONS
For treatment of depression, there are many options, including tricyclic antidepressants (desipramine, nortriptyline, protriptyline, amoxapine, maprotiline, imipramine, trimipramine, doxepin), MAO inhibitors (tranylcypromine, phenelzine, isocarboxazid), other serotonin reuptake inhibitors (paroxetine and sertraline), and stimulants such as methylphenidate. The appropriate drug varies from person to person and depends on age, physical health and condition, and other drugs being concurrently used.

# OXAZEPAM

### BRAND NAME (MANUFACTURER)
Serax (Wyeth-Ayerst)

### TYPE OF DRUG
Psychoactive–tranquilizer

### USED FOR
Oxazepam is used for the short-term relief of anxiety, including anxiety associated with depression. It is also used to treat withdrawal symptoms of alcoholism.

### GENERAL INFORMATION
Oxazepam is a member of a class of psychoactive drugs called benzodiazepines. Benzodiazepines are the most commonly used antianxiety drugs because they are fairly safe, they rapidly reduce the symptoms of anxiety, and they do not have to be taken on an ongoing basis in order to be effective. All benzodiazepines cause dose-related suppression of the central nervous system, varying from slight impairment to deep sedation.

Oxazepam is a short-acting benzodiazepine, which means that the drug is rapidly eliminated from the body. This reduces the risk that the drug will cause a "hangover" effect the day after it is taken. It also reduces the risk the drug will accumulate in the body to high levels that may cause side effects.

Like other benzodiazepines, oxazepam can cause dependency. Withdrawal symptoms may include convulsions, tremors, abdominal pain, muscle cramps,

vomiting, sweating, restlessness, perceptual disturbances, and insomnia. The risk of dependency is increased in people with a history of alcoholism, drug use, or marked personality disorder. However, clinical studies show that oxazepam is less likely to cause addiction than diazepam, lorazepam, alprazolam, or triazolam.

Oxazepam is available as tablets and capsules for oral administration.

### TREATMENT
The dosage of oxazepam should be adjusted for each individual. As with other psychoactive drugs, the minimum effective dosage should be used to reduce the risk of side effects. The dosage is generally started low and increased as necessary and tolerated.

For treatment of mild-to-moderate anxiety, the usual adult dosage is 10 to 15 mg, taken three or four times a day. For severe cases, the dosage may be doubled. Older people generally receive 10 mg, three or four times a day, to be increased as necessary to 15 mg per day.

### CAUTIONS AND WARNINGS
Oxazepam should not be used by people who know they are allergic to it. Oxazepam depresses the central nervous system. People taking the drug should not drive an automobile or operate dangerous machinery.

Because of their increased risk of side effects, people with a history of low blood pressure should take the drug with caution.

### SIDE EFFECTS
People rarely stop using oxazepam because of side effects. Transient mild drowsiness is common for the first few days of therapy. If it persists, the dosage of the drug should be reduced. In a few rare instances, dizziness, vertigo, headache, or fainting has occurred after taking the drug. Occasionally, the drug may cause excitement or stimulation during the first two weeks of therapy. Rarely, allergic reactions, nausea, vomiting, lethargy, swelling, slurred speech, tremor, changes in sex drive, white blood cell deficiency, and liver toxicity occur.

### PREGNANCY/BREAST-FEEDING
Oxazepam has not been formally studied in pregnant women. However, other benzodiazepines have caused serious birth defects when taken by pregnant women. Pregnant women are encouraged to discuss the benefits and potential risks of oxazepam with their physician before deciding to use the drug.

HIV may be passed from a woman to her child through breast milk. In areas where nutritionally sound alternatives are readily available, breast-feeding is discouraged for HIV-positive women. Oxazepam is excreted in breast milk and causes sedation in infants. Because of the potential risk of the drug, women should consider alternatives to breast-feeding while taking it.

**USE IN CHILDREN**

Children over twelve years of age can use the lowest adult dosage, to be increased as necessary and tolerated. Little data are available regarding the use of the drug for children under twelve. The drug is not recommended for children under the age of six years because it has not been formally studied in them.

**USE IN THE ELDERLY**

Elderly people are more susceptible to the dose-related side effects of the drug and should use the reduced dosages listed above.

**DRUG INTERACTIONS**

Oxazepam can cause additive central nervous system depression when used with anticonvulsants, antihistamines, alcohol, and other drugs that produce central nervous system depression. Cimetidine, isoniazid, and valproic acid may increase oxazepam levels in the blood, potentially increasing the risk of side effects. Oxazepam may reduce the effectiveness of oral contraceptives and increase the risk of phenytoin toxicity. Use of oxazepam together with lithium can cause serious reductions in body temperature.

**FOOD INTERACTIONS**

None reported.

**OTHER DRUGS USED FOR SIMILAR CONDITIONS**

Many different benzodiazepines are available for prescription use. They include lorazepam, diazepam, chlordiazepoxide, temazepam, flurazepam, and triazolam, among others. The drugs differ somewhat in the side effects they produce, their potencies, the time it takes them to work, and the tendency for them to cause withdrawal symptoms. Generally, oxazepam is considered to be one of the safer benzodiazepines.

Buspirone is an antianxiety medication that is not part of the benzodiazepine class. It is not addictive and is less likely to be sedating or to impair mental and physical alertness in people who take it. On the other hand, it needs to be taken many times each day and it is not effective for many people.

# PAROXETINE

**BRAND NAME (MANUFACTURER)**

Paxil (SmithKline Beecham)

**TYPE OF DRUG**

Psychoactive–antidepressant

**USED FOR**

Paroxetine is primarily used for the treatment of mental depression. It is also used to treat obsessive-compulsive disorder.

**GENERAL INFORMATION**

Paroxetine belongs to a class of antidepressants known as serotonin reuptake inhibitors. It is chemically unrelated to tricyclic, tetracyclic, or other known classes of antidepressants. It has become widely used because it is effective and tends to have fewer side effects than older antidepressants.

Antidepressant medications are usually taken over long periods. It generally takes ten days of treatment before steady levels of paroxetine are built up in the blood, and it may take equally long for the drug to have an effect on depression. In some people, it may take considerably longer.

Paroxetine accumulates in the body's tissues with prolonged use, and the drug may stay in the body for weeks after discontinuing therapy. It is especially important to wait at least two weeks after stopping the drug before taking an antidepressant that is a monoamine oxidase (MAO) inhibitor (e.g., phenelzine or tranylcypromine). Similarly, paroxetine should not be taken for at least two weeks after an MAO inhibitor is discontinued.

In prolonged use, tolerance to paroxetine may develop over time, and the drug may lose its effectiveness.

**TREATMENT**

The recommended initial dose is 20 mg taken once a day, usually in the morning. Some people who do not respond to this dose may respond to dose increases, in 10 mg per day increments, up to a maximum of 50 mg per day. The dose increases should occur no more often than once a week.

The recommended initial dose for the elderly, debilitated, and/or people with kidney or liver impairment is 10 mg per day. In these people, the daily dose may be increased as necessary but should not exceed 40 mg.

**CAUTIONS AND WARNINGS**

Paroxetine should not be used by anyone with a known allergy to it. The drug is broken down by the liver and excreted by the kidneys. People with liver or kidney disease should take it with caution. In a small number of people who suffer from mania, paroxetine causes a reactivation of the condition. Paroxetine should be used with caution by people with a history of seizure disorders.

**SIDE EFFECTS**

Twenty-one percent of volunteers in clinical trials of paroxetine quit using the drug because of side effects. The most common side effects include nausea, sleepiness, insomnia, increased sweating, tremors, anxiety, agitation, abnormal ejaculation, diarrhea, dry mouth, and vomiting. Less common side effects include flushing, increased salivation, cold or clammy skin, dizziness, blood pressure changes, swelling, coldness in the hands or feet, rapid heartbeat, weakness, loss of coordination, headaches, acne, hair loss, dry skin, difficulty swallowing, stomach gas, joint pains, muscle pains, cramps and

weakness, abnormal thinking patterns, blurred vision, bleeding between periods, weight changes, and lymph swelling.

### PREGNANCY/BREAST-FEEDING
Paroxetine has not been formally studied in pregnant women. In animal studies, the drug did not cause fetal harm, but it is not known whether this would be true for humans. Pregnant women are encouraged to discuss the benefits and potential risks of paroxetine with their physician before deciding to use the drug.

HIV can be passed from a woman to her child through breast milk. In areas where nutritionally sound alternatives are readily available, breast-feeding is discouraged for HIV-positive women. Paroxetine is excreted in human milk. Because of the potential toxicity of the drug, women are encouraged to consider alternatives to breast-feeding while using it.

### USE IN CHILDREN
Paroxetine is not recommended for children because its safety and effectiveness have not been formally studied or established for them.

### USE IN THE ELDERLY
Paroxetine is metabolized more slowly in the elderly than in younger people, and their blood levels of the drug are higher for a given dosage. Consequently, elderly people often require lower doses of the drug.

### DRUG INTERACTIONS
Paroxetine combined with tryptophan may cause headache, nausea, sweating, and dizziness. It is recommended that the two drugs not be taken together. Serious and fatal reactions may occur if paroxetine and monoamine oxidase (MAO) inhibitors are taken together. Paroxetine may increase the blood thinning effect of warfarin. Cimetidine may increase paroxetine blood levels. Phenobarbital or phenytoin may decrease paroxetine blood levels.

Combinations of paroxetine with nortriptyline, amitriptyline, imipramine, desipramine, fluoxetine, thioridazine, propafenone, flecainide, or encainide may require dose adjustments of either drug used in the combination. Paroxetine may decrease procyclidine blood levels.

### FOOD INTERACTIONS
Paroxetine may be taken with or without food.

### OTHER DRUGS USED FOR SIMILAR CONDITIONS
A number of other drugs are available for the treatment of depression. Fluoxetine and sertraline are other effective serotonin reuptake inhibitors. Monoamine oxidase inhibitors that are useful as antidepressants are tranylcypromine, phenelzine, and isocarboxazid. Tricyclic antidepressants include amoxapine, desipramine, nortriptyline, amitriptyline, and doxepin.

Each person may react differently to different antidepressants. The choice of drug usually depends on the individual's response to the drug, the drug's effectiveness, and side effects. People who do not benefit from one type of antidepressant may respond to another.

# PERPHENAZINE

**BRAND NAME (MANUFACTURER)**
Trilafon (Schering)
Perphenazine + Amitriptyline: Etrafon (Schering); Triavil (Merck)

**TYPE OF DRUG**
Psychoactive–antinausea, antivomiting, antipsychosis drug

**USED FOR**
Perphenazine is used to treat severe nausea and vomiting. It is also used to treat the symptoms of psychosis.

**GENERAL INFORMATION**
Perphenazine belongs to a class of psychoactive drugs called phenothiazines. Although the mechanism by which phenothiazines work is unknown, they have potent effects on the central nervous system and other organs. They can reduce blood pressure, stop seizures, control nausea and vomiting, and control the symptoms of psychosis, a mental disorder characterized by difficulty thinking, recognizing reality, and acting rationally.

Perphenazine is available as tablets, oral concentrate, and solution for injection. It is also available in a number of combination products with the tricyclic antidepressant amitriptyline.

**TREATMENT**
The dosage is individualized and adjusted for each person's response. As with all psychoactive drugs, the lowest effective dose should be used to reduce the risk of side effects. The drug is generally started at a low dosage and increased as necessary and as tolerated. Adults usually take 8 to 16 mg a day, in divided doses for the treatment of nausea and vomiting. Doses up to 24 mg per day may be necessary. As soon as possible, the dosage should be reduced. Higher doses are used for the treatment of psychosis.

The oral concentrate should not be mixed with beverages containing caffeine (coffee, cola, etc.), tannic acid (tea), or pectinates (apple juice). It may be diluted with water, saline, homogenized milk, carbonated orange or pineapple drinks, apricot, prune, orange, tomato, or grapefruit juices.

**CAUTIONS AND WARNINGS**

Perphenazine should not be used by anyone with a known allergy to it. It should also not be used by people in comas, those with fevers above 104°F, suspected or established brain damage, liver damage, or suppressed bone marrow activity (as may occur when using AZT, ganciclovir, alpha interferon, or other drugs).

Perphenazine may increase the risk of seizures and should be used with caution in people with a history of seizures and those experiencing alcohol withdrawal symptoms.

Perphenazine may impair the mental and physical abilities necessary to operate an automobile or dangerous machinery.

Phenothiazines elevate blood levels of prolactin, a hormone involved in the production of breast milk. Because many breast cancers are stimulated by prolactin, perphenazine may aggravate existing breast cancers, but there is no evidence that it increases the risk of developing breast cancer.

People exposed to phosphorus insecticides or extreme heat should use perphenazine with caution because of the risk of serious side effects.

**SIDE EFFECTS**

Drowsiness, stuffy nose, dizziness, blurred vision, tremors, and constipation are common side effects of perphenazine.

Tardive dyskinesia is a special neuromuscular side effect of phenothiazines. It is characterized by potentially irreversible, involuntary muscle movements that usually involve the tongue, face, mouth, lips, jaw, torso, and extremities. Although the side effect occurs most frequently among the elderly (especially elderly women), it is not possible to predict whether an individual will develop the disorder. The risk of the side effect and the likelihood it will be irreversible are believed to be increased with increased duration of treatment and cumulative dose.

Other neuromuscular side effects of phenothiazines include agitation, insomnia, muscle spasm, difficulty swallowing, and shuffling gait.

Antipsychotic drugs, including perphenazine, can cause a potentially fatal side effect called neuroleptic malignant syndrome. The syndrome is characterized by high fever, muscle rigidity, altered mental status, irregular pulse or blood pressure, and abnormal heart rhythms. If these symptoms occur, the drug should be stopped and a physician contacted immediately.

Other side effects of perphenazine include low blood pressure or fluctuations in blood pressure, weight change, swelling in the extremities, allergic reactions, high fever, darkening of the skin, impaired vision, muscle weakness, and liver damage. In some cases, the drug has caused deficiencies in white blood cell counts.

**PREGNANCY/BREAST-FEEDING**

Perphenazine has not been formally studied in pregnant women. It is usually not prescribed during pregnancy because its effects on the fetus are uncertain. Pregnant women are encouraged to discuss the benefits and potential risks of perphenazine with their physician before deciding to use the drug.

HIV can be passed from a woman to her child through breast milk. In areas where nutritionally sound alternatives are readily available, breast-feeding is discouraged for HIV-positive women. Perphenazine is excreted in human milk, but its effects on nursing infants are not well understood.

**USE IN CHILDREN**

Perphenazine is not recommended for children under twelve, because its safety and effectiveness in this population have not been studied or established.

**USE IN THE ELDERLY**

Older adults may be more susceptible to the side effects of the drug and may require reduced doses.

**DRUG INTERACTIONS**

Perphenazine and other central nervous system depressants (narcotic analgesics, alcohol, antihistamines, sleeping pills, tranquilizers, and some antidepressants) may enhance the depressing effect of each other.

Use of alcohol with perphenazine may result in severe low blood pressure.

Antacids (including those in ddI tablets or powder) may interfere with absorption of perphenazine into the body. Perphenazine should be taken one hour before or after taking an antacid.

**FOOD INTERACTIONS**

Perphenazine may be taken with or without food. Caffeine may interfere with the effects of perphenazine and should be avoided while taking the drug.

**OTHER DRUGS USED FOR SIMILAR CONDITIONS**

For treatment or prevention of nausea and vomiting, several types of drugs are available. Drugs used include metoclopramide, antihistamines (e.g., dimenhydrinate, meclizine, and promethazine), phenothiazines (e.g., prochlorperazine or thiethylperazine), granisetron, or ondansetron. The different types of drugs differ significantly in their side effects, and the choice of therapy is often determined by the side effects for which an individual is at risk.

# PROPRANOLOL

**BRAND NAME (MANUFACTURER)**

Inderal (Wyeth-Ayerst)

Propranolol + Hydrochlorothiazide: Inderide (Wyeth-Ayerst)

**TYPE OF DRUG**
Psychoactive–beta-blocker

**USED FOR**
Propranolol is used most often for the treatment of high blood pressure, angina, and abnormal heart rhythms. It is also used to treat the symptoms of anxiety and to prevent migraine headaches.

**GENERAL INFORMATION**
Propranolol was the first beta-blocker available in the United States. Beta-blockers are drugs that interfere with nerve signals transmitted by the chemical norepinephrine. They reduce the force and speed of the heartbeat and prevent dilation (widening) of certain blood vessels. These actions reduce the workload on the heart, relieve the muscle tremors that often accompany anxiety, and reduce the blood pressure in the brain to prevent migraines.

Propranolol is available as tablets, long-acting capsules, and solution for injection.

**TREATMENT**
The dosage of propranolol must be individualized. When used orally, common dosages range from 40 to 320 mg per day. Dosages in the lower end of the range are usually prescribed for anxiety or the prevention of migraines. Angina, hypertension, and irregular heart rhythms are generally treated with higher dosages.

**CAUTIONS AND WARNINGS**
Propranolol should not be used by anyone with a known allergy to it. It should also not be used by anyone with certain heart conditions such as congestive heart failure.

People with angina who abruptly stop propranolol may experience heart attacks or more severe angina. When discontinuing the drug, its dosage should be tapered off with the guidance of a physician.

In general, people with bronchial diseases such as bronchial asthma, chronic bronchitis, or emphysema should not use propranolol because the drug may cause severe difficulty in breathing.

Because propranolol affects the body's sugar metabolism, it should be used with caution in people with diabetes or hypoglycemia (low blood sugar). Propranolol may mask certain clinical signs of thyroid disease and interfere with thyroid function tests. Similarly, propranolol may interfere with tests for glaucoma.

Because of the risk of side effects, propranolol should be used with caution in people with impaired kidney or liver function.

### SIDE EFFECTS
Lethargy and cold hands and feet are common side effects of propranolol. Less common side effects include irregular heartbeat, heart failure, low blood pressure, light-headedness, insomnia, weakness, fatigue, mental depression, visual disturbances, hallucinations, nightmares/vivid dreams, disorientation, short-term memory loss, emotional swings, clouded senses, nausea, vomiting, stomach irritation, cramping, diarrhea, constipation, allergic reactions, difficulty breathing, bone marrow toxicity, hair loss, dry eyes, and impotence.

### PREGNANCY/BREAST-FEEDING
Propranolol has not been formally studied in pregnant women. In animal studies, it caused spontaneous abortions when administered at ten times the maximum human dose. It is not known whether the drug causes birth defects in humans. Pregnant women are encouraged to discuss the benefits and potential risks of propranolol with their physician before deciding to use the drug.

HIV can be passed from a woman to her child through breast milk. In areas where nutritionally sound alternatives are readily available, breast-feeding is discouraged for HIV-positive women. Propranolol passes into breast milk, but at normal doses, side effects in nursing babies are uncommon.

### USE IN CHILDREN
The oral form of propranolol is used in children. The usual pediatric dosage range is 2 to 4 mg per kg of body weight per day, in two equally divided doses. Doses above 16 mg per kg per day should not be used in children.

### USE IN THE ELDERLY
No changes in dosage or administration are required for older adults.

### DRUG INTERACTIONS
Propranolol may intensify the effects of reserpine, potentially causing severe side effects. Haloperidol used in combination with propranolol may cause low blood pressure and heart attack.

Propranolol may increase blood levels of chlorpromazine, antipyrine, lidocaine, and theophylline. Chlorpromazine and cimetidine may increase propranolol blood levels. Phenytoin, phenobarbitone, indomethacin, and rifampin may reduce blood levels of propranolol.

Aluminum hydroxide antacids and alcohol interfere with the absorption of propranolol into the body.

### FOOD INTERACTIONS
To maintain the most consistent blood levels of propranolol, it should be taken the same time every day on an empty stomach.

### OTHER DRUGS USED FOR SIMILAR CONDITIONS
Other beta-blockers include sotalol, timolol, carteolol, and penbutolol. For treatment or prevention of nausea and vomiting, a number of different types

of drugs are available. These include metoclopramide, antihistamines (e.g., dimenhydrinate, meclizine, and promethazine), phenothiazines (e.g., prochlorperazine or thiethylperazine), and serotonin reuptake inhibitors (e.g., granisetron or ondansetron). The different types of drugs differ significantly in their side effects, and the choice of therapy is often determined by the side effects for which an individual is at risk.

# PROTRIPTYLINE

### BRAND NAME (MANUFACTURER)
Vivactil (Merck)

### TYPE OF DRUG
Psychoactive–tricyclic antidepressant

### USED FOR
Protriptyline is used for the relief of symptoms of mental depression.

### GENERAL INFORMATION
Protriptyline belongs to a class of drugs known as tricyclic antidepressants. It is chemically unrelated to other classes of antidepressants, including monoamine oxidase (MAO) inhibitors. It is thought to work by increasing the concentrations of neurotransmitters called serotonin and norepinephrine in the brain.

Tricyclic antidepressants are usually taken over long periods. It takes weeks for steady levels of protriptyline to build up in the blood, and it may take up to a month for the drug to have an effect on depression.

Protriptyline is available as tablets for oral administration.

### TREATMENT
To prevent side effects, the dosage of the drug should initially be low and increased as necessary until improvement, as long as there are no serious side effects.

The recommended initial dosage for treatment of depression in adults is 15 to 40 mg a day, divided into three or four doses. When satisfactory improvement has been reached, the dosage should be reduced to the smallest amount that will maintain relief of the symptoms. Lower doses (15 mg per day to start) are recommended for elderly adults.

### CAUTIONS AND WARNINGS
Protriptyline should not be used by anyone with a known allergy to it. It should also not be used by people recovering from heart attacks. Because of the risk of serious side effects, protriptyline should not be used in combination with antidepressants of the monoamine oxidase (MAO) inhibitor class.

When protriptyline replaces an MAO inhibitor for treatment of depression, a minimum of fourteen days should elapse after stopping the MAO inhibitor before starting therapy with protriptyline. Protriptyline should be started cautiously with a gradual increase in dose until a response is achieved.

Protriptyline should be used with caution in people with a history of seizures, difficulty urinating, or glaucoma. People with thyroid disease or those receiving thyroid medication should not use protriptyline because of the risk of heart toxicity.

Protriptyline may increase the hazards of concurrent electroshock therapy. Similarly, when possible, the drug should be discontinued several days before surgery.

Protriptyline may impair the mental and physical abilities necessary to drive an automobile or operate dangerous machinery.

Rapidly stopping protriptyline may cause withdrawal symptoms, including nausea, headache, and a sickly feeling.

**SIDE EFFECTS**

The most common side effects of protriptyline include rapid heartbeat, fainting when getting up quickly, sedation, blurred vision, disorientation, confusion, hallucinations, muscle spasms, seizures, dry mouth, constipation, difficulty urinating, and sensitivity to bright light or sunlight.

Other potential side effects include heart attack, stroke, changes in blood pressure, palpitations, delusions, anxiety, restlessness, agitation, panic, nightmares, numbness, tingling or pain in the extremities, weakness, fatigue, headache, allergic reactions, bone marrow toxicity, nausea, vomiting, loss of appetite, stomach upset, diarrhea, peculiar taste, blackened tongue, impotence, changes in sex drive, jaundice, hair loss, weight change, frequent urination, altered blood sugar levels, and increased perspiration.

**PREGNANCY/BREAST-FEEDING**

Protriptyline has not been formally studied in pregnant women. Protriptyline crosses the placenta. There have been reports of birth defects when the drug was taken during the first three months of pregnancy and severe side effects in newborns whose mothers took the drug during delivery. Pregnant women are encouraged to discuss the benefits and potential risks of protriptyline with their physician before deciding to use the drug.

HIV can be passed from a woman to her child through breast milk. In areas where nutritionally sound alternatives are readily available, breast-feeding is discouraged for HIV-positive women. Protriptyline is excreted in human milk. Because of the potential toxicity of the drug for newborns, women are encouraged to consider alternatives to breast-feeding while taking it.

**USE IN CHILDREN**

Protriptyline is not recommended for children because its safety and efficacy in children have not been formally established.

**USE IN THE ELDERLY**

Older adults may be more susceptible to the side effects of protriptyline. If they use the drug, it is usually at reduced dosages, as described above.

**DRUG INTERACTIONS**

Protriptyline may interfere with the effect of blood pressure medications such as guanethidine or clonidine. Taking protriptyline and thyroid drugs together may intensify the effects of both drugs.

Oral contraceptives and cigarette smoking may decrease the effect of protriptyline. Estrogens can increase or decrease the effect of protriptyline.

Bicarbonate of soda, acetazolamide, quinidine, and procainamide may increase the effect of protriptyline. Methylphenidate, cimetidine, and phenothiazines (perphenazine, prochlorperazine, etc.) may increase blood levels of protriptyline, potentially increasing the risk of its side effects.

Protriptyline may increase the effect of other central nervous system depressants including alcohol, sleeping pills, narcotic pain relievers, tranquilizers, barbiturates, and antihistamines.

**FOOD INTERACTIONS**

Protriptyline may be taken with or without food.

**OTHER DRUGS USED FOR SIMILAR CONDITIONS**

For treatment of depression, there are many options, including other tricyclic antidepressants (desipramine, amitriptyline, nortriptyline, amoxapine, maprotiline, imipramine, trimipramine, doxepin), MAO inhibitors (tranylcypromine, phenelzine, isocarboxazid), serotonin reuptake inhibitors (fluoxetine, paroxetine, and sertraline), and stimulants such as methylphenidate. The appropriate choice varies from person to person and depends on age, physical health and condition, and other drugs being used at the same time.

Desipramine is often the first choice among tricyclic antidepressants because it is effective and has relatively few side effects in most people. Protriptyline is more likely to cause abnormal heart rhythms or low blood pressure and to aggravate agitation and anxiety than other antidepressants.

# SERTRALINE

**BRAND NAME (MANUFACTURER)**

Zoloft (Roerig/Pfizer)

**TYPE OF DRUG**
Psychoactive–antidepressant

**USED FOR**
Sertraline is widely used to treat the symptoms of mental depression. It is also used to treat obsessive-compulsive disorder.

**GENERAL INFORMATION**
Sertraline belongs to a class of antidepressants known as serotonin reuptake inhibitors. It is chemically unrelated to tricyclic, tetracyclic, or other known classes of antidepressants. It has become widely used because it is effective and tends to have fewer side effects than other older antidepressants.

Antidepressant medications are usually taken over long periods. It takes a week or more before steady levels of sertraline are in the blood, and it may take equally long for the drug to have an effect on depression. Sertraline accumulates in the body's tissues with prolonged use, and the drug may stay in the body for weeks after discontinuing therapy. It is especially important to wait at least two weeks after stopping sertraline before taking an antidepressant that is a monoamine oxidase (MAO) inhibitor (e.g., phenelzine or tranylcypromine). Similarly, sertraline should not be taken for at least two weeks after an MAO inhibitor is used.

**TREATMENT**
Sertraline is initiated at a dose of 50 mg per day. If there is no response, the dose may gradually be increased up to 200 mg per day as tolerated and needed. Dose changes should not occur any more frequently than once a week. Lower doses of sertraline may be required in people with reduced liver function.

**CAUTIONS AND WARNINGS**
Sertraline should not be taken by anyone with a known allergy to it. The drug is broken down by the liver and excreted by the kidneys. People with liver or kidney disease should take it with caution. In a small number of people who suffer from mania, sertraline may worsen their condition.

**SIDE EFFECTS**
The side effects that occur most frequently are dry mouth, headache, dizziness, tremors, nausea, diarrhea, fatigue, insomnia, difficulty ejaculating, and sleepiness. Each of the side effects occurred in more than 10% of people taking the drug in clinical trials.

Other side effects of sertraline include increased sweating, heart palpitations, twitching, rash, constipation, stomach upset, vomiting, changes in appetite, hot flushes, fever, increased thirst, agitation, nervousness, anxiety, impaired concentration, abnormal vision, menstrual disorders, back pain, ringing in the ears, and changes in taste.

### PREGNANCY/BREAST-FEEDING

Sertraline has not been formally studied in pregnant women. In animal studies, it did not cause fetal harm, but it is not known whether this is true for humans. Pregnant women are encouraged to discuss the benefits and potential risks of sertraline with their physician before deciding to use the drug.

HIV can be passed from a woman to her child through breast milk. In areas where nutritionally sound alternatives are readily available, breast-feeding is discouraged for HIV-positive women. It is not known whether sertraline is excreted in human milk, but because of the potential toxicity of the drug for newborns, women are encouraged to consider alternatives to breast-feeding while using it.

### USE IN CHILDREN

Sertraline is not recommended for children because its safety and effectiveness in children have not been formally studied or established.

### USE IN THE ELDERLY

Sertraline was studied in several hundred elderly people in clinical trials. In general, the side effects reported were similar to those seen in younger people. Sertraline is metabolized about 40% more slowly in elderly people, possibly because of the reduced liver and kidney function that occurs with aging. Therefore, it takes longer for sertraline to build up to steady levels in the blood of elderly people (two to three weeks compared to one week for younger people), which may mean it takes longer for the drug to work.

### DRUG INTERACTIONS

Sertraline may prolong the effects of diazepam and other benzodiazepines. Serious and fatal reactions may occur if sertraline and monoamine oxidase (MAO) inhibitors are taken together.

Sertraline may increase the effect of warfarin or digoxin, requiring dose adjustments of those two drugs. It may also affect blood levels of lithium and tolbutamide.

### FOOD INTERACTIONS

Food increases the rate of uptake of sertraline into the body, and it may slightly increase the total amount of the drug absorbed. Nevertheless, the most consistent drug levels in the blood occur when sertraline is taken on an empty stomach.

### OTHER DRUGS USED FOR SIMILAR CONDITIONS

A number of other drugs are available for the treatment of depression. Fluoxetine and paroxetine are other serotonin reuptake inhibitors that are effective. MAO inhibitors that are useful as antidepressants are tranylcypromine, phenelzine, and isocarboxazid. Tricyclic antidepressants include amoxapine, desipramine, nortriptyline, amitriptyline, and doxepin.

Each person may react differently to different antidepressants. The choice of drug usually depends on the individual's response to the drug, the drug's effectiveness, and side effects. People who do not benefit from one type of antidepressant may respond to another.

# TEMAZEPAM

**BRAND NAME (MANUFACTURER)**
Restoril (Novartis)

**TYPE OF DRUG**
Psychoactive–sedative

**USED FOR**
Temazepam is used for the short-term treatment of insomnia.

**GENERAL INFORMATION**
Anxiety, depression, and many medications can cause sleep problems in people with HIV infection. Temazepam is a member of a class of psychoactive drugs called benzodiazepines. All of these drugs reduce anxiety or cause drowsiness to some degree. Compared with other benzodiazepines, temazepam is relatively long-acting and is useful for people who wake up too early. Its primary disadvantage is that it can cause a hangover, making the person using the drug feel drowsy and/or light-headed the following day.

Temazepam is available as capsules for oral administration.

**TREATMENT**
The usual adult dose of temazepam is 15 mg, taken before bedtime. Doses as small as 7.5 mg or as high as 30 mg may be appropriate for some people. In elderly or debilitated people, 7.5 mg is the recommended starting dose until individual response is known.

**CAUTIONS AND WARNINGS**
Temazepam should not be used by people who know they are allergic to it or other benzodiazepines (such as diazepam, lorazepam, chlordiazepoxide, alprazolam, oxazepam, triazolam or flurazepam).

Sleep disorders may be symptoms of other physical or psychiatric problems. Eliminating the underlying cause of sleeplessness, if it can be determined, may be a better long-term solution to the problem. If people do not respond within seven to ten days of treatment with temazepam, there may be another underlying illness. Worsening insomnia or the appearance of new abnormalities of thinking or behavior may be the consequence of an unrecognized psychiatric or physical disorder.

The smallest effective dose should be used because some of the side effects are dose-related. Elderly people are especially susceptible to dose-related side effects of the drug. Similarly, the drug should be used with caution in people with a history of kidney disease, liver disease, chronic breathing insufficiency, or sleep apnea (stoppage of breathing during sleep).

Like other benzodiazepines, temazepam can cause dependency. Withdrawal symptoms may include convulsions, tremor, abdominal pain, muscle cramps, vomiting, sweating, restlessness, perceptual disturbances, and insomnia.

Temazepam depresses the central nervous system. People taking the drug should not drive an automobile or operate heavy machinery.

### SIDE EFFECTS

The most common side effects of temazepam are dizziness and daytime drowsiness. Other side effects that occurred in more than 1% of people taking the drug in clinical trials included lethargy, hangover, anxiety, diarrhea, euphoria, weakness, confusion, and vertigo. Less frequently, allergic reactions, loss of appetite, loss of balance, heart palpitations, backache, vomiting, burning eyes, amnesia, and hallucinations were reported.

### PREGNANCY/BREAST-FEEDING

Temazepam may cause serious birth defects and should be avoided during pregnancy. If taken near the time of delivery, the drug may cause sedation and reluctance to feed in the newborn baby. Newborns from mothers who take temazepam during pregnancy may suffer withdrawal symptoms.

HIV can be passed from a woman to her child through breast milk. In areas where nutritionally sound alternatives are readily available, breast-feeding is discouraged for HIV-positive women. Because of the potential toxicity of the drug, women using it should consider alternatives to breast-feeding.

### USE IN CHILDREN

Temazepam is not recommended for children because its safety and efficacy in children have not yet been demonstrated.

### USE IN THE ELDERLY

Older adults may be more susceptible to the side effects of temazepam and generally receive reduced doses. Because the drug is long-lasting, it is generally not prescribed for elderly people. Another, shorter-acting benzodiazepine called oxazepam is often prescribed instead when elderly people require help sleeping.

### DRUG INTERACTIONS

Temazepam may intensify the effect of other central nervous system depressants, including alcohol, narcotic pain relievers, antihistamines, barbiturates, and some antidepressants.

Oral contraceptives, cimetidine, disulfiram, probenecid, isoniazid, and macrolide antibiotics (azithromycin, clarithromycin, or erythromycin) may increase blood levels of temazepam, potentially increasing the risk of its side effects. Cigarette smoking, rifampin, and theophylline may reduce temazepam blood levels.

Temazepam may increase blood levels of AZT, phenytoin, or digoxin, potentially increasing the risk of side effects of these drugs. Temazepam may decrease blood levels of levodopa.

Benzodiazepines used with clozapine have sometimes led to respiratory failure. Temazepam should be stopped for at least a week before starting clozapine.

### FOOD INTERACTIONS
Temazepam may be taken with or without food.

### OTHER DRUGS USED FOR SIMILAR CONDITIONS
A number of drugs are available for treatment of insomnia. Barbiturates such as secobarbital or phenobarbital are occasionally used. More commonly, sedatives such as triazolam, lorazepam, diazepam, or promethazine are used. There is no definitive treatment for insomnia. The choice of drug will primarily depend on which drugs can be tolerated, the side effects for which a person is at risk, and which drugs prove to be effective for the individual.

# THIORIDAZINE

### BRAND NAME (MANUFACTURER)
Mellaril (Novartis); Mellarzine (Major)

### TYPE OF DRUG
Psychoactive–phenothiazine antipsychotic

### USED FOR
Thioridazine is primarily used to treat the symptoms of psychosis. It is also used to treat depression and anxiety, especially in older adults. In children, it is used to treat hyperactivity that results in impulsivity, difficulty sustaining attention, aggression, wide emotional swings, and poor tolerance for frustration.

### GENERAL INFORMATION
Thioridazine belongs to a class of psychoactive drugs called phenothiazines. Although the mechanism by which they work is unknown, they have potent effects on the central nervous system and other organs. They can reduce blood pressure, stop seizures, control nausea and vomiting, and control the symptoms of psychosis, a mental disorder characterized by difficulty thinking, recognizing reality, and acting rationally.

Thioridazine is particularly useful in treating the elderly because it is less likely to cause abnormal shaking movements than other phenothiazines. Its major disadvantage is that it can cause vision problems when taken at high doses for long periods.

Thioridazine is available as tablets, oral solution, and oral suspension.

### TREATMENT

The dosage is individualized and adjusted for each person's response. As with all psychoactive drugs, the lowest effective dose should be used to reduce the risk of side effects. The drug is generally started at a low dosage and increased as necessary and as tolerated. For treatment of psychosis in adults, the starting dose is usually 50 to 100 mg, taken three times a day, with a gradual increase to a maximum of 800 mg daily if necessary. As soon as possible, the dosage should be reduced.

The initial adult dosages for treatment of depression and anxiety, agitation, tension, sleep disturbances, or fear is 25 mg taken three times a day. The total daily dosage usually does not exceed 200 mg.

### CAUTIONS AND WARNINGS

Thioridazine should not be used by anyone with a known allergy to it. It should also not be used by people in comas or those with severely elevated or suppressed blood pressure.

People with a history of seizures or experiencing alcohol withdrawal should use phenothiazines with caution as it may increase the risk of seizures.

Thioridazine may impair the mental and physical abilities necessary to operate an automobile or dangerous machinery.

Phenothiazines elevate blood levels of prolactin, a hormone involved in the production of breast milk. Because many breast cancers are stimulated by prolactin, thioridazine may aggravate existing breast cancers, but there is no evidence that it increases the risk of developing breast cancer.

Thioridazine should be used with caution by people who are exposed to phosphorus insecticides or extreme heat because of the risk of serious side effects.

### SIDE EFFECTS

The most common side effects of thioridazine include drowsiness, dry mouth, and stuffy nose. Less frequently, blurred vision, muscle stiffness, loss of balance, dizziness, abnormal shaking or tremors, constipation, nausea, vomiting, diarrhea, loss of color, allergic reactions, and fainting occur. Hyperactivity, lethargy, restlessness, and headache have been rarely reported.

Tardive dyskinesia is a special neuromuscular side effect of phenothiazines. It is characterized by potentially irreversible, involuntary muscle movements that usually involve the tongue, face, mouth, lips, jaw, torso, and extremi-

ties. Although the side effect occurs most frequently among the elderly (especially elderly women), it is not possible to predict whether an individual will develop the disorder. The risk of the side effect and the likelihood that it will be irreversible are believed to be increased with increased duration of treatment and cumulative dose.

Antipsychotic drugs, including thioridazine, can cause a potentially fatal side effect called neuroleptic malignant syndrome. The syndrome is characterized by high fever, muscle rigidity, altered mental status, irregular pulse or blood pressure, and abnormal heart rhythms. If these symptoms occur, the drug should be stopped and a physician contacted immediately.

### PREGNANCY/BREAST-FEEDING
Thioridazine has not been formally studied in pregnant women. In limited clinical use, it has prolonged labor when taken near delivery. Pregnant women are encouraged to discuss the benefits and potential risks of thioridazine with their physician before deciding to use the drug.

HIV can be passed from a woman to her child through breast milk. In areas where nutritionally sound alternatives are readily available, breast-feeding is discouraged for HIV-positive women. Thioridazine may pass through breast milk and cause side effects in newborns. Because of this potential toxicity, women are encouraged to consider alternatives to breast-feeding while using the drug.

### USE IN CHILDREN
Thioridazine is not intended for children under two years of age. For children between two and twelve years of age, dosages range from 0.5 to 3.0 mg per kg of body weight per day. The dosage is usually started at 10 mg two or three times a day and increased as necessary and tolerated.

### USE IN THE ELDERLY
Older adults may be more susceptible to the side effects of thioridazine, and they may require reduced dosages. However, thioridazine is less likely than many other phenothiazines to cause side effects in elderly people.

### DRUG INTERACTIONS
Thioridazine may intensify the effects of other central nervous system depressants, including alcohol, antihistamines, narcotic pain relievers, sedatives, and barbiturates. Thioridazine may also intensify the effects of atropine or phosphorus insecticides.

Thioridazine greatly increases blood levels of propranolol, potentially increasing the risk of its side effects. Concurrent use of pindolol and thioridazine have resulted in higher blood levels of both drugs.

### FOOD INTERACTIONS
None reported.

**OTHER DRUGS USED FOR SIMILAR CONDITIONS**

Haloperidol and a number of other phenothiazines (including chlorpromazine, fluphenazine, perphenazine, and prochlorperazine) are used to treat symptoms of psychosis. For the treatment of depression or anxiety, a wide variety of different types of drug are available. The choice of drug usually depends on the disorder, the overall condition of the individual, and other drugs being concurrently taken.

# TRIAZOLAM

**BRAND NAME (MANUFACTURER)**

Halcion (Pharmacia & Upjohn)

**TYPE OF DRUG**

Psychoactive–sleeping agent

**USED FOR**

Triazolam is used for the short-term treatment of insomnia.

**GENERAL INFORMATION**

Anxiety, depression, and many medications can cause sleep problems in people with HIV infection. Triazolam is one of the most widely used sleeping pills in the United States, primarily because it eliminates the next-day "hangover" caused by many other sleeping medications.

Triazolam is a member of a class of psychoactive drugs called benzodiazepines, all of which reduce anxiety or cause drowsiness to some degree. They differ mostly in the extent of their effects. Triazolam, especially at higher doses, appears to cause more memory problems than other benzodiazepines. There have also been reports of violent behavior and psychosis after using the drug, but it is not known whether or not the drug actually caused the behavior.

Like other benzodiazepines, triazolam can cause dependency. Withdrawal symptoms may include convulsions, tremor, abdominal pain, muscle cramps, vomiting, sweating, restlessness, perceptual disturbances, and insomnia. Some people taking the drug will experience withdrawal symptoms between doses. The risk of dependence is increased in people with a history of alcoholism, drug use, or marked personality disorders.

Triazolam is available as tablets for oral administration.

**TREATMENT**

The recommended dose for most adults is 0.25 mg at bedtime. A dose of 0.125 mg may be adequate for some people. A dose of 0.5 mg should only be used

for people who do not respond adequately to a lower dose. Lower doses are recommended for elderly or disabled people.

**CAUTIONS AND WARNINGS**

Triazolam should not be used by people who know they are allergic to it or other benzodiazepines (such as diazepam, lorazepam, chlordiazepoxide, alprazolam, oxazepam, temazepam, or flurazepam).

Sleep disorders may be symptoms of other physical or psychiatric problems. Eliminating the underlying cause of sleeplessness, if it can be determined, may be a better long-term solution to the problem. If people do not respond within seven to ten days, there may be another underlying illness. Worsening insomnia or the appearance of new abnormalities of thinking or behavior may be the consequence of an unrecognized psychiatric or physical disorder.

The smallest effective dose should be used because some of the side effects are dose-related. Elderly people are especially susceptible to dose-related side effects of the drug. Similarly, the drug should be used with caution in people with a history of kidney disease, liver disease, chronic pulmonary insufficiency, or sleep apnea (stoppage of breathing during sleep).

Triazolam depresses the central nervous system. People taking the drug should not drive an automobile or operate heavy machinery.

**SIDE EFFECTS**

Triazolam may cause behavioral changes. It is difficult to determine if the changes are caused by the drug, are spontaneous, or are the result of some underlying illness.

Respiratory depression and sleep apnea have infrequently been reported in people with breathing disorders.

The most common side effects of triazolam are drowsiness, dizziness, or light-headedness. Another common side effect is loss of coordination.

An overdose can occur when a person takes as little as 2 mg of triazolam, which is four times the recommended maximum dose. Symptoms include confusion, impaired coordination, slurred speech, coma, and in some cases death.

**PREGNANCY/BREAST-FEEDING**

Triazolam may cause fetal damage and should be avoided during pregnancy. HIV can be passed from a woman to her child through breast milk. In areas where nutritionally sound alternatives are readily available, breast-feeding is discouraged for HIV-positive women. Newborns from mothers who take triazolam during pregnancy may suffer withdrawal symptoms. Because of the potential toxicity of the drug, women should consider alternatives to breast-feeding while taking it.

### USE IN CHILDREN

The safety and effectiveness of the drug have not been studied in children under eighteen.

### USE IN THE ELDERLY

Elderly or debilitated people should start at a low dose, 0.125 mg per day, to decrease the risk of oversedation, dizziness, or impaired coordination. The maximum dose for elderly or debilitated people is 0.25 mg per day.

### DRUG INTERACTIONS

Triazolam produces additive central nervous system depression when used with anticonvulsants, antihistamines, alcohol, and other drugs that produce central nervous system depression.

Triazolam should not be used with delavirdine, indinavir, itraconazole, ketoconazole, nelfinavir, ritonavir, or saquinavir as this may lead to serious side effects.

Caution is advised when triazolam is administered to people receiving erythromycin and clarithromycin, since they may decrease the plasma clearance of triazolam.

### FOOD INTERACTIONS

Triazolam may be taken with or without food.

### OTHER DRUGS USED FOR SIMILAR CONDITIONS

A number of drugs are available for treatment of insomnia. Barbiturates such as secobarbital or phenobarbital are occasionally used. More commonly, sedatives such as lorazepam, diazepam, or promethazine are used. There is no definitive treatment for insomnia. The choice of drug will primarily depend on which drugs can be tolerated, the side effects for which a person is at risk, and which drugs prove to be effective for the individual.

# TRIFLUOPERAZINE

### BRAND NAME (MANUFACTURER)

Stelazine (SmithKline Beecham)

### TYPE OF DRUG

Psychoactive–phenothiazine antipsychotic/antianxiety drug

### USED FOR

Trifluoperazine is used to treat the symptoms of psychotic disorders and for the short-term management of anxiety.

### GENERAL INFORMATION

Trifluoperazine belongs to a class of psychoactive drugs called phenothiazines. Although the mechanism by which they work is unknown, they have

potent effects on the central nervous system and other organs. They can reduce blood pressure, stop seizures, control nausea and vomiting, and control the symptoms of psychosis, a mental disorder characterized by difficulty thinking, recognizing reality, and acting rationally.

Trifluoperazine is available as tablets, solution for injection, and concentrate for oral administration.

**TREATMENT**

The dosage of trifluoperazine must be adjusted for each person's response. Most people use the tablets. The injectable solution is usually reserved for hospitalized patients, and the concentrate is designed for severe conditions when oral medication is preferred but the tablets are impractical.

As with all psychoactive drugs, the lowest effective dose should be used to reduce the risk of side effects. The drug is generally started at a low dosage and increased as necessary and as tolerated. For treatment of psychosis in adults, the starting dose is usually 2 to 5 mg, taken two times a day, with a gradual increase as necessary. Most people respond to 15 to 20 mg a day, but some people require as much as 40 mg per day. For treatment of anxiety in adults, the usual dosage is 1 to 2 mg, taken twice daily, up to a maximum of 6 mg per day. The drug should not be taken for longer than twelve weeks for the treatment of anxiety.

**CAUTIONS AND WARNINGS**

Trifluoperazine should not be used by anyone with a known allergy to it or any other phenothiazine drug. It should also not be used by anyone with severe central nervous system depression, severe bone marrow suppression, or liver damage.

Trifluoperazine may impair the mental and physical abilities necessary to operate an automobile or dangerous machinery.

Phenothiazines elevate blood levels of prolactin, a hormone involved in the production of breast milk. Because many breast cancers are stimulated by prolactin, trifluoperazine may aggravate existing breast cancers, but there is no evidence that it increases the risk of developing breast cancer.

Trifluoperazine should be used with caution by people who are exposed to phosphorus insecticides or extreme heat because of the risk of serious side effects.

Trifluoperazine concentrate contains sodium bisulfite and should be used with caution in people with sulfite allergies.

The antivomiting effect of trifluoperazine may mask the symptoms of other drugs and may obscure the diagnosis and treatment of other conditions such as intestinal obstruction, brain tumor, and Reye's syndrome.

Trifluoperazine should be used with caution in people with glaucoma because the drug can exacerbate the condition. Trifluoperazine may increase the risk of seizures and should be used with caution in people with a history of seizures.

## SIDE EFFECTS

Drowsiness, dizziness, skin reactions, rash, dry mouth, insomnia, irregular periods, fatigue, muscular weakness, loss of appetite, abnormal lactation, blurred vision, or involuntary muscle movements may occur in people taking trifluoperazine.

Tardive dyskinesia is a special neuromuscular side effect of phenothiazines. It is characterized by potentially irreversible, involuntary muscle movements that usually involve the tongue, face, mouth, lips, jaw, torso, and extremities. Although the side effect occurs most frequently among the elderly (especially elderly women), it is not possible to predict whether an individual will develop the disorder. The risk of the side effect and the likelihood that it will be irreversible are believed to be increased with increased duration of treatment and cumulative dose.

Antipsychotic drugs, including trifluoperazine, can cause a potentially fatal side effect called neuroleptic malignant syndrome. The syndrome is characterized by high fever, muscle rigidity, altered mental status, irregular pulse or blood pressure, and abnormal heart rhythms. If these symptoms occur, the drug should be stopped and a physician contacted immediately.

## PREGNANCY/BREAST-FEEDING

Trifluoperazine has not been formally studied in pregnant women. In limited clinical experience it has caused severe side effects in the newborns of women who took the drug during pregnancy. In addition, in animal studies it caused birth defects when administered at high doses. Pregnant women are encouraged to discuss the benefits and potential risks of trifluoperazine with their physician before deciding to use the drug.

HIV can be passed from a woman to her child through breast milk. In areas where nutritionally sound alternatives are readily available, breast-feeding is discouraged for HIV-positive women. Phenothiazines are known to pass into human milk. Because of the potential toxicity of the drug, women are encouraged to consider alternatives to breast-feeding while using it.

## USE IN CHILDREN

Trifluoperazine is used in children older than six years of age. The dosage of the drug should be adjusted for the weight of the child and the severity of the symptoms. The starting dosage is 1 mg administered once or twice a day. The dosage should gradually be increased until the symptoms are controlled or side effects become troublesome.

**USE IN THE ELDERLY**

In general, the elderly use the lower range of adult doses because they may be more susceptible to the side effects of the drug. The initial dose should be low and increased even more gradually than for younger adults.

**DRUG INTERACTIONS**

Trifluoperazine may intensify the effect of other central nervous system depressants, including alcohol, antihistamines, narcotic pain relievers, tranquilizers, and sedatives.

Phenothiazines, including trifluoperazine, may interfere with the action of blood thinners such as warfarin or drugs used to treat blood pressure (e.g., guanethidine). Use of propranolol together with trifluoperazine may increase blood levels of both drugs, potentially increasing the risk of side effects.

Use of trifluoperazine with thiazide diuretics may increase the risk of severe low blood pressure.

Phenothiazines may increase the risk of seizures, requiring dosage modifications of anticonvulsant drugs, such as phenobarbital, phenytoin, or carbamazepine. Trifluoperazine may increase blood levels of phenytoin, potentially increasing the risk of its side effects.

**FOOD INTERACTIONS**

Trifluoperazine may be taken with or without food. The oral concentrate should be diluted in tomato or fruit juice, milk, orange syrup, carbonated beverages, coffee, tea, or water. Semisolid foods such as soup or puddings may also be used.

**OTHER DRUGS USED FOR SIMILAR CONDITIONS**

Haloperidol and a number of other phenothiazines (including chlorpromazine, fluphenazine, perphenazine, and prochlorperazine) are used to treat symptoms of psychosis. For the treatment of anxiety, a wide variety of different types of drug are available, including the benzodiazepines (alprazolam, chlordiazepoxide, diazepam, lorazepam, or oxazepam). Phenothiazines, including trifluoperazine, are generally not the first drug used to treat anxiety because their side effects are more severe than those of the benzodiazepines. Ultimately, the drug chosen depends on the disorder, the overall condition of the individual, and other drugs being concurrently taken.

# VENLAFAXINE

**BRAND NAME (MANUFACTURER)**
Effexor (Wyeth-Ayerst)

**TYPE OF DRUG**
Psychoactive–antidepressant

**USED FOR**
Venlafaxine is used to treat depression.

**GENERAL INFORMATION**
Venlafaxine is an antidepressant chemically unrelated to other antidepressants such as the tricyclics or monoamine oxidase (MAO) inhibitors. Venlafaxine is thought to work by increasing the concentration of a number of different neurotransmitters in the brain.

Venlafaxine is available as tablets for oral administration.

**TREATMENT**
The recommended starting dose of venlafaxine is 75 mg per day, taken in two or three divided doses. As needed and tolerated, the dose may be increased up to 150 mg or 225 mg per day. When increasing the dose, increments of up to 75 mg per day should be made at intervals of at least four days. People with kidney or liver disease may need to take reduced dosages.

When discontinuing venlafaxine, the risk of withdrawal symptoms is lowest if the drug is tapered off slowly. The drug should be discontinued under the guidance of a physician.

When switching from an MAO inhibitor antidepressant, at least fourteen days should elapse between stopping the MAO inhibitor and starting venlafaxine. Similarly, venlafaxine should be stopped for seven days before starting an MAO inhibitor antidepressant.

**CAUTIONS AND WARNINGS**
Venlafaxine should not be used by anyone with a known allergy to it. Taking venlafaxine along with MAO inhibitors may cause severe, potentially fatal side effects.

Because venlafaxine causes increased blood pressure, people taking the drug should have their blood pressure monitored routinely.

In people with a history of mania, venlafaxine may induce manic episodes.

Although venlafaxine did not impair thinking or motor skills in clinical trials, people taking the drug should refrain from driving or operating dangerous machinery until they are reasonably certain the drug does not cause drowsiness or sedation in them.

### SIDE EFFECTS

The most common side effects of venlafaxine include nausea, constipation, loss of appetite, drowsiness, dry mouth, dizziness, insomnia, nervousness, headache, weakness, sweating, abnormal ejaculation, and diarrhea. Less common side effects include vomiting, anxiety, tremors, confusion, blurred vision, and impotence.

### PREGNANCY/BREAST-FEEDING

Venlafaxine has not been formally studied in pregnant women. In animal studies, it did not cause fetal harm, but it is not known whether the same would be true in humans. Pregnant women are encouraged to discuss the benefits and potential risks of the drug with their physician before deciding to use it.

HIV can be passed from a woman to her child through breast milk. In areas where nutritionally sound alternatives are readily available, breast-feeding is discouraged for HIV-positive women. It is not known whether venlafaxine is excreted in human milk. Because of the potential toxicity of the drug, women are encouraged to consider alternatives to breast-feeding while using it.

### USE IN CHILDREN

Venlafaxine is not recommended for use in those under eighteen years of age, because the safety and effectiveness of the drug for them have not yet been established.

### USE IN THE ELDERLY

In clinical trials, no overall differences in safety or effectiveness were observed between older and younger adults. However, older adults may be more susceptible to the side effects of the drug and may require reduced doses.

### DRUG INTERACTIONS

The use of venlafaxine and MAO inhibitors greatly increases the risk of serious, potentially fatal side effects.

### FOOD INTERACTIONS

The manufacturer recommends taking venlafaxine with food.

### OTHER DRUGS USED FOR SIMILAR CONDITIONS

For treatment of depression, there are many options, including tricyclic antidepressants (desipramine, amitriptyline, protriptyline, amoxapine, maprotiline, imipramine, trimipramine, doxepin), MAO inhibitors (tranylcypromine, phenelzine, isocarboxazid), serotonin reuptake inhibitors (fluoxetine, paroxetine, and sertraline), and stimulants such as methylphenidate. The appropriate choice varies from person to person and depends on age, physical health and condition, and other drugs being concurrently used.

# VACCINES

A vaccine is a substance administered to produce or increase an immune response against a particular disease. It is usually given before a person has contracted the disease in hopes of preventing the infection or reducing its severity. Vaccines have traditionally been used to fight viral infections because so few effective antiviral drugs have been available.

In the past, most vaccines consisted of weakened or dead viruses which, when injected, stimulate immune responses. With most such vaccines, there is always some concern, however, that a person injected with a weakened (but still live) virus might contract the disease the vaccine was designed to prevent. Modern recombinant DNA technology has offered a solution to this risk. Now most vaccines are made from pieces of viruses grown in bacteria, yeast, or mammalian cells. Because the entire virus necessary to cause disease is not present, these new vaccines are much safer to use.

Some researchers believe that vaccines may also be useful in treating viral disease. These vaccines, called "therapeutic" vaccines, may stimulate a better immune response in people already infected with a virus, possibly serving as a catalyst to help the immune system keep the virus in check. Therapeutic HIV vaccines are currently being studied.

The following vaccines are profiled in this section:
- hepatitis A vaccine
- hepatitis B vaccine
- influenza vaccine

At the end of the section, some experimental vaccines are briefly described. The HIV-specific experimental vaccines include:
- gp120 vaccines
- gp160 vaccines
- HIV immunogen
- p24 vaccines

Experimental vaccines for other microorganisms that cause opportunistic infections in people with HIV are also being studied and are briefly described at the end of this section.

# HEPATITIS A VACCINE

**BRAND NAME (MANUFACTURER)**
Havrix (SmithKline Beecham); Vaqta (Merck)

**TYPE OF DRUG**
Vaccine

**USED FOR**
Hepatitis A vaccine is used to prevent infection and symptomatic disease caused by hepatitis A.

**GENERAL INFORMATION**
Hepatitis A is one of five known hepatitis viruses that cause a systemic infection and potentially serious liver damage. The other viruses are hepatitis B, C, D, and E. Hepatitis A is not known to cause chronic infection, but it is a serious disease in adults. It can cause flu-like symptoms as well as serious gastrointestinal symptoms that may prevent someone with the disease from eating. It may also cause serious liver damage. It is estimated that six people in every ten thousand who contract hepatitis A will die.

There is no clear evidence that hepatitis A causes more severe disease or affects HIV disease progression, but even in people with healthy immune systems, hepatitis A in adults is worth preventing.

Two similar hepatitis A vaccines have been developed and approved by the FDA. Both contain purified virus that has been killed with the chemical formalin. In large-scale clinical trials (one included more than forty thousand children), the vaccines were 95% to 100% effective in preventing symptomatic disease for at least one year. It is expected that the protection should last from five to ten years, but long-term studies have not been completed.

**TREATMENT**
Hepatitis A vaccine is administered by injection into a muscle. Primary immunization for adults consists of a single dose. Primary immunization for children (two to eighteen years of age) consists of two smaller doses given one month apart. A booster dose is recommended anytime between six and twelve months after the primary immunization to ensure the highest response.

In people with an impaired immune system, including people with HIV infection, more vaccine doses may be necessary to obtain an adequate response.

**CAUTIONS AND WARNINGS**
Anyone who develops an allergy to the vaccine after the first injection should not receive additional injections.

As with all immunizations, the body's immune system must mount a response to the hepatitis A vaccine for it to be effective. Consequently, each vaccine may be less effective when administered in the later stages of HIV infection because the immune system cannot mount an effective response.

Administration of the hepatitis A vaccine may transiently stimulate HIV replication, although the clinical importance of this finding is not clearly understood.

**SIDE EFFECTS**

In clinical trials, the vaccines were well tolerated. In more than a hundred thousand injections, no serious adverse reactions were noted. Pain, redness, or tenderness at the injection site were occasionally reported.

**PREGNANCY/BREAST-FEEDING**

No information is available about the value or risks of immunizing pregnant women with hepatitis A vaccines. In all likelihood, the inactivated vaccine will be safe for use in pregnant women like all other inactivated vaccines.

HIV can be passed from a woman to her child through breast milk. In areas where nutritionally sound alternatives are readily available, breast-feeding is discouraged for HIV-positive women. Hepatitis A antibodies are excreted in human milk, and may provide some protection to breast-fed infants.

**USE IN CHILDREN**

In clinical trials, the drug was both safe and effective for children between one and sixteen years of age.

**USE IN THE ELDERLY**

Although there is little information available regarding the use of hepatitis A vaccines in elderly people, it is likely that the drug will be safe and effective for them.

**DRUG INTERACTIONS**

None reported.

**FOOD INTERACTIONS**

Because the vaccine is administered by injection, food does not affect absorption of the drug.

**OTHER DRUGS USED FOR SIMILAR CONDITIONS**

Immune globulin can provide temporary protection (on the order of a few months) against infection with hepatitis A. Realistically, they are useful only during an epidemic or when traveling to an area where the virus is prevalent. In contrast, the vaccine should provide protection from infection for years.

Hepatitis A is often transmitted through food or water contaminated with feces. Thorough hand washing, safe food-handling practices, and good sanitation are effective measures to prevent spread of the virus.

# HEPATITIS B VACCINE

**BRAND NAME (MANUFACTURER)**

Engerix-B (SmithKline Beecham); Recombivax HB (Merck)

**TYPE OF DRUG**

Vaccine

**USED FOR**

This vaccine is used to prevent infection caused by all known types of hepatitis B. It is routinely used for infants in the United States and people of all ages in areas where hepatitis B is prevalent. Health care workers are often vaccinated because they have a high risk of exposure from the people they treat.

**GENERAL INFORMATION**

Hepatitis B is one of at least five hepatitis viruses that cause a systemic infection and potentially serious liver damage. The other viruses are hepatitis A, C, D, and E. The incubation period for hepatitis B is relatively long—six weeks to six months may elapse between exposure and onset of clinical symptoms.

It has been estimated that 170 million people worldwide are carriers for hepatitis B. After initial infection, hepatitis B causes chronic hepatitis in 5% to 10% of infected people. For HIV-positive individuals, the situation is worse. One study found that more than 20% of HIV-positive men exposed to hepatitis B developed chronic infection, and HIV-positive individuals with chronic infection tend to have higher levels of replicating virus in their blood.

Alpha interferon is the only approved therapy for hepatitis B. It has about a 40% response rate in the general population, but response rates are much lower in people co-infected with HIV. The likelihood of response appears to be dependent on the health of the immune system and the extent of liver damage when therapy begins.

Two genetically engineered hepatitis B vaccines have been approved for use by the FDA. They are made by recombinant DNA technology, so no live virus is used and the vaccination cannot cause hepatitis B.

The vaccine is generally given in three injections over six months and is effective in preventing the disease in 95% of the general population. The vaccine is somewhat less effective in HIV-infected people, possibly because a weakened immune system is less effective at raising a response. In a clinical trial of seventy HIV-positive people, a fourth injection with the vaccine improved the response. More than 84% of the study participants who received all four injections began producing antibodies to hepatitis B, a sign of protection against infection.

**TREATMENT**

The vaccine is intended for intramuscular injection, but people who cannot tolerate injections into muscle tissue may have the drug injected subcutaneously (under the skin).

There are different dosages of hepatitis B vaccine, depending on the use. For example, one high-dose formulation is for people undergoing kidney dialysis.

Another lower-dose formulation is available for children, high-risk infants, and adults.

The typical vaccination schedule consists of three doses. The second dose is injected one month after the original injection, and the third dose is injected six months after the first. The standard dose is 2.5 to 10 micrograms (mcg) depending on age and risk of infection. People undergoing dialysis receive a 40 mcg dose. HIV-positive people often receive the 40 mcg dose as well.

## CAUTIONS AND WARNINGS

The vaccine is produced in yeast. It should not be used by people who are allergic to yeast. People who develop an allergy to the vaccine after any of the injections should not receive additional injections.

Administration of hepatitis B vaccine may transiently stimulate HIV replication, although the clinical importance of this finding is not clearly understood.

## SIDE EFFECTS

No serious side effects were reported in clinical trials. Pain, redness, or swelling at the injection site were reported following 17% of injections. Other side effects were reported after 15% of injections and included fatigue, weakness, headache, malaise, nausea, diarrhea, or upper-respiratory infection.

## PREGNANCY/BREAST-FEEDING

This inactivated vaccine is safe for use in pregnant women. The antibodies that the body develops in response to vaccination are excreted in human milk, but they are unlikely to cause harm to infants.

## USE IN CHILDREN

Hepatitis B is transmitted from infected mothers to their children at a rate of 90% to 100%, and in 90% of these infected infants the disease becomes chronic. The vaccine is well tolerated and highly effective in children and it is routinely given to infants and children of all ages. Maternally transferred antibodies or passively administered antibodies against hepatitis B do not interfere with the active immune response to the vaccine in newborns.

## USE IN THE ELDERLY

No changes in dose or administration are recommended for elderly people.

## DRUG INTERACTIONS

None reported.

## FOOD INTERACTIONS

Because the vaccine is administered by injection, it is unlikely that food would interfere with the absorption of the drug in the body.

## OTHER DRUGS USED FOR SIMILAR CONDITIONS

Immunoglobulins pooled from individuals infected with hepatitis B have been shown to be effective in preventing transmission of the virus or reducing symp-

toms of the disease. However, the protective effect of these immunoglobulins is short-lived.

## COMMENTS
Hepatitis B vaccine is only useful if used before a person is infected with the virus. Those infected with the virus already produce antibodies against it, and vaccination may not be effective. One exception is newborn children. Infants who receive the vaccine after exposure to the virus during labor may effectively respond to the vaccine.

# INFLUENZA VACCINE

## BRAND NAME (MANUFACTURER)
Fluzone (Connaught)

## TYPE OF DRUG
Vaccine

## USED FOR
Influenza vaccine is used to prevent influenza (the flu), a respiratory infection characterized by aches and fever.

## GENERAL INFORMATION
Influenza vaccine consists of flu virus that has been grown in eggs and then purified and inactivated. The preparations are changed each year based on the different strains of the virus most likely to be encountered during the flu season.

People with HIV are at increased risk for the flu and should be vaccinated each year before the beginning of the flu season. Because the vaccine is not 100% effective, partners and caregivers of those infected with HIV should also use the vaccine to reduce the risk of transmitting influenza to them. Because the use of vaccines of this type sometimes causes transient increases in HIV viral load, some physicians have worried vaccination might be harmful to HIV infected people. Studies which have examined this, however, have shown that any increase in viral load is temporary and is much less likely to harm the patient than a bout of the flu.

## TREATMENT
Influenza vaccine is recommended for anyone over six months of age who is at increased risk of influenza because of age or underlying medical conditions. Initial immunization requires two doses. A single dose of the vaccine is generally recommended for previously vaccinated children and adults. The vaccine is administered before the beginning of flu season, ideally during mid-October to November in the United States.

**CAUTIONS AND WARNINGS**

People who develop an allergic reaction the first time they receive an influenza vaccination should not receive subsequent vaccinations. Because the vaccine is produced from viruses grown in eggs, people who are allergic to eggs should not use it either.

In general, anyone with a high fever should not be administered the vaccine until his or her temperature returns to normal.

As with all immunizations, the body's immune system must mount a response to the influenza vaccine for it to be effective. Consequently, the vaccine may be less effective when administered in the later stages of HIV infection because the immune system is suppressed and cannot raise an effective response.

**SIDE EFFECTS**

The most frequent side effects of influenza vaccine are pain or tenderness at the injection site. Less frequently fever, malaise, or muscle pain may occur, especially in people who have not previously received the vaccine. Rarely, serious allergic reactions to the vaccine or to the residual egg protein may occur.

**PREGNANCY/BREAST-FEEDING**

Influenza vaccine is considered safe for pregnant women. Pregnant women who have health conditions that increase their risks for influenza-related complications should be vaccinated regardless of the stage of pregnancy.

HIV can be passed from a woman to her child through breast milk. In areas where nutritionally sound alternatives are readily available, breast-feeding is discouraged for HIV-positive women. The antibodies developed in response to influenza vaccination are excreted in human milk, and they may provide some protection against influenza in the child.

**USE IN CHILDREN**

Children under the age of nine who have never been vaccinated should receive two doses of vaccine at least one month apart to maximize the chance of successful immunization. In the United States, the first dose is usually administered sometime after September (before the beginning of flu season). It is recommended the second dose be administered before December.

**USE IN THE ELDERLY**

Most fatalities due to influenza occur in elderly people. People over sixty-five years of age are encouraged to receive the vaccine every year.

**DRUG INTERACTIONS**

Intravenously administered immune globulin may interfere with the effectiveness of influenza vaccine. The vaccine should not be administered within three months of receiving the immune globulin.

**FOOD INTERACTIONS**

Because influenza vaccine is administered by injection, food does not affect the absorption of the vaccine.

**OTHER DRUGS USED FOR SIMILAR CONDITIONS**

A number of cold and flu medications are used to treat the symptoms of the flu. None of these medications will prevent a person from contracting the illness.

**COMMENTS**

A few years ago, a small study suggested that influenza vaccine may transiently stimulate HIV replication. Although the study was small and the results were contradicted by other studies, many people with HIV decided not to get flu shots. As with every medical decision a person must make after becoming HIV positive, the decision whether or not to use the flu vaccine requires considering a number of tradeoffs. In this case, the possibility of temporary increased HIV replication due to the vaccine must be weighed against the damage that can be caused by actually contracting the flu, which usually causes sustained increases in viral load.

# VACCINES —

## EXPERIMENTAL

The following vaccines are being tested for HIV and other infections. Generally, they are not widely available; most can be obtained only when participating in clinical trials. Experimental HIV vaccines are described first followed by vaccines used for other infections.

**HIV THERAPEUTIC VACCINES**

Traditionally, vaccines are given to uninfected people to prevent disease or to diminish the strength of an infection. Today, vaccines are being explored as potential therapies for a variety of diseases, particularly AIDS. A number of therapeutic vaccine studies are under way to determine if treatment can boost the immune system and protect against disease development and progression.

Several HIV therapeutic vaccines are being tested in infected people whose immune systems are still intact. They include gp120 vaccines, gp160 vaccines, p24 vaccines, and HIV immunogen (Remune). Although therapeutic vaccines have been shown to work in an AIDS-like disease in monkeys, there is little evidence at this point that therapeutic HIV vaccines slow the progression of AIDS in people.

### GP120 AND GP160 VACCINES

gp120 and gp160 are thought to be key proteins on the surface of HIV viral particles. The vaccines to them do not carry viral RNA, but they do stimulate the immune system to produce antibodies to HIV viral particles. At the current time, no data suggest that gp120 or gp160 vaccines can prevent HIV infection or favorably alter the course of disease. Studies of preventive gp120 vaccines continue in some foreign countries.

### HIV IMMUNOGEN

HIV immunogen (Remune) is a vaccine made from whole HIV viral particles that are inactivated with a chemical that strips the viral envelope away from the proteins and RNA inside. Presumably, the virus should not be able to infect cells after inactivation. Preliminary results have shown no improvements in CD4+ cell counts or reductions in viral load (HIV RNA) in people receiving the HIV immunogen compared to people receiving a placebo.

### P24 VACCINES

p24 is a major core protein of HIV viral particles. It is not "visible" to the immune system until the virus invades a cell and releases its RNA and protein contents inside. p24 vaccines are designed to induce an immune response to this protein, which is essential for the replication of HIV.

# OTHER VACCINES

In addition to vaccines against HIV, a number of other experimental vaccines are being developed and tested for people with AIDS to prevent or treat specific opportunistic infections. They include vaccines against cryptococcus, cytomegalovirus, and herpes simplex virus.

# ANTIRETROVIRAL STRATEGIES

**BY BEN CHENG, MARTIN DELANEY, AND REENA LAWANDE**

## INTRODUCTION

HIV (Human Immunodeficiency Virus) is a virus that infects and takes over certain cells of the immune system that are important in fighting disease. The virus then uses these cells to make new copies of itself, which then go on to infect other cells. This causes the infected cells to function improperly and die prematurely, weakening the immune system and permitting the development of opportunistic infections (opportunistic infections are infections that "take the opportunity" to flourish when the immune system is damaged by HIV). The immune system is very complex and researchers do not yet know all the ways HIV, the immune system, and opportunistic infections interact. The overall goal of antiviral therapy is to slow or stop this process, and thereby slow or stop the progression of HIV disease and the destruction of the immune system. While other approaches to combating HIV infection have been proposed and tested, thus far only antiviral therapy has been proven to slow disease progression and extend life. A balanced approach to understanding and making decisions about antiretroviral therapy must include knowledge of the benefits, risks and limitations of existing therapies, as well as the prospects for improvements offered by combination therapies and newer drugs.

## THE GOAL OF ANTIVIRAL THERAPY

Once HIV was identified as the cause of AIDS, stopping or slowing the reproduction of the virus became a major scientific goal. Significant progress has been made, yet uncertainty remains about when to start and when to switch or combine antiretroviral therapies. Also, the failure of existing drugs to remain effective for long periods of time is sometimes misunderstood as meaning that the drugs don't work at all. Making wise decisions about the use of antiviral therapies requires understanding the benefits and risks of therapies, good communication with a knowledgeable physician, and proper use of various laboratory tests. In recent years, the advent of better drugs and combination therapy has made it possible for the first time to develop long-term strategies for antiviral management of HIV. The objectives of antiretroviral therapy should be:

- To prevent immune system destruction and thereby prevent or delay disease progression and death;

- To lower viral levels (HIV RNA) below the limit of detection of the currently available tests (or as low as possible)—this may take from three to six months to achieve;

- To extend, as much as possible, the utility of the currently available antivirals. This means using the various options in wise combinations, rigorously adhering to the regimens prescribed to prevent or delay the development of drug resistance, and thinking ahead regarding how choices about antiviral therapy today might effect future use of therapies.

## WHY USE ANTIVIRAL THERAPIES?

The reasons for using antiviral therapies are fairly clear despite doubts and frustrations raised by the inability of early single drug therapies to produce long-term benefits.

When a person is first infected with HIV, high virus levels develop that are often accompanied by symptoms and a decline in the number of CD4+ T cells. The immune system, without the use of antiviral therapies, succeeds in producing a dramatic, but incomplete, suppression of the virus. In most cases CD4+ cell counts return partially toward normal levels and a person usually regains full clinical health for many years. New studies demonstrate that even during this time of seemingly good health, there is an aggressive battle waged on a daily basis between HIV and the immune system. In addition to immune dysfunction caused by HIV, over time, the immune system is overwhelmed by the virus' rapid and constant activity.

Considering these points, it makes sense to attempt to slow down or stop the replication of HIV as much and for as long as possible. A number of drugs have been shown to significantly reduce levels of virus found in the blood (viral load), and these drugs almost always cause some rise in CD4+ cell counts (one common measure of immune health) indicating some degree of response in the immune system. Conversely, antiretroviral drugs that fail to reduce viral load also generally fail to improve measures of immune health such as CD4+ cell counts. There is a clear relationship between increased levels of HIV found in blood (viral load) and more advanced disease states and increased risk of disease progression. As a general rule, the more virus being produced in the body, the more rapidly disease progresses. Also, the less virus that is produced, the less opportunity it has to change, or "mutate," and become more dangerous. Several studies have now shown that when viral load is reduced and CD4+ cell counts increase for 24 weeks or longer, disease progression and death are delayed.

The challenge for antiretroviral drug developers is to develop therapies that produce a long-lasting reduction in viral load in both blood and tissue

sites in the body where HIV accumulates. Antiviral therapies must do this, however, without causing serious toxicity or interfering excessively with a person's quality of life. Many researchers believe that unless virus replication can be controlled, other efforts at rebuilding immune health will ultimately fail.

Although antiretroviral therapies impair HIV's ability to replicate, they are not a cure since these drugs have not been shown to totally eradicate the virus from the body. Over time, the virus mutates or changes itself enough so that it is no longer affected by these drugs. This process, called viral resistance, is likely to happen with almost all antiretroviral drugs to some degree. Many scientists fear that it will not be possible to fully eradicate the virus from the body, no matter how good the drugs become or how early treatment is started. It is still clear, however, that suppressing the virus lengthens survival time, and it may be possible with truly effective therapy to live out a normal life span despite HIV infection.

## WHEN SHOULD I START TREATMENT?

There is much debate about when to start anti-HIV therapy, which therapies to start, and in what combinations. Should treatment be used immediately when people first learn they are infected, or should it be "saved" until there are changes in immunologic or virologic parameters or until symptoms of HIV develop? These and other questions need to be considered when deciding when and which combinations to use. When deciding when to start, switch, or change antiviral regimens there are generally three medical or biological factors to consider:

- What is happening with the virus (HIV RNA) levels;
- What is happening with measures of immune health (particularly CD4+ cell counts);
- What is happening clinically (e.g., symptoms of HIV disease or recurrent health conditions despite treatment).

Using treatment is not just a matter of medical or biological factors. Several additional factors must be considered, including:

- A person's readiness and willingness to commit to constant, long-term use of therapy;
- The impact therapy will have on quality of life;
- How long therapies can last, and whether or not there will be new and better drugs to replace them when they eventually fail;
- A person's relative risk of disease progression in the short, medium, and long-term.

There is no single, absolute answer to the question of when to start antiviral treatment. Some researchers and physicians believe that everyone who is HIV infected, regardless of viral load, symptoms, or CD4+ counts should be on treatment. Some believe people should begin therapy when their CD4+ counts fall below 500 or their viral load exceeds 10,000-20,000 copies of virus. Others believe that only people with symptoms of HIV disease should consider anti-HIV therapy. One note of agreement is that most researchers and physicians believe that the decision to start anti-HIV therapy should be guided by looking at clinical health and measures of both CD4+ cell counts as well as viral load (HIV RNA levels). Increasingly, information suggests that the new viral load tests (or HIV RNA tests), coupled with CD4+ cell counts, together provide the most accurate tool to monitor the risk of HIV disease progression. The most commonly used viral load tests are Roche's PCR (polymerase chain reaction) test (also known as the Amplicor HIV Monitor Test), Chiron's bDNA (branch DNA test, also known as Quantiplex), and Organon Teknika's NASBA (nucleic acid sequence based amplification) test. For more information on viral load tests, call the Project Inform Hotline and ask for the *Diagnostics Fact Sheet*.

Recently, the U.S. Department of Health and Human Services released a set of Guidelines for the Use of Antiretroviral Agents in the Treatment of HIV-Infected Adults and Adolescents. These guidelines are summarized in Table 1 at the end of this chapter. In short, they suggest that most HIV-infected people should be treated. The one general exception is regarding people with the combination of high CD4+ counts (above 500) and low viral load (below 20,000 copies of virus). In this population, the Federal Guidelines recommend "observing" the person and continuing diagnostic testing. However, the Guidelines acknowledge that this is just one approach and that some will still prefer to offer treatment, even in this population.

The new Federal Guidelines do not argue that all patients must be tested. Instead, they describe the recommendations of the researchers, but also point out that patients and physicians must take many other facts into consideration, such as the person's readiness to start treatment and concerns about long-term toxicity and drug resistance.

## HIT HARD, HIT EARLY?

A number of researchers are suggesting using a "hit hard, hit early" strategy for people known to be in or just beyond the acute-infection stage—a period of flu-like illness which often occurs a month or so after initial infection with HIV. Immediate treatment is already offered to people who have recently been exposed to HIV, such as health care workers stuck by an infected needle. Increasingly, researchers are interested in testing three-, or four-

drug combinations (including protease inhibitors) in these people. The hope of aggressive treatment is to either stop the infection altogether, or at least minimize the potential for long-term damage by lowering viral load.

Lack of data make it unclear if the "hit hard, hit early" philosophy is always right for everyone. Some questions around this strategy include:

- Should all HIV-infected people, regardless of CD4+ cell levels or viral load, be treated immediately with the most potent multi-drug combinations? Some scientists believe this is appropriate or at least warrants further study. Others fear that even the best therapies will not work indefinitely and using them too early in relatively healthy people, or people with very low viral loads, might use up our best weapons in many people before they are truly needed.

- In some people, will 2-drug combinations like AZT+3TC be sufficient to sustain low viral load? In this case, does adding a protease inhibitor help in any way? While this approach might, in a small percentage of cases, achieve the goal of lowering viral levels below the limit of detection, it still might not be the best way to extend the use of currently available options. For example, using 3TC in this fashion quickly results in the development of 3TC resistance.

- Do people with low viral loads, say fewer than 5,000 copies of HIV RNA, require any therapy at all? If viral load drives disease progression, why use therapy when viral load is already low? Does using therapy simply expose the patient to the risk of toxicity and create the opportunity to develop viral resistance, without adding any measurable clinical benefit? Or, on the other hand, might using a powerful combination early on make it possible to suppress the disease for the longest possible period or even permanently? These questions remain unanswered.

There are many opinions but very little hard data. Plenty of data show that most HIV-infected people will live longer with therapy, even if there is no precise way to determine when to start. There are other data, however, that indicate that a small subset of HIV-infected people (less than 5%) fare very well for long periods (more than 15 years) without therapy. Some researchers argue that intervening with therapy could, theoretically, upset this balance in such people. But it may be equally valid to test therapy in such people to see whether, with a little more help, the body might be able to rid itself permanently of any risk of symptomatic disease. For now, both views are equally valid and in need of research.

Not all people have access to the same treatment options and different people respond differently to individual drugs. The options include existing approved drugs and combinations, experimental drugs accessed through clinical trials

and expanded access programs, and other unapproved drugs. Even though all studies which have compared two- vs. three-drug combinations have concluded that people fare better on the triple combinations, not everyone has access to three drugs. Still others can't tolerate three drugs, or can't find three drugs they haven't used up before.

One thing is certain: How these drugs are used is critical. Developing an effective treatment strategy requires taking what is known from clinical studies and, what we know about how HIV causes immune destruction (pathogenesis), and combining it with expert opinion. Several factors should be considered:

- Successful long-term use of therapies is more important than short-term gains. It is possible to get short-term benefits at the cost of wasting potential long-term benefits.

- People who are being treated for the first time have the greatest number of options and generally have the best possible response to therapy. It is critical to think of the long-term picture when choosing options. A strategy should provide long-term benefits from the chosen therapies while preserving options for future use. An example of an *ineffective* strategy would be to begin therapy using single drugs or modest combinations that merely reduce, but do not fully suppress, viral replication. Such a strategy does little more than waste the drugs being used by employing them in a way that leads to rapid development of viral resistance.

- Reducing viral load as low as possible, preferably below the level of detection with the current tests, should be the goal of anti-HIV therapy. Drugs and combinations which have a larger, more consistent, and longer-lasting effect in reducing viral loads and increasing CD4+ cell counts are likely to produce longer-lasting clinical and survival benefits. People with HIV RNA levels below the limit of detection have a significantly longer-lasting response than people with detectable viral loads. When therapy fails to reduce viral load below the limit of detection, it is usually a sign that the therapy will fail over the next several months. Today, most available viral load tests measure reliably down to 400 or 500 copies of virus. Any number below this is considered "undetectable." However, new tests (not yet widely available) will soon make it possible to measure as low as 20 copies of virus. Studies have already shown that people who reach "undetectable" levels on this new test will have a longer-lasting effect from therapy than those who only reach the limit of detection on the older tests.

- The question of whether everyone should be treated immediately has not yet been fully answered. Theoretically, the sooner HIV replication

is reduced or stopped, the better. But this goal must be measured against possible side effects of long-term therapy; long-term interference with quality of life; and the risk of using options prematurely. An individual's ability to take the medications correctly also has an impact (see "Quality of Life Issues" on page 552). Both the "very aggressive" and the "less aggressive" approaches can be supported as matters of reasonable personal choice. For now, neither has been proven right for all situations.

- Lessons from treating tuberculosis show that it is important to change or add two new therapies at the same time. This will help combat viral resistance to the drugs. Just adding a protease inhibitor on top of an existing therapy regimen that is not suppressing HIV RNA to below the limit of detection is unlikely to produce the dramatic results seen in the clinical studies. The best results in clinical studies have always come when two or more new drugs are started at the same time. It might be possible to achieve the necessary degree of viral suppression in some situations by changing only one drug when viral load is low (below 5,000 copies HIV RNA). However, in other instances, far less consistent results have been shown than changing two drugs simultaneously.

- The use of treatment that is only partially effective speeds the development of viral resistance. If a treatment reduces viral load but still permits a measurable level of viral activity, the virus that is still present is capable of mutating and developing resistance to that treatment. When a 3-drug combination doesn't quite succeed in stopping measurable viral activity, many researchers believe it may be wise to either change two of the drugs, or perhaps add a fourth drug. It makes sense to try and fully suppress viral replication if this can be done with a reasonable quality of life. When this goal cannot be achieved, people should realize they can still benefit from therapy and that longer-term solutions may become apparent when additional therapies are available.

- Using a drug exactly as prescribed is critical to success. Using an inadequate dose, reducing the dose below the prescribed level, or failing to take the drug at regularly spaced intervals will increase the risk of developing viral resistance. If intolerance or side effects develop, it is often better to try to overcome the side effects than to immediately change the regimen. If side effects aren't manageable, it is better to temporarily stop the drug rather than reduce its dose. This runs counter to common clinical practice with the nucleoside analogue reverse transcriptase inhibitors or NARTIs (e.g., AZT, ddI, ddC, d4T, and 3TC), in which physicians routinely lowered doses as a way of dealing with side ef-

fects. The fastest way to develop resistance to antiviral drugs is to use them at an inadequate or inconsistent dose level.

## WHAT THERAPY SHOULD I USE?

Ideally, the best drug combination to use would be the one that is most successful in reducing viral load below the limit of detection for the longest time, while preserving quality of life. In the real world, what is best for the individual is sometimes different from what works best in a clinical trial. Some drugs and combinations are clearly more potent than others. In some instances, the differences between various combinations are not clearly defined, largely because comparative studies have not been done. Drug manufacturers try to avoid conducting studies that make direct comparisons. While this may be good for them, it often leaves the patient in the dark. Still, a reasonable amount of data is available which allows us to conclude that some drugs are "highly active" antivirals and some are less active. In general, the most effective combination therapy regimens contain at least two "highly active" antivirals, usually added to a third drug of similar or lesser potency but which works in a different way. Within the realm of combinations with adequate overall potency, other factors become important in selecting a therapy regimen.

### QUALITY OF LIFE ISSUES

Tolerance can be as important as the potency of a drug. If you can't take a drug consistently as prescribed, its potency is irrelevant. Lack of adherence to the protocol will quickly contribute to the development of drug-resistant mutations of HIV. When choosing a combination, consider the daily pills count (antiretrovirals, drugs for opportunistic infections, and everything else), when they will be taken, whether they can be taken with other medications, and whether they can be taken with food.

It is easiest to combine drugs that require similar conditions for their use (with food, without food, etc.). Otherwise, one's life becomes dominated by drug schedules. Also, it is best to avoid mixing drugs with similar side effects, though sometimes this is impossible. And it is critical to learn about possible drug interactions before mixing any of these drugs together. To help with understanding these issues, Project Inform has Fact Sheets on each of the antiretrovirals as well as an extensive *Drug Interactions Fact Sheet*.

Quality of life would improve if combination therapies restore the immune system enough to make it possible for people to eliminate the need for preventative medicines, such as TMP/SMX (Bactrim or Septra) for PCP, etc. Limited clinical experience suggests that some people who have a good response to antiviral therapy can safely go off preventive therapies they have used previ-

ously, but the majority of others cannot. For now, there is no way to predict who will and won't be successful. Therefore, for now, stopping the use of preventive therapies is an unwarranted gamble and preventive treatments should be continued.

## TARGETS FOR THERAPY

Various antiviral drugs work by targeting different stages in the reproduction of new copies of HIV. No drug has proven to do a perfect job in stopping its target of HIV viral activity. Researchers believe the most effective approach to therapy combines drugs which target two or more different stages of the virus's reproductive cycle. That way, even if one step isn't completely blocked, treatment can still work by blocking another step in the cycle. Perhaps the effective therapies will someday prove to be ones which block several steps all at the same time. For now, the available antivirals are capable of stopping two different steps in the viral life cycles (reverse transcription and protease clipping), and there are two different ways of stopping reverse transcription.

### REVERSE TRANSCRIPTASE INHIBITORS

The first general class of antiviral drugs is called *reverse transcriptase inhibitors*. Reverse transcriptase inhibitors interfere with HIV's ability to combine its genetic material with that of the cells it infects. For now, there are two different types of drugs which do this, in somewhat different ways. The most common approach is found in drugs called nucleoside analogue reverse transcriptase inhibitors. Examples of NARTIs include AZT (zidovudine and Retrovir), ddI (didanosine and Videx), ddC (zalcitabine and Hivid), d4T (stavudine and Zerit), and 3TC (lamivudine and Epivir), all of which are approved by the Food and Drug Administration (FDA). NARTIs were the first to be tried against HIV because they were better understood and better proven than other antiviral approaches. Also, at least three of the nucleoside analogues—AZT, 3TC, and d4T—are effective in crossing the blood-brain barrier and therefore helpful in managing HIV-associated dementia. For more information on these specific drugs, please call the Project Inform National HIV/AIDS Treatment Hotline. Other NARTIs that are in development include 1592U89 and MKC-442.

A second approach is found in the category called non-nucleoside reverse transcriptase inhibitors (NNRTIs). These work at the same step of viral replication as the NARTIs, although they use a different mechanism. The NNRTIs are generally effective in crossing the blood-brain barrier and may be useful in managing HIV-associated dementia. Examples of NNRTIs include nevirapine (Viramune) and delavirdine (Rescriptor) which are approved by the

FDA. Other NNRTIs that are in development include DMP 266, and S1153. For more information on specific NNRTIs, please call the Project Inform Hotline.

A third approach, called nucleotide analogue reverse transcriptase inhibitors, is currently undergoing clinical trials.

### PROTEASE INHIBITORS

The second general class of antiviral drugs is called *protease inhibitors.* These drugs work at a later stage of the virus' life cycle, after the virus has successfully infected the cell and attempts to make new copies of itself. Currently, none of the approved protease inhibitors are effective in crossing the blood-brain barrier. However, newer protease inhibitors may be effective in crossing the blood-brain barrier. Examples of protease inhibitors include saquinavir (Invirase), ritonavir (Norvir), indinavir (Crixivan), and nelfinavir (Viracept), all of which are approved. Other protease inhibitors that are in clinical development include 141W94 (VX 478), DMP-450, PNU-140690, BMS-234475, and ABT-378. For more information on specific protease inhibitors, please call the Project Inform HIV/AIDS Treatment Hotline.

Other approaches, some of which are in clinical testing, will try to inhibit HIV from replicating at other stages in its life cycle.

### CELLULAR TARGETS

Unlike all other antiviral drugs, which target the virus itself, this class of compounds inhibits factors inside the cell that are necessary for viral replication. Attacking cellular targets, instead of targets on the virus itself, offers hope of slowing or avoiding viral resistance because the cellular target does not rapidly mutate like the virus. In general, these drugs work by suppressing compounds inside the cell that the virus needs to replicate. In the laboratory setting, this requires only a small reduction in the level of these compounds, not enough to hurt the cell's own reproductive cycle or function. The most researched of this class of drugs is called hydroxyurea (HU).

### NUCLEOSIDE ANALOGUE CONSIDERATIONS

The five available nucleoside analogues have different side effects and have different levels of activity when used in combination.

Resistance to 3TC occurs almost universally in people who use it for 2 months or longer when the drug is used alone or in a typical two-drug combination. When 3TC is used initially in an effective three-drug combination, typically including a protease inhibitor, the treatment regimen usually suppresses viral load below the limit of detection. This appears to suppress the development of resistance to 3TC, which allows the drug to then make a large and long-lasting contribution to therapy. Once resistance is present though, 3TC

loses its ability to directly produce large reductions in viral load. As a result, most researchers and the new Federal Guidelines argue against using two-drug combinations like AZT + 3TC or d4T + 3TC as first-line therapy. Instead, these make excellent and long-lasting contributions when employed as part of a 3-drug regimen. In short, 3TC has a lot to offer, but only if it is used wisely.

The best results from combinations using AZT + 3TC + protease inhibitors (or any other combinations) seem to occur in people who initiate all three drugs for the first time or for people who initiate at least two of the drugs for the first time when they start the protease inhibitor.

A recent study of AZT + d4T in people who have been on prolonged AZT therapy showed that people on this combination fared significantly worse than people who received AZT + ddI, d4T alone, or ddI alone. A second study also tested the AZT + d4T combination but in people who had not taken any prior antiretroviral drugs. This study found that people on the AZT + d4T combination did not fare any worse than people receiving other antiretroviral regimens. The use of other combinations should be seriously considered before initiating this particular combination.

Some NARTIs, like ddI, d4T, and ddC, have the potential for creating similar side effects. Therefore, many researchers believe it is unwise to combine them, fearing that the combination will increase the risk of the side effects common to both drugs. Therefore, a good general rule is to try to mix drugs with different, rather than overlapping, side effects.

As with any other class of drugs, the most effective combinations will include drugs that do not have cross resistance, that is, resistance to one does not confer resistance to the other. Among NARTIs, AZT and d4T have somewhat different patterns of resistance than ddI, ddC, and 3TC, while ddI, ddC, and 3TC have at least some degree of overlap when resistance develops. Resistance to 3TC may affect a person's response to ddI, for example, but is unlikely to affect AZT or d4T.

Since many people have used some or all of the NARTIs previously, the choice of a drug in this class when starting three-drug combination therapy is often dictated by a person's individual drug history. The most potent NARTIs to use in combination are likely to be those that haven't been used before, or that have been used for the shortest time.

NON-NUCLEOSIDE REVERSE TRANSCRIPTASE INHIBITOR CONSIDERATIONS

The NNRTIs have very potent activity against HIV. However, these drugs can be rendered ineffective by a single, easily attained mutation in HIV. They can go from being highly potent to totally ineffective in a short time unless a wise strategy is used to prevent the development of resistance.

The NNRTIs should not be used alone or in two-drug combinations. Even in a 3-drug combination, it is important that all three drugs be new to the user.

A potential role for the NNRTIs may be for people with early stage HIV disease, where the results have been very encouraging. By using an NNRTI early in place of a protease inhibitor in a 3-drug combination, it may be possible to save the protease inhibitors for later use. If, instead, people begin immediately using a protease combination, there are few or no places left to turn when the resistance eventually develops to the protease inhibitor since there is some cross-resistance between all currently available protease inhibitors. In contrast, use of a 3-drug combination including an NNRTI does not cause development of mutations which could lead to resistance to protease inhibitors.

Some data suggest that most NNRTIs can be combined with protease inhibitors. In some cases, the combination may even permit or require reducing the dose of the protease inhibitor. To date, only one small clinical trial has yet been conducted employing such a combination but the outcome was highly positive.

The NNRTIs are metabolized (broken down) using the same enzyme that is used by the protease inhibitors and many of the common drugs used to prevent and treat opportunistic infections. Make sure your physician knows about all the medications that you are taking to reduce the risk of drug side effects and to better manage potentially harmful drug interactions.

## PROTEASE INHIBITOR CONSIDERATIONS

The four available protease inhibitors are radically different drugs. Each has a unique blend of activity, side effects, and drug interactions and must be selected carefully. Only a highly active protease inhibitor should be considered as first-line therapy.

As with the NNRTIs, make sure your physician knows about all the medications that you are taking to reduce the risk of drug side effects and to better manage potentially harmful drug interactions.

Indinavir has relatively few and infrequent side effects but can be complex to use. It must be taken three times daily, one hour before or two hours after eating any full meals. This requires people to plan their day and meal schedule around the drug. For some, this is quite intrusive. However, the restriction about food only applies to meals which include a high fat content. Low fat snacks can be taken with indinavir without harm. Taking indinavir with ddI can be particularly difficult because of the complicating food restrictions of both drugs.

Ritonavir is an easier alternative for people with busy schedules because it is taken only twice a day and *should* be taken with food. However, this is offset by a very high rate of initial unpleasant side effects (nausea, vomiting, diarrhea, numbness, etc.). Such side effects can cause as many complications for people as dietary restrictions. Also, ritonavir needs to be kept refrigerated otherwise it will lose its antiviral effects. Many people who choose ritonavir abandon it within 60 days because of these side effects. Ritonavir also has many interactions with other drugs that can complicate dealing with opportunistic infections and other difficulties associated with HIV. Ritonavir and indinavir are highly cross-resistant (resistance to one causes resistance to the other) and both are partially cross-resistant to saquinavir and possibly nelfinavir.

Saquinavir may be easy to take and have few side effects, but these benefits are completely offset by the poor level of antiviral activity in the initial, "hard gel capsule" version of this drug. Also, recent data have made it clear that initial use of saquinavir can lead to cross-resistance to indinavir (and probably to ritonavir and nelfinavir). Similarly, use of the current flawed version of saquinavir will also damage the ability of a person to later benefit from the improved version of the drug, likely to become available in 1998. Once the new version of saquinavir, the "soft gel" formulation marketed under the tradename "Fortovase," is available, it will be possible to reevaluate the role of saquinavir. It will then likely become a truly useful protease inhibitor. Until that time, however, it should not be used as a first-line protease inhibitor in 3-drug combinations. The principal valid use of the original version of saquinavir is as part of a double protease inhibitor combination with ritonavir. Recent studies combining saquinavir with nelfinavir have all employed the new, as yet unavailable formulation, so it is unclear whether the old version can be successfully combined with nelfinavir (or indinavir).

Nelfinavir is taken three times a day with food and has a moderate frequency of side effects (primarily diarrhea) that are generally manageable. Little information is available on the long-term use of this drug. The degree of cross-resistance between nelfinavir and the other protease inhibitors is still not known. Agouron Pharmaceutical, the manufacturers of nelfinavir, claims that there is little cross-resistance if nelfinavir is used first; however, many researchers believe that the incidence of cross-resistance will be quite significant. Some researchers also question whether the optimum dose of nelfinavir has yet been determined. They typically recommend using a dose somewhat higher than the current recommendations on the label, though they acknowledge that this results in a higher frequency of side effects.

# HOW DO I KNOW IF TREATMENT IS WORKING?

The goal of antiretroviral therapy is to reduce HIV RNA levels below the limit of detection with the current viral load tests or at least to fewer than 5,000 HIV RNA copies. When the new, more sensitive viral load tests become available, the goal will be to fall below the limit of detection on those tests, which measure down to 20 copies of virus or less. The indications of a treatment effect vary somewhat depending on the stage of disease. However, not everyone is able to bring their viral load levels to below the limit of detection or to fewer than 5,000 HIV RNA copies. For these people the minimum change in viral load that indicates the therapies are active is a three-fold reduction (0.5 log) in HIV RNA levels. However, many physicians believe you need at least ten-fold reduction (1 log) to have a real impact on disease progression. People with lower CD4+ cell counts and high HIV RNA measures may find that viral levels drop more slowly over time. Anecdotal experience suggests that among people in more advanced disease decreases in HIV RNA happen slower (three to six months).

# WHEN IS IT TIME TO CHANGE?

The Federal Guidelines recommend that people switch or add new therapies when their HIV RNA levels return to baseline (or within 1- to 3-fold of pre-therapy levels). "Baseline" means the level of virus prior to beginning a new therapy regimen. Other researchers believe that this recommendation is not aggressive enough and recommend people switch or add therapies if their HIV RNA levels are more than 3-fold higher than their previous results, signaling the onset of viral resistance. Others fear that changing therapy too quickly might cause a person to cycle through all the available drugs too quickly and leave him or her with no further options. In any case, the decision to switch or add therapies should be based on two viral load tests spaced about two weeks apart. A common infection such as the flu, or even a vaccine shot, can increase HIV RNA levels temporarily. Prior to making dramatic adjustments in regimens, factor in how other health considerations may be affecting the viral load test results and if necessary, wait and get another HIV RNA test before making decisions.

# THE FUTURE OF THERAPY

The future of antiretroviral therapy is likely to concentrate on the search for better combinations of new and existing drugs. Most researchers expect the combination of potent drugs with different mechanisms of action and different resistance patterns will have the most long-lasting antiviral response. Better drugs, however, doesn't necessarily mean that the drugs will be more potent, since many of the current combination regimens seem to be about as

potent as therapy can get. Better drugs will be easier to use, have fewer dietary restrictions, fewer and less severe side effects and drug interactions, and may require less frequent dosing.

Other antiviral approaches in study include antisense and drugs that inhibit the integrase enzyme, the tat gene, the rev gene, the binding of HIV to the CD4+ cell, the zinc finger of HIV and cyclophilin (inhibits fusion of infected and uninfected cells).

## COMMENTARY

In addition to overall general health and quality of life factors, both CD4+ cell counts and viral load must be considered when making decisions about starting antiretroviral therapy or when considering switching therapies. In most studies, as would be expected, there is a direct inverse correlation (when one goes down the other goes up) between viral load and CD4+ cell counts as more virus means more CD4+ cells being infected and destroyed. There are some individuals, who despite substantial decreases in HIV RNA levels, continue to experience CD4+ decline. In these cases it is important for health care providers to conduct more extensive diagnosis to see if some other condition is affecting CD4+ cell counts, such as common or even not so common infections.

Ideal combination strategies call for the use of fresh new drugs to be started at the same time. This is readily achievable for people beginning therapy for the first time but far more difficult for those who have used many therapies. Existing therapies can sometimes be juggled to achieve the desired effect. At other times, this may be impossible. For some people, the best choice may sometimes be to delay using protease inhibitors or other new therapies until there are enough new drugs available to initiate an ideal combination (e.g., at least two drugs never previously used by the individual). For most people, this will seldom be more than a year away as several new therapies are on the horizon. But getting there will require some people to resist the urge to jump to each new drug as soon as it is available. This shift toward long-term thinking is the true hallmark of this second decade of anti-HIV therapy. It must become a part of everyone's thinking. The alternative is the perpetuation of the short-term benefits and long-term failures characteristic of the last decade's approach to therapy.

All of this emphasizes the importance of a recent study which showed that people who received medical care from physicians with a great deal of experience treating HIV infection actually lived longer than those who saw less experienced physicians. The complexity of treating HIV has changed dramatically in the last year and the demands on the knowledge of physicians have increased proportionally. Whatever medical strategy a person chooses,

it should begin with finding a physician who is experienced in treating HIV and who is wise enough to continue studying and learning from new developments in HIV research.

# FEDERAL RECOMMENDATIONS BY STAGE OF DISEASE

### ADVANCED STAGE DISEASE
All people with AIDS should be treated. When initiating therapy for opportunistic infections at the same time as initiating antiviral therapy, special care should be taken to avoid drug interactions. When a patient experiences an opportunistic infection, he or she should not normally be taken off antiviral therapy.

### SYMPTOMATIC, REGARDLESS OF CD4+ CELL COUNTS
All should be treated after consideration of the issues affecting treatment choices.

### ASYMPTOMATIC WITH CD4+ COUNTS ABOVE 500
There are two unproven approaches to treatment in early, asymptomatic people: aggressive and conservative. For people with CD4+ cell counts above 500 and a low viral load, there is no available data to suggest which approach results in longer survival. Very early, aggressive treatment might lead to longer life. Or conversely, it might lead to using up the limited supply of therapies too early in the course of disease by triggering the development of resistance earlier than necessary. In addition to the general principles and patient preferences, the Guidelines recommend that physicians take into account the relative risk of disease progression people face based on viral load.

### ASYMPTOMATIC WITH CD4+ COUNTS BELOW 500
All should be treated after consideration of the issues affecting treatment choices.

### ACUTE INFECTION
If infection is suspected, test for HIV viral load. Many, but not all, experts recommend treatment if the test is positive, even at low levels. They believe this offers the chance of changing the entire later course of HIV disease in the person. However, people should be made aware of all the potential risks and benefits of such early treatment. The true long-term effect of immediate treatment is unknown because current studies are not yet complete. Some experts also recommend treatment for all people who were infected within the previous six months. Similarly, immediate treatment is recommended for people with suspected exposure due to accidents in the health care setting.

# Maintaining Adherence to Highly Active Antiretroviral Therapies

**BY PROJECT INFORM STAFF**

Highly active antiretroviral therapy (HAART) has brought new hope and new challenges to people living with HIV. However, if these treatments are not used properly (i.e., doses are repeatedly skipped, taken at lower than prescribed dosages, or not taken at scheduled intervals), drug resistance will almost certainly develop more rapidly and the potential benefits of combination therapy can be lost. Moreover, resistance to one therapy may also result in decreased effectiveness of other therapies of the same class (cross-resistance). This is particularly true in regard to protease inhibitors. The development of high level resistance to any one of these drugs almost certainly conveys some degree of resistance to all the other drugs of this type. Adhering to a treatment regimen is difficult under the best of circumstances. Studies have shown that even health care providers can find it difficult to take a simple course of antibiotics as directed. The new triple combinations used with HIV disease typically require that a person take a dozen or more antiviral pills per day with specific timing and dietary requirements. When a person must also use preventive or maintenance doses of drugs for opportunistic infections, the total daily pill count soars. Keeping track of one's medication alone becomes a major activity. It's little wonder that many people have trouble keeping up with the program.

Preliminary data from one clinical trial suggest that as many as 12% of the study population missed one dose in the preceding day, 11% the day before that. At least two other recent clinical trials reported that nearly all of the people who failed to achieve and sustain a viral load below the limit of detection had significantly deviated from their prescribed treatment regimen for a month or more. There are many possible explanations for failure to adhere to the treatment regimen. A recent study by the University of California Center for AIDS Prevention Studies (CAPS) showed that, of those people who admitted missing one or more doses:

- 40% said they simply forgot
- 37% slept through a dose
- 34% were away from home
- 27% had changed their therapy routine

- 22% were busy
- 13% were sick
- 10% were experiencing side effects
- 9% were depressed.

There appears to be little debate about the fact that it is difficult to maintain perfect adherence to today's complex treatment regimens. It is somewhat less clear what degree of non-adherence is tolerable and how quickly it contributes to drug failure. Most of all, it is not entirely clear what to do about it, though many useful strategies are evolving over time.

## INITIATING THERAPY

Engaging in complicated courses of long-term treatment doesn't feel natural to most people. However, this challenge is not unique to people with HIV. Millions of people have learned to cope with diseases requiring complex, long-term management, such as diabetes. Whether or not you feel you are able to commit and adhere to a treatment regimen may be one factor to consider, along with lab results and clinical condition, in determining the appropriate time to begin highly active antiretroviral therapy (HAART). Giving careful thought to what benefits you hope to get from treatment, how you will evaluate the benefit, and how you might manage side effects will be helpful. Some people try a "dry run" before beginning therapy, taking empty gel caps on the prescribed schedule while sticking to the required dietary requirements.

Perhaps the first and most important aspect of adherence lies in choosing the right therapy in the first place. Drugs differ widely in:

1. Whether they can be taken with or without food
2. How many times per day they must be taken
3. What other drugs they can and cannot be successfully used with
4. Their side effects and how they make a person feel
5. Whether you have access to the facilities needed for storage (for example, refrigeration for supplies of ritonavir [Norvir]).

Similarly, people differ widely in their personal habits and needs. A few examples:

- Some people are bound to rigid schedules defined by their employment, such as hourly workers.
- Some people have loose and constantly changing schedules or routinely move in and out of different time zones, such as many airline workers.
- Some people are unable to work and their schedules are dictated by a seemingly endless string of medical appointments.
- Some have children, elderly parents, or partners to care for as well.

- Some have people around them all the time to help remind them of their medication schedules, while others are alone and must rely on timers, pill boxes, and other devices.
- Some people suffer from wasting syndrome, which makes eating difficult and critical; others have no dietary problems but don't eat on a regular schedule.
- Finally, some people have to deal with other challenging life issues such as substance abuse or homelessness.

To find a treatment regimen you can live with, it is necessary to reconcile the two sets of requirements: yours and the drug's. People who lead busy, but largely unstructured lives might prefer drugs that can be taken easily with or without food and thus more easily fit in with their changing daily routines. Others whose time is tightly structured by job requirements might find it easier to accept more demanding drug schedules and therefore can select a regimen purely on the basis of its expected potency. People who have trouble eating or who are struggling with weight loss might wish to avoid drugs which can't be taken with foods. People who must take a large number of other drugs for treatment or prevention of opportunistic infections might avoid antivirals that have the highest number of drug interactions or require the greatest number of pills per day.

The goal is to select a regimen you believe you can live with, one that fits with who you are and how you live. There are, of course, no perfect choices in this regard. Some people may seek a regimen that most easily fits their lifestyle, while others may be willing to adapt their lifestyle in hopes of getting the most potent possible treatment. Also, the more HIV medications you have used previously, often the fewer choices you have about what to use next. Thus, often in more advanced disease, prior history with the drugs tends to dictate what can and can't be done.

## MAINTAINING THERAPY

Once a regimen has been selected, sticking to it requires planning, support, and commitment.

### PLANNING

Stable access to drugs is a critical requirement for effective use. People cannot adhere to a regimen if they do not have continuous access to the drugs. While it may sound obvious, many or even most people taking HIV medications sometimes find themselves running short of one or another treatment. This is almost always a consequence of poor planning. Skipping doses when you run out of a drug temporarily is still skipping doses, with all the consequences. Thus, it is best to try to plan to never have less than a week's supply of your

entire medication needs on hand. Remember also that some drugs require much different storage than others, so part of your planning must address the storage requirements. Once storage is addressed, it is often helpful to put aside an entire week's supply the first time the drugs are delivered, and then use only the remaining supply. This will also create an "emergency stash" should unforeseen circumstances cause your basic supply to run short. The "stash" should be rotated or replaced once a month to keep it fresh.

Keeping a steady supply of your prescriptions requires close coordination with your doctor and your pharmacist. When using sources like the AIDS Drug Assistance Programs or patient assistance programs sponsored by pharmaceutical companies, which are potential sources of drug access, more of the burden falls on you to make sure you order supplies as the program requires. But the main point is always to stay at least a week ahead of your needs. Your care provider should work closely with you to ensure access.

People with varying lifestyles may differ in their ability to adhere to a treatment regimen. People dealing with major life problems such as active drug use or homelessness face the most difficult challenges adhering to a treatment regimen. But that doesn't mean that adherence is impossible. Studies have shown that people with depression are also more likely to have difficulty taking their treatments consistently. If you suffer from depression and are considering treatment, consult a mental health professional as well as your regular provider. Outside of depression, there are very few reliable predictors of nonadherence. In reality, only you can make the decision as to whether you are ready and committed enough to maintain a steady course of treatment. If you are not ready or in a position to make a serious attempt at adherence, you might be better off to delay treatment. This option doesn't jeopardize your ability to use treatment effectively some time later in the future. In contrast, the misuse of treatment, through inconsistency or poor adherence, can indeed jeopardize future options by encouraging development of drug resistance that affects entire classes of anti-HIV therapy.

## SUPPORT

Establishing a good working relationship with your provider is critical for maintaining adherence to a treatment regimen. A provider should be knowledgeable in the current standards of care for treating HIV and should be willing to spend time to thoroughly explain the benefits and challenges of treatment.

After the decision to start treatment has been made, it is important to clarify your treatment regimen with your physician. Knowing what medications you are taking and why will help to better understand the importance of adherence. One survey indicated that the vast majority of people were unclear of their treatment regimen only ten minutes after consulting with their physi-

cian. Some people understood the dosage but were confused about dietary restrictions. Others were unclear on the correct dosage or the timing of the doses. Since dietary adjustment can be difficult at first, it is important to know what and when you can and cannot eat. Just as important, try to understand exactly what is meant by the dietary requirements. For example, many people interpret the requirements for indinavir (Crixivan) as saying that the drug should not be taken with food, which can be difficult for many people. The actual dietary requirement is that it shouldn't be taken with fatty foods. Light snacks and non-fat foods can be taken with the drug without concern. Similarly, the requirements for nelfinavir (Viracept) are often interpreted as meaning that it *must* be taken with food, when in fact the label says only that it *can* be taken with food. In some cases, there is a genuine medical need to take a drug with or without food, while in other cases, such as the use of ritonavir (Norvir), use with foods is recommended only to minimize side effects or unpleasant aftertaste.

A useful technique for understanding a treatment regimen is writing down instructions and repeating them back to the care provider, then checking them again with a pharmacist when you pick up or order the drugs. Use the team approach; your physician, nurse, pharmacist, and other health care providers can all be helpful with initiating and supporting effective therapy. Researchers have noted that people who actively foster a friendly and supportive relationship with medical office staff get better service from their providers. Bringing another person (family member or friend) to appointments ensures that there are two people to ask questions and get information.

Ask the doctor to be clear about potential side effects and how they may be managed. Being mentally prepared for possible side effects can make them easier to manage if they occur. Make an agreement with your care provider as to what the process will be if you experience a difficult side effect. Knowing that you will have timely contact with a provider may provide reassurance that side effects will be managed efficiently. It is also important to find out from your physician what to do if you miss a dose. If you do miss a dose, find out if you should make it up or simply take the next one. Also, note the missed dose and the reason for missing. There may be a strategy you can employ to avoid missing future doses. If you are not able to take all the drugs in your combination, don't take a partial dose. Contact your care provider immediately. If necessary, stop all of the drugs in your combination therapy until you are able to take a complete dose again.

## COMMITMENT

At the initiation of therapy, most people question what "adherence" means. It is important to keep an adequate level of drug in your blood stream 24

hours a day in order to prevent the development of resistance. Each time a dose is missed, the blood level of the antiviral drugs falls below the minimal necessary amount for several hours, creating a temporary opportunity for the selection and growth of drug-resistant strains of virus. There are no data telling us exactly when resistance to drugs begins, but there is plenty of evidence that people who are adherent to their treatment regimens have a better and more sustained antiviral response. While no single episode of a skipped or late dose is likely, by itself, to trigger resistance, the more often such episodes occur, the more likely resistance becomes.

## STRATEGIES FOR ADHERENCE

Some of the following strategies and tools have worked for many people taking triple combination therapy:

- Integrating your treatment regimen into your daily routines. Most people find it easier to fit their medications into their lives, rather than scheduling their lives around their medications. Use a daily activity, one that you do every day without fail, to prompt you to take medications. Take your medications before the activity; it's easier to remember.

- Counting out all your medications in daily doses for a week at a time. Use a pill box or a nail organizer from a hardware store to hold each dose. Setting up the weekly pill box must become a routine weekend duty. Medications can also be divided daily by dose and put in separate canisters (some people use film canisters) marked with the dosage times. Some people put each canister near the place they will take a dose. For example, put the morning dose by the coffee pot, evening by the television set. This is more difficult with drugs that need refrigeration.

- Keeping a checklist for doses taken with a space to note how you are feeling.

- Using an electronic pill box or beeping alarm to remind you when to take medications. The downside of these mechanisms is that the currently available electronic pill boxes are too small and the alarms may be too obvious.

- Using a daily planner, especially at the start of a new treatment regimen. Inserting medication requirements in a planner, as if they were appointments, can be a useful reminder for many people. Still others use hand-held computers and inexpensive electronic organizers with scheduling functions to remind themselves of their daily medication needs. Electronic devices of this type can be purchased for less than $50.

- Evaluating your treatment regimen about two weeks after you start. It may take a few weeks of experimenting to figure out how best to schedule both your medications and other events in your life. For this reason it

may be useful to start a "dry run" of therapy, allowing time to adjust routines prior to actually taking the drugs.

- Planning ahead for weekends and vacations. People often miss doses when they are away from home. For most people, weekends are different from their normal weekday routine so it is important to plan ahead. Take into account the changed environment. Will you feel comfortable with your normal routine or will you need other strategies?

- Keeping all your medications with you when traveling. Baggage containing medication can be lost or delayed.

- Planning ahead for privacy if you need to hide the fact that you are taking medication. If you are not able to take your medication openly, try to find at least one person with a similar problem with whom you can discuss strategy. Some examples might be adjusting your lunch or break schedule to ensure privacy or keeping water in your bedroom at all times.

- Keeping a diary—include whatever is important to you: when you took treatment, reason for missed dose, how you feel, etc. Keeping a record like this serves as a reminder of how well, or poorly, you are doing with adherence.

- Using your support network to remind you of your medication requirements. Some people select a "treatment buddy" who can make daily reminder phone calls.

- Setting up a support network for your emotional needs as well. It's difficult to take treatment and also deal with daily stress, whether it be taking care of children, working, or dealing with illness.

These strategies may not work for all individuals. Because of cultural, gender, and socio-economic differences, some suggestions are more appropriate for some people than others. Different issues are more important in some settings than others. For example, in the Latino community, many individuals reported that people they knew might not be able to reveal their HIV status or their use of medications. This places much greater emphasis on planning ahead for moments of privacy each day. For people struggling with lack of housing, active drug use, or untreated mental health conditions, the strategies for successful treatment will often go beyond what we cover here. Still, even under the most challenging situations, people have daily routines which can be used as triggers for the use of medications.

Adherence strategies can and must vary from person to person and group to group. However the most effective method of ensuring success is motivation and commitment to a treatment regimen, along with the recognition that it is possible to accommodate the need for long-term treatment. It may take

several attempts before you find the approach that works best for you, but people with other life-threatening chronic illnesses have long demonstrated that it can be done. As an elderly woman with diabetes said at a recent Project Inform Town Meeting, "If you want to live, you'll find a way to do it."

## COMMENTARY

Perhaps the greatest way in which adherence to HIV treatments differs from adherence in other chronic illnesses is the lack of immediate symptoms or consequences when adherence fails. In diabetes, for example, failure to adhere can quickly result in insulin shock or even death. In HIV disease, the effects of non-adherence are slow to appear, but nonetheless deadly. This lack of a rapid feedback or response places more of the burden for adherence on the intellect and a bit less on the immediate reaction of the body. A person with HIV infection must take a long-term view in order to have a long-term future.

Adherence is also a challenge to the many support systems for people with HIV. Managed care and other economic changes in the medical field have left providers with less time to spend educating patients. Moreover, most health care providers have little or no training in the self-adherence tools that might help people who are undertaking a new treatment regimen. Training will be needed both in HIV treatments and tools of self-compliance. Some pharmaceutical companies already offer "adherence training" programs which have been developed for other illnesses. They are just now beginning to pilot test their use in HIV disease.

There are few effective structures in the HIV care and service industry to support people taking treatment effectively, such as treatment support groups and treatment-knowledgeable case managers. Many working in the HIV service field have been operating from a model of disability and death. The transition to supporting people who are living longer with complex treatments and social needs will require planning and shifts, not only in programs, but in paradigms.

The best long-term solutions must ultimately go beyond helping the individual adhere to the schedules demanded by the drugs. Instead, they must begin to focus on making better therapies and longer-lasting formulations that are easier to use, more easily absorbed, have fewer side effects and drug interactions, and maintain more consistent drug levels in blood. This work is already well under way and studies have already begun on treatments which may require only once per day dosing. The final solution, of course, is an outright cure to the disease, one which not only results in eradication of HIV and immune restoration, but no further need for medication. The prospects for this kind of solution are, unfortunately, less certain.

# Project Inform's Guide to the Management of Opportunistic Infections

**BY MICHAEL WRIGHT AND PROJECT INFORM STAFF**

The following chart is intended as a general guide to managing opportunistic infections. Obviously, it can't substitute for a detailed discussion of each infection, and anyone dealing actively with one or more of these infections should call the Project Inform Treatment Information Hotline for more comprehensive information and then consult with his or her primary care provider.

If the standard drug for prevention or treatment fails, it may be necessary to try various experimental therapies. The prophylaxis and treatment of opportunistic infections is not an exact science and often requires a certain amount of complicated trial and error to determine the best regimen for a particular patient.

There is often a noticeable gap between the therapies prescribed by experienced clinicians with large HIV practices and those prescribed by clinicians with less HIV experience. On occasion, patients may need to bring experimental therapies to the attention of providers who haven't previously prescribed them.

The availability of various medications referenced on this chart can be problematic. A limited number are approved for specific HIV use; others are approved for non-HIV use but may be prescribed for HIV applications. Most are available either through clinical trials, expanded-access, or compassionate-use programs. The access individuals have to prescription drugs may vary widely according to whether their health care is provided by private insurers or by government agencies.

As more drugs have become available for the treatment and prevention of opportunistic infections, more awareness of possible drug interactions has become necessary. Most people are already aware of the interaction between AZT and ganciclovir, which results in increased bone-marrow suppression, but many other drug interactions exist. For a complete list of potential HIV drug interactions, see the drug interactions chart.

---

*MICHAEL WRIGHT WAS A LONG-TERM PROJECT INFORM VOLUNTEER WHO INITIATED PROJECT OPPORTUNISTIC INFECTION.*

| OPPORTUNISTIC INFECTION | SYMPTOMS OF ACTIVE INFECTION |
|---|---|
| *Mycobacterium avium complex* (MAC or MAI) a bacterial infection | **General:** persistent fever, night sweats, fatigue, weight loss, chronic diarrhea, anemia, thrombocytopenia (low platelets), abdominal pain, weakness, dizziness, nausea. Also, enlarged lymph glands (frequently on one side), enlarged liver and spleen, and soft tissue masses (especially in the thighs). May be **organ-specific** or **disseminated.** |
| Tuberculosis (TB) a bacterial infection | Similar to MAC. May be pulmonary (lungs), or extra-pulmonary (other organs) especially meningitis. Cough, weight loss, night sweats, fatigue, fever, swollen lymph nodes, or organ specific symptoms. Can occur at any CD4+ cell range. |
| Candidiasis (Thrush) a fungal infection | **Mouth or esophagus:** white patches on gums, tongue or lining, pain and difficulty swallowing. Loss of appetite. **Vagina:** itching, burning, vaginal discharge. |
| Cryptococcosis (Cryptococcal Disease) a fungal infection | Meningitis most common: mild headache and intermittent fevers. Progressive malaise, nausea, fatigue, loss of appetite. Altered mental status, seizures (rare). May also cause a form of pneumonia (mimicking PCP, sometimes occurring at the same time as PCP). Disseminated infection of multiple organs, may cause skin lesions. |
| Histoplasmosis a fungal infection | Fever, weight loss, skin lesions, difficulty breathing, anemia, lymphadenopathy (swollen lymph nodes). May cause pneumonia. |
| Cryptosporidiosis a protozoal infection | Diarrhea with frequent watery stools, abdominal cramping, nausea, vomiting, fatigue, flatulence (gas), weight loss, loss of appetite, constipation. Dehydration and electrolyte imbalances (sodium and potassium). |
| *Pneumocystis carinii* pneumonia (PCP) a protozoal infection | Fever, dry nonproductive cough, difficulty breathing, weight loss, night sweats, fatigue, elevated serum LDH (a liver enzyme). |

| DIAGNOSTIC PROCEDURES | TREATMENTS (TX) FOR ACTIVE INFECTION |
|---|---|
| Can be difficult to diagnose. Lab Tests: blood culture, sputum culture, stool culture, organ tissue biopsy and culture. Often treated prior to definitive diagnosis if smear positive for Acid Fast Bacilli (AFB). Elevated alkaline phosphatase may indicate MAC infection. | Clarithromycin 500mg BID or Azithromycin 500–600 mg/day (monitor for resistance) in combo with at least one of the following: **Ethambutol, Ciprofloxacin, Rifabutin** (monitor clarithromycin blood levels). **Amikacin (IV), Sparfloxacin** (CT)(various combos in CT). |
| PPD skin test with greater than 5mm reaction. Chest X-ray, sputum smear, culture, and sensitivity, blood, bone marrow or liver cultures. See April '92 *PI Perspective*. | Treat with at least 3 oral drugs: **Isoniazid (INH), Pyrazinamide (PZA)** and **Rifampin;** when resistance suspected add **Ethambutol;** if treatment failure or intolerant **Streptomycin (EA)** or **Amikacin** &/or **L-ofloxacin** or **Sparfloxacin.** Monitor for drug resistance. |
| **Mouth and Vagina:** visual exam, smear and culture. **Esophagus:** usually treated presumptively, confirmed by biopsy culture. | Fluconazole, Nystatin, Clotrimazole Troches or cream, Ketoconazole, Itraconazole, ABLC. Vaginal: First try yogurt and/or vinegar douche, garlic, then topical creams, then oral systemic drugs. |
| Testing for cryptococcal antigen (CRAG) on serum, cerebral spinal fluid (CSF), India ink stain on CSF. Chest X-ray for pneumonia. With altered mental status, seizures or other neurological problems CT scan or MRI scan should be done to rule out other factors, followed by lumbar puncture (spinal tap). | Fluconazole (oral or IV). **Amphotericin B** with or w/o **5-flucytosine (5-FC) (ampho** B often used first, particularly in severe cases with **5-FC** followed by **Fluconazole**). **ABLC, ABCD, liposomal ampho B** (CT). **Itraconazole** (CT). **Dexamethasone +** ampho B for patients. w/ high cranial pressures. |
| May be difficult to diagnose. Blood and sputum culture, bone marrow biopsy and culture, lymph node biopsy or skin lesion biopsy. Chest X-ray. | **Itraconazole, Amphotericin-B (IV), Fluconazole. ABLC, ABLC, liposomal ampho B.** |
| Stool tests (often repeated tests are necessary), bowel biopsy, endoscopy. May be infected but asymptomatic. | No standard Tx. **Azithromycin** oral or IV (CT, CU). **Paromomycin (humatin),** bovine colostrum (CT), **Immuno-C** (CT), **NTZ** (CT) (CU). **Octreotide** (and others for symptoms only). Nutritional therapies. |
| Chest X-ray, sputum induction*, gallium scan, bronchoscopy*.<br><br>* Requires special stain to identify organisms. | Systemic Tx preferred. **TMP/SMX** {(IV or oral) same as **Bactrim, Septra,** co-trimoxozole}; **Pentamidine** (IV); **Dapsone** with or without **Trimethoprim** (CT) (EA). **Atovaquone** for mild to moderate PCP, **Trimetrexate** IV; **Primaquine** (BC) with **Clindamycin.** Corticosteroids might be added to any of the above in moderate to severe cases. |

| OPPORTUNISTIC INFECTION | SYMPTOMS OF ACTIVE INFECTION |
|---|---|
| Toxoplasmosis (Toxo/*toxoplasma gondii*) a protozoal infection | Encephalitis most common: altered mental state (lethargy, confusion, delusional behavior), paralysis on one side of body, seizures, severe headaches that do not respond to pain killers, fever, coma. May also cause symptoms outside CNS, notably in lungs, heart, and eyes. |
| Cytomegalovirus (CMV) a viral infection | **Retinitis:** blurry vision leading to blindness. **Esophagitis:** pain and difficulty swallowing, ulcerations. **Colitis:** fever, diarrhea, abdominal pain, wasting. **Pneumonia** (rare): usual pneumonia symptoms (see PCP). |
| Herpes Simplex Virus Varicella Zoster Virus viral infections | Painful blisters, ulcers, itching on the lips (**HSV-1**), anus, and/or genitals (**HSV-2**). Shingles on body in Herpes Zoster (**Varicella Zoster Virus or VZV**). VZV is a reactivation of chicken pox and usually occurs on legs or torso. |

| OPPORTUNISTIC INFECTION | PROPHYLAXIS (PX) AND MAINTENANCE (MX) OPTIONS |
|---|---|
| *Mycobacterium avium complex* (MAC or MAI) a bacterial infection | Risk of MAC increases when CD4+ count is <75 or 5%, Px: **Rifabutin** FDA approved for Px at 300mg/day or **Clarithromycin** FDA approved for Px at 500 mg 2x/day (resistance may be an issue) and **Azithromycin** 1,200 mg/week. Combination of **azithromycin + rifabutin** may be more effective than either drug alone. May also prevent resistance to the drugs. Mx: required after treatment for active disease. Treatment doses may be required. NOTE:*TB skin test before prophylaxis* |
| Tuberculosis (TB) a bacterial infection | TB risk increases with PPD skin test of >5 mm reaction, or history of positive PPD. Mx/Px: **Isoniazid** 300 mg. (Take w/ Vitamin B$_6$) for 1 year (CT). **Rifampin** 450–600 mg (by weight) w/ **Pyrazinamide** 50 mg/day (CT). |

| DIAGNOSTIC PROCEDURES | TREATMENTS (TX) FOR ACTIVE INFECTION |
|---|---|
| Should do baseline Toxo antibody titer (when first diagnosed with HIV) to verify past exposure. Usually treated presumptively if MRI scan shows brain lesions and antibody positive; also, brain biopsy to rule out lymphoma. Can do tissue culture and CSF. Requires special stain to identify. If Toxo-negative, avoid cat feces and undercooked meat and fish. | Always treat with combination therapy. **Pyrimethamine** with any of the following:<br>  - **Sulfadiazine**.<br>  - **Clindamycin**.<br>  - **Sulfadiazine & Clindamycin** (CT).<br>  - **Azithromycin** (CT) (EA).<br>  - **Sulfadiazine & rIFN Gamma** (CTP).<br>**Atovaquone** (CT). Folinic acid supplement should be used. |
| Should do baseline CMV antibody titer to verify past exposure. For retinitis, an "Amsler Grid" or Teich test can be self-administered to check for early vision loss, followed by a professional retinal examination. For other types of CMV, biopsy, and endoscopy. | **Ganciclovir** (**DHPG**) (IV), **Foscarnet** (IV), **Ganciclovir Implants** (intraocular), **IV Cidofovir**. Combo of **Ganciclovir** and **Foscarnet**, **Intravitreal Cidofovir** for retinitis. **ISIS 2922**, **GEM 132** (antisense) for retinitis (CT). **GW1263** for retinitis (CT), **proganciclovir** (CT). |
| Visual exam, tissue biopsy, and culture. (HSV Esophagitis may also occur, and appears similar to CMV or candida). | **Acyclovir** (oral or IV), **Valacyclovir** (oral), **Famciclovir** (oral). If acyclovir-resistant, **Foscarnet** (IV) or topical **Trifluridine** (**TFT**), topical **Cidofovir** (CT), cidofovir (CT) or topical **Foscarnet** (CT). |

| POSSIBLE SIDE EFFECTS | DRUG INTERACTIONS (AND NOTES) |
|---|---|
| **Rifabutin:** rash, fever, GI distress, hemolysis, decreased WBC & platelets, uveitis, joint pain. **Ethambutol:** liver toxicities, vision changes, vomiting, diarrhea. **Clofazimine:** skin discoloration, itchy, dry skin, rash. **Ciprofloxacin:** nausea, diarrhea, vomiting. **Amikacin:** kidney, liver toxicity, hearing loss. **Clarithromycin:** nausea, reversible hearing loss. **Azithromycin:** Nausea, loose stools, and hearing loss. **Sparfloxacin:** Photosensitivity. | Avoid alcohol with liver-toxic drugs. **Rifampin**, **Rifabutin**, **Clarithromycin** affects many drugs metabolized through liver including **protease inhibitors**. May also affect **Methadone** metabolism. **Ciprofloxacin:** avoid **antacids**. **Cyclosporine** or **Probenecid**: monitor kidney functions. **Amikacin:** avoid **ampho-B**, diuretics, penicillins. **Clindamycin:** avoid erythromycin. **Clarith.:** can reduce **AZT** levels by one-third. **Rifabutin** can reduce **Clarith.** blood levels by 50%. |
| **Isoniazid:** peripheral neuropathy and liver toxicity. **Rifampin:** liver & kidney toxicity, rash, discoloration of body fluids. **Pyrazinamide:** liver toxic, nausea, vomiting, diarrhea. **L-Ofloxacin:** GI disturbances, nausea, headache, and insomnia. | Infection control important with active TB. Yearly testing important, as TB epidemic spreads. **Isoniazid:** avoid **antabuse**, **Ketoconazole**, tuna fish; monitor liver. See above for **Rifampin & Amikacin**. **Ethambutol:** avoid co-administration with *Aluminum salts (ALOH)* |

| OPPORTUNISTIC INFECTION | PROPHYLAXIS (PX) AND MAINTENANCE OPTIONS |
|---|---|
| Candidiasis (Thrush) a fungal infection | Risk increases as CD4s fall <75 or 5%. Px thought preferable to dealing with active infection by some but fluconazole resistance becoming an issue. Px: **Fluconazole** 100–200 mg/day. Mx: **Fluconazole** 50–200 mg/day. **Vaginal:** Any CD4+ count, Px and Mx same as Treatment. Use topical or troches before systemic Px. |
| Cryptococcosis (Cryptococcal Disease) a fungal infection | Risk increases as CD4s fall < 75 or 5%. Cryptococcal antigen tests should be done regularly. If positive, follow with cultures. Px: **Fluconazole** 100–200 mg/day. Mx important indefinitely: **Fluconazole** 200–400 mg/day. **Amphotericin B** appears inferior to **fluconazole** as Mx. Consider **Itraconazole** 200 mg/day but has poor penetration into CNS. |
| Histoplasmosis a fungal infection | Risk increases as CD4s fall < 75 or 5%. No Px regimens being studied. Mx: **Itraconazole** 200 mg twice a day better than **Fluconazole** 600 mg/day. |
| Cryptosporidiosis a protozoal infection | Risk increases as CD4s fall < 75 or 5%. However, as in Tx, there is no consensus on an effective Px regimen. Some physicians report possible Px success with **Paromomycin** (humatin) and **Azithromycin** (ANH). |
| *Pneumocystis carinii* pneumonia (PCP) a protozoal infection | Px if symptomatic and CD4 <300, or if asymptomatic and CD4 <200 or 20%. Prefer oral drugs for Px or Mx, unless not tolerated (some success in desensitizing), then use **Aerosol Pentamidine (AP)** (300mg/month). Post-PCP, if CD4 < 50 and symptomatic, aggressive docs/patients combine oral with AP. Oral: **TMP/SMX:** one dbl strength tablet 3x/wk, or once daily. **Dapsone:** 100 mg 3x/wk or once daily. **Primaquine** 15 mg 3x/wk. **Atovaquone** (CT). |
| Toxcoplasmosis (Toxo/*toxoplasma gondii*) a protozoal infection | At risk if positive toxo antibodies and CD4+ count <250 or 20%. Tx/Mx: **Pyrimethamine** 25–50 mg/day with **Sulfadiazine** 2–4gm/day, and **Leucovorin** 10–50 mg/day, if needed. **Dapsone:** 100 mg 2x/week. **Atovaquone:** promising, but not currently in trials for Toxo Px. In a recent CPCRA study, **Pyrimethamine** <u>was</u> <u>not</u> effective as **Px** but is still good for Tx and Mx. Best bet for Px is **TMP/SMX**, possibly **Dapsone**. |

| POSSIBLE SIDE EFFECTS | DRUG INTERACTIONS (AND NOTES) |
|---|---|
| **Nystatin:** diarrhea, gastrointestinal upset with high doses. **Fluconazole:** nausea &/ or headache, rare liver reactions, abdominal pain. **Itraconazole:** similar. **Ketoconazole:** can be toxic to liver (fatal), headache, drowsiness, dizziness. *Monitor for resistance to these drugs.* | **Fluconazole:** avoid **Hismanal, Seldane, Warfarin, Rifampin,** oral contraceptives, **Cimetidine, Dilantin, Hydrochlorothiazide,** and **Sulfonylureas. Itra & keto: Seldane, Hismanal, Antacids & ddI,** take 2 hrs. apart. **Clotrimazole:** raises liver function tests. **Flu & Itra** may interact with **clari** and **rifabutin.** |
| **Fluconazole:** see above. **Amphotericin B:** damage to kidneys (fluid loading may reduce this; monitor BUN and creatinine levels), anemia, chills, fever, headache, vomiting, diarrhea, cramping, low blood pressure, and abnormal heartbeat. **ABLC, ABCD,** and **liposomal ampho B** reportedly less toxic. **Flucytosine** (5-FC): nausea, diarrhea, vomiting, severe bone marrow suppression, liver toxicity. **Itraconazole:** see above. | See above for **Fluconazole. Amphotericin B:** avoid steroids, some antineoplastics; may be synergistic with **Flucytosine;** requires frequent monitoring of various blood levels; some side effects treatable. **Flucytosine,** requires close monitoring of blood, kidney, and liver functions. |
| See above for **Fluconazole, Itraconazole,** and **Amphotericin B.** | See above for **Fluconazole, Itraconazole,** and **Amphotericin B.** Histoplasmosis is most common in the river valleys of Midwest, especially Kansas. |
| **Paromomycin:** nausea, reversible kidney toxicity, and hearing loss. **Spiramycin:** vomiting, colitis. **Azithromycin:** see MAI. **Atovaquone:** nausea, rash and fever and increased liver function tests. **Octreotide:** nausea, diarrhea, malabsorption, headache. | **Atovaquone:** Take with fatty foods for proper absorption. |
| **Pentam** (IV): Low blood pressure and high blood sugar, low blood counts, elevated kidney and liver function tests, nausea, and pancreatitis. **AP:** cough, shortness of breath, pancreatitis. **TMP/SMX:** High rates of mild to severe allergic side effects: rashes, itching, nausea, fever, leukopenia, vomiting. **Dapsone:** similar allergic reactions, severe anemia (with G6PD deficiency), sensitivity to sunlight, headache, neuropathy. **Atovaquone:** see above. | **TMP/SMX:** interacts with **Warfarin, Sulfonylureas, Methotrexate, Phenytoin, thiazide diuretics,** and **Cyclosporine.** Some physicians "desensitize" patients to **TMP/ SMX** by starting with very low doses and gradually increasing. **Dapsone:** do not take within 2 hrs. of **ddI** as it will not be properly absorbed. **Atovaquone:** see above. **Pentam.** with **ddI:** monitor for pancreatitis. ** |
| **Pyrimethamine:** marrow suppression leading to anemia (monitor semiweekly). Use caution with convulsive disorders. Anemia risk in patients with G6PD deficiency. **Sulfadiazine:** skin rashes (sometimes severe) and itching, nausea, fever, leukopenia. **Clindamycin & azithromycin:** see MAC. **Atovaquone:** see Cryptosporidiosis. **TMP/ SMX and Dapsone:** see PCP. | **Pyrimethamine:** leucovorin (folinic acid) may be given to decrease bone marrow suppression, particularly at high doses. **Pyrimethamine** may not be well absorbed with **ddI. Clindamycin:** avoid **Erythromycin. Atovaquone:** unknown at this time. ** |

| OPPORTUNISTIC INFECTION | PROPHYLAXIS (PX) AND MAINTENANCE OPTIONS |
|---|---|
| Cytomegalovirus (CMV) a viral infection | At risk if positive CMV antibodies and CD4+ count <75 or 5%. Long-term Mx necessary with Retinitis: **Ganciclovir** 5–10 mg/kg daily (Mx), **Cidofovir** (5 mg/kg every other week) (Mx). Switch to **Foscarnet** if resistance develops. **Oral ganciclovir** (3 g/day) Px/Mx. |
| (Herpes Simplex Virus, Varicella Zoster Virus) viral infections | Mx if recurrent HSV with **Acyclovir** 200–400 mg 2 to 4x/day. Higher doses if resistant (very high with HZV); possible extreme cases: monthly **Foscarnet** induction. **Famciclovir, Valacyclovir.** |

Legend:
*When taking broad-spectrum antibiotics, monitor for fungal infections
< = less than
> = greater than
ANH = approved for non-HIV-related conditions
BC = buyer's club

BID = twice a day
CD4+ = T4 helper cell
CT = clinical trial
CTP = clinical trial pending
CU = compassionate use
EA = expanded access
IV = intravenous

| POSSIBLE SIDE EFFECTS | DRUG INTERACTIONS (AND NOTES) |
|---|---|
| **Ganciclovir (DHPG):** reversible neutropenia, thrombocytopenia, confusion, disorientation, anemia, fever, rash, abnormal liver function tests. **Foscarnet:** may be highly damaging to the kidneys, anemia, nausea, penile ulcerations in uncircumcised men. Serum creatinine and electrolyte level monitoring essential and can prevent irreversible damage. | **Ganciclovir: G-CSF** and **GM-CSF** can be used to decrease neutropenia (low white blood cells). When combining with **AZT** or other neutropenic drugs blood monitoring is essential; dose reduction or discontinuation could be necessary. Concurrent administration of saline solution has been reported to help prevent **Foscarnet's** renal toxicities. **Ganciclovir** and **ddI:** monitor for pancreatitis. |
| **Acyclovir:** nausea, diarrhea, headache, skin rash. **Foscarnet:** see CMV. **Trifluridine (TFT):** transient burning & stinging. | **Foscarnet:** see CMV.<br><br>** When taking broad spectrum antibiotics, monitor for fungal infections |

Legend:
mg = milligrams
Mx = maintenance therapy
Px = prophylaxis (prevention)
Tx = treatment

# YOU AND YOUR DOCTOR

**BY SHARON LEE, MD**

One of the most important decisions facing an individual who learns he or she is HIV-infected is the choice of a primary care physician. Loneliness and isolation as well as fear and disbelief are just some of the distressing emotions expressed by many newly diagnosed people. Finding the right doctor can help lessen some of those feelings as well as set a person living with HIV on the road toward the best possible care.

After the first shock of receiving a diagnosis, the next step is to choose an HIV-knowledgeable doctor who can be trusted. The doctor-patient relationship is an intimate partnership that requires matching several traits. As in other relationships, you may be lucky and stumble upon a good doctor. More likely, finding a doctor will take research and some legwork. (Note: Insurance plans often limit your choice of both doctors and hospitals. Make sure you read and understand your health insurance plan if you have one.)

## HOW TO FIND A DOCTOR

Your family doctor may provide the best referral to a physician experienced in HIV care. If the diagnosis was made at a health clinic, a laboratory, or another health provider's office, counselors, doctors, or nurses on-site can often provide names of physicians who specialize in HIV/AIDS.

In addition, many communities have AIDS service organizations that provide physician referrals. If your city or town doesn't have such an organization, see the Resource Guide at the back of this book. Also check with hospitals that are known to treat people with HIV disease in the largest nearby community. If you are searching for access to a specific experimental drug, pharmaceutical companies may be able to provide the names of doctors who are involved in a clinical study or trial and treat people with HIV in your locale. Another source for clinical-trials information is 1-800-TRIALS-A, a federally sponsored referral source. Local health departments or medical societies can provide referrals. Finally, friends who may have firsthand information about specific doctors are an excellent resource when seeking a provider.

## QUALIFICATIONS TO SEEK IN A PHYSICIAN

There are two primary qualifications to look for when choosing your doctor: knowledge of HIV disease and the ability to communicate with you.

It is crucial to locate an HIV-experienced medical provider. Many doctors have had limited exposure to some of the specific disease processes that oc-

cur as well as the highly specialized, and sometimes experimental, treatments used to combat them. They may be excellent doctors for non-HIV-infected patients, but you will want a doctor who

- has treated a significant number of people with HIV/AIDS before.
- keeps up-to-date on the latest research findings.
- is informed about FDA-approved therapies and experimental treatments.
- is affiliated with a respected and convenient hospital.
- is generally well-regarded by his or her HIV-infected patients.

Ideally, it's also important to choose a doctor who is board certified in either family practice, internal medicine, infectious diseases, or a related specialty, and who has a wide range of contacts for additional referrals.

Once you've satisfied that checklist, here are some questions to ask a prospective doctor:

- How aggressive an approach will he or she take with your illness? (This should be matched with your own preferences.)
- Can the doctor enroll you in new drug trials or new research protocols?
- Will he or she monitor use of alternative and unproven therapies (such as vitamin therapies, homeopathy, or nutritional interventions) if you choose to use them?
- Will your doctor follow your wishes with regard to ending life support?
- What is his or her general style? (It's important that the doctor be willing to work with you in the manner you choose.)

It is critical to have a high level of trust, confidence, and comfort with your doctor. If you cannot discuss personal questions or issues, you may want to find a doctor with whom you can communicate more honestly and directly—and who can do so with you. Often, these attributes may not be found in one doctor. In some instances, a collaboration between your family doctor and an AIDS clinician may provide the necessary balance.

Finally, will the doctor listen to your concerns and respect your decisions, especially with regard to whom you designate as medical power of attorney (the person who makes your medical decisions in the event you are not able to)? Some doctors are uncomfortable talking with a same-sex partner or refuse to recognize a homosexual partner as a legitimate equivalent to a spouse or family member. If you choose a friend or lover rather than a family member, it's important to be sure the doctor will respect this decision.

## MAXIMIZING THE DOCTOR-PATIENT RELATIONSHIP

After identifying a physician, a number of questions remain to be answered:

- What general parameters are there for calls? For visits?

- What warrants an emergency visit or immediate evaluation?

- What kind of frequency does he or she recommend for routine visits and what do they consist of?

Remember, when it comes to you and your health, there is no such thing as a stupid question.

In establishing a relationship with a health care provider, it's essential to share your past medical history, family health history, and any specific health-related issues (such as smoking or drug use). Try to complete a candid health history before the consultation so there will be more time for you to discuss other issues with your doctor.

Over the years, Project Inform has developed the following guidelines to help maximize your relationship with your doctor:

- Start the education process at home. Learn as much as you can about HIV infection, therapies, and treatment strategies before you see the doctor. Overtaxed doctors rarely have the time to instruct people in the fundamentals of HIV disease, and most welcome working with people who learn on their own.

- Decide on the relationship style that works best for you. People have different ways of relating to their physicians, and those styles may vary over time or for different illnesses. For example, some people prefer that their doctors take an authoritative stand because it makes them feel secure. Others view the physician as a specialist called in to advise them on a particular problem. Still others seek a collaborative relationship in which both doctor and patient weigh the pros and cons of a treatment strategy before decisions are made. If you know what relationship style you prefer, tell your doctor.

- Prepare for appointments. While it only takes a few minutes to make a list of key questions for your doctor, it's important to plan and organize yourself ahead of time. List questions. Outline problems. Make notes on information you want. Be sure to note any changes in the dosage or drugs you are taking. Note any deviation from your treatment plan. Both patient and physician benefit when a visit is well planned.

- Discuss treatment requests in a spirit of mutual respect. For a variety of reasons, many physicians don't recommend unapproved treatments. Some take a conservative view and don't see any point in using unproven remedies. Some are concerned with legal questions, while oth-

ers simply feel uncomfortable dealing with little-known products. It's not unusual that some aspects of the usual patient/physician role may be reversed when unapproved treatments are discussed. Under these circumstances, people with HIV disease often take the more active role in reviewing and selecting treatments.

In initiating such a discussion, the patient should describe what's known about a treatment and why he or she wants to use it—while listening to the doctor's feedback. You might ask, "What will it take for you to feel comfortable with what I want to do? More careful monitoring? Reviewing the decision in a month or two? More review of available data? Discussion with other physicians? A statement releasing you from liability?" Similarly, the physician might ask, "What can I do to help you better understand the risks and why I'm concerned with what you want to do?" or "What other options, if any, have you considered?" or "Will you wait while I review the matter more carefully?" Sometimes it is possible to find new alternatives that neither party had expected before the discussion began.

Whether or not agreement is reached on the use of a treatment, cooperation is essential between doctor and patient. The physician should continue to monitor the patient with appropriate examinations and lab tests; the patient, in turn, should heed reasonable warnings based on the monitored findings.

If, in the final analysis, a physician doesn't feel comfortable agreeing with the use of an unapproved treatment strategy, and a patient is equally firm in his or her convictions, then physician and patient must question whether it is possible to continue a mutually respectful relationship. Often, it is possible to maintain the relationship while disagreeing and continuing to talk about the differences. The decision to change your doctor, always an option, should be reached only as a last resort, when it is clear that the parties cannot accept each other's approach to a treatment strategy.

Most physicians treating HIV infection are sensitive, caring individuals who respond emotionally to their patients—whether or not they show it. If you find you do not like the way he or she is managing your care, speak up. Feel free to discuss your expectations, concerns, and needs and be prepared to listen. As in every relationship, this partnership is a two-way street.

# How to Manage
# Medications

**BY JOHN GILMORE, MD**

Because of the complex nature of HIV, many people living with HIV take a variety of drugs to fight fungi and viruses, to strengthen immune systems, control cancers, as well as to fight pain and depression. They may also take vitamins and food supplements. Keeping track of medications can be a daunting task for anyone and is an especially challenging one for a person who is quite ill.

Yet, managing medications is key to successful treatment management. Each medication has specific indications for when and how it should be taken, whether or not it should be taken with food, and how it interacts with other medications. It's also important to pay attention to the time lapse between administration of the medication and when it takes effect, especially if there are adverse side effects. If so, share this information with your health care provider.

Before starting a new medication or beginning treatment with a new doctor, it is vital to review all medications currently being taken. Some health care providers suggest "brown bagging"—literally putting all medications, including complementary therapies and supplements, into a sack and taking them to the doctor. Or, bring in a list of current medications for the physician to review.

## THE IMPORTANCE OF COMMUNICATION

The best treatment management—avoiding overtreatment or undertreatment—results from an ongoing dialogue between patient and physician. Decisions about when to start a medication, stop one, or adjust the timing or dose of a specific treatment (or combination) require keen observations, careful attention to detail, and for the provider, the full weight of his or her experience in treating people with HIV disease. Frank discussions of side effects, suspected allergies, feelings of depression and lethargy, are important. If feeling poorly, ask, "Is it the medication or the disease that makes me feel this way?" Often a change in dosage or a substitute medication can make a profound difference in the way people feel.

Not surprisingly, it is when the patient and the health care provider most need to communicate that the obstacles become the greatest. A patient may be delirious or irrational with fever, dehydration, pain, or fear. The physician may be preoccupied with diagnostic decision-making, consulting with specialists, securing non-licensed therapies, and juggling the demands and

needs of other patients. An honest dialogue is especially important because HIV infection is a dynamic threat and as a result, treatment options and recommendations should undergo continual reevaluation and revision. In summary, the best treatment strategy will result from real-life patient experience combined with the accumulated expertise of an experienced physician with access to clinical and research specialists, along with a pharmacist who can provide the most current information regarding treatments.

In this era of managed care, doctors often experience the same kind of frustration as their patients about the lack of time in an office visit. As a general rule, patients and physicians should not assume that each knows what medications are being taken or remembers what was last discussed in an office visit. Being organized when you see your doctor is critical to maximize the time available. To help achieve a productive dialogue, here is a checklist of questions and information to be exchanged between you and your doctor.

## PATIENTS SHOULD ASK DOCTORS

- What does this medication treat? Is it a prophylaxis (preventive for opportunistic infection or other symptom) or HIV treatment? Why am I taking it?
- When should I begin taking this medication?
- How often? (what time of day) Over what period of time? (days, weeks, months, forever)
- How do I take it? (orally, on empty/full stomach, injection, suppository)
- What should I expect from it?
- What side effects should I be aware of? (common, less common, rare)
- What reactions are important enough to call you (the doctor) about?
- Will this medication interfere with other medications or therapies I'm using?
- What monitoring—blood tests, lab work, etc.—will be necessary with it and how frequently?
- What should I do if I forget to take it—double up? Skip it?
- Is there a generic brand? By what other names is it known? Is it okay to substitute one of these?

## TELL YOUR DOCTOR

- About any allergies you have for example, medicines or foods.
- Any known drug intolerances.

- About all the medications you are taking, including alternative therapies or protocol studies you are participating in.
- Any noticeable benefits or adverse side effects.
- Any feelings of discouragement or resistance to continuing a particular regimen. Depression and altered states of mind may be indications of a drug reaction—get a reality check.
- Any disagreement you have with his or her recommendations–and your basis for that disagreement.
- About other treatments that you feel might be helpful. Your doctor can't read everything, so mention what you've learned from other providers, friends, consumer/activist literature, and medical journals.
- Any changes you've made in your treatments or medication regimen.
- About any financial or other problems in getting medications (see Resource Guide at the back of this book for buyers' clubs, etc.)

Following are two charts to help manage a variety of medications. The first chart has been filled out by a person with HIV in consultation with a physician. The second chart is blank and can be reproduced and enlarged at your local copy shop. Ask your doctor or pharmacist for other versions. Keep it where you and your caregiver can easily find it, and be sure to take it with you whenever you visit your doctor.

Patient Name: John Doe  Doctor: Maria Smith  Phone: (415) 555-1212  Allergies: Demerol Penicillin

| DRUG | HOW TO TAKE | WHAT IT IS FOR | SPECIAL INSTRUCTIONS | POSSIBLE SIDE EFFECTS | COMMENTS |
|---|---|---|---|---|---|
| Biaxin 500 mg Clarithromycin | 1 tablet daily | MAI prophylaxis | | Metallic taste, stomach upset | If stomach upset, can take with food. Do not take with Seldane |
| Septra DS TMP/SMX 160/800 mg | 1 tablet daily | PCP prophylaxis | Important to take daily. Take with plenty of water | Allergic reaction such as rash, itching, photosensitivity, stomach discomfort | Use sunscreen SPF -15 or above if out in the sun for prolonged periods |
| Folate 1 mg | 1 tablet daily | Vitamin supplement | | | |
| Megace Megestrol acetate 40 mg/ml | 20 ml (4 tsp) (800 mg) every morning | Appetite stimulant | | Weight gain, nausea, vomiting, edema, rash | |
| Diflucan 100 mg Fluconazole | 1 tablet daily | Fungal or yeast infection | | Stomach upset | |
| Paxil 20 mg Paroxetine | 1 tablet daily | Depression | | Headache, insomnia, drowsiness, stomach upset | Takes approximately 2 weeks to see full effect |
| Lomotil Diphenoxylate Atropine 2.5 mg | 1 tablet as needed for diarrhea | Diarrhea | DO NOT exceed 8 tablets per day | Constipation, drowsiness, dizziness | |

Patient Name:

Doctor:

Phone:

Allergies:

| DRUG | HOW TO TAKE | WHAT IT IS FOR | SPECIAL INSTRUCTIONS | POSSIBLE SIDE EFFECTS | COMMENTS |
|------|-------------|----------------|----------------------|----------------------|----------|
|      |             |                |                      |                      |          |
|      |             |                |                      |                      |          |
|      |             |                |                      |                      |          |
|      |             |                |                      |                      |          |
|      |             |                |                      |                      |          |
|      |             |                |                      |                      |          |
|      |             |                |                      |                      |          |

# DEVELOPING A WEIGHT MAINTENANCE AND NUTRITION STRATEGY

**BY BRENDA LEIN**

Weight loss and malnutrition are common problems associated with HIV disease. Weight loss can begin and become severe anywhere across the spectrum of CD4+ counts. Wasting is defined as an unexplained loss of 10% or more of a person's normal lean body mass. There are people who report wasting despite a very high level of CD4+ cells, but the risk of wasting and serious malnutrition increases dramatically when CD4+ cell counts fall below 100. The body's ability to absorb nutrients and maintain lean body mass is associated with general good health and the ability to fight disease.

There are many approaches to managing nutrition and wasting. A comprehensive treatment strategy for managing HIV/AIDS should include a component on nutrition, and weight should be monitored with the same watchful eye as CD4+ cell counts and other laboratory parameters. Early intervention in weight loss is critical. Specialists note that the difference between successful treatment of an opportunistic infection and treatment failure can often depend on a few pounds of weight.

There are many options for prevention and treatment of weight loss and different approaches may be needed across the spectrum of disease. Someone who is healthy with no obvious signs of weight loss will probably develop a very different kind of weight maintenance strategy than someone experiencing significant weight loss. Similarly, weight loss due to gastrointestinal distress, diarrhea, or other HIV-related conditions may require different interventions than weight loss that is due to chemotherapy or drug interactions. Finding a nutrition and weight stabilization program that adapts to both lifestyle and nutritional needs is critical for success. The following are a few points to consider:

- *Evaluate nutrition and exercise as part of a comprehensive, early intervention treatment strategy for HIV.*
- *Employ rigorous diagnosis and appropriate treatment for causes of weight loss.*
- *When necessary, consider using nutritional and vitamin supplements to replenish deficiencies.*
- *Follow reasonable guidelines for "safer" food preparation.*

- *Learn the pros and cons of various intervention options.*

The overall goal of a comprehensive strategy for controlling HIV is to prolong life and improve quality of life for the long term. A nutritional and weight maintenance component to this strategy may help to reduce symptoms of HIV, reduce side effects of therapies, increase energy, improve general health and overall feeling of well-being, and strengthen the body's ability to fight disease.

## EVALUATE NUTRITION AND EXERCISE AS PART OF A COMPREHENSIVE, EARLY INTERVENTION STRATEGY

The importance of nutrition and maintaining lean body mass cannot be overstated. Good nutrition, combined with exercise, not only relieves stress, which is proven to be immune suppressive, but also provides a solid foundation to optimize the potential benefits of HIV therapeutic regimens.

Most physicians and people living with HIV do not recognize early signs of weight loss. Careful monitoring of weight, periodic laboratory evaluations looking for vitamin and hormone deficiencies, and an aggressive nutritional and exercise program can help prevent wasting and malnutrition. Nutritionists who specialize in HIV can be helpful in guiding the development of a comprehensive weight maintenance program. While complex solutions like total parenteral nutrition (TPN) can sometimes correct severe wasting, the cost is often unacceptably high, both in dollars and risks of side effects or risks associated with treatment. Whenever possible, it is far better to take action to correct nutritional problems before they become severe. This may mean intervening with improved diet, appetite stimulants, or weight gain supplements before weight loss becomes unmanageable.

Like any basic program, your strategy for coping with nutritional and exercise needs should be reevaluated periodically, adapting strategies to your body's changing needs. Two people at the same stage of wasting may use completely different approaches depending on their willingness to exercise and work at a nutritional program. Someone willing to follow a workout regimen and careful diet may rebound from wasting by simply adopting better eating habits. Someone who is less inclined to invest in an exercise regimen and finds it more difficult to follow a careful dietary plan may require more invasive intervention, ranging from the use of appetite stimulants and supplements to TPN. Both individuals might successfully rebound from wasting, but each intervention regimen reflects individual lifestyle factors and choices. There are pros and cons to each option. Weigh the risks and benefits to develop a realistic plan to prevent or reverse wasting.

Many people who are experiencing weight loss feel frail and shy away from strenuous activity. They may have a tendency to feel depressed, which can be linked to malnutrition. The feelings often get in the way of maintaining a regimen of good nutrition and exercise. This perpetuates a cycle. It's important to remember even if you feel frail, you are not. Your body is much more resilient than you may feel!

## EMPLOY RIGOROUS DIAGNOSIS AND TREATMENT FOR CAUSES OF WEIGHT LOSS

HIV and many related conditions cause weight loss, fatigue, loss of muscle mass, and chronic diarrhea. The gastrointestinal tract is a major site of early HIV infection, and for many bacterial, viral, fungal, and parasitic infections which can contribute to weight loss once a damaged immune system lets such organisms grow unchecked.

Some health professionals conduct repeated tests to identify the cause of diarrhea and weight loss. Others only treat symptoms and never attempt to identify the cause. It is important to do both. Aggressive diagnosis should be accompanied by aggressive treatment. Diagnosing and treating unexplained weight loss and diarrhea can be difficult as there are often multiple causes operating at the same time. An infectious agent, like a parasite, might be identified but treatment may only reduce and not resolve the problem. This might be because the parasite was "masking" another infection and additional diagnostic and treatment procedures may be required to deal with the underlying problem. Similarly, wasting is sometimes due to poor absorption, a condition in which the tissue and cells lining the intestinal tract have lost the ability to properly take up nutrients. If this is the case, it can have a major impact on which treatments are selected. Finding the cause or causes of weight loss or diarrhea is always critical to finding the right solution. Treating symptoms, without understanding the underlying causes, can sometimes do more harm than good.

## CONSIDER NUTRITIONAL AND VITAMIN SUPPLEMENTS TO REPLENISH DEFICIENCIES

Studies have shown that two phenomenon are present at all stages in HIV disease, even when CD4+ counts are high and there are no apparent signs or symptoms of disease: (1) the virus is always actively replicating, and (2) there is some evidence of nutritional deficiency. Many people attempt to give the body an edge over the virus by complementing their diet with vitamins and other nutritional supplements. This may not only help correct minor nutritional deficiencies, but may also strengthen the body's natural immune defenses. Much research still needs to be done to fully document vitamin and

nutritional deficiencies across the spectrum of HIV disease and the degree to which supplements correct these problems. Nonetheless, a reasonable level of vitamin and nutritional supplementation to replenish deficiencies just makes common sense.

Vitamin and nutritional supplements should not be used to replace food. Whenever possible, increasing vitamin intake through improved eating habits is preferable. For people on strict budgets, living on disability or other assistance programs, vitamins and other supplements are often too expensive. Some people spend hundreds of dollars per month on such products. This is probably unwarranted in most situations as there is little data to support the use of "mega" doses of vitamins and supplements in AIDS. Some counties have programs which help cover the cost of alternative therapies and supplements. To find out if programs exist in your area, call your local health department.

Vitamin supplementation, like nutrition and exercise regimens, should be reevaluated periodically. In the course of HIV disease, the body appears to be less able to absorb nutrients, and thus it may be useful to take using amino acids and other enzyme supplements which promote the digestion of food. In this instance, it is unclear whether taking larger doses of supplements produce any added benefit. Some physicians who specialize in the use of vitamins and supplements recommend intravenous administration when absorption is a problem. This is not such a far-fetched idea, as conventional TPN formulas have always included vitamin supplements in the mix. Similarly, some hospitals include intravenous vitamin supplements when patients are restricted from oral food intake.

A "brown bag medical checkup" is an important part of health monitoring. Each time you visit your health care provider, throw all the medications you take, intermittently and regularly, into a bag. Include vitamins, herbs, nutritional supplements, and prescribed medications. Ask your doctor to have a pharmacist conduct a personalized review of your therapies for safety, appropriateness, compatibility, and instructions for use. This will help avoid drug interactions and may help figure out which drugs are causing side effects. Just because something is available over-the-counter or perceived as "alternative," it does not mean it is nontoxic or safe to take with other therapies. Also, be sure to see the chapter on drug interactions.

## GUIDELINES FOR "SAFER" FOOD PREPARATION

Not many people consider food and food preparation as a prevention against opportunistic infections or as a tool for supporting a healthy immune system, but avoiding certain foods and the careful handling of food may help prevent infections which further tax the immune system. Some guidelines include:

- Wash fruits and vegetables thoroughly as this can remove many organisms, such as *mycobacterium avium* complex (MAI or MAC), which are found in soil. Use a vegetable brush to remove soil and chemical residues.

- Avoid eating fresh vegetables and salads at restaurants or anywhere else where you can't be certain that the products are washed adequately to meet your needs.

- Avoid eating raw eggs and foods containing raw eggs. In recent years there have been thousands of cases of salmonella poisoning from Caesar salad made with raw eggs. If you choose to eat salads at restaurants (despite these guidelines), be sure to ask whether raw eggs are used in salad dressings and other foods.

- Cook meat thoroughly at at least 140°F. Avoid "pink" meat, including rare steaks and burgers, uncooked meat and sushi. Diseases such as salmonella, toxoplasmosis; and parasites are found in raw and undercooked chicken, beef, pork, and fish.

- Use different cutting boards for foods which will be cooked and those served raw. For example, salads that are prepared on a cutting board that has just been used for preparing meat can become contaminated by organisms in the meat.

- Wash hands, kitchen utensils, and cutting boards frequently and thoroughly during food preparation, avoiding meat juices from contaminating cheese, vegetables, and other foods. When possible, use different cutting boards for raw and cooked food.

- Keep kitchen appliances, shelves, countertops, refrigerators, freezers and utensils clean, and wash sponges and towels frequently. Wash sponges and towels after each use if possible. Proper food storage and cooking can help reduce risk of food-borne diseases.

- Wash all utensils and your hands with soap and water between handling one food and handling another in order to help prevent cross-contamination.

- Boil drinking water between 1 and 5 minutes to avoid cryptosporidiosis.

- Thaw meats in the refrigerator rather than open air, keeping the refrigerator temperature at 40°F or lower.

## LEARN THE PROS AND CONS OF VARIOUS INTERVENTION OPTIONS

Like all other aspects of HIV/AIDS treatment, there is no free lunch when it comes to the intervention options for nutrition and wasting. There are a number of products and approaches which are helpful for many people, but no guaranteed solutions for every possible situation. Likewise, there is a fair amount of hype and misinformation about various approaches. Nutritional supplements and vitamins are often promoted aggressively, whether or not there are adequate data to support the claims made for them. There are varying degrees of effectiveness, and varying side effects of each drug. A good rule is to remember that what works for one person in one situation may not work for the next person. The best solution is to form your own opinions after collecting as much information as possible.

Finally, good nutrition and maintaining lean body mass are core components of a comprehensive HIV treatment strategy. Weigh the pros and cons of available options and develop a nutrition and weight maintenance strategy that fits your lifestyle. Consult a nutritionist who specializes in HIV for guidance in developing a comprehensive strategy. Interventions are available if wasting becomes a problem, but as with almost every aspect of HIV, preventing the problem is the best solution.

# ALTERNATIVE AND HOLISTIC THERAPIES

**BY CHARLES STEINBERG, MD**

## INTRODUCTION

In exploring all the treatments for HIV disease, many individuals examine approaches outside of standard mainstream therapies. In fact, various studies indicate between a quarter and three-quarters of people living with HIV have employed some form of alternative treatments. Because HIV is a life-threatening illness where conventional medicine has not found a cure, alternative approaches—including ancient traditional healing modalities, spiritual approaches, foreign pharmaceuticals, homeopathy, and East Indian spices—have been widely used to combat this disease and its symptoms. Stories of remarkable success and failure have been documented. At the same time, rip-offs abound.

This chapter describes the elements that an individual may consider in devising a comprehensive, holistic, aggressive approach to fight HIV. This approach focuses on body, mind, and spirit and incorporates general health maintenance, nutritional factors, and alternative therapies. A person living with HIV can learn about these approaches from a variety of practitioners, then integrate them with standard medical care in collaboration with an HIV-experienced physician. No endorsement of any particular or specific program or product is intended or should be inferred. Scientific studies are discussed when available. Use the same criteria to evaluate "natural" approaches as you would for standard therapy drugs. Just because a treatment is "natural" doesn't mean it has no potential toxicity or adverse effects. As always, potential toxicity, cost, and availability need to be balanced with a treatment's potential effectiveness.

## GENERAL HEALTH MAINTENANCE

A solid foundation for better health is achieved by making some well-known—indeed common sense—lifestyle choices. These steps are the basics of any healing plan and should be taken before any specific alternative product or modality is contemplated.

*CHARLES STEINBERG, MD, HAS WORKED FOR OVER A DECADE WITH PEOPLE WITH HIV TO COMBINE AND INTEGRATE TRADITIONAL MEDICAL CARE WITH COMPLEMENTARY THERAPIES. HE IS THE FOUNDER OF THE NATIONAL CONFERENCE ON AIDS, MEDICINE AND MIRACLES, AND A HOLISTIC CLINIC IN BOULDER, COLORADO, CALLED WELLSPRING PARTNERS.*

### NUTRITION

People living with HIV need a higher-protein, lower-fat, nutrient-rich diet with frequent, regular meals including fresh fruits and vegetables, complete proteins, whole grains, less sweets, and less highly refined foods. A good diet for someone with HIV has multiple protein sources such as lean meat, cheese, fish, chicken, nuts, and yogurt. While it is possible (yet difficult) for someone with HIV to get adequate and complete proteins in a vegetarian diet, strict macrobiotic diets have usually not benefited individuals with HIV. Several servings daily of fruits, grains, and a variety of vegetables are also important for a balanced diet. Small, frequent meals make it easier for the body to digest food than does a single, large portion.

Studies show that even asymptomatic HIV-positive individuals, very early in the course of disease, can have decreased absorption of nutrients, so that the recommended dietary allowances (RDAs) are often inadequate. People with HIV, from the beginning of their illness, need more of the basic nutrients than others to compensate for poor absorption. Compensating for poor absorption is crucial since maintaining a stable weight, especially lean body mass (muscle and organ weight), directly correlates with survival. "Fat" weight doesn't help.

### EXERCISE

Physical exercise has a demonstrated value for improving health and as a supportive HIV treatment. For people living with HIV who are symptom free, vigorous regular aerobic exercise, lasting thirty to forty-five minutes, three to four times per week, provides a solid cardiovascular workout. Examples of this aerobic exercise include running; biking; dancing; aerobics classes; swimming; cross-country skiing; roller-blading; games like soccer, racquetball, or basketball; and use of cardiovascular machines such as StairMasters, stationary bikes, NordicTracks, or treadmills. Many people "cross-train" with a variety of activities to keep up their interest and motivation.

An aerobics program conditions the heart and lungs, combats depression by raising endorphin levels, and in several studies actually raised CD4+ counts (an indicator of the strength of the immune system). One study showed fewer opportunistic infections and better coping with stress in a group of regular exercisers. However, marathons and other extreme endurance workouts have sometimes weakened a person's immune system. Resistance exercises (using weights or machines) build muscle mass, help preserve lean body weight, and promote better health.

For those who are symptomatic or recovering from illness, it's important to discuss a specific exercise program with your health care provider. Physical therapists are trained to help develop rehabilitation programs. Regard-

less of your health status, always begin exercise gently and build slowly. In almost all cases, any exercise is better than none at all.

### RELAXATION

Life is stressful. Having HIV disease is very stressful. Being a patient is stressful. Fear, loss, grief, and financial trouble can all be stressful. Studies show that people with HIV benefit from some form of structured daily relaxation, whether it's yoga, music, deep breathing, muscle relaxation, meditation, or tai chi. Multiple studies reported at recent international AIDS conferences have shown that regular relaxation decreases depression, improves attitude, and improves specific laboratory measurements of immune function. Other studies have shown that high levels of stress can weaken the immune system, which may lead to increases in symptoms and infections.

### SUBSTANCE-ABUSE TREATMENT

An obvious lifestyle change for any person living with HIV is to consider ending any form of substance abuse. Overall health and the strength of the immune system are significantly improved when certain substances are avoided. Terminating these substances may be one of the most difficult challenges an individual can face. Addiction is its own life-threatening illness.

Cigarette smoking has been correlated with increased problems with *Pneumocystis carinii* pneumonia (PCP), as well as more frequent cases of cryptococcal meningitis (a fungal infection). Elimination of cigarette smoking restores the lungs' ability to cleanse themselves within just a few weeks, with lung function continuing to improve over time.

There is diversity of opinion regarding marijuana use. Marijuana smoke has an impact on the lungs similar to tobacco smoke, and some studies have shown marijuana to be slightly injurious to the immune system. Yet its appetite-stimulating effect (the "munchies") has helped people who don't eat enough gain weight. If you are considering marijuana use, talk to your physician about its risks and benefits.

Chronic use or overuse of alcohol and hard drugs poisons the same organs (brain, liver, and immune cells) that HIV attacks. Studies show cocaine and narcotics may increase viral replication. In my practice when patients have quit alcohol or hard drugs, the improvement in their health has been obvious to them and to me and is reflected in their lab values, including their CD4+ counts.

## SUPPORTIVE ACTIVITIES

While there is no hard data linking support groups or the role of a positive attitude with increased survival, people living with HIV disease frequently

attest that these activities are associated with a higher quality of life and greater optimism about the future.

The value of being in a support group has been researched in cancer patients, with one study reporting that being in a group for a year doubled the survival time for women with breast cancer. Similar studies of HIV support groups are in progress and may show significant value. People with HIV who attend support groups initially receive assistance in coping with their feelings of shock and denial as they deal with their diagnosis. They often encounter people who are surviving and thriving with this disease. Groups also serve as a forum for sharing new information on treatments and resources, as well as provide time for problem-solving. Individuals often have the opportunity to build a support network that extends outside of the group meeting that may help meet emotional needs for friendship and intimacy. All this occurs in a context of talking through the difficult issues raised by HIV: who and when to tell about one's HIV status, family issues, career changes, dating, sex, love, and one's personal search for the meaning of life. Support groups also provide time for healing activities, such as singing, meditation, and the use of imagery.

### POSITIVE ATTITUDE

The overall attitude a person with HIV takes toward his or her illness also makes a difference. For instance, the notion of the patient as "helpless victim" can be replaced by a model of one who is actively involved in his or her health care and is educated and empowered to make treatment choices. Researchers in a relatively new field, psychoneuroimmunology, are studying the connections between thought, feeling, and the immune system. It seems that what we tell our bodies about our health or illness can impact the progression or outcome of a disease.

The placebo effect is the best-known example of this process. Studies show that when someone believes a medicine will be effective, as many as 40% of those taking the placebo (a sugar pill with no active ingredients) will realize a positive effect. Likewise, if someone believes the illness to be a death sentence, this result may be more likely to come true. Studies of the characteristics of long-term AIDS survivors show that most have a positive outlook and believe that their actions will make a real difference.

## VITAMINS AND SUPPLEMENTS

The use of vitamins and supplements is a highly individualized choice, with some people using none and others taking literally dozens of capsules and tablets a day. As of yet, no hard scientific data are available from controlled clinical trials reporting which vitamins and supplements, and what doses,

are best for people with HIV disease. Several recent observational studies have been published showing delayed disease progression in individuals with increased intake (from food or supplements) of various vitamins, including vitamin A, B$_6$, C, E, thiamine, riboflavin, niacin, and beta-carotene. Vitamins should always be taken with food, with the exception of carnitine and NAC (two amino acids that are better absorbed on an empty stomach). If you are serious about using nutritional supplements, work closely with a nutritionist experienced with HIV.

## ACUPUNCTURE AND CHINESE HERBS

Chinese medicine is an ancient method of healing used by over 20% of the world's population, with an emphasis on treating the whole person, not just a particular disease. For instance, two people with HIV disease might receive very different Chinese-medicine treatment plans geared to each individual's strengths, weaknesses, imbalances, and lifelong patterns.

In spite of this highly individualized approach of Chinese medicine, protocols have been established to test standard herbal formulations and acupuncture treatments in HIV disease. In several studies, formulas with astragalus, lingustrum, ginseng, licorice, and other Chinese herbs have shown effectiveness against various symptoms such as fatigue, sweats, weight loss, diarrhea, and skin rashes. These herbs have not been documented to improve lab values.

Some people choose to add one of the standard combination herbal formulas based on astragalus to their treatment regimen. Others who want to go further should work with a practitioner of Chinese medicine experienced with HIV. There are many ways to combine these approaches with standard medical practices. In fact, remedies from Chinese medicine can often relieve the side effects from standard prescription drugs.

## HERBS AND "NATURAL" PHARMACEUTICALS

From the outset of the epidemic when no approved drugs existed, people living with HIV viewed herbal remedies as drugs from nature. Some of the products were general "immune enhancers" or antivirals by reputation, others were more specifically focused against HIV. Initial recommendations were made based on folklore and anecdotal information. Now a few have been studied scientifically. People often mistakenly believe "natural" means safe. For all potential HIV treatments, potential risk and benefit must be balanced.

### COMPOUND Q

Compound Q is an intravenous medicine that comes from the root of the Chinese cucumber plant. It is used in China as a cancer therapy and to induce abortions. Imported into the United States and sold through buyers' clubs for HIV disease, compound Q is administered through intravenous infusion,

given by physicians willing to work with unapproved products or by "underground" clinics staffed by knowledgeable laypeople.

Compound Q is different from other antivirals, which slow the spread of the virus to uninfected cells; instead, compound Q kills already infected cells. Practitioners hope that compound Q will greatly reduce the viral load, allowing the immune system to repair itself. Currently, there is wide variation in dosages being used (one or two vials up to twenty vials), the frequency of administration (weekly to monthly), and the duration of the infusion (two to twenty-four hours). In various studies, CD4+ stabilization has been achieved in some patients, with dramatic increases for a few. Data from a moderate sized trial of compound Q showed little impact of the therapy on viral levels or CD4+. Though study results have not been encouraging, some people in the community claim benefit and continue using the therapy.

Common side effects, such as muscle aches and fatigue, are reduced by beginning anti-inflammatory drugs like ibuprofen before the infusion. There is a rare life-threatening side effect—an emergency allergic reaction—called anaphylaxis. Benadryl pretreatment, either orally or intravenously, may lessen this risk. There have been reports of serious central nervous system side effects (disorientation, hallucinations, and coma) that may be prevented, with pretreatment with Decadron and by screening out individuals with low CD4+ counts. Anyone with a CD4+ count under 100 should approach compound Q with great caution. If used, this compound must be administered by someone experienced with it and prepared for the emergency treatment of anaphylaxis.

### HYPERICIN

Hypericin is an extract from the flower St. John's Wort, and produced synthetically, with reputed broad-spectrum antiviral effects against HIV, herpes, cytomegalovirus, and Epstein-Barr. It provides several good examples of our growing understanding about herbal medicines. Originally, people with HIV took St. John's Wort, the herb itself, since there was test-tube evidence that hypericin stopped HIV replication. Later, it was seen that hypericin levels from the orally administered herb were less than 1% of the test-tube levels that showed antiviral effects. A study was begun with much higher intravenous doses of hypericin but was stopped quickly because of liver toxicity and light-sensitive skin rashes. A "natural" concentrate, administered orally, has been developed, but data are sketchy. Hypericin clearly requires further study.

### ECHINACEA AND OTHER IMMUNE SYSTEM STIMULANTS

Several natural products stimulate the immune system, such as echinacea, Viscum album or mistletoe, goldenseal, shiitake mushrooms, acemannen or aloe, and garlic. While each product has a theoretical basis for boosting CD4+ counts, these stimulants require further research in people with HIV. The

complexities of the interactions between HIV and the immune system are so great that the idea of "stimulating the immune system" is clearly an over-simplification. A stimulus to CD4+ cells might help the body or might lead to increased viral replication. Boosting some of the immune system's chemical messengers (cytokines) may help the body, while boosting others may lead to disease progression. As a result, immune-stimulating herbs have become controversial in HIV therapy, and some experts advise against them.

Similarly, if substances like garlic and pau d'arco contain "natural" antibiotics and antifungals, there are still considerations about changing the balance of the body's normal "flora" (the natural balance of bacteria and fungi) as well as the possibility of developing resistance as with standard treatments for HIV. Clinical trials are in progress for some of these products, which should help answer some of these questions.

### CURCUMIN

Curcumin is one of the elements in tumeric, a spice used to make curry. Along with several other compounds, it slows HIV replication in test tubes. Results of trials in humans are pending, but the appeal is great because of curcumin's low price and easy availability.

### SHARK CARTILAGE

The soft bones of sharks contain natural antibiotics and other substances that may slow the growth of a tumor's new blood-vessel formation (an angiogenesis inhibitor). Because shark cartilage smells foul, is difficult to take orally, causes nausea, and is poorly absorbed in the stomach, it is usually administered as a retention enema. It has been studied in small numbers of people and was shown to be effective in a few cases.

### BLUE-GREEN ALGAE

Blue-green algae grows wild on the surface of an Oregon lake and is sold as an amino acid and mineral-rich nutrient. It is claimed to be a tonic that can energize both the body and the mind. People report increased energy on this supplement, and in the early days of high AZT doses it seemed to help some people avoid AZT-induced anemia. Researchers at the National Cancer Institute found certain substances (sulfolipids) from other algae species that inhibit HIV in the test tube, but this result has not been found with blue-green algae.

### KOMBUCHA

Kombucha is a living, growing colony of fungal and bacterial elements also known as the Manchurian mushroom. Rapid growth in kombucha's popularity resulted from early positive press and because it is readily available. It is brewed and taken as a tea, with supposed immune-enhancing and antibi-

otic properties. There are a few dramatic stories of improvement in HIV illness, and frequent reports of increased energy and mental clarity. A concern of some specialists is that other potentially disease-causing germs, such as the mold aspergillus, may also be growing in the brew. In addition, if it does contain antibiotic substances, there is concern over the development of resistance. Individuals with low CD4+ counts should be wary and discuss taking this treatment with their physician.

### LICORICE

Licorice root has long been used as an anti-inflammatory treatment, and also as a tonic and treatment for low blood pressure. It is used in many Chinese herbal mixtures, while in Japan, glycyrrhizin, the extract from the root, is used as an intravenous pharmaceutical with documented effectiveness against hepatitis B. Most of the research done with licorice has come from Japan. In a handful of small studies it has shown benefit in HIV infection with decreases in fatigue and light-headedness and small lab improvements. It showed particular value for people with liver problems. Side effects include high blood pressure, fluid retention, and cardiac problems.

## PHYSICAL AGENTS

A variety of therapies have been tried against HIV that are best described as physical agents. For instance, blood has been exposed outside the body to certain wavelengths of light and to heat. People have tried hyperbaric chambers (used to treat the bends in scuba divers) and heating the body or the blood. So far these and other methods have not shown any consistent scientific value, but several are popular in certain alternative-therapy circles.

### DNCB

DNCB, di-nitrochlorobenzene, is a sensitizing chemical used in photography that has been an underground AIDS therapy since the beginning of the epidemic. It was first used as a localized treatment for Kaposi's sarcoma (KS), with individual lesions being painted at regular intervals. After five years its use began to wane because of the lack of consistent results, but recently DNCB has reemerged as an immune-enhancing therapy that is not just for KS. On a weekly basis, people paint DNCB on themselves in a two-to-four-inch patch on their forearm, using a gradually weaker solution as the body's sensitivity increases. It creates a poison-ivy-like reaction varying from an itchy red area to painful blisters like a serious burn. The theory behind DNCB is that it will activate the immune system to fight HIV. There have been some bad rashes from DNCB, and no hard data support its use.

**OZONE**

Ozone is an unstable form of oxygen that is commercially used to kill bacteria. In theory it works because high oxygen levels are toxic to many microbes. Thus a belief developed that ozone might kill HIV. Ozone is administered intravenously, rectally, and through ex-vivo infusion (blood is drawn from the body, mixed with ozone, and then reinfused) in people with HIV. The obvious flaw in this theory is that 99% of HIV in the body is not in the blood but tucked away in the lymph nodes, inside cells, and in other organs. While no good data support its use, ozone therapy has strong supporters, and people travel far and spend large sums of money to try it.

**HYPERTHERMIA**

There is a belief in "natural" healing that fever is the body's way to fight infection. Before the discovery of antibiotics, syphilis was treated by giving a patient malaria to induce high fevers. In the late 1980s, several reports concluded that hyperthermia (heating of the blood) as a treatment for HIV had no value, and its use was not allowed in the United States. As a result, clinics were set up outside the United States where several people died from the treatment. Hyperthermia treatment centers still exist, but no clear, documented data support the use of this therapy in HIV. Scientifically, it faces the same objection as ozone therapy—only a tiny and insignificant amount of the overall HIV viral load exists as free virus in the blood. Most of the HIV is incorporated inside cells or body tissue, where such treatments are unlikely to have any effect.

# HOMEOPATHY

Homeopathy is an approach to healing that is popular in Europe and has many followers in the United States. It has been used by people living with HIV because it is nontoxic. Homeopathy is diametrically opposed to Western medicine. In Western medicine, disease is usually attacked head-on—specific antibiotics kill specific bacteria. Homeopathic approaches try to treat "like with like." Homeopaths seek to find substances that cause the symptoms to be treated and administer them to the patient in a diluted form. This approach is intended to stimulate the body's own internal healing mechanisms.

Many people living with HIV report significant reduction of their symptoms using homeopathic remedies. A published study in the pediatric literature showed homeopathy effective in treating diarrhea (not HIV-related) in children in Nicaragua. This was the first double-blind study to document the effectiveness of homeopathy. As a result, homeopathy's popularity and this recent research has begun to challenge the medical establishment's bias against homeopathy.

Homeopathic remedies are said to be inactivated by the consumption of alcohol, coffee, certain foods, and drugs. If an individual decides to use homeopathy, he or she should work closely with an experienced HIV practitioner, so that drugs of clearly proven value are not eliminated.

## HANDS-ON THERAPIES

Touch was among the earliest healing humans did for one another. Infants experience the healing, soothing value of their mother's or father's touch. Studies have shown how much better premature babies do if they are regularly held and not just left in incubators. It is natural that touch has come to be an important aspect of AIDS treatment.

### MASSAGE

In many locales, massage programs are available to people with HIV and AIDS. Massage provides muscle relaxation, improved circulation of blood and lymphatics, comfort, and a heightened sense of well-being. It has also helped with the edema associated with Kaposi's sarcoma. Massage may affect people in a deep and personal way. During a session an individual's attention is directed inward, where he or she may discover stress or other areas of inner discomfort. For some individuals, massage provides the unique experience of being touched again after developing an "untouchable" disease. Emotional issues of isolation, loss, loneliness, guilt, and shame may emerge and be dealt with during massage.

### CHIROPRACTIC

Chiropractic offers similar benefits to massage through a different model of body healing. Many people believe that its emphasis on spinal manipulation and alignment helps with structural problems and pains. While it is not a specific HIV therapy, some people use it as a general approach to improved well-being.

## OTHER PHYSICAL THERAPIES

Therapeutic touch is a popular therapy included in some nurses' training. Healing is promoted by the application of gentle touch, which theoretically "moves energy" through the body. Reiki is a similar technique. These techniques offer touch, comfort, and support, and many people feel helped by them. To date there is little scientific data on any of these approaches regarding HIV, but generally people show an improvement in quality of life, rather than longevity.

## PSYCHOTHERAPY, SPIRITUAL, AND METAPHYSICAL APPROACHES

HIV-positive individuals are challenged by emotional and spiritual issues from the time they first learn of the infection. These challenges include dealing with a life-threatening disease, as well as the ongoing issues in life itself: career, love, family, sexuality, relationships, and self-esteem. People living with HIV compress decades of emotional and spiritual issues into a few short months or years. As a result, many individuals report that counseling has resulted in significant psychological benefits.

Much of the work to improve the quality of life of the HIV-positive individual has been done in the spiritual realm. Many churches and temples have stepped forward to offer support, love, and service. The books and tapes of Ram Dass (*Be Here Now* and *The Only Dance There Is*), Stephen Levine (*Who Dies*), Elizabeth Kubler-Ross (*On Death and Dying*), Gerald Jampolsky (*Love Is Letting Go of Fear*), Bernie Siegel (*Love, Medicine and Miracles*), and others have been widely read in the AIDS community. These authors attempt to offer individuals answers in their search for inner peace and deeper meaning. While these approaches provide greater peace through understanding and faith, their effect on the immune system awaits further study.

### MEDITATION

Meditation is the practice of focusing and quieting the mind, by remaining in a state of inner awareness. It is a crucial component of many Eastern spiritual paths. Some people living with HIV use meditation or other relaxation exercises as the beginning of their work with imagery and healing visualizations. Creating inner pictures that are focused on healing, such as imagining stronger and more numerous CD4+ cells, or rashes disappearing, may be a way the mind can assist the body in healing. Work with people with cancer has suggested such imagery has definite value. For example, people with cancer have learned to imagine that their tumors are shrinking, or that their cancer cells are being eaten up Pac-Man–style by their immune cells. They visualize their bodies growing stronger, and their immune systems winning out over the disease.

At a minimum these positive images help create a more positive attitude. Researchers in psychoneuroimmunology are currently trying to confirm a physiological benefit from visualization.

## CONCLUSIONS

An individual considering alternative treatments should consider several basic principles:

- Create Your Own Program. No one can do everything. Decide what works for you in conjunction with your primary care physician and follow through. Avoid treatment envy. ("Look what he's doing, I want to try it.") Avoid treatment bashing. ("It didn't work for me, so why are you wasting your time?")

- Work with Your Physician. Develop a trusting, mutually respectful, collaborative relationship with an HIV-experienced health care professional. Review your plans and revisions together on a regular basis.

- Watch Out for the Red Flags of Fraud. Beware of treatments with remarkable claims such as a "cure" or promotions like "it's only available outside the country," its contents are "secret," "it heals many different things like AIDS, cancer, aging, and arthritis," "there is only one source for this treatment," and "there is a conspiracy to suppress this therapy." Be a cautious, educated consumer. (See the next chapter, "How to Avoid Fraud and Exploitation.")

- Do Not Limit Yourself to One Therapy. One treatment approach need not automatically exclude another (unless you're in a clinical trial with certain restrictions). Some physicians without knowledge of an alternative modality may discourage its use simply because it is unfamiliar to them. An alternative practitioner might downplay the value of standard medical care as not holistic or discourage medications as toxic or unnatural. Question a practitioner in any field who tells you, "For this to work you have to stop all your other therapies." Many individuals combine very different modalities into an optimal health plan. Get the information you need to make an informed decision about what works best for you.

- Keep Hope Alive. Years ago AIDS activist Michael Callen described the one common link in the long-term survivors he had interviewed: hope. Now, with expanding knowledge of how the virus causes disease, with new tools to measure disease progression, and new treatments from standard and alternative practices, there is, indeed, much to be truly hopeful about. Similarly, Project Inform has stated for years that "hope is the most potent therapy for HIV disease, and false hopelessness and despair are the most destructive pathogens."

# How to Avoid Fraud and Exploitation

**BY MARTIN DELANEY**

AIDS, like some forms of cancer, is a disease that is seen as having no known cure. At best, standard treatments for AIDS are a mixed bag, each having a variety of pros and cons. In the cancer world, a thriving underground exists offering "cures" and treatments based on unproven (often disproven) and conflicting theories, with many promising "miraculous" improvements beyond the power of standard treatments (and often with the promise of few or no side effects).

In AIDS, at least two types of "underground" networks have evolved. One is the familiar turf of the "buyers' clubs," community-based groups that strive to improve access to legitimately promising treatments and reduce their cost. But a second underground exists that offers many kinds of treatments and "cures" with little or no scientific basis. The Project Inform Treatment Hotline receives a steady stream of calls about mysterious treatments that don't have or invite FDA evaluation or scientific validation, but that are nonetheless being promoted to the public with claims of efficacy. Over the years, Project Inform has examined hundreds of such products and claims, ranging from genuinely interesting new approaches to mystery formulas purportedly delivered from the flight decks of flying saucers.

Assessing these claims, separating the plausible from the truly crazy, is more difficult than it might sound. Almost all of them offer some form of evidence and some satisfied users (typically people with AIDS who are convinced they have benefited). There is little point in arguing with people who report increases in their CD4+ counts, who "feel much better," or who "recovered miraculously" and truly believe that their latest treatment discovery is directly responsible for their newly felt well-being. The last thing they want to hear is someone, least of all a treatment advocacy group like Project Inform, questioning their experience.

Ideally, some authoritative and unbiased agency would examine all these purported treatments and their practitioners. California and several other states have established AIDS fraud task forces in an effort to address this issue. The Food and Drug Administration already has the authority to control the sale of products and the claims made about them, and several state and local agencies

---

*MARTIN DELANEY IS FOUNDING DIRECTOR OF PROJECT INFORM. THIS ARTICLE FIRST APPEARED IN THE PI PERSPECTIVE.*

have varying degrees of responsibility in this area as well. Information sources, such as Project Inform, try to offer some consumer guidance since we are often the first to learn of these new therapies and promotions. Once in a rare while, some obvious charlatan is arrested or sued. But in recent years, promotions of fraudulent treatments have grown considerably, perhaps because standard treatments have failed to cure the disease. Unfortunately, many people assume that if a particular product is on the store shelves, it must have some legitimate use. In fact, consumers should always be on guard and learn as much as they can on their own about the medications and treatments they choose, because regulatory resources are spread thin.

Evaluating potential treatments is not easy. If it were, there would be little need for complicated and expensive clinical trials. Even among treatments in FDA-approved clinical trials, researchers differ greatly about what's promising and what isn't. But, in dealing with claimed "cures-of-the-week," judgments are sometimes easier to make, since precise evaluations aren't necessary. Often, all that's needed is a general determination of whether or not something has a rational and responsible basis. What follows is a short guide to the kinds of evidence that count, and don't count, in evaluating such treatments, as well as a guide to the warning signs of possible AIDS fraud.

## WARNING SIGNS

Some forms of evidence offered on behalf of a new treatment are almost always considered questionable, if not misleading. When these are the principal kinds of evidence offered on behalf of a treatment, it is a sign that something is wrong or at least warrants caution and more careful examination.

### TESTIMONIAL EVIDENCE

The most common form of questionable promotion comes in the form of personal testimony from people who are not scientifically trained. Personal testimony is indeed seductive. It's always impressive to hear from a real person that a treatment has been successful. If it worked for him or her, why not me? But personal reports of success, which is often fleeting, unfortunately don't provide reproducible evidence. No matter how unlikely, unscientific, or transparently mercenary a new treatment may be, there will always be true believers who are evangelical, often innocently so, in their enthusiasm for it.

How is it possible that well-meaning people might believe a product is benefiting them if the treatments are not really effective? There are some obvious, and some subtle, reasons why almost everything seems to work for somebody. One is the power of positive thinking. People in clinical trials who think they're getting a toxic drug often experience the known side effects of the drug, even though they are receiving a placebo. Likewise, people who think they're getting a beneficial drug often get better, at least for a while, even

though the drug may later be proven to have no overall effect. These are not imaginary events—the people involved often experience measurable, objective changes. But they are not always due to the treatment. The so-called placebo effect is very real. Because it is such a powerful force, elaborate procedures are used in clinical trials to separate it from the genuine effects of treatment. This is not to say that placebo effects are unreal or happen only in the mind, but that such effects must be distinguished from proven drug effects if we are to effectively determine the value of any particular therapy.

Sometimes, perceived benefits are also proportional to the cost of claimed treatment. The higher the price paid or the more difficult the pursuit, the better the perceived response—at least for a while. People who have made a big investment, emotionally or financially, in a purported treatment may, at a minimum, feel increased energy and well-being. They also have a proportionally larger need to justify their investment.

Some perceived treatment benefits may be a result of pure chance. No one fully understands or can predict the "natural course" of HIV disease. In treated and untreated people, CD4+ levels rise and fall, symptoms come and go, and there are long periods of stabilization as well as periods of precipitous decline, all without any obvious and visible explanation or cause. Simply put, HIV infection is a highly variable condition. People who lack broad experience in AIDS often think a miracle has occurred the first time they give a patient their magic elixir and some lab values improve or the person goes on to live a normal life—for a while. To them, the results seem obviously attributable to the treatment. To someone new to AIDS—patient or practitioner—simple stabilization of disease often looks like a breakthrough because many people expect HIV infection to be a state of constant, obvious decline leading to death. As any long-term HIV veteran will confirm, this is rarely the case.

Another source of confusion for people with HIV disease is that even if a treatment doesn't do what is claimed, it might do "something." Therapies containing vitamins, herbs, or food supplements, while not necessarily having any special anti-HIV effect, might remedy other common deficiencies in some people. It's a hit-or-miss process, of course, unless specific medical needs are first diagnosed, but there is no question that many auxiliary or "complementary" therapies can produce beneficial effects. But treatment of symptoms or a generalized feeling of well-being should not be mistaken as a cure for HIV infection.

### EMOTIONAL APPEALS

A second inadequate approach for judging the value of a proposed treatment is the sincerity or presentation skills of the person promoting it. Few outright con artists are working in AIDS, and almost all practitioners believe

fervently in their own products and solutions. However, without the rigorous discipline of clinical research studies, it is far too easy for promoters to fall into the trap of focusing their attention on any result that can be interpreted as positive while overlooking or dismissing any or all evidence to the contrary. Their sincerity isn't in question, only the value of the product and their objectivity in evaluating it. It's even quite common for promoters to act and sound more sincere than well-trained physicians and researchers, largely because they are willing to make greater promises of success and thus inspire greater hope, while the true researcher is bound by more realistic expectations and the FDA.

### UNVERIFIABLE DATA

A common source of misinformation is the use of studies or proposed studies in developing countries or other locations where the data cannot be verified. It is no fault of doctors in Africa, Latin America, or the Caribbean that they may not have the same medical resources available to them as researchers in developed nations. And, it is entirely possible that serious research can be done in these places. But all too often, so-called "studies" reported from such locations are just treatment observations collected under uncontrolled conditions, with inferior laboratory facilities. Not surprisingly, many of these efforts are sponsored by entrepreneurs from developed countries who are more concerned about promoting products (and making a profit) than seriously evaluating them. Such people aggressively promote their wares and theories to impoverished third-world medical practitioners, governments, and patients after they have been booted out of the developed nations. These third-world nations are sometimes quick to work with such offers simply because they bring some degree of medical support and funding as a side benefit. The track record of medical research in developing countries is not good, and such research has not led to any promising HIV treatments now under study in developed countries. In most developed countries, research must meet more rigid standards, making it harder for promoters to make false claims with dubious data.

## THE RED FLAGS OF MEDICAL FRAUD

The need to guard against medical fraud and misinformation is particularly important for people with HIV and AIDS because the consequences of mistakes can be so great. A wrong turn while fighting HIV disease can be an unforgiving and sometimes fatal error. Consider some of the following warning signs that hint at the presence of questionable treatments or practitioners.

### EXORBITANT PRICES/EXORBITANT CLAIMS

Charging exorbitant prices for a treatment that has not been proven effective by serious scientific study is always suspect. Legitimate research

studies generally are free to volunteers, and most ethical physicians do not charge participants for wholly unproven therapies. There are some exceptions. Occasionally, an unavoidably expensive but legitimately promising therapy might be made available by some doctors before trials are completed. At the very least, there should always be a rational explanation of any high costs. In general, the more a treatment costs, the more evidence one should demand in advance.

Similarly, a promoter who makes exorbitant claims for a product should be approached with great skepticism. Claims that a product "makes patients go negative on the HIV test," "cures" anything, or "greatly strengthens the immune system" in nonspecific ways are all highly suspect. No known treatment has been shown to do any of these things. Often, lurking behind such claims are misunderstandings or misstatements about HIV and the diagnostic tests used to measure its progress.

### LACK OF SUPPORTING EVIDENCE

People with AIDS have few opportunities to recover from medical mistakes and must learn to demand as much information as possible about any new treatment. This is especially true if the promoter of the treatment is asking the person to step outside the boundaries of approved medical practice. This doesn't mean that everything "unapproved" is necessarily bad, but only that when people cross the line away from "approved" therapies, they need to assume a defensive and careful posture, since the normal protections from fraud and error no longer apply.

Anyone promoting an unknown remedy should be prepared to demonstrate a solid body of evidence as to how and why it works, and what the user can reasonably expect. In this sense, any product that has not previously been tested in well-designed clinical trials and is being promoted as "treatment" rather than research is automatically suspect. If there are no legitimate, verifiable clinical trials of a product, or a sound body of laboratory or animal data, it's good to start asking tough questions (or head for the exit sign). When confronted with questions, fraudulent promoters have been using the same excuses for decades, including:

*"We don't have the resources to do research."*

*"We're too busy saving lives, so we don't have time to collect data."*

*"The medical system (or the AMA or the NIH, or the government) is totally biased against us."*

*"We can't follow up with data collection because our patients all get well and don't come back."*

*"We don't need studies—it's obvious it works. Just look at the testimonials."*

*"Do you want studies or do you want to live?"*

*"There are dozens of studies. You'll just have to look them up yourself.
But if we don't get started now, you'll lose your chance."*

### UNIVERSAL CLAIMS

In general, claims of multidisease efficacy are almost always a warning
sign. For instance, any claim that a treatment works both for AIDS and various kinds of cancer should automatically be suspect. Although it is sometimes
true that a drug or treatment is found to have value in treating two or more
diseases, claims of outright cure for utterly different diseases make no sense.
Simplistic-sounding, unconventional theories of AIDS, medicine, or biology
are often used to explain why the same treatments will work for radically
different diseases. These claims are seldom more than the product of market-
ing—not medical—skill.

### THE WRONG CREDENTIALS

A promoter or practitioner claiming an HIV remedy but whose area of spe-
cialization is far removed from AIDS should generally be suspect. The average cardiologist or radiologist didn't learn about AIDS in medical school. Practitioners without previous achievements or a degree in the field of medicine
are extremely unlikely to unravel the complexities of HIV disease. Every month,
Project Inform receives packages sent by electricians, physicists, inventors,
spiritualists, crystal healers—even flying saucer contactees—outlining miracle
"cures." The "cures" make sense to their promoters only because they know
so little about AIDS and medical research. Many of them live in worlds and
systems of their own making.

Similarly, promoters who cite articles in unrelated or obscure publications
or research performed at obscure institutions should be suspect. Vitamin maga-
zines, physics journals, or medical journals no one has ever heard of, whatever their virtues, have no established expertise in HIV research questions.
References to institutions or research centers with impressive titles that can't
be verified should set off alarm bells.

### THE BIG SECRET

Question any practitioner who insists on keeping secrets or who insists that
patients keep secret any aspect of a claimed treatment program. There is no
legitimate reason why people shouldn't be told exactly what they'll be getting
and how it's supposed to treat HIV. In fact, this is a legal requirement. Concern
about patent protection is sometimes claimed as a reason for secrecy, but it is
a false one.

### FOREIGN LOCATIONS

Promoters offering treatments that require travel to foreign countries should
be suspect. Legitimate studies in other countries are usually filled by local

people; people attempting to enroll in an overseas trial should be wary if the treatment in question isn't being studied in the United States. Moreover, promising and legitimate treatments approved or under study overseas can often be imported for personal use; generally, what's being studied seriously in any other country is also being studied in your own. There is no reason to believe that high-priced treatments from Switzerland, Germany, or Peru are any more promising than the myriad of magical "cures" offered here. Every country has its share of snake-oil dispensers. Over the years, Project Inform has received dozens of reports from people who were persuaded to go overseas for costly treatments. Sometimes, they were even given falsified lab reports claiming success, only to see their lab values mysteriously collapse again when their doctor at home repeated the tests.

## USE COMMON SENSE AS A GUIDE

The most important thing to keep in mind for someone seeking treatment is to use common sense. People with HIV disease often feel desperate and feel they have little to lose, but a moment's clear thought should reveal that someone who wants to infuse you in Tijuana with an expensive, mysterious, and vaguely defined substance has probably not solved the great medical puzzle of our time. There is indeed a lot to lose when people go from one questionable treatment to another; it's a lot like playing the lottery (but with even less chance of winning).

The saddest and most dangerous thing about cures-of-the-week, however, is not the money they extract from vulnerable people or the shattered sense of hope when they fail: it's the harm they do to people who could benefit from other readily available treatments but who let their precious time run out pursuing fly-by-night cures. All too often the fraudulent practitioner does everything possible not only to sell his or her own product, but to dissuade individuals from the use of conventional, better-proven medical approaches. When people abandon their regular medications to try a treatment that has virtually no chance of benefiting anyone, they're risking an irreversible decline. Some people feel they've exhausted everything that can be done with standard anti-HIV medication, but far more, in a futile search for home-run drugs, neglect the currently available options and the limited but useful benefits they bring.

Unfortunately, there is no "cure" for AIDS now, only maintenance and preventive treatments and combinations that buy time until a cure can be found. In the meantime, the cures-of-the-week will keep coming over the hills in waves, beyond anybody's capacity to keep track of them. People will continue to go running to Mexico, Bavaria, and to shady practitioners all over America, lured by the promise of miracles. Money can be the least important thing to be lost.

# CLINICAL TRIALS AND EXPERIMENTAL THERAPIES

**BY STEVEN G. DEEKS, MD AND PAUL A. VOLBERDING, MD**

## INTRODUCTION

In the early 1980s, the medical and scientific communities were not prepared to tackle the unexpected AIDS epidemic. The slow, methodical path that experimental therapies went through from initial conception to final approval was clearly inadequate. Efforts of community groups, such as Project Inform, led to significant changes in the way clinical research is performed. Still, as the second decade of the epidemic unfolds, many aspects of clinical trials, such as the use of placebos in some studies, remain a part of good clinical research. They also remain a source of confusion, frustration, and at times, anger among people living with HIV.

What is a clinical trial? How do you get into a trial? What are the pros and cons of volunteering to be a research subject? These are some of the questions about clinical research that are answered in the following pages. This information should allow you to make a more informed decision regarding clinical trial participation.

## WHAT IS A CLINICAL TRIAL?

A clinical trial is a study conducted with volunteers. Clinical trials usually involve the testing of a new drug, but they may study a new treatment strategy or even a new diagnostic test. The primary purpose of most studies is to determine if a new medication is safe and/or effective.

Before being researched in humans, most experimental approaches first undergo extensive studies in the laboratory and in animals. If a therapeutic approach shows promise, it then enters clinical trials, where the new therapy is studied in humans. Initial studies are designed to determine if it is safe and well-tolerated. Later studies are designed to determine if the therapy is effective. For every drug that makes it through the approval process, thousands of others are tested and rejected along the way.

## WHAT TYPES OF CLINICAL TRIALS ARE THERE?

In general, there are three types of clinical trials, referred to as Phase I, II, and III. Phase I trials are designed to determine if a drug is well tolerated (i.e., safe) and what concentrations of the drug are typically achieved in blood (that is, the drug's pharmacokinetics). During Phase I trials, humans are of-

ten exposed to the experimental therapy for the first time. These trials are usually small (fewer than twenty to thirty people), short (two to four weeks) and intense (requiring frequent visits and blood draws). Phase I studies often look at a number of doses of a new drug, trying to identify the minimum effective dose as well as the maximum tolerated dose. In these types of trials, the chances of receiving the "optimal" dose of a drug is slim, yet some studies will offer what is determined to be an "optimal" dose of the drug to trial participants once the study is over. When participating in a Phase I study, individuals should weigh the potential risks of receiving a suboptimal dose (e.g., the development of resistance to the particular drug or class of drug) to the potential benefits of gaining early access to a new therapeutic approach. In later phases of drug testing there is more information about the potential for a therapy to be beneficial as well as more information about possible side effects of a therapy. The approach being studied may turn out to have no beneficial effects, it may be discovered that it is harmful or it might be the next wonder drug. Participating in a Phase I study typically involves more risk-taking by an individual, with little to no information on the effect of the drug in humans.

If a drug proves to be reasonably well tolerated, it then moves into Phase II trials. Although highly variable, these trials typically last three to twelve months and involve one hundred to two hundred people. Phase II trials are designed to determine if the new drug is well tolerated over longer periods of time. They are also designed to gather information on the effectiveness of a new therapy. For example, in trials involving new antiretroviral therapies, Phase II trials may look for evidence that the new drug reduces the amount of HIV in the blood (the viral load) or increases the CD4+ (or T-helper) cell count. Information about the side effects of a drug and preliminary information about a drug's impact on viral load or CD4+ cell counts will often be available to people considering participation in a Phase II study. Moreover, Phase II trials often study two different doses of a drug, both of which are believed to have activity. The chances of receiving a potentially beneficial dose of a drug is much greater in a Phase II study compared to Phase I studies. Participation in a Phase II study still involves risks, although less than in Phase I studies. It may be discovered that a drug has longer-term side effects than what was observed in shorter Phase I studies. Conversely, it may be shown that longer-term use of the drug in question results in greater and more prolonged impact on health markers.

A drug that continues to show promise after Phase II moves into Phase III clinical trials. These trials are very large (sometimes over a thousand people) and may last one to three years or longer. They are designed to prove that a new therapy is as effective or more effective than the standard therapy. Drugs that successfully complete Phase III testing are then reviewed by the FDA for

final approval. While not free of risk, Phase III studies are probably the least risky studies to participate in and the least time intensive in terms of the number of required visits to a research site. Typically in Phase III studies, participants can receive information about a drug's side effects and potential benefits and they are most likely to receive an active dose of the study drug. Even still, in the history of drug development, therapies which were believed to be beneficial based on Phase I and II studies have proved to be harmful when in the larger Phase III studies. Even after a drug receives approval by the FDA, it may still be studied in large clinical trials, called post-marketing studies. These trials often involve several thousand volunteers and typically compare different treatment strategies or regimens to see if one approach produces greater benefit than another.

## WHO RUNS THE CLINICAL TRIAL?

Most trials take place at specialized research centers, such as a university clinic. However, some trials, particularly Phase III trials, may take place in private doctors' offices. Each research site has a "principal investigator" who is ultimately responsible for overseeing the study. Before volunteering for a clinical trial, try to meet one-on-one with the principal investigator. In reality, the person you will get to know best is often the research nurse. He or she coordinates the day-to-day administration of the trial and is often the person whom you will first contact. The research nurse also provides support and continuity of care to people enrolled in trials.

Beware of clinical trials that take place in resort locations and/or charge individuals to participate. Nearly all clinical trials in HIV do not charge individuals to participate. On the contrary, some trials pay participants or reimburse for transportation and/or child care. If a trial pays for participation, often, although not always, this may be a signal that a volunteer is being asked to assume some greater risk or discomfort. Therefore, if a trial pays participants, take extra care to gather information about the potential risks of the approach being studied as well as what is required of trial participants.

## WHAT ARE THE PROS OF CLINICAL TRIALS?

There are many reasons to enroll in a clinical trial. Often clinical trials are the only way to gain access to promising new drugs early in their development. Clinical trials may be an affordable way to receive prohibitively expensive drugs or diagnostic testing. They are also a good resource for learning more about HIV and other approaches to treatment. In general, clinical trials provide medication, checkups, and laboratory work at no cost to the participants. However, for reasons outlined below, many clinical trials do not guarantee that you will receive the new therapy.

The most important reason to consider clinical trials is to help other people living with HIV. In the past decade, significant progress has been made in the fight against HIV, largely because of the efforts of countless HIV-positive individuals who have volunteered for clinical trials. Currently, many promising new drugs are in development. Only through rapid testing in well-designed clinical trials will these drugs be able to move forward toward approval.

## WHAT ARE THE CONS OF CLINICAL TRIALS?

Volunteering for a clinical trial requires significant sacrifices. Studies sometimes require frequent visits to the study center, with schedules that are more strict than those of primary care providers. Invasive testing may be required, ranging from frequent blood draws to bone marrow biopsies. The new therapy may prove to have significant and unexpected toxicities, with side effects that may outweigh any potential benefit. Indeed, there is always a chance that the experimental therapy may not work or may even hurt you. Clinical trials tend to have strict guidelines, limiting access to other experimental therapies. Sometimes, they even limit your ability to participate in future trials. There's also the possibility that you will be receiving a placebo rather than the new treatment, or perhaps a dose of the new treatment that's too low or too high. Finally, by taking a new drug daily, and by making frequent visits to an AIDS research center, many otherwise healthy people find that they now have constant reminders of their disease.

Not all clinical trials are well-designed or ethical. In HIV disease, clinical trials have moved forward despite information suggesting one treatment arm of a study was superior to another. Last year results from a large study showed that people receiving triple-drug therapy lived longer than those receiving therapy with a two-drug regimen of AZT + 3TC. Despite preliminary information that the three-drug regimen containing a potent protease inhibitor was more effective, a significant number of people were left on the two-drug regimen to progress in their disease and die for the sake of the study. Not all clinical trials are equal and therefore it is important that independent sources of information are sought out about the clinical trial and the regimens being studied prior to participating in research.

## WHO CAN JOIN CLINICAL TRIALS?

Clinical trials are typically open to anyone, as long as the individual meets certain eligibility requirements. These requirements vary from trial to trial. In general, potential research subjects must be relatively healthy and able to comply with the demands of being in a trial. The ability to understand the clinical trial and give informed consent (see below) is also required. Many trials have specific participation requirements based on CD4+ cell counts or viral load levels.

## ARE TRIALS OPEN TO WOMEN AND CHILDREN?

Since most therapies will be given to women and men, it is important that women enroll in clinical trials. Unfortunately, in the past women have been discriminated against in clinical research, mainly due to pregnancy-related concerns. This was done to protect the fetus from potentially harmful new drugs. These strict regulations are gradually changing. Most clinical trials today actively encourage women to enroll, as long as they are not pregnant or nursing. Adequate birth control is almost always required both for men and women.

Because children are very different from adults, most therapies need to be tested separately in children. Therefore, completely independent clinical trials are made available for children infected with HIV. A child's parent or guardian must provide informed consent before a child can enroll in a trial.

## WHY DO TRIALS EXCLUDE SO MANY PEOPLE?

The exclusionary nature of many clinical trials is one of the more controversial areas in HIV-related research today. It is also the source of tremendous frustration for many people who have been willing to enter trials, only to be rejected because their CD4+ cell count is too high or too low, or because they have taken AZT or some other drug in the past.

Because of the cost of clinical research and the urgency surrounding new HIV therapies, researchers design trials so that questions can be answered as quickly as possible. This often requires that a specific population be studied.

Prior to receiving full FDA approval, novel anti-HIV drugs) must demonstrate that they either delay disease progression or prolong survival. If these drugs were to be studied in people with CD4+ counts greater than 500, it would require over five years to demonstrate effectiveness. Currently, the quickest way to study these types of therapies is in people with lower CD4+ counts, thereby excluding a large number of people.

Likewise, it is difficult to demonstrate the effectiveness of a new drug in people who have had extensive exposure to similar drugs in the past. These people may be less sensitive to newer therapies, thereby raising the chance that a truly effective new drug may not be approved. For this reason, trials involving protease inhibitors (and other novel anti-HIV drugs) exclude people who have been extensively treated with drugs such as zidovudine (AZT), didanosine (ddI), or zalcitabine (ddC). These strict eligibility requirements are currently being reevaluated by researchers and will hopefully become less of a barrier in the future.

## WHY ARE PLACEBOS SOMETIMES GIVEN IN TRIALS?

The AIDS epidemic has seen many promising new therapies that later fail to demonstrate effectiveness in larger numbers of people. Part of the problem

is the unpredictable nature of HIV disease. For unclear reasons, some HIV-positive individuals become progressively more ill, while others remain stable and some even appear to improve spontaneously.

For these reasons, it is often difficult to demonstrate effectiveness of a new therapy. Scientifically, the best way to do this is to compare a new treatment with a placebo, or a "sugar pill." Placebos are pills that are designed to look like and taste like a new drug, but have no therapeutic value. By comparing the new drug with the placebo, researchers hope to prove that a drug is effective and safe.

In AIDS research, placebos are used less frequently now because most HIV-related problems have an effective therapeutic regimen. If an approved therapy is available, then researchers will compare the new therapy to the standard one. Placebos are therefore not needed. However, sometimes placebos are used in addition to standard therapy. In these trials everyone will receive standard therapy in combination with either a new treatment or a placebo. This ensures that everyone will receive treatment and provides a way to get information about a new therapy.

## WHY ARE CLINICAL TRIALS "BLINDED" AND "RANDOMIZED"?

Researchers and participants are naturally biased; it's part of human nature. When a new therapy is available, everyone has high hopes that it will prove to be more effective than standard therapies. This bias toward the new drug can be powerful and may lead to false conclusions that a new therapy is indeed effective. To avoid this, study participants and researchers remain "blinded" to which therapy is being given. This means that neither the researchers nor the patients know what drug is being given on an individual basis.

The decision as to who receives the experimental therapy and who receives the placebo or standard therapy is made by a computer in a process referred to as randomization. In this way, everyone in a clinical trial has the same chance of receiving the experimental therapy. The "double-blinded, randomized" aspect of clinical research can be frustrating for patients and caregivers, but it remains a critical component of most trials.

## WHAT IS INFORMED CONSENT? WHO PROTECTS MY RIGHTS?

Clinical research is tightly regulated. Before initiating a clinical trial, researchers must first obtain approval from a Committee on Human Research (CHR). This committee is also sometimes referred to as the Institutional Research Board (IRB). The CHR is an independent board whose sole mission is to protect your rights as a research subject. The FDA also regulates each clinical trial.

One of the most important responsibilities of the CHR is to review the consent form that you will sign. This form must discuss in detail all aspects of the trial, particularly side effects. It should also inform you of your alternatives to participation (e.g., other drugs used to treat similar conditions), warn you of potential drug interactions between the study drug and other commonly used medications, and explain what will be required of you during the research (e.g., frequency of visits to the research facility and required procedures—such as blood work or invasive procedures). Before joining a study, you should read and understand this form completely. This process is referred to as giving informed consent. As a research subject, you always have the right to withdraw your consent, which means you can drop out of any study at any time. The name and phone number of a contact person from the CHR or IRB will be listed in the informed consent. If you have any questions about the study that you feel are not being fully addressed by the principal investigator or study nurse, you should feel free to call the CHR/IRB contact person. Moreover, it is a good idea to discuss the study and the consent form with a health care provider who is not associated with the study. *Remember, you have the right to withdraw from a clinical trial at any time and for any reason.*

## WHAT ARE MY RESPONSIBILITIES AS A SUBJECT?

Enrolling in a clinical trial is a significant commitment. You should expect to stay in the trial for the entire period (if possible), agree to inform the researchers of all medications you are taking, and take the study medications as prescribed. You need to understand that if you do not comply with the study requirements, you might weaken the quality of the data and slow down final approval of potentially beneficial therapies. Because studies will sometimes exclude the use of other medications, it may be difficult for an individual to participate in a trial and optimally manage HIV disease at the same time. Typically, the researchers must justify not allowing the simultaneous use of certain medications. This means that the study drug may be dangerous to use with the medication being excluded, or it may mean that use of the other medication will make it difficult to evaluate the effects of the study drug. If you are participating in a study where there are drug exclusions that you do not understand, you may want to talk to the research staff, call the CHR/IRB contact person and/or seek assistance from the Community Advisory Board for the research site if the site has one.

## WHAT ARE THE IMPORTANT QUESTIONS TO ASK BEFORE ENTERING A CLINICAL TRIAL?

Before enrolling in a clinical trial, you need to ask the principal investigator and/or research nurse a series of questions. We recommend writing them

down first and not signing the consent form until you are completely satisfied with the answers. At a minimum, the following questions should be asked:

- What is the prior experience with the drug? What side effects have occurred?
- What are my chances of receiving the drug? If I receive a placebo, will I have access to the drug after the trial is over? For how long?
- How many pills a day will I be asked to take?
- If I become sick, will I be asked to drop out of the study? Will I then have access to the new drug?
- If I become sick from the drug, will I be treated and will my care be paid for by the study?
- When will I be informed if I received the new drug? When will I learn the results of the trial?
- Will enrolling in this trial limit my access to other drugs? How might this affect my participation in future trials?
- What role will my own primary care provider have?
- How often will I have to visit the clinic? How long will each visit be?
- Will I be given the results of laboratory and other diagnostic procedures conducted (e.g., resistance testing, biopsy results, viral load information)? When?
- Are there independent sources of information about the trial or therapy?
- Are there other ways, other than this study, to access the therapy?

## HOW DOES SOMEONE ENROLL IN CLINICAL TRIALS?

If, after considering all the pros and cons, you decide to enroll in a clinical trial, you should first discuss it with your primary care provider. You then need to contact the research nurse. If you appear to qualify, you will be asked to visit the clinic for a screening exam. This will involve a detailed evaluation by a physician, as well as blood tests. If you remain eligible, you may be asked to make one or two more visits before the study begins. Women will often be asked to have urine pregnancy tests periodically. Many studies will ask you to come back after the study is completed, mainly to see if any long-term side effects have developed.

Volunteering to be a research subject can be a challenging decision. Hopefully, the information outlined here will allow you to make a more informed decision. People with AIDS are now living longer, healthier lives, largely due to the clinical trials that have been completed. Still, there may be a long way to go before we have a cure. By volunteering for a clinical trial, you can make significant contributions to this goal.

# EXPANDED ACCESS, COMPASSIONATE USE, PARALLEL TRACK, AND TREATMENT IND

The FDA has approved several mechanisms for distributing experimental drugs before those drugs are approved for general sale. When a promising new drug is intended to treat a life-threatening illness that is not curable by other means, it is important that the drug be made available to patients in need as quickly as possible—often before all the required studies are completed. Programs that make a new drug available to the public prior to its full approval are called expanded access.

The three general mechanisms for expanded access to a promising new drug are: compassionate use, parallel track, and treatment IND. They differ primarily in when they are used in the overall cycle of drug testing and development. All are primarily designed for use with new drugs that treat life-threatening illnesses for which there is no approved cure or completely satisfactory treatment.

### COMPASSIONATE USE

This mechanism can be used to provide a new drug to individuals upon the request of their physicians. In effect, this approach makes each person's use of the drug a kind of clinical study in which the physician must follow a protocol and report results. Compassionate use can be requested at almost any time after a drug has undergone early safety testing. In effect, compassionate use represents a one-time exception for each individual who gets a drug in this fashion. For several reasons, this approach is not widely used and is seldom permitted or recommended by the FDA. In general, it requires a considerable amount of paperwork and effort for each individual case. Perhaps more importantly, researchers believe that little is learned about the efficiency of a drug when used in this fashion; it exposes patients to unknown risks and has little chance of helping them because too little is yet known about how to use the drug.

### PARALLEL TRACK

This mechanism was created in 1990 in response to concerns raised by AIDS advocates. Parallel track does not change or reduce the number of studies required before a drug can be offered for sale, but it permits the creation of a second channel, or "parallel track," that distributes the drug while it is still

being studied in clinical trials. Parallel track is designed to allow people who cannot participate in clinical trials to have access to the experimental drug being studied. A drug can be distributed on a parallel track during Phase II trials. Parallel track programs are generally restricted to certain classes of patients based upon their state of disease progression. Tens of thousands of people with AIDS have received new drugs under parallel track programs. These programs almost always provide the drug at the manufacturer's expense, and as a consequence a parallel track can only be created when a manufacturer is willing to fund it.

### TREATMENT IND

This mechanism is generally used somewhat later in the development of a drug. Typically, a treatment IND (investigational new drug) is granted after researchers have concluded that a drug is safe and very likely effective, but before completion and approval of the final paperwork that accompanies drug approval. In effect, treatment IND bridges a relatively short gap at the end of a drug's development, making it available to the public while the manufacturer and the FDA complete the final regulatory requirements, which can take from several months to a year or longer.

For information on how to find experimental-treatment sites nationwide, see the Resource Guide at the back of this book.

# PROJECT INFORM'S DRUG INTERACTION CHART

**BY BEN CHENG**

As more drugs have become available to treat HIV and prevent or treat opportunistic infections and HIV-related malignancies, the potential for drug interactions has become an increasing concern. Not only does every therapy have potential side effects, but how each therapy might augment or diminish the benefit of another must be considered when making treatment decisions. Many people are taking a wide variety of therapies simultaneously—ranging from experimental and approved antivirals and prophylaxis for opportunistic infections to complementary approaches and over-the-counter medications. How therapies interact is not always considered and may play a major role in the success of any plan for managing HIV disease. The following are some guidelines to help decrease the likelihood of drug interactions.

## MEDICATION REVIEW

- Each time you see your health care professional, put all your medications, including over-the-counter and complementary products, in a bag and have your health care provider conduct a review of your medicine for safety, appropriateness, compatibility, and instructions for use. Or, bring in a complete list of current medications.

- Each time you are given a prescription for a new medication, ask your health care provider if it will work safely with the other therapies you are on.

- Talk to your health care provider about making a "medicine checkup" part of your regular visits, and discuss how best to monitor for the potential effects of drug interactions. Bring the Project Inform Drug Interaction Chart with you to your appointment.

Drug interactions can take different forms and may occur immediately or may take weeks to develop. Potential interactions may prohibit the use of two therapies together, while in other instances careful monitoring is sufficient to detect emergency problems, which can guide treatment decisions to avoid complications. Interactions can occur when one therapy affects how another is absorbed, broken down (metabolized), distributed, or excreted in the system. Interactions can also occur when one therapy alters the effect of another. A common form of drug interaction can occur when two drugs have similar potential toxicities. For example, both ddI and ddC can cause peripheral neuropathy, a tingling or pain in the legs, hands, or feet. Because of the

similar toxicities of the two drugs, it is recommended that they not be used together as this may increase the potential for neuropathy. Similarly, both AZT and ganciclovir, a treatment for CMV, may cause bone-marrow suppression, which results in anemia. With the addition of a third drug, G-CSF (also called Neupogen), this drug interaction may be managed, however.

The issue of drug interactions is of increasing concern as a number of different drugs are being used and proposed for the prevention of multiple opportunistic infections (OIs). Multiple OI prevention brings the issue of drug interactions to a critical head. It is possible that OI drug interactions may cause more harm than good in some regimens. For example, one drug could reduce blood levels of another drug, which may lead to the development of drug-resistant organisms. In other words, drug interactions could result in the development of a disease that is not responsive to standard treatment. It is also possible that the added toxicity of taking numerous therapies outweighs their potential benefit for preventing disease. For these reasons, health care providers and people living with HIV should carefully choose OI prevention regimens, monitor for drug interactions and other side effects, and make informed decisions about combination therapies and OI prevention approaches.

Unfortunately, most drug interaction studies look at only two drugs, and most people with HIV take many drugs. As a result, little is known about how all the commonly used drugs interact. For this reason, ACTG (AIDS Clinical Trials Group) and CPCRA (Community Programs for Clinical Research on AIDS) are proposing to conduct new studies to determine the benefits of preventing all the major opportunistic infections versus the potential toxicities and drug interactions from the commonly used therapies against them (fluconazole, rifabutin, clarithromycin, azithromycin, TMP/SMX, dapsone, oral ganciclovir, and valacyclovir).

In the meantime, it is important to discuss potential drug interactions with a health care provider and a pharmacist. Before starting a new therapy, be it approved, experimental, or complementary, factor in the potential for drug interactions and possible side effects. Not everyone experiences side effects of drugs, and many problems of drug interactions may be managed by careful monitoring and adjusting of dose or discontinuing of therapy as needed.

The following chart should only be used as a guide for *potential* drug interactions. Some of these interactions have been reported in medical literature while others are purely anecdotal. While some of these interactions may occur in some people, they may not occur in everybody. Interactions are dependent on the amount of drug in the bloodstream. The higher the amount of drug in the bloodstream, the greater the chance of toxicity. This chart was compiled from package inserts, anecdotal reports, discussions with pharmacologists and physicians who treat HIV disease, and information from pharmaceutical companies.

**141W94 (VX-478) PLUS...**

| Indinavir | Increases 141W94 levels by 63% in blood |

**ACYCLOVIR (ZOVIRAX) PLUS...**

| Atovaquone | May decrease atovaquone levels |
| AZT | Increased antiviral activity in test tubes |
| Interferon-alpha | Increased antiviral activity in test tubes |
| Probenecid | Increases acyclovir levels |

**ADEFOVIR (BIS-POM PMEA) PLUS...**

| D-carnitine | Should not be taken together |
| Food | Increases adefovir levels |
| Isoniazid | Increases risk of side effects |
| Rifampin | Increases risk of side effects |

**AMPHOTERICIN B (FUNGIZONE) PLUS...**

| Amikacin | May increase risk of kidney toxicity |
| Antineoplastics | May increase risk of kidney toxicity and low blood pressure |
| AZT | May increase risk of bone marrow toxicity |
| Cidofovir | Should not be used together. Increases risk of kidney toxicities |
| Corticosteroids | May decrease potassium levels and increases risk of cardiovascular toxicity |
| Cyclosporine | May increase risk of kidney toxicity |
| ddC | May increase ddC levels and increase risk of peripheral neuropathy |
| Digitalis | May increase risk of cardiovascular toxicity |
| Fluconazole | May interfere with the activity of amphotericin B |
| Flucytosine(5-FC) | Increased antifungal activity in test tubes but increases risk of bone marrow toxicity |
| Foscarnet | May decrease number of red blood cells and increases risk of kidney toxicity |
| Ganciclovir | May increase risk of bone marrow toxicity |
| Itraconazole | Decreases itraconazole levels and may interfere with the activity of amphotericin B |
| Ketoconazole | May interfere with the activity of amphotericin B |
| Pentamidine (IV) | May increase risk of kidney toxicity |

| | |
|---|---|
| Probenecid | May increase amphotericin B levels and decrease amphotericin B clearance |

**ANTINEOPLASTICS PLUS...**

| | |
|---|---|
| Amphotericin B | May increase risk of kidney toxicity and low blood pressure |
| AZT | May increase risk of bone marrow toxicity |
| ddC | May increase risk of peripheral neuropathy |
| ddI | May increase risk of peripheral neuropathy |
| Ganciclovir | May increase risk of bone marrow toxicity |
| Interferon-alpha | May increase risk of bone marrow toxicity |
| Pentamidine | May increase risk of bone marrow toxicity |
| TMP/SMX | May decrease number of red blood cells and neutrophils |

**ATOVAQUONE (MEPRON) PLUS...**

| | |
|---|---|
| Acetaminophen | May decrease atovaquone levels |
| Acyclovir | May decrease atovaquone levels |
| AZT | Increases AZT levels by 35% in blood |
| Benzodiazepines | May decrease atovaquone levels |
| Cephalosporins | May decrease atovaquone levels |
| Fatty foods | Increases atovaquone levels |
| Fluconazole | May increase atovaquone levels |
| Laxatives | May decrease atovaquone levels |
| Prednisone | May increase atovaquone levels |
| Rifampin | Decreases atovaquone levels by 50% in blood |

**AZITHROMYCIN (ZITHROMAX) PLUS...**

| | |
|---|---|
| Antacids | Need to be taken two hours apart or results in decreased azithromycin levels |
| Cyclosporine | May increase cyclosporine levels |
| Food in stomach | May decrease azithromycin levels (only azithromycin capsules) |
| Phenytoin | May increase phenytoin levels |
| Rifabutin | May increase rifabutin levels |
| Theophylline | May increase theophylline levels |
| Warfarin | May increase warfarin levels |

**AZT (ZIDOVUDINE, RETROVIR) PLUS...**

| | |
|---|---|
| Acyclovir | Increased antiviral activity in test tubes |
| Adriamycin | May increase risk of bone marrow toxicity |
| Amphotericin B | May increase risk of bone marrow toxicity |
| Antineoplastics | May increase risk of bone marrow toxicity |
| Atovaquone | Increases AZT levels by 35% in blood |
| Clarithromycin | Decreases AZT levels by 12% in blood |
| Dapsone | May increase risk of bone marrow toxicity |
| ddC | Increased antiviral activity in test tubes. May increase risk of pancreatitis |
| ddI | Increased antiviral activity in test tubes |
| Delavirdine | Increased antiviral activity in test tubes |
| d4T | May decrease antiviral activity |
| Fluconazole | Increases AZT levels by 74% and may increase fluconazole levels |
| Flucytosine | May increase risk of bone marrow toxicity |
| Food in stomach | May decrease AZT levels |
| Foscarnet | Increased antiviral activity in test tubes. May decrease number of red blood cells |
| Ganciclovir | Increases AZT levels (oral ganciclovir) and may increase risk of bone marrow toxicity |
| Indinavir | Increased antiviral activity in test tubes, increases AZT levels by 17-36% in blood |
| Interferon-alpha | Increased antiviral activity in test tubes and may increase risk of bone marrow toxicity |
| Lamivudine (3TC) | Increased antiviral activity in test tubes |
| Methadone | Increases AZT levels by 50% in blood |
| Nelfinavir | Decreases AZT levels by 35% in blood |
| Nevirapine | Increased antiviral activity in test tubes |
| Pentamidine | May increase risk of bone marrow toxicity |
| Pentoxifylline | May increase risk of bone marrow toxicity |
| Phenytoin | May decrease phenytoin and AZT levels |
| Probenecid | Increases AZT levels |
| Pyrimethamine + sulfadiazine | May increase AZT levels and may increase risk of bone marrow toxicity |
| Ribavirin | Decreased antiviral activity in test tubes |
| Rifabutin | Decreases AZT levels by 32% in blood |

| | |
|---|---|
| Rifampin | May decrease AZT levels |
| Ritonavir | Decreases AZT levels by 25% in blood. Increased antiviral activity in test tubes |
| Saquinavir | Increased antiviral activity in test tubes |
| TMP/SMX (Bactrim/Septra) | May decrease number of red blood cells and neutrophils. May increase AZT levels and decrease AZT clearance (high dose TMP/SMX) |
| Valproic Acid | Increases AZT levels by 80% in blood |
| Vinblastine | May increase risk of bone marrow toxicity |
| Vincristine | May increase risk of bone marrow toxicity |

**CIDOFOVIR (VISTIDE) PLUS...**

| | |
|---|---|
| Aminoglycosides | Should not be used together. Increases risk of kidney toxicities |
| Amphotericin B | Should not be used together. Increases risk of kidney toxicities |
| Foscarnet | Should not be used together. Increases risk of kidney toxicities |
| Pentamidine IV | Should not be used together. Increases risk of kidney toxicities |
| Probenecid | Needs to be taken together to reduce the risk of kidney toxicities |

**CIPROFLOXACIN (CIPRO) PLUS...**

| | |
|---|---|
| Antacids | Needs to be taken two hours apart otherwise decreases ciprofloxacin levels |
| Caffeine | May increase caffeine levels |
| Cyclosporine | May increase risk of elevated serum creatinine |
| ddI | Needs to be taken two hours apart otherwise may decrease ciprofloxacin levels |
| Food in stomach | Decreases ciprofloxacin levels |
| Iron supplements | Needs to be taken two hours apart otherwise may decrease ciprofloxacin levels |
| Probenecid | Increases ciprofloxacin levels |
| Sucralfate | Needs to be taken two hours apart otherwise may decrease ciprofloxacin levels |
| Theophylline | May increase theophylline levels |
| Warfarin | May increase warfarin levels |

| Zinc-containing multivitamins | Needs to be taken two hours apart otherwise may decrease ciprofloxacin levels |
| --- | --- |

### CLARITHROMYCIN (BIAXIN) PLUS...

| | |
| --- | --- |
| Anticoagulants | May increase anticoagulants effect. Monitor pro-thrombin time |
| Astemizole | Should not be taken together, may increase risk of cardiovascular toxicity |
| AZT | Decreases AZT levels by 12% in blood |
| Carbamazepine | Increases carbamazepine levels. Monitor carbamazepine levels |
| Cisapride | Should not be taken together, may increase risk of cardiovascular toxicity |
| Cyclosporine | May increase cyclosporine levels |
| Delavirdine | Increases delavirdine levels by 31% and increases clarithromycin levels by 100% (but decreases 14-hydroxy clarithromycin levels by 75%) in blood |
| Digoxin | May increase digoxin levels. Monitor digoxin levels |
| Indinavir | Increases clarithromycin levels by 53% and indinavir levels by 29% in blood |
| Loratadine | May affect loratadine and clarithromycin levels |
| Nevirapine | May affect nevirapine and/or clarithromycin levels |
| Phenytoin | May increase phenytoin levels |
| Rifabutin | May increase rifabutin levels by up to 80% and decrease clarithromycin levels by up to 50% in blood. Increases risk of painful eye inflammation, arthritis, joint pain, tenderness or pain in muscles |
| Rifampin | Decreases clarithromycin levels by 120% in blood |
| Ritonavir | Increases clarithromycin levels by 77% and increases ritonavir levels by 12% in blood |
| Terfenadine | Should not be taken together, may increase risk of cardiovascular toxicity |
| Theophylline | Increases theophylline levels. Monitor theophylline levels |
| Triazolam | May increase triazolam levels |
| Trimetrexate | May affect trimetrexate and/or clarithromycin levels |
| Warfarin | Monitor prothrombin time |

**CLINDAMYCIN (CLEOCIN) PLUS...**

| | |
|---|---|
| Erythromycin | Should not be taken together |
| Kaolin-pectin | Should be taken two hours apart otherwise decreases clindamycin levels |
| Neuromuscular blocking agents | May increase neuromuscular blocking effect |

**CLOFAZIMINE (LAMPRENE) PLUS...**

| | |
|---|---|
| Dapsone | May decrease effectiveness of clofazimine |
| Fomivirsen | May increase risk of ocular toxicity |
| Food in stomach | Increases clofazimine levels |

**CYCLOSERINE (SEROMYCIN) PLUS...**

| | |
|---|---|
| Alcohol | May increase risk of seizures |
| Ethionamide | May increase risk of central nervous system related toxicity |
| Isoniazid | May increase risk of central nervous system related toxicity |
| TB drugs | May decrease B-12 and folic acid levels, and may decrease number of red blood cells |

**DAPSONE PLUS...**

| | |
|---|---|
| AZT | May increase risk of bone marrow toxicity |
| Clofazimine | May decrease effectiveness of clofazimine |
| ddC | May increase risk of peripheral neuropathy |
| ddI | Needs to be taken two hours apart otherwise dapsone has no activity |
| Delavirdine | May increase dapsone levels |
| Ganciclovir | May increase risk of bone marrow toxicity |
| Nevirapine | May affect dapsone and/or nevirapine levels |
| Probenecid | May increase dapsone levels and decrease dapsone clearance |
| Pyrimethamine | May increase risk of bone marrow toxicity |
| Rifabutin | May decrease dapsone levels |
| Rifampin | Decreases dapsone levels by 7- to 10-fold in blood |
| Saquinavir | May increase dapsone levels |
| TMP/SMX | Increases trimethoprim levels by 1.5-fold and increases dapsone levels by 1.5-fold in blood |

| Trimethoprim | Increases trimethoprim levels by 1.5-fold and increases dapsone levels by 1.5-fold in blood |

## DDC (ZALCITABINE, HIVID) PLUS...

| | |
|---|---|
| Aminoglycosides | May increase ddC levels and increase risk of peripheral neuropathy |
| Amphotericin B | May increase ddC levels and increase risk of peripheral neuropathy |
| Antacids | Decreases ddC levels by 25% in blood |
| Antineoplastics | May increase risk of peripheral neuropathy |
| AZT | Increased antiviral activity in test tubes. May increase risk of pancreatitis |
| Chloramphenicol | May increase risk of peripheral neuropathy |
| Cimetidine | Increases ddC levels by 36% in blood |
| Cisplatin | May increase risk of peripheral neuropathy |
| Dapsone | May increase risk of peripheral neuropathy |
| ddI | Should not be used in combination. Significantly increased risk of peripheral neuropathy |
| Disulfiram (Antabuse) | May increase risk of peripheral neuropathy |
| Ethionamide | May increase risk of peripheral neuropathy |
| Food in stomach | May decrease ddC levels |
| Foscarnet | May increase risk of kidney toxicity and peripheral neuropathy |
| Hydralazine | May increase risk of peripheral neuropathy |
| Iodoquinol | May increase risk of peripheral neuropathy |
| Isoniazid | May increase risk of peripheral neuropathy |
| Maalox | Decreases ddC levels by 25% in blood |
| Metoclopramide | Decreases ddC levels by 10% in blood |
| Metronidazole | May increase risk of peripheral neuropathy |
| Pentamidine (IV) | May increase risk of peripheral neuropathy and pancreatitis |
| Phenytoin | May increase risk of peripheral neuropathy |
| Probenecid | Increases ddC levels by 50% in blood |
| Ribavirin | May increase risk of peripheral neuropathy |
| Saquinavir | Increased antiviral activity in test tubes |

**DDI (DIDANOSINE, VIDEX) PLUS...**

| | |
|---|---|
| Alcohol | May increase risk of pancreatitis |
| Antineoplastics | May increase risk of peripheral neuropathy |
| AZT | Increased antiviral activity in test tubes |
| Cimetidine | Needs to be taken two hours apart |
| Ciprofloxacin | Needs to be taken two hours apart otherwise may decrease ciprofloxacin levels |
| Dapsone | Needs to be taken two hours apart otherwise dapsone has no activity |
| ddC | Should not be used in combination. Significantly increased risk of peripheral neuropathy |
| Delavirdine | Needs to be taken an hour apart otherwise decreases delavirdine levels. Decreases delavirdine levels by 22% and decreases ddI levels by 20% in blood |
| d4T | Increased antiviral activity in test tubes |
| Food | Decreases ddI levels |
| Ganciclovir (IV) | Increases ddI levels by up to 65% in blood. May increase risk of pancreatitis |
| Ganciclovir (oral) | Increases ddI levels by up to 80% and ddI decreases oral ganciclovir levels by up to 20% in blood. May increase risk of pancreatitis |
| Indinavir | Increased antiviral activity in test tubes. Indinavir should be taken 1 hour before taking ddI or 2 hours after taking ddI |
| Ketoconazole | Needs to be taken two hours apart otherwise may significantly decrease ketoconazole levels |
| Lamivudine | Increased antiviral activity in test tubes |
| Nevirapine | Increased antiviral activity in test tubes |
| Pentamidine (IV) | May increase risk of pancreatitis |
| Quinolones | Needs to be taken two hours apart otherwise quinolone has no activity |
| Ranitidine | Needs to be taken two hours apart |
| Ribavirin | Increased antiviral activity in test tubes |
| Ritonavir | Decreases ddI levels by 13% in blood |
| Saquinavir | Increased antiviral activity in test tubes |
| Tetracyclines | Should not be used together |

## DELAVIRDINE (RESCRIPTOR) PLUS...

| | |
|---|---|
| Alprazolam | Should not be taken together, increases risk of serious side effects |
| Antacids | Needs to be taken an hour apart otherwise decreases delavirdine levels by 48% in blood |
| Astemizole | Should not be taken together, increases risk of serious side effects |
| AZT | Increased antiviral activity in test tubes |
| Barbiturates | May decrease delavirdine levels |
| Carbamazepine | May significantly decrease delavirdine levels |
| Cimetidine | May decrease delavirdine levels |
| Cisapride | Should not be taken together, increases risk of serious side effects |
| Clarithromycin | Increases delavirdine levels by 31% and increases clarithromycin levels by 100% (but decreases 14-hydroxy clarithromycin levels by 75%) in blood |
| Cyclosporine | May increase cyclosporine levels |
| Dapsone | May increase dapsone levels |
| ddI | Needs to be taken an hour apart otherwise decreases delavirdine levels. Decreases delavirdine levels by 22% and decreases ddI levels by up to 20% |
| Digitalis | May increase digitalis levels |
| Diltiazem | May increase diltiazem levels |
| Erythromycin | May increase delavirdine levels |
| Ethinyl Estradiol | May increase ethinyl estradiol levels |
| Fluconazole | Increases delavirdine levels by 21% in blood |
| Fluoxetine | Increases delavirdine levels by 50% in blood |
| Food (high fat) | May decrease delavirdine levels |
| Hydrocortisone | May increase hydrocortisone levels |
| Indinavir | Increases indinavir levels between 50-100% |
| Itraconazole | May increase itraconazole and delavirdine levels |
| Ketoconazole | Increases delavirdine levels by 50% in blood |
| Lidocaine | May increase lidocaine levels |
| Loratadine | May increase loratadine levels |
| Lovastatin | May increase lovastatin levels |
| Midazolam | Should not be taken together, increases risk of serious side effects |

| Nifedipine | May increase nifedipine levels |
|---|---|
| Phenobarbital | May significantly decrease delavirdine levels |
| Phenytoin | May significantly decrease delavirdine levels |
| Prednisolone | May increase delavirdine levels |
| Prednisone | May increase prednisone and delavirdine levels |
| Progesterone | May increase progesterone levels |
| Quinidine | May increase quinidine levels |
| Ranitidine | May decrease delavirdine levels |
| Rifabutin | Decreases delavirdine levels significantly and increases rifabutin levels |
| Rifampin | Should be taken together otherwise delavirdine levels significantly decreased |
| Ritonavir | Slight decrease in delavirdine levels |
| Saquinavir | Increases saquinavir levels by 5-fold and decreases delavirdine levels by 24% in blood. May increase risk of GI side effects and LFTs |
| Terfenadine | Should not be taken together, increases risk of serious side effects |
| Testosterone | May increase testosterone levels |
| Triazolam | Should not be taken together, increases risk of serious side effects |
| Trimetrexate | May affect trimetrexate and/or delavirdine levels |
| Warfarin | May increase warfarin levels |

**D4T (STAVUDINE, ZERIT) PLUS...**

| AZT | May decrease antiviral activity in test tubes |
|---|---|
| ddI | Increased antiviral activity in test tubes |
| Ganciclovir | May increase risk of pancreatitis |
| Indinavir | Increases d4T levels by 25% in blood |
| Nelfinavir | Increased antiviral activity in test tubes |
| Pentamidine (IV) | May increase risk of pancreatitis |

**DMP 266 PLUS...**

| Food | Increases DMP 266 levels between 10-50% in blood |
|---|---|
| Indinavir | Decreases indinavir levels by 37% in blood |

**ETHIONAMIDE (TRECATOR) PLUS...**

| | |
|---|---|
| Cycloserine | May increase risk of central nervous system related toxicity |
| ddC | May increase risk of peripheral neuropathy |
| Isoniazid | May increase risk of encephalopathy (dysfunction of the brain) and may increase isoniazid levels |

**FLUCONAZOLE (DIFLUCAN) PLUS...**

| | |
|---|---|
| Astemizole | Should not be taken together, may increase risk of cardiovascular toxicity |
| Atovaquone | May increase atovaquone levels |
| AZT | Increases AZT levels by 74% and may increase fluconazole levels |
| Benzodiazepines | May increase benzodiazepine levels |
| Cimetidine | Decreases fluconazole levels by 13% in blood |
| Cisapride | Should not be taken together, may increase risk of cardiovascular toxicity |
| Coumarin | May increase prothrombin time |
| Cyclosporine | Increases cyclosporine levels by 92% in blood |
| Delavirdine | Increases delavirdine levels by 21% in blood |
| Ethinyl Estradiol | Increases ethinyl estradiol levels by 38% in blood |
| Glipizide | Increases glipizide levels by 49% in blood |
| Glyburide | Increases glyburide levels by 44% in blood |
| Hydrochlorothiazide | Increases fluconazole levels by 45% in blood |
| Indinavir | Decreases indinavir levels by 19% in blood |
| Isoniazid | May decrease fluconazole levels |
| Levonorgestrel | Increases levonorgestrel levels by 25% in blood |
| Loratadine | May affect loratadine and/or fluconazole levels |
| Phenytoin | Increases phenytoin levels by 88% in blood |
| Ranitidine | May decrease fluconazole levels |
| Rifabutin | May increase rifabutin levels by up to 80% in blood. Increase risk of painful eye inflammation, arthritis, joint pain, tenderness or pain in muscles |
| Rifampin | Decreases fluconazole levels by 23% in blood |
| Ritonavir | Increases ritonavir levels by 12% in blood |
| Sulfonylurea oral hypoglycemic drugs | Increase risk of low blood sugar levels |

| | |
|---|---|
| Terfenadine | Should not be taken together, may increase risk of cardiovascular toxicity |
| Theophylline | Increases theophylline levels by 21% in blood |
| Tolbutamide | Increases tolbutamide levels by 26% in blood |
| Trimetrexate | May affect trimetrexate and/or fluconazole levels |
| Warfarin | May increase prothrombin time |

**FLUCYTOSINE (ANCOBON) PLUS...**

| | |
|---|---|
| Amphotericin B | Increased antifungal activity in test tubes but increases risk of bone marrow toxicity |
| Antacids | Need to be taken two hours apart otherwise flucytosine will have no effect |
| AZT | May increase risk of bone marrow toxicity |
| Cytosine arabinoside | May decrease antifungal activity |
| Ganciclovir | May increase bone marrow toxicity |
| Interferon-alpha | May increase risk of bone marrow toxicity |
| Sorivudine | Should not be used together. Can cause severe bone marrow suppression |

**FOMIVIRSEN (ISIS 2922) PLUS...**

| | |
|---|---|
| Chlorpromazine (Thorazine) | May increase risk of ocular toxicity |
| Clofazimine | May increase risk of ocular toxicity |
| Ethambutol | May increase risk of ocular toxicity |
| Fluconazole | May increase risk of ocular toxicity |
| Thioridazine | May increase risk of ocular toxicity |
| Trifluoperazine | May increase risk of ocular toxicity |

**FOSCARNET (FOSCAVIR) PLUS...**

| | |
|---|---|
| Aminoglycosides | May increase risk of kidney toxicity, requires careful monitoring |
| Amphotericin B | May decrease number of red blood cells and increases risk of kidney toxicity, requires careful monitoring |
| AZT | Increased antiviral activity in test tubes. May decrease number of red blood cells |
| Cidofovir | Should not be used together. Increases risk of kidney toxicity |

| | |
|---|---|
| ddC | May increase risk of kidney toxicity and peripheral neuropathy |
| Imipenem-Cilastin | May increase risk of central nervous system toxicity (seizures), monitor closely |
| Pentamidine (IV) | May increase risk of low blood sugar levels and kidney toxicity, monitor closely |
| Probenecid | May increase foscarnet levels |

**GANCICLOVIR (CYTOVENE) PLUS...**

| | |
|---|---|
| Amphotericin B | May increase risk of bone marrow toxicity |
| Antineoplastics | May increase risk of bone marrow toxicity |
| AZT | Increases AZT levels (oral ganciclovir) in blood and may increase risk of bone marrow toxicity |
| Dapsone | May increase risk of bone marrow toxicity |
| ddI | Oral ganciclovir may increase ddI levels by up to 80% and oral ganciclovir levels may be decreased by up to 20% in blood. IV ganciclovir may increase ddI levels by up to 65% in blood. May also increase risk pancreatitis |
| d4T | May increase risk of pancreatitis |
| Flucytosine | May increase risk of bone marrow toxicity |
| Food | Increases ganciclovir levels (oral ganciclovir) in blood |
| Interferon-alpha | May increase risk of bone marrow toxicity |
| Pentamidine | May increase risk of bone marrow toxicity |
| Probenecid | May increase ganciclovir levels and decrease ganciclovir clearance |
| TMP/SMX | May increase risk of bone marrow toxicity |

**INDINAVIR (CRIXIVAN) PLUS...**

| | |
|---|---|
| 141W94 (VX-478) | Increases 141W94 levels by 63% in blood |
| Alcohol | May increase risk for kidney stones |
| Astemizole | Should not be taken together, increases risk of serious side effects |
| AZT | Increased antiviral activity in test tubes, increases AZT levels by 17-36% in blood |
| Benzodiazepines | May increase benzodiazepine levels |
| Cisapride | Should not be taken together, increases risk of serious side effects |

| | |
|---|---|
| Clarithromycin | Increases clarithromycin levels by 53% and indinavir levels by 29% in blood |
| ddI | Increased antiviral activity in test tubes. Indinavir should be taken 1 hour before taking ddI or 2 hours after taking ddI |
| Delavirdine | Increases indinavir levels between 50-100% |
| d4T | Increases d4T levels by 25% in blood |
| DMP 266 | Decreases indinavir levels by 37% in blood |
| Ethinyl Estradiol | Increases ethinyl estradiol levels by 24% in blood |
| Fatty foods | Decreases indinavir levels. Indinavir should be taken 1 hour before eating or 2 hours after eating |
| Fluconazole | Decreases indinavir levels by 19% in blood |
| Grapefruit juice | Decreases indinavir levels by 26% in blood |
| Isoniazid | Increases isoniazid levels by 13% in blood |
| Itraconazole | May affect indinavir and/or itraconazole levels |
| Ketoconazole | Increases indinavir levels by 68% in blood |
| Lamivudine | Decreases lamivudine levels by 6% in blood |
| Midazolam | Should not be used together, increases risk of serious side effects |
| Nelfinavir | Increases indinavir levels by 51% and increases nelfinavir levels by 83% in blood |
| Nevirapine | Decreases indinavir levels by 27% in blood |
| Quinidine | Increases indinavir levels by 10% in blood |
| Rifabutin | Increases rifabutin levels by 204% and decreases indinavir levels by 32% in blood |
| Rifampin | May increase rifampin levels. Should not be used together |
| Ritonavir | Increases indinavir levels by 800% in animals |
| Saquinavir | Increases saquinavir levels between 4.6- and 7.2-fold |
| Terfenadine | Should not be used together, increases risk of serious side effects |
| TMP/SMX | Increases trimethoprim levels by 19% in blood |
| Triazolam | Should not be used together, increases risk of serious side effects |

**INTERFERON-ALPHA (INTRON-A, ROFERON-A) PLUS...**

| | |
|---|---|
| Acyclovir | Increased antiviral activity in test tubes |

| Antineoplastics | May increase risk of bone marrow toxicity |
| AZT | Increased antiviral activity in test tubes and may increase risk of bone marrow toxicity |
| Flucytosine | May increase risk of bone marrow toxicity |
| Ganciclovir | May increase risk of bone marrow toxicity |
| Pentamidine | May increase risk of bone marrow toxicity |
| Pyrimethamine | May increase risk of bone marrow toxicity |

**ISONIAZID (INH) PLUS...**

| Acetaminophen | Decreases acetaminophen metabolism |
| Adefovir | Increases risk of side effects |
| Alcohol | May increase risk of isoniazid associated hepatitis |
| Antacids | Should be taken two hours apart otherwise isoniazid will have no effect |
| Carbamazepine | Decreases carbamazepine metabolism |
| Corticosteroids | Increases isoniazid metabolism and decreases isoniazid levels |
| Cycloserine | May increase risk of central nervous system toxicity |
| ddC | May increase risk of peripheral neuropathy |
| Ethionamide | May increase risk of encephalopathy (dysfunction of the brain) and may increase isoniazid levels |
| Fluconazole | May decrease fluconazole levels |
| Food in stomach | May decrease isoniazid levels |
| Indinavir | Increases isoniazid levels by 13% in blood |
| Itraconazole | May decrease itraconazole levels |
| Ketoconazole | Decreases ketoconazole levels. Should not be taken together |
| Phenytoin | Decreases phenytoin metabolism |
| Rifampin | May increase risk of liver toxicity |
| Sulfonylureas | May increase risk of high blood sugar levels |

**ITRACONAZOLE (SPORANOX) PLUS...**

| Amphotericin B | Decreases itraconazole levels and may interfere with activity of amphotericin B |
| Antacids | Decreases itraconazole levels, should be taken 2 hours apart |
| Astemizole | Should not be taken together, may increase risk of cardiovascular toxicity |

| | |
|---|---|
| Benzodiazepines | May increase benzodiazepine levels |
| Cimetidine | Decreases itraconazole levels |
| Cisapride | Should not be taken together, may increase risk of cardiovascular toxicity |
| Cola beverage | Increases itraconazole levels |
| Coumarin | Enhances anticoagulant effects |
| Cyclosporine | Increases cyclosporine levels |
| ddI | Decreases itraconazole levels, should be taken 2 hours apart |
| Delavirdine | May increase delavirdine and itraconazole levels |
| Digoxin | Increases digoxin levels |
| Food in stomach | May increase itraconazole levels |
| Indinavir | May affect itraconazole and/or indinavir levels |
| Isoniazid | May decrease itraconazole levels |
| Loratadine | May affect loratadine and/or itraconazole levels |
| Lovastatin | Should not be used together, may increase risk of side effects |
| Midazolam (oral) | Should not be taken together, may increase risk of side effects |
| Nevirapine | May affect nevirapine and/or itraconazole levels |
| Omeprazole | Decreases itraconazole levels |
| Phenytoin | Decreases itraconazole levels and may increase phenytoin levels |
| Quinidine | Increases risk of ototoxicity |
| Ranitidine | Decreases itraconazole levels |
| Rifabutin | May increase rifabutin levels and may decrease itraconazole levels |
| Rifampin | Decreases rifampin levels and may decrease itraconazole levels |
| Ritonavir | May significantly increase itraconazole levels |
| Saquinavir | May increase saquinavir levels |
| Simvastatin | Should not be used together, may increase risk of side effects |
| Sulfonylurea oral hypoglycemic drugs | May increase risk of low blood sugar levels |
| Tacrolimus | Increases tacrolimus levels |

| | |
|---|---|
| Terfenadine | Should not be taken together, may increase risk of cardiovascular toxicity |
| Triazolam | Should not be taken together, may increase risk of side effects |
| Warfarin | May increase prothrombin time and increase anticoagulant effects |

### KETOCONAZOLE (NIZORAL) PLUS...

| | |
|---|---|
| Alcohol | May increase risk of nausea, vomiting, low blood pressure |
| Amphotericin B | May interfere with the activity of amphotericin B |
| Antacids | Should be taken two hours apart otherwise may decrease ketoconazole levels |
| Astemizole | Should not be taken together, increases risk of cardiovascular toxicity |
| Benzodiazepines | May increase benzodiazepine levels |
| Cimetidine | Should be taken two hours apart otherwise may decrease ketoconazole levels |
| Cisapride | Should not be taken together, may increase risk of cardiovascular toxicity |
| Coumarin | May enhance the anticoagulant effects of coumarin. The anticoagulant effect should be carefully monitored |
| Cyclosporine | May increase cyclosporine levels |
| ddI | Should be taken two hours apart otherwise may significantly decrease ketoconazole levels |
| Delavirdine | Increases delavirdine levels by 50% in blood |
| Digoxin | May increase digoxin levels. Digoxin levels should be carefully monitored |
| Indinavir | Increases indinavir levels by 68% in blood |
| Isoniazid | Should not be taken together, may significantly decrease ketoconazole levels |
| Loratadine | Increases loratadine levels by 300% in blood |
| Methylprednisolone | May increase methylprednisolone levels |
| Midazolam | Increases midazolam levels. Should not be used together |
| Nelfinavir | Increases nelfinavir levels by 35% in blood |
| Nevirapine | May affect nevirapine and/or ketoconazole levels |
| Omeprazole | Decreases ketoconazole levels |
| Phenytoin | May affect both ketoconazole and phenytoin levels |

| | |
|---|---|
| Prednisolone | May increase prednisolone levels |
| Ranitidine | Should be taken two hours apart otherwise may decrease ketoconazole levels |
| Rifabutin | May decrease ketoconazole levels |
| Rifampin | Significantly decreases ketoconazole levels. Should not be used together |
| Ritonavir | May significantly increase ketoconazole levels |
| Saquinavir | Increases saquinavir levels by 3-fold in blood |
| Sulfonylurea oral hypoglycemic drugs | May increase risk of low blood sugar levels |
| Tacrolimus | May increase tacrolimus levels |
| Terfenadine | Should not be taken together, increases risk of cardiovascular toxicity |
| Testosterone | May decrease testosterone levels |
| Triazolam | Increases triazolam levels. Should not be used together |
| Trimetrexate | May affect trimetrexate and/or ketoconazole levels |
| Warfarin | May increase prothrombin time |

**LAMIVUDINE (3TC, EPIVIR) PLUS...**

| | |
|---|---|
| Amantadine | May affect lamivudine and/or amantadine levels |
| AZT | Increased antiviral activity in test tubes |
| Cimetidine | May affect lamivudine and/or cimetidine levels |
| ddI | Increased antiviral activity in test tubes |
| Ethambutol | May affect lamivudine and/or ethambutol levels |
| Indinavir | Decreases lamivudine levels by 6% in blood |
| Nelfinavir | Increases lamivudine levels by 10% in blood |
| Ranitidine | May affect lamivudine and/or ranitidine levels |
| TMP/SMX | Increases lamivudine levels by 44% in blood |

**NELFINAVIR (AG 1343, VIRACEPT) PLUS...**

| | |
|---|---|
| Astemizole | Should not be used together, increases risk of cardiovascular toxicities |
| AZT | Decreases AZT levels by 35% in blood |
| Cisapride | Should not be used together, increases risk of cardiovascular toxicities |
| d4T | Increased antiviral activity in test tubes |
| Ethinyl Estradiol | Decreases ethinyl estradiol levels by 47% in blood |

| | |
|---|---|
| Food | Increases nelfinavir levels |
| Indinavir | Increases indinavir levels by 51% and increases nelfinavir levels by 83% in blood |
| Ketoconazole | Increases nelfinavir levels by 35% in blood |
| Lamivudine | Increases lamivudine levels by 10% in blood |
| Midazolam | Should not be used together, increases risk of cardiovascular toxicities |
| Norethindrone | Decreases norethindrone levels by 18% in blood |
| Rifabutin | Increases rifabutin levels by 207% and decreases nelfinavir levels by 32% in blood |
| Rifampin | Decreases nelfinavir levels by 82% in blood |
| Ritonavir | Increases ritonavir levels by 9% and increases nelfinavir levels by 152% in blood |
| Saquinavir | Increases saquinavir levels by 4-fold and increases nelfinavir levels by 18% in blood |
| Terfenadine | Should not be used together, increases risk of cardiovascular toxicities |
| Triazolam | Should not be used together, increases risk of cardiovascular toxicities |

**NEVIRAPINE (VIRAMUNE) PLUS...**

| | |
|---|---|
| Amoxicillin | May increase risk of rashes and Stevens-Johnson syndrome, requires careful monitoring |
| Astemizole | May affect astemizole and/or nevirapine levels |
| AZT | Increased antiviral activity in test tubes |
| Cimetidine | Should not be taken together, may decrease nevirapine levels |
| Clarithromycin | May affect clarithromycin and/or nevirapine levels |
| Clavulanic acid | Should not be used together during the first 6 weeks of taking nevirapine |
| Dapsone | May affect dapsone and/or nevirapine levels |
| ddI | Increased antiviral activity in test tubes |
| Dicumarol | Should not be used together, may increase dicumarol levels |
| Erythromycin | Should not be taken together, may increase risk of liver toxicity |
| Ethinyl Estradiol | May decrease ethinyl estradiol levels |

| | |
|---|---|
| Glucocorticoids (systemic) | May increase rate of metabolism of glucocorticoids |
| Indinavir | Decreases indinavir levels by 27% in blood |
| Itraconazole | May affect nevirapine and/or itraconazole levels |
| Ketoconazole | May affect nevirapine and/or ketoconazole levels |
| Oral contraceptives | May decrease effectiveness of oral contraceptives |
| Phenytoin | May decrease nevirapine levels. May also increase rate of metabolism of phenytoin |
| Prednisone | May affect prednisone and/or nevirapine levels |
| Rifabutin | May affect rifabutin and/or nevirapine levels |
| Rifampin | May affect rifampin and/or nevirapine levels |
| Ritonavir | Decreases ritonavir levels by 11% in blood |
| Saquinavir | Decreases saquinavir levels by 27% in blood |
| Steroids | May increase rate of metabolism of steroids |
| Terfenadine | May affect terfenadine and/or nevirapine levels |
| Ticarcillin | May increase risk of Stevens-Johnson syndrome, requires careful monitoring |
| TMP/SMX | Should not be initiated together for the first 4-6 weeks. May increase risk of rashes |
| Tolbutamide | Should not be taken together, may increase risk of toxicity |
| Trimetrexate | May affect trimetrexate and/or nevirapine levels |
| Warfarin | Should not be used together, may raise warfarin levels |

**PENTAMIDINE (PENTAM) PLUS...**

| | |
|---|---|
| Amphotericin B | May increase risk of kidney toxicity |
| Antineoplastics | May increase risk of bone marrow toxicity |
| AZT | May increase risk of bone marrow toxicity |
| Cidofovir | Should not be used together. Increases risk of kidney toxicity |
| ddC | May increase risk of peripheral neuropathy and pancreatitis |
| ddI | May increase risk of pancreatitis |
| d4T | May increase risk of pancreatitis |
| Foscarnet | May increase risk of severe low blood sugar levels and kidney toxicity, requires careful monitoring |
| Ganciclovir | May increase risk of bone marrow toxicity |

| Interferon-alpha | May increase risk of bone marrow toxicity |

**PROBENECID (BENEMID, COLBENEMID) PLUS...**

| | |
|---|---|
| ACE Inhibitors | Increases ACE inhibitor levels |
| Acetaminophen | Increases acetaminophen levels |
| Acyclovir | Increases acyclovir levels |
| Aspirin | Increases aspirin levels |
| AZT | Increases AZT levels |
| Barbiturates | Increases barbiturates levels |
| Benzodiazepines | Increases benzodiazepine levels |
| Bumetadine | Increases bumetadine levels |
| Cidofovir | Needs to be taken together to reduce the risk of kidney toxicities |
| Clofibrate | Increases clofibrate levels |
| ddC | Increases ddC levels by 50% in blood |
| Famotidine | Increases famotidine levels |
| Furosemide | Increases furosemide levels |
| Indomethacin | Increases indomethacin levels |
| Ketamine | Increases ketamine levels |
| Ketoprofen | Increases ketoprofen levels |
| Lorazepam | Increases lorazepam levels |
| Meclofenamate | Increases meclofenamate levels |
| Methotrexate | Increases methotrexate levels |
| Naproxen | Increases naproxen levels |
| Penicillin | Increases penicillin levels 2- 4-fold and increases risk of side effects |
| Pyrazinamide | Reduces activity of probenecid |
| Rifabutin | May increase rifabutin levels |
| Rifampin | Increases rifampin levels |
| Sulfonamide | Increases sulfonamide levels |
| Sulindac | Increases sulindac levels and reduces activity of probenecid |
| Theophylline | Increases theophylline levels |
| Thiopental | Increases thiopental levels |

**PYRIMETHAMINE (DARAPRIM, FANSIDAR) PLUS...**

| | |
|---|---|
| AZT | May increase AZT levels and increase risk of bone marrow toxicity |
| Chloroquine | May increase risk of bone marrow toxicity |
| Dapsone | May increase risk of bone marrow toxicity |
| Interferon-alpha | May increase risk of bone marrow toxicity |
| Lorazepam | Increases risk of liver toxicity |
| Para-aminobenzoic acid | May decrease pyrimethamine levels |
| Sulfonamides | May increase risk of bone marrow toxicity |
| TMP/SMX | May decrease number of red blood cells |

**RIFABUTIN (MYCOBUTIN) PLUS...**

| | |
|---|---|
| Analgesics | May decrease effectiveness of analgesics |
| Anticoagulants | May decrease effectiveness of anticoagulants |
| Azithromycin | May increase rifabutin levels |
| AZT | Decreases AZT levels by 32% in blood |
| Barbiturates | May decrease effectiveness of barbiturates |
| Clarithromycin | May increase rifabutin levels by up to 80% and decrease clarithromycin levels by up to 50% in blood. Increases risk of painful eye inflammation, arthritis, joint pain, tenderness or pain in muscles |
| Corticosteroids | May decrease corticosteroid levels |
| Cyclosporine | May decrease cyclosporine levels |
| Dapsone | May decrease dapsone levels |
| Delavirdine | Decreases delavirdine levels significantly and increases rifabutin levels |
| Diazepam | May decrease effectiveness of diazepam |
| Disopyramide | May decrease effectiveness of disopyramide |
| Estrogen | May decrease effectiveness of estrogen |
| Ethinyl Estradiol | May decrease ethinyl estradiol levels |
| Fluconazole | May increase rifabutin levels by up to 80% in blood. Increases risk of painful eye inflammation, arthritis, joint pain, tenderness or pain in muscles |
| Indinavir | Increases rifabutin levels by 204% and decreases indinavir levels by 32% in blood |

| Itraconazole | May decrease itraconazole levels and increase rifabutin levels |
| --- | --- |
| Ketoconazole | May decrease ketoconazole levels |
| Methadone | May decrease effectiveness of methadone |
| Mexilitine | May decrease effectiveness of mexilitine |
| Nelfinavir | Increases rifabutin levels by 207% and decreases nelfinavir levels by 32% in blood |
| Nevirapine | May affect rifabutin and/or nevirapine levels |
| Probenecid | May increase rifabutin levels |
| Progesterone | May decrease effectiveness of progesterone |
| Quinidine | May decrease quinidine levels |
| Ritonavir | Should not be taken together, may increase toxicity risk |
| Saquinavir | Decreases saquinavir levels by 40% in blood |
| Sulfonylureas (oral hypoglycemia drugs) | May decrease sulfonylurea levels |
| Theophylline | May decrease theophylline levels |
| Trimetrexate | May affect trimetrexate and/or rifabutin levels |
| Verapamil | May decrease effectiveness of verapamil |

**RIFAMPIN (RIFADIN) PLUS...**

| Adefovir | Increases risk of side effects |
| --- | --- |
| Analgesics | May decrease effectiveness of analgesics |
| Anticoagulants | May decrease effectiveness of anticoagulants |
| Atovaquone | Decreases atovaquone levels by 50% in blood |
| AZT | May decrease AZT levels |
| Barbiturates | May decrease effectiveness of barbiturates |
| Clarithromycin | Decreases clarithromycin levels by 120% in blood |
| Corticosteroids | May decrease corticosteroid levels |
| Cyclosporine | May decrease cyclosporine levels |
| Dapsone | Decreases dapsone levels by 7- to 10- fold in blood |
| Delavirdine | Should be taken together otherwise delavirdine levels significantly decreased |
| Diazepam | May decrease effectiveness of diazepam |
| Digitalis | May decrease effectiveness of digitalis |
| Disopyramide | May decrease effectiveness of disopyramide |
| Estrogen | May decrease effectiveness of estrogen |

| | |
|---|---|
| Ethinyl Estradiol | May decrease ethinyl estradiol levels |
| Fluconazole | Decreases fluconazole levels by 23% in blood |
| Food in stomach | May decrease rifampin levels |
| Halothane | May increase risk of liver toxicity |
| Indinavir | May increase rifampin levels. Should not be used together |
| Isoniazid | May increase risk of liver toxicity |
| Itraconazole | May decrease itraconazole levels |
| Ketoconazole | Significantly decreases ketoconazole levels. Should not be used together |
| Methadone | May decrease effectiveness of methadone |
| Mexilitine | May decrease effectiveness of mexilitine |
| Nelfinavir | Decreases nelfinavir levels by 82% in blood |
| Nevirapine | May affect rifampin and/or nevirapine levels |
| Probenecid | Increases rifampin levels |
| Progesterone | May decrease effectiveness of progesterone |
| Quinidine | May decrease quinidine levels |
| Ritonavir | Decreases ritonavir levels by 35% in blood |
| Saquinavir | Decreases saquinavir levels by 80% in blood. Should not be used together |
| Sulfonylureas (oral hypoglycemic drugs) | May decrease sulfonylurea levels |
| Theophylline | May decrease theophylline levels |
| Trimetrexate | May affect trimetrexate and/or rifampin levels |
| Verapamil | May decrease effectiveness of verapamil |

**RITONAVIR (ABT-538, NORVIR) PLUS...**

| | |
|---|---|
| Alfentanil | May significantly increase alfentanil levels |
| Alprazolam | Should not be taken together, may increase toxicity risk |
| Amiodarone | Should not be taken together, may increase toxicity risk |
| Amitriptyline | May increase amitriptyline levels |
| Amlodipine | May significantly increase amlodipine levels |
| Astemizole | Should not be taken together, may increase toxicity risk |
| Atovaquone | May decrease atovaquone levels |
| AZT | Decreases AZT levels by 25% in blood. Increased antiviral activity in test tubes |

| | |
|---|---|
| Benzodiazepines | Should not be taken together, may increase risk of toxicity |
| Bepridil | Should not be taken together, may increase risk of toxicity |
| Bromocriptine | May significantly increase bromocriptine levels |
| Buproprion | Should not be taken together, may increase risk of toxicity |
| Carbamazepine | May significantly increase carbamazepine levels |
| Chlorpromazine | May increase chlorpromazine levels |
| Cisapride | Should not be taken together, may increase risk of cardiovascular toxicity |
| Clarithromycin | Increases clarithromycin levels by 77% and increases ritonavir levels by 12% in blood |
| Clofibrate | May decrease clofibrate levels |
| Clomipramine | May increase clomipramine levels |
| Clonazepam | May increase clonazepam levels |
| Clorazepate | Should not be taken together, may increase risk of toxicity |
| Clotrimazole | May increase risk of side effects |
| Clozapine | Should not be taken together, may increase risk of toxicity |
| Codeine | May decrease codeine levels |
| Cyclosporine | May significantly increase cyclosporine levels |
| ddI | Decreases ddI levels by 13% in blood |
| Delavirdine | Slight decrease in delavirdine levels |
| Desipramine | Increases despramine levels by 145% in blood |
| Dexamethasone | May significantly increase dexamethasone levels |
| Dexfenfluramine | May increase dexfenfluramine levels |
| Diazepam | Should not be taken together, may increase risk of toxicity |
| Dihydroergotamine | Should not be used together, may increase risk of toxicity |
| Diltiazem | May significantly increase diltiazem levels |
| Diphenoxylate | May decrease diphenoxylate levels |
| Disipramine | Increases disipramine levels by 240% in blood |
| Disopyramide | May increase disopyramide levels and increase cardiac and neurological side effects |

| | |
|---|---|
| Divalproex | May decrease divalproex levels |
| Dronabinol | May increase dronabinol levels |
| Encainide | Should not be taken together, may increase risk of toxicity |
| Ergotamine | Should not be taken together, may increase risk of toxicity |
| Erythromycin | May significantly increase erythromycin levels |
| Estazolam | Should not be taken together, may increase risk of toxicity |
| Ethinyl Estradiol (birth control pills) | Decreases ethinyl estradiol levels by 40% in blood. Should use barrier method for contraception |
| Ethosuximide | May increase ethosuximide levels |
| Etoposide | May increase etoposide levels |
| Felodipine | May significantly increase felodipine levels |
| Fentanyl | May significantly increase fentanyl levels |
| Flecainide | Should not be taken together, may increase toxicity risk |
| Fluconazole | Increases ritonavir levels by 12% in blood |
| Fluoxetine | Increases ritonavir levels by 19% and may increase fluoxetine levels |
| Flurazepam | Should not be taken together, may increase toxicity risk |
| Fluvastatin | May significantly increase fluvastatin levels |
| Food | Increases ritonavir levels |
| Haloperidol | May increase haloperidol levels |
| Hydrocodone | May increase hydrocodone levels |
| Hydromorphone | May decrease hydromorphone levels |
| Imipramine | May increase imipramine levels |
| Indinavir | Increases indinavir levels by 800% in animals |
| Isradipine | May significantly increase isradipine levels |
| Itraconazole | May significantly increase itraconazole levels |
| Ketoconazole | May significantly increase ketoconazole levels |
| Ketoprofen | May decrease ketoprofen levels |
| Ketorolac | May decrease ketorolac levels |
| Lamotrigine | May decrease lamotrigine levels |
| Lidocaine | May significantly increase lidocaine levels |
| Loperamide | May decrease loperamide levels |
| Loratadine | May significantly increase loratadine levels |

| | |
|---|---|
| Lorazepam | May reduce lorazepam levels |
| Lovastatin | May significantly increase lovastatin levels |
| Maprotiline | May increase maprotiline levels |
| Mefloquine | Increases mefloquine levels by 300% in blood |
| Meperidine | Should not be taken together, may increase toxicity risk |
| Methadone | May significantly increase methadone levels |
| Methamphetamine | May increase methamphetamine levels |
| Metoclopramide | May decrease metoclopramide levels |
| Metoprolol | May increase metoprolol levels |
| Metronidazole | May increase toxicity risk (ritonavir liquid only) |
| Mexiletine | May increase mexiletine levels and increase cardiac and neurological side effects |
| Miconazole | May significantly increase miconazole levels |
| Midazolam | Should not be taken together, may increase toxicity risk |
| Morphine | May decrease morphine levels |
| Naproxen | May decrease naproxen levels |
| Nefazadone | May significantly increase nefazadone levels and increase cardiac and neurological side effects |
| Nelfinavir | Increases ritonavir levels by 9% and increases nelfinavir levels by 152% in blood |
| Nevirapine | Decreases ritonavir levels by 11% in blood |
| Nicardipine | May significantly increase nicardipine levels |
| Nifedipine | May significantly increase nifedipine levels |
| Nimodipine | May significantly increase nimodipine levels |
| Nisoldipine | May significantly increase nisoldipine levels |
| Nitrendipine | May significantly increase nitrendipine levels |
| Nortriptyline | May increase nortriptyline levels |
| Ondansetron | May increase ondansetron levels |
| Oxazepam | May decrease oxazepam levels |
| Oxycodone | May increase oxycodone levels |
| Paclitaxel | May increase paclitaxel levels |
| Paroxetine | May increase paroxetine levels |
| Penbutolol | May increase penbutolol levels |
| Pergolide | May increase risk of side effects |
| Perphenazine | May increase perphenazine levels |
| Pimozide | Should not be taken together, may increase toxicity risk |

| | |
|---|---|
| Pindolol | May increase pindolol levels |
| Piroxicam | Should not be taken together, may increase toxicity risk |
| Pravastatin | May increase pravastatin levels |
| Prednisone | May increase prednisone levels |
| Propafenone | Should not be taken together, may increase toxicity risk |
| Propofol | May decrease propofol levels |
| Propoxyphene | Should not be taken together, may increase toxicity risk |
| Quinine | May significantly increase quinine levels |
| Quinidine | Should not be taken together, may increase toxicity risk |
| Rifabutin | Should not be taken together, may increase toxicity risk |
| Rifampin | Decreases ritonavir levels by 35% in blood |
| Risperidone | May increase risperidone levels |
| Saquinavir | Increases saquinavir levels by about 20-fold in blood |
| Sertraline | May significantly increase sertraline levels |
| Simvastatin | May significantly increase simvastatin levels |
| Sulfamethoxazole | Decreases sulfamethoxazole levels by 20% in blood |
| Tacrolimus | May significantly increase tacrolimus levels |
| Tamoxifen | May significantly increase tamoxifen levels |
| Temazepam | May decrease temazepam levels |
| Terfenadine | Should not be taken together, may increase toxicity risk |
| Theophylline | Decreases theophylline levels by 43% in blood |
| Thioridazine | May increase thioridazine levels |
| Timolol | May increase timolol levels |
| TMP/SMX | Decreases sulfamethoxazole levels by 20% and increases trimethoprim levels by 20% in blood |
| Tramadol | May increase tramadol levels |
| Trazodone | May increase trazodone levels |
| Triazolam | Should not be taken together, may increase toxicity risk |
| Trimethoprim | Increases trimethoprim levels by 20% |
| Trimipramine | May increase trimipramine levels |
| Venlafaxine | May increase venlafaxine levels |
| Verapamil | May significantly increase verapamil levels |
| Vinblastine | May increase vinblastine levels |
| Vincristine | May increase vincristine levels |
| Warfarin | May increase warfarin levels |

| Zolpidem | Should not be taken together, may increase toxicity risk |
|---|---|

### SAQUINAVIR (INVIRASE) PLUS...

| | |
|---|---|
| Astemizole | Should not be taken together, may increase toxicity risk |
| AZT | Increased antiviral activity in test tubes |
| Calcium Channel Blockers | May increase calcium channel blocker levels |
| Carbamazepine | May decrease saquinavir levels |
| Clindamycin | May increase clindamycin levels |
| Dapsone | May increase dapsone levels |
| ddC | Increased antiviral activity in test tubes |
| ddI | Increased antiviral activity in test tubes |
| Delavirdine | Increases saquinavir levels by 5-fold and decreases delavirdine levels by 24% in blood. May increase risk of GI side effects and LFTs |
| Dexamethasone | May decrease saquinavir levels |
| Food | Increases saquinavir levels |
| Grapefruit juice | Increases saquinavir levels |
| Indinavir | Increases saquinavir levels between 4.6- and 7.2-fold |
| Itraconazole | May increase saquinavir levels |
| Ketoconazole | Increases saquinavir levels by 3-fold in blood |
| Nelfinavir | Increases saquinavir levels by 4-fold and increases nelfinavir levels by 18% in blood. |
| Nevirapine | Decreases saquinavir levels 27% in blood |
| Phenobarbital | May decrease saquinavir levels |
| Phenytoin | May decrease saquinavir levels |
| Quinidine | May increase quinidine levels |
| Rifabutin | Decreases saquinavir levels by 40% in blood |
| Rifampin | Decreases saquinavir levels by 80% in blood. Should not be used together |
| Ritonavir | Increases saquinavir levels by about 20-fold in blood |
| Terfenadine | Should not be taken together, may increase toxicity risk |
| Triazolam | May increase triazolam levels |

### SORIVUDINE (BROVAVIR) PLUS...

| | |
|---|---|
| 5-fluorouracil (5-FU) | Should not be used together. Can cause severe bone marrow suppression |

| Flucytosine (5-FC) | Should not be used together. Can cause severe bone marrow suppression |

**SULFADIAZINE PLUS...**

| AZT + pyrimethamine | May increase AZT levels and increase bone marrow toxicity |
| Sulfonylureas (oral hypoglycemic drugs) | May increase risk of low blood sugar levels |
| Warfarin | Increases prothrombin time |

**TMP/SMX (BACTRIM, SEPTRA) PLUS...**

| Antineoplastics | May decrease number of red blood cells and neutrophils |
| AZT | May decrease number of red blood cells and neutrophils. May increase AZT levels and decrease AZT clearance (high dose TMP/SMX) |
| Dapsone | Increases trimethoprim levels by 1.5 fold and increases dapsone levels by 1.5 fold in blood |
| Diuretics | May decrease number of platelets |
| Ganciclovir | May increase risk of bone marrow toxicity |
| Indinavir | Increases trimethoprim levels by 19% in blood |
| Lamivudine | Increases lamivudine levels by 44% in blood |
| Nevirapine | Should not be initiated together for the first 4-6 weeks. May increase risk of rashes |
| Phenytoin | May increase phenytoin levels |
| Pyrimethamine | May decrease number of red blood cells |
| Ritonavir | Decreases sulfamethoxazole levels by 20% and increases trimethoprim levels by 20% in blood |
| Theophylline | May increase theophylline levels |
| Warfarin | May increase prothrombin time |

**TRIMETREXATE (NEUTREXIN) PLUS...**

| Acetaminophen | May affect trimetrexate and/or acetaminophen levels |
| Cimetidine | May affect trimetrexate and/or cimetidine levels |
| Clarithromycin | May affect trimetrexate and/or clarithromycin levels |
| Delavirdine | May affect trimetrexate and/or delavirdine levels |
| Erythromycin | May affect trimetrexate and/or erythromycin levels |

| | |
|---|---|
| Fluconazole | May affect trimetrexate and/or fluconazole levels |
| Itraconazole | May affect trimetrexate and/or itraconazole levels |
| Ketoconazole | May affect trimetrexate and/or ketoconazole levels |
| Nevirapine | May affect trimetrexate and/or nevirapine levels |
| Ranitidine | May affect trimetrexate and/or ranitidine levels |
| Rifabutin | May affect trimetrexate and/or rifabutin levels |
| Rifampin | May affect trimetrexate and/or rifampin levels |

**EXPLANATION OF SIDE EFFECTS:**

Anemia = decrease in red blood cells

Neutropenia = decrease in neutrophils

Thrombocytopenia = decrease in platelets

Nephrotoxicity = kidney toxicity

Hypokalemia = decrease in potassium levels in blood

Uveitis = painful inflammation of the uveal tract (structures of the eye)

Arthralgia = joint pains

Myalgia = tenderness or pain in muscles

Encephalopathy = dysfunction of the brain

CNS = central nervous system

LFTs = Liver Function Tests

Hypoglycemia = abnormally low levels of glucose in blood

Hyperglycemia = increase of blood sugars

Hypocalcemia = abnormally low levels of calcium in blood

Granulocytopenia = abnormal reduction in granulocytes in blood

Prothrombin time = a test of blood clotting time

Stevens-Johnson syndrome = dilation of blood capillaries that results in redness and lesions all over the skin. Eyes and mouth may become swollen leading to inability to eat. Sometimes fatal.

# PROJECT INFORM'S NATIONAL HIV/AIDS TREATMENT HOTLINE

The toll-free Project Inform National HIV/AIDS Treatment Hotline is the only nationwide hotline service dedicated to providing information about the treatment of HIV and AIDS. The Project Inform hotline is so highly regarded that the Centers for Disease Control, the San Francisco AIDS Foundation, the national AIDS Hotline, and other AIDS service organizations' hotlines regularly refer their callers to us for treatment information.

Staffed by trained volunteers, the Hotline receives 45,000-50,000 calls per year, and serves as a gateway to other Project Inform services and publications. Callers can request Project Inform publications, get clarification on news reports about treatment options, and receive an objective, reliable "second opinion" to counter rumors, hype, and hysteria.

Volunteers, many who are HIV-positive, staff the Hotline six days per week (Monday through Friday, 9 a.m.-5 p.m., and Saturday, 10 a.m.-4 p.m. Pacific Time). All Hotline volunteers are trained to answer questions regarding the latest treatments for HIV, associated opportunistic infection information, and HIV-related services across the country. Callers may access the toll-free Hotline at (800) 822-7422 nationwide; or (415) 558-9051.

# GLOSSARY

**A**

**ACUPUNCTURE:** An ancient technique of traditional Chinese medicine that stimulates or disperses the natural flow of energy within the body. The technique consists of piercing the skin at specific points of the body with a thin needle.

**ACUTE:** Rapid in onset; severe, life-threatening. The opposite of persistent, chronic, or long-term.

**ADJUVANT:** Any substance (i.e., treatment) that enhances the immune-stimulating properties of an antigen or a vaccine or the pharmacological effect of a drug.

**ADMINISTRATION (ROUTE OF ADMINISTRATION):** How a drug or therapy is introduced into the body, e.g., intravenously or orally.

**AEROSOLIZED:** A form of administration in which a drug, such as pentamidine, is turned into a fine spray or mist by a nebulizer and inhaled.

**AIDS (ACQUIRED IMMUNE DEFICIENCY SYNDROME):** The most severe manifestation of infection with the human immunodeficiency virus (HIV). The Centers for Disease Control and Prevention lists numerous opportunistic infections and neoplasms that, in the presence of HIV infection, constitute an AIDS diagnosis. In addition, a CD4+ count below 200 in the presence of HIV infection constitutes an AIDS diagnosis.

**AMOEBIASIS:** Infection with amoebas, especially Entameba histolytica.

**ANALGESIC:** Agent that reduces pain without reducing consciousness. Aspirin is an analgesic.

**ANAPHYLAXIS:** A systemic allergic reaction to a drug or other antigen that results in life-threatening respiratory distress usually accompanied by shock and collapse of blood vessels.

**ANEMIA:** A condition that occurs if the blood cannot carry enough oxygen to nourish tissues. Common symptoms of anemia are fatigue, headaches, and shortness of breath. Anemia may be caused by too few red blood cells or too little hemoglobin or both.

**ANGIOGENESIS:** The formation of new blood vessels; the induction of the growth of blood vessels from surrounding tissue into a solid tumor.

**ANTIBIOTIC:** A chemical substance that kills or inhibits the growth of bacteria; Antibiotics are used to treat infectious diseases caused by bacteria.

**ANTIBODIES:** Proteins in the blood that seek out and attach to foreign substances in the blood, marking them for destruction by other components of the immune system.

**ANTICOAGULANT:** A substance that delays or counteracts blood clotting.

**ANTIFUNGAL:** A substance that kills or inhibits the growth of a fungus.

**ANTIGEN:** A substance that, when introduced into the body, is capable of inducing the production of a specific antibody.

**ANTI-INFLAMMATORY:** A substance that counteracts or suppresses inflammation. Swelling and redness are consequences of inflammation. there are two types of anti-inflammatory drugs: steroids, such as cortisone, and non-steroidal agents, such as aspirin.

**ANTINEOPLASTIC:** Inhibiting or preventing the proliferation of tumor (cancer) cells.

**ANTIOXIDANT:** Substance that may prevent free radicals (chemicals with free electrons; oxidants) from causing cell damage. Examples of antioxidants are vitamins A, C, and E.

**ANTIPROTOZOAL:** Drugs or other therapies that kill or inhibit the multiplication of single-celled microorganisms called protozoa.

**ANTIRETROVIRAL:** A substance that stops or suppresses the activity of a retrovirus such as HIV. AZT, ddC, ddI, indinavir, ritonavir, and nevirapine are examples of antiretroviral drugs.

**ANTISENSE:** A strand of nucleic acid that will bind to a specific DNA or RNA sequence, interfering with the function of that gene.

**ANTIVIRAL:** A substance or process that destroys a virus or suppresses its replication.

**ARC (AIDS RELATED COMPLEX):** A term once used to describe some HIV-related symptoms but no AIDS-defining diagnosis. These may include recurrent fevers, unexplained weight loss, swollen lymph nodes, and/or fungus infection of the mouth and throat. Today, such conditions are more commonly called HIV infection.

**ARTHRALGIA:** Pain in a joint.

**ASPERGILLOSIS:** A disease caused by a fungus. It can cause lesions of the skin, ear, eye socket, nasal sinuses, lungs, and sometimes the bones, brain, heart, kidneys, or spleen. Symptoms include fever, chills, difficulty breathing, and coughing up blood. If the infection reaches the brain, it may cause dementia.

**ASSAY:** A test.

**ATROPHY:** A wasting or decrease in size.

**AUTOIMMUNE DISEASE:** A disease in which the immune system attacks an individual's own tissues.

**B**

**B LYMPHOCYTES (B CELLS):** One of the immune-system cell types; B cells fight infection primarily by making antibodies. During infections, these cells are transformed into factories that make thousands of antibodies against a foreign substance. This transformation occurs through interactions with various types of CD4+ cells and other components of the immune system.

**BACTERIA:** A group of microscopic organisms that cause disease when they infect someone.

**BDNA:** An assay used to directly detect the presence and amount of a particular nucleic acid. In people with HIV, the test can be used to detect HIV RNA in a blood sample and to determine the amount of viral RNA present.

**BETA-2 MICROGLOBULIN:** This blood test shows how fast cells are being killed by HIV. High beta-2 microglobulin levels occur in a variety of diseases and cancers. While elevated beta-2 is not specific to HIV, there is a correlation between this marker and the progression of HIV disease.

**BILIRUBIN:** A pigment produced by the liver. It is measured as an indication of the health of the liver.

**BIOAVAILABILITY:** The rate and extent to which a substance is absorbed and circulated in the body.

**BIOPSY:** Removal and laboratory examination of tissue from the living body.

**BLOOD-BRAIN BARRIER:** A barrier between brain blood vessels and brain tissues. The barrier controls what goes into the brain. Some drugs cannot cross this barrier, making brain infections difficult to treat.

**BONE MARROW:** Soft tissue located in the cavities of the bones where blood cells are formed, including erythrocytes (red blood cells), leukocytes (white blood cells), and platelets (particles involved in blood clotting).

**BONE MARROW SUPPRESSION:** A condition that can be caused by certain drugs. It leads to a decrease in white blood cells, red blood cells, and platelets. This can lead to bleeding or infections.

**BRONCHOSCOPY:** Insertion of a thin, flexible tube into the lungs through the nose or mouth. Often used as a diagnostic tool for PCP.

**BURKITT'S LYMPHOMA:** A malignant cancer of lymph tissue. Epstein-Barr virus has been isolated from Burkitt's lymphoma and is suspected as a causative agent.

**C**

**CACHEXIA:** Profound ill health or malnutrition.

**CANCER:** A large group of diseases characterized by uncontrolled growth and spread of abnormal cells.

**CANDIDA:** A yeast-like fungus commonly found in the mouth, skin, intestinal tract, and vagina. It can become clinically infectious in immune-compromised people.

**CANDIDIASIS:** A fungal disease caused by Candida, commonly seen in people with suppressed immune systems. It is most commonly seen as white patches in the mouth (known as thrush) or as a white discharge from the vagina, but the fungus can cause disease all over.

**CATHETER:** A semipermanently installed tube used to inject fluids into the body.

**CDC:** The Centers for Disease Control and Prevention. A federal health agency that is a branch of the Public Health Service.

**CD8+ (T8):** A protein embedded in the cell surface of cytotoxic T lymphocytes.

**CD4+:** A protein embedded in the surface of helper T lymphocytes.

**CD4+ COUNT:** Also known as the CD4+ lymphocyte count or T4 cell count, it is the most commonly used marker to determine HIV progression. HIV infects and depletes CD4+ cells, which help fight infections. T lymphocytes include both CD4+ (helper) cells and CD8+ (cytotoxic) cells. A significant drop in the CD4+ count reflects damage to the immune system.

**CELL:** The smallest independent unit of an organism. A cell is composed of cytoplasm and a nucleus and is surrounded by a membrane or wall.

**CHANCROID:** A sexually transmitted disease caused by Haemophilus ducreyi, characterized by painful sores on the genitals.

**CHEMOTHERAPY:** The treatment of disease by chemical agents; usually refers to cancer treatment.

**CHINESE MEDICINE:** Chinese medicine is based on treatments that enhance the body's natural immunity and eliminate or reduce the potency of pathogens (external harmful organisms). Traditional Chinese medicine includes the use of herbs and acupuncture.

**CHRONIC:** Continuous or ongoing.

**CLINICAL:** Pertaining to or founded on actual observation and treatment of patients, as distinguished from theoretical or basic science.

**CMV:** Cytomegalovirus, a herpes infection that is the third leading cause of death in people with AIDS. It can manifest in the eyes (CMV retinitis), the brain (CMV encephalopathy), the lungs (CMV pneumonia), the colon (CMV colitis), or other parts of the body.

**CNS (CENTRAL NERVOUS SYSTEM):** Composed of the brain, spinal cord, and its coverings (meninges).

**COFACTORS:** Substances, microorganisms, or characteristics of individuals that might influence the progression of a disease or the likelihood of becoming ill.

**COLPOSCOPY:** Examination of the cervix or vagina by means of an instrument with a magnifying lens that can be inserted into the vagina.

**COMBINATION THERAPY:** The use of two or more drugs as treatment. Also, the use of two or more types of treatment in combination, alternately or together.

**COMPARISON TRIAL:** A trial in which experimental drugs are tested against each other or against an approved drug.

**COMPASSIONATE USE:** A method of providing experimental drugs to sick patients who have no other treatment options. Usually, case-by-case approval must be obtained from the FDA for compassionate use of a drug.

**COMPLETE BLOOD COUNT (CBC):** Series of tests including red and white blood cell counts, hemoglobin, and cell volume measurement.

**CONTINUOUS INFUSION:** Uninterrupted introduction of fluid other than blood into a vein.

**CONTRAINDICATION ("TO INDICATE AGAINST"):** A specific circumstance when a certain treatment should not be used.

**CONTROLLED TRIALS:** Trials in which one group gets an experimental drug and another group gets either a placebo or an approved drug therapy. Participants usually do not know which group they are in.

**CREATININE:** A protein found in muscles and blood and excreted by the kidneys in the urine. The level of creatinine in the blood and urine provides a measure of kidney function.

**CRYPTOCOCCAL MENINGITIS:** A fungal infection of the brain and spinal cord. Symptoms include severe headache, dizziness, nausea, weight loss, vision disorders, and mental deterioration. Inflammation with headache, blurred

vision, confusion, dizziness, nausea, anorexia, depression, agitation, or slurred speech are common symptoms.

**CRYPTOSPORIDIOSIS:** A protozoal opportunistic infection whose main symptom is prolonged diarrhea that leads to weight loss.

**CRYPTOSPORIDIUM:** A protozoan parasite found in the intestines of animals that may be transmitted to humans by direct contact with an infected animal or by eating contaminated food or water. The parasite grows in the intestines and may cause severe chronic diarrhea in people with HIV disease.

**CYTOKINE:** A protein produced by white blood cells that acts as a chemical messenger between cells.

**CYTOTOXIC:** An agent or process that is toxic to cells that results in suppression of function or cell death.

**D**

**DEMENTIA:** Chronic intellectual impairment (loss of mental capacity) with organic origins that affects a person's ability to function in a social or occupational setting.

**DENDRITIC CELLS:** Cells containing dendrites, threadlike or branched extensions on nerve cells. Dendrites are the surfaces of the nerve cell that receive signals from other cells.

**DIAGNOSIS:** The determination of the presence of a specific disease or infection usually accomplished by evaluating clinical symptoms and laboratory tests.

**DIARRHEA:** Abnormally frequent, loose, or watery stools.

**DISSEMINATED:** Spread throughout the body.

**DIURETIC:** A drug or other agent that promotes excretion of urine resulting in the loss of water from the body.

**DNA (DEOXYRIBONUCLEIC ACID):** A complex molecule that is the carrier of genetic information. HIV can insert itself into a cell's DNA and use cellular mechanisms to make copies of itself.

**DOSAGE:** The size, frequency, and number of doses.

**DOSE:** The amount of a drug that is given at one time.

**DOSE RANGING:** A drug trial in which two or more doses of a given drug are being tested against each other to determine which dose works best and is the least harmful.

**DOUBLE-BLIND:** A type of drug trial in which people are divided into different groups. One group takes the experimental drug and other groups take

different doses, the standard therapy, or a placebo. Neither the researchers nor the people in the trial know who is taking what until the trial is over.

# E

**EARLY INTERVENTION:** Taking action to do something about your health before your immune system becomes seriously weakened by HIV and you develop opportunistic infections. Early intervention with antiviral drugs like AZT has been shown to help people live longer.

**EFFICACY:** Effectiveness.

**ELISA (ENZYME-LINKED IMMUNOSORBENT ASSAY):** A laboratory test to determine the presence of antibodies to HIV in the blood.

**ENCEPHALITIS:** A general term denoting inflammation of the brain.

**ENDOSCOPY:** Viewing the inside of a body cavity with a device using flexible fiber optics.

**ENZYME:** A protein that makes chemical reactions proceed at a faster rate, without itself being consumed in the reaction.

**EPSTEIN-BARR VIRUS (EBV):** A herpeslike virus that causes one of the two kinds of mononucleosis (the other is caused by CMV).

**ERYTHROCYTES:** Red blood cells whose primary function is to carry oxygen to cells.

**EXPANDED ACCESS:** A general term for methods of distributing experimental drugs to people who are unable to participate in ongoing clinical trials and have no other treatment options. Specific types of expanded-access mechanisms include parallel track and compassionate use.

**EXPERIMENTAL DRUG:** A drug that has not been approved for use as a treatment for a particular condition.

# F

**FDA:** Food and Drug Administration, the federal agency responsible for regulating the testing and sale of pharmaceutical drugs and food products.

**FIBROSIS:** Formation of fibrous tissue; e.g., pulmonary fibrosis is chronic inflammation that results in progressive fibrosis in the air sacs of the lungs, which interferes with their function and may lead to severe breathing difficulties.

**FLOATERS:** Floating dark spots within the field of vision. They can be caused by CMV retinitis, but also appear in some persons as a normal part of aging. An HIV-knowledgeable eye doctor can make a correct diagnosis.

**FUNGUS:** A general term used to denote a class of microbes including mushrooms, yeast, and molds. Fungi cause infections such as oral and vaginal thrush and cryptococcal meningitis.

## G

**GAMMA GLOBULIN:** A group of blood proteins that contain most of the blood-borne antibodies.

**GASTROENTERITIS:** Inflammation of the lining of the stomach and intestines.

**GASTROINTESTINAL:** Relating to the stomach and intestines.

**GENE THERAPY:** The process of using or manipulating genes to treat disease.

**GENITAL INFECTIONS:** Recurrent yeast infections in the vagina, or warts or ulcers on the penis, rectum, labia, or cervix.

**GP41:** A glycoprotein ("sugar-covered" protein) inserted in the HIV viral envelope.

**GP120:** A protein found on the surface of the HIV particle. gp120 is the foundation for several of the older approaches to making an HIV vaccine.

**GP160:** A glycoprotein ("sugar-covered" protein) made from the HIV RNA. After synthesis, it is cleaved into gp120 and gp41, two glycoproteins inserted in or on the HIV envelope.

**GRAY BABY SYNDROME:** A potentially fatal condition in newborns, especially premature infants, caused by a reaction to chloramphenicol and characterized by an ashen gray skin color, listlessness, weakness, and low blood pressure.

**GROWTH FACTORS:** A growth factor is responsible for regulating cell proliferation (rapid and repeated reproduction), function, and differentiation. Different growth factors elicit different responses from different cell types, such as stimulating cell growth, enhancing cell survival, initiating cell migration, and stimulating the secretion of tissue-specific hormones.

## H

**HAIRY LEUKOPLAKIA:** A whitish, slightly raised lesion that appears on the side of the tongue. Thought to be related to Epstein-Barr virus infection, it was not observed before the HIV epidemic.

**HELPER-SUPPRESSOR RATIO:** The ratio of helper (CD4+) cells to CD8+ cells.

**HELPER T CELLS (T4, CD4+):** A subset of T cells that carry the CD4+ receptors that are essential for activating antibody production, cytotoxic T cells, and other immune responses.

**HEMATOCRIT:** A laboratory measurement that determines the percentage of packed red blood cells in a given volume of blood.

**HEMOGLOBIN:** The protein in red blood cells responsible for carrying oxygen.

**HEMOPHILIA:** An inherited disease that prevents the normal clotting of blood.

**HEPATITIS:** A viral liver disease that can be acute or chronic and even life-threatening, particularly in people with poor immune systems. Several different viruses cause hepatitis. These include hepatitis A, B, C, and D. Hepatitis A is easily transmitted through food and casual contact. Hepatitis B is sexually transmitted. It is less clear how hepatitis C is transmitted, but it is common among people living with hemophilia and injection-drug users.

**HERPES SIMPLEX VIRUS I (HSV I):** A virus that causes cold sores or fever blisters on the mouth or around the eyes and can be transmitted to the genital region. Stress, trauma, other infections, or suppression of the immune system can reactivate the latent virus.

**HERPES SIMPLEX VIRUS II (HSV II):** A virus causing painful sores of the anus or genitals that may lie dormant in nerve tissue and can be reactivated to produce the symptoms. HSV II may be transmitted to a baby during birth.

**HERPES VARICELLA-ZOSTER VIRUS:** A herpes virus that causes chicken pox in children and may reappear in adulthood as herpes zoster (shingles). Shingles consist of painful blisters on the skin that follow nerve pathways.

**HICKMAN CATHETER:** A flexible, needle-shaped tube that can be surgically placed in a large blood vessel and held in place for long periods of time.

**HISTAMINE:** A hormone/chemical transmitter involved in local immune responses, in regulating stomach-acid production, and in allergic reactions.

**HIV DISEASE:** A variety of symptoms and signs found in people who are HIV-positive. These may include recurrent fevers, unexplained weight loss, swollen lymph nodes, and/or fungus infection of the mouth and throat. Also commonly described as symptomatic HIV infection.

**HODGKIN'S DISEASE:** A malignant cancer of lymph tissue. Symptoms include swollen lymph glands, wasting, weakness, fever, itching, night sweats, and anemia. This disease is treated with radiation and chemotherapy.

**HOLISTIC MEDICINE:** System of health care based on the concept of the "whole" person as one whose body, mind, spirit, and emotions are in balance with the environment.

**HYPERSENSITIVITY:** An allergic reaction; the body reacts with an exaggerated immune response to drugs or other substances.

**HYPERTHERMIA:** A treatment that consists of artificially raising the body's temperature. Using tubes inserted in an artery and a vein in the thigh, blood is withdrawn, heated outside the body with a heat exchanger, and then put back into circulation.

**I**

**IMMUNE DEFICIENCY:** A breakdown or inability of certain parts of the immune system to function, making a person susceptible to certain diseases that he or she would not ordinarily develop.

**IMMUNE RESPONSE:** The activity of the immune system against foreign substances.

**IMMUNE SYSTEM:** The cells, tissues, and circulating proteins of the body that recognize foreign agents or substances, neutralize them, and recall the response later when confronted with the same challenge.

**IMMUNITY:** A natural or acquired resistance to a specific disease. Immunity may be partial or complete, long-lasting, or temporary.

**IMMUNIZATION:** To protect against disease by vaccination, usually with a weak form of the agent that causes illness. People are usually immunized against a disease by getting vaccinated, although having a disease one time usually prevents or "immunizes" you from getting it again. This may not always be true with people who are HIV-positive.

**IMMUNOMODULATOR:** Any substance that strengthens the immune system and helps the body fight off opportunistic infections or other diseases that attack people with HIV or AIDS.

**IMMUNOSUPPRESSION:** A state of the body in which the immune system is damaged and does not perform its normal functions. Drugs or result from certain diseases (such as HIV infection) may induce immunosuppression.

**IMMUNOTHERAPY:** Treatment aimed at reconstituting an impaired immune system.

**IN VITRO (LATIN FOR "IN GLASS"):** An artificial environment created outside a living organism, e.g., a test tube or culture plate, used in experimental research to study a disease or process.

**IN VIVO (LATIN FOR "IN LIFE"):** Studies conducted within a living organism, e.g., animal or human studies.

**INCLUSION/EXCLUSION CRITERIA:** The medical or other reasons why a person may or may not be allowed to enter a trial. For example, some trials do not allow pregnant or nursing women to join, others do not allow people taking certain drugs, and others exclude people with certain illnesses.

**INCUBATION PERIOD:** The time between the initial exposure to infection and the appearance of the first symptom or sign of disease.

**IND (INVESTIGATIONAL NEW DRUG):** A license given by the FDA which permits a company or a researcher to conduct clinical studies of a new drug in humans. An IND is an exemption of the Food, Drug and Cosmetics Act.

**INDICATION:** Purpose for which a drug is intended, e.g., pentamidine is indicated for PCP.

**INFORMED CONSENT:** Type of protection available to people entering a drug trial. Before entering a trial participants must sign a consent form that contains an explanation of (a) why the research is being done; (b) what researchers want to accomplish; (c) what will be done during the trial and for how long; (d) what risks are involved in participating in the trial; (e) what benefits can be expected from the trial; (f) other treatments available; and (g) the right to leave the trial at any time.

**INFUSION:** The slow injection of a substance (medication, food supplements, etc.) into an individual's vein. This procedure can be continued over many hours, days, or even months.

**INHIBITOR:** A chemical or other substance that inhibits or blocks something from happening.

**INTERACTION:** Change in the body's response to one drug when another is taken. A drug interaction may increase the effect or one or both drugs, decrease the effect of one or both drugs, or cause toxicity.

**INTERFERON:** A substance that is produced when the body senses an infection with a virus. Interferon is released to coat uninfected cells so that they don't become infected. There are three main classes of interferon: alpha, beta, and gamma.

**INTERLEUKIN:** A natural blood cytokine that helps immune-system cells communicate.

**INTESTINAL MALABSORPTION:** A condition in which the nutrients found in food are not absorbed by the body. It can lead to malnutrition and weight loss.

**INTRALESIONAL:** Injected directly into a lesion.

**INTRATHECAL:** Injected into the fluid surrounding the spinal cord.

**INTRAVENOUS (IV):** Injected directly into the veins.

**INTRAVITREAL:** Injected directly into the eye.

**ITP (IDIOPATHIC THROMBOCYTOPENIA PURPURA):** A condition in which the body produces antibodies against platelets, which are particles involved in blood clotting. ITP is common in HIV-infected people and often manifests as bruising and purplish spots.

## K

**KAPOSI'S SARCOMA (KS):** A tumor of the wall of blood vessels. Usually appears as pink to purple, painless spots on the skin, but may also occur internally in addition to or independent of lesions.

**KARNOFSKY SCORE:** A subjective score from 0 to 100 assigned by a physician to describe a person's mental function and ability to perform tasks.

**KILLER T CELLS:** A class of immune-system cells that kill cancer and virus-infected cells.

## L

**LATENCY:** The period when an organism is in the body but is not producing any ill effects.

**LESION:** Any pathological or traumatic damage to tissue, which may cause a loss of function of the affected or surrounding tissue.

**LUMBAR PUNCTURE:** A procedure in which fluid from the lumbar region of the spinal cord is tapped for examination, also known as a spinal tap.

**LYMPH NODES:** Small, bean-sized organs of the immune system, distributed widely throughout the body. Lymph fluid is filtered through the lymph nodes, in which all types of lymphocytes take up temporary residence. Antigens that enter the body find their way into lymph or blood and are filtered out by lymph nodes or the spleen, for elimination by the immune system.

**LYMPHADENOPATHY:** Swollen, firm, and possibly tender lymph glands. The cause may range from a temporary infection to lymphoma (cancer of the lymph nodes).

**LYMPHOCYTIC INTERSTITIAL PNEUMONIA (LIP):** A type of pneumonia that affects 35% to 40% of children with AIDS. Children with HIV who have LIP are diagnosed as having AIDS.

**LYMPHOMA:** A cancer of the cells that are responsible for normal immune function. Symptoms may include lymph-node swelling, weight loss, and fever.

# M

**MACROPHAGE:** A scavenger cell specializing in the ingestion of large particulate matter, especially harmful bacteria. The macrophage may be a reservoir for HIV.

**MAGNETIC RESONANCE IMAGING (MRI):** A noninvasive diagnostic technique that can provide information on the form and function of internal tissue and organs of the body.

**MAINTENANCE THERAPY:** Use of a treatment or treatments after the disease has been brought under control to prevent recurrent disease. Unless maintenance therapy is used against PCP pneumonia, for example, the disease will probably occur again.

**MALABSORPTION SYNDROME:** Decreased intestinal absorption resulting in loss of appetite, muscle pain, and weight loss.

**MALIGNANCY:** A tumor or cancer.

**MENINGITIS:** Inflammation of the brain and spinal cord.

**MOLLUSCUM CONTAGIOSUM:** A skin disease caused by a virus that causes small, rounded tumors. They are persistent but have no other general symptoms.

**MUCOUS MEMBRANE:** A moist layer of tissue that lines body cavities or passages that have an opening to the external world, e.g., the lining of the mouth, nostrils, or vagina.

**MULTIPLE ALLERGIC REACTIONS:** Increased severity of reactions (fever, rash, swelling, itching) to insect bites or common medications such as sulfa or penicillin.

**MYALGIA:** Muscle pain.

**MYCOBACTERIUM AVIUM COMPLEX (MAC or MAI):** A disease caused by an organism found in soil and dust particles. In people with HIV disease, it can spread through the bloodstream to infect many parts of the body. Symptoms of MAC include prolonged wasting, fever, fatigue, and enlarged spleen. It is usually found only in individuals who have CD4+ counts less than 100.

**MYCOSIS:** Any disease caused by a fungus.

**MYELOSUPPRESSION:** The suppression of bone marrow activity, which can cause anemia, increased risk for infection, or increased risk of bleeding.

# N

**NASBA (NUCLEIC ACID SEQUENCE-BASED AMPLIFICATION):** An assay used to detect HIV RNA in a blood sample and to determine the amount of viral RNA present.

**NAUSEA:** An unpleasant sensation in the abdomen (like carsickness or seasickness) that often leads to vomiting.

**NEOPLASM:** An abnormal and uncontrolled growth of tissue; a tumor.

**NEPHROTOXICITY:** Toxic or destructive to kidney cells.

**NEUROLEPTIC MALIGNANT SYNDROME (NMS):** A rare, sometimes fatal, reaction to certain psychoactive drugs; the syndrome is characterized by high fever, muscle rigidity, and in severe cases, coma.

**NEUROPATHY:** Any abnormal, degenerative, or inflammatory state of the peripheral nervous system; symptoms include numbness, tingling, or pain in the extremities.

**NEUTROPENIA:** A low number of neutrophils in the blood. Neutrophils are white blood cells important in defending the body against infections.

**NEUTROPHIL:** A white blood cell that plays a central role in the immune system. Neutrophils are the immune system's main defense against bacterial infections.

**NIGHT SWEATS:** Extreme sweating that happens during sleep. Night sweats are considered a symptom of HIV only when the body is drenched. Slight sweating is not a symptom.

**NON-HODGKIN'S LYMPHOMA (NHL):** Cancer of the lymph tissue, commonly characterized by painless enlargement of one or more lymph nodes.

**NON-NUCLEOSIDE REVERSE TRANSCRIPTASE INHIBITOR:** A drug that interferes with reverse transcription but is not chemically similar to the building blocks of DNA (nucleosides).

**NUCLEIC ACIDS:** Large, naturally occurring molecules composed of chemical building blocks known as nucleotides. DNA and RNA are nucleic acids.

**NUCLEOSIDE ANALOGUE:** A synthetic compound similar to one of the components of DNA or RNA; a general type of antiviral drug, e.g., acyclovir and AZT.

## O

**OFF-LABEL:** A drug prescribed for conditions other than those approved by the FDA.

**OPEN-LABEL:** A type of drug trial in which researchers and participants know who is taking the experimental drug or the treatment being given.

**OPEN TRIAL:** A drug trial is "open" when doctors and participants know which drug is being administered, as opposed to a double-blinded trial in which they do not know (some may receive a test drug or placebo) until the trial is over.

**OPPORTUNISTIC INFECTIONS (OI):** Certain illnesses (such as PCP) that people with AIDS can get and that can be life-threatening. People with healthy immune systems do not usually get these illnesses, even though most people have the organisms that cause these illnesses in their body. Only when the immune system is damaged can the organisms take advantage of the "opportunity" of this weakened state and cause damage.

**ORAL (PO):** Taken by mouth as a pill or liquid.

## P

**PANCREATITIS:** Inflammation of the pancreas, which can produce severe pain and debilitating illness.

**PARALLEL TRACK:** A system of distributing experimental drugs to individuals who are unable to participate in ongoing clinical trials.

**PARASITE:** A plant or animal that lives and feeds on or within another living organism. Does not necessarily cause disease.

**PATHOGENESIS:** The process by which an infectious agent or metabolic disorder causes disease or harm in the body.

**PELVIC INFLAMMATORY DISEASE (PID):** Inflammation of the pelvic area, which may lead to tubal scarring, infertility, or ectopic pregnancy. The most common symptom is pain in the lower abdomen. Additional symptoms may include fever, cervical tenderness, and/or abnormal vaginal discharge. PID is usually caused by untreated sexually transmitted infections, such as chlamydia or gonorrhea.

**PERIPHERAL NEUROPATHY:** A disorder of the nerves, usually involving the hands, feet, arms, and legs. Symptoms may include numbness, a tingling or burning sensation, sharp pain, weakness, and abnormal reflexes. In severe cases, paralysis may result.

**PHASE I STUDY:** Safety testing; the first step in human testing of a drug. Designed to evaluate toxicity at different dose levels. Takes place with a small number of participants.

**PHASE II STUDY:** Small-scale trials for determining drug efficiency and toxicity in humans. Proceeds only if Phase I studies show toxicity to be within acceptable levels.

**PHASE III STUDY:** Large-scale trials for determining drug efficiency in humans. Designed to back up information gathered in Phase I and II testing. Also compares the drug to other agents, either alone or in combination.

**PLACEBO:** A substance that has no effect on the body (often referred to as a sugar pill) that is given to one group in a placebo-controlled trial. In placebo-controlled drug studies, a placebo is given to one group of participants, while the drug being tested is given to another group. The results obtained in the two groups are then compared.

**PLACEBO EFFECT:** A change that occurs after a placebo is taken due to the expectations of the patient.

**PLAGUE:** Severe, acute, or chronic bacterial infection caused by Yersinia pestis.

**PLATELET:** A cellular particle involved in blood clotting. HIV can decrease platelets and cause bleeding and other disease. A normal platelet count is between 200,000 and 400,000.

**PNEUMOCYSTIS CARINII PNEUMONIA (PCP):** A protozoal infection of the lungs; the most common life-threatening opportunistic infection in AIDS patients.

**POLYMERASE CHAIN-REACTION TEST (PCR):** A very sensitive test for the presence of specific DNA or RNA fragments. Commonly used to detect and quantify HIV viral load.

**PROPHYLACTIC DRUG:** A drug that helps to prevent a disease or initial infection. For example, Bactrim is a prophylactic treatment for PCP.

**PROPHYLAXIS:** Taking a drug to prevent an illness.

**PROTEASE:** A substance that breaks down proteins. When first made in a cell, a number of HIV proteins are joined together. HIV protease breaks them into functional proteins. Protease inhibitors interfere with this stage in the HIV life cycle, showing the progression of viral infection.

**PROTEIN:** Proteins are organic compounds made up of amino acids and are a major constituent of plant and animal cells.

**PROTOCOL:** A detailed plan that states a drug trial's rationale, purpose, drug dosages, length of treatment, how the drug is given, and who may participate (inclusion/exclusion criteria).

**PROTOZOA:** A group of one-celled animals, a few of which cause human disease.

**P24 ANTIGEN:** A protein fragment of HIV. The p24 antigen test detects this fragment. A positive result for p24 suggests that HIV is multiplying.

**PULMONARY:** Pertaining to the lungs.

**R**

**RADIATION THERAPY:** A treatment for cancer using radiation produced by a machine.

**RESISTANCE:** The ability of a microorganism to overcome a drug. For example, after long-term use of AZT, strains of HIV develop in the body that are no longer suppressed by this drug and are therefore said to be resistant to AZT.

**RETINA:** The light-sensitive tissue in the back of the eyeball that sends images to the brain.

**RETINITIS:** Inflammation of the retina.

**RETROVIRUS:** A class of viruses with RNA as its genetic material (e.g., HIV).

**REVERSE TRANSCRIPTASE:** A retroviral enzyme that is capable of copying RNA into DNA, an essential step in the life cycle of HIV. AZT, ddI, and ddC work by inhibiting reverse transcriptase.

**REYE'S SYNDROME:** A rare and sometimes fatal disease of childhood, most often as part of chicken pox or a viral upper-respiratory infection. It is characterized by vomiting, liver toxicity, acute brain swelling, loss of consciousness, and seizures.

**S**

**SALVAGE THERAPY:** Treatment for individuals who don't respond to or who can't take other treatments for a condition.

**SEPSIS:** A serious condition caused by uncontrolled growth of bacteria in the blood. This condition can lead to septic shock, a sudden drop in blood pressure, changes in heart rate, and temperature.

**SGOT AND SGPT:** Blood tests that measure liver enzymes to see if the liver is damaged.

**SIDE EFFECTS:** The action or effect of a drug other than that desired. The term usually refers to undesired or negative effects, such as headache, skin irritation, or liver damage. Experimental drugs must be evaluated for both immediate and long-term side effects.

**SINUSITIS:** Inflammation of the sinuses.

**SPINAL TAP:** See Lumbar puncture.

**STAPHYLOCOCCUS:** A genus of anaerobic bacteria, some of which cause local lesions and severe systemic opportunistic infections.

**STD:** Sexually transmitted disease, such as syphilis, gonorrhea, herpes, hepatitis, and others.

**STEM CELLS:** Cells from which all blood cells are derived. Bone marrow is rich in stem cells.

**STEVENS-JOHNSON SYNDROME:** A sometimes fatal syndrome that is characterized by severe lesions on the skin or mucous membranes. The lesions may be gray or white. The syndrome may include inflammation or perforation of the tissues of the eye, leading to blindness. The syndrome may also include symptoms in the lungs, gut, heart, and kidneys.

**STOMATITIS:** Swelling of the mouth or throat, which is usually painful. Some drugs, such as ddC, may cause this condition.

**SUBCLINICAL INFECTION:** An infection, or phase of infection, without readily apparent symptoms or signs of disease.

**SUBCUTANEOUS:** Giving a drug by injecting it under the skin.

**SUPERANTIGEN:** Foreign materials, such as toxins, produced by infectious microorganisms. Superantigens have the ability to activate many different T cells, resulting in large amounts of cytokine production and large-scale activation of the immune system. This activation may result in shock. Many toxins that cause food poisoning in humans are superantigens.

**SUPPRESSOR T CELLS:** T cells that turn other T cells off; CD8+ cells.

**SURROGATE MARKERS:** A measurement used to assess stage of disease or general health. In HIV disease, CD4+ cells, a marker of immune status, and HIV "viral load," a measurement indicating viral activity, are commonly used surrogate markers. Once a laboratory marker, such as CD4+ or HIV-RNA PCR, is definitely correlated to disease progression, it is then considered a clinical marker.

**SYMPTOMS:** Any perceptible, subjective change in the body or its functions, as reported by the patient, that indicates disease or phases of disease.

**SYNERGISM/SYNERGISTIC:** An interaction between two or more agents (e.g., drugs) that produces an effect that is greater than the sum of their individual effects.

**SYSTEMIC:** Affecting the whole body.

**T**

**T CELLS:** White blood cells that play an important part in regulating the immune system. All cells are derived from the bone marrow, and where they mature will determine their function. T cells mature in the thymus, whereas B cells mature in the bone marrow. There are two major types of T cells, CD4+ (T4) and CD8+ (T8) cells. Each type of cell has subsets that perform different functions. CD4+ cells can be TH1, TH2, or TH0 cells, each of which supports different types of immune responses. CD8+ cells are often cytotoxic cells, which seek out and destroy virally infected cells.

**T-HELPER CELL:** CD4+ cells. CD4+ cells trigger and stimulate the immune response. The normal range for T-helper cells is 500 to 1,500.

**T-KILLER CELL (CYTOXIC T CELLS):** A type of white blood cell that kills foreign organisms after being activated by T-helper (CD4+) cells.

**TARDIVE DYSKINESIA:** Involuntary movements, generally of the muscles in the face or mouth. It is usually the consequence of long-term administration of certain psychoactive drugs.

**THIAZIDES:** A group of related chemicals that stimulate secretion of urine resulting in loss of water from the body; diuretics. Thiazides are used for the treatment of swelling due to congestive heart failure or chronic liver or kidney disease.

**THROMBOCYTOPENIA:** A decreased number of blood platelets, particles important for blood clotting.

**THRUSH:** A fungal infection of the vagina, mouth, or throat that usually causes white spots or blotches. Thrush is caused by infection by Candida.

**TOXIC REACTION:** A poisonous or unwanted reaction to a vitamin, drug, or other substance. A toxic side effect is when a helpful medicine also causes some damage to the blood or body. Toxicity is a measurement of how much damage may be caused.

**TOXOPLASMOSIS:** An opportunistic infection caused by the protozoan Toxoplasma gondii. It frequently causes encephalitis (inflammation of the brain). Toxoplasmosis may also involve the heart, lungs, adrenal glands, pancreas, and testes.

**TUBERCULOSIS (TB):** An infection caused by Mycobacterium tuberculosis, usually in the lungs. Treatment consists of the administration of a combination of bacterial drugs for long periods of time.

**TUMOR NECROSIS FACTOR (TNF):** A protein produced by macrophages that modulates the immune response. By itself, TNF destroys cancer cells. TNF can cause fever, chills, fatigue, headache, and inflammation. TNF causes weight loss and is associated with KS progression and increased HIV replication.

**U**

**UVEITIS:** Inflammation of number of tissues in the eye.

**V**

**VACCINE:** A shot or shots that prevent a disease. Another kind of vaccine, therapeutic vaccines, are in development and being studied. These vaccines may help fight HIV even after someone has been infected.

**VAGINAL CANDIDIASIS:** Infection in the vagina caused by Candida. Symptoms include pain, itching, redness, and white patches in the vaginal wall. Much more common and more difficult to treat in women with HIV infection.

**VIRAL LOAD:** The quantity of virus measurable in blood serum or other fluid or tissue.

**VIREMIA:** The presence of virus in the bloodstream.

**VIRUS:** The smallest known infectious organism. A group of infectious agents characterized by their inability to reproduce outside a living cell.

**W**

**WASTING SYNDROME:** Progressive, involuntary weight loss associated with advanced HIV infection.

**WESTERN BLOT:** A laboratory test for the presence of specific antibodies.

**WHITE BLOOD CELLS:** Part of the immune system that protects the body against foreign substances such as disease-producing microorganisms.

# HIV/AIDS PREVENTION/ TREATMENT/INFORMATION RESOURCES

Project Inform encourages people living with HIV to make their healthcare decisions in conjunction with their supporters and health care providers on the basis of information from reliable, responsible resources. The following resource list will help in this process. Project Inform does not necessarily endorse the information which these information providers may recommend. The choice is yours.

Whether you are reading an HIV newsletter, talking to a hotline operator, reading a pharmaceutical company advertisement, or listening to your doctor, a friend or coworker, remember—you are the person who must ultimately live with your decisions. You have a right to choose. What's best for another may not be best for you. Maybe there are other options. As always in health care, beware of those telling you what you *should* do. Be alert for fraud. Get a second or third opinion. Seek out support from people you trust.

We encourage you to call Project Inform's National HIV/AIDS Treatment Hotline to speak with trained hotline volunteers who are personally familiar with many of the questions you may be facing.

## NATIONAL ORGANIZATIONS

The following telephone numbers for nationwide resource groups can be useful in locating or double-checking local resources. Many state AIDS hotlines' (800) numbers are available only within the state or a given area code. If you are not able to reach a hotline through the numbers provided, call (800) information at (800) 555-1212, the CDC, or Project Inform's hotline.

**ACTIS/AIDS CLINICAL TRIALS INFORMATION SERVICE**
(FDA Approved Trials)
(800) TRIALS-A
(800) 874-2572
FAX (301) 738-6616
Spanish spoken
Hearing impaired:
TTY/TDD (800) 243-7012

**ATIS/AIDS TREATMENT INFORMATION SERVICE**
(FDA Approved Treatments)
(800) HIV-0400
(800) 448-0400
FAX (301) 738-6616
Spanish spoken
Hearing impaired: TTY/TDD
(800) 243-7012

## (CDC) NATIONAL HIV AND AIDS HOTLINE

(800) 342-2437
Spanish: (800) 344-7432
Hearing impaired:
TTY/TDD: (800) 243-7889
Information and referrals on all aspects of HIV/AIDS treatment and services. Open 24 hours a day, 365 days a year.

## (CDC) CENTERS FOR DISEASE CONTROL AND PREVENTION

National AIDS Clearinghouse
(800) 458-5231
FAX (800) 738-6616
Referrals to organizations, services, prevention, funding, publications. Information on clinical trials, treatment, and research on HIV and other infectious diseases.

## COMMUNITY PROVIDER AIDS TRAINING (CPAT)

(800) 933-3413
7:30 A.M. - 5 P.M. PT
24 hour Voice Mail
National HIV telephone consultation service for health care providers

## HANDI/NATIONAL HEMOPHILIA FOUNDATION

Hemophilia and AIDS/HIV Network for the Dissemination of Information
(800) 424-2634
English, ext. 3051
Spanish, ext. 3054

## HIV NIGHTLINE/CRISIS HOTLINE

(415) 434-2437
Open from 5 P.M. to 5 A.M. PT
Spanish: (415) 989-5212
Hearing impaired:
TTY/TDD (415) 781-2228
California only: (800) 273-2437
Spanish: (800) 303-7432

## NATIONAL INSTITUTES OF HEALTH (NIH)

Information line AIDS clinical trials
(800) AIDS-NIH
(800) 243-7644

## NATIONAL ASSOCIATION OF PEOPLE WITH AIDS (NAPWA)

(202) 898-0414

## NATIONAL HOSPICE ORGANIZATION

(800) 658-8898
Advocacy for the needs of terminally ill.

## NATIONAL LIBRARY OF MEDICINE

(800) 638-8480
Free info packet on on-line AIDS databases: AIDSLINE/HIV-related organizations; AIDSTRIALS/protocol info on trials listed through ACTIS; and AIDSDRUGS/treatments.
Also Medline database, Grateful Med software/Lonesome doc/Toxnet and PDQ

## NATIONAL NATIVE AMERICAN AIDS PREVENTION CENTER HOTLINE

(800) 283-2437

## NATIONAL SEXUALLY TRANSMIT-TED DISEASE HOTLINE

(800) 227-8922

## PLANNED PARENTHOOD FEDERA-TION OF AMERICA, INC

(212) 541-7800

## PROJECT INFORM NATIONAL HIV/AIDS TREATMENT HOTLINE

(800) 822-7422
(415) 558-9051

## STATE HIV/AIDS REFERRAL HOTLINES

Contact the HIV/AIDS Referral Hotline in your state to seek referrals for local services; volunteerism; advocacy groups; safer sex guidelines; medical care; your state's AIDS Drug Assistance Program (ADAP); services for women, people of color, youth, gay, lesbian, bisexual, and transgendered people; benefits; substance abuse treatment programs; support services; food; housing; therapy; etc.

Many toll-free (800) numbers include words, in most instances we have provided the numerical equivalent for AIDS (2437).

**ALABAMA**
(800) 228-0469

**ALASKA**
(800) 478-2437, (907) 263-2050

**ARIZONA**
(602) 265-2437

**ARKANSAS**
(800) 342-2437

**CALIFORNIA**
(800) 367-2437, (415) 863-2437

**COLORADO**
(800) 333-2437, (303) 692-2720

**CONNECTICUT**
(800) 203-1234

**DELAWARE**
(800) 422-0429

**DISTRICT OF COLUMBIA**
(202) 332-2437

**FLORIDA**
(800) 243-7101, (850) 681-9131

**GEORGIA**
(800) 551-2728, (404) 876-9944

**HAWAII**
(800) 321-1555, (808) 922-4787

**IDAHO**
(800) 677-2437, (208) 345-2277

**ILLINOIS**
(800) 243-2437, (773) 404-8726

**INDIANA**
(800) 848-2437, (317) 926-7470

**IOWA**
(800) 445-2437, (515) 244-6700

**KANSAS**
(316) 264-2437

**KENTUCKY**
(800) 840-2865

**LOUISIANA**
(800) 992-4379, (504) 944-2437

**MAINE**
(800) 851-2437, (207) 775-1267

**MARYLAND**
(800) 638-6252, (410) 333-2437

**MASSACHUSETTS**
(800) 235-2331, (617) 536-7733

**MICHIGAN**
(800) 872-2437, (810) 547-3783

**MINNESOTA**
(800) 248-2437, (612) 341-2060

**MISSISSIPPI**
(800) 826-2961, (601) 936-6959

**MISSOURI**
(800) 533-2437

**MONTANA**
(800) 233-6668

**NEBRASKA**
(800) 782-2437, (402) 552-9260

**NEVADA**
(800) 842-2437, (702) 687-4800

**NEW HAMPSHIRE**
(800) 752-2437, (603) 271-4502

**NEW JERSEY**
(800) 624-2377, (793) 926-7443

**NEW MEXICO**
(800) 545-2437

**NEW YORK**
(800) 872-2777, (800) 828-3280

**NORTH CAROLINA**
(800) 342-2437

**NORTH DAKOTA**
(800) 472-2180

**OHIO**
(800) 332-2437

**OKLAHOMA**
(800) 535-2437

**OREGON**
(800) 777-2437

**PENNSYLVANIA**
(800) 662-6080

**RHODE ISLAND**
(800) 726-3010

**SOUTH CAROLINA**
(800) 322-2437, (803) 737-4110

**SOUTH DAKOTA**
(800) 592-1861, (605) 773-3364

**TENNESSEE**
(800) 525-2437, (615) 741-7500

**TEXAS**
(800) 299-2437, (512) 490-2538

**UTAH**
(800) 366-2437, (801) 487-2323

**VERMONT**
(800) 995-8567

**VIRGINIA**
(800) 533-4148

**WASHINGTON**
(800) 272-2437, (360) 586-3887

**WEST VIRGINIA**
(800) 995-3746

**WISCONSIN**
(800) 334-2437

**WYOMING**
(800) 675-2698

## CANADIAN ORGANIZATIONS

**COMMUNITY AIDS TREATMENT
INFORMATION EXCHANGE**
(416) 944-1916
(800) 263-1638

**PACIFIC AIDS RESOURCE CENTER**
(604) 687-2437

**CANADIAN PUBLIC HEALTH ASSO-
CIATION**
(613) 725-3434

## CANADIAN HIV/AIDS HOTLINE NUMBERS

**ALBERTA**
(800) 772-2437

**BRITISH COLUMBIA**
(800) 665-4347

**MANITOBA**
(800) 782-2437

**NEW BRUNSWICK**
(800) 561-4009

**NEWFOUNDLAND**
(800) 563-1575

**NORTHWEST TERRITORIES**
(800) 661-0795

**NOVA SCOTIA**
Call collect (902) 425-2437

**ONTARIO**
English (800) 668-2437
French (800) 267-7432

**PRINCE EDWARD ISLAND**
(800) 314-2437
(902) 566-2437

**QUEBEC**
**(800) 463-5656**

**SASKATCHEWAN**
(800) 667-6876

**YUKON**
(800) 661-0507

## NATIONAL HIV/AIDS PUBLICATIONS

**AIDS MEDICINES IN
DEVELOPMENT**
Pharmaceutical Manufacturers
Association
Communications Division
1100 15th Street, NW
Washington, DC 20005
(202) 835-3400

**AIDS TREATMENT NEWS**
P.O. Box 411256
San Francisco, CA 94141
(415) 255-0588
(800) 873-2812
Published twice-monthly by John
James, reports on developments in
treatments for HIV, opportunistic
infections, and issues related to
research and treatment access. Call
for subscription rates.

**AIDS WEEKLY PLUS AND
AIDS THERAPIES**
C. W. Henderson
P.O. Box 830409
Birmingham, AL 35283
(800) 633-4931
*AIDS Weekly Plus*, a newsletter with
short abstracts of AIDS-related news
items, journal articles, conference
reports, and *AIDS Therapies*, a 200-
page binder with monthly updates.

**BEING ALIVE NEWSLETTER**
3626 Sunset Boulevard
Los Angeles, CA 90026
(213) 667-3262
Also *Women Alive* and information
in Spanish

**BETA (BULLETIN OF EXPERIMEN-
TAL TREATMENTS FOR AIDS)**
P.O. Box 426182
San Francisco, CA 94142-6182
(800) 959-1059
Monthly Newsletter also in Spanish
Also *Positive News/Noticias
Positivas*, lower literacy in English
and Spanish

**FAACTS (FACTS ON ALTERNATE
AIDS COMPOUNDS AND TREAT-
MENTS)**
111 Gates Street
San Francisco, CA 94110
(415) 648-1357
Provides summaries and reprints
from the scientific and popular press
concerning emerging treatments for
HIV disease. Nominal fee

**NOTES FROM THE UNDERGROUND**
PWA Health Group
150 West 26th Street
Suite 201
New York, NY 10001
(212) 255-0520
FAX (212) 255-2080
E-mail: pwahg@aidsnyc.org
Bi-monthly

**PI PERSPECTIVE**
Project Inform
1965 Market Street, Suite 220
San Francisco, CA 94103
(800) 822-7422
HIV treatment newsletter. Comes out
three times per year

**POSITIVELY AWARE**
Test Positive Aware Network
1258 West Belmont Avenue
Chicago, IL 60657-3292
(773) 404-8726
Monthly newsletter

**POZ MAGAZINE**
Subscription Department
P.O. Box 1965
Danbury, CT 06813
(800) 9-READ-POZ
(800) 973-2376
Editorial offices:
Box 1279, Old Chelsea Station,
New York, NY 10113
Bi-monthly magazine for HIV-
infected and affected individuals

**STEP PERSPECTIVE**
Seattle Treatment Education Project
127 Broadway East, #200
Seattle, WA 98102
(206) 329-4857
Treatment newsletter published three
times per year

**TAGLINE**
200 East 10th Street, #601
New York, NY 10003
(212) 260-0300
Monthly Treatment Newsletter

**TREATMENT ISSUES**
Gay Men's Health Crisis/GMHC
129 West 20th Street
New York, NY 10011
(212) 337-3505
Monthly treatment newsletter

**TREATMENT REVIEW**
AIDS Treatment Data Network
611 Broadway, Suite 613
New York, NY 10012
(800) 734-7104
Monthly treatment newsletter

## HIV/AIDS WEBSITES

**AIDS EDUCATION GLOBAL INFORMATION SYSTEM (AEGIS)**
http://www.aegis.com

**AIDS RESEARCH INFORMATION CENTER, INC.**
http://www.critipath.org/aric/

**AIDS TREATMENT DATA NETWORK**
http://www.aidsync.org

**ALL THE VIROLOGY ON THE WWW**
brought to you by the Gary Lab
http://www.tulane.edu/dmsanders/garryfavweb.html

**BETA**
http://www.staf.org/beta.html

**THE BODY**
http://www.thebody.com/cgi-bin/body.cig

**THE COMMUNITY AIDS TREAT-**

**MENT INFO EXCHANGE**
http://www.catie.ca

**GMHC**
http://www.gmhc.org

**HIV INSITE**
http://hivinsite.ucsf.edu

**IMMUNET**
http://www.immunet.org

**MARTY HOWARD'S HIV/AIDS HOMEPAGE**
http://www.smartlink.net/m~martinjh/

**PROJECT INFORM**
http://www.projinf.org

**PWA HEALTH GROUP**
http://www. aidsnyc.org

## BUYERS' CLUBS

Buyers' clubs are small businesses or non-profit agencies created to help HIV-infected people access and purchase some kinds of therapies at a reduced cost. Each club or business is different and offers its own group of products for sale. Products available can sometimes include discounted vitamins and herbs, unapproved and alternative therapies, imported drugs not licensed for sale in the United States, and (rarely) bootleg versions of new or experimental drugs. Though most such organizations operate with high integrity and genuine concern for the HIV-infected community, they are unregulated and there are no guarantees about the usefulness of the treatments they sell. Nonetheless, many buyers' clubs perform an important role in providing access to special therapies at a reasonable cost.

### ARIZONA

**BEING ALIVE BUYERS' CLUB**
AIDS Project Arizona
Phoenix
(602) 265-2437

**SOUTHERN ARIZONA AIDS FOUNDATION**
Tucson
(520) 322-6226

## CALIFORNIA

**HEALING ALTERNATIVES**
San Francisco
(415) 626-4053

**CFIDS AND FIBROMYALGIA HEALTH RESOURCE**
Santa Barbara
(800) 366-6056

**LIFELINK**
Grover Beach
(888) 433-5266
(805) 473-1389

**EMBRACE LIFE**
Capitola
(800) 448-1170
(408) 464-7444

## COLORADO

**DENVER BUYERS' CLUB**
PWA Coalition of Colorado
Denver
(303) 329-9379

## DISTRICT OF COLUMBIA

**CARL VOGEL FOUNDATION**
Washington
(202) 638-0750

## FLORIDA

**AIDS MANASOTA**
Sarasota
(941) 954-6011

**HEALTH LINK**
Fort Lauderdale
(954) 565-8284

**WHOLESALE HEALTH**
Fort Lauderdale
(954) 764-1587

## GEORGIA

**AIDS TREATMENT INITIATIVES**
Atlanta
(404) 874-4845

## MASSACHUSETTS

**BOSTON BUYERS' CLUB**
Boston
(800) 465-5586
(617) 266-2223

## NEW YORK

**DIRECT AIDS ALTERNATIVE INFORMATION RESOURCES (DAAIR)**
New York City
(888) 951-5433
(212) 725-6994

**PWA HEALTH GROUP**
New York City
(212) 255-0520

## CANADA

**CANADIAN NUTRITION CLUB**
Ottawa
(800) 996-8466
(613) 284-0076

**SUPPLEMENTS PLUS**
Toronto
(800) 387-4761
(416) 977-3088

## STATE AIDS DRUG ASSISTANCE PROGRAMS (ADAP)

State AIDS drug assistance programs (ADAPs) were originally established with federal dollars to make AZT available to people with HIV disease who could not afford it or get it through their health care plan. As the epidemic has progressed and more therapies have become available, the programs have provided a wider variety of therapies. ADAPs are intended to serve the treatment needs of people who do not have private insurance or whose insurance doesn't cover the cost of AIDS drugs. ADAPs are administered on a state level, and eligibility and the list of specific drugs provided vary greatly from state to state. For eligibility criteria and a listing of the drugs covered on your state's AIDS drug assistance program, call the local information line listed. Because these numbers may change, call the Project Inform Treatment Information Hotline for an update when necessary.

**ALABAMA**
(334) 206-5364

**ALASKA**
(907) 276-1400

**ARIZONA**
(602) 230-5819

**ARKANSAS**
(501) 661-2292

**CALIFORNIA**
(916) 327-6784

**COLORADO**
(800) 858-2437

**CONNECTICUT**
(860) 424-5144

**DELAWARE**
(302) 428-2538

**DISTRICT OF COLUMBIA**
(202) 724-5206

**FLORIDA**
(904) 487-3684

**GEORGIA**
(404) 657-3100

**HAWAII**
(808) 732-0315

**IDAHO**
(208) 334-6526

**ILLINOIS**
(217) 524-5983

**INDIANA**
(317) 920-3190

**IOWA**
(515) 284-0245

**KANSAS**
(913) 296-0201

**KENTUCKY**
(502) 564-6539

**LOUISIANA**
(504) 568-7474

**MAINE**
(207) 287-5060

MARYLAND
(410) 767-6535

MASSACHUSETTS
(800) 228-2724

MICHIGAN
(517) 335-9333

MINNESOTA
(612) 297-3344

MISSISSIPPI
(601) 960-7723

MISSOURI
(573) 751-6470

MONTANA
(406) 444-3565

NEBRASKA
(402) 471-2937

NEVADA
(702) 687-4800

NEW HAMPSHIRE
(603) 271-4502

NEW JERSEY
(609) 984-6125

NEW MEXICO
(505) 827-2335

NEW YORK
(518) 459-1641

NORTH CAROLINA
(919) 733-6298

NORTH DAKOTA
(701) 328-2378

OHIO
(614) 466-6669

OKLAHOMA
(405) 271-4636

OREGON
(503) 731-4438

PENNSYLVANIA
(717) 772-6057

RHODE ISLAND
(401) 464-2183

SOUTH CAROLINA
(803) 737-4110

SOUTH DAKOTA
(605) 773-3737

TENNESSEE
(615) 741-7308

TEXAS
(512) 490-2510

UTAH
(801) 538-6495

VERMONT
(802) 241-3064

VIRGINIA
(804) 225-3897

WASHINGTON
(801) 538-6096

WEST VIRGINIA
(304) 558-2950

WISCONSIN
(608) 267-5287

WYOMING
(307) 777-5800

# PHARMACEUTICAL PAYMENT ASSISTANCE PROGRAMS

Some of these programs provide a free supply of drugs or diagnostic tests to people with HIV who don't have insurance and can't qualify for other programs. Others provide a payment cap on expensive drugs. (After a certain dollar amount has been spent within a given year, the program will provide the drug for free.) In almost all cases, you need to have your doctor call these numbers. You will not be able to sign yourself up. You may be able to speed the process by calling for eligibility information and forms.

**ACYCLOVIR (ZOVIRAX)**
Herpes simplex, herpes zoster
**Glaxo Wellcome Co.**
Contact: HIV Patient Assistance Program
(800) 722-9294

**ALPHA INTERFERON (INTRON A)**
KS, ano-genital neoplasms
**Schering-Plough Corp.**
Contact: Reimbursement Information Services
(800) 521-7157

**ALPHA INTERFERON (ROFERON-A)**
KS, ano-genital neoplasms
**Hoffmann-La Roche, Inc.**
Contact: Reimbursement Assistance
(800) 443-6676

**AMITRIPTYLINE**
Peripheral neuropathy
**Hoffman-La Roche, Inc.**
Contact: Reimbursement Assistance
(800) 285-4484

**AMPHOTERICIN B LIPOSOMAL (ABELCET)**
Aspergillosis
**The Liposome Company, Inc.**
Contact: Financial Assistance Program
(800) 335-5476

**AMPHOTERICIN B ORAL SUSPENSION (FUNGIZONE)**
Fungal Infections
**Bristol-Myers Squibb Co.**
Contact: Reimbursement and Assistance
(800) 272-4878

**ATOVAQUONE (MEPRON)**
PCP, toxoplasmosis, cryptosporidiosis, microsporidiosis
**Glaxo Wellcome Co.**
Contact: Patient Assistance Program
(800) 722-9294

**AZITHROMYCIN (ZITHROMAX)**
Toxoplasmosis, MAC, cryptosporidiosis
**Pfizer Inc.**
Contact: Premier Research
(800) 438-1985

**BDNA (BRANCH CHAIN DNA) (QUANTIPLEX)**
Viral load test
**Chiron**
Contact: Reimbursement Assistance
(800) 755-7533

**BLEOMYCIN (BLENOXANE)**
KS, lymphoma
**Bristol-Myers Squibb**
Contact: Reimbursement and Assistance
(800) 272-4878

**CIDOFOVIR (HPMPC) (VISTIDE)**
CMV retinitis
**Gilead Sciences**
Contact: Support Services
(800) 445-3235

**CIPROFLOXACIN (CIPRO)**
Bacterial infections
**Bayer Pharmaceuticals**
Contact: Indigent Patient Program
(800) 998-9180

**CLARITHROMYCIN (BIAXIN)**
MAC
**Abbott Laboratories**
Contact: Patient Assistance
(800) 688-9118

**CLINDAMYCIN (CLEOCIN)**
PCP, toxoplasmosis
**Pharmacia & Upjohn**
Contact: Patient Assistance
(800) 242-7014

**CLOFAZIMINE (LAMPRENE)**
MAC
**Novartis Pharmaceuticals**
Contact: Patient Assistance Program
(800) 257-3273

**DAUNORUBICIN LIPOSOMAL (DAUNOXOME)**
KS
**NeXstar**
Contact: Reimbursement Hotline
(800) 226-2056

**DELAVIRDINE (RESCRIPTOR)**
HIV infection
**Pharmacia & Upjohn**
Contact: Patient Assistance Program
(800) 711-0807

**DIDANOSINE (DDI) (VIDEX)**
HIV infection
**Bristol-Myers Squibb Co.**
Contact: Reimbursement and Assistance
(800) 788-0123

**DOXORUBICIN LIPOSOMAL (DOXIL)**
KS
**Sequus Pharmaceuticals**
Contact: Patient Assistance Program
(800) 375-1658

**DRONABINOL (MARINOL)**
Weight loss
**Roxane Laboratories**
Contact: Patient Assistance Program
(800) 274-8651

**ERYTHROPOIETIN**
AZT-related anemia
**Amgen**
Contact: Reimbursement and Safety Program
(800) 272-9376

**ERYTHROPOIETIN (PROCRIT)**
AZT-related anemia
**Ortho Biotech**
Contact: Procritline
(800) 553-3851

**ETHAMBUTOL (MYAMBUTOL)**
MAC
**Wyeth-Ayerst Lederle Laboratories**
Contact: Patient Assistance Program
(800) 568-9938

**FAMCICLOVIR (FAMVIR)**
Herpes simplex, herpes zoster
**SmithKline Beecham**
Contact: Access to Care Program
(800) 366-8900 x5767

**FLUCONAZOLE (DIFLUCAN)**
Fungal infections
**Pfizer Inc.**
Contact: Diflucan Patient Assistance
Program
(800) 646-4455

**FOSCARNET (FOSCAVIR)**
CMV retinitis
**Astra Pharmaceuticals**
Contact: Foscavir Assistance, Reimbursement
(800) 488-3247

**G-CSF (NEUPOGEN) FILIGRASTIM**
Neutropenia
**Amgen**
Contact: Reimbursement &
Safety Program
(800) 272-9376

**GANCICLOVIR IMPLANT (VITRASERT)**
CMV retinitis
**Chiron Vision**
Contact: HTA Associates
(800) 843-1137

**GANCICLOVIR INTRAVENOUS (CYTOVENE)**
CMV disease
**Hoffmann-La Roche**
Contact: HIV Therapy Assistance Program
(800) 285-4484

**GANCICLOVIR ORAL (CYTOVENE)**
CMV retinitis: maintenance and prevention
**Hoffman-La Roche**
Contact: HIV Therapy Assistance Program
(800) 285-4484

**GM-CSF (LEUKINE) (SARGAMOSTIM)**
Neutropenia
**Immunex Corporation**
Contact: Patient Assistance Program
(800) 334-6273

**HUMAN GROWTH HORMONE (SEROSTIM)**
Weight Loss
**Serono Laboratories**
Contact: Patient Assistance Program
(888) 628-6673

**HYDROXYUREA (HYDREA)**
HIV Infection
**Bristol-Myers Squibb Co.**
Contact: Reimbursement and Assistance
(800) 272-4878

**INDINAVIR (CRIXIVAN)**
HIV infection
**Merck Pharmaceuticals**
Contact: Crixivan Support Program
(800) 850-3430

**ITRACONAZOLE (SPORANOX)**
Histoplasmosis
**Janssen Pharmaceutica, Inc.**
Contact: Patient Assistance Program
(800) 544-2987

**KETOCONAZOLE (NIZORAL)**
Fungal infections
**Janssen Pharmaceutica, Inc.**
Contact: Patient Assistance Program
(800) 544-2987

**LAMIVUDINE (3TC) (EPIVIR)**
HIV Infection
**Glaxo Wellcome Inc.**
Contact: HIV Patient Assistance Program
(800) 722-9294

**MEGESTROL ACETATE (MEGACE)**
Weight loss
**Bristol-Myers Squibb**
Contact: Megace Temporary Assistance
Program
(800) 272-4878

**NELFINAVIR (VIRACEPT)**
HIV infection
**Agouron Pharmaceuticals**
Contact: VIRACEPT Assistance Program
(888) 777-6637

**NEVIRAPINE (VIRAMUNE)**
HIV infection
**Boehringer Ingelheim/Roxane**
Contact: Roxane Reimbursement Services
(800) 274-8651

**OCTREOTIDE ACETATE (SANDOSTATIN)**
Diarrhea
**Novartis Pharmaceuticals**
Contact: Patient Assistance Program
(888) 455-6655

**OXANDROLONE (OXANDRIN)**
Weight loss
**Bio-Technology General Corporation**
Contact: Quantum Express
(800) 741-2698

**PARAMOMYCIN (HUMATIN)**
Cryptosporidiosis
**Parke-Davis**
Contact: Patient Assistance
(800) 223-0432

**PCR TEST (POLYMERASE CHAIN REACTION) (AMPLICOR)**
Viral load test
**Roche Diagnostics**
Contact: Patient Assistance Program
(888) 837-8727

**PENTAMIDINE (NEBUPENT)**
PCP prophylaxis
**Fujisawa, USA, Inc.**
Contact: Nebupent Reimbursement Service
(800) 888-7704 x 8607

**PYRIMETHAMINE (DARAPRIM)**
Toxoplasmosis
**Glaxo Wellcome Inc.**
Contact: HIV Patient Assistance Program
(800) 722-9294

**RIFABUTIN (MYCOBUTIN)**
MAC
**Pharmacia & Upjohn**
Contact: Patient Assistance Program
(800) 366-5570

**RITONAVIR (NORVIR)**
HIV Infection
**Abbott Laboratories**
Contact: Program Coordinator
(800) 659-9050

**SAQUINAVIR (INVIRASE)**
HIV Infection
**Hoffman-La Roche**
Contact: HIV Therapy Assistance Program
(800) 282-7780

**STAVUDINE (D4T) (ZERIT)**
HIV infection
**Bristol-Myers Squibb Co.**
Contact: Patient Assistance Program
(800) 788-0123

**TESTOSTERONE (TESTODERM)**
Hypogonadism
**Alza Pharmaceuticals**
Contact: Ron Qualia, HIV Account Specialist
(800) 321-3130

**TMP/SMX (BACTRIM)**
PCP prophylaxis, acute PCP
**Hoffmann-La Roche**
Contact: Oncoline Reimbursement Assistance
(800) 443-6676

**TMP/SMX (SEPTRA)**
PCP prophylaxis, acute PCP
**Glaxo Wellcome Co.**
Contact: HIV Patient Assistance Program
(800) 722-9294

**TRIMETREXATE (NEUTREXIN)**
PCP treatment
**U.S. Bioscience**
Contact: Financial Assistance
(800) 887-2467

**WINRHO SD (IVIG)**
ITP
**Univax Biologics, Inc.**
Contact: Patient Assistance Program
(800) 789-2099

**ZALCITABINE (DDC) (HIVID)**
HIV infection
**Hoffmann-La Roche**
Contact: Assistance Program
(800) 285-4484

**ZIDOVUDINE (AZT) (RETROVIR)**
HIV infection
**Glaxo Wellcome Inc.**
Contact: HIV Patient Assistance Program
(800) 722-9294

# PROJECT INFORM NATIONAL BOARD OF GOVERNORS

**Robert Schooley, MD**
Infectious Disease Division
University of Colorado
Denver, CO

**Erik Sterling**
The Sterling/Winters Company
Los Angeles, CA

**Paul Volberding, MD**
UCSF AIDS Program
San Francisco General Hospital
San Francisco, CA

**Irv Weissman, MD**
Stanford University,
School of Medicine
Palo Alto, CA

**Jason Winters**
The Sterling/Winters Company
Los Angeles, CA

# PROJECT INFORM BOARD OF DIRECTORS

**Curtis Ingraham**
*Co-chair*

**Ken Turner**
*Treasurer*

**Susan Brautovich**
**Diane Cenko**
**Martin Delaney**
**Tom Downing**
**Brenda Freiberg**
**Linda Grinberg**

**Tom Kelley**
*Co-chair*

**Gregory Horowitt**
*Secretary*

**Steve Hutnick**
**Barry Krost**
**Peter Minichiello**
**Rod O'Neal**
**Bill Sprick**
**Tim Wu**

# PROJECT INFORM STAFF

**Dawn Averitt**
*Information and Advocacy Associate*

**Annette Brands, MFCC**
*Executive Director*

**Ben Cheng**
*Asst. Director, Information Dept.*

**Ryan Clary**
*Treatment Action Network Coor.*

**Ben Collins**
*Program Services Director*

**Martin Delaney**
*Founding Director*

**Camilla Dickinson**
*Administrative Assistant*

**Sabine Dolle**
*Constituent Services Manager*

**Anne Donnelly**
*Public Policy Director*

**David Evans**
*Outreach Coordinator*

**Ellen George**
*Office Manager*

**Barry Harrison**
*Accountant*

**Judy Hogan**
*Outreach Coordinator*

**Brenda Lein**
*Director of Information and Advocacy*

**David Mills**
*Development Associate*

**Hunter Morey**
*Hotline Assistant*

**Mark Owens**
*Volunteer Coordinator*

**Reuel Sherwood**
*Constituent Services Assistant*

**Tom Teasley**
*Director of Development*

**Eric Whitney**
*Hotline Manager*

**David Wood**
*Information Coordinator*

# ACKNOWLEDGMENTS

The staff and volunteers at Project Inform work hard under enormous pressures and with a great sense of urgency. This new and improved edition of *The HIV Drug Book* is a reflection of our commitment to help those living with HIV, their lovers, families, and caregivers deal with the sometimes overwhelming task of getting the information necessary to make the best treatment decisions possible. In this new, second edition of *The HIV Drug Book*, the Project Inform staff took over the responsibility for all aspects of the writing and production for the book, creating dozens of new drug profiles and updating and revising the material carried over from the original edition. In addition, the staff added several new articles critical to the proper use of combination therapies and the new class of drugs known as protease inhibitors. All of this work reflects the commitment of the Project Inform staff and Board to keep this book up to date with the rapidly changing scene of AIDS treatment research.

This time around, staff members also performed all the editing, formatting, and layout functions themselves, sometimes building upon and sometimes revising the first edition based on feedback from purchasers. Though this second edition resembles the first, it is in many ways a new book. Like most other Project Inform publications, it is difficult to say who wrote what because of the collective way in which the staff works. Everything is a joint effort, the result of many layers of writing and review, reflecting the input of all the people in the Information and Advocacy Department and anyone else at Project Inform who wanted to have input.

## GRATEFUL ACKNOWLEDGMENT IS MADE TO:

Martin Delaney, founding director of Project Inform, BRENDA LEIN and BEN CHENG, who are the core of the Information and Advocacy arm of the organization, oversaw all aspects of the creation of this second edition. Ben Cheng developed the new drug profiles and along with Martin and Brenda, contributed to many of the new articles. All three reviewed and edited each other's work, as is our custom, and made the decisions about what to include.

REENA LAWANDE, a highly skilled intern at Project Inform, worked tirelessly as an editor, reviewer, and research assistant. Additionally, she developed new drug profiles and contributed to many of the new articles. Without her help and dedication, the staff would have been

overwhelmed and incapable of meeting the deadline. Reena's contribution was particularly remarkable in that, unlike staff, she received no paycheck for work.

DAVID WOOD, also of the Information Department, oversaw the dismantling of the original edition and, along with Martin Delaney, performed the reassembly and layout revisions of the new edition.

ANNETTE BRANDS, Executive Director of Project Inform, provided the planning, resources, and support needed by the staff and managed the relationship with the publisher.

Finally, once again we acknowledge those who contributed to the first edition of the book, which provided the framework upon which this version is based:

BETSY NOLAN, the project manager for the first edition of *The HIV Drug Book,* was the heart and soul of the first edition. As everyone involved knows well, without Betsy and the countless ways in which she contributed, there would be no *HIV Drug Book*. Quite literally, her determination, more than anything else, made this book happen.

STEVEN PETROW, first edition editor who guided the original project from its inception.

BRIAN KEARNEY, principal author of first edition drug profiles, who displayed his enormous talent and intelligence in assembling all the knowledge of Project Inform's ten years of treatment information into these pages.

POCKET BOOKS, which not only supported this project right from the beginning, but also gave unstintingly of its time and expertise. Thanks to all at Pocket Books who supported the 2nd edition of *The HIV Drug Book.*

TOM BECKMAN, the former PI Board President whose conversations inspired Betsy Nolan to call for the creation of this book. Tom died just as the first manuscript was completed.

THE BOARD OF DIRECTORS, THE CONSTITUENTS, AND THE VOLUNTEERS OF PROJECT INFORM , whose continual support and enthusiasm for the mission of Project Inform make all our work possible

September 1997

# In Memoriam

**SO MANY HAVE DIED IN THIS EPIDEMIC...**

In the first edition of this book, we were able to list many of the special friends and supporters who helped make the work of Project Inform—and this book—possible. Today, just a few years later, the number of names who now meet that description has become too large to list. Instead, we dedicate this new edition of *The HIV Drug Book* first to all those who have supported our work but lost their lives, and secondarily to the millions worldwide who have succumbed to this plague.

Due to the recent advances in AIDS research, it is popular for people today to act as if the AIDS epidemic is somehow winding down. Sadly, this is not the case. Certainly, most of the advances in HIV/AIDS treatment and prevention are not remotely available to the vast majority of HIV-infected people worldwide. But even for those who can access the best and most expensive new therapies, today's advances are by no means a cure. They have indeed brought wonderful relief for many from the pain and suffering of AIDS, but unfortunately, it is but a reprieve, not a lasting solution. Until we find the means to literally cure the disease, it will continue to loom over the heads of all those infected, whether in urban centers of the United States or the plains of Africa. The AIDS epidemic will not be over until it is over for everyone. As of today, it is over for no one.

# INDEX

This index contains all drugs mentioned anywhere in this book. They are listed separately under every known name of each drug. The Index also includes the names of the diseases the drugs are intended to treat. It is a simple, single level alphabetical index

# About Project Inform

Project Inform, established in 1985 as a national, non-profit, community-based HIV/AIDS treatment information and advocacy organization, serves HIV-infected individuals, their caregivers, and their healthcare and service providers through its national, toll-free treatment hotline, the *PI Perspective,* and other information publications, educational Town Meetings, on-line services, and research and drug access advocacy programs. All information is available free of charge; donations are strongly encouraged. For more information, contact the Project Inform National HIV/AIDS Treatment Hotline. An electronic version of this material is available on Project Inform's website.

Project Inform
205 13th Street
San Francisco, CA 94103

| | |
|---|---|
| TREATMENT HOTLINE: | 800-822-7422 (toll-free) or |
| | 415-558-9051 (in the San Francisco Bay Area and internationally) |
| HOTLINE HOURS: | Monday – Friday, 9 a.m. – 5 p.m. and |
| | Saturday, 10 a.m. – 4 p.m. (Pacific Time) |
| OFFICE TELEPHONE: | 415-558-8669 |
| FAX: | 415-558-0684 |
| E-MAIL: | info@projinf.org |
| WWW: | http://www.projinf.org |

Readers are invited to respond with their comments, suggestions, criticisms, or requests for additional information to *The HIV Drug Book* at the address listed above.